The Revelation of Imagination

From Homer and the Bible through Virgil and Augustine to Dante

✦

William Franke

NORTHWESTERN UNIVERSITY PRESS
EVANSTON, ILLINOIS

Northwestern University Press
www.nupress.northwestern.edu

Printed in the United States of America

10 9 8 7 6 5 4 3 2 1

Library of Congress Cataloging-in-Publication Data

Franke, William, author.
The revelation of imagination : from Homer and the Bible through Virgil and Augustine to Dante / William Franke.
pages cm.
Includes index.
ISBN 978-0-8101-3119-4 (cloth : alk. paper) — ISBN 978-0-8101-3182-8 (pbk. : alk. paper) — ISBN 978-0-8101-3120-0 (ebook)
1. Revelation in literature. 2. Religion and literature. 3. Bible as literature. 4. Homer. Odyssey. 5. Virgil. Aeneis. 6. Augustine, Saint, Bishop of Hippo. Confessiones. 7. Dante Alighieri, 1265–1321. Inferno. I. Title.
PN49.F653 2015
809.93382—dc23

2015017407

∞ The paper used in this publication meets the minimum requirements of the American National Standard for Information Sciences—Permanence of Paper for Printed Library Materials, ANSI Z39.48-1992.

The Revelation of Imagination

For Margaret Doody

CONTENTS

PREFACE

The Approach

The humanities represent a special kind of knowledge involving interpretation and judgment that is vital to our existence both individually and together in society. Their mission has been variously defined in the course of history, and the curriculum has altered accordingly. I attempt to focus on what is enduring and perennial rather than accommodated to the agenda of the moment. The humanities embody a kind of wisdom or philosophy and, I believe, something of a "revelation" that I have wanted to bring to conscious reflection in detailed readings of some of the most thought-provoking texts of the Western intellectual tradition.

This book grows out of a lecture course on "Great Books of the Western Tradition" that I have given at Vanderbilt University beginning in the 1990s and into the ensuing millennium. The course frames readings of representative classic works of literature within a general theory of the humanities that I developed under the influence of German hermeneutic thought about the *Geisteswissenschaften* (human sciences) conjugated with French linguistic and critical theory. This theoretical background is married to a vision of poetry as prophecy and even as prayer, which is itself the result of crossing an enthusiasm for English Protestant poets—particularly Blake, Milton, Spenser, and Herbert—with a passion for Dante and the Italian Catholic tradition through Vico and Manzoni. My approach has been nurtured, furthermore, by assiduous cultivation of Greek *paideia* and of the Latin rhetorical tradition as matrices of the *artes liberales*.

Drawing on these backgrounds, the book endeavors not only to offer re-actualized readings of representative humanities texts: in addition, these literary-critical meditations are linked together by an overarching argument concerning the peculiar nature of knowledge in the humanities. The book reflects philosophically on what constitutes vital insight and ultimately the experience of truth in this domain of culture. This reflection outlines, most importantly, a way of articulating the connection of humanities knowledge with what may, in various senses, be called "divine revelation." Such revelation entails the sort of inspiration to which poets since Homer have laid claim, as well as that proper to revealed religion in the Bible. Both kinds of inspiration have traditionally been designated in different, but related, senses as "prophetic." A hybrid approach to the notion of prophecy, therefore, is central to the argument of the book.

The book can be read as critical interpretation and commentary on a core selection of classic humanities texts—but also as a philosophical theory that ponders the claim of imaginative literature to become prophetic revelation. In the latter respect, it consists not so much in abstract propositions about prophetic poetry as in thoughtful formulations of the theoretical premises inherent and operative in the practice of prophecy in these poems. The book is bound to be taken in one or the other of these directions by different types of readers, depending on what they are looking for and on how they are trained and accustomed to read and think. The ambiguity itself, however, between exegesis and theory serves to point us toward what lies beyond this very distinction and at its origin—to what can be neither simply read by traditional philological methods nor be directly thought out by the conceptual methods of philosophy, but must rather be "revealed."

This is why we require a kind of theology of literature (or literary theology), though one that can only be critical: not any positive, dogmatic system, but rather an opening to the infinite "space of literature" and to its untrammeled exploration by the imagination. When poetry attains to this level of prophetic revelation, literature provides, in effect, what I call a metacritique of epistemology—a reflection on the foundations of knowledge that precedes and surpasses all possible philosophical analysis. Such critique shows why all rational grounding of knowledge fails to reach the sources of our insight and of our very being. At this depth, origins can only be imagined. The imagination is called in to take over in grounding—or at least in backgrounding—knowledge, where critical reason runs up against limits that it cannot surpass.

The ground covered here corresponds to only the first semester of the Great Books sequence that I have taught at Vanderbilt. I plan eventually to prepare for publication a sequel, the working title of which is "Mythopoiesis in a Scientific Age." It takes up the study of representative humanities texts from the Renaissance, beginning with *Hamlet*, and moves through the modern and contemporary periods. These works are placed in a theoretical framework that complements the one used in the present volume for reading ancient and medieval literature and extends it toward a more comprehensive philosophy of revelation in the humanities.[1]

---

1. This aim, meanwhile, although not abandoned, has been displaced and differently fulfilled by *Secular Scriptures: Modern Theological Poetics in the Wake of Dante* (Columbus: Ohio State University Press, 2016]); *Poetry and Apocalypse: Theological Disclosures of Poetic Language* (Stanford: Stanford University Press, 2009); and *Poetics of Revelation: From Ancient Theological Hermeneutics to Modern Linguistic Epistemologies* (in course of preparation).

In the present volume I attempt to draw from the best of what thinkers and scholars have written in commenting on these works in order to re-propose sometimes familiar interpretations from an angle that brings out why they are enduringly important and illuminating. With regard to classics of this stature, it is often most worthwhile to concentrate on understanding what they have long been appreciated for in a way that elucidates why they continue to be relevant for us today rather than to strain to present only views that are purportedly brand-new. When these works are actually grasped in their pertinence to our present situation and its questions, then their meaning originates in our own reading of them informed by tradition and imagination. On this basis, our interpretations are "original" in the sense that matters most.

The Argument

In its central argument, the book demonstrates that literature of this order—literature that aspires to become the conscience and indeed the consciousness of a whole civilization, or even of civilization as a whole—is essentially "prophetic." Such literature endeavors to reveal the heart of human life and history in a perspective that is never past. However beholden to tradition it may be, this perspective is always original because it draws from and even helps to constitute the original source of inspiration that invents a history and a human identity in the first place. Past, present, and future are but interchangeable vantage points on a disclosure of truth that remains the origin of the world within which such truth has been articulated, into which it speaks, and upon which it can continue to work transformatively into the future. At this level of originality—which is not to be confounded with mere novelty, although it opens the greatest opportunities for innovation—every insight, whether cast in the mode of the past, present, or future, can have a "prophetic" bearing: it can become what in poetic tradition has often been styled "divine vision."

Literature expressing such insight can and should, I argue, be understood as "revelation" still today. Poetry that attains to this height of prophetic vision asks to be embraced as a species of revealed understanding or awareness that reaches beyond all rationally grounded knowledge in order to sound its sources in the creative springs of reason itself. This outlook, then, is implicitly a literary theology: it claims that inspired poetry can open up a kind of comprehensive vision of—or relation to—reality as a whole and thereby fathom its normally inaccessible depths. Such vision peers into the world in its creative emergence and calls to be understood as, in effect, a participating in the mind of God.

However, it is only the limits and impossibility of objective sight and knowledge of God that frees the imagination to explore unfettered its own sources and the grounds of all that is—and thus to inhabit and animate the theological dimension of the infinite. So what we have to do with here is more precisely a critical negative theology of literature. Positive theological doctrines and images serve as metaphorical means for interpreting otherwise unfathomable heights and depths of experience and for scrutinizing (or at least relating to) the otherwise impenetrable enigma of existence.

Such, in barest abstract, is the thesis that will be developed here in five steps corresponding to five epoch-making works in the Western intellectual tradition. Each chapter presents a global reading of the work in question. In each case, poetry, or more exactly *poiesis*, is revealed as prophecy, and the meaning of both of these terms is renegotiated through recognizing their intrinsic relationship. Virgil stands at the center of this renegotiation and Dante at its culmination, while the Bible serves as its matrix. Homer's *Odyssey* and Augustine's *Confessions* are less obviously prophetic-poetic texts, and yet the crucial lineaments of the whole tradition emerge into clarity by reading them in this light. The light from Troy and that radiating from Jerusalem and eventually Rome, for all their decisive differences, blend into one light as refracted through these chief beacons of the Western humanities.

Acknowledgments

My thanks go in the first place to all the students who have engaged with me in adventurous study and reflection on these and other humanities texts. I thank particularly my former teaching assistants in the Comparative Literature Program at Vanderbilt University—many now professors in their own right—who have been invaluable partners in dialogue: Gian Balsamo, Claudia Baracchi, Alan Bourassa, Donald Holman, Madalena Vucicozici, Rachel Roth, Ken Himmelman, Lara Newborn, Laura Matter, Patricia Crespo, Michael Reid, Scott Hubbard, Xiaolun Qi, Shaun Haskins, and Jennifer Krause. I dedicate this book to all those who have been my students—and at the same time my teachers—in the humanities, but especially to the one who was our leader in crucially formative years.

Throughout the book, translations not otherwise attributed are my own.

Versions of some segments from the chapters have been previously published as articles in periodical literature or in collections of essays. My thanks are due to the publishers for permission to reprint in revised form material from the following:

1. "Involved Knowing: On the Poetic Epistemology of the Humanities." *The European Legacy: Towards New Paradigms* 16, no. 4 (2011): 449–69 (http://www.tandfonline.com).
2. "From the Bible as Literature to Literature as Theology: A Theological Reading of Genesis as a Humanities Text." *Interdisciplinary Humanities* 29, no. 2 (2012): 28–45.

3. "The Exodus Epic: Universalization of History through Ritual." In *Universality and History: The Foundations of Core*, ed. Don Thompson, Darrel Colson, and J. Scott Lee, 59–70. Lanham, Md.: University Press of America, 2002.
4. "Prophecy as a Genre of Revelation: Synergisms of Inspiration and Imagination in the Book of Isaiah." *Theology* 114, no. 5 (2011): 340–52.
5. "Gospel as Personal Knowing: Theological Reflections on Not Just a Literary Genre." *Theology Today* 68, no. 4 (2011): 413–23.
6. "Writings and Revelation: Literary Theology in the Bible." *Theology and Literature* 28, no. 4 (2014): 1–16.
7. "Homer's Musings and the Divine Muse: Epic Song as Invention and Revelation." *Religion and Literature* 43, no. 3 (2011): 1–29.
8. "Virgil, History, and Prophecy." *Philosophy and Literature* 29 (2005): 73–88.
9. "On Doing the Truth in Time: The *Aeneid*'s Invention of Poetic Prophecy." *Arion: A Journal of Humanities and the Classics* 19, no. 1 (2011): 53–63.
10. "The Secondariness of Virgilian Epic and Its Unprecedented Originality." *College Literature: A Journal of Critical Literary Studies* 40, no. 1 (2013): 11–31.
11. "War and Tragedy and the Fate of the Spoken: Virgil's Secularization of Prophecy." *College Literature: A Journal of Critical Literary Studies* 41, no. 4 (2014): 25–40.
12. "Augustine's *Confessions* and the Transcendental Ground of Consciousness: or How Literary Narrative Becomes Prophetic Revelation." *Philosophy and Literature* 38, no. 1 (2014): 204–22.
13. "The Interpretive Journey and the Allegory of Reading: Introduction to the *Inferno* as a Humanities Text." In *Uniting the Liberal Arts: Core and Context*, ed. Bainard Cowen and J. Scott Lee, 75–82. Lanham, Md.: University Press of America, 2002.
14. "Dante's *Inferno* and the Poetic Revelation of Prophetic Truth." *Philosophy and Literature* 33, no. 2 (2009): 252–66.
15. "Paradoxical Prophecy: Dante's Strategy of Self-Subversion in the *Inferno*." *Italica* 90, no. 3 (2013): 343–64.
16. "Deep Hermeneutics of Complicity and Conversion in *Inferno* IX–XVII." *University of Toronto Quarterly* 82, no. 1 (Winter 2013): 1–19.
17. "Dante's Deconstruction and Reconstruction of Prophetic Voice and Vision in the Malebolge (*Inferno* XVIII–XXV)." *Philosophy and Literature* 36, no. 1 (2012): 111–21.
18. "The Death and Damnation of Poetry in *Inferno* XXXI–XXXIV: Ugolino and Narrative as an Instrument of Revenge." *Romance Studies* 28, no. 1 (2010): 27–35.
19. "Canonicity, Creativity, and the Unlimited Revelation of Literature." *Partial Answers: Journal of Literature and the History of Ideas* 12, no. 1 (2014): 1–24.

The Revelation of Imagination

Introduction

✦

Involved Knowing

On the Poetic Epistemology of the Humanities

I. Method and Truth in the Humanities

What kind of knowledge, if any, do the humanities represent? Posing epistemological questions concerning the nature and conditions of knowledge in the disciplines that come under this rubric might seem hopelessly remote from probing classic works of literature and their remarkably rich and revelatory contents. Yet theoretical awareness and self-reflectiveness are integral to almost any authentic knowledge and insight in this domain. To begin, therefore, with some broad theoretical considerations concerning the study of the humanities is already a way of embarking on them.[1]

The question of the kind of knowledge the humanities entail might be approached through exploring either the history or the method of these disciplines. Logically, the question of method demands to be taken up first. But even to speak of "method" in the humanities betrays an, in some ways, inappropriate bias. For knowledge in the humanities is not per se methodical. To the extent that we feel the need to establish at the outset the right method of research, our conception of the humanities is under the sway of the scientific disciplines with which they share the liberal arts curriculum in our academic institutions of higher learning. While in science a sound method supposedly guarantees true results and is theoretically necessary to arrive at certainty of the truth, the experience of truth in the humanities, for example,

1. In introducing a special issue of *Daedalus* 138 (2009) dedicated to "Reflecting on the Humanities," the editors Patricia Meyer Spacks and Leslie Berlowitz similarly write: "The essays assembled here enact as well as reflect the humanities" (5).

in and through a work of art, may be more likely to come about rather as an epiphany and in the most *un*methodical, incalculable ways.[2]

Not cognitive knowledge alone but aesthetic sensibility and moral feeling, emotional empathy and imaginative vision, along with many other types of intelligence and awareness, are intrinsic to all that is known in the humanities. This means that knowledge in the humanities is contextual and relational, and therefore also historical and even personal. A unique personal history is necessarily the context for all knowledge that is one's own and that can truly be called human knowledge. Given this inextricably historical character of humanities knowledge, history and method are closely intertwined and practically inseparable.

There are a few verses by the eighteenth-century English poet William Blake which for me personally, since undergraduate days, have stood out as a sort of motto over the gate of entry into the field of the humanities:

> For a tear is an intellectual thing
> And a sigh is the sword of an angel king
> And the bitter groan of the martyr's woe
> Is an arrow from the Almighty's bow.[3]

It is enough to hang on to just the first verse for its suggestiveness concerning what may be considered the objective of the kind of study undertaken in the humanities, namely, the attempt to learn to think with and through feelings and in light of images, and to cultivate what in tradition has often been called "the intelligence of the heart." In putting it that way, I am echoing the seventeenth-century French philosopher Blaise Pascal, who wrote that the heart has its reasons which reason does not understand ("Le coeur a ses raisons, que la raison ne connaît point," *Pensées* 277, Brunschvicg ed.). Our objective, in other words, less like the Bible's and more like Plato's, is to attain to that kind of thinking—or approach that level of understanding—where knowledge and love are one, or where the will's desire for the good coincides with the intellect's passion for truth. And if we also heed the aesthetic aspects of this intelligence, we can state further that both of these longings—desire for the good and passion for the true—coalesce in the love of the beautiful.

That truth and goodness unite in beauty is a seminal idea, for example, in "The Oldest System-Program of German Idealism," which is attributed

---

2. This contrast between the experience of truth in the humanities and methodical knowing in science is a fulcrum for Hans-Georg Gadamer's humanities-based "hermeneutic" philosophy in *Wahrheit und Methode* (Tübingen: J. C. B. Mohr, 1960), translated by Joel Weinsheimer and Donald Marshall as *Truth and Method* (New York: Crossroad, 1989), 2nd ed. rev.

3. William Blake, *The Complete Poetry and Prose of William Blake*, ed. David W. Erdman (Berkeley: University of California Press, 1982).

variously to Hegel, Schelling, and Hölderlin: "Finally the idea that unites all, the idea of *beauty*, this word taken in its higher Platonic sense. I am now persuaded that the highest act of reason, the act in which it comprehends all ideas, is an aesthetic act and that *truth and goodness* are kin to each other *only in beauty.*"[4] Such wholeness of vision, in which our faculties of theoretical cognition, moral discernment, and aesthetic appreciation interpenetrate, has been a hallmark of the humanities throughout their history.

I state the objectives in what are, admittedly, somewhat lofty and elusive terms partly because of a doubt as to whether objectives can or should be stated very fully or precisely at the outset of any study in the humanities. The requirement of fixing one's objectives before one even begins belongs rather to the methodology of science as a technology for achieving practical aims and—even more problematically—expresses the demands of an information-crazy culture based on clear-cut bites of unambiguous data. Such a culture actually preserves little or nothing of the genuine scientific spirit of search for knowledge by experience and through inquiry into the unknown, but only the mechanical, calculating aspects of science as exploited in technologies of mass production. Such mindless applications are unlike real scientific endeavor, which is nothing if not a richly human enterprise.

The very procedure of specifying objectives and positing methodical steps to achieving them entails assumptions that are not altogether appropriate to learning in the humanities—nor even to actual scientific discovery. The ideal of total clarity and transparency of aims demanded by at least a certain interpretation of scientific method and procedure abstracts from the temporality of human understanding and inquiry and from the way in which all human knowledge is embedded in experience in time and, more concretely, in the histories of persons. In its specifically human meaning and dimension, the goal of all our experience remains perpetually a mystery beholden to a time beyond time and beyond scientific comprehension. It is a time when all things shall be revealed and "all flesh shall see it together" (Isaiah 40: 5), as intimated by the biblical voice that is so pervasively infused all through the Western humanities tradition.

For the sake of conformity to the unrelenting demand to define objectives, we might say, for instance, that the objective of study of the humanities is to develop critical thinking. We cannot help but hope that precisely that will come about. Nevertheless, our ultimate goal is not to acquire another power or to hone another skill to enable us better to dominate the information that

4. Georg Wilhelm Friedrich Hegel, *Werke*, vol. 1 (Frankfurt: Suhrkamp, 1979), 235. "Zuletzt die Idee, die alle vereinigt, die Idee der *Schönheit*, das Wort in höherem platonischen Sinne genommen. Ich bin nun überzeugt, daß der höchste Akt der Vernunft, der, indem sie alle Ideen umfaßt, ein ästhetischer Akt ist und daß *Wahrheit und Güte nur in der Schönheit* verschwistert sind." Hölderlin further elaborates on this idea in a lyrical vein in *Hyperion*.

occupies such a large place in our culture and consciousness, but rather to open up new worlds of experience, that is, to open ourselves up—in Blake's words, once again—to "infinite worlds of delight," to "Eternity ever expanding in the bosom of God, which is the Human Imagination" (Blake, *Jerusalem* 5: 20).

Study of the humanities does not aim to give us just another capability for manipulating the world after our own designs, so as to make it conform yet more conveniently to our wishes or "objectives": it aims to give us another world, in fact, infinite worlds. Rather than striving to achieve preconceived objectives, we advance toward human intelligence through an intensely energetic letting be, and in doing so we ourselves are changed. Our objective is to respond fully to the possibilities of being human as they have been mediated to us, among other ways, by "great books" of our tradition. What we, in the end, most profoundly desire belongs to the search itself rather than being just its goal or result. We need *not* to know exactly what we want out of it in order to genuinely—and most profitably—study the humanities. For the goal of human endeavor conceived as its potential fulfillment belongs to the mystery in question: it is to be freshly discovered and revised all along the way rather than being determined and presupposed from the outset.

Indeed, our question must be not what do we want out of this type of study and out of the texts that we study in it so much as: What do they want of us? This involves treating our texts as partners in dialogue rather than just as specimens for analysis. Only in this way do we allow them to effectively make their claim upon us. Only so can we respond to the possibilities of human being as they have been construed and conveyed to us by presumptive "great books," ones that have gained recognition as monumental classic works of our tradition. We interrogate them in order to be ourselves interrogated. The question is: What do these works call us to be and see and do? What do they invite and challenge and enable us to become?

Human existence has, and indeed *is*, a multiplicity of possibilities which call for realization. We are constantly contemplating these possibilities for our own lives as we work through the possibilities for human existence that are represented in our readings in the humanities. My proximate goal as pedagogue is to mediate (or, as Socrates would say, play the midwife) in allowing these texts to speak to us, to waken us to the sense of the possibilities for existence that are in us and which we are. One can be qualified for doing this only by virtue of one's own experience of these texts matured through a long-standing, exacting discipline and devotion to the study of the humanities. The pedagogue's knowledge of the matter of the humanities is not different in kind from the beginning student's, but it has been painstakingly trained in ways that may prove to be of service in leading others down the path of discovery of the human and imaginative worlds embodied in these texts.

II. Contextual-Relational Knowing versus Scientific Objectivity

What, then, are the humanities? In terms of academic disciplines, one straightforward, inevitable answer, given the usual structure of university instruction, is that they are the third division in the threefold breakdown of the liberal arts curriculum: science / social sciences / humanities. This approach, however, can cause distortions in our understanding of the humanities by allowing them to fall under the shadow cast over the liberal arts curriculum as a whole by the monolith of the scientific paradigm. Humanities in this scheme tend to be treated by assimilation as a further field for the application of the scientific method of knowing. Christened thus "the human sciences"—literally *les sciences humaines*, as they are called in French, or "the sciences of the spirit," *die Geisteswissenschaften*, as German says—the objective of the humanities would seem to be to extend knowledge by adapting the methods of natural science to a different kind of subject matter—no longer nature or numbers, but "humanity" in the full breadth of its creative self-expression in history and culture. The tendency to treat the humanities as a peculiar, less exact, less potent, less certain, less reliable, and less lucid kind of scientific pursuit is very strong in the academy. For we think we know what scientific knowledge is and believe that we can define it.[5]

Yet, understood according to the scientific paradigm, the humanities are denatured. For humanity is not an object. We *are* human—in all the irreducible facets of our subjectivity. A common way of expressing the presumed privilege and superiority of scientific knowledge is to state that science is "objective knowledge." However, human beings cannot be known as objects. To gain knowledge of human beings, one must actually participate in human experience and know it from within, personally, as a subject, rather than only analyze it detachedly and objectively from without. Indeed, all human knowledge is necessarily self-knowledge, at the same time as it is knowledge of whatever type of objects. The ancient motto "know thyself" (γνῶθι σεαυτόν) inscribed over the oracle of Apollo at Delphi, as recorded by Pausanias in his second-century A.D. *Description of Greece* (10.24.1), expresses in the form of an injunction a condition that is fundamental and imperative to all genuinely human knowing: in all knowledge in the humanities, we experience ourselves. This includes our possible selves—that is, the possibilities for our existence. In fact, the possibilities for existence and self-understanding available in our culture today have, to a considerable extent, been forged by works such as those studied in our humanities curriculum. We can, therefore,

5. See, for example, the keynote address by Edward O. Wilson, "How to Unify Knowledge," with its argument that "all of knowledge . . . can be united by a continuous skein of cause-and-effect explanation," in *Unity of Knowledge: The Convergence of Natural and Human Science*, ed. Antonio R. Damasio (New York: New York Academy of Sciences, 2001).

extend our understanding of why we think and feel the way we do about things by discovering the attitudes and insights that define our intellectual horizons in their emergence in these texts. Only this awareness enables us either to refuse or to freely choose such perspectives.

Scientists themselves today generally recognize the naivety of belief in objective knowledge, but we seem not to be in possession of any clear and convincing alternative to it. Due to lack of understanding of the nature of the knowledge proper to the humanities, we no longer know what genuine knowledge is, if it is not "objective" in the scientific sense. We can only imagine that the alternative must be subjective and arbitrary ideas that are really not worthy to be honored with the name of "knowledge" at all. We have become progressively less aware of the traditional sort of pursuit of knowledge as an endeavor to assimilate *oneself* to the true and real by identification with universal human ideals, yet such was the nature of knowing practiced as a spiritual exercise for millennia before the advent of science in the modern sense.[6] Accordingly, we can aim through this type of study to come back into touch with ancient and medieval approaches to human learning that had not yet forgotten this broader meaning of knowledge in relation to the subject that knows—what used to be called the "soul"—as an integral part of being in and belonging to a cosmos from which the individual had not yet been extracted and expelled.

All that is being said here about human knowing actually applies, only a little less directly and obviously, to scientific knowing as well, for science, too, is nothing if not a human activity of knowing. Rather than understanding the humanities as "human sciences," we can just as well understand the sciences as human endeavors. While science likes to abstract from this inescapable human element—from the fact that, whenever knowledge takes place, there is always *someone* who knows—the humanities dwell upon and accentuate precisely this human factor. They bring forward into the light of truth the human conditions surrounding all knowledge, including scientific knowledge. And, in this light, it is clear that the objectivity of science comes at the expense of an awareness of the humanly contingent conditions and contexts

6. Pierre Hadot's *Exercices spirituels et philosophie antique* (Paris: A. Michel, 2002 [1981]), translated by Michael Chase as *Philosophy as a Way of Life: Spiritual Exercises from Socrates to Foucault*, ed. Arnold I. Davidson (Oxford: Blackwell, 2007 [1995]), represents a seminal effort to recuperate this ancient approach to knowledge. Hadot is joined in this endeavor by Giovanni Reale, *Sagezza antica: Terapia per i mali dell'uomo d'oggi* (Milan: Raffaello Cortina, 1995); Jean Greisch, *Expérience philosophique, exercices spirituels et thérapie de l'âme* (Paris: Institut Catholique de Paris, 1996); André-Jean Voelke, *La Philosophie comme thérapie de l'âme: Etudes de philosophie hellénistique* (Paris: Cerf, 1994); and Martha C. Nussbaum, *The Therapy of Desire: Theory and Practice in Hellenistic Ethics* (Princeton, N.J.: Princeton University Press, 1994).

that impinge upon every actual instance of knowing. To express cognizance in its wholeness as an all-embracing awareness of the circumambient conditions of knowing, which include also the being of the knower, beyond the narrow focus on objects of science or *scientia*, the ancients used the term *sapientia* or "wisdom." Knowledge, not just of facts but also of oneself and one's limitations, and of the meaning of the world in relation to oneself, is the goal of the humanities expressed in this term "wisdom." The better part of wisdom is knowing that in knowing anything at all humanly, we always know also ourselves, including our limits and our possible selves in their scarcely fathomable variety.

All this is to say that the humanities consist in relational or personal knowing more than in objective, methodological knowledge. In other words, we ourselves are involved in what we know, and this character of personal involvement is crucial to the nature of such knowing. This applies, I would suggest, to all knowledge, in the humanities and in the sciences alike, with the difference that in the humanities we do not try to eliminate—or, at least, to limit as much as possible—this personal involvement that underpins our knowing. Instead, this irreducibly personal dimension is opened up and explored and developed in the course of interpreting, for example, a painting or a poem or a prayer. The humanities thus attain a more comprehensive point of view, and in the end we need to understand science, too, as fundamentally a human undertaking that is dependent on imagination and the poetry of its discoveries in order to be meaningful.[7]

In fact, science, or its ancestor "natural philosophy," in a direct line of descent, began as poetry. The earliest Greek philosophers, the "physicists" of Ionia on the Anatolian coast in Asia Minor in the sixth century B.C., thinkers such as Thales, Anaximander, Anaximenes (of the Milesian school), and Heraclitus of Ephesus, together with those active at the other rim of the Greek world in the colonies of the southern Italian peninsula, including Parmenides of Elea, Pythagoras of Crotone, and Empedocles of Agrigento, wrote their observations on nature and the world wholly or partly in verse (or at least in highly poetic, metrical prose) and, in effect, as poems of the universe, artworks expressing its intrinsic Logos. This serves as a reminder of the originally poetical character of science at its earliest stages. Conversely, the first poems are, at the same time, essays in natural philosophy, typically in mythic form. Mythologies in Greece and the world over represent the earliest

7. Among philosophers and scientists reconnecting science with humanities matrices are Jean-Marie Besnier, Hervé Le Guyader, Etienne Klein, and Heinz Wismann, *La Science en jeu* (Arles, Fr.: Actes sud, 2010). Wismann argues that modern science, in abandoning substance for function, derives from Christian paradigms of Incarnation and Eucharist, in which substance is constituted by relations.

attempts to formulate a comprehensive understanding of the world in which humans live: they constitute the earliest encyclopedias of knowledge.

The fact that knowledge is assembled into encyclopedic form, particularly in epic poetry, hints at the holistic character of knowledge in the humanities. Etymologically, the word "en*cyclo*paedia" contains the notion of a cycle or comprehensive circle of subjects of study, in addition to the idea of the education of children, *paedeia* in Greek. It is by comprehending matters in their furthest ramifications and implications, and in their widest contexts, that the type of knowledge characteristic of the humanities fulfills itself. As the encyclopedic model suggests, humanities knowledge strives to be knowledge in the round that encompasses things whole. Emblematic of this is the fact that the epic poems constituting the backbone of traditional humanities classics are all works that in various ways are encyclopedic in scope.

The basis of education in the ancient Greek world from the sixth century B.C. was Homer. The first prerequisite to being a cultivated individual was knowing Homer by heart. Homer was generally esteemed to be the source and sum of all knowledge and wisdom. Ancient philosophers such as Numenius and Porphyry relay the widespread conviction that Homer was a philosopher. This qualification included his being also a theologian, one who revealed sublime and even divine truths in the manner of Plato. Moreover, according to Quintilian, he was "familiar with all the arts" (*Institutio oratoria* 12, 11, 21). Even as late as the Reformation, the humanist Philipp Melanchthon (1497–1560) states that the description of Achilles's shield in book 18 of the *Iliad* laid the foundations for astronomy and philosophy. The *Iliad* was traditionally read as an instruction manual for kings and princes, with invaluable lessons on such matters as war and statecraft. The *Odyssey*, on the other hand, was studied and revered as an authoritative encyclopedia of information about domestic life and all the arts appertaining thereto. Thus, between them, the Homeric poems were considered to contain the whole of knowledge of the most necessary sort. Seen this way, the poems laid claim to being a compendium of all the arts and sciences, as well as of the deepest philosophical and theological sources of wisdom.[8]

The philosophical allegorization of epic that had grown up around Homer already in antiquity continued especially with relation to Virgil in the Middle Ages. In the Neoplatonic tradition of Macrobius and Servius, Virgil was

8. A guide throughout my discussion of the ancient and medieval tradition of the liberal arts is Ernst Robert Curtius's *Europäische Literatur und Lateinisches Mittelalter* (Bern: Francke, 1948), 206, trans. Willard R. Trask as *European Literature and the Latin Middle Ages* (New York: Bollingen, 1952). I have also profited particularly from Roland Barthes, "L'Ancienne rhétorique: Aide mémoire," *Communications* 16 (1970): 172–223, and from Henri Irénée Marrou, "Les Arts libéraux dans l'antiquité classique," in *Arts libéraux et philosophie au moyen âge* (Montréal: Institut d'études médiévales, 1967).

viewed as a universal polymath and magician, the master of all knowledge, natural and supernatural.[9] This example of the epic poet was to be emulated in subsequent literary history most completely by Dante, who endeavored to gather into the encyclopedic form of his poem, the *Divine Comedy*, essentially all that was known of human history and culture and to frame it within a comprehensive knowledge of the whole of the cosmos bound together by an intuition of its final Ground, God. This work even includes frequent excursuses on current scientific topics such as embryology, meteorology, the astronomy of moon spots, geometrics, and optics. Dante's own model, of course, to an even greater extent than Virgil, was the Bible. Holy Writ had an even stronger claim to be deemed the paragon of encyclopedias. For the Christian Middle Ages this book was *the* book, the very archetype of the Book, containing all possible books—at least virtually—in its purported character as a total, unified system of knowledge. As a revelation of the Mind of God, the Bible was held to express the original template for the entire Creation.

An incomparably important predecessor to Dante in his totalizing synthesis of traditions by the power and originality of his literary form is Saint Augustine. Augustine's *Confessions*, like Dante's *Commedia*, represent a sort of summa of fundamental philosophical and theological knowledge in the form of an autobiographical narrative. Augustine also wrote other encyclopedic works, including a theological interpretation of universal history: his *De civitate Dei* (*The City of God*). But most interesting to us in the present context is not the system of doctrines that he was to lay out from the Christian vantage point he finally attained through his conversion so much as the autobiographically recorded path that he followed in order to reach his theological vision. The way the two sorts of knowledge, the personal and the systematic, fit together and indeed fuse in tradition, as again in Dante's visionary journey through the three realms of the afterlife, is itself highly instructive concerning the nature of knowledge in the humanities—not to mention in any possible science whatsoever. The personal and poetic search along the path of their respective intellectual-existential journeys is clearly indispensable to the doctrinal knowledge that is ultimately gained by both Dante and Augustine alike.

The universality of poetry, its being the original form of expression of all knowledge, is grounded in the facts that all knowledge is humanly situated and that every human situation can be sounded by poetry. In every

9. Macrobius, *Saturnalia* (Stuttgart: Teubner, 1994), trans. Percival Vaughan Davies (New York: Columbia University Press, 1969), and Servius, *In Virgilii Carmina Commentarii*, ed. Georgius Thilo and Hermannus Hagen (Hildesheim: Georg Olms, 1961), in the fourth century are important sources for this view of Virgil. See Domenico Comparetti, *Virgilio nel medioevo* I (Livorno, 1895), rpt. ed. Giorgio Pasquale (Florence: La Nuova Italia, 1955).

instance, knowledge belongs to *someone* endowed with a particular disposition and placed in specific circumstances. As such, this knowledge can best be expressed by poetry. While science in the modern epoch has tended to dictate paradigms to all disciplines, historically the liberal arts and knowledge generally emerge rather from religious and artistic modes of experience that almost always find expression first in poetic genres. Poetry, as the affectively charged representation of a world, embodies, at the earliest stages of culture, the sort of universality that tends to be accorded only to science later on—at least in the age of the technological domination of society and of its forms of communication. Giambattista Vico, with his *Scienza nuova* (1744), was instrumental to the modern rediscovery of "poetic sapience" at the origins of human culture as the most universal, all-embracing form of knowledge. Vico's "new science" in some sense echoes Aristotle, who already in antiquity, from quite a different type of scientific perspective, had underscored the preeminent capability of poetry to disclose the universal, in which alone true knowledge consists (*Poetics* 1451b).

This means, for example, that the fundamental importance and basic human interest of astronomy—its universal value—might be captured more effectively by a poem than by any astrophysical formula. The words of a poetic text like Psalm 8 communicate the overwhelming wonder of a human being in the face of the mystery of the universe. And just that feeling of awe, in all its immediacy, is what lies at the source of all meaningful astronomical inquiry:

> When I consider the heavens,
> the work of thy fingers,
> the moon and the stars, which thou hast ordained,
> What is man that thou art mindful of him,
> or the son of man, that thou visitest him?

Admittedly, it is possible to obtain from astronomical science much more precise information about the stars and their properties than what is given in these verses. But does that added technical knowledge—for instance, statistics concerning the stars' orbits and material densities—enhance the human being's actual experience of cognitive encounter with the phenomena of the heavens? Does it heighten the sense of belonging to an infinitely fascinating cosmos and the rapt wonderment through which the heavens are perceived as divinely made, or as participating in and as manifesting the mystery of Creation? It certainly could. The technical precisions of modern knowledge of astronomy are nothing if not awe-inspiring. Still, those who love science will not overlook its human dimension and rootedness. Otherwise, we risk suffering an immense human loss for the sake of a merely instrumental gain of "technical" expertise. Knowledge, humanly considered, is valuable in proportion to the intensity and richness of the relationships it enables.

In stressing the human significance and originally poetical character of all knowledge, whether personal or systematic, I wish to valorize scientific inquiry and research in a new and vigorous way rather than to diminish or disparage it. Science is without doubt one of the most thought-provoking gnoseological adventures of the human race in modern times and, in certain respects, of all time. It is the apotheosis of the speculative odyssey that began in Greece in the sixth century B.C. with the first recorded meditations of the pre-Socratic philosophers on the general nature of things.[10] The incalculable complexity and order of Creation, as it has been progressively discovered by the more and more powerful instruments of science—from the microscope to the atomic particle accelerator to the laser beam—fill those who consider it with amazement and coerce minds like Newton's and Einstein's, not to mention many more of humbler capacity, to see evidence that God does not just play dice with the universe. Yet, in order to be this provocative revelation of the infinitely rich and intricate mystery of existence, science needs to retain a sense of the human significance of what it discovers through probing by means of its methods and instruments ever further the facts and the very matter of nature.

Consideration of how epic poetry and pre-Socratic philosophy served as matrices for proto-scientific patterns of thinking makes it clear that the history of science emerges from the history of the humanities. Accordingly, my purpose is not at all to denigrate science but rather to integrate it into the whole spectrum of human knowledge so as to bring out its original unity with human culture broadly construed. The predominant tendency to view all the various disciplines of the liberal arts as species or subspecies of scientific knowledge, more or less rigorous and pure, is practically irresistible. It is one more symptom of the cultural hegemony that science has achieved in our technocratically managed, technologically driven and dependent civilization. However, I am proposing that we can equally well view the humanities and their pursuit of a wisdom that reflects understanding oneself in relation to the general order or disorder of things as embodying the spirit that pervades the entire gamut of the liberal arts. By inducing to empathetic participation in the experience of discovery rather than inculcating a detached domination over positively given fields of objects, the humanities most fully realize the values and virtues of all forms of liberal learning, including the scientific.

Typically, the sciences objectify. They bring into sharp focus a certain field of objects, yet they can tend to block out the human situation that is comprehended by the peripheral vision characteristic of the humanities with their sensitivity to the unfocused, background factors that count so much in determining the overall significance of any experience. In human knowing, there is always a subject who cannot be completely focused as object, but who is

10. The far-reaching destiny of this adventure is profoundly traced by Martin Heidegger, *Early Greek Thinking* (New York: Harper and Row, 1975).

indirectly expressed in countless ways—as intimated, for example, by the tenor of a discourse and the affective nuances of its language, or as conveyed by color and perspective in painting, or by subtle orchestration of emotional tonalities in music. And this is poetry. In humanities studies, we always need to ask what the human meaning and value of a given form or instance of knowledge is, for that is what makes it matter to human beings. Some sort of subjective view and knowledge of the world is expressed even in performance of a musical instrument, or in the choreographing of a dance, or in the crafting of artifacts.[11]

An example from classical poetry can serve to illustrate the ineradicably relational and personal aspects of knowledge that loom into the foreground in humanities texts. Homer recounts with pathos the drama of the encounter between Hector and Andromache, in which Andromache pleads with her husband not to go out to battle, where he is going to be killed by Achilles and so leave her a widow and her son an orphan. Like any human experience, this encounter is not per se a fully determinate object of knowledge, a discrete entity, one and the same for all concerned. Andromache's predicament is apprehended through her personal history and is expressed in terms of personal symbols: they are first her own, and then they belong to any reader who becomes involved in interpreting her story. As its appropriations in later literature, for example, by Baudelaire in "Le Cygne" ("Andromaque, je pense à vous . . .") suggest, this drama is bound to mean something different to every individual. Homer's Andromache pleads movingly with Hector:

> "Dearest,
> your own great strength will be your death, and you have no pity
> on your little son, nor on me, ill-starred, who soon must be your widow;
> for presently the Achaians, gathering together,
> will set upon you and kill you; and for me it would be far better
> to sink into the earth when I have lost you, for there is no other
> consolation for me after you have gone to your destiny—
> only grief; since I have no father, no honoured mother.
> It was brilliant Achilleus who slew my father, Eëtion,
> when he stormed the strong-founded citadel of the Kilikians,

11. Particularly feminist criticism has pointed in this direction, for example, Hilary Rose, "Hand, Brain and Heart: A Feminist Epistemology for the Natural Sciences," *Signs: Journal of Women in Culture and Society* 9, no. 1 (1983); and Sarah Harding and Merrill Hintikka, eds., *Discovering Reality: Feminist Perspectives on Epistemology, Metaphysics, Methodology and Philosophy of Science* (Dordrecht: Reidel, 1983). Along comparable lines, Kenneth L. Wilson and Florin Lowndes propound an "integrative epistemology" in "Heart-Thinking: An Archetypal Epistemology for the Humanities and the Sciences," *International Humanities Journal* 1 (2003): 1–12.

> Thebe of the towering gates. He killed Eëtion
> but did not strip his armour, for his heart respected the dead man,
> but burned the body in all its elaborate war-gear
> and piled a grave mound over it, and the nymphs of the mountains,
> daughters of Zeus of the aegis, planted elm trees about it.
> And they who were my seven brothers in the great house all went
> upon a single day down into the house of the death god,
> for swift-footed brilliant Achilleus slaughtered all of them
> as they were tending their white sheep and their lumbering oxen;
> and when he had led my mother, who was queen under wooded Plakos,
> here, along with all his other possessions, Achilleus
> released her again, accepting ransom beyond count, but Artemis
> of the showering arrows struck her down in the halls of her father.
> Hektor, thus you are father to me, and my honoured mother,
> you are my brother, and you it is who are my young husband.
> Please take pity upon me then, stay here on the rampart,
> that you may not leave your child an orphan, your wife a widow,
> but draw your people up by the fig tree, there where the city
> is openest to attack, and where the wall may be mounted."
>
> (*Iliad* 6.404–34, Lattimore trans.)

Everyone experiences the scene described by Andromache in a personal way, as projected onto their own existence. Each of us has our own horizon of possibilities, past and future, and each of us understands Andromache's predicament by reference to what for us personally would constitute loss of that which is most vital to us—the central relationship or core or unifying concern of our lives. Understanding the experience of others entails mapping its crucial features onto the coordinates of our own personal experience. In this sense, human experience calls to be understood from the inside rather than only as an object of analysis.

Just such a pitiful portrait of the widow of a fallen warrior being led away captive, like Andromache, recurs only a little later in the *Odyssey*. The bard Demodocus's singing of the tragedy of Troy causes Odysseus, in disguise among the Phaeacians, to break into torrential weeping, "As a woman wails embracing her husband who has fallen before his own city and people, defending the city and its children from the day of doom" (*Odyssey* 8.521–31, Cook trans.). Odysseus is moved by these heart-rending tales to divulge his identity and even to elaborate it poetically in the riveting recital of his travels related in books 9 through 12. This moment demonstrates how he is provoked and changed personally through representations in poetry—by which means he then continues to forge his own legendary persona.

Odysseus's harrowing and transformative tears in reaction to poetic images turn up again at a later stage in tradition in Aeneas's contemplation, on a temple in Carthage, of murals representing the already legendary battles before Troy's gates. Aeneas discovers here the "tears of things" ("lacrimae rerum"), which speak of universal human experiences that are communicated, especially by poetry and art, across languages and cultures. By representing the "tears of things," and thus treating objects as subjects, poetry expresses and actually contributes to "making" things what they really are, humanly and affectively. It is in some such sense that Blake, too, can speak of a tear as an "intellectual thing." By freeing the subjective valences of things that are cemented into representations of objects, poetry releases their affects to flow from age to age. It becomes thereby the medium of a transmission of experience through intelligible symbols that reveal humanity to itself in a perspective that is constitutive of its history. The history evoked here is that of the human heart or mind and of how it is "touched by mortal things" ("sunt lacrimae rerum et mentem mortalia tangunt," *Aeneid* 1.462).

To this extent, the process of knowledge in the humanities is closer to the activity of reading than to direct, sensorial perception. Classical science tends to understand all knowledge on the model of the perception of an object. The object to be known is what it is wholly apart from the knower and the question of *who* he or she is. Knowers simply open their "eyes" and perceive what is objectively in front of them. In reading, on the other hand, the text in front of the reader's eyes does not become known, except as it is assimilated into the reader's own interior world: it is reformulated in the reader's memory and imagination, and this subjects the text to all manner of influences from the reader's own individual existence and personal concerns.

Indeed all knowledge, including scientific knowledge, when approached from the distinctive point of view of the humanities, is in crucial ways more like reading than like sensory perception. For all knowledge is humanly conditioned and situated. Traditionally, science has wished to forget, or at least to delimit, the effects of this situatedness by an intense, narrow focus on the object alone. However, a subject is the condition of possibility of having an object in the first place. "Subject" and "object" are nothing if not correlative terms. The subject is constantly reading himself or herself into the object, and this encounter and interaction with the object in turn is necessary to constitute the subject.[12]

Today, more than ever, we need a broader perspective than that of the hard sciences taken in and for themselves, a perspective that recognizes aspects of reality that cannot be objectified and subjected to scientific scrutiny without distortion. After all, why is technology increasingly achieving dominion over the earth and destroying the physical, together with the human, environment in so many appalling ways? The name "Chernobyl," conjuring up the specter of a transcontinental nuclear disaster, is perhaps most apt to suggest

12. The philosophical underpinnings of such awareness are investigated especially by phenomenological currents of thought and criticism in the wake of Edmund Husserl and Maurice Merleau-Ponty.

some of the more sensational aspects of this pervasive catastrophe. But there are "accidents" all the time, such as calamitous oceanic oil slicks, that prove disastrous for the earth, and these are relatively isolated incidents compared with the constant polluting every day that accumulates and exacerbates, among other problems, the greenhouse effect threatening to make our planet uninhabitable. We see everywhere, moreover, the deliberate, rampant ravaging of the natural environment by urbanization, the defacing and complete disappearance of coastlines crammed with construction, or again the all-too-conspicuous eyesore of river banks heaped with the wreckage and waste of industrial production and consumption.

Such spectacles appall our sight. However, this tragedy occurs even earlier and more insidiously within the human spirit that endures subjection to a view of the natural world as consisting in mere material objects available for manipulation, with loss of the human dimension—and a fortiori the divine one—which characterizes the world as it is revealed in innumerable works of the tradition of the humanities. The effects of this crisis of the spirit have become manifest over and over again in the arts and culture of the twentieth century and beyond—for example, in Dada and surrealism, in existentialism, in the ecology movement, in religious revivals east and west, including "new age" religions and naturist cults. All in various ways represent a revolt against the invincible automatization that implacably advances in the ever more highly technologized civilization of our present historical era—the disturbing aftermath of the second millennium and troubled embarkation upon the third.[13]

Because the outlook of science and technology can view only objects, it eclipses the dimension of the infinite and indefinable that is present in whatever is human—for example, in the infinite value of a single human life. All that can be specified as an object never adds up to the human individual, nor can it begin to exhaust the mystery of personal identity, not to mention that of the divine person of which the human is held traditionally to be a reflection or "image." Science cannot pick it up on the radar screen or stethoscope or X-ray machine or electroencephalograph. For it is no object but rather belongs irreducibly to the being of a subject. The light of science can make perceptible only objects, but objects can be objects only in relation to subjects, which a

13. A peculiarly prescient philosophical reflection on this catastrophe is found in Martin Heidegger, "Die Frage nach der Technik," in *Vorträge und Aufsätze* (Pfullingen: Neske, 1954), trans. as "The Question Concerning Technology," in *Basic Writings*, ed. David Krell (New York: HarperCollins, 1993). It is developed into an ecological philosophy by his student, Hans Jonas, *Das Prinzip Verantwortung: Versuch einer Ethik für die technologische Zivilisation* (Frankfurt: Insel, 1979), trans. H. Jonas and David Herr as *The Imperative Responsibility: In Search of Ethics for the Technological Age* (Chicago: University of Chicago Press, 1984).

certain conventional, mainstream science tends, nevertheless, inevitably to reduce to the status of just objects among other objects.[14] Poetry, conversely, tends to animate objects, to treat all things as subjects. The sea takes on personality as Neptune, trees are inhabited by nymphs named dryads, the air by sprites, heaven and earth become Uranos and Gaia, "the hills leap like rams," and "the earth rejoices in the Lord," at the sound of his coming.

As these quotations and allusions illustrate, humanities texts are almost without exception also religious texts.[15] This is the case at least in the sense that they take some sort of stand concerning the whence and wherefore of human existence, but often also more specifically through the express imagination of divinity. For humanity does not exclude divinity but is defined rather in relation to it. Humanity, from earliest times in virtually all known cultures, has conceived of itself vis-à-vis some form of divinity. In one way or another, virtually all the classic works of the humanities tradition happen to propose what may be understood as profoundly religious visions of life.[16]

Although religion may mean very different things, this ineluctable involvement with religion in some guise is even more evident close to the origins of the humanities tradition. Homer is the source book of Greek religion at a stage when religion is undifferentiated from myth. Virgil elaborates a theological justification of the political empire of Rome, a theodicy—even as he simultaneously questions and undermines it. Dante adopts classical tradition and programmatically Christianizes it by reinterpreting classical figures and myths as anticipations and foreshadowings of revealed Christian truth. The calling or summons to fullness of human vision and experience is conceived in all these texts as issuing from some kind of at least quasi-divine source such as the poet's Muse. The Bible and Augustine's *Confessions*, finally, are religious classics par excellence. This apparent inseparability of humanity

14. This paradigm of science, of course, is increasingly outdated and contested, even within the sciences themselves, beginning perhaps most vigorously from the life sciences. Some insights into the paradigm shift can be gleaned from David Ray Griffin, ed., *The Reenchantment of Science: Postmodern Proposals* (New York: SUNY Press, 1988).

15. Overtly anti-religious works such as Nietzsche's *The Antichrist* or Freud's *The Future of an Illusion* attack specific forms of religiosity and propose alternative ways of envisioning and relating to life as a whole, and in this sense they are still, at least negatively, "religious" in their scope of vision. For a compelling religious reading of atheist philosophers Nietzsche, Marx, and Freud, see Merold Westphal, *Suspicion and Faith: The Religious Uses of Modern Atheism* (New York: Fordham University Press, 1998).

16. Examples of how this is being rediscovered by critical theory in our "post-secular age" can be found in Mark Knight and Louise Lee, eds., *Religion, Literature, and the Imagination: Sacred Worlds* (London: Continuum, 2010).

and divinity calls for elucidation—it constitutes a vital topic for reflection within studies in the humanities.

To sum up what has been said here on the threshold of this study in the humanities: we are involved in what we know. Science necessarily forgets and abstracts from this subjective condition of all our knowledge in the *interests* of universality, objectivity, and disinterestedness. But note the contradiction. Science, too, stems from human interest, and it never transcends this starting point as its indispensable condition.[17] Science is no less humanly involved than any other type of knowledge, even though for methodological reasons it undertakes to filter and separate out this human element from its object of study. Humanities studies, in contrast, move this human element on to center stage: they underscore the human conditionedness of all knowledge and therewith also its generally subjective dimensions and aspects.

The point here is not to diminish the importance nor to challenge the integrity of science but rather to see science in its essential unity with human concerns and endeavors. For this purpose, we can do no better than to turn to the history of education. Having characterized the specificity of human knowledge in descriptive terms, most succinctly as "involved" knowing, and having brought out its resistance to being measured by the standards of scientific method, we must now open a deeper perspective into the historical development of this sort of knowledge. In doing so, we will continue to view the knowledge specific to the humanities in its relation to the scientific knowledge that apparently contrasts with human knowing but actually develops only within and from it. Science and its methods can become a threat to human knowing only if the distinctive character of knowledge in the humanities is not understood and respected.

III. Vicissitudes of the Liberal Arts in the History of Education

When we lengthen our historical perspective and take a look at how humanities, arts, and science have positioned themselves relative to one another throughout the history of education in the Occident, what we find is an original inseparability and virtual indifferentiation of science (*episteme*) and art (*techne*). Originally, the Greek word for "art," τέχνη, meant all types of human activity as rational—that is, inasmuch as they involve some form of knowing. Medicine thus qualifies as a prime example of an "art," since it is based on knowledge of the microcosm of the human body and its humors in relation to the harmonies of the macrocosm, or the universe as a whole. This is certainly what it was for its ancient founders, eminently Hippocrates (fifth

17. Jürgen Habermas, *Erkenntniss und Interesse* (Frankfurt: Suhrkamp, 1968), trans. as *Knowledge and Human Interests* (Cambridge, Eng.: Polity, 1987).

century B.C.).[18] The same goes for astronomy and even mathematics. In fact, Aristotle writes of "mathematical arts" and "poetic science." The two, science and art, are so much a part of the same thing that the Greek words for them can be used sometimes interchangeably.

This near equivalence is preserved at least covertly and unconsciously today in our word "technology." Although technology seems to us to be automatically associated with science, so that we speak in one breath of "science and technology," this word tellingly sinks its roots back into the Greek word for "art"—namely, *techne*. On reflection, this need not surprise us, since science and its objectivity are necessarily rooted in human concern and involvement such as the arts express with peculiar translucency and power. Even a physical object or artifact reveals itself to us only in relation to our existence, with its specific exigencies and interests, as *for* something, as defined by a network of relations that confer its being and human meaning upon it, and to this extent even physical science cannot escape a certain measure of "art." Whether they are considered scientific or artistic, human modes of knowing are also modes of relating; they express an existential relationship to the things with which they are concerned.[19] Arts and sciences are indeed in this sense one and have, accordingly, been joined in the curriculum of the liberal arts since antiquity.

The sort of knowledge that characterizes the humanities as at once *techne* and *episteme*, as both art and science, has been pursued throughout the history of education under the heading of the "liberal arts." Liberal arts programs embrace both science and humanities. This is so because both are pursued together as essentially human forms of intellectual development and enrichment of persons. In this frame of general education, all knowledge is seen as fundamentally human, and in this sense the liberal arts as a whole can be understood as hinging on the humanities: all are ultimately for the sake of the development of the human individual. This orientation of the arts and sciences becomes especially perspicuous in a historical perspective.

---

18. Andrzej Szczeklik, *Catharsis: On the Art of Medicine*, trans. Antonia Lloyd-Jones, foreword by Czesław Miłosz (Chicago: University of Chicago Press, 2005) revives this outlook from within the practice of medicine today. The same challenge is taken up also by Edmund D. Pellegrino in his numerous works on medical humanities, bioethics, and the philosophy of medicine, starting from *A Philosophical Basis of Medical Practice: Toward a Philosophy and Ethic of the Healing Professions*, coauthored with David C. Thomasma (New York: Oxford University Press, 1981).

19. Martin Heidegger's analysis of human existence (*Dasein*, Being-there) as Being-in-the-world is based on relation to worldly beings' readiness-to-hand (*Zuhandenheit*), or their being adapted to use, as prior to their presence-at-hand (*Vorhandenheit*), or their just being objectively there, provides a penetrating philosophical elucidation of this ontological condition. See *Sein und Zeit* (Tübingen: Niemeyer, 1963 [1927]), 69–76 and 106, trans. J. Macquarie and E. Robinson, *Being and Time* (New York: Harper and Row, 1962).

The traditional canon of the liberal arts as it came to be fixed in late antiquity for the whole of the Middle Ages, embraces seven disciplines: Grammar, Rhetoric, Dialectics, Arithmetic, Geometry, Music, and Astronomy.[20] The first three of these disciplines were grouped together and known as the Trivium. All are in various ways language arts and cultivate verbal skills. The four remaining disciplines—making up the Quadrivium—are all quantitative in nature instead. Music, too, was treated as a science of numbers and proportions and even as a pure mathematics: it was every bit as quantitative—or abstract and exact—as astronomy, which concerned measurements of heavenly bodies and their motions.

The Seven Liberal Arts

Trivium	*Quadrivium*
Grammar, Rhetoric, Dialectics	Arithmetic, Geometry, Music, Astronomy
(verbal arts)	(quantitative arts)

Speculation on the rank and sequence of the various liberal arts was rife from ancient times, all through the Middle Ages, and on into the Renaissance. Indeed it remains in different guises a burning issue still today. At stake here is the selection and valuation of the types of study the young are trained in, and thus the basic outlook imparted to mature individuals—the very mentality imprinted by a civilization on those whose minds it forms and nurtures. One idea that was frequently broached from early on is that the language arts constitute the necessary basis for all further learning. The *word* thus assumes a leading role as the enabling factor and the originating source of knowledge. Grammar, the art of writing, accordingly, was conceived as the foundation of all the arts and, consequently, of all knowledge. It could even be taken to reveal the origins and essences of things themselves. Theological support for this idea was found in the biblical doctrine of Creation by the Word (Genesis 1 and John 1:1–3), which declares the divine Word to be at the very origin of the existence of all things. One great champion of grammar, for example, Isidore of Seville in the seventh century, in his encyclopedic *Etymologiarum*, analyzed the names of things etymologically in order to discover inherent in them the intrinsic natures of the things named. In this perspective, the complex interconnections between love (*amor*), death (*mors*), and bitter (*amer*) could all be found written into the respective (Latin) words for these things, the names of which seem to suggest their intimate relations. All reality in this manner was conceived of as revealed immanently in language.

---

20. This roster was established especially by Martianus Capella's *On the Marriage of Philology and Mercury* (*De nuptiis Philologiae et Mercurii*, 439 A.D.), which became a standard textbook in the Middle Ages.

According to another variant, the integrating factor of all knowledge and education could be found in the art of persuasion, namely, rhetoric. Thus Quintilian—following Cicero's ethical-philosophical slanting of the art of oratory—exalted the perfect orator or rhetorician as the consummate master of all fields of knowledge. In the same manner, the third member of the Trivium, dialectics, the art of discerning the truth by logical analysis, was considered by philosophers in the lineage of Plato as furnishing the only reliable criterion of true knowledge as against opinion. All of these views make the Trivium, or one particular branch of it, primary as the noblest part and the true basis of all learning.

However, it was also possible to emphasize rather the preliminary status of the first three disciplines in the series in order to claim greater prestige for the Quadrivium as comprising the higher disciplines furnishing substantive knowledge, for which the verbal disciplines were considered as merely a propaedeutic. More generally, this reflects the split between linguistic and mathematical approaches to learning that has created tensions in every age, just as it continues to do still today. Plato, for example, took mathematics as the model of true knowledge and associated poetry with illusory images. On his authority, ever since antiquity, philosophy has often asserted its hegemony over poetry, which is charged with purveying merely pleasing fictions or even malicious lies. The battle between literature-based, poetic knowledge and more logically rigorous and rational forms of knowledge is perennial. Plato's banishment of the poets from his ideal Republic (book 10), on grounds that their representations are too far removed from the truth, set a precedent that history has frequently repeated. In the high Middle Ages, a predominantly rhetorical culture based on literary study was again challenged by the newer proto-scientific and systematic reasoning that asserted itself in the shape of Scholasticism. Humanities learning, which flourished, for example, in the school of Chartres during the twelfth century, was eventually superseded by the dialectical theology emanating from the University of Paris in the thirteenth century.[21]

The pattern of conflict between proponents of classical literary tradition and advocates of various forms of rational critique continued in the Renaissance. A great age for this debate is reached with the humanism of the Italian Renaissance. Scholars such as Coluccio Salutati (1331–1406), Leonardo Bruni (1370–1444), and Giovanni Pontano (1426–1503) attempted to recuperate the sense of all knowledge as fundamentally poetic in nature.[22] The

21. John Marenbon, "Humanism, Scholasticism and the School of Chartres," *International Journal of the Classical Tradition* 6, no. 4 (2000): 569–77; R. W. Southern, *Scholastic Humanism and the Unification of Europe, I, Foundations* (Oxford: Blackwell, 1995).

22. A powerful contemporary proponent of this philosophical tradition is Ernesto Grassi, *Rhetoric as Philosophy: The Humanist Tradition* (University Park: Pennsylvania State University Press, 1980).

pendulum swings back again with the founding of modern science, emblematically in Francis Bacon's *Novum Organum* (1620). This work establishes a logic of scientific inquiry on the basis of observation and experimentation guided by the principle of induction. No less influentially, René Descartes's *Discourse on Method* (1637) rejects the whole tradition of learning handed down in words from generation to generation in order to begin building the impregnable edifice of certain, deductive knowledge anew on the foundation of the individual inquirer's own clear and distinct perceptions. Indeed, the whole history of education can be viewed schematically as playing out the tensions between poetic or literary learning and culture, on the one hand, and technical, scientific types of knowledge on the other. While Plato (429–347 B.C.) banishes most poets from his Republic, for other ancient thinkers, like the almost exactly contemporary Isocrates (436–338 B.C.), poets are the key educators, those who are able to lead the soul through images to truth. The tensions between the more humanistic and the more scientific orientation of studies today—felt acutely, for example, at the level of university budgetary allocations—are the prolongation of this ancient rivalry that turns sometimes into deadly strife.

Just as hotly debated as the relative rank among the various liberal arts was their place, as a group, within the overall order of knowledge. Were the liberal arts, taken together, to serve as preparation for some higher type of study, such as philosophy or theology, or law, or could they be considered to be an end in themselves, even the ultimate attainment of knowledge or culture, and hence, at least in the medieval view, of human perfection? Hugh of St. Victor, followed by Thomas Aquinas, makes the *artes* a propaedeutic for philosophy, while for Saint Bonaventure all arts and sciences depend directly on theology and ultimately on revelation for their unity, clarity, and completeness.[23] The idea of taking theology as "the ultimate 'social science' " is not without its advocates still today. John Milbank argues indeed that theology, as God's imparted self-knowledge, must lay claim to being solely capable, on its own terms, of discerning completely the truth concerning the universe and human beings' existence within it and thus to being the one form of knowledge that can correctly position all the others.[24]

Efforts to co-opt the liberal arts into some other program of education for which they would serve as a foundation began early. However, the intention

---

23. Hugh of St. Victor, *Eruditio Didascalica*, in *Patrologia Latina*, vol. 176, ed. J.-P. Migne (Turnholti: Brepols, 1862); Bonaventure, *De reductione artium ad theologiam*, ed. Sister Emma Thérèse Healy (Saint Bonaventure, N.Y.: Franciscan Institute, 1955), 2nd ed.

24. John Milbank, *Theology and Social Theory: Beyond Secular Reason* (London: Blackwell, 2006 [1990]), 6. See also Milbank's "The Conflict of the Faculties: Theology and the Economy of the Sciences," in *The Future of Love: Essays in Political Theology* (Eugene, Ore.: Cascade, 2009), 301–15.

was not necessarily to instrumentalize the liberal arts, so that their practical value could be cashed out for purposes extraneous to themselves, so much as to continue in their spirit of liberal learning for its own sake carried over into further spheres of intellectual endeavor or of concrete life. For Galen (c. 130–c. 210 A.D.), in the tradition of Hippocrates, the arts were preparatory to the study of medicine, but medicine entailed a complete and even a contemplative knowledge of the general order of the cosmos. For Vitruvius, in the first century B.C., the arts readied the student for studying architecture, which was conceived of as the all-embracing framework of knowledge, since the works and activities of all the arts and sciences, and of civilization as a whole, needed to be situated somewhere within the spaces defined by architecture.

Similar sorts of subordination of the liberal arts have occurred for religious motives in the myriad syntheses since antiquity of Judeo-Christian with classical Greco-Roman tradition. For Philo, Clement, and Origen in the first and second centuries in Alexandria, as well as for church fathers in the Roman tradition up to Carolingian times, and then particularly for Alcuin (735–804), the liberal arts were the necessary prerequisite for advanced studies in philosophy and theology. Already this might suggest, at least ambiguously, their being understood as techniques valuable for their utility in application to some purpose beyond themselves. But this is certainly not the understanding of their nature that is most proper to the liberal arts as such—unless we understand them as being integrated in this way into the highest, omnicomprehensive forms of knowledge represented by medicine, architecture, philosophy, or theology, and thus as participating in the ultimate ends of humanity.

Inherent in the very words *artes liberales* is the idea that these studies are essentially not subservient but free and autonomous and valuable for their own sake quite apart from their professional and pragmatic applications. Aristotle so defines them in book 8, chapter 2 of the *Politics*. In Seneca's statement, famous in antiquity, the *artes liberales* are those arts whose purpose is *not* to make money (Letter 88). This notion, at its purest, involves a sort of contemplative ideal, whereby knowledge taken for itself is esteemed as the highest value for humans. Aristotle established this value of knowledge for its own sake by defining metaphysics as "first philosophy" and explaining that its being studied for the sake of nothing else beyond itself was the greatest distinction and honor possible for any type of knowing (*Metaphysics*, book 1, chapter 2). In this perspective, the highest form of human life is the intellectual one, quite independently of any instrumental value that the uses of the intellect may have. The act of intellection, coinciding with love—in essence a purely intellectual act for Plato—is the most perfect human activity, and to achieve it is to participate even in divinity in the Platonic and especially the Neoplatonic conception.

The liberal arts, when studied for their own sake, thus partake of the kind of knowing considered as in itself the supreme realization of being human. The idea of their forming a continuum with philosophy and theology—each of which, in its own way, also claims to be first and final knowledge—actually validates the ideal that the liberal arts should incarnate knowledge as an end in itself. Taken in their radical freedom as liberal study, the "humanities" tend to transcend all given frameworks and all set definitions of human ends and purposes. They thereby open knowledge to speculative scrutiny and to creative reinvention. Such speculative pursuit of knowledge in the humanities opens up and probes the question of what lies beyond—or at least of what globally determines—the horizon of the human. In this sense, liberal studies can be understood as intrinsically philosophical and even as implicitly theological. The free exercise of knowledge in any field whatsoever (whether geometry or music or grammar) is a way of contemplating the general order of things from a particular perspective: every aspect or dimension of the cosmos reveals, from a certain angle of vision, the nature of the entire ensemble. In this outlook, the ultimate ground or raison d'être of all things can be fathomed analogically through each specific kind of liberal study in relation to some special subject matter. Each subject is pursued freely and as unlimited in its potential for illuminating and fulfilling individuals by relating them to reality as a whole.

Without this dimension of a vocation to free contemplation of all that is, the personal and human character of all real, concrete knowledge would be eclipsed: it would become instrumentalized and would serve merely as a tool for some extrinsic and pragmatic purpose bound inevitably to material interests. Indeed, the dominant tendency in modern times is to construe the liberal arts as serviceable tools or as preparatory exercises. Math and science, as well as English, can be necessary and useful training for further technical and professional specialization. College catalogs typically state that training in the study of the liberal arts is "fundamental" because it is "the basis of all professional study" (Vanderbilt University Catalogue, 1991).

This type of statement can easily be misleading and risks marginalizing the spirit of the humanities, which—properly understood—animates the whole spectrum of the liberal arts. Unless it is made clear that the liberal arts prepare for professional study only indirectly by forging whole individuals capable of applying their talents in whatever ways they choose and by instilling in them the pure passion to learn, this view reflects the demise of belief in liberal learning and in the intellectual life it enables as itself the highest activity of which a human being is capable. It eventually leads to the abandonment of study of the liberal arts for other types of "training," which will undoubtedly be proved by statistics to be more effective preparation for careers in our ever more technical working world. Nevertheless, such results and their implications also continue to be a subject of vigorous debate. It is often ably argued that precisely the mental flexibility of a non-vocational, non-technical study of liberal arts is most apt to empower young minds to adapt to situations and technologies that change faster than instructional programs can be revamped.[25]

Science and humanities alike within the liberal arts curriculum have, since antiquity, had as their purpose not so much technical mastery and the objective knowledge of facts as individual development and the enhancement of human cultural life. The word in ancient Greek for education was *paideia*—the cultural forming of children.[26] In German, the word for education or culture is *Bildung*, and it concerns the disciplined building up of persons into full realization of their human potential. Science is part of this. It belongs to the concerted program of development of the whole individual. Only in this context do the sciences remain connected with and mindful of their own final meaning and purpose. To this extent, the humanities have set the tone for the liberal arts since earliest times. It was never completely forgotten in antiquity that the humanities, or more broadly the liberal arts, according to their most proper calling, were to be viewed as a kind of *haute culture* without further purpose or ulterior motives—the priceless culture of a free person. For Cicero, the art of living, *ars vivendi*, was the only one worth learning. By their own original conception, all the liberal arts are valuable to the extent that they teach—together with whatever specific technical instruction—this art of living.

For Augustine, in his challenging dialogue *De ordine*, written at Cassaciacum in 386 A.D., shortly after his conversion to Christianity and while he was still very close to his first profession as a teacher of rhetoric, all the liberal arts are taught "partly for their use in life, partly for knowledge and contemplation of things" ("artes illae omnes liberales, partim ad usum vitae, partim ad cognitionem rerum contemplationemque discantur"). It is, moreover, "very difficult to pursue them except for someone who ingeniously from very youth has been constantly and insistently devoted to their practice" ("usum earum assequi difficillimum est nisi ei qui ab ipsa pueritia ingeniosissimus instantissime atque constantissime operam dederit").[27]

25. See Martha C. Nussbaum, *Cultivating Humanity: A Classical Defense of Reform in Liberal Education* (Cambridge, Mass.: Harvard University Press, 1997) for contemporary perspectives on the continuing value of classical education, as well as on the need for adaptations. *Not For Profit: Why Democracy Needs the Humanities* (Princeton, N.J.: Princeton University Press, 2010) accentuates and updates her case. Harry R. Lewis, *Excellence Without a Soul: Does Liberal Education Have a Future?* (New York: Public Affairs, 2007) is a clarion call to defend this model of education.

26. Werner Jaeger, *Paedeia: Die Formung des grieschichen Menschen* (Berlin: W. de Gruyter, 1934), trans. Gilbert Highet as *Paedeia: The Ideals of Greek Culture* (New York: Oxford University Press, 1939).

27. Augustine, *De ordine*, ed. Silvano Borruso (South Bend: St. Augustine's Press, 2007), 2.16.44.

Drawing particularly on Cicero's *Tusculan Disputations*, Augustine portrays reason (and by implication philosophy) as the origin of the liberal arts and of human society in general. Building on this foundation, reason recognizes itself at work in the creation of the sciences and is led by this critical reflection to *self*-knowledge and eventually to the knowledge of God and his providence as the ground of reason itself and as the supreme rational principle governing the universe.

Augustine's system of the order of knowledge gears it all consistently toward self-knowledge and intellectual "conversion."[28] The theological implications of this kind of knowledge are insisted on throughout the *De ordine*, which has been recognized as the first philosophical exposition of the systematic unity and progression of the seven liberal arts.[29] For Augustine, all studies in every domain of nature and culture illuminate the nature and freedom of the divine reason beyond human ken that is manifest analogically in the order of things throughout the universe. The ultimate aim of such study is nothing less than the blessed life, as Augustine makes explicit in the contemporaneous dialogue *De vita beata* (386).[30]

Accordingly, each liberal art should be understood not just as a separate discipline unto itself but as a way of contemplating the universe as a whole and so of seeing each kind of knowledge in relation to all the others. Each liberal art is open to every other and, in fact, to all fields of knowledge as complementary lenses for contemplating the whole cosmos together with the place of the individual knower within it. All knowledge is relational and without intrinsic limits—and, in this sense, ultimately "religious" in scope and tenor. Liberal arts do not just add a few enticing ornaments of a more frivolous kind to the technical training that would be the real business of higher education. They are rather the soul of education as it has been understood throughout the Western tradition. They offer an initiation into a whole approach to living through awareness of self as vitally related to others in the overall order of things in the universe.

Transmitting Augustine's vision, John Scott Eriugena (c. 810–c. 877) underscores the speculative purport of liberal learning and its leading to an all-encompassing theological wisdom. He conceives of "the seven disciplines

28. Michael Patrick Foley, *The "De ordine" of St. Augustine* (Ann Arbor, Mich.: UMI, 2006).

29. Ilsetraut Hadot, *Arts libéraux et philosophie dans la pensée antique: Contribution à l'histoire de l'éducation et de la culture dans l'antiquité* (Paris: Vrin, 2005 [1984]), 101–36.

30. Augustine's seminal role in the comprehensive idea of education propounded here is further sounded by Henri I. Marrou, *Saint Augustin et la fin de la culture antique*, 4th ed. (Paris: Boccard, 1958), and in *Augustine and Liberal Education*, ed. Kim Paffenroth and Kevin L. Hughes (Aldershot, Eng.: Ashgate, 2000).

which philosophers call liberal" as "symbols of the plenitude of intelligible contemplation, in which God and creatures are most purely known" ("Septem disciplinas, quas philosophi liberales appellant, intelligibilis contemplativae plenitudinis, qua Deus et creatura purissime cognoscitur, significationes esse astruit"). He affirms that, "just as many waters from diverse sources flow together and run into the bed of a single river, so the natural and liberal disciplines are gathered and run together into one and the same figure of internal contemplation, that supreme fountain of all wisdom, which is Christ, thence to meander among diverse theological speculations" ("Ut enim multae aquae ex diversis fontibus in unius fluminis alveum confluunt atque decurrunt, ita naturales et liberales disciplinae in una eademque internae contemplationis significatione adunantur, quem summus fons totius sapientiae, qui est Christus, undique per diversas theologiae speculationes insinuate").[31] Such contemplation of the intrinsic unity of knowledge as a whole was the Augustinian legacy that would continue to develop throughout the Middle Ages, particularly from the Carolingian Renaissance forward.[32]

The humanities in this view emerge as the lifeblood of the liberal arts. We have at least glimpsed a perspective hailing from antiquity in which liberal education in the humanities appears as the vital center of all learning rather than as peripheral and as merely preparatory to vocational training. Of course, this latter goal may also be achieved at the same time and in the best way. We have seen emerge, on counts both of method and history, the claim of the humanities to be an autonomous form of universal knowing. The humanities offer their own kind of wisdom, which is not to be supplanted by any technique or system: it has proved to be indispensable to the working and to the very sense of the whole system of knowledge as it has evolved down to our own modern predicament. Humanities knowledge even stakes a claim to being considered the pinnacle of this whole edifice of knowledge—a claim that great books courses aim to test and defend. These reflections must suffice to suggest preliminarily the paramount importance of this traditional form of cultivation to the health and development of a humanity that exceeds the dimensions of all possible objects of scientific analysis and opens upon the mystery and infinity of all that is—upon what from age to age has been conceived of persistently in terms of "the divine."

31. Eriugena, *Super caelestem hierarchiam* I, in *Patrologia latina* 122, pp. 139–40. *Patrologiae Cursus Completus: Series Latina* (Paris: J. P. Migne, 1844–64).

32. Marie-Thérèse d'Alverny, "La sagesse et ses sept filles: Recherches sur les allégories de la philosophie et des arts libéraux du IXe au XIIe siècle," in *Mélanges dédiés à la mémoire de Félix Grat* (Paris: Pecqer-Grat, 1946), 1: 245–78.

Chapter 1

✦

Humanities Tradition and the Bible

I. The Bible as Exemplary Humanities Text

Certain distinctive qualities of knowledge in the humanities were understood more profoundly, or at least more intriguingly, in antiquity and the Middle Ages than they are today. This applies particularly to the knowledge conveyed through literary texts. The nature of such knowledge has in some ways been obscured through the scientific approach of modern philology. With the rise of modern empirical science as the dominant paradigm for knowing, texts are taken as specimens for analysis and are dissected according to the will and criteria of a knowing subject considered to be wholly external to them. Previously, it was possible for the text to exercise sovereign authority in determining its own meaning and in interrogating the reader and potentially challenging the reader's insight and very integrity.

Bound up with this sovereignty, the poetic text was capable of assuming a theological aura. This is most evident and explicit in the case of the Bible as paradigmatic text. However, before the secularist turn of culture in modernity, certain other literary texts, too, were attributed a quasi-prophetic authority and revelatory power. They were treated as authoritative sources of an event of truth in a sense that we are now in a position to recover thanks to what can be called the post-secular turn of postmodern culture.[1] Part of my purpose in what follows is to extend from the Bible to the humanities fields and literature more broadly an approach freed from secularist dogmas that reduce texts to inert objects for our examination, thereby exorcizing their authoritative voices and preempting their ability to speak to us and so to structure the encounter with the reader in their own way.

---

1. Post-secularity has been discussed most intensively in theology and philosophy, for example, in *Post-Secular Philosophy: Between Philosophy and Theology*, ed. Phillip Blond (London: Routledge, 1998). Concerning specifically the Bible, see Hans W. Frei, *The Eclipse of Biblical Narrative: A Study in Eighteenth and Nineteenth Century Hermeneutics* (New Haven, Conn.: Yale University Press, 1974).

Rather than understanding the humanities as some lesser kind of science, a clumsy application of scientific method to a more recalcitrant sort of material, I propose to understand the whole liberal arts curriculum (which traditionally included the language arts of grammar, rhetoric, and dialectic, but also the quantitative sciences of geometry, arithmetic, astronomy, and music) from the point of view of the humanities. Seen from this angle, liberal learning in science and arts alike shows up as driven by the human interests that motivate all search for knowledge. Such knowledge, moreover, as is clearest in the case of the knowledge gained through humanities texts, turns out always to be in some way self-knowledge—a knowing of one's own limits and of one's place in the overall scheme of things. This is what used to be called "wisdom"—or, in the Latin humanist tradition, *sapientia*.

Taken as reflecting on ourselves, humanities texts are not objects of scientific analysis so much as partners in dialogue. If this is so, their meaning must change over the course of history, for it depends essentially on how they are read by diverse readers who exist in changing historical contexts. Reading is a process of projection, of finding oneself and one's human concerns in the world projected by the text, as well as of mapping the text's concerns onto one's own world of experience.[2] Even if the text, as a sequence of markings, stays literally the same, humanity or the individual reader, the other partner in the dialogue, undergoes continual change. The text's meaning changes, accordingly, with each new interpreter and with each new era of interpretation, and this mobility belongs to its own internal life and structure. The dimension of reading, taken as intrinsic to the text, lends it its dynamism and living significance.

The Bible is arguably the most eminent example of this life-process inherent in a work that is passed down from generation to generation. It embodies the relationship of Israel to its past and to its tradition not as an artifact available for objective analysis but as a partner in dialogue. The Bible, moreover, presents itself as a dialogue between divinity and human beings interpreting their common life as a response to God's calling. There is thus also an explicitly theological frame for the "dialogue" within the Bible between numerous different phases and strata of a people's history. This history extends far beyond biblical times and indeed all the way to our own contemporary world, since in each period the dialogue has to be renewed on the basis of new situations and sensibilities, both within faith communities themselves

2. Paul Ricoeur theorizes this process in his general *Interpretation Theory: Discourse and the Surplus of Meaning* (Fort Worth: Texas Christian University Press, 1976), as well as specifically with regard to the Bible in *Figuring the Sacred: Religion, Narrative, and Imagination* (Philadelphia: Fortress, 1995) and *Essays on Biblical Interpretation*, ed. Lewis S. Mudge (Philadelphia: Fortress, 1980).

and in their broader cultural contexts.[3] This history must always be appropriated anew in every age in order to achieve its full meaning. Only so may it truly be said that the Word "became flesh and dwelt among us" (John 1:14).

This phrase has specific doctrinal meaning when read in the context of particular confessional communities, such as churches, but it also announces a general interpretive principle: the meaning of tradition is experienced only in its application to life in the present. This application is carried out by countless communities in different contexts and, in the end, also by single individuals. Individuals must appropriate the words of Scripture—make them "flesh" and give them a meaning in terms of their own lives.

As the "Word of God," therefore, the Bible provides a uniquely privileged model for humanities texts, specifically for their establishing a dialogue with the reader, the one to whom they are addressed. The very notion of the book as such—as authoritative, as not just an object among objects, but as circumscribing and transcending them, and as the voice of Truth—is intimately bound up with the example of the Bible and with the influence it has exerted down through the ages. In religious and in secular spheres alike, the Bible is somehow not on a par with other books. And yet the Bible, as a "great book" in this tradition of texts embodying a revelation of truth living in history through reinterpretation in continually changing contexts, is exemplary of what holds for the rest as well: we can and, I submit, should learn to read other great books of imagination as revelatory in a similar sense. This book, proverbially *the* Book, is absolutely fundamental, not only to religion but also to the whole secular tradition of Western humanities, which it thereby exposes as far from purely secular after all. Divine revelation in the Bible, rather than being lost or denied, is compellingly realized through its endless worldly transmogrifications as interpreted from age to age and across cultures.

Despite its unrivaled authoritativeness, this imposing book, perhaps more than any other, has undergone continuous transformation. In the first place, this is so because the Bible is deeply enmeshed in the process not only of linguistic but also of cultural translation. To begin with just the linguistic level, it is without question the most translated of all books. It has been translated into virtually every written language, as well as being the object of an endless

3. Reflection on the worldwide variation of readings over time is proposed by *La Bible: 2000 ans de lectures*, ed. Jean-Claude Eslin (Paris: Desclée de Brouwer, 2003). Further intra- and extra-biblical perspectives are found in *Die Bibel im Dialog der Schriften: Konzepte intertextueller Bibellektüre*, trans. as *Reading the Bible Intertextually*, ed. Stefan Alkier, Richard B. Hays, and Leroy A. Huizenga (Waco, Texas: Baylor University Press, 2009). In a literary-critical vein, see Piero Boitani, *Ri-Scritture* (Bologna: Mulino, 1997), trans. Anita Weston as *The Bible and Its Rewritings* (Oxford: Oxford University Press, 1999).

succession of different translations into the same language, as in the case of English.

Translation into English, which has been continuous from Anglo-Saxon times, began to approach familiar forms with the work of William Tyndale in the early sixteenth century. This translation, together with other sixteenth-century translations, like Miles Coverdale's and the Geneva Bible, became the basis for the translation commissioned by King James I of England known as the Authorized Version (1611). Widely accepted as standard, it was at various times revised, and by the nineteenth century, when earlier manuscripts had been discovered and numerous errors of translation detected, a revision was undertaken that produced the Revised Standard Version.[4]

Translation in a cultural sense, more importantly, is constitutive of the ongoing tradition of the Bible. It is, in effect, undertaken already within the Bible itself, signally by Saint Paul, who says that he became all things to all men so that by all means he might save some (1 Corinthians 9:22). Indeed the Bible is not, like science, cast into mathematical language that is the same for all everywhere. The Bible, by its very nature, speaks into the particular situations of individuals and their specific cultures, tailoring its message to what they are ready to receive and understand. This phenomenon is already reflected internally to the work itself again by Paul in his preaching to the Athenians, as recorded in the Acts of the Apostles.

Paul begins by citing the Greek philosophical conception of God's unknowability as expressed in the inscription TO THE UNKNOWN GOD that he happened to see on an altar in the city as he was being led to the Areopagus by philosophers who were eager to have this "babbler" explain his strange new doctrine. Against their avowed ignorance, Paul proclaims the self-revelation of God in Christ: "Whom therefore ye ignorantly worship, him declare I unto you" (Acts 17:22ff.). Paul casts his message in terms that answer to and challenge the Greeks' philosophical culture. He works from their admission of the vanity of their search for God, who remains an Unknown to the intellect alone. Shifting the ground out from under them, Paul affirms that the one true God has revealed himself in history—specifically in the messianic event of Jesus the Christ, in his death and resurrection for the salvation of the world. Paul's speech is thus conscious of itself as a humanities text in exactly the sense I have been at pains to define: its meaning depends on and must be adapted to how it can be received and interpreted by its hearers, who change and will continue to change on an ongoing basis into the future.

---

4. The process of revision has continued further. Nevertheless, I prefer to draw quotations from the Authorized Version for the most part because its memorable phrasing and resonant diction have indelibly stamped the English language and its literature. On this sinuous history, see Alister E. McGrath, *In the Beginning: The Story of the King James Bible and How It Changed a Nation, a Language, and a Culture* (New York: Doubleday, 2001).

This outward-reaching, self-transforming character of the Bible is not to be taken for granted. Another "great book" of monotheistic religion, the Qur'an, is characterized precisely by its *un*translatability. In principle, the message of Islam can be communicated only in Arabic. The Name of God—*Allah*—cannot be properly spoken in any other language. In the faith tradition it spawned, the Qur'an is held typically to be a purely divine revelation that was given whole and intact to Mohammed without any human mediation. Read in this way, the Qur'an repels attempts to interpret it in terms of its history and to examine its process of formation. It is deemed to be forever unchanging in form and content and is to be learned and recited verbatim, even by students who do not understand Arabic and so cannot interpret its meaning.[5]

The Bible, in contrast, comes to us swaddled in a complicated and fascinating history of composition that needs always to be unraveled and that continues to be woven as the book continues to be interpreted in new historical situations. At the base of it all are the Hebrew Scriptures, the sacred books of Israel, which are themselves a whole library of diverse kinds of literature: τα βίβλια means literally "the books." They are traditionally classified as Law, Prophecy, and Writings, and these are only the most general categories into which the Bible's varied component books break down.[6]

All these Scriptures, which to Jesus of Nazareth were sacred, indeed, the Word of God, were taken over by his followers and reinterpreted as alluding to and culminating in the Christ event. This event's beginning with the birth from a virgin was interpreted, for example, as the fulfillment of the prophecy of Isaiah 7:14: "Behold, a virgin shall conceive, and bear a son, and shall call his name Immanuel." This interpretation may, however, be erroneous in linguistic terms, since the word "parthenos" (παρθένος) or "maiden" in the Greek translation of the Bible, the Septuagint, which is quoted by Matthew 1:22–23, translates Isaiah's Hebrew word "'almah," which means simply "young girl." Luke 1:27 also calls Mary a virgin, but he too is working from the Septuagint, and so it seems that the whole story might have been generated by a mistranslation.

---

5. The broad contrast drawn here, relaying current prejudices, would require, of course, qualification and scholarly refinement considering the diverse currents within Islam, for which see Lenn E. Goodman, *Islamic Humanism* (Oxford: Oxford University Press, 2003). Let me also stress that my crude attempt to mark a difference between the Bible and the Qur'an in their relation to history is not a value judgment. It does not mean to detract from the mystical beauty or the prophetic power and truth of either work. We have everything to learn, furthermore, from the different approach to revelation in Muslim tradition that we still know far too scantly.

6. For subtle generic distinctions in literary terms, see David Damrosch, *The Narrative Covenant: Transformations of Genre in the Growth of Biblical Literature* (San Francisco: Harper and Row, 1987).

Yet the issue is not nearly so simple, since the "original" Hebrew text is itself reconstructed from the Masoretic text that dates only from the sixth century A.D. and was finally established by Aaron Ben Asher as late as 925 A.D. The discovery of the Dead Sea Scrolls in 1947 has shown that the Greek Septuagint (third century B.C.) may occasionally be even closer than the Masoretic text to these more ancient versions of the Hebrew Scriptures. Moreover, many earlier glosses on Isaiah also understood him to be prophesying a virgin birth. There was thus an ancient tradition that formed the basis for the Septuagint translators' understanding "'almah" to mean "virgin." The term has evidently shifted in meaning over time and may, after all, have originally connoted virginity.[7]

The prophecy of a virgin birth testifies, in any case, to a belief deeply rooted in the early Christian Church that plays itself out in the Christian appropriation of Jewish Scripture. The Christian communities began developing a literature of their own openly centered on Christ, who was interpreted as the foundation stone: "the stone that the builders rejected has become the corner-stone" (Psalm 118:22). The narratives of the life of Christ—the Gospels—became the core of the New Testament. This is the ensemble of books that are explicitly about the revelation of God in Christ. Together with the Hebrew Scriptures (*Tanakh*), taken as the Old Testament, they form the Christian Bible.

Jesus in the Gospels steps forth as an interpreter and renewer of the revelation of the Hebrew Scriptures. He affirms continuity with this tradition as the bedrock for his revolutionary message in the Sermon on the Mount: "Think not that I am come to destroy the law, or the prophets: I am come not to destroy, but to fulfill" (Matthew 5:17). But he also, in the same speech and repeatedly, underlines the rupture of his own words with tradition: "Ye have heard that it was said by them of old time . . . But I say unto you . . . ." Precisely this process of reinterpretation from within (practically a form of "immanent critique") constitutes the backbone of biblical tradition. And, in this respect, the Bible provides an especially privileged model for humanities texts, to the extent that they are continually in the process of rewriting themselves. This follows inevitably from their being intrinsically addressed to a reader: they thereby establish a dialogue between the reader's present and what has been handed down from the past.

The far-reaching significance of the Bible's translatability resides in the inexhaustibly productive and *re*productive potential of this book as a literature that can be lived. It interprets human experience by the light of divine revelation, which is itself in every instance a humanly situated idea with

7. Raymond E. Brown, *The Birth of the Messiah: A Commentary on the Infancy Narratives in the Gospels of Matthew and Luke*, new ed. (New York: Doubleday, 1999), 143–53.

unlimited different possible meanings.[8] This will be demonstrated in different ways by selections from the Bible exemplifying the imaginative genres of myth, epic history, prophecy, apocalyptic, Writings, and Gospel. Each new genre develops creative forms that incorporate and build upon those of its predecessors in progressively constructing the overall revelation through imagination of the "divine Word."

Pursuant to recent revolutions in literary theory, in which the very possibility of meaning has been seen to be generated by the differential nature of the linguistic sign, "revelation" can newly be understood as a poetic no less than a religious category. In some crucial respects, these two types of revelation might well be construed as overlapping or even as coinciding with one another. Rather than considering literary form to be extraneous to religious content and considering the linguistic medium to be purely instrumental to conveying a revelation of transcendent meaning, it has become imperative to apprehend the content of the form and to explore poetic form's own intrinsic capacities and propensities to deliver a revelation that might well be considered to be theological in the sense most pertinent for many types of readers today. This chapter aims, in its own speculative way, to reflect on a constellation of literary genres within the Bible and to demonstrate in new ways their intrinsic aptness for communicating something of what has traditionally been held to be divine revelation.

The ongoing interpretation of human experience through the shifting lens of revelation in tradition is played out in exemplary fashion from the very beginning of the Bible. Genesis proffers an interpretation of the meaning of the cosmos and of humanity's place within it. It does this particularly in the form of myth, the myth of Creation. The significance of this myth is disclosed anew in each succeeding historical period as a result of contact with new situations that bring out relative constants of human experience from novel angles and in new relations.

II. The Genesis Myth: Existence as Revelation

The prevailing literary genre of Genesis, at least in the primeval history or prehistory contained in the stories of Creation, Fall, and Flood (chapters 1–9), is myth, μύθος in Greek, which means literally "word," "speech," or "story." I use the word "myth" neutrally as a description of literary type or genre and absolutely without prejudice as to the actual or possible truth of its contents.

8. Newly emerging possibilities for construing the Bible's claim to "inspiration" and its status as "revelation" are explored in relation to traditional disciplines such as biblical studies and church history by Terrence E. Fretheim and Karlfried Froehlich, *The Bible as Word of God in a Postmodern Age* (Minneapolis, Minn.: Fortress, 1998).

I consider myths specifically as stories that objectify fundamental conditions of existence and interpret their human significance.[9] Genesis may be about something that happened in the past to certain individual human beings who lived and died long ago, but it is also about a universal condition that belongs to us all. The narrative invites us to interpret ourselves as being created in God's image—and also as fallen away from the original, ideal perfection of our being. In interpreting Genesis as "myth," we discover its narrative to be not only about what happened once upon a time, "in the beginning," but also about what is a reality for us today.

Genesis is about essential conditions of existence as we experience them in everyday life. These conditions are embodied in imaginative form in its narratives. Humankind and the human condition are represented symbolically as a particular individual named "Adam." This becomes the name for humanity as a whole, first as it exists in its original, perfect, intact state, and then as fallen. The technique employed here by the Hebrew imagination is to represent the whole human condition concretely as a particular individual, the first: Adam. Adam serves as Archetype of the human race. Myths are necessary forms of expression for existential realities of this order. They are found in the analogical imagination of primordial cultures the world over. Especially where faculties of abstract thought have not yet developed or become dominant, the general significance of human existence cannot be expressed except in such a symbolic language.

What, according to biblical revelation, is the nature of the relation between God and humanity, between humanity and nature, between man and woman? The biblical doctrines on these matters are embodied in the vivid scenes of Genesis, chapters 1–3 that are not *only* about one individual—Adam, by name. His very name tells us that they also refer to the whole human race: "Adam" in Hebrew is the common noun "man," *'adam*, used as a proper name. This clearly is the way Saint Paul understood it in fashioning what became a normative doctrine for Christian churches. The foundation for the notion of original sin that was to be developed later by Saint Augustine was laid down by Paul through his interpretation of Genesis 3: "Wherefore, as by one man sin entered into the world, and death by sin; and so death passed unto all men, for that all have sinned . . ." (Romans 5:12). The universality of Adam's sin for Paul corresponds to, and seems to be made necessary by, the universality of Christ's act of redemption: "death reigned from Adam until Moses, even over them that had not sinned after the likeness of Adam's transgression, who is the figure of him that was to come. . . . For if by one man's offence death reigned by one; much more they which receive abundance of grace and of the gift of righteousness

9. This is not to deny or even diminish the ideological determination of such "objectifications," which is effectively underscored by Bruce Lincoln, *Discourse and the Construction of Society: Comparative Studies of Myth, Ritual, and Classification* (New York: Oxford University Press, 1989).

shall reign in life by one, Jesus Christ" (Romans 5:14–17). Paul reads Adam's sin as universal in order that Christ's resurrection may also count as a universal cosmic event redeeming all humankind (1 Corinthians 15:20–23).

The doctrine of original sin often constitutes a stumbling block for modern readers, who typically find it to be repugnant. It arouses the furor of believers and non-believers alike because of the seemingly blatant injustice and illogicality of holding all humans responsible and making them guilty for the sin of just one man. But if in Adam is symbolized the contingent, precarious existential condition of all humans—a condition inducing them to wish to be autonomous, lords of themselves, no longer subject to any higher authority than their own—then Adam's sin stands for our response to a predicament that inevitably affects us all. As finite creatures, we are not self-sufficient. Our condition is one of dependence, of subjection to biological and psychological needs, and of conscious, indeed anxious awareness of them to boot.

We are determined, furthermore, as ambiguously within and at the same time above nature, and as gendered. All this is also represented in the Genesis account of a man who needs a companion but cannot find one among the animals that he is given to name. And this condition is intimately bound up with our susceptibility to sin. We sin, fundamentally, because we would like to evade our condition of dependency and its attendant deficiencies so as to be like God—indeed *be* God—that is, be perfectly self-sufficient, autonomous Lords of our own lives, not to mention of those of others.

Our dependent, vulnerable condition leads us into temptation, furthermore, by luring us into not respecting the divisions upon which the whole order of Creation is based—from the moment that God banishes chaos by separating the light from the darkness, the waters that are above the firmament from those below it, the dry land from the sea, and so on. Our ever-renewed attempts to transgress the limits set for man, to "become like gods, knowing all"—in the serpent's words of temptation to Eve—are all prefigured in the first, the archetypal human sin. A little later in the narrative, the building of the Tower of Babel, "whose top is in the heavens," again expresses a failure to accept the separation of heaven from earth, a separation upon which the creation is founded. Refusal to accept the human condition and its limits—in other words, the human desire to be and to supplant God—is exposed as the universal root of sin. It is repeatedly represented in narrative form in the first eleven chapters of Genesis, as well as throughout the rest of the Bible—sometimes in more explicit, less mythic form. Adam's "original" difficulty in this predicament and his susceptibility to failure is reenacted, furthermore, by each one of us every day. The disease of a will in this way tending to transgress the boundaries set for it by its Creator constitutes, if not original sin, at least *our* original sinfulness—or rather our *disposition* to sin. This wayward, insubordinate will is itself the constitutive corruption of human nature that is engendered by Adam's sin—or that, more exactly, is objectified mythically *as* his sin together with its consequences.

My purpose here is not to unravel the theological conundrums of the doctrine of original sin but simply to recognize Genesis as an interpretation of the universal meaning of human life, first as created in its original, ideal perfection, and then as it actually exists in a fallen state. In the interpretation of existence in Genesis, all creation is ordered to and dependent on God: it is as it pleases Him that it should be. This is affirmed and reaffirmed in the refrain: "and God saw that it was good," which rings repeatedly through the narrative. Moreover, according to this account of Creation, humanity is its crowning glory. Standing in direct and privileged relation to God, as made in his own image, the human being is a sort of delegate, a sovereign in turn, God's viceroy, who is granted dominion over the earth. This, at least, is *one* of the interpretations that the Bible offers of human beings' place in Creation, the one suggested particularly by Genesis 1 and taken up in lyric form in Psalm 8, which places humans "a little lower than the angels," with all other created things "under their feet."

There is another, in some ways quite different, interpretation given already in the second chapter of Genesis. This second account is anthropocentric. It *begins* with the creation of man, whereas in Genesis 1 humanity is created at the end of a series of six days of Creation. In Genesis 2, moreover, Creation is effected not by the word, as in Genesis 1 ("And God *said*, Let there be light, etc."): man is created rather by being molded from the earth, the way clay is molded by a potter, making for a much less hieratic, more naturalistic account of man's origin. This diversity generates a dialectic of views about the human condition already within the first two chapters of Genesis. Woman is portrayed in Genesis 2:20–25 as created after man, as springing derivatively out of his side. In contrast, in chapter 1 woman is the symmetrical mirror image of man and is created together with man in the image of God: "So God created man in his own image, in the image of God created he him; male and female created he them" (1: 27). Together these accounts may reflect the experience of woman as man's spiritual partner and peer, when not his adversary—as fully his equal by nature but also, at the same time, institutionally and socially, subordinate.[10]

If this were a science text, we would expect it to tell us unequivocally the facts about what happened "in the beginning." But in reading it as a humanities text, we are interested not so much in what it says, truly or falsely, about a remote past as in what it says about relationships in which we participate presently. The failure to make this distinction has fed raging controversies in the history of interpretation of the Bible centered typically upon this Creation

10. See Robert Alter, *The Art of Biblical Narrative* (New York: Basic Books, 1981) for this suggestion and others helpful to the reading offered here. Also highly illuminating is Leon R. Kass, *The Beginning of Wisdom: Reading Genesis* (Chicago: University of Chicago Press, 2003), who reads the story as a philosophical anthropology interpreting our human and sexual nature.

story. However Creation may have happened, in fact and in detail, once upon a time, Genesis communicates a wealth of understanding concerning the human condition—and thereby of *self*-understanding potentially valid for us still today. The Bible, as a humanities text, thus asks to be read not just as a document about what happened in time past but as a word and, moreover, a "truth" living in the present, "the word of life." It becomes even, in a sense, by dint of constant reinterpretation and renewal, a word of "eternal" life—as in Peter's confession to Christ: "thou hast the words of eternal life" (John 6:68). Hence the necessity of translation and re-translation—and of reinterpretation and reappropriation—in order that its truth take root and germinate in each new culture and individual life with which it comes into cross-fertilizing contact.

Whether or not Genesis is a factual account of what happened "in the beginning," we need to give a practical priority to the significance of the relationships represented in it rather than to purportedly historical facts pertaining exclusively to the past. For these relationships obtain, in ever-evolving form, still today and at any time. The Bible has always been understood in relation to the human contexts in which it is lived and relived; it is thereby newly discovered, interpreted, and applied in every new present.[11] In this crucial respect, it represents an essential paradigm for humanities texts as vital negotiations between past sedimentations of culture and present social pressures. Precisely this type of interaction between the ages produces continual innovation—and occasionally continental shifts—in the history of interpretations.

Layers of Tradition in the Creation Story

Tensions and contradictions in the Creation story emerge when we ask questions such as, What is the sequence of creation? Is man created last, after the lower orders of the animals and as the crowning glory of Creation, or first, before them all? What about woman's Creation? Is she made together with man, symmetrically in a single act, or after him, and indeed after the other animals are brought first to Adam to be named? Where is man created, inside the Garden or outside of it? By what means is Adam created? Is he uttered into existence simply by the divine Word or is he formed out of the dust (*adamah*) of the ground into which life is breathed?

The apparent incompatibilities between these, at any rate, differing accounts compel us, following well over a century of critical scholarship on the Bible, to distinguish between several different traditions and even to conjecture different documents that have been woven together in the Creation story as we have it. We can distinguish two stories right away, one in chapter 1, in which the six days of Creation culminate in the Creation of man

11. This emerges strikingly from later literary re-creations such as those inventoried by David Jasper and Stephen Prickett, *The Bible and Literature: A Reader* (Oxford: Blackwell, 1999), 65–79.

and woman together simultaneously, and the other in chapter 2 (starting from verse 4), in which Creation practically begins with man. In this second account, the other creatures are made first after man, and woman is then made out of a rib taken from his side by God, who has put him into a deep sleep. As analyzed by scholars, the Creation story is thus already a composite of antecedent traditions. This supposition makes it possible to explain a number of inconsistencies between the first two chapters by distinguishing various strata of the Creation story as composed in different times and places by different authors expressing distinct theological visions.[12]

Genesis 1, read as a humanities text in the mythic mode, has a vision of its own: we must attempt to discern what it is saying about the significance of the universe and of human life. Its distinctive style already tells us a great deal. The numerically measured, rhythmic unfolding of the event over seven days is embodied in a formulaic language enriched by constant repetition and refrains ("And God said . . . and it was so"; "And the evening and the morning were the first . . . the second . . . the third day," "And God saw that it was good"). Such rhythmically repeated refrains magnify the glory of Creation as a harmoniously appointed, ceremonious composition. The sense of a decorous procession in stately parade of all things in order, according to their kinds, is conveyed by the even, paratactic syntax, in which phrase after phrase begins with "and," giving each statement full and equal dignity. This writing is organized by parallel clauses saturated with repetitions that are cumulative and of graduating intensity. The chapter is, in effect, a solemn celebration of Creation wrought in a grand literary style. The successive presentation in a series of seven days leading up to the Sabbath makes the Creation itself a kind of liturgy, the first of all time, replete with blessings ("And God blessed them and said unto them, Be fruitful and multiply and replenish"). The universe is a temple of God, with the moon and sun as its lights, the greater light to rule the day and the lesser light to rule the night.[13]

---

12. A classic formulation of this "source-critical" hypothesis dates from Julius Wellhausen, *Prolegomena zur Geschichte Israels* (1878). Specific hypotheses concerning documents are still very much in question in biblical scholarship. The model I evoke is based on Martin Noth, *Überlieferungsgeschichte des Pentateuch* (1948), trans. B. W. Anderson as *A History of Pentateuchal Traditions* (Englewood Cliffs, N.J.: Prentice-Hall, 1972) and used, for example, by Antony F. Campbell and Mark A. O'Brien, *Sources of the Pentateuch: Texts, Introductions, Annotations* (Minneapolis, Minn.: Fortress Press, 1993). This heuristic model helps to isolate a few fundamental differences in the handling of ostensibly the same stories. A useful introduction is Richard Elliot Friedman, *The Hidden Book in the Bible: The Discovery of the First Prose Masterpiece* (San Francisco: HarperSanFrancisco, 1999).

13. This description, absorbing traditional interpretations of Genesis 1–3, is guided by Robert Alter's magisterial reading of the two different biblical Creation stories in *The Art of Biblical Narrative*, 142–47.

This hieratic vision of the Creation in Genesis 1 belongs, appropriately enough, to a strain of the Genesis tradition that is attributed by scholars to priestly writers working presumably at Jerusalem. Numerous scholars place it during the captivity in Babylon in the sixth century B.C. This magnificent panorama highlighting the Creator's sovereignty and the perfect order and coherence of the Creation would undoubtedly have been inspiring and reassuring for a people living in distress and exile. It would be a tribute to the creative splendor and resilience of their faith even during times of severest tribulation. Other scholars have placed it earlier, even as early as the ninth century B.C. In any case, given its priestly origin, the document used by the final editor of Genesis as we have it in this opening chapter has been labeled by scholarship as the "P document."[14]

Compared with this priestly version of Creation and its exalted, sacralizing cosmogony, the account in chapter 2, which is continuous with the story of the Fall in chapter 3, is more earthy in character. It describes man as molded by God from the dust of the ground. It is assigned by some scholarship to the so-called "J document," supposed to have originated in Judah in the period of the divided kingdom (922–722 B.C.). Its various parts were identified, in the first instance, by their reference to God as Jahweh (Yahweh, or better: YHWH), sometimes transliterated as *Jehovah*. This distinguished it from the "E document," supposed to have been composed during the same period, but in the northern kingdom of Israel (also called "Ephraim") before its fall to the Assyrian empire in 722 B.C. Furthermore, in this document, God is referred to as *Elohim*, a form of the generic word for God (*El*), presumably in the belief that God had been designated by his proper name (YHWH) only since the revelation to Moses (see Exodus 6:2–3).

In the J account of Creation, we find ourselves in the midst not of a liturgical ritual but of a materially imagined encounter with an anthropomorphic God. Somewhat clumsily concrete, the "voice" of the Lord "walks" in the garden in the cool of the day (Genesis 3:8). In this author's vision, moreover,

14. This so-called documentary hypothesis has again become a subject of considerable scholarly controversy and has, since the upheavals of the 1970s, often been declared to be no longer believed. See, for example, *Abschied vom Jawisten: Die Komposition des Hexateuch in der jüngsten Diskussion*, ed. Jan Christian Gertz, Konrad Schmid, and Markus Witte (Berlin: Walter de Gruyter, 2002). However, much recent scholarship marks a swing back toward accepting it in modified forms. Richard Elliott Friedman, *The Bible with Sources Revealed: A View into the Five Books of Moses* (San Francisco: HarperSanFrancisco, 2003) assembles evidence in its favor. Mark McEntire, *Struggling With God: An Introduction to the Pentateuch* (Macon, Ga.: Mercer University Press, 2009), 11–24, and J. N. Aletti and J. L. Ska, eds., *Biblical Exegesis in Progress* (Rome: Istituto Pontificio, 2009), confirm that the documentary hypothesis leaves many open questions and disputes but remains influential as a model for understanding the Bible's composition.

humanity remains close to nature rather than in a position of domination over it. Man is formed out of the dust of the ground and is animated by a physical breathing into his nostrils of the "breath of life" rather than being created purely by the word and in God's immaterial "image." Man has, moreover, a clear function binding him to the earth: he is supposed to till the ground. He is placed in the Garden "to dress it and to keep it" (Genesis 2:17). This account is more natural and less ritualized. Its language reflects not the formal balance and symmetry of the cosmos, as in the bird's-eye view of Genesis 1, so much as the complex interweave of the world as seen from within and below. Materials and motivations mix together in the dense opacity of a mysterious life and inscrutable destiny marked by the inexplicable catastrophe of the Fall from perfection. The predominantly "hypotactic" syntax, complicated by subordinate clauses beginning with "before," "but," "when," "for," "then," is dense and ramified, branching out and twisting round: it contorts the orderly, evenly measured flow of the "paratactic" syntax (and . . . and . . . and) that rhythmically scores chapter 1.

The closer relation with nature goes hand in hand with a somewhat more childlike relation to God. In the first version of Creation, as already suggested, Man is its crowning glory and represents God within it, whereas in the second version man is a weak creature in need of help and in mostly passive roles, as when he is put to sleep so that a rib may be taken out of his side and be formed into his female counterpart. Also, not the abstract, ideal symmetry of "male and female created He them" (1:27), but an apparent derivativeness of woman from man—Eve emerging out of Adam's side—is graphically embodied in their physical origins. God himself, in this version, is closer to nature and humanity, acting like a potter molding clay to create man, instead of as a spirit moving over the water and creating solely by his divine Word. The whole account is more anthropocentric: the Creation is seen *not* vertically from above, in a sovereign panoptic vision that can survey all levels of the universe, but rather from the level of the ground and from the point of view of man on the earth.

Like the P document, the J document is conceived of as a strand that extends further and can be detected running all through the book of Genesis and indeed throughout the whole Pentateuch (the first five books of the Bible). It is readily recognizable by its vivid, concrete, bodily imagination of human life and its anthropomorphic conception of God. The divine and the human are not quite completely separate in J's mythical depiction of the era of the giants, the *Nephilim* (6:4), who are produced by the sons of God mating with the daughters of men. The mythic proportions of the lifespan of the patriarchs descended from Adam, several of whom, like Methuselah, live to be over 900 years old, make them into people unlike us, for whom a mere 70 years, "three score and ten," is the common measure (Psalm 90:10). The J author, moreover, is often wildly unpredictable and enigmatic. It is J who writes, "Enoch walked with God; and he was not, for God took him" (Genesis 5:24). The divine mystery impersonated in the unaccountable character of Yahweh is full of exuberance and blessing and also of "terrifying extravagances," such as the attempt upon Moses's life by God himself (Exodus 4:24). J delivers an uncanny narrative full of irony and paradox.[15]

The J account also displays to particular advantage the concreteness of the Hebrew language and consequently of the thought it expresses always in terms of physical phenomena such as bodily organs and functions. For example, the word *ruah* for "spirit" derives from the word for "wind" (Genesis 1:2) or for "breath" (Psalm 104:30; see also Jeremiah 34:14). Intellect and emotion both have their seat in the "heart" (*lev*), as in the phrase: "and every imagination of the thoughts of his heart was only evil continually" (Genesis 6:5). This contrasts with the faculties of abstraction in which the Greek language excels and which it uses for conceiving intellectual essences such as the soul. The physical immediacy of the Hebrew language guides the J writer into dense regions of inextricable confusion riddled with all the contradictions of terrestrial existence.

We see, then, that the two different—howsoever complementary—stories say some rather different things about the significance of the cosmos and human life. The one highlights the symmetrical orderliness of the Creation seen from God's point of view, while the other envisages the concrete, corporeal involvement of human life in a natural environment rather than just in a symbolic order: it exposes complex nexuses of causation and the moral dilemmas that they entail. This diversity illustrates how humanities texts from the beginning inevitably produce—and are produced by—the diverse meaning for different interpreters of facts that are humanly significant. Significance is inevitably manifold because human beings are many and diverse, and the significance of things can never be clearly abstracted from these concrete individuals and the particularities of their existence. The different, and in some respects incompatible, accounts of Creation in Genesis 1 and 2 might seem problematic if we take them as factual accounts of a unique historical event. Read as humanities texts, on the other hand, they testify to the rich variety and contradictoriness of human experience itself in its evolving metamorphoses.[16]

In the narratives of Creation, Fall, and Flood, various ways of understanding human existence are embodied in objective form. Particularly poetry, with

15. For a provocative hypothesis on the J writer, see Harold Bloom's commentary and introduction to *The Book of J* (New York: Grove Weidenfeld, 1990), translated from the Hebrew by David Rosenberg, quotation, 317.

16. A good sense of the shifting multivocity of meanings accreting around the opening chapters of Genesis in the interpretive tradition can be acquired from Elaine Pagels, *Adam, Eve, and the Serpent* (New York: Random House, 1988); and from Gary A. Anderson, *The Genesis of Perfection: Adam and Eve in Jewish and Christian Imagination* (Louisville, Ky.: Westminster John Knox, 2001).

its figurative objectifications, is apt to express human experience of the relations between humanity and God, humanity and nature, man and woman. One of the cardinal principles for the interpretation of humanity offered in Genesis is the idea of sin. As it is portrayed in the primeval history comprised in chapters 1 through 11 of Genesis, before the ancestral history that begins with the call of Abraham in Genesis 12, sin consists fundamentally in usurping upon God's authority. It is first committed when humans disobey the commandment not to eat of the fruit of the tree of the knowledge of good and evil, which allegedly makes one "like God, knowing good and evil" (3:5). It is through not respecting the divisions that constitute the very order of Creation that evil comes about once again when the mixed marriages between the sons of God and the daughters of men engender giants and, as a result, violence in the earth (6:1–7). Sin thereby emerges as a transgression against the clear separation of humanity from divinity. By wanting to be "like God," humans collapse the fundamental divisions on which Creation, as described in the first chapter of Genesis, is erected.

Creation itself is conceived basically as the use of language for making distinctions. All the verbs for creating in Genesis 1:1–5, of which God is the subject, have this sense: created, divided, called, said. Creation is essentially a system of verbally instituted differences. The attempt of mortals to lift themselves up to the height of God, dramatized in the original sin of Adam and Eve eating the apple so as to become "like gods," is repeated in the construction of the Tower of Babel. Here it is the power of the word—at least of a unified word intelligible to all—that is taken away from man as punishment and as surety of his keeping to the subordinate place assigned him in the order of Creation. The word, at the same time, is also the power by which man and everything else is created. It is the word that enables man to participate in community with God and to share in the divine life. However, the word also transcends man and can even be taken away from him (or be turned into an unintelligible babble), if he does not respect the transcendent authority on which it is grounded.

Creation by the Word—Theory and Theology

In addition to its pivotal role in Genesis in the Hebrew Bible, the motif of Creation by the Word also forms the starting point for Christian revelation in the Gospel of John: "In the beginning was the Word [ὁ Λόγος], and the Word was with God, and the Word was God. All things were made by him [the Word], and without him was not anything made that was made" (1:1). The word is thereby given a metaphysical status as the origin and cause of all that is. Thematically, language is the bridge between God and Creation, just as formally the language of Genesis embodies the order by which and in which God creates. In its symmetry and progressiveness, the narrative of Creation incarnates and in some sense even institutes the order of Creation itself.

Creation by the Word offers a warrant for believing that the natures of things are ultimately revealed by their verbal interpretations. The word interprets the being of the thing it names. The passage describing Creation recognizes the constitutive role of language in the very making of the world. Language is not merely an adventitious, extra something supervening upon a world already fully determined in its ontological constitution before and without respect to the advent of language. Instead, all that exists is called into being by the Creator Word. Humanity's being made in God's image expresses itself particularly in Adam's possessing speech and using words to name creatures, thereby echoing God's use of the Word in Creation. The animals are brought to Adam "to see what he would call them" (2:19). The originally divine faculty of naming is handed on to Adam made in God's image and establishes Adam's relation of dominion over the things of the world. It makes him a kind of co-creator. His creative use of this verbal faculty might even be taken as a means of expression and fulfillment of the divine injunction to Adam and Eve: "Replenish the earth and subdue it" (1:28).

Humanity rules and is productive on earth essentially by the power of the word—the very power through which God creates. We will focus recurrently throughout our investigation on how humanity's relation to the world in its origin and essence is embodied in an act of naming that exercises and releases a divinely creative power over things. This is a power, however, that transcends humanity and is subject to greater powers of creation than its own—powers that humans can only attempt to correspond to and mirror, or mediate. This is one level of insight that the inherently linguistic and literary viewpoint of humanities studies is especially apt to bring to focus and to foster: interpretation by the word is the means and the very medium of study in the humanities. Such study therefore finds a matrix in the story of Creation, where the word is revealed symbolically as instrumental to the very being and making of the universe.[17]

Crucial to our predicament today is understanding that the creative power given us especially through language, as the origin of human *techne*, is not just an arbitrary power to manipulate the world at will but is rather embedded within an overall order of creation that surpasses us and that remains beholden to other and higher powers than our own will to dominate. Such is

17. Literary-theoretical underpinnings of this revelation by the creative word are probed in David G. Firth and Jamie A. Grant, eds., *Words & the Word: Explorations in Biblical Interpretation & Literary Theory* (Downers Grove, Ill.: InterVarsity, 2008). Leonard L. Thompson, *Introducing Biblical Literature: A More Fantastic Country* (Englewood Cliffs, N.J.: Prentice-Hall, 1998) similarly emphasizes "the world-creating power of language" (5) revealed in the Bible. German-Jewish language philosophy is applied to the exegesis of Genesis 1–12 in a speculatively original fashion by Mendel W. Tronk, *Wesen und Ursprung der Sprache: Eine Untersuchung* (Berlin: Frieling, 1995).

at least one vital lesson to be drawn from the Genesis text as applied in our contemporary context, given the unprecedented risks brought about by our all too uncontainable capabilities for manipulation of our biopolitical environment and for the technological reconstitution of our very bodies. This might seem to be a purely secular reading of a literary text. However, there is arguably a kind of theological sense here as well simply in the acknowledgment of dependence on a higher power than human powers alone. This respect for an order of things beyond human making is an urgent message borne by Genesis as a humanities text in our apocalyptic times of the eclipse of nature and the destruction of the very conditions of life through unbounded exploitation and unguided deployment of human technology and industry.

Theology, in the sense intended here, is not a set of doctrines given in advance and circumscribing the meaning assigned to the text but rather an inherent dimension of the text itself in its humanly uncircumscribable potential to signify: such significance reaches beyond our will and even comprehension. This "theological" sense emerges as an uncontrollable and incalculable address coming from or through the text itself. As such, the text is allowed to challenge the reader and every method of reading, as well as to critique every context in which readers might wish to definitively place it, so as to control and contain it.

Theology, in this type of reading, is not imposed externally on the text. Instead, reading the text radically as literature opens up a theological dimension of transcendence beyond human control from within the text itself. Accordingly, reading the Bible theologically here means reading it nondogmatically—as free not only of ecclesiastically normed interpretation but also of secular norms: secular dogmas, too, with their embedded doctrines, dictate what texts and language and human subjects are supposed to be, delimiting what they are allowed to mean and do. The model of the Bible serves to alert us to this possibility that the word itself in the literary text might be allowed to speak in its intrinsically "theological" character as a word with infinite and open meaning—as unconstrained by the limited capacities of any finite, intending subjects and their culturally specific hermeneutic apparatus.

What comes from the "text itself," of course, is received and assimilated variously into one's own world of culture and into one's personal vision of truth. Although the type of reading I practice in these pages gives authority to the text and even receives the text's own voice as "theological," it is nevertheless to be understood as belonging to the sort of philosophically leveraged critical readings that have flourished in the wake of the new departures of literary theory in recent decades.[18] "Theology" functions here as a hermeneutic that can serve like structuralism or deconstruction or psychoanalysis or

18. A good sampling of such theoretical approaches is presented by Regina Schwartz, ed., *The Book and the Text: The Bible and Literary Theory* (Oxford: Blackwell, 1990).

feminism or Marxism to define an overall approach to the world, one which is integrated with how we understand texts and events and, more broadly, our "life-world."

Regina Schwartz suggests that, starting from the time of the Reformation, theology "went underground" for several centuries, in flight from scientific-historical criticism of the Bible, but that today "theology . . . is returning in the guise of theory" (*The Book and the Text*, 12). Schwartz acutely assesses the Pandora's box opened by the new engagement of biblical studies with literary-theoretical discourse, noting that biblical history (including the issue of what history is) and biblical authority (including the authority of the text) can no longer be cordoned off from literary theory and its radical questioning of historicity and textuality as such. Our understanding of the ways in which history and text may serve as vehicles of truth and revelation have been—and are being—challenged and in practice radically transformed.

Previously, the historical-critical examination of the Bible, considered as scientific philology or research, was kept separate from matters of faith and theology, but that is no longer possible in the face of the theory revolution that affects our approach to interpretation of texts and history and existence generally, and without any such disciplinary limits. As Schwartz lucidly recognizes, "questions of faith are matters of theory" (14). This implicit dependence of theology on theory underwrites the interdisciplinary and ultimately extra-disciplinary readings that I offer, putting forward a theory of humanities texts, exemplarily the Bible, as "theological" revelation. Conversely, these readings illustrate the implicit dependence of theory on theology—or more precisely on the literary theology that I propound. As a discourse on the unconditioned, this "theology" is itself unconditioned by disciplinary limits. Particularly, as we are about to see, the ontology of history (what it is) is penetrated by theory and therefore also by "theology" in this sense of discourse open without disciplinary divisions to the infinity of all possible relations—Word without end.

III. The Exodus Epic: History and Ritual

Read as religious myth, Genesis represents fundamental conditions of human existence in the form of a narrative about a couple of characters, Adam and Eve, who stand for the whole human race. Such interpretation of the "truth" of Genesis in no way precludes belief in Adam and Eve as having been real people, particular individuals—the first—but it maintains that the story, at any rate, also reaches far beyond them as single individuals in order to represent something about the universal condition of humankind. This, as we saw, is how Saint Paul reads it: for Paul, in Adam "all have sinned" (Romans 5:12). Such an interpretation enables us to read Genesis as being not only about what happened in a remote past but also about us and our present relationships. We find ourselves exposed in this text as subject to certain factors—signally freedom and its infirmity—that determine our being human. This human condition is embodied archetypally in Adam and Eve. Precisely in this sense, Genesis can be understood as belonging to the genre of "myth."

The second book of the Bible, Exodus, on the other hand, can best be assimilated to another literary genre, namely, epic history. An epic is the story of the origin of a people. It focuses on some founding event in which a people becomes a cohesive group with a collective life and thereby constitutes itself as a nation. This event is memorialized in the nation's traditions and gives the people its sense of having an identity. The founding event of the nation, its heroic origin, furnishes it with an image also of its future destiny. The purpose for which a certain people came into being illuminates its national history as a whole and offers guidance for each step on the way toward fulfillment of the future promised and foreshadowed already in its beginnings.[19]

In actual fact, a variety of traditions are likely to coalesce around any event that comes to be chosen as the unifying symbol for the origin of the nation. The Trojan War, as recounted by the Homeric epics, emerged in this way as the founding event of Greek national consciousness. The Greek world's ideals of human excellence and heroism were given a compelling imaginative representation by the Homeric epics that became normative for diverse Hellenic city-states and for the entire civilization which they spawned. Similarly, the Roman people's sense of a unique historical mission and even of a cosmic purpose was concentrated into the image of Aeneas as conqueror and founder that was cast by Virgil's *Aeneid* into enduring, monumental form. Chivalric poems such as *Beowulf* and the *Chanson de Roland* had comparable functions in defining a distinctive civilization for medieval England and France, as did the *Nibelungenlied* in German-speaking lands and the Icelandic sagas in Scandinavia.

All these epics embody interpretations of idealized historical events that express the ethos of a people. They tell what a certain people has been enabled to become through the actions of its heroes, as well as revealing proleptically what that people will be called to realize in the challenges facing it in the future. It is important to distinguish the language of myth from the language of epic so that the very different truth claims appropriate to these diverse genres can be discerned and respected and appreciated. Myth at its most proper and paradigmatic sounds deep, timeless, ultimately unanswerable questions like: Where did the universe come from? What is humanity's purpose in being here? Why is there suffering and death? Epic history answers to another set of questions concerning not the general conditions of human existence but rather the historical identity of a people. What sets them apart

19. For epic as a genre, see Northrop Frye, *Anatomy of Criticism: Four Essays* (Princeton, N.J.: Princeton University Press, 1957), 315–26.

from all other peoples of the earth? How did they come to band together in the first place? What are their distinguishing characteristics, their special virtues and talents, as well as their defects and weaknesses, their nemesis? What should they aspire collectively to achieve? While great epics very often enfold mythological cosmogonies and cosmologies, their specificity as epic demands to be understood in terms of the category of history and of the distinctive historical mission of a certain people.

What, then, is history? Of all that happens, those events become historical that leave a trace in the memory of a people because of their having significance for this people as a whole. "History" always consists in events being understood in accordance with a certain significance. But the "true" significance of events is recognized always only retrospectively: only in the sequel does the full meaning and purport of an event become manifest. Viewed from a historical distance, certain events take on value as emblematic and as standing for crucial junctures of a people's past. One event may even become a symbol for all the rest.

In a way something like this, we might surmise, the Exodus became the founding event of the Hebrew nation. Indeed, the very name "hebrew" seems originally to have designated not so much an ethnicity as a social class, the lowest.[20] The Hebrews may not have been a distinct people at all prior to the Exodus event. In other words, it is conceivable that the very existence of a Hebrew people may be more a result of the Exodus as the formative narration of the Hebrew nation than an independent and antecedent fact. This phenomenon of narrative proving instrumental in the production of nationhood has become more transparent to us through its modern manifestations, especially in postcolonial societies.[21]

The process of making a history, and through it a people, is exemplified by the way that, from among many memories, the Exodus emerged symbolically as the crucial event for the Jews.[22] Crossing the Jordan, conquering the Canaanites, waging victorious military campaigns against neighboring peoples, deliverance from invasions, and successful resistance in the face of foreign empires—these and other such scenarios became confirmations of God's special favor and tutelage of Israel as revealed originally and most powerfully by the Exodus. The Hebrews, both as individuals and in groups,

20. See Gerhard von Rad, *Theologie des Alten Testaments* (Munich: Kaiser, 1965–66), "Die Herausführung aus Ägypten," 189ff., trans. by D. M. G. Stalker as *Old Testament Theology: The Theology of Israel's Historical Traditions* (Louisville, Ky.: Westminster John Knox, 2001).

21. See, for example, Homi K. Bhabha, ed., *Nation and Narration* (New York: Routledge, 1990).

22. See Martin Buber, "Holy Event (Exodus 19–27)," in *On the Bible: Eighteen Studies by Martin Buber* (New York: Schocken, 1968), and Étienne Charpentier, *Pour lire L'Ancien Testament* (Paris: Cerf, 1983), 32.

experienced their God as a liberator and savior in manifold ways. But the central symbol of all these diverse experiences of the event of liberation became, and remained, the Exodus.[23] The Jews generally could identify with this story as describing what was essential in their experience of being freed by the God of their faith from those who oppressed them.

The book of Exodus—at least in certain of its strata—clearly goes back to an earlier stage in Israel's history than the Creation stories in Genesis.[24] The liberation from Egypt, placed by scholars in the thirteenth century B.C., would have been a necessary precondition for the formation of a people and a history of Israel in the first place. As the founding event of this holy nation, the Exodus would have been necessary first to constitute Israel as a people with a distinctive consciousness of itself, specifically with an identity pivoting on its singularly privileged relationship with God. The image of God as Creator in Genesis in many ways appears to be a development of the image of God as Liberator in Exodus. The imagery of "dividing" gives the two a common imaginative and structural basis: the dividing of the Red Sea could easily have served as prototype for the divisions (light from darkness, etc.) by which the God of Genesis creates.

From the point of view of historical anthropology, philosophical reflection about origins (in the form of myth) usually comes only after communal life and a cultic matrix have been established and have evolved to a considerable level of sophistication. Only at this stage do the speculative questions that are probed in Genesis come into their own. The origins of the cosmos and the philosophical issues of humanity's place and relations within it would in all likelihood have been treated somewhat later than the historical origins of the people and the effective constituting of the nation. From this perspective, Exodus, even more than Genesis, comes "in the beginning" of the story of the Hebrew people and their religion.

The Hebrew people constantly returned to and meditated on the Exodus as their founding event in order to reaffirm their identity in the present and as directed toward the future. The national self-image forged by the Exodus was in this manner reinterpreted in correspondence with each new situation and its present exigencies in every successive epoch of Hebrew history. Religious truth—specifically the experience of being saved by God—cannot be only a historical fact pertaining to the past: it must also be lived in the present. The narrative of the Exodus sets this event of salvation up as a norm for the

23. Exodus is discussed as "paradigmatic" history by Eric Voegelin, *Israel and Revelation* (Baton Rouge: Louisiana State University Press, 1956); and Walter Brueggemann, *An Introduction to the Old Testament: The Canon and Christian Imagination* (Louisville, Ky. : Westminster John Knox, 2003) builds on a similar idea.

24. Von Rad, *Theologie des Alten Testaments*, "Die Anfänge," 17ff., and "Die Herausführung aus Ägypten" opens this historical perspective.

present and derives laws from it. Moreover, the Exodus celebrates this event in ritual and liturgical forms, thereby preserving it as an active inspiration and living ideal. All the rememorative reflections upon the Exodus event, including its ritual repetition in liturgical celebration in subsequent times, are in this connection actually a continuation of the event.

Exodus is an especially perspicuous example of a text that exposes its own use of history for purposes of a people's self-affirmation through ritualistic commemoration of its birth as a nation. The injunction to such liturgical repetition is written into the narrative of the event itself: "And this day shall be unto you for a memorial; and ye shall keep it a feast to the Lord throughout your generations; ye shall keep it a feast by an ordinance for ever" (Exodus 12:14). The text is constantly concerned with re-actualizing the event it recounts in the present and even in the future: the people addressed in it are not only the original witnesses or hearers in the desert, but also future generations: "your children's children."

Thus the book is expressly attentive not just to the event it relates but also to the process of memorializing it through which history is lived and continually *re*lived: "And it shall be when thy son asketh thee in time to come, saying, What is this? that thou shalt say unto him, By strength of hand the Lord brought us out from Egypt, from the house of bondage" (Exodus 13:14). Hence also the reiterated injunctions to remember that are interpolated directly into the midst of the event as narrated: "And Moses said unto the people, Remember this day, in which ye came out from Egypt, out of the house of bondage" (Exodus 13:3).

With reference to Passover rites, such as sprinkling blood with a branch of hyssop upon lintels and doorposts so that the Lord will "pass over" their houses and strike down only the Egyptians, the text enjoins, "You shall observe this rite as a perpetual ordinance for you and your children . . . And when your children ask you, 'What do you mean by this observance?' you shall say, 'It is the Passover sacrifice to the Lord, for he passed over the houses of the Israelites in Egypt, when he struck down the Egyptians but spared our houses' " (Exodus 12:24–27). The book of Exodus in this way explicitly anticipates its own history of effect (literally *Wirkungsgeschichte*, with its retrospective illumination): history is told for the purpose of embodying a significance of vital importance for the present and for the future times in which it is going to be recited and re-actualized.

The description of the "original" event in Exodus is, in fact, at many points, transparent to innumerable subsequent events of re-actualization in the form of cultic commemoration. The theophany on Mount Sinai, as described in Exodus 19–24, in which the Ten Commandments are given (20:2–17), followed by the Covenant Code (20:22–23; 33), reads for the most part as a description of the ceremony of renewal of the covenant that was performed periodically by the Hebrews in ensuing centuries. Such a ceremony at Schechem, for example, is recorded in Joshua 24 and is reflected in projective remembrance in the closing chapters of Deuteronomy (27–33). Just such acts of ritual repetition in cultic celebration appear to have been superimposed upon the original experience of the Exodus and, in some instances, to have been written right into the account of the Exodus event itself. The meteorological phenomena of cloud and thunder surrounding the sanctuary of the mountain on which the holy event takes place in Exodus 19:16–19 (see also 20:18) become indistinguishable from clouds of incense and trumpet blasts in ritual celebrations restaging the event for later generations. The narrative tends in this way to conflate the original theophany with its liturgical reenactments.[25]

At the heart of the book, the verse sequence known as the Song of Moses manifestly displays this structure of ritualized use of history in the process of commemoration that creates and maintains national identity by renewing it in each successive age. There is constant alternation between verses pertaining to the specific past event, on the one hand, and more general celebrations of the power and goodness of the Lord, on the other.[26] The opening verse declares that the Lord has triumphed gloriously by throwing horse and rider into the sea. The following verses build on this unique event of the past: they extend it toward a larger field of applications in later times and indeed as a lesson for all time. The second verse reads:

> The Lord is my strength and my song,
> and he is become my salvation:
> he is my God, and I will prepare him an habitation;
> my father's God, and I will exalt him.

Nothing in these lines has anything to do specifically with Moses, Pharaoh, or crossing the Red Sea. But these verses express something essential about the God revealed in Exodus for all subsequent generations. The succeeding verses of the Song of Moses make reference to the itinerary of the Israelites among the peoples of Edom, Moab, Canaan, and even to their passing into the promised land and to the building there of a temple. All of this took place long after the event of escape by passing through the sea—the event that the Song ostensibly commemorates. In this manner, the crossing of the Red Sea is

25. As James Plastras, *The God of Exodus: The Theology of the Exodus Narratives* (Milwaukee, Wis.: Bruce, 1966) indicates: "The Sinai narrative tells the story of Israel going to meet her God, but it is not just the story of the first generation of Israelites. It is the story of Israel in every generation. It was the story of the current generation who, even as they listened to the narrative, felt themselves standing at the foot of Sinai ready to listen to the voice of God in the liturgical celebration: 'Oh, that *today* you would hear his voice' (Ps 95[94]: 7)" (21).

26. The first group comprises verses 1, 4–5, 8–10, 12–17; the second, verses 2–3, 6–7, 11, 18. See Charpentier, *Pour lire l'Ancien Testament*, 30.

projected upon Israel's future: her future, seen in this event's light, is already reflected back into the victory Song itself.[27]

The incipit of the Song of Moses, in Exodus 15:1—

> I will sing to the Lord, for he hath triumphed gloriously:
> the horse and his rider hath he thrown into the sea

—is to be counted as among the oldest compositions in the whole Bible. It seems very possible that the sequence of verses comprising the song contains, in poetic form, the germ of the narrative that eventually became the full-blown story of the Exodus.[28] There is a hint that these opening verses may very well be older than the rest of the song, since they appear repeated again verbatim a little later in the chapter, but this time labeled as "Miriam's Song" (15:21). This suggests that they may have existed independently and antecedently to the narrative and that they were already known by another name when they came to be integrated into the Song of Moses and therewith into the narrative recounting the crossing of the Red Sea in chapters 14 and 15. They may even have been composed by an eyewitness to the event—only later to become the originating cell of Moses's Song and thereby perhaps of the entire Exodus epic.[29]

Critical analysis of Exodus has enabled scholars to distinguish different layers of tradition in the climactic event of the crossing of the Red Sea.[30] In one account, Jahweh fights side by side with the Israelites; in another he acts only by his word. The first is attributed to the oldest strand of the narrative traditions woven together in Exodus, the J document, in which God is called "Jahweh."[31] It is sometimes dated to the tenth century B.C. in Jerusalem under the united monarchy. It represents God anthropomorphically as performing such acts as looking down from the pillar of fire and cloud on the Egyptian army so as to throw it into panic by clogging the wheels of its chariots (14:

27. Robert Alter, in *The Art of Biblical Narrative*, speaks here of a "telescoping" of history.

28. This commonplace in Exodus scholarship is treated by Plastras, *The God of Exodus*, 166.

29. Compare Martin Buber, *Moses: The Revelation and the Covenant* (New York: Harper and Row, 1958), 74.

30. In addition to Charpentier, *Pour lire L'Ancien Testament*, 33, see Jean Louis Ska, *Le Passage de la mer: Étude de la construction, du style et de la symbolique d'Ex 14, 1–31* (Rome: Biblical Institute, 1986).

31. The very idea of a pre-exilic J document has been effectively questioned since F. V. Winnett, *The Mosaic Tradition* (Toronto: University of Toronto Press, 1949). Since the 1970s, it has been abandoned by many scholars, as we noted in the previous section. Nevertheless, much higher biblical criticism has been turning back to modified forms of the documentary hypothesis, as is remarked by Bernard Renaud, *La Théophanie du Sinai: Ex 19–24* (Paris: J. Gabalda, 1991), 7.

24–25). This is the God that, like a potter, formed man from the dust of the ground in Genesis 2.

The second account is assigned to the P document elaborated by priestly writers in exile in Babylon during the sixth century B.C. This is the source of the priestly theology that left such a clear stamp on Genesis 1, in which God creates by his Word. In the J version, the Lord fights for Israel like a warrior, having driven the sea back by a strong east wind (14:14; 14:21). In the P version, the waters divide under Moses's arm stretched out in a priestly gesture at God's command (14:16). The saying-doing sequence (14:4, 8) and the saving act construed as a "dividing," separating, and making holy are exactly homologous to the creative act in the priestly version of the Creation in Genesis 1. Both idioms for describing the event may appear spliced together in a verse like 14:21: "Then Moses stretched out his hand over the sea [Priestly]. The Lord drove the sea back by a strong east wind all night, and turned the sea into dry land [Yahwist]; and the waters were divided [Priestly]."

We can never objectively know what actually happened in the Exodus event—and not only because of its being in a remote past, but also because of the nature of religious experience itself as witness rather than objective fact. Nevertheless, we can read and interpret the significance that was attributed to the Exodus in later epochs. And whether we take the J version or the P version, the meaning is that God is revealed as the Liberator of his people. It is the soul of a people—as constituted by their historical memory—that finds expression in this event. Either set of "facts" serves to illustrate the fundamental event, which is a passage not just from one side of the Red Sea to the other, but from fear to freedom. The manifest miracle is the inner transformation, at least from the perspective of the later reenactments, in which the miracle is never over but occurs ever anew.

This type of miraculous event becomes the model for New Testament miracles, where indeed its logic becomes more explicit and deliberate. For example, the return of sight to the eyes of the two blind men in Matthew 9:27–31 is presented as a confirmation and a sign of the primary miracle that has occurred already within their hearts: "When he entered into the house, the blind men came to him; and Jesus said to them, Do you believe that I am able to do this?' They said to him, 'Yes, Lord.' Then he touched their eyes and said, 'According to your faith be it unto you.' And their eyes were opened." Their spiritual blindness has been healed already in the instant in which they believe in Jesus, the light of life, and the recovery of sensible sight only ratifies this healing, sealing it with an outward sign.

The miraculous crossing of the Red Sea leads to the theophany and the giving of the Law on Mount Sinai. God's saving act of dividing the waters is completed by the giving of the Law that divides good from evil. In order to truly become God's special people, and thus be made different from others, Israel must internally appropriate what has befallen it externally. The difference that makes Israel a "chosen people" must be constituted by its own will as a people. For this purpose, the divine law must be not an imposition restricting freedom so much as a way of living liberty itself. Psalm 119 beautifully articulates this sense of the Law as *itself* Israel's salvation and its ardent love ("O, how I love thy law!" v. 97) rather than only representing an arduous discipline necessary for meriting a reward.

The freedom of the people is expressed par excellence in the history that it remembers and chooses to tell about itself. Genuinely historical significance belongs to the sphere of freedom, not just of fact. In this sense, every aspect of the Exodus epic tells us something about the national identity of the people that adheres to this account of its origins. It is clear, for example, that the stories of Moses's birth and youth are meant to show how he, as the protagonist of the Exodus epic, was providentially favored for the purpose of relieving his people's oppression. His being saved by "coincidence" in the ark of bulrushes—distantly echoing Noah's ark—by Pharaoh's daughter hints that God has chosen Moses to lead his people to safety from the Egyptian menace: we discern providence in what appears to be chance. His very name, with its reference to his having been "drawn out of the water," points forward to the Red Sea crossing that draws a whole people out of the watery chaos to salvation, as well as pointing backward to the Flood as a preceding event in which God's salvation was made manifest to Noah.

In each case, allusion is made to God's providential saving of his chosen people. Moses is portrayed as defending the weak against injustice—the Hebrew against the Egyptian, or Jethro's daughters against the shepherds at the well. In different ways, all the elements of the story set him up for his role as defender of his people and representative of God. Not wholly unrelated, the burning bush that is not consumed (3:2) seems to be saying that God is eternal and yet also intensely present in time; holy and mysterious, potentially violent, yet preserving even in his violence.[32] Something like this seems to be symbolized also by the rainbow that follows upon the Flood. But at the center of all these motifs and manifestations, God's paternal care and saving action on behalf of his chosen people is demonstrated in the event that reveals and interprets the meaning of them all—the Exodus.

What I am proposing is that Exodus as a whole be read not as if it were, in some crude form, a documentary history of a unique event in the past, but rather as a witness to the Hebrew people's faith throughout the ages. As such, it represents not objective but personal and relational knowing. A people's sense of being and living in relation to God in all the vicissitudes of its history, its conviction of being cared for and guided, is expressed in the form of epic narrative growing up around its most significant and obsessive memory

32. Martin Buber, "The Burning Bush (Exodus 3)," in *On the Bible: Eighteen Studies by Martin Buber* (New York: Schocken, 1968).

traces. These crystallizations of memory then engender further expressions in narrative and in lyric traditions.[33]

It is patent that the narrative and even the laws laid down in the book of Exodus reflect historical conditions pertaining to the time(s) of the book's writing at least as much as to the supposed time of the Exodus event itself. In defining the essential norms for national life, the exigencies of later periods are just as relevant as those proper to the time in which the story is set. The laws actually reflect a number of different phases of society based, for example, on successive nomadic and agricultural economies. By its heterogeneous and "geologically" stratified nature, the book of Exodus exposes the way in which its own task is not just to record facts but rather to interpret a sense of national identity as founded upon the relationship with a God who is active as liberator in history, yet also in the present. This liberation is something that must be experienced ever anew by every successive generation.

The text of Exodus eminently exemplifies and highlights how epic narrative does not merely recount an event in the historical past but rather displays the process of memory at work in preserving the event and its founding significance by enabling new meaning to accrue to its various features on the basis of lived realities as they are encountered in ensuing epochs. Critical-historical analysis reveals that many of the age-old, traditional feasts of the Hebrew calendar year were given new meaning by being attached to the Exodus event. Certain of these feasts were quite generally part of the culture of the ancient Near East in which the Hebrews resided. In particular, nomadic peoples of the Near East practiced the sacrifice of a lamb, with spraying of blood on lintels or tents, in order to ward off evil spirits. This custom receives historically specific meaning in the Exodus narrative as a sign for the Angel of the Lord to "pass over" those houses, when smiting the first-born in the land of the Egyptians.

Or again, farmers in the spring, as part of a fertility rite, would celebrate the feast of unleavened bread, discarding old yeast before taking in a new harvest. Exodus's prescriptions for unleavened bread read very cogently as a reinterpretation of such ritual practices in coordination no longer with the cycle of nature but with a historical event. In the context of the Exodus, the readiness to escape in a hurry from Pharaoh's impending pursuit is adduced as the original motivation for this practice that is then ritually repeated in remembrance. Take, for instance, a verse like: "And they baked unleavened cakes of the dough which they brought forth out of Egypt, for it was not leavened; because they were thrust out of Egypt, and could not tarry, neither had they prepared for themselves any victual" (12:39). This has all the

33. Walter Benjamin's writings concerning memory and history, including those in *Angelus Novus* (Frankfurt: Suhrkamp, 1966), theoretically illuminate the legacy of this especially Jewish sensibility for living memory, which continues down to recent times.

appearances of an after-the-fact etiological gloss on a well-established ritual practice.[34]

Such passages interpreting the reasons for ritual practices as connected with the Exodus event strongly suggest that the exigency of memorializing and keeping alive its religious meaning in the present reacted upon the account of the "original" event. The Decalogue itself, which supposedly was given word for word to Moses and inscribed in stone on Mount Sinai, shows signs of having been subjected to interpretation resulting in interpolations in subsequent ages. Formally, the commandments can be broken down into concise prescriptions plus explanatory glosses. For example, the last of the commandments dealing with duties to God enjoins simply, "Remember the Sabbath day, and keep it holy" (20:8). But the following explanation—"For in six days the Lord made heaven and earth, the sea, and all that is in them, and rested the seventh day; therefore the Lord blessed the Sabbath day and hallowed it" (20:11)—evidently depends on the Priestly account of Creation in Genesis 1, which is presumably much later. Surely the practice of the Sabbath antedates this justification given for it.

The whole of the Pentateuch (the first five books of the Bible) consists in reinterpretation of traditions—legal, covenantal, ritual, and cultic—in narrative terms and with reference to the all-embracing frame of a national salvation history based on the Exodus. The cultic prescriptions in Exodus 25–31 and 35–40, which are supplemented by the laws of the Holiness Codes in Leviticus 17–26, are given not only for a nomadic people in constant migration, such as the Hebrews were after fleeing from Egypt and while wandering in the desert: this is where the giving of these prescriptions is set narratively, but they are clearly adapted also to later periods in Israel's history. They deal with the fruit of the harvest and with slaves and much else reflecting more mature stages in the development of Hebrew civilization. Still, all this variety of legislation is shaped by the guiding concept of Israel as a holy people, separated unto the Lord. And Israel first defined and constituted itself as such a people through the Exodus event. Similarly, the account, in the Book of Numbers, of the forty year sojourn in the wilderness of Sinai reflects the life and crises of the monarchy, the exile in Babylon, and even later periods, all within the narrative framework of the aftermath of the Exodus.

This process continues in the book of Deuteronomy, which means "second law," following upon the law first given through Moses in the Exodus. Deuteronomy does not only reiterate the Decalogue and Covenant Code: it also thoroughly reinterprets these and other traditions in an effort to recover an

34. See also 12:26 and 13:14. A number of such presumable adaptations of festival traditions are pointed out by the notes to the Oxford Annotated Bible (New York: Oxford University Press, 1962). Jeffrey J. Niehaus, *Ancient Near Eastern Themes in Biblical Theology* (Grand Rapids, Mich.: Kregal, 2008) further illuminates such appropriations.

acute sense of a special vocation for the Israelite nation. Deuteronomy *preaches* the laws. It is, moreover, cast as Moses's farewell address. Moses is presented no longer as high priest but as prophet. This reflects a shift in the spiritual leadership of Israel and a need to go deeper than mere ritual repetition and achieve a revolutionary renewal of the inspired Word. Deuteronomy proposes a direct experience of God's saving acts in the proclamations of prophecy. This book also advocates reform of worship by means of the centralization of the cult. On the whole, it represents a return to Mosaic traditions, with a zeal to revive their original theological meaning in order to reform and restore Israel morally and religiously, while at the same time adapting these traditions to the very different requirements of an evolving society.[35]

The process of ritual reinterpretation is evident already in the oldest strands of Old Testament tradition, for example, in the primitive Hebrew creed of Deuteronomy 26:5–10: "A Syrian ready to perish was my father, and he went down into Egypt, and sojourned there with a few, and became there a nation, great, mighty, and populous" (see also Deuteronomy 4:32ff.). This creedal statement links the offering of first fruits with the Jewish Passover ritual built around the commemoration of the Exodus event: "and the Lord brought us out of Egypt with a mighty hand and an outstretched arm. . . . And now, behold, I have brought the first fruits of the land, which thou, O Lord, hast given me" (Deuteronomy 26:7–10).

Israel based its faith on historical events—especially on the event of the Exodus as the founding event of its national history. History as a genre is the means through which a people construct their heritage so as to establish their sense of identity as distinct from other peoples. This beginning of historical, revealed religion separates Israel from other ancient peoples and their nature-based religions, and it is a momentous novelty in the history of world religions. Feeling oneself to be specially chosen is particularly necessary to an infantile understanding of love. Later, the same love can be recognized as universal in its own intrinsic nature. In this manner, the religion of the "chosen people" evolves toward the realization, particularly with the prophets, that God intends to save not only the Jews but all humanity.

The book of Exodus, as read down through the ages, remains open to a dimension of continuing experience of "exodus" in myriad forms by all peoples. The process of liturgical reenactment and re-actualization has, in fact, extended the founding event far beyond its original matrix and even beyond the boundaries of Hebrew culture. Particularly the Christian religion and specifically the Christ event, especially as celebrated in the Easter liturgy, are themselves founded on the commemoration of the Exodus. Christ, the paschal sacrifice, the sacrifice that saves, is figured as the Passover lamb

35. Deuteronomy's pivotal role in the memnotechnics of the Bible is highlighted by Jan Assmann, *Das kulturelle Gedächtnis: Schrift, Erinnerung und politische Identität in frühen Hochkulturen* (Munich: C.H. Beck, 1997).

instituted by the Exodus. In Christian reinterpretation, this sacrifice is linked not just with escape from bondage in Egypt but more universally with liberation from the slavery of sin. Hence Paul sees the Exodus as prefiguring salvation in Christ: he interprets the passage through the sea as a figure for baptism—the sacrament that cleanses Christians from sin by immersion in water and the Spirit. He explicitly states that these things happened to Israel in the Exodus in order to serve as examples or "types" "for us": they are written down for our instruction or "admonition" (1 Corinthians 10:1–11).

Accordingly, in medieval exegesis, the Exodus becomes the paradigm text for illustrating the fourfold senses of Scripture. Beyond the *literal* sense of the narrative, which recounted the actual historical event of Moses leading the Israelites out of Egypt, the Exodus was understood allegorically in three further, spiritual senses: it was the type or prefiguration of Christ's freeing of the human race from the power of its enemy, Satan, according to its *typological* sense; in its *moral* sense, the Exodus represented the escape of the individual human being from the bondage of sin; and, according to its *anagogical* sense, it signified the delivery of the soul out of this world of time into eternity.[36] These are ways in which the Exodus story opens into an ongoing event of Redemption experienced in various guises by later generations and even in other religions.

If, then, epic history concerns the founding event of a people with a distinct identity and historical destiny, we can return to the question of what history is in the particularly revealing form in which we find it realized in the book of Exodus. For this book, especially when analyzed into its various layerings of tradition, shows with exemplary clarity how history consists essentially in the interpretation of the past as a means for understanding the present—and with a view to envisaging the future. No history is simply a neutral account of what happened long ago. Every history is written in a historical context of its own that determines inescapably what can be considered to be true and important—or even just intelligible—in the present. History concerns contingent happenings, such as a certain journey from Egypt to Israel, rather than necessary and universal structures of existence, like human creatureliness and ontological dependence. Such universal conditions are apt, rather, to be represented symbolically as myth. But, like myth, and indeed like every form of literature and of human knowledge generally, history treats what is not only an object but involves also a human subject.

Revealing of this subject-object hybridity is the fact that we use the word "history" in two senses. "History" (1) in the sense of what happened is the

---

36. This technique of the fourfold exegesis of scripture, as it developed in the Middle Ages, is studied in detail by Henri de Lubac, *L'Éxégèse médiévale: Les quatre sens de l'écriture* (Paris: Aubier, 1959), trans. E. M. Macierowski as *Medieval Exegesis*, 4 vols. (Grand Rapids, Mich.: Erdmans, 1998). The Exodus is used by Dante to illustrate these four senses of scripture in *Convivio* 2.i.

object of "history" (2) or historiography in the sense of the recounting and reconstruction of the past. But, in reality, the two interpenetrate and are inseparable from each other. For history is nothing, if not a dialogue or interaction between events and their recounting. History consists fundamentally not in the bald facts of what happened but in the living significance of events as they are remembered and retold. This meaning in the present for those who remember or, more exactly, memorialize events is thrown into vivid relief by humanities texts and exemplarily by the book of Exodus, which takes us near to the "original" sources of biblical tradition.

IV. Prophecy as Inspired Interpretation of History

So far, we have seen that revelation, whether of fundamental conditions of human existence (myth) or of the founding event of a nation (epic history), cannot abstract from the present moment and the particular situation of those for whom it occurs. Revelation occurs for them, moreover, specifically in and through their own acts of interpretation. To this extent, revelation of a mythic or of a historical past is always also *self*-revelation in which latter-day interpreters find their own reality mirrored and disclosed in the past as refracted by the newly breaking light of actual experience. Revelation inevitably involves this present dimension of the interpreters' lived experience, in which the event of revelation occurs—or rather *re*curs—presently.

Prophecy, the next genre to which we turn, continues and intensifies the process of actualizing or contemporizing revelation in present acts of interpretation that mythic and historical imagination in their different ways already embody and exemplify. Cast in the generic mould of prophecy, divine revelation is formulated as the present utterance of God in person. Since revelation in the biblical sense can only be realized in the present tense of a living relationship with God, myth and history are finally fulfilled in their revelatory meaning as the purportedly "divine" disclosure of human life only in prophecy. For prophecy speaks as if directly from God's own point of view and even in his own voice.

The whole Bible is "prophetic" in the sense that it is all divine revelation, all "the Word of God." However, the narrower sense of "prophecy," as a distinct genre among others in the Bible, turns upon a specifically prophetic rhetoric that makes fully explicit the hypothesis that God is speaking and that he is personally addressing his people. In narrative genres, such as the Creation myth and the Exodus epic, this first-person address of God to humans remains almost entirely implicit. But the oracular form used in prophecy formally reports God's own speech directly. This is often indicated explicitly by phrases such as "Thus saith the Lord" or "Hear ye the word of the Lord." For example, the beginning of the Book of Isaiah first announces that the Lord has spoken and then moves into an actual address from the Lord God as "I":

> Hear, O heavens, and give ear, O earth:
> for the Lord hath spoken,
> *I* have nourished and brought up children,
> and they have rebelled against me.
>
> (Isaiah I:2)

This opening welds a reprise of Genesis 1:1 ("In the beginning, God created the heavens and the earth") together with a direct address from God, who speaks in the first person as "I." It also alludes to the history of God's relationship with his people and to their rebelliousness, as is often recalled in Exodus, for example, in the incident of the golden calf (Exodus 32).

Pro-phecy (from the Greek φάσις—assertion, via the Latin *fateor*—confession) means "speaking out" and, in effect, is a speaking *for* ("pro") God. Hence the broad sense in which the whole of the Bible, as the "Word of God," is prophetic. But the books that are labeled "prophetic" in the stricter sense of the word render this fact explicit: they attempt to dramatically realize the divine voice. The vocative is the fundamental mode of prophetic address. It is nominally God in the first person who directly addresses his people in prophetic discourse. The statements that result are very aptly called "oracles."

In content, prophecy is about (re)interpreting for the present the meaning of revelation as it has been crystallized in tradition. Thus a vital task of the prophets was to revive in their contemporary relevance certain hoary religious traditions, such as those of Creation and Exodus, that had grown cold and become *mere* history and empty ritual. The prophets aimed to bring back—in all its urgency for the present, with its decisions and dilemmas—the demand of God for justice and therewith for reform and repentance. This phenomenon of returning to and revitalizing religious traditions can be documented within the Bible preeminently in relation to the Exodus narration. A great deal of prophetic influence is channeled into Deuteronomy, the "second law," in which the original Mosaic Law from Exodus is re-proposed, but as adapted to new historical conditions and as ardently preached.[37] Not mere exterior actions of ceremony and cultic sacrifice, but a heart sincerely moved in its depths and turned (literally "con-verted") to God, was demanded by the prophets.

The basis for the prophet's interpretation of history, including contemporary history, is a personal relationship with God. This is established for Isaiah in the account of his vocation or calling. Chapter 6 dramatically describes Isaiah's vision of the King, the Lord of hosts, seated on his throne on high and surrounded by ministering and worshipping seraphim. It culminates in sending the prophet on his mission, after his lips have been touched with a

37. Von Rad's studies of Deuteronomy in *Old Testament Theology: The Theology of Israel's Historical Traditions* are pioneering in this regard.

live coal and thus purified. This, in effect, authorizes the prophet to interpret history as if from the divine point of view. This was implicitly the case in Exodus, too: Moses is its "author," and his authority is based on his being the prophet who functioned as mediator in Israel's relationship with God at that crucial juncture in its history. But now a formal change comes about. In prophecy, God is speaking. The "pro-phet" is one in whom God directly speaks, and this makes for the formal difference between the prophetic and the "historical" books, which nevertheless are tellingly subsumed as the "former prophets," suggesting the broader sense in which they, too, are prophetic, albeit less explicitly so, since they lack the form of direct first-person address from the Almighty.

The books that are properly prophetic in the strict sense by virtue of their rhetorical form as oracles in which God directly speaks take on also a more pronounced poetical character. Prophecy addresses specific historical agents and situations, yet its poetic form also generalizes its messages beyond their original contexts. This has been shown effectively in relation to Isaiah, chapter 1, by Robert Alter.[38] Our main purpose in what follows is to explore the implications of the *poetic form* of prophecy as exemplified chiefly by the prophet Isaiah.

As we move into the genre of prophecy in biblical literature, the interpretation of the historical past or of mythic origins in terms of present experience and its significance is not left behind: it becomes even more urgent. It becomes clear at this point that myth and history as employed from the beginning of the Bible have been implicitly a kind of prophecy. Prophecy presents, once again, the Creator God, "who has measured the waters in the hollow of his hand / and marked off the heavens with a span" (Isaiah 40:12), as well as the Lord of history, "who brings princes to naught, / and makes the rulers of the earth as nothing" (40:23). Prophecy recapitulates these mythological and historical motifs from the Genesis and the Exodus traditions, but it attempts to reinterpret them as relevant to and prescriptive for a contemporary context. Each new present predicament needs to be dealt with through recollection of these traditions, and the prophets make this exigency programmatic. In prophecy, furthermore, history and myth are clearly revealed as human mediations of divine revelation, such as the Bible as a whole represents. Interpretation of history, as well as of fundamental conditions of human existence, can be determined not as matters of objective fact but only in a dimension of freedom, of free response to the call of God that the prophet makes to be heard again, beseeching and pleading for genuine faith in the God who has revealed himself in history and Creation.

Thus prophecy incorporates and redeploys the sorts of historical and mythic discourses that we have already considered, but in prophecy the

38. Robert Alter, *The Art of Biblical Poetry* (New York: Basic Books, 1985), 142ff.

present horizon of significance—which we have already stressed as decisive for all interpretation, whether historical or mythic or symbolic—is brought directly into view. Present threats of destruction and promises of deliverance are overtly the prophet's theme. He aims expressly to act within and impinge upon the present predicament of the nation. He is not just saying what will inevitably happen—any more than the biblical historian is saying merely what, as a matter of fact, took place. He is provoking an examination of conscience and is attempting to influence behavior by bringing about a certain self-understanding in which his people will recognize itself as God's chosen people. In this way, prophecy is an even more highly evolved and explicit example than we have had so far of how humanities texts reinterpret tradition so as to realize its truth in the present—and thereby also in a fashion that is exemplary for all ages.

Oracular Form and Poetic Power in Isaiah

Prophecy formally is the speech of God cast into oracles announced by the prophet, who serves as spokesperson or mouthpiece. A model for this relationship is the way Aaron served as "mouth" for Moses, who was as "God" to him (Exodus 4:14–16). Accordingly, prophecy is distinguished first by its vocative character. It is addressed to Israel, and to other human agents, as audience. It modulates from invective to accusation and satire; it employs sarcasm and name-calling, as well as the more positive modes of comforting, praising, and promising. But in all of these moods, the poetic form of these utterances serves to maintain also a high degree of indeterminacy for what God says.[39] It is especially this poetic character of prophetic oracles that makes them fit to communicate *God*'s message and gives them universal scope and meaning.

The "oracles" in which prophecy principally consists typically speak to specific historical situations and agents. They address, for example, a city with an invader approaching: the people are accused of apostasy or corruption and are enjoined to understand the immanent catastrophe as a condign punishment for their sins. By such means, prophecies make a powerful argument and urgent appeal for immediate reform. Prophecies are not general maxims or logical reflections but spontaneous eruptions of difficult truth—disclosures of God and of his demands for justice in concrete crises. However, they also have a tendency to exceed the requirements of their immediate historical situations. They are not just recipes for practical reform. Particularly

39. Walter Brueggemann, *Theology of the Old Testament: Testimony, Dispute, Advocacy* (Minneapolis, Minn.: Fortress, 2005) also pertinently emphasizes that prophets "speak most often with all the elusiveness and imaginative power of poetry" (625). He develops this insight in his *The Prophetic Imagination*, 2nd ed. (Minneapolis, Minn.: Fortress, 2001).

their poetic form promotes prophetic oracles to messages of much more general purport and far-reaching significance: they become religiously valid revelations of the eternal fidelity of God and of the ways of his providential involvement in history. Transfigured into poetry, the historically specific messages of prophecy take on paradigmatic significance for human societies and individuals. In chapter 14 of the book of Isaiah, for example, the prophecy against the king of Babylon is elaborated with such imaginative amplitude and power as to transform its subject into an archetype of evil. From "How hath the oppressor ceased! the golden city ceased!" this passage modulates into a cosmological register, evoking forces of good and evil in the universe:[40]

> How art thou fallen from heaven, O Lucifer, son of the morning!
> how art thou cut down to the ground, which didst weaken the nations!
> For thou hast said in thine heart, I will ascend into heaven,
> I will exalt my throne above the stars of God:
> I will sit also upon the mount of the congregation,
> in the sides of the north;
> I will ascend above the heights of the clouds;
> I will be like the most High.
>
> (Isaiah 14:12–14)

Similarly ranging from the specific to the symbolic, the "servant of the Lord" in Isaiah can sometimes be identified with the historical king of the Persians, Cyrus, who is called by name, for example, in 44:28 and 45:1. Cyrus served the Lord in bringing about the fall of the Babylonian Empire in 539 B.C., thereby freeing subject peoples like Israel to return home out of exile. And yet too narrow and exclusive an identification of such figures in prophecy runs the risk of compromising their manifold resonances in later history. The suffering servant of Isaiah 53 will come to be recognized, for instance, anachronistically, as Christ redeeming our sins through his Passion:

> But he was wounded for our transgressions,
> he was bruised for our iniquities:
> the chastisement of our peace was upon him;
> and with his stripes we are healed.
>
> (Isaiah 53:5)

40. Compare the reading of this passage offered by Alter, *The Art of Biblical Poetry*, 146. Deeper in the background here is the stylistic analysis of Isaiah by Hermann Gunkel, generally recognized as the founder of "form-criticism." Pages 34–70 from his *Die Propheten* (Göttingen: Vandenhoeck & Ruprecht, 1917) are translated by James L. Schaaf and excerpted in David L. Petersen, ed., *Prophecy in Israel: Search for an Identity* (Philadelphia: Fortress, 1987), 22–73.

The poetry of such figures resides not least in their miraculously elastic identity, which enables unexpected connections to be made later in history, as the Crucifixion narratives richly attest, with their manifold allusions to Isaiah.

The form of prophecy itself, by using the specific and concrete to communicate something more ideal and general, is eminently poetic. Such poetic language is necessarily the form required for communicating the Word of God in God's own voice by direct discourse. For such communication entails expression of what in principle transcends all determinate objects and all literal expression in language. How could God speak in any one finite voice except provisionally and poetically? Poetry achieves an indeterminacy of language that opens upon infinity. This does not exclude precision and concreteness: on the contrary, these qualities are necessary, and in any case highly conducive, to poetic expression. Still, all determinate, literal meaning in poetry is but a gesture beyond itself toward a meaning that is metaphorical, or open and infinite. Literal meaning is not denied but is transfigured into another, an unbounded register of significance.

It is not easy to say what poetry is, but one good way to experience it in certain of its peculiarly formidable powers is simply to read the book of Isaiah aloud in the King James Version. The sublimity of the conception of God, who remains, of course, undefined and out of sight, is expressed in the measureless intensity of the language that flows from the unattainable height of his sovereignty. Such language asserts the Lord's authority over life and death and affirms his visceral passion for his people. The prophet's poetic afflatus makes for breath-taking strophes such as:

> All flesh is grass,
> and all the goodliness thereof is as the flower of the field:
>
> The grass withereth, the flower fadeth:
> because the spirit of the Lord bloweth upon it:
>
> surely the people is grass.
> The grass withereth, the flower fadeth:
> but the word of our God shall stand for ever.
>
> (Isaiah 40:6–7)

It may be necessary to read several chapters consecutively before, by virtue of its cumulative effect, the poetry builds to its full momentum and succeeds in conveying unshakeable conviction. A steady concentration is required in order to feel oneself swept up by the rapid clip of the verses in their rhythmic swelling to sublime intimations that communicate not concepts so much as a cloudy sense of an overwhelming presence. This poetry evokes fear and awe by exposing the littleness of all that is human and worldly as compared with the greatness of God that rings through lines like those describing the Day of Judgment:

> Enter ye into the rock,
> and hide thee in the dust,
> for fear of the Lord, and for the glory of his majesty.
> The lofty looks of man shall be humbled,
> and the haughtiness of men shall be bowed down,
> and the Lord alone shall be exalted in that day.
>
> (Isaiah 2:10–11)

The language is lofty and exalted and yet, at the same time, unaffected and immediate, using whatever homely metaphors may be ready to hand: "the ox knoweth his owner, the ass his master's crib," "a heritage for hedgehogs," "And the daughter of Zion is left as a cottage in a vineyard, as a lodge in a garden of cucumbers." Such language retains its jagged edges, as the imagery itself insists: "To go into the clefts of the rocks, and into the tops of the ragged rocks." For all its classical poise and rhetorical polish, the style manages to remain remarkably abrupt and rough. Sudden epiphanies of recognition tend to interrupt any effort at methodical development.

Crude images of unrefinement and wildness only add to the raw power and force of such poetic diction, which describes princely palaces abandoned to moles and bats, to briers and thorns, to wild asses. A small handful of recurrent motifs—chastisement, forgiveness, restoration, exaltation, and rejoicing—make up the repertoire of these poems and are made to pass through imponderable intensities of emotion. It does not necessarily matter at first exactly what is being denounced or exulted over: the degree of affect alone is a revelation in its own right. At the emotional height from which such conceits spring forth, they seem inevitable, however fanciful and far-fetched:

> It is he that sitteth upon the circle of the earth,
> and the inhabitants thereof are as grasshoppers;
> that stretcheth out the heavens as a curtain,
> and spreadeth them out as a tent to dwell in.
>
> (Isaiah 40: 22)

Exactly appropriate, pungent images make for memorable phrases that become proverbial, such as the "drop in the bucket" and "small dust in the balance" (40:15), the heavens "rolled together as a scroll" (34:4), and "they shall beat their swords into plowshares, and their spears into pruninghooks" (2:4). Every image flashes out with the rapidity of lightning. The imagination makes always an immediate leap to the concrete. No coldly calculated analyses of moral corruption in Israel but rather excruciatingly detailed description of a horridly diseased body:

The whole head is sick, and the whole heart faint.
From the sole of the foot even unto the head there is no soundness in it;
But wounds, and bruises, and putrifying sores:
They have not been closed, neither bound up, neither mollified
with ointment

(Isaiah 1:5–6)

The dimension of poetry is essential to humanities texts in general, given their relative freedom from the contexts in which they originate and their susceptibility to being reappropriated ever again in new and different circumstances. Aristotle noted that poetry possesses the universality of truth that is lacking to history (*Poetics*, chapter 7). And this is why poetry is essentially the medium of tradition—that is, of truth that must be found over and over again by succeeding generations and so establish its universality. In this manner, the fundamental indeterminacy of meaning in poetic language becomes instrumental to the inexhaustible life of the traditional text.

The Raptures of Isaiah: Their Influence Down to Jesus and Beyond

The book of Isaiah particularly illustrates how revelation is achieved in and through poetic language. Universalization of meaning can be achieved when historically specific oracles directed toward designated agents in given historical settings are cast into poetic form. This is especially evident in Isaiah's prophecies and is part of the reason why Isaiah has lent itself so well to Christian appropriations. Indeed, the drive toward the universalization of revelation lies at the heart of this book, even at a thematic level: the theme of opening faith in Israel's God to all peoples is, perhaps more than anything else, what makes it one book. Compiled together under the name "Isaiah" in our Bibles are the works of at least three distinguishable prophets: preexilic (second half of the eighth century B.C.), exilic (just before 539 B.C.), and post-exilic (530–510 B.C.).[41] But the universal opening of revelation and salvation to the Gentiles is ecstatically announced already in "First Isaiah," which comprises basically chapters 1–39. In the second chapter of the book, we read: "And it shall come to pass in the last days, that the mountain of the

41. This picture has been made even more complex through the theories of growth by accretion, according to which the prophetic books are perhaps accumulations of writings attached to the name of the original prophet who founded what was at first only an oral tradition. See Jacques Vermeylen, *Du prophète Isaïe à l'apocalyptique: Isaïe, I–XXXV*, 2 vols. (Paris: J. Gabalda, 1977–78), and Luis Alonso Schökel, "Isaiah," in *The Literary Guide to the Bible*, ed. Robert Alter and Frank Kermode (Cambridge, Mass.: Harvard University Press, 1987), 165–83.

Lord's house shall be established in the top of the mountains, and shall be exalted above the hills; and all nations shall flow unto it" (2:25).

A universal redemption not only of history but also of nature is envisaged in the prospect of a return to Edenic peace and amity among all creatures:

> The wolf also shall dwell with the lamb
> and the leopard shall lie down with the kid . . . .
> They shall not hurt nor destroy
> in all my holy mountain:
> for the earth shall be full of the knowledge of the Lord,
> as the waters cover the sea.
>
> (Isaiah 11:6–9)

In "Third Isaiah," the note of universality is again struck in the triumphant chapters 60–63, beginning "Arise, shine; for your light has come, and the glory of the Lord has risen upon you . . . Nations shall come to your light, and kings to the brightness of your dawn." But the generalization of revelation through poetic universality is realized perhaps most convincingly of all by Second Isaiah (chapters 40–55), from whom the phrase "I will also give thee as a light to the Gentiles" (49:6 and 42:6) is borrowed by Luke 2:32 and woven into the Song of Simeon and therewith into the liturgy of the Chirstian church. This promise of universal human enlightenment through the Jewish messiah has, in fact, been recited throughout the centuries in the Roman Catholic monastic liturgy at the end of each day at the office of compline, the last of the seven canonical hours.

"Second" Isaiah, moreover, is particularly prized for its unsurpassable expression of sheer exaltation. "Sing, O barren, thou that didst not bear; break forth into singing" (54:1). The emotions are of an intensity that transcends any specific situation and becomes exemplary of sheer unadulterated glorying and exultation. The feelings expressed are not necessarily bound to any single series of events. One requires at first no complex and differentiated understanding of the historical context and causes of these sentiments: in their intensity alone they are immediate, irresistible, and overwhelming.

> Sing, O ye heavens; for the Lord hath done it:
> shout, ye lower parts of the earth:
> break forth into singing, ye mountains,
> O forest, and every tree therein:
> for the Lord hath redeemed Jacob,
> and glorified himself in Israel.
>
> (Isaiah 44:23)

Isaiah is by common consent the lyrical apogee of the prophetic books and therewith of at least a certain type of poetry in the Bible. Perhaps only the book of Job has been equally praised for the matchless excellence of its poetry. These judgments hold surprisingly well for readings both in Hebrew and in English. The King James Version of the book of Isaiah ranks among the very greatest poetic masterpieces of English literature. But not only does Isaiah, with its rare poetic distinction, come first in the corpus of the prophets (*Nebiim*) in the Hebrew Bible: Isaiah also has a special role in anticipating and announcing the Christian Gospel. It is in Isaiah that we read:

> How beautiful upon the mountains
> Are the feet of him that bringeth good tidings,
> That publisheth peace;
> That bringeth good tidings of good,
> That publisheth salvation . . .
>
> (Isaiah 52:7ff.)

Isaiah's uncannily evangelical power is graphically illustrated in Acts of the Apostles 8:26–39, where it is by explaining passages from Isaiah that the apostle Philip converts the Ethiopian court eunuch, who leaps down from his chariot to receive baptism immediately.

In the Gospels, Jesus himself has special regard for Isaiah: he reads from this book publicly in the synagogue (Luke 4:16–21). The Gospel writers pick up on a host of its prophecies, centrally the description of the suffering servant (Isaiah 52:13ff.), with whom Jesus in his Passion is identified. Not surprisingly, then, Isaiah also furnishes an abundance of source texts for later liturgical and artistic celebrations of the Gospel story, some very popular, such as Handel's *Messiah*. This book distinguishes itself by the way it contributes to the realization of tradition—namely, through the perennial reprise of traditional motifs relived in fresh contexts and as disclosing their truth anew. The book thus bridges between epochs and unifies history. The poetic quality of the text is surely not accidental or irrelevant to this result: it is perhaps principally poetry that enables this process of synthesis by virtue of its polysemousness and the inexhaustible fertility of its meanings. Certainly the deep, humanly moving power of poetry motivates a continual return to verbal traditions for the sake of their reappropriation in new historical predicaments.

Isaiah's lyrical rapture is essential, moreover, to revelation as "out of this world." It is by the transports of poetry that a dimension of existence beyond representation—the invisible, unrepresentable divine transcendence—can be intimated. Poetry can give us a fleeting sense of eternity, as in Rimbaud's "L'éternité." Poetry in the Hebrew prophets, as in poets of all ages, runs up against the limit of the inexpressible. But prophecy motivates this formal limit of poetry thematically in terms of its primary subject matter—God. The sublimity of God revealed by Isaiah resides in what is *not* revealed about him. To this extent, Isaiah has no express theology and no articulated idea of God, except that he is incomparably higher than any idea we can possibly have of him: "To whom then will ye liken God? or what likeness will ye compare unto him?" (40:18). The inaccessible height of God's transcendence, which can make him a hidden God, a *Deus absconditus* (45:15), is definitively expressed by Isaiah:

> For my thoughts are not your thoughts,
> neither are your ways my ways, saith the Lord.
> For as the heavens are higher than the earth,
> so are my ways higher than your ways,
> and my thoughts than your thoughts.
>
> (Isaiah 55:8–9)

This gap between our thoughts and God points toward the passage beyond representation altogether: it points toward a total rupture with the world as we know it, and thereby toward "apocalypse."

From Prophecy to Apocalyptic

Prophecy interprets history and existence in the light of revelation. It interprets them explicitly *into* the present, in which challenges must be faced courageously and decisions must be made, not least about faith. But even while addressing the ever so specific situations of a people undergoing all manner of tribulation, prophecy also delivers messages whose validity is much wider and potentially unbounded. Prophecy speaks out of its particular historical situation to all times with a universal message claiming to reveal the God of history and the cosmos. This it does eminently by virtue of its poetic form. Isaiah eminently displays how poetry is used to directly represent the oracular speech of God.

Prophecy can perhaps best be defined as the poetic interpretation of history in the light of revelation. In a prophetic perspective, history is lived in the present and is the mirror of the future. For the biblical prophets, history is providentially ruled by the one eternal God who acts with one purpose from the beginning of time to the end. In this way, the vulgar meaning of prophecy as foretelling the future can be comprehended within the definition of prophecy as inspired interpretation of history. But *fore*sight is only one dimension of the *in*sight into history—into its purpose and destiny—that is realized much more completely by prophecy in the deeper sense of the word.

Predicting the future is perhaps the most sensational aspect of prophetic vision. For there seem to be other, natural ways of knowing the past and the present but not the future, since the future has not yet happened, nor been experienced. Yet, for Isaiah the prophet, knowing the future is probably not different in kind from knowing the whole dispensation of the divine will from the foundations of the world:

> Have ye not known? have ye not heard?
> hath it not been told you from the beginning?
> have ye not understood from the foundations of the earth?
> (Isaiah 40:21)

The prophets do often project their oracles into the past in order to make them anticipate cataclysmic events. Second Isaiah "predicts" the campaigns of Cyrus the Persian, culminating in the fall of Babylon in 538 B.C., when they are already underway. The book of Daniel was written between 167 and 164 B.C., under the persecution of the Hellenistic Seleucid Emperor Antiochus IV Epiphanes that led to the Maccabean revolt in the aftermath of the Greek control of Palestine by the successors of Alexander the Great, who had died in 323 B.C. The author—"Daniel"—assumes the name of a persona from a much earlier age, the Babylonian captivity in the sixth century B.C., in order to project forward, with the sureness of hindsight, already accomplished facts. But this only further confirms that rather than being prediction of the future, prophecy is essentially interpretation of history in such a way as to reveal its divine significance, its meaning from the point of view of God.

Only because the past and future are embraced together in the present—God's eternal present—can the prophet "see" the future. Understanding history enables the prophet to discern the essential shape of things to come. It is not by magic, not by command over an otherwise inaccessible field of objects, that the prophet sees the future. It is rather by identifying with God through grace and inspiration to such an extent that his interpretations themselves become instrumental to the realization of the divine purpose in history. Prophets prophesy the future because they anticipate and participate in it—and indeed even help to bring it about. They situate themselves within the horizon of the revelation of God and his providential plan, making its implications compellingly evident to human beings. This is why prophecy leads inevitably to apocalypse, where the interpretation of history reveals the final sense of history as a whole beyond the limits of history as such. This sense might thus be said to issue out of the womb of eternity, into whose secret depth the vision of apocalypse darkly penetrates.

By virtue of its centrifugal energies, driving toward ever greater scope and significance, prophecy tends to lead to a projection from history into eternity. And this takes it to the threshold of apocalypse. The book of Isaiah, from its very beginning, is about the imminent judgment of God and "the Day of the Lord": the "last days" are announced (2:2). The sequence commencing "Enter into the rock" (2:10) already imagines the cataclysm of the Lord coming in his majesty, "When he ariseth to shake terribly the earth." But it is particularly chapters 24–27, together with 34–35—known respectively as the great and little Isaiah apocalypses—that have been recognized as constituting veerings into actual apocalyptic.

To an even greater extent, the book of Daniel is distinguished among the prophetic books for modulating from prophecy into apocalyptic. This becomes especially clear and explicit in the final chapters, 10–12. An angel-like "man" (Daniel 10:5) comes to Daniel to make him understand what is to befall his people "in the latter days." This is a vision "for days yet to come" (Daniel 10:14). In apocalyptic, history is interpreted from the point of view not only of divine revelation but specifically of the revelation of its end. The purpose of the book of Daniel as a whole is significantly different from that of the prophets and is to be understood rather as specifically apocalyptic. Daniel does not directly address his people in order to exhort or reprove and chastise them. He writes to encourage and provide comfort and reassurance in times of dire hardship by promising an imminent intervention on the part of God in defense of his people. A triumphant finale to all their tribulation in the present is discerned as waiting in the wings: in an already encroaching future, the time of the end will erupt and usher in the advent of eternity.

Apocalyptic is concerned not so much with reform, or with relations within this world. The focus is no longer on God's becoming effectively present in history through the actions of human beings: it shifts to the other world and to God's action to overthrow the historical order as such. Exotic allegorical visions adumbrate this transformation. The revelations to Daniel are ones that Daniel himself does not understand (12:8); they are sealed up in a book until the time of the end (12:4). There is no longer the visionary transparency enjoyed by the prophets as interpreters of the divine. This is signified also by the introduction of mediators like the angels Gabriel and Michael. They are an index, as Shemaryahu Talmon explains, of "the unbridgeable chasm which increasingly separates man from the divine sphere. In the biblical past, a prophet could bring God's word to man. Now, the seer requires a celestial interpreter to explain his visions to him. Mediator upon mediator intervenes between man and God. And even then the meaning of the revelation may remain hidden."[42] In the second half of Daniel, that is, in chapters 7–12, after the court stories of chapters 1–6, very late prophetic and now more properly apocalyptic writing tends to narrow and restrict the interpretive faculties of the prophet, who becomes more a mechanical mouthpiece for relaying purportedly objective facts about the future.

These apocalyptic visions are mostly concerned, in various guises, with the succession of empires in the ancient world as leading to total corruption and disaster and, finally, reversal in the reign of God. After Egypt and Assyria, world empire will pass to Babylon (607 B.C.), to Medes/Persians (539 B.C.), to Greece (331 B.C.), and to Rome (30 B.C.). This succession is encoded into the series of metals (gold, silver, bronze, iron/earth) composing the sections of the statue in Nebuchadnezzar's dream (Daniel 2). Daniel also elaborates

42. Shemaryahu Talmon, "Daniel," in *The Literary Guide to the Bible*, 350.

the images of beasts rising from depths with numerous heads and a speaking horn that will reappear in the Christian apocalypse par excellence, the Revelation of Saint John the Divine. There is a whole genre of inter-testamental apocalypses (2 Esdras, 2 Baruch, 1 Enoch, etc.) spouting this sort of inebriating imagery with its surreal scenographies.

Yet it is important that apocalyptic not be limited to or centered upon these fantastic visions; neither should the apocalyptic mode be confined to the specific genre that fosters them. The prophets and even the Gospels are themselves already intrinsically apocalyptic, or at least "eschatological," in the sense of envisaging the end ("eschaton," in Greek). The apocalypses per se often tend to degrade poetic vision into a factual rhetoric of revenge. But apocalyptic moments within prophecy, as it occurs in both the Old Testament and the New, envision the end in its intrinsic connection with the present and in the tension of the fateful decisions that the present exacts. Rather than attempting to declare in pseudo-factual rhetoric, in the style of the inter-testamental apocalypses, what will unfailingly come to pass, Gospels and prophets alike invite to living within a vision of the end that enables humans to work for realizing the highest possibilities of their present. Such apocalyptic and eschatological moments throughout the Bible are open to receiving the revelation of God through the interpretive mediation of humans rather than formalizing it into a fixed code of images and a set repertoire of dramatic disasters. In this way, apocalyptic, too, rather than appearing only as the final unveiling of a supposedly unequivocal, positive truth participates in revelation as it is progressively discovered through the unfolding of the Bible.[43]

The idea of apocalyptic revelation is a very challenging one within the framework of human and historical study. It threatens history with annihilation and is therefore often rejected by the historical (when not outright historicist) outlook of a great part of contemporary cultural criticism.[44] But considered in light of the nonobjective nature of knowledge in the humanities, apocalyptic belongs essentially to the Western intellectual tradition as a whole—at its limit. It is surely no objective knowledge of events, but nevertheless it seems to be a necessary structure of the striving to come to full knowledge of oneself, since this requires transcending the self and every manifest phenomenon of the world that can be seen.[45]

43. I elaborate these theses in theoretical terms in *Poetry and Apocalypse: Theological Disclosures of Poetic Language* (Stanford, Calif.: Stanford University Press, 2009), 8–19.

44. David G. Roskies, *Against Apocalypse: Responses to Catastrophe in Modern Jewish Culture* (Cambridge, Mass.: Harvard University Press, 1984).

45. The widely felt human need for apocalyptic access to worlds unseen is confirmed by comparison, beyond Western traditions, with Mayan, Himalayan, Siberian, and other cultures in John Leavitt, ed., *Poetry and Prophecy: The Anthropology of Inspiration* (Ann Arbor: University of Michigan Press, 1997).

V. Writings and Revelation

We have now seen how myth, history, and prophecy can all be used as vehicles of religious revelation. But what of consciously literary art? The prophets, in spite of all their poetic imagery and rhetoric, spoke in God's name and delivered oracles as direct speech in God's own voice. In the Writings (Ketubim in Hebrew), human voices expressing human concerns emerge and present themselves as such: they explore the affective and volitional dimensions of human existence. Whereas in the Prophets, in accordance with the formal structure of the oracle, God speaks to humans, in the Writings it is human beings who are speaking to and about God. Perhaps most conspicuously, the Psalms speak for humanity: they speak from and of its hopes and fears. They voice its miseries and triumphs, its sense of comfort or guilt or trust or doubt referred directly to a divinity in relation to which all human experiences are lived and articulated. Typically these voices are addressed to God, who is praised and revered, feared, pleaded with, thanked, complained to, quarrelled with, and queried. The human voices of the Writings, moreover, are of different types of "radical" (the root, or generative source, of discourse in a situated communication). While most often in the prayer of the Psalms an anonymous, universal human voice is speaking, usually in a communal and sometimes also liturgical language, in Ecclesiastes a highly self-conscious "I" steps forward and identifies himself as a distinct and indeed very distinguished individual.

With the vector of communication reversed with respect to prophecy, the Writings open in myriad new directions. We have humanity speaking to and about God in a great variety of literary forms, including prayer (Psalms), lament or threnody (Lamentations), philosophical meditations (Ecclesiastes), love lyrics (Song of Songs), drama (Job), and wise sayings (Proverbs). Such diversity of artistic forms is deployed in order to explore the inexhaustible *human* dimensions and depth of the experience of God. This has, in effect, already been the case, indirectly yet inevitably, in Myth, History, and Prophecy: each genre in its own way is based on human mediation of divine revelation. But now a more self-consciously human and artistic sifting of the meaning of the experience deposited in Israel's traditions is brought into the foreground and elaborated. Without attenuating the claim to deliver a revelation from and of God, the Writings, for the first time, give us the full sense of humanity expressing itself directly in its own voice and sometimes even in an outspokenly personal way.

Of course, in all that we have read so far, humanity could not help but express itself. Nonetheless, the requirements of the previous genres relegated the expression of human sentiment and sensibility to the margins as epiphenomena. What the experience felt like to the human beings involved was, at least in principle, secondary. The human voice was muted or masked in a variety of ways in the preceding genres: behind the voice of God in prophecy;

in favor of the (purported) facts themselves in history; in deference to impersonal, universal conditions of existence in myth. In the Writings, the sphere of subjective human experience, on the part both of a people and of individuals, is opened up to being probed and articulated with all the deliberate aesthetic self-consciousness of a highly refined literary art.

How are the experiences of God, history, and existence of human beings in the world actually lived? What feelings are produced and how can they be expressed? Human subjectivity—individual and collective—opens in the Writings as a further dimension in which revelation is discovered and progressively unfolds. Still, even as overtly human expression, this part of the Bible is equally to be considered God's Word. In the Writings, it becomes fully transparent that human and divine agencies are to be conceived of as collaborating and even as coinciding in the composition of the Bible: the two types of agent are indeed figured as coauthoring it. What binds all these human, often all-too-human, modes of expression together is their function as divine revelation. In the Writings, even artistic exploration of the human experience of the world and the psyche in relation to God is presented as inspired by faith and as revelatory of manifold intimate aspects of a personal God. The embrace of such writings as divine revelation and as equal in status to oracles spoken in the voice of the Almighty expresses the intuition that God is present in all of Creation, including human creations—and perhaps also the realization that any representation of divinity inevitably participates in a degree of fiction.

Existential Crisis in Ecclesiastes

Ecclesiastes (in Hebrew *Qohelet*, meaning "Preacher," "Speaker," or sometimes "Teacher") presents a very personal author with his private palaces, parks, forests, fruit trees, and hundreds of concubines. The strong sense of individuality and even of intimately personal experience, with its usually tacit satisfactions and frustrations, makes Ecclesiastes a book that many readers are apt to feel close to today. Perhaps an even more strikingly modern aspect—and a direct consequence of this high degree of subjective self-consciousness—is that Ecclesiastes expresses doubts about the meaning of life. The sense of life's absurdity, its meaninglessness, its "vanity," resonates with more recent types of thinking like existentialism or the "philosophy of the absurd" that epitomize the modern era. In fact, it has often been debated whether and why this book should have been canonized and included in the Bible at all, since to many it seems more expressive of existential *Angst* and despair than of religious faith. An editor of the Oxford Annotated Bible (1991), for instance, introduces the work with the comment that, "Ecclesiastes contains the reflections of a philosopher rather than a testimony of belief. The author seeks to understand by the use of reason the meaning of human existence and the good which man can find in life" (805). And yet, somehow, the religious communities that have revered this book for millennia have found sustenance for their faith in it. Otherwise, it would never have been included in the Bible in the first place, and indeed it has played an important—even if not unproblematic—role in the religious reflection of the faithful throughout the centuries.

The hypothesis of the reading I wish to propose here is that Ecclesiastes is a very powerful, albeit somewhat indirect, testimony of faith. The philosophical reflections it offers, leading always inescapably to the conclusion that all is vanity, are meant to show not the futility of life itself but rather the inability of philosophy to understand it. They thereby point beyond philosophy to faith as necessary to any adequate understanding of the world and of human existence. The reader must therefore allow for a reversal of the book's overt assertions—a reversal that is realized by a subtle rhetorical strategy. The effectual meaning of the book is to be gathered not directly from what it affirms, namely, that "all is vanity," but rather from the manifest vanity of philosophical reasoning itself. Such thinking cannot discover any lasting value in existence and therefore keeps coming back compulsively to the conclusion that all is vanity. It is the vanity of philosophy—and of everything as seen in the view of philosophy—that is played out and proved by the text's repeated, syllogistic assertions of "vanity." These insistent assertions display *their own* vain absurdity. The text exhibits the fallacy of philosophy as a merely human endeavor to know all things in their true meaning and purport ("All things have I seen in the days of my vanity," Ecclesiastes 7:15) and consequently to be the master of one's own life. What presumably has always been felt, at least obscurely, by those who read the book through the lens of their religious faith, is that it is a reductio ad absurdum not of existence itself but of the type of egocentric philosophical ratiocination that sets itself up as the judge of life and its worth and then can find therein only vanity.

In this way, the book demonstrates the vanity not of life as God created it but of human reason in its presumption to know the meaning of life and to understand the final end of things—which, so far as natural reason can see, can only be death. The Teacher's affirmations of vanity, for example, in Ecclesiastes 2:20–21 or 7:15, are subtly undercut by an irony that exposes these statements themselves—and the form of judgment they represent—as vain. We cannot but notice, for example, the self-enclosed, self-referential style of the Teacher's circuit of reasoning. He quotes himself, in a self-satisfied tone, even in declaring his deep dissatisfaction: "I said to myself, 'I have acquired great wisdom, surpassing all who were over Jerusalem before me; and my mind has had great experience of wisdom and knowledge' " (1:16). That is certainly a dangerous affirmation to make about oneself. By whose standards does the speaker esteem himself so savant? Evidently, he has assumed his own standards and judgment as definitive and absolute. In the context of the whole Bible, which constantly inculcates reliance on God rather than on oneself, we cannot but sense the perhaps inadvertent irreverence and arrogance of this blind self-assurance.

What better illustration of how it is folly to be wise—as Thomas Gray was to write—than this sort of solipsistic dialogue of the self with itself. The circularity of this reasoning is made explicit at the linguistic surface by a rhetoric of talking to oneself: "I said to myself, 'Come now, I will make a test of pleasure; enjoy yourself.' But again, this also is vanity" (Ecclesiastes 2:1). In this way, "Solomon" in his greatness, as described in chapter 2, comes across as afflicted by colossal self-absorption, and his pessimism can be seen to be a consequence not of the order of things in the universe but of his narrowly self-centered perception of it—as representative of human egocentricity in general.

The existential sickness unto death expressed in Ecclesiastes's philosophy of despair, then, is not shown to be the only—or even the natural or necessary—response to life as it is given in the human condition. It is the outcome rather of the Teacher's own all too typically human egocentrism and reliance on self rather than on God as the foundation for his judgment. The vainly egotistical logic of the Teacher's reasonings communicates to everything it touches a pessimistic spin. Thus the fact that, upon dying, we leave all that we have accumulated to someone else who did not labor for it provides one more reason for despondency in this characteristically self-involved utterance: "So I turned and gave my heart up to despair concerning all the toil of my labors under the sun, because sometimes one who has toiled with wisdom and knowledge and skill must leave all to be enjoyed by another who did not toil for it. This also is vanity and a great evil" (2:20–21). All this labor and toil of the ego is shown quite conclusively to be vanity. The speaker wants to possess the fruits of those labors himself rather than let them be inherited by someone else. More generally, he wants to be his own master and raison d'être rather than acknowledging that the purpose of his existence is determined by a radically other being, namely, God, who surpasses his understanding and who beholds the true meaning of things, even where the preacher himself can see no meaning at all.

The book opens with observation of the cycles of time from a detached point of view and advances the judgment that "all is vanity" and a striving after wind. But what really proves vain, by the showing of these circuitous verses, is the self-referential pattern of reasoning itself: futile is the endeavor to judge life by the standards of human reason rather than adapting and adjusting reason to life as it is given in the Creation. It is the philosopher's detached remoteness, pretending to survey all things and to sift their meaning, as if from the omniscient vantage point of God, which makes them appear vain to him. As actually lived, and thus as seen from within time and its involvements, things are not vain at all. When things are done in their own proper time, they are filled with poignancy and purpose. From this point of view, everything, whether happy or sad, is just as it should be:

> To everything there is a season,
> And a time to every purpose under the heaven:
> A time to be born, and a time to die;
> A time to plant, and a time to pluck up that which is planted;
> A time to kill, and a time to heal;
> A time to break down, and time to build up;
> A time to weep, and a time to laugh;
> A time to mourn, and a time to dance;
> A time to cast away stones, and a time to gather stones together;
> A time to embrace, and time to refrain from embracing;
> A time to get, and a time to lose;
> A time to keep, and a time to cast away;
> A time to rend, and a time to sew;
> A time to keep silence, and a time to speak;
> A time to love, and a time to hate;
> A time of war, and a time of peace.
>
> (Ecclesiastes 3:1–8)

These verses express a spirit of acceptance of time and its cycles rather than of judgment and of what Nietzsche was later to call "revenge" against time and its "It was"—the ostensibly unchangeable fixity of the past (*The Gay Science*, book 4, aphorism 341). They accept that man's consciousness is time-bound and that he must be guided by the times and seasons with their changes rather than endeavor to judge by any other standard of his own that presumes to transcend them. The temptation to do so is constant, yet the attempt is doomed to fail, for its time-boundedness marks the absolute difference between human and divine knowledge. As stated in verses following close upon those given above, "He," that is, God, "has made everything suitable in his time; moreover he has put a sense of past and future into their minds, yet they cannot find out what God has done from the beginning to the end" (Ecclesiastes 3:11). Human beings have "eternity" or "a sense of the past and the future" or "the world" (*ha-olam*) in their heart: they possess a faculty of reflection that enables them, in effect, to transcend the present and to synoptically overview the succession of times. Yet humans do not have the key to time's meaning, they cannot see beyond its furthest limits so as to know the final purpose of things. They must accept time's terms, hence mortality. But once they do, they can indeed have much profit from life: "I know that there is nothing better for them than to be happy and enjoy themselves as long as they live" (Ecclesiastes 3:12).

This optimistic morality, which is evidently in contradiction with the Teacher's pessimism, is explicitly articulated in clusters of verses and occasional passages that point up the limits of his rigorous philosophy of vanity. Life can be rapturously affirmed, even without reasons, by anyone who accepts to abide within its mortal limits: "In the day of prosperity be joyful, and in the day of adversity consider; God has made the one as well as the other, so that mortals may not find out anything that will come after them" (Ecclesiastes 7:14). Only the last clause endeavors to snare what is a heartily positive, all-accepting outlook in the nets of nihilistic mistrust. An originally sanguine version could conceivably have been modified by an editorial intervention in order to jerk this verse back into line with the philosophy of pessimism expressed in the statement of vanity that frames the preacher's teaching as a whole. Originally the thought may have resembled that of another verse that stands as an unqualified affirmation of life without any reasons but rather simply as an immediate, indisputable perception: "Truly the light is sweet, and a pleasant thing it is for the eyes to behold the sun" (Ecclesiastes 11:7). The following verse reads plausibly as a later addition in order to force this irrepressible effusion of cheerfulness back toward a formally negative conclusion: "But if a man live many years, and rejoice in them all; yet let him remember the days of darkness; for they shall be many. All that cometh is vanity" (11:8). Is there not something mechanical or perfunctory about this inevitable, obligatory melancholy?

The first thought—"Truly the light is sweet, and a pleasant thing it is for the eyes to behold the sun"—is pure joy, and it is simply given with no caveats. It is a joy not in anything produced by our own thought or possessed through our own labor. The Teacher, in typically human fashion, had attempted to construct his own happiness in life, and he found it a toilsome task and full of vexation. But this is because he tried to be the master of life and its joys and pains rather than accepting whatever comes as given from God, taking the good with the bad. What seems bad or unpleasant to us is evidently still good in the sight of God, which surpasses our own outlook. In fact, man's work on earth is not to be calculated and judged by us, but rather to be performed in a spirit of exhilaration in life and of open acceptance of its mystery. Then all is not vanity but is rather filled with significance that is perhaps sometimes terrible as well as delightful. But in any case, it is not experienced merely as vanity.

Chapter 11, on balance, suggests that one must live with confidence in life and its returns—"Cast thy bread upon the waters: for thou shalt find it after many days" (Ecclesiastes 11:11)—and without worrying about or calculating the final outcome of it all, which, in any event, is unknowable to mortals. Too much worrying and reflection will rob one of vitality and, in effect, prevent one from living and producing:

> He that observeth the wind shall not sow;
> and he that regardeth the clouds shall not reap.
> As thou knowest not what is the way of the spirit,
> nor how the bones do grow in the womb
> of her that is with child:
> even so thou knowest not the works of God who maketh all.

> In the morning sow thy seed,
> and in the evening withhold not thine hand:
> for thou knowest not whether shall prosper,
> either this or that, or whether they both shall be alike good.
>
> (Ecclesiastes 11:4–7)

Reason wants to see beyond time and keeps asking, what do you have in the end? To which the answer, of course, is nothing, nothing but death. Therefore, all is vanity. This is inevitably the answer for reason that reflects itself, by its powers of abstraction, out of the actual, living involvements of existence. And yet, life is full of immanent meaning for human beings involved in its manifold processes: "for everything there is a time . . . ." In chapter 12, at the very climax of the book, even death—to take the most challenging theme of all to interpret in any perspective other than that of vanity—is viewed immanently as a process unfolding from within life. As such, far from reducing all to the one abstract significance of "vanity," death is full of untold, mysterious meaning as expressed by the many vital and vigorous suggestions of the poetry:

> Remember now thy Creator in the days of thy youth, while the evil days come not, nor the years draw nigh, when thou shalt say, I have no pleasure in them; while the sun, or the light, or the moon, or the stars, be not darkened, nor the clouds return after the rain: In the day when the keepers of the house shall tremble, and the strong men shall bow themselves, and the grinders cease because they are few, and those that look out of the windows be darkened, And the doors shall be shut in the streets, when the sound of the grinding is low, and he shall rise up at the voice of the bird, and all the daughters of musick shall be brought low; Also when they shall be afraid of that which is high, and fears shall be in the way, and the almond tree shall flourish, and the grasshopper shall be a burden, and desire shall fail; because man goeth to his long home, and the mourners go about the streets: Or ever the silver cord be loosed, or the golden bowl be broken, or the pitcher be broken at the fountain, or the wheel broken at the cistern. Then shall the dust return to the earth as it was: and the spirit shall return unto God who gave it.
>
> (Ecclesiastes 12:1–7)

The "strong men" bowing down here represent the hunched-over shoulders of old age; the few grinders ceasing to work, an advancing toothlessness; the darkened windows, a loss of sight, and so on. For here we contemplate death not just as an absolute limit, but from within time. Hence the piquant, humanly rich allegorical figure conveying an intimate sense of the ailments of age, its dreary infirmities and ghastly disfigurements—yet vividly pictured in their lively and stark significance and human drama. The passage can inspire desire to live with redoubled intensity the limited time that is given to mortals before the dimming and closing off of the senses and slackening of the appetites (taking the loosening silver cord and the broken golden bowl sexually, as Blake suggests) to the shakiness of the limbs of the elderly and the lightness of their sleep broken at the sound of a bird. When death itself is not simply reasoned about in the abstract, as the final reduction to vanity, but is viewed immanently and is lived through in the graphic unfolding of its process of decline, it turns out to be very moving and expressive, full of pathos and poetic meaning in every detail. It is not all pretty, but it is in any case not just vanity.

Especially the poetry of chapters 3, 11, and 12, which are written largely in verse form, expresses this alternative point of view. Such poetic vision does not stand outside of life so as to judge it by rational, human standards but is rather immersed within the stream of its continuing process. Wisdom is conceived at the end of the book, in effect, as relational knowing: “Let us hear the conclusion of the whole matter: Fear God, and keep his commandments: for this is the whole duty of man” (Ecclesiastes 12:13). Just as in Proverbs, “The fear of the Lord is the beginning of knowledge” (1:7). A right relationship with one’s Maker rather than howsoever ingenious insight acquired by one’s own lights is what alone is apt to make a human being truly wise.

Although this “pious conclusion” has often been said to be tacked on in order to give an orthodox meaning to a rebellious book, it seems just as arguable that this conclusion somewhat more curtly and explicitly expresses what the book’s poetry as a whole persuades us to believe. It may actually be certain pessimistic deductions and syllogisms that have been tacked on in search of “consistency” and due to fundamental lack of understanding of the book’s poetic mode of argument and its deeply ironic rhetoric. Ultimately, this book means the opposite of what it repeatedly and programmatically says, for the philosophical statements discredit themselves: as the text performs them, they illustrate *their own* vanity. This performed reversal gives a measure of the freedom and flexibility that revelation takes on in the Writings. It suggests how the human voice can lend itself to becoming a vehicle of God’s Word, in spite of and even *because of* its inability to directly state the truth of that Word. Precisely this inadequacy enables the truth about human limits to be revealed beyond what the words themselves can say.

Read in this way, this work is the converse of prophecy: it reveals by the unmistakable inadequacy and even irreverence of its human words rather than by the incontrovertible authority of direct divine speech. Human beings, except when inspired extraordinarily by God, do not see the world from a prophetic perspective—and knowing this is wisdom. As a profoundly ironic text turning on a rhetorically performed reversal, Ecclesiastes teaches us our human limits (together with God’s infinite, incomprehensible superiority) and the necessity of acting on faith rather than just relying on our own reasoning. As such, and because it teaches this indirectly—not by means of pious statements, but by their apparent opposite—Ecclesiastes has been wondrous in its workings and has been cherished by countless readers in all ages, perhaps especially by those struggling with doubt and yet arduously in search of faith.

The Song of the Senses

The Song of Songs has remained an enigma for scholarly efforts to define its original form and purpose. It is sometimes taken to be a dramatic poem, one which could be reconstructed by assigning groups of verses to a cast of characters including the Shulamite, King Solomon, and Choruses made up of the Brothers and Daughters of Jerusalem. Another hypothesis is that it is rather an anthology of love poems, all independent compositions.[46] In any case, the human voice breaks irrepressibly into a multiplicity of expressions in this work. The speakers in the Song are inherently multiple and differentiated, without any preestablished, unitary self-identity. The perennial question in interpretation of the Song of Songs is whether this multiplicity harmonizes into an ultimate unity that transcends its isolated ejaculations. If there is such a unity, furthermore, might it indicate a transcendent, divine love beyond all the merely sensual impulses that are so frankly expressed and made so palpably manifest? The context of the Song within the biblical canon has exerted constant pressure throughout the ages in precisely this direction of interpretation. Hence the persistent determination to read the Song as a dialogue between God and his people, or between Christ and the church, or the bridegroom and his bride, and therefore as a discourse revealing a love that is realized ultimately as a union of humanity with divinity. Such allegorical interpretation has kept the most celebrated exegetes—from Origen to Saint Bernard—busy for millennia producing massive volumes of commentary.[47]

I would like to be receptive to the intuitions on which this tradition of commentary is based and, at the same time, to read the Song of Songs radically in its essence as poetry[48]—and therefore also as exceeding any particular confessional appropriation. Poetry in its intrinsic indeterminacy, given the characteristic polysemousness of metaphorical expression, signifies infinitely: taken to its limits, poetry opens itself to signifying the Infinite. It is, therefore, no accident that this love poetry has lent itself so well to being read as an

46. A. Robert, "Le genre littéraire du Cantique des Cantiques," *Revue biblique* 52 (1943–44): 192–213; Marcia Falk, *Love Lyrics from the Bible: A Translation and Literary Study of the Song of Songs* (Sheffield: Almond, 1982).

47. For contemporary transmissions and transformations of this tradition, see especially Jean-Louis Chrétien, *Symbolique du corps: La tradition chrétienne du Cantique des Cantiques* (Paris: Presses Universitaires de France, 2005), and Anne-Marie Pelletier, *Lectures du Cantique des Cantiques: De l'énigme du sens aux figures du lecteur* (Rome: Editrice Pontificio Biblico, 1989).

48. Compare Patrick Hunt, *Poetry in the Song of Songs: A Literary Analysis* (New York: Peter Lang, 2008).

allegory of divine, that is, of infinite love. Perhaps all radically poetic language tends to speak of such Love. It is important to recollect this potential of poetry for absolute meaning (or even perhaps for attaining an absolute beyond meaning, where sense turns into pure sensation) in an age where poetic language is more often taken to be subversive of all unified order. Poetry is that, too, especially when pursuing the Rimbaldian project announced in the famous "Lettres du voyant," according to which "the poet becomes a seer by a long, immense, and deliberate derangement *of all the senses*" ("Le poète se fait voyant par un long, immense et raisonné dérèglement de *tous les sens*").[49] But precisely its unruliness and spontaneity are laden with the suggestion that poetry's uncanny beauty and power devolve from a transcendent order that it expresses in a way which remains beyond rational calculation.

If the object of the Song of Songs is to express divine love exceeding human comprehension, it does so by representing an absolute degree of human or sensual love. One might speak here, with Luce Irigaray, of a "sensible transcendental." It is the limitlessness of the love in question precisely in its total sensual abandon, devoid of any specific doctrinal content, that makes it comparable to divine love. Love is absolute and its own authority in this universe. Love must be allowed absolute freedom to do its own pleasure, without being conditioned externally:

> I charge you, O ye daughters of Jerusalem,
> by the roes, and by the hinds of the field,
> that ye stir not up, nor awake my love, till he please.
> (Song of Songs 3:5)

It is unabashedly sensual, sexual love that is being celebrated. The veil of a highly figurative language, depicting, for example, the mound of Venus as a mountain of myrrh and frankincense, only makes more exquisite and provocative a dramatic and, above all, erotic climax such as the following:

> I sleep, but my heart waketh:
> it is the voice of my beloved that knocketh, saying,
> Open to me, my sister, my love, my dove, my undefiled:
> for my head is filled with dew,
> and my locks with the drops of the night.
> I have put off my coat; how shall I put it on?
> I have washed my feet; how shall I defile them?
> My beloved put in his hand by the hole of the door,
> and my bowels were moved for him.

---

49. Arthur Rimbaud, letter to Paul Demeny, May 15, 1871. Such a conception of poetry is developed by Julia Kristeva, *La révolution du langage poétique* (Paris: Seuil, 1974).

I rose up to open to my beloved;
and my hands dropped with myrrh,
and my fingers with sweet smelling myrrh,
upon the handles of the lock.

(Song of Songs 5:2–5)

The unchecked exaltation of the senses, the uncircumscribed intensity of pure sensation, is the most appropriate human vehicle for expressing the unlimited intensity of divine love. Paradoxically, in this way the senses in their own purity and absoluteness can suggest what transcends sense-experience altogether. The experience of the senses is perhaps what comes closest in an analogical sense to the experience of God. The total exposure and vulnerability and the enrapturing ecstasy of sex have across untold ages and in numerous different art forms been seen as like the religious rapture of the direct experience of God. Bernini's sculpture in the Cornaro chapel in Santa Maria della Vittoria in Rome depicting Saint Teresa pierced by a glowing shaft and in an attitude often interpreted as expressing orgasm is emblematic of this surprising coincidence of spirituality with sensuality wrought to its uttermost.

If this unabashed sensuality is seen and admitted, the Song raises the question of the place of sensual love in the economy of redemption and salvation. The image of the love of the bridegroom for the bride and vice versa became, in fact, a canonical figure for divine love. It recurs in the penultimate chapter of the book of Revelation, with "new Jerusalem, coming down from God out of heaven, prepared as a bride adorned for her husband" (21:2). Can precisely sensual attraction and erotic exultation become something holy? Without any special qualifications? Sensual love per se is life and energy, innocent of good and evil, and as such it is wholly good like Creation before the Fall. Sensation is per se infinite, in the sense that it is without conceptual definition and limit. It is precisely the unqualified, unlimited nature of this love as pure sensation that suggests and signifies divinity, the Infinite. And this significance of sensation is expressed best in poetry because of the latter's relative indeterminacy, its intentionality reaching beyond all that its words concretely and pragmatically designate.

The innocence presupposed by the unchecked, unself-conscious abandonment to sensual excitement expresses itself further in a certain flouting of boundaries that normally demarcate legitimate from forbidden love. By virtue of poetic license, a certain ambiguously incestuous urge can be freely and innocently avowed:

O that thou wert as my brother,
That sucked the breasts of my mother!
When I should find thee without, I would kiss thee;
Yea, I should not be despised.
I would lead thee, and bring thee into my mother's house,

who would instruct me; I would cause thee to drink
of spiced wine of the juice of my pomegranate.
(Song of Songs 8:1–2)

The same incestuous suggestion surfaces in the epithet "my sister, my bride," which occurs in 5:1 and 4:9: "You have ravished my heart, my sister, my bride, you have ravished my heart with a glance of your eyes." Such employment of "brother" and "sister" is perhaps just formulaic and customary, a literary convention for signifying closeness or affinity. Nevertheless, the straightforward literal sense also is released to work poetically on the imagination. The effect is to suggest that nothing is impure in this ideal garden of love and poetry. The universal desire moving toward unity, ultimately of all in one, knows no boundaries. Love, as return to origin—which is paradigmatically the case with love for God as the transcending of all separateness through the *unio mystica*—is inherently a sort of metaphysical incest. It is fulfilled here in the ultimate realization of an absolute poetry, where everything is totally open to everything else: indeed all things are ambiguously identified with one another. This becomes explicit and programmatic in Symbolist poetics, with Baudelaire and Mallarmé,[50] but it may be at work at some level in poetry generally and not least here in the poetry of the Song of Songs.

The elusiveness of this poem as a drama—the difficulty of pinning down the exact scenario and the dramatis personae—frees it from social and moral categories. It is the innocence of sensual love, pure sensation without reflection, as in the Garden of Eden, that makes it redolent of holiness. The indeterminacy of poetic language creates the possibility of undoing all constraints of law and social mores. Therefore language is completely freed and takes on a life of its own in this poem that upstages any field of reference to extra-linguistic realities. This is typical of poetic language, particularly at its most flamboyant or baroque. The similes, being elaborate and somewhat far-fetched, tend to overpower what they stand for and so to catapult us into a realm of pure metaphor.

Thy hair is a flock of goats,
That lie along the side of Gilead.
Thy teeth are like a flock of ewes,
Which are come up from the washing;
Whereof every one hath twins,
And none is bereaved among them.
Thy temples are a piece of pomegranate
Behind thy veil.
(Song of Songs 6:5–7)

50. I develop this idea in "The Linguistic Turning of the Symbol: Baudelaire and His French Symbolist Heirs," in *Baudelaire and the Poetics of Modernity*, ed. Patricia Ward (Nashville, Tenn.: Vanderbilt University Press, 2000), 28–40.

Many conceits, like the comparison of the neck to "the tower of David builded for an armoury, whereon there hang a thousand bucklers, all shields of mighty men" (4:4), by a certain ostentation and sometimes even preposterousness, highlight language itself as the main theme. Descriptions like "thy nose is as the tower of Lebanon / Which looketh toward Damascus" (7:4) no longer help us to visualize the referential object more exactly; they rather substitute a new register of meaning for what is literally envisaged. The thematic object becomes a pretext for the image rather than the image being a means of representing its object.[51]

A taste for extravagance and luxurious stylization may be thought to belong in the first place simply to a certain oriental aesthetic that characterizes the poem. But the often somewhat shockingly non-naturalistic imagery makes sense also, if not in terms of the object, then at least in terms of emotions projected onto it, as, for example, in the description of the beloved woman as "terrible as an army with banners" (Song of Songs 6:4, 10). Though the beloved is elsewhere described as attractive and inviting, certainly there is something fearful in the experience of love and its overpowering passions that rob one of one's sovereignty and self-control and make one vulnerable.

In descriptions wrought to the breaking point, the poetic medium of the Song declares, finally, the ineffability of its subject. The obvious stretching of the imagery to an extreme hints at the poet's impotence to adequately express the theme. This could hardly help but be the case where this theme is divine love. The absolute experience of love, represented by pure sensuality, fosters an absolute experience of language, which in its purity is silence, the silence of pure sensation. And that is sacred.

Theoretical-Theological Conclusion

These are but summary indications of how the Writings contribute to an understanding of the poetic nature of religious revelation as it has been developed here through reading some books from the biblical Writings as humanities texts. Such a reading has been proposed not against the claim of these writings to be divine revelation, but as a way of suggesting what this might mean in human and in literary terms. Such a reading is "theological," not in a dogmatic sense, but rather in its discovery of *theos* as inhering in *logos*. A certain sense of divinity can be found reflected in the language humans use to express the deepest roots of their existence and consciousness.

51. Robert Alter suggests that in the comparisons in which this desire is expressed, the second term of the comparison flaunts metaphor "by pushing its frame of reference into the foreground" (*Art of Biblical Poetry*, 197) rather than using metaphor to point to and sharpen its referent. This analysis follows I. A. Richards's theory of metaphorical language in *The Philosophy of Rhetoric* (Oxford: Oxford University Press, 1965).

A transcendent reality or sphere of experience has been discovered particularly in the unfathomable opening of meaning in poetry to a dimension of indeterminacy. Theology is then proposed as a discourse that interprets this dimension imaginatively through exploring the existential experience vis-à-vis an unutterable ground or groundlessness of our being and of all that is.

Kindred reflections along the lines of a literary theology contemplating and speculating on certain inherently theological latencies of language have been proposed notably by Paul Ricoeur in his reading of selected texts from the Bible. Ricoeur similarly emphasizes "those quite striking features of indetermination" which give poetic language a sort of transcendence of all pragmatic contexts of communication. With reference specifically to the Song of Songs, he writes of "the tendency of the whole metaphorical interplay unfolded by the poem to free itself from its proper referential, that is, sexual, function."[52] This enables him to valorize the ancient and medieval allegorical interpretations of the poem (which are typically dismissed in modern historical-critical interpretation) as nevertheless pertinent reinvestments of the semantic potential of the poem and its metaphors in other, later historical and interpretive contexts.

Ricoeur refers to an "enclave of innocence" in the Song of Songs in which erotic love can connect itself with the "theologically approved" innocence of Genesis 2 and specifically with man's jubilation over the woman whom God has made from him and then given to him to be his companion (2:23). This intertextual linking of Song of Songs with the story of the Creation of woman suggests "the theological character of these two texts where God is not named or referred to" (299). God is the more imposingly present as unnamed.

Thus Ricoeur, too, proposes a "theological" reading that conjugates ancient allegorical tradition with modern "naturalistic" readings of the book as simply an erotic dramatic poem. Its theological import is found within the poem's own autonomous and secular meaning as literature, but this meaning cannot be narrowly identified with any literal sense fixed by the supposedly original intention of the author(s) as it might be reconstructed by historical-critical methods. Instead, the poetry opens up a space of indetermination, which is the space that theology can interpret most intriguingly—with its self-subverting reference to an infinite God who remains always indeterminable in merely human language and consciousness.[53] This "space" could also be conceived of as a "moment" that calls to be interpreted theologically, a moment of unlimited openness in the realization of the meaning of the text that allows it to be informed by relation to the Infinite—or, quasi-equivalently, by infinite relations.

52. Paul Ricoeur and André LaCocque, *Thinking Biblically: Exegetical and Hermeneutical Studies* (Chicago: University of Chicago Press, 1998), 268.

53. Ricoeur discusses the unnamable divine Name as a "limit-expression" in *Figuring the Sacred*, 228–30.

Ricoeur finds in the Song of Songs "a reconciliation between the sexual and the sacred" (*Thinking Biblically*, 298) and therefore also between the secular and the theological. He also concurs with the general approach being advocated in these pages in finding, beyond literary form, something that it cannot convey except by canceling itself out and gesturing toward what is beyond logos: "reread in light of Genesis, the Song of Songs becomes a religious text insofar as we can hear in it the word of a silent, unnamed God, who is not discerned owing to the force of attestation of a love caught up in itself" (299). *Theos* is thus revealed as logos but also as always finally beyond logos: the mystery of the Father remains intact even in the revelation of the Word in the Son. This has been the "spirit" of the Hebrew Scriptures all along in their forcing the word to its limits and opening it to its own unfathomable beyond. This Spirit will be revealed in its full purport as divine Person in the word of the Gospel.

VI. Gospel as Personal Knowing

At first glance, the Gospel would seem to be a kind of biography, the life story of Jesus of Nazareth. Moreover, to the extent that it purports to be a true story about events among a certain people in a particular historical time and place, it might also be assimilated superficially to history. In fact, much research into the Gospels has traditionally taken the form of the search for "the historical Jesus."[54] But these resemblances to other genres are deceptive, for the Gospel is in crucial respects sui generis. Gospel, considered as a literary genre, is not to be confounded with biography or historiography. Its purpose is not to recount the facts of Jesus's life per se, but to show what he meant for his disciples. Specifically, it shows how he revealed God to them in himself and thereby became their Savior. The Gospel witnesses to the power of Jesus to transform human lives and give them a new meaning. Gospel means literally "good news" (from Old English *god*, good, and *spel*, message or story—like *Spiel* in German, used also in English: "a long spiel"). And indeed it is good news that is meant to change people's lives: it proclaims a message of salvation rather than simply telling a story or a history for its own sake.

---

54. Albert Schweitzer, *The Quest for the Historical Jesus: A Critical Study of Its Progress from Reimarus to Wrede*, trans. W. Montgomery (London: A. & C. Black, 1910), originally *Geschichte der Leben-Jesu-Forschung* (Tübingen: J.C.B. Mohr, 1906). Contemporary continuations of this quest include John Dominic Crossan, *The Historical Jesus: The Life of a Mediterranean Jewish Peasant* (San Francisco: Harper and Row, 1991), and John P. Meier, *A Marginal Jew: Rethinking the Historical Jesus* (New York: Doubleday, 1991).

If the Gospels only presented the objective facts of Jesus's historical existence, they would not be able to say what is most important about him, for that is revealed only by his significance in the lives of the people whom he meets and who believe in him. It is his life-transforming power for the individuals who were changed by their belief in him that is supremely important, indeed miraculous. His followers were given new hope and were empowered to love in previously unattainable ways, ways for which they could not possibly have accounted otherwise. A purely factual account of Jesus's life—100 percent certain and demonstrated—would never be able to witness to the experience of this sort of power. A historian could, at most, tell us about a man, whereas those who believed in Jesus personally perceived and experienced God. The idea that Jesus was a divine being, the Son of God—how could that ever be an observable fact and be recorded as such? How can such a conviction even be meaningful, except within the context of a personal relationship? If you look, you see a man. And if you insist on looking for objective, empirical proof of his being something else, you will never know what Jesus meant to those who knew him and followed him and loved him and believed in him and found in him their salvation.

To appreciate the Gospels accurately, even just as literature, we need to read them not as transparent to the historical Jesus, but as testimonies of faith.[55] This makes it to a large degree futile to inquire: did it really happen that way? What is being recorded fundamentally is how Jesus was *experienced*. To understand the Gospels as gospel—as the unique literary form and genre of religious testimony that they are—we need rather to ask: what meaning does that which is recounted have for those who experienced and perhaps *still* experience it? This is the meaning that can be interpreted and reexperienced as true in the present by readers in all ages, hence also by us still today. The Gospel is based on witness to purportedly historical happenings, yet it is fully unveiled never as naked history but rather always only for those who have made the commitment and decision of faith. Indeed, if humanities texts generally give us history and tradition always mediated by present reality and beliefs, this is acutely true in the case of the Gospels. For intrinsic to the Gospels as a genre is a further purpose beyond simply recording something that happened in the past: they deliver their testimony in order that the reader or hearer of the word of the Gospel might believe in turn and be saved. Their message is directed toward an actualization of God's saving grace through Jesus in the lives of hearers and readers *now*—in the present tense of the Gospel as it is proclaimed—even in being read to oneself.

---

55. This approach has frequently been championed also in theological interpretation, perhaps most influentially by Rudolph Bultmann, *Theologie des Neuen Testaments,* 9th ed. (Tübingen: J.C.B. Mohr, 1984 [1948]), trans. Kendrick Grobel as *Theology of the New Testament* (New York: Scribner, 1955).

If the Gospel is also in some sense a history, it is best understood as a *prophetic* type of history. For what is at stake is a living of history in the present and in light of a divine revelation of its meaning. Such revelation takes up a point of view outside the sequence of past events, one not attainable from within that series. The Gospels are indeed prophetic in the way that the whole Bible is prophetic, namely, in the sense that by recounting history they reveal something beyond history, what in a certain traditional language of faith is called eternity. This is something which cannot be grasped as an objective fact in the order of the past or the future; it can only be lived and fathomed in the infinite freedom and openness of the present. As such, it is not fully formed and determinate but is rather in the process of determining all facts in their deepest significances. History in this way opens to "eternity." Yet this eternal dimension of significance to human life cannot be experienced as anything positively given. It is projective rather than positive, and it claims the whole individual in the intimate sphere of personal experience and decision. The revelation of Jesus Christ cannot be approached without such directly personal engagement.

To this extent, it is clear that the Gospel concerns what we have called personal knowing.[56] It is fundamentally not about facts but about their significance. It aims at opening up personal lives to possibilities beyond their parameters as ordinarily perceived. The knowledge of Jesus, in particular of Jesus as God, is inseparable from what people experience *about themselves* in relation to him. This experience occurs in the present and as decisive for the whole of their lives projected into the future without limit—and in this sense, for all eternity.

To appreciate the different sorts of personal significance that can be conveyed by the Gospel as a genre, it is important to distinguish a variety of subgenres operating within it. Examples of these subgenres include the miracle story, the controversy (against the scribes and Pharisees, for instance), and the parable.

A parable is a comparison developed in story form, usually to the end of inducing the auditor to make a judgment on him- or herself. The parable told by the prophet Nathan to King David in 2 Samuel 12 illustrates this well. It is told as a means of stirring up David's conscience against himself for having had Uriah the Hittite placed in the front lines of battle to be killed, so that he, David, might possess Uriah's wife, Bathsheba. Nathan recounts that a rich man, in order to dress a meal for a wayfarer, instead of using his own livestock took from a poor man his ewe lamb, his one and only, which he carried in his bosom. When David's indignation is kindled, provoking him

---

56. An illuminating discussion of some of the wider epistemological ramifications of such knowing is Michael Polanyi, *Personal Knowledge: Towards a Post-Critical Philosophy* (London: Routledge, 1998 [1958]).

to cry out angrily for the offender's death, Nathan concludes dramatically: "Thou art the man!"

This example vividly illustrates how the effectual meaning of a parable arises out of and speaks into the specific situation of its hearers. These situations actually change over the course of the process of transmission of the Gospels. Especially the conclusions or lessons drawn from parables tend to shift from being about the Kingdom of God—when Jesus tells them to the crowds—to being about Jesus himself when they are retold by the Gospel writers. In the light of Easter, their sense is transformed from being theological to being Christological. They may even become ecclesiological in the light of Pentecost, when the Holy Spirit is bestowed in order to constitute the church (Acts 2:1–41). For example, the marriage-feast parable addressed to the Pharisees in Matthew 22:1–14 is taken by Luke 14:15–24 as addressed to Christians. Whereas for Jesus the good news was the advent of the Kingdom of God, for the writers of "the Gospel of Jesus Christ" (Mark 1:1), Jesus himself becomes the good news. He is himself the central event of the new world that he announces—which may not be how he originally presented it. And it is an even further extrapolation to understand the wedding banquet to be the church, which did not yet exist at the time of Jesus's original telling of the parable.

In their quest for the historical Jesus, scholars seek to reconstruct Jesus's preaching and ministry as it took place around 30 A.D. However, this is only one of several types of study of the Gospels, each endeavoring to gain access to a different level of their meaning and significance for subsequent generations. Another type of study focuses on the stage immediately after Jesus's ministry—on the oral elaboration of the Jesus tradition, from about 30 to 50 A.D. This material is studied particularly by the discipline of *form criticism*, which undertakes to reconstruct the kerygma, the essential proclamation of the Christian message of salvation, together with the liturgy and catechisms of the earliest churches as transmitted in oral *forms*, before they were deposited in the documents of the New Testament and apocrypha.[57]

After this period, the first written traditions would have begun to crystallize, and attempts to isolate them constitute another discipline known as *source criticism*. This discipline constructs, for example, the hypothesis of a Q document (from the German *Quelle*—source) comprising the sayings of Jesus common to Matthew and Luke but not found in Mark. Such a text seems to have been available to Matthew and Luke, since they repeat large sections of Jesus's teaching, agreeing with each other almost verbatim, although also with certain characteristic inflections of their own. Then sometime after 70

57. Martin Dibelius, *Die Formgeschichte des Evangeliums* (Tübingen: Mohr, 1919), trans. Bertram Lee Woolf as *From Tradition to Gospel* (Cambridge: J. Clarke, 1971).

A.D. the written Gospels began to appear, and establishing the derivations and transmission of the manuscripts is the business of *redaction criticism.*

	Jesus's life	oral traditions	written traditions	manuscript transmission
A.D.	30	50	70	
	historical research	form criticism	source criticism	redaction criticism

If we pay attention to how they write about Jesus, we can discover the significance that the traditions conveying Jesus's words and deeds had for each of the several Gospel writers and for the communities to which they belonged. For all the Gospel writers, that significance was that he was divine, and thus a miracle: their lives were changed by him, they experienced redemption and salvation. But it is also possible to finely distinguish between the various writers and their very distinct experiences of Jesus reflecting their different communities and cultural backgrounds, as well as their different theological agendas.

The Gospel according to Matthew is characterized, in the first place, by its conspicuous Jewishness. It was evidently written by and for Christians converted from Judaism. This appears from the outset in its special emphasis on genealogy and on Jesus's Davidic ancestry. Whereas Mark declares Jesus in his opening sentence to be the "son of God," Matthew opens by identifying Jesus as "the Messiah, the son of David." The first two chapters of Matthew, moreover, establish the pattern of reading every detail of Jesus's life as a fulfillment of Old Testament prophecy. This can be verified for events of the Gospel from the virgin birth of the Messiah—understood as having been foretold by Isaiah (7:14)—to his coming out of Bethlehem, as predicted by Micah (5:2), to the going down to Egypt, which Matthew links to a verse of Hosea: "Out of Egypt I have called my son" (1: 11). Similarly, the slaughter of the innocents is read by Matthew (2: 18) in correspondence with the weeping and lamentation in Ramah of Rachel for her children, spoken of by Jeremiah (31:15).

This pattern continues throughout the Gospel according to Matthew with repeated references—they are much more insistent in Matthew's version of the Gospel—to the Jewish Scriptures, most often to Isaiah and the Psalms, as proof texts. The procedure becomes fully explicit when, for example, Matthew adds to an account of Jesus's miraculous healings: "This was to fulfill what had been spoken through the prophet Isaiah, 'He took our infirmities and bore our diseases' " (8:17). The same appeal to fulfillment of Isaiah's prophecies is made with reference to the chosen servant of the Lord and the oracle "I will put my Spirit upon him" in Matthew 12:17 (see further

4:14–16; 12:17–21; 13:35; 21:4–5; 27:9–10). Other clear indications of intimate involvement in Jewish affairs and in their rival communities are the mission to Israel (10:6, 23), the story of the Canaanite woman (15:21–28), and the bitterness against the scribes and Pharisees (23:1–36; 12:1–14, etc.). At Jesus's Roman trial, Matthew adds the dream of Pilate's wife, thus deepening the guilt of the Jews as contravening a supernatural sign.

Sharply polemical against the unconverted Jewry of his day, Matthew's message is that Jesus is the fulfillment of the Law and the Prophets represented symbolically by Moses and Elijah, with whom Jesus appears transfigured on Mount Tabor. His face shines like the sun (17:2), just as did Moses's when he came down from Mount Sinai, bearing the tablets of the Law (Exodus 34:29–35). This hints that Jesus recapitulates in his own life the history of the Israelites coming up out of Egypt and wandering forty years in the desert. His forty days fasting in the wilderness, where he is tempted by the devil (chapter 4), are immediately followed by the proclamation in the Sermon on the Mount, starting from chapter 5, of what in effect is a new covenant with God that fulfills the covenant made with Moses on Mount Sinai. In showing that the revelation of God is now fully vested in Jesus, Matthew nevertheless always carefully articulates the emergence of the new faith from the matrices of Judaism.

The Gospel according to Matthew is also distinguished as characteristically Jewish by the weight given to Jesus's teachings. His quintessentially rabbinical activity gives priority to the word, just as in the priestly story of the Creation in Genesis. More about Jesus's teaching is learned from Matthew than from any other Gospel writer. The teachings are concentrated into five great discourses (echoing the fivefold division of the books of Moses in the Pentateuch) that define the basic structure of this Gospel: the Sermon on the Mount in chapters 5–7; the commissioning of the disciples sent upon missions in chapter 10; seven parables of the kingdom of heaven in chapter 13; the rule of life for a community of disciples in chapter 18:1–20; and the apocalyptic discourse in chapters 24–25. The alternation of such discursive passages with narrative sequences is repeated throughout this Gospel as a whole. This divides the Gospel according to Matthew roughly into words and deeds: Jesus's preaching is followed by his enactment of the Kingdom of God (again paralleling the Creation paradigm: "And God said . . . and it was so").

The greatest of these discourses is the Sermon on the Mount, in which Jesus takes up and fulfills the teaching of the Law delivered by Moses from Mount Sinai. It begins with the beatitudes, which define a new kind of existence still immersed in the suffering of the world and yet placed also in relation to God and therefore "blessed." The beatitudes condense the core meaning and message of the Gospel and present it as an intensification and interiorization—but not an abrogation—of the Jewish Law and Scriptures. This is stated explicitly in the ensuing antitheses of chapter 5, beginning:

"Think not that I am come to destroy the law or the prophets; I have come not to destroy but to fulfill" (5:17).

A related distinguishing characteristic of Matthew among the Gospels is that the role of the church is particularly pronounced. As the so-called "ecclesiological Gospel," Matthew bears the communitarian stamp of its Jewish origins. Its religion is conceived as the religion of a people. The fundamental experience of the Messiah occurs particularly in community worship. Indeed, Matthew's Jesus all along is the Risen Lord celebrated in the liturgy—far more than just the man Jesus peregrinating around Palestine. All these distinctive traits, and the biases they embody, come out by comparison of the accounts of given incidents and exchanges with the other synoptic writers, each marked by its own specific theology and cultural background.

Whereas Mark leads us to discover first the man Jesus of Nazareth, Matthew presents the glorified Lord right from the prostrations of the Magi in adoration before the infant Jesus ("they knelt down and paid him homage," 2:11). The same gesture is repeated in closing this Gospel of the risen Christ with the disciples' prostration before the resurrected Jesus on the mountain in Galilee (28:17). Matthew's Jesus, moreover, is hieratic and solemn. He has a plethora of titles such as "King of Israel," "Son of David." At his Jewish trial, Jesus foretells his coming in glory as the Son of Man. Jesus presents himself, moreover, explicitly as the beloved Son of his Father (11:27) and is repeatedly recognized as such by his disciples (14:33; 16:16), whereas in Mark the disciples never seem able to grasp his messianic identity.

Matthew eliminates the emotion and ignorance attributed to Jesus by Mark. Jesus's impotence as a prophet without honor in his own country ("he could there do no mighty work") according to Mark 6:5 is attenuated by Matthew to the acknowledgment: "And he did not many mighty works there because of their unbelief" (13:58). Matthew consistently accentuates Jesus's power. Matthew's Passion narrative (chapters 26–27) begins with Jesus's foretelling of his Crucifixion. From this point forward, Jesus is in control of the unfolding drama. He interprets the woman's pouring of costly ointment on his head in a house in Bethany as an anointing for his burial (26:6–12). He is like a priest celebrating the sacrifice of the Mass. The last supper is framed by Jesus's announcement of Judas's betrayal and of Peter's denial of him. He is conscious of himself as fulfilling the Scripture (26:31). The agony in the garden of Gethsemane shows Jesus's human side and vulnerability, though he is still master of the situation—unlike his sleep-prone disciples, to whom he is able to announce, just before the event, that his betrayer is at hand (26:45–46). Even when he is arrested, Jesus has the power to summon twelve legions of angels, but he declines to use it (26:53) and rather practices the non-resistance that he has preached.

Matthew also streamlines the miracle stories, eliminating much realistic detail and presenting the disciples as much more like Christians of his own time, so as to suggest how Jesus continues his work of salvation in the community currently. A perspicuous example of this is the healing of Peter's mother-in-law. Mark 1:29–30 tells of this incident as part of a visit to Capernaum. Jesus exerts power physically, actually taking the woman by the hand and lifting her up. Luke 4:38–39 has organized a sequence of exorcisms within the day's work at Capernaum and, accordingly, turns this healing into an exorcism in which Jesus "rebukes" the fever and "immediately she rose and served them." The word "immediately" here represents a certain enhancement with respect to Mark: it heightens the wonder of the miracle. But Matthew 8:14–15 gives this healing a different narrative setting altogether as one of ten miracles following the Sermon on the Mount. He concentrates the story on Jesus alone, eliminating the secondary personages and details. Jesus no longer needs to be told of the illness, nor is he beseeched to heal it. He simply "saw" the woman lying sick and "touched" her hand so that the fever left her, "and she rose and served him." Mark and Luke conclude that she served "them" (the disciples), but Matthew insists that she served *him*. This, in effect, simplifies the story to make the mother-in-law a symbol of the resurrected church serving its glorified Lord.[58]

Similar tendencies in Matthew to sacrifice incidental narrative detail in order to more sharply focus the central significance of Christ for the church can be documented by comparison of the synoptic accounts of the Stilling of the Storm (Matthew 8:23–27; Mark 4:35–41; Luke 8:22–25). The disciples are swamped by the waves in a violent storm—σεισμὸς, suggesting a seismic eruption, which is symbolic of the end of the world. They wake and implore Jesus, saying, "Save, Lord; we are perishing." The Greek Κύριε σῶσον ("Save, Lord") was a liturgical formula in the early church, very much like *Kyrie eleison* ("Lord, have mercy"). It makes audible the church's pleading for help and salvation. Matthew thus allows us to descry the contemporary experience of the early church at worship beneath the narrative of Jesus's acts with his original disciples. The former is the experience out of which his narration arises and in which it remains embedded.

Such experience is the locus of religious truth experienced as always present in the revelation of Jesus as alive in the faith community and thus always the believer's contemporary: it makes the Gospel the perfect paradigm of a humanities text. The truth of such texts happens all over again, ever again, in the event of their reading and interpretation. In liturgy and worship, Jesus is revealed as the risen Lord and as with his Church always "even unto the end of the world" (Matthew 28:20).

One must experience Jesus in the present in order to believe in the truth of the Gospel story. Especially the present experience of the death and

58. Such a parallel reading of this and other miracles in the synoptic Gospels is proposed by Étienne Charpentier, *Pour lire le Nouveau Testament* (Paris: Cerf, 1981), where numerous other commonplaces of New Testament scholarship evoked in these pages are conveniently summarized.

resurrection of Jesus remains the literally crucial event out of which the whole of the Gospel is conceived. This event and its being relived every day—*hodie resurrexit* ("He is risen today"), as the Easter liturgy has it—establishes the frame for the Gospel portrait of Jesus's life as a whole.

The Gospels Begin from Easter

As a testimony of faith in the risen Lord, the Gospels begin essentially from Easter. That is when the protagonist is finally revealed in his true identity and as establishing the Kingdom of God. Previously, apart from exceptionally privileged moments, such as Peter's confession at Caesarea Philippi ("Thou art the Christ, the son of the living God," Matthew 16:13ff.), this identity had been closely guarded as the "messianic secret."[59] Even after the revelation to Peter at Caesarea Philippi, the secret is reinstated immediately: "Then he sternly ordered his disciples not to tell anyone that he was the Messiah" (16:20). When asked why he speaks in parables in public, Jesus replies, "To you it has been given to know the secrets of the kingdom of heaven, but to them it has not been given" (Matthew 13:11). It is only with the Easter event, comprising Christ's death and resurrection, followed up by Pentecost and the pouring out of the Spirit, that the good news of Jesus Christ as the Son of God is ripe to be publicized beyond the circle of his intimates and disciples. From that point forward, everything is seen in a new light with the help of the Holy Spirit. Yet Matthew's whole Gospel is written from precisely this point of view *after* the Christ event. The Messianic secret so crucial to the drama that Mark creates is divulged by Matthew, but still only for those who have ears to hear, thus in correlation with an inward condition.

The Easter experience is behind and within everything recounted by Matthew even about Jesus's earthly existence: all the memories of him are transfigured in the light of Easter. Upon Easter are leveraged not only the New Testament's celebrations of the risen Christ and the preaching of salvation through him, but also the narratives—especially Matthew's—about his earlier life and mission: all point toward the Paschal mystery as the story's climax and consummation.

Particularly significant, then, is the way that the Gospels represent the Easter event itself narratively. There are basically two sets of images used to express the mystery of Easter: return to life and Ascension to glory. The first is a before/after schema serving to affirm continuity between the earthly and the exalted Jesus. The second is a high/low schema emphasizing the radical otherness of the resurrected life.[60] He is both the same Jesus come back again

59. William Wrede, *Das Messiasgeheimnis in den Evangelien* (Göttingen: Vandenhoeck & Ruprecht, 1901), trans. J. C. G. Greig as *The Messianic Secret* (Cambridge: J. Clarke, 1971).

60. Compare Charpentier, *Pour lire le Nouveau Testament*, 39.

(resurrected) and yet totally different, transfigured (exalted, glorified). These are two complementary faces of the same mystery.

Matthew does not actually narrate any ascension, as do Luke (24:50–53; see also Acts 1:9–11) and Mark (16:19, in the so-called Longer Ending), but the apparition of Jesus after his resurrection in Matthew presents a glorified, perhaps already ascended Christ. In fact, seeing the resurrected Jesus on the appointed mountain in Galilee already requires faith: "And when they saw him, they worshipped him: but some doubted" (Matthew 28:17). Neither is he given fish to eat, as in the case in the other synoptic Gospels, in token of his physicality prior to the Ascension. Rather, Jesus "came" (28:18) to his disciples, even though they were already bowed down before him. Evidently he "came" in some other sense besides the merely physical one, since according to the narrative he is already standing there before them. As the one who comes, Jesus is assimilated to the Son of Man in Daniel 7:13 and to Christ at the Second Coming as he is invoked at the end of the Book of Revelation ("Even so, come, Lord Jesus," 22:20).

Matthew portrays Jesus as he is in and for his church. Matthew enables us to discern not only the superimposition of the present experience of Christ in the faith community upon the past, the "history" of Jesus: he clearly brings out also the anticipation in the church of the future fulfillment of the Kingdom that is to be definitively accomplished at Christ's Second Coming. It is already announced in Jesus's ministry—"The Kingdom of God is at hand"—and is actually inaugurated by the Easter event, as marked by the earthquake and the rending of the veil of the temple (Matthew 27:51) along with other apocalyptic signs. Jesus's death is the beginning of the end of the world. His resurrection is the beginning of the Kingdom of God, as suggested by the *general* resurrection that commences with his death and resurrection. Thus, immediately after Jesus's death on the Cross and the attendant earthquake, "the graves were opened; and many bodies of saints which slept arose, and came out of the graves after his resurrection, and went into the holy city, and appeared unto many" (Matthew 27:52–53). These are clear signs that the afterlife of the saints in New Jerusalem has already begun.

Matthew is the Gospel writer who actually develops the idea of the church as an eschatological community, the Kingdom of God. The Gospel according to Mark, in its original form, breaks off abruptly with the Resurrection at 16:8. John is not interested in the historical church. His Jesus says, "My kingdom is not of this world" (18:36). Luke reserves his ecclesiology for a second work, the Acts of the Apostles. Only at the very end of the Gospel according to Luke, at the breaking of bread, that is, in the celebration of the sacrament of the Eucharist, is Jesus recognized as the risen Lord by the pilgrims to Emmaus (Luke 24:13–35). But Matthew's Jesus all along stands in the light of Easter, in which the glorified Lord is recognized and worshipped by his community. The Easter event is apocalyptic and casts present life, the daily life of the church, in the light of the end-time.

If Easter guides the story all along, the Resurrection is really where the Gospel of the Kingdom begins. But this is to say, again, that the Gospel begins with faith, for to perceive the resurrected Jesus requires faith. This is evident even at Jesus's final appearance on the mountain in Galilee, where some doubted (Matthew 28:17). This difference among witnesses implies that the Gospel revelation is not a wholly objective event but depends rather on how different individuals perceive and receive it. The miracle takes place, at the deepest level, inside people and manifests itself in the transformation of their lives. The *physical* healing, for example, of the two blind men in Matthew 9:27–30, is added as a sign of the *spiritual* recovery of sight accomplished already in their acceptance of Jesus as Savior: "According to your faith be it unto you" (see also Matthew 9:1–8). Prophecy in general works in this way—not by imposing an inevitable fate or solid fact, but by inviting to the realization of possibilities of life through interpreting the past with a view to the future in the freedom of the present. The Gospels in this perspective are paradigmatic for humanities texts as calling to be constantly re-actualized: they live a resurrected life themselves in each successive age. They are animated by being appropriated and lived anew, thanks to interpretations in which their potential for truth is newly tapped into and revealed.

These select observations on the Gospel according to Matthew have been offered in an attempt to give some sense of how the Gospels represent a consummate work of interpretation, where the facts of Jesus's life are recounted not for their own sake but as a testimonial of faith and for the purpose of revealing an overarching order of significance, a providential plan for history and redemption. As such, moreover, the Gospel works as interpellation—it calls all who hear to conversion of life in light of the truth it discloses. Near the end of his Gospel, John states explicitly that everything in it is written to the end that its hearers or readers might believe "that Jesus is the Christ, the Son of God; and that believing ye might have life through his name" (20:31). Beyond this common purpose, the differences between the various Gospels highlight how different writers and communities inflect and nuance the Gospel message in ways reflecting their own cultures and concerns. Precisely this variability according to context serves to reveal a meaning that is not limited to any one historical moment but rather transcends its own time and is prophetic. Like prophetic works generally, the Gospels reveal the end of history, its ultimate destination and purpose—of course, always from within specific historical limits, and yet as if these limits were miraculously suspended.

Chapter 2

✦

Homer's Musings and the Divine Muse

Preamble: Epic Song as Invention and Revelation

The idea of revelation is generally recognized as belonging more to the study of the Bible than of Homer. The Bible uses genres such as myth (especially in Genesis) and epic history (Exodus), as well as prophecy (Isaiah et al.), in order to communicate what it proposes as a revelation of God and his providential acts on behalf of his chosen people and, eventually, of all humankind. Of these genres used in the study of the Bible, it is immediately evident that the mythic and epic forms belong equally to the *Odyssey*. For, on the one hand, the Homeric poems are the primary thesaurus of Hellenic myth (taking myth, once again, in the sense of "story" that represents essential conditions of human existence). And, on the other hand, the Greeks identified with the Homeric tales and found in them their own heroic origins as an historical people: in this sense the poems are epic history.

Furthermore, although it may be somewhat less obvious, the Homeric poems are also prophetic. While they are not exactly prophecy in the biblical sense of the term, still, in their own way, they are interpretation of the history (or at least the story) of the Trojan War and its aftermath in the light of a divine revelation: everything in them is seen from the perspective of the divine Muse. The very first words of the *Odyssey*—"Tell me, Muse, of the man . . ." (Ἄνδρα μοι ἔννεπε, Μοῦσα)—invoke divine assistance in retelling the story of Odysseus.[1] The bard, in Homer's representation, is a "divine singer" (θεῖος ἀοιδὸς, IV, 17), one "inspired by the god" (ὁρμηθεὶς θεοῦ, VIII, 499).

1. I quote the English translation of Albert Cook, *The Odyssey* (New York: Norton, 1967). It has the advantage of corresponding in its numeration of the verses with the Greek text, for which I use *The Odyssey of Homer*, ed. W. B. Stanford, 2 vols., 2nd ed. (London: Macmillan, 1959).

In these terms, Homer himself, at the dawn of Greek literature, presents his poetic vision as divinely inspired.[2]

The Muses can be read as a kind of shorthand for the divine knowledge of truth claimed by the poet, a godly power of being present at all times and places, particularly to the heavenly and historical events recounted in the poem.[3] One of the clearest statements of this is found in the *Iliad*, book 2, lines 484–493, where, in introducing the catalogue of ships, the Muses are invoked because they are present to and know all, unlike mortals, who only hear reports or rumor. Hence George Dimock can state that "through them [the Muses] he [the poet] has direct access to everything just as it happened, whereas human tradition is indirect, scant, and fast fading."[4] And yet this higher power is nevertheless continuous with human faculties. There is typically an ambiguity in bardic singing between its actually being of divine origin or inspiration and its merely *resembling* a work of the gods. This comes out in the praise Odysseus lavishes on Demodocos, Homer's alter ego among the Phaeacians:

> "Indeed it is pleasant to listen to such a singer
> As this one is, who resembles the gods in his voice" (θεοῖς ἐναλίγκιος αὐδήν)
>
> (*Odyssey* 10.3–4)

It may be possible to detect in the relative autonomy of the bard as represented in the *Odyssey* a degree of emancipation from the total dependence of the poet on the inspiring deity found in the *Iliad*. This new orientation emerges also in the increased attention paid to the poet's individuality.[5] In

2. Useful treatments, amidst the vast specialized bibliography on this subject, include Graham Wheeler, "Sing, Muse . . . : The Introit from Homer to Apollonius," *Classical Quarterly* 52, no. 1 (2002): 33–49; Jenny Strauss Clay, *The Wrath of Athena: Gods and Men in the Odyssey* (Princeton, N.J.: Princeton University Press, 1983), 9–25; and Simon Goldhill, *The Poet's Voice: Essays on Poetics and Greek Literature* (Cambridge, Eng.: Cambridge University Press, 1991), 1–68.

3. The idea of the Muses as possessing "memory" that is omniscient and divinatory of "that which is, that which will be, and that which was," as well as deciphering the invisible by a word with magical-religious power, is studied broadly in Greek tradition by Marcel Detienne, *Les Maîtres de vérité dans la grèce archaïque* (Paris: Maspero, 1967); and by Jean-Pierre Vernant, *Mythe et pensée chez les grecs: Études de psychologie historique* (Paris: Maspero, 1965).

4. George E. Dimock, *The Unity of the Odyssey* (Amherst: University of Massachusetts Press, 1989), 6. Also revealing in this regard is Andrew Ford's analysis of "*Audê*: Human Voice" and "*Thespis*: Divine Speaking" in *Homer: The Poetry of the Past* (Ithaca, N.Y.: Cornell University Press, 1992), 172–97.

5. See Franco Montanari, *Introduzione ad Omero*, 2nd ed. (Florence: Sansoni, 1992), 111–12.

the *Odyssey*, the alternatives of human versus divine creation are felt to be not mutually exclusive but rather different degrees of the same thing. The difference between human and divine agency may sometimes not even be discernible. The poet himself, inspired by the Muse, is also "self-taught" (αὐτοδίδακτος). Another Homeric bard, Phemios of Ithaca, states both the human and divine provenance of his singing in the very same breath:

> "I am self-taught, and a god has planted all kinds
> Of lays in my mind."
>
> (*Odyssey* 22.347–48)

The same ambiguity is hinted at also in the way Odysseus gives "praise above all mortal men" to the bard Demodocos. He says that Demodocos sings of the war in Troy and of all that the Achaeans acted and endured and suffered, "as though you had somehow been there yourself or heard one who was" (8.491). This exceptional narrative capacity and authenticity compels Odysseus to infer that "either a Muse, a child of Zeus, has taught you, or Apollo" (8.488). To his mind, this uncanny human capability of making poetry cannot but be explained as a divine gift—though the language of "teaching" (ἐδιδαξε) also implies a degree of participative assimilation at the receiving end.

The inspiration of the Muses is the most obvious point at which Homer presupposes something of the order of revelation and prophecy. At the same time as it is an invention by the poet, such inspired discourse is understood to be interpretation of history from a privileged point of view—that of the gods. Dimock cogently elucidates this overlapping of divine and human agency in miraculous creations like poetry: "Given the idea that the remarkable in human life, including brilliant or crucial or otherwise impressive language or speech, often comes from the gods, it is utterly natural that a culture like the Greeks' should hypostatize the Muses or some similar divine agent as the source both of the power and of the content of its poetry" (*The Unity of the "Odyssey,"* 7).

Dimock explains, furthermore, that what Homer feels to be his Muse is essentially what we would understand to be his own imagination: "The Muse, in our terms, sets him free to compose fiction; but we must not forget that both he and his audience considered this fiction to proceed from the very mouth of Truth" (*Unity*, 8). This intimation of the immanence of divinity in the creation of fiction is a powerful way of experiencing the human potentiality and openness for revelation of the divine as constitutive of the human poetic imagination. Dimock thus suggests how, in the specific case of Homer, human interpretation, even in the highly spontaneous, inventive forms of poetic imagination, can serve as the necessary channel for what is understood to be, in effect, divine revelation, even if it does not reproduce historical fact in a documentary sense: "If the largest part of the re-creation is, from our point of view, unhistorical, it is nonetheless what a great mind—Homer's—passionately believes to have happened, controlled by his sense of the way the world actually works" (*Unity*, 8).

The Muses stand for the revelation of divinity that lies at the origin of humanities tradition generally: in some sense, their "message is equated with that of creative tradition."[6] In this way, it becomes possible to read biblical and pagan texts together in a perspective of literature—and particularly of poetry—as revelation.

Our reading of selections from the Bible as a prophetic work has already brought out the extent to which revelation of the divine is mediated by poetic forms and human performances. The discovery of humanity in these texts takes place in a light which is at the same time revelatory of an otherness—of what we do not know how to name except as "divine." Humanity is understood in this tradition as made "in God's image." However, we have been especially interested in the ways in which not just the specific religious content of biblical faith, but the forms of poetic interpretation themselves, entail this co-implication of the human and the divine. The disclosure inherent in the interpretive process itself, especially in its linguistic and textual incarnation, embodies essential structures and dynamics of revelation. Certain "transcendental" aspects of the event of understanding in language motivate and even necessitate the sort of theological interpretation of this occurrence of disclosure that is represented directly and explicitly in mythic and imaginative forms in the Bible and in Homer alike.[7]

For alongside biblical revelation, a widely divergent and yet strangely similar testimony to the intimate closeness and indeed coincidence of religious revelation and *poiesis* or human "making" can be gathered from Homer at the other source-spring of Western humanities, the Greco-Roman tradition. All life is represented in Homer as, at least covertly, invested with an aura of divinity. At any moment, this higher world can shine forth and penetrate so as to appear in and through nature and events in the human world. These events

6. Gregory Nagy, *The Best of the Achaeans: Concepts of the Hero in Archaic Greek Poetry* (Baltimore: Johns Hopkins University Press, 1979), 16. See, further, Nagy's "Ancient Greek Poetry, Prophecy, and the Concepts of Theory," in *Poetry and Prophecy: The Beginnings of a Literary Tradition*, ed. James L. Kugel (Ithaca, N.Y.: Cornell University Press, 1990). Certain limitations in the "human realization" of what is, nevertheless, the "divine gift" of song are stressed by William G. Thalmann, *Conventions of Form and Thought in Early Greek Epic Poetry* (Baltimore: Johns Hopkins University Press, 1984).

7. The speculative tradition of hermeneutic thought is rich in reflection on transcendental structures of thought and communication that invite theological interpretation of disclosure through discourse in general. Classic texts by religious thinkers from Schleiermacher to Tillich and Scharlemann touching on this nexus between communication and revelation are gathered in *Hermeneutical Inquiry*, ed. David E. Klemm (Atlanta: American Academy of Religion, 1986), vol. 1.

then suddenly turn into theophany—a manifestation of the immortal world become momentarily visible within the terrestrial sphere. Homer's world generally is touched and illumined by just such an aura of enchantment.

Homer is indeed an indispensable source for Greek religion, which is understood, accordingly, as an aesthetic religion. It is born with and as poetry. The implications of this were suggested by Hegel already in his *Phenomenology of Spirit*.[8] Divinity is represented as immediate and objective. Rather than clouded intimations of the divine transcendence, with its mysterious inwardness as conveyed by the biblical sublime, we have fully externalized, objectified representations of divine beings.[9] The dominant Western spirit of secularism—privileging an objective, outer world that will eventually be investigated by science—can already be discerned as present in embryo and as a destiny in the Homeric poems, particularly in the *Odyssey*. Apprehending theological revelation as inherently poetic—as accessible to human making in objective form by the instrumentality of language—leads ineluctably in the direction of discovering and affirming human autonomy and a secular worldview.

David Bouvier maintains that the *Odyssey* brings about a "relativization" of the divine inspiration of the singer by human tradition and technique. The bard's song no longer figures as an absolute given ("donnée absolue") of the Muses: "divine inspiration cannot be systematically recognized; it is no longer an absolute given, but can be judged by technical criteria—perhaps even be confounded with the simple human knowing of a witness well-informed about the facts."[10] Bouvier suggests that Homer identifies not with the traditional *aoidos* as represented by Phemios, Demodocos, and Clytemnestra's anonymous singer, who is banished to a deserted island to perish (3.267ff.), but with Odysseus, who is said to be "like a singer." The *Odyssey*'s claim to divine inspiration is projected, accordingly, onto the human ingenuity and

8. "Die Kunstreligion," in Hegel, *Phänomenologie des Geistes*, chapter VII, section B.

9. Erich Auerbach, "Odysseus's Scar," in *Mimesis: The Representation of Reality in Western Literature*, trans. Willard Trask (Princeton, N.J.: Princeton University Press, 1953), 3–23. Auerbach's development of these observations has been critiqued by Adolf Köhnken, "Die Narbe des Odysseus: Ein Beitrag zur homerisch-epischen Erzähltechnik," *Antike und Abendland* 22 (1976): 101–14. Further reconsiderations are offered by William Whallon, "Biblical Poetry and Homeric Epic," in *Parnassus Revisited: Modern Critical Essays on the Epic Tradition*, ed. Anthony C. Yu (Chicago: American Library Association, 1973), 214–20.

10. David Bouvier, "Le Pouvoir de Calypso: A propos d'une poétique odysséenne," in *La Mythologie et l'Odyssée: Hommage à Gabriel Germain*, ed. André Hurst and Françoise Létoublon (Geneva: Droz, 2002), 69–85. Citation, 80: "l'inspiration divine ne peut être systématiquement reconnue; elle n'est plus une donnée absolue mais peut être jugée au nom de critères techniques—peut même être confondue avec le simple savoir humain d'un témoin bien informé des faits."

inventiveness embodied in Odysseus himself. Odysseus no longer invokes the Muses: he is rather the champion of a verbal mastery and technical knowledge of arranging words poetically, a "combinatory intelligence" in the art of ordering language.

Bouvier argues, in effect, that the *Odyssey* achieves what I will call a secularization of the divine inspiration of the singer. In this new form of poetic inspiration—new especially with respect to the *Iliad*—the technical aspects of singing are foregrounded. Such a thesis is, in fact, argued for by Herwig Maehler, who emphasizes in addition, however, that in the *Odyssey* the singer—and Odysseus himself, when he becomes a tale-teller—can "enchant" (θέλγειν). This is a capacity reserved for the gods in the *Iliad*, where bards' songs induce merely "enjoyment" (τέλπειν).[11] In gaining a measure of autonomy from the gods in the *Odyssey*, the bards become more recognizably "divine"—θεῖον, used of Demodocos (8.43) and Phemios (16.252; 23.133, 143) and the singer at the wedding of Menelaos's children (4.17)—now in the sense more of their own free, creative self-expression and its unaccountably astonishing power.

The force of song to hold spellbound and move to tears and even to bewitch is not diminished. It is rather augmented, but it is now no longer a work wrought exclusively by the gods. The bard attracts attention in his own right and becomes more than an instrument or mouthpiece: "he presents what matters to him personally," and "he is evidently proud of his own creative power."[12] Song can be shaped by human beings and can be exercised in relation to interests that are more commonly human—like desire for accurate knowledge of current news. Even the Sirens' Song entices not by means of magic or miracles but simply by offering complete information concerning what happens on earth (12.184–91). Song thus realizes its divine powers more fully in becoming more completely human. The *Odyssey* proposes a new, more human model of poetry as no longer turned toward the past and death, as are the Muses of the *Iliad*.[13] To the extent that the inhuman Sirens still echo and emulate the *Iliad*'s Muses, Odysseus must escape from their uncanny and paralyzing incantation. Of course, it is thanks to the goddess Circe's warning that he is able to do so—hence, again, the double (seemingly contradictory) message concerning human autonomy and divine action as mutually enabling dimensions of reality that reciprocally call on one another.

Thematically, the *Odyssey* is about a struggle to liberate an autonomous human sphere from domination by the gods. Odysseus asserts his human

11. Herwig Maehler, "The Singer of the *Odyssey*," in *Schrift, Text und Bild: Kleine Schriften* (Munich: K. G. Sauer, 2006), 10. See also George B. Walsh, *The Varieties of Enchantment: Early Greek Views of the Nature and Function of Poetry* (Chapel Hill: University of North Carolina Press, 1984), 3–21.

12. Maehler, "The Singer of the *Odyssey*," 2, 3.

13. Pietro Pucci, *The Song of the Sirens: Essays on Homer* (Lanham, Md.: Rowman and Littlefield, 1998), 1–9.

independence by developing resources of his own through *techne*—art. And he adheres, furthermore, with tenacity to his own will to live his mortal life for its own sake. This decisive secularization of the ends and means of earthly existence itself represents a revelation and metamorphosis of the divine light animating human life. It is by secularization—by human power or autonomy coming into conscious possession of itself—that divinity is revealed in the world of the *Odyssey*. This freedom that spontaneously arises in humanity is given us from we know not where: unfathomable, infinite powers are accordingly objectified by Homer as gods.

Homer seems unable even to conceive of gods and mortals except as in relation to each other and as mutually revealed in the inspired perspective of poetry. He, of course, stages the inveterate conflict between divine sovereignty and human autonomy as epitomized in Odysseus's struggle against Poseidon. Yet the influence of divinities, considered in its effects as poetic event and performance rather than just at the level of the plot, so far from constraining human agency, frees this agency to come into its own. Odysseus's striving against the gods, more than anything else, makes him godlike. Generally, the superhuman force attained by a man or woman is what manifests divine presence and activity in human affairs.[14]

The *Odyssey* thus reveals not so much the loss of the divine, or of a metaphysical dimension of existence, but rather this higher reality's being recognized as present and operative in certain exceptional registers of human activity and awareness. Seen thus, divine agency can become ambiguously identified with human actions rather than only standing outside and in opposition to them. Indeed, the secularization of revelation—or taking humanity as the locus and even, in some sense, as the source of revelation—is already implicit in the idea that the divine Muses should be daughters of Mnemosyne, *Memory*, a human faculty crucial to poetic invention. So Odysseus's *memory* of the prophetic revelations of Circe counts as divinely inspired ("a god himself shall remind you," she says in 12.38). It seems that memory, the mind, such as humans experience it in their peculiarly temporal and synthetic experience of the world, is in and of itself something divine: it is the source of an epiphany of divinity within the world.

Religious myth is the vocabulary Homer possesses for attempting to understand the mystery experienced in being human. Other languages, including that of science, can be invented, but theological myth is the language that has

---

14. The coexistence of divine and human agency in Homer is treated by Albin Lesky, *Göttliche und menschliche Motivation im homerischen Epos* (Heidelberg: Carl Winter, 1961). Also still useful is Ove Jörgensen, "Das Auftreten der Götter in den Büchern ι–μ der Odyssee," *Hermes* 39 (1904): 357–82. E. R. Dodds, *The Greeks and the Irrational* (Berkeley: University of California Press, 1951) initially opposes the "religious" and the "psychological" explanations of human action, but underlines nevertheless that the latter is "overdetermined" (7).

been found and used more or less spontaneously in virtually the whole range of primordial cultures to probe and articulate the horizon of human existence as it is first experienced. Much argument about religion runs dry if it assumes that the question is whether God or the gods objectively exist. The gods have always been a way of expressing a transcendent mystery about human life that as such is unobjectifiable, and their expression in the objectifications of poetry is neither true nor false in any sense decidable in abstraction from the language of their appearance itself: the objectifications of myth are a necessity of representation in language of a transcendent reality.[15]

Revelation is shown in the *Odyssey* to be something very human in a way different from but uncannily similar to the disclosure of the Bible. The divine reveals itself in the *Odyssey* always ambiguously. This leaves a space for human beings to make their own decisions and to freely appropriate their own experience rather than simply submitting to the divine decree and dispensation of things. The divine is no longer left as unrepresentable in its sheer transcendence. Revelation entails a necessary mediation on the part of human beings. This means also that revelation is actualized in new ways concretely in the human situations in which it is interpreted by human beings attempting to see their lives and history through it.

What has always been so remarkable to moderns about the Greeks—especially the archaic Greeks, as reflected in the works of Homer—is first and foremost this seeing of the gods as present in all things, together with the visionary freshness and splendor that this divine vision makes manifest. Precisely this has been celebrated by hosts of Hellenic scholars and interpreters from Winckelmann to Goethe, Hölderlin, and Hegel—to mention only some high points leading up to German Romantic Hellenism—and still by Nietzsche. In Homer, countless scholars and poets have rediscovered a premodern world that is not yet disenchanted, one where all nature is revealed as alive with a divine life. This has been analyzed as "mythic thought" and brought suggestively into relation with metaphorical language.[16] It has been

15. The ancient traditions rationalizing Homer's gods by interpreting them allegorically as poetic expressions that are neither true nor false begin with Theagenes of Rhegium (late sixth century B.C.) and continue through the Sophists and Aristotle. They are usefully reviewed by D. C. Feeney, *The Gods in Epic: Poets and Critics of the Classical Tradition* (Oxford: Clarendon, 1991), especially 5–56.

16. For example, by Ernst Cassirer, *Sprache und Mythos: Ein Beitrag zum Problem der Götternamen* (Leipzig: B. G. Teubner, 1925), trans. Susanne K. Langer as *Language and Myth* (New York: Dover, 1946); and Bruno Snell, *Die Entdeckung des Geistes: Studien zur Entstehung des Europäischen Denkens bei den Griechen* (Hamburg: Claassen, 1955), trans. T. G. Tosenmeyer as *The Discovery of the Mind: The Greek Origins of European Thought* (New York: Harper and Row, 1960).

continually rediscovered in perennial revivals of Homer, especially in the wake of Giambattista Vico (1668–1744).

Vico dedicated the entire third book of *La scienza nuova* (1744), his revolutionary new philosophy of cultural history, to the "Homeric question." Homer represented for him a primitive, prerational stage of human thought and culture. It was therefore a stage peculiarly apt to show the powers of unbridled imagination, as well as of uninhibited sensation and feeling. Vico argued that Homer's knowledge is of a primordial, unreflective kind and that precisely this enables it to be universal and original. In this special sense, poetry embraces all knowledge before it becomes highly differentiated and abstract, and Vico understood such poetry to be the language of the gods.[17] Following him, Herder and the German Romantics found Homer's attunement to a transcendent dimension of existence, which he objectified metaphorically as the gods, to be the key to an inimitable religious "revelation" ("Offenbarung") in his works.[18] This idea is actually a very old one that had been developed especially within the ambit of Neoplatonic allegorical interpretations of Homer as theologian, for example, by Porphyry in his *Homeric Questions* and *The Cave of the Nymphs* (*De antro nympharum*).[19]

As the earliest Greek literature, and because of their own intrinsic quality, the Homeric poems have always represented in Western tradition the purity and infancy of poetic vision—the *iuventus mundi*. For Schiller, Homer was the archetype of naive as opposed to sentimental poetry: the objectivity of the world is presented in its overwhelming fascination, without the inward-directed reflections of the self-conscious poet that were to become the norm among the Romantics.[20] Sharing something of the same vision of Homer, Goethe famously commented, "I confess it no longer seems a poem but Nature itself."[21]

Yet we should not forget that Homer himself is undoubtedly the heir of a long tradition. What is first about "Homer," or more precisely the *Iliad* and the *Odyssey*, is that they count, with certain qualifications, as the first (Greek)

---

17. Giambattista Vico, *Scienza nuova* (Bari: Laterza, 1942), conclusion of paragraph 836.

18. See, for example, Friedrich Schlegel, *Über das Studium der griechischen Poesie* (1797), and August Wilhelm Schlegel, *Geschichte der klassischen Literatur* (Stuttgart: Kohlhammer Verlag, 1964), 99–139.

19. Porphyry, *The Cave of the Nymphs*, trans. Robert Lamberton (Barrytown, N.Y.: Station Hill, 1983). See also Lamberton's *Homer the Theologian: Neoplatonist Allegorical Reading and the Growth of the Epic Tradition* (Berkeley: University of California Press, 1986).

20. Friedrich Schiller, *Über naive und sentimentalische Dichtung* (1795; Stuttgart: Reclam, 1952).

21. *Briefwechsel zwischen Schiller und Goethe* (Jena: Eugen Diederichs Verlag, 1905), no. 424 (February 16, 1798), vol. 2, 48–49.

poetry to be written down and so preserved. The formulaic language, as a hint of an originally oral form of the poem, alludes manifestly to an extended period of incubation during which the linguistic materials of the epics in formation were being elaborated and refined. The idealized past studded with the heroes of the Trojan War that the poems represent may be placed in the twelfth century B.C. in the Mycenaean period of the Bronze Age of Greece. "Homer," then, names the bard, or possibly group of bards, responsible for the final crafting of preexisting oral traditions into the poems in their present written shape, which dates from closer to the eighth century B.C.

The formulaic language of the poems is itself an immediately palpable index of orality, suggesting oral recitation as the original medium in which the poems were composed.[22] Formulas were necessary for mnemonic purposes, since the bard composed extemporaneously before a live public. Certain fixed units, for example, proper names joined with stereotyped epithets, were metrically the right fit in certain positions in the dactylic hexameter verse, and so tended to be used, sometimes even with apparent indifference to their thematic appropriateness. Antinoos, the most insolent among the suitors, might happen to be called "godlike," even when he least deserves it. Formulaic technique could thus result in what Milman Parry called "illogical use of epithets."[23] This gives the poem a character of naïveté: it seems not always to be aware of what it is saying. Nevertheless, for all its direct simplicity and ingenuousness, the poem is constructed with consummate artfulness. The artistry simply is not all at the level of the poet's self-conscious control of meaning in the service of surface coherence. It evidently exceeds the measure of any one mind. Conscious artistry and its unpredictable inventiveness, moreover, become crucial themes within the story. Odysseus's self-consciousness of his creative powers is vital to his success and even to his very survival.

This growth in creative self-consciousness is something that the ensuing reading of the work will attempt to show in detail. But so far, anticipating and reaching beyond all such thematic leads, it has been opportune to suggest how the revelation of a transcendent order in the world belongs to human excellence and poetic prowess and even to the very discursive fabric of the

22. Milman Parry, *The Making of Homeric Verse: The Collected Papers of Milman Parry*, ed. Adam Parry (Oxford: Oxford University Press, 1971). Fundamental to understanding Homer as oral poetry is also A. B. Lord, *The Singer of Tales* (Cambridge, Mass.: Harvard University Press, 1960). The implications of this perspective have been followed further by Gregory Nagy in *Poetry as Performance: Homer and Beyond* (Cambridge, Eng.: Cambridge University Press, 2000) and *Homeric Questions* (Austin: University of Texas Press, 1996), and by Ruth Scodel, *Listening to Homer: Tradition, Narrative, and Audience* (Ann Arbor: University of Michigan Press, 2002).

23. Milman Parry, "The Traditional Epithet in Homer," in *The Making of Homeric Verse*, especially 22–23.

Odyssey: revelation, even divine revelation, is achieved by eminently human and poetic means. The Homeric poems were the revelation of a visionary perception of life and nature—indeed they still *are* that, or claim to be, for every new audience: "speak to *us too*, Muse" (εἰπὲ καὶ ἡμῖν, 1.10). Vital to this quality of enchantment is the fact that the gods have not yet fled from the midst of human existence. And yet, precisely a struggle to escape the constant manipulations of the gods so as to live human life on its own terms emerges as a central theme of the poem. The *Odyssey* shows us the mythic world in crisis vis-à-vis the new and emergent powers of individual ingenuity and self-shaping. It charts the development of new forms of human empowerment such as the arts and especially technology. But it shows the new human powers as themselves once again a revelation of divinity now *in human form*—and not simply the banishment of divinity from the human universe.

Odysseus takes on value as an exemplar with remarkably long historical reach of the struggle toward an autonomous human consciousness choosing its own destiny and yet choosing from destinies allotted by the Fates. As Keld Zeruneith recalls, at the end of Plato's *Republic* (620c-d), Odysseus's soul's free choice of a lot for the next life is also a choice of a divine principle or *daimon*. Socrates, too, was represented by Plato as inhabited and frequently prompted to action by his *daimon*. Odysseus's divinely human freedom thus establishes an archetype of human autonomy that is still valid for Socratic free self-reflection, which accordingly still acknowledges the gods. "And in this respect, Socrates becomes a completely developed model for the internalization and spiritualization that Odysseus anticipates."[24] Divine power is internalized and spiritualized in and as human freedom. In these terms, the secularizing development of Greek thought and culture can be traced from early epic to classical philosophy.

The secular is sometimes defined as a neutral realm between the sacred and the profane.[25] Such a realm is important for societies that are religiously pluralistic: they require a rule of law that can be binding for all, independently of the binding claims of individual religions. This situation clearly obtains in Saint Augustine's world under the Roman Empire, but it is not yet the case in the world of the *Odyssey*. "Secularization" in Homer's context means rather that the divine is manifest in the worldly. The paradox I am pointing to is that as the human becomes more independent of the divine, it realizes itself in forms that make it less distinguishable from the divine. There is not the breach between two worlds, human and divine, that will come about later and create the zone of the secular in between. There is rather a unity of vision

24. Keld Zeruneith, *The Wooden Horse: The Liberation of the Western Mind from Odysseus to Socrates*, trans. from the Danish by W. Glyn Jones (New York: Overlook, 2007), 561.

25. Robert A. Markus, *Christianity and the Secular* (Notre Dame, Ind.: University of Notre Dame Press, 2006).

that embraces both human and divine dimensions—a unity that envisions the human as reaching to the divine. The assertion of the autonomy of the human is well underway, but without the cleavage that ruptures the unified plane of action between gods and mortals. Instead, both categories of beings (or super-beings) are distilled from the same imaginative ether.

I. The Telemachy: Growing Up and Growing with the Gods (*Odyssey*, Books 1–4)

The question of the relation of gods and mortals is placed center stage from the poem's beginning, in the prologue and in the Council in Heaven. Both highlight the relation between supernatural fate and human responsibility as an overarching issue of the epic. The argument of the *Odyssey* embraces what is logically a kind of contradiction: we are completely at the mercy of higher powers, and at the same time we choose our actions and are therefore responsible for them. The Council of the gods in the proem in book 1 affirms human responsibility, even in contriving to manipulate human actions and events. The gods spin the thread for Odysseus to return to his home. Zeus commands: "let all of us here carefully devise his return so he may arrive" (1.76–77). And yet Odysseus still has to achieve it by nearly superhuman exertions of his own. When Zeus insists that humans are responsible for their own wretchedness, Athena suggests that this may not be so in Odysseus's case. Zeus replies that he has not forgotten Odysseus and brings up past god-offending deeds by the hero as the cause of his misfortune. Nevertheless, he begins devising plans for enabling Odysseus to return home.

The struggle to carve out one's human identity, which is central to the whole epic, is resolved not on the plane of human action alone, but only at a level where human agency is intersected by the divine. In general in Homer, it is only when the god or demon arouses the hero to action that he is able to act decisively and win the day. Human life is constantly envisioned by Homer as negotiated with the higher powers that integrate all its forces. If in the Bible we see how knowledge of the divine is inextricably bound up with forms of human self-knowledge, in Homer, conversely, we see how human self-knowledge is mediated by divine revelation. We begin to see this in the *Odyssey* with Telemachos—the son in quest of his father and of his own manhood.

The first four books of the *Odyssey*, known as "the Telemachy," defer the introduction of the epic's protagonist by beginning the story with his son. Yet they also project the end that is to be realized, specifically the war at the end of the epic, as this very name suggests: *telos*—"end" and *machy*—"combat" (see 3.215ff.). These books prefigure the main issue in microcosm, moreover, also at the narrative level, for Telemachos's search for his father, which is also a search for his own identity and self-knowledge, mirrors Odysseus's journey of self-discovery in order to come home to himself. In particular, Telemachos must learn the implications of human mortality that so dominate the understanding that Odysseus comes to have of himself.

Telemachos's problem of identity is caused first and foremost by the *disappearance* of his father. In his own words:

> "As it is, the storm winds have snatched him off without glory.
> He is gone, vanished and unperceived, and has left me
> Pains and laments."
>
> (1.241–43)

This uncertainty caused by Odysseus's being neither certifiably dead nor alive seems to open Telemachos to a dimension of experience higher than that of objective empirical fact, for it makes him sensitive rather to unseen presences and even to intimations of the gods.

The way that human awareness at the limit of its own potential approaches divinity in its powers of apprehension is eminently illustrated by the encounter between Telemachos and Athena in book 1. Athena arouses Telemachos to consciousness: her divine power frees him from his paralysis and melancholy. After her disguised intervention, he shows himself to be empowered vis-à-vis the suitors and Penelope. Athena has revived the image of Odysseus in him, and he begins to identify with it, whereas previously his image of his father had been dead and occulted. Indeed, his father is literally "hidden" by "Calypso" (from καλύψειν—to cover over or hide). Athena reassures him that his race will not be "nameless" (1.223) and exhorts him to earn the praise of posterity, like Orestes, who avenged his father's murder (1.297–302). Only after this is Telemachos able to say his father's name—the significance of which the whole epic will gradually unfold—in telling his mother that she should not forbid Phemios to sing and celebrate her husband: "*Odysseus* is not alone to have lost his day of return / in Troy" (1.354). Letting Odysseus come back celebrated in song is a first step to his being reborn in the minds and hearts of his own family. Telemachos must first choose to be Odysseus's son, to embrace his father's legend, in order to accept reports that Odysseus lives and to receive them as divine oracles of a truly live possibility.

The miracle of Athena coming to him is revealed in Telemachos primarily as a sudden accession of amazing strength in his own heart. As soon as she is done,

> She flew upward like a bird. Into his spirit
> She had put strength and courage. She put him in mind
> Of his father more than before. When he thought it over,
> He was amazed in his spirit; he thought she was a god.
>
> (1.320–23)

This sets up a correlation between the outward miracle and the inner state that demands it. In fact, the psychological logic of the scene strongly insinuates that he saw her *because* he needed and wanted to see his father. Telemachos is the first to see Athena come to the palace in the guise of Mentes; indeed, he is practically the only one to take notice:

> Godlike Telemachos was by far the first to see her
> For he sat among the suitors, crushed in his own heart,
> Seeing his noble father in his mind, if from somewhere
> He would come and make those suitors scatter through the halls,
> So that he himself might have honor and command his own goods.
> Thinking this over while seated with the suitors, he sighted Athena.
> (1.113–18)

Telemachos's acute attunement to the goddess's appearing is an extension of his psychological need to recover a living image of his father in order to grow into his own stature as a man. This could explain why Athena's prophecy of Odysseus's immanent return is deliberately spoken as a kind of wild hypothesis rather than as assured by the indubitable authority of the gods:

> "Well, I will now tell you a prophecy, how the immortals
> Cast it in my heart, and how I think it will end,
> Though I am not a prophet, and have no clear skill with birds."
> (1.200–202)

This message is meant to awaken Telemachos, to catapult him into active seeking after his father: uncertainty is an enabling condition of such search.

Telemachos must search for his identity and discover his father inwardly, since there is no outward surety. All supposed facts in this matter are equivocal:

> "My mother calls me the son of the man. But I myself
> Do not know. No one has ever been certain of his father."
> (1.215–16)

This doubt and heartache opens an inward space of imagination, which is also the space where divinity operates in the midst of the human. It is the uncertainty and necessity of the search that launch Telemachos on the voyage that will introduce him to his father's world, where he is to recover his own identity.

The continuity between the human and the divine is underscored by the fact that instead of giving authoritative, divinely guaranteed revelations, Athena orders Telemachos:

"To fit out the ship that is best with twenty oarsmen
And go in search of your father who has been gone so long,
On the chance some mortal may tell you of him, or you hear from Zeus
The voice that best of all brings report to men."

(1.280–83)

This is to open an adventure of discovery rather than to close it off by categorically declaring the facts about the father through divine revelation flat out. Athena works by instilling in Telemachos a certain image of his father as an inflictor of pain and punishment: he is depicted "seeking a man-killing drug" (1.261). For this is the key to Telemachos's finding the spirit of the father whom he has lost not only physically but also in his own mind—by forgetting or being unable to accept the reality that Odysseus represents. She evokes Odysseus specifically in the guise of a warrior, a predator, an avenger:

"Would that he came now to the outer doors of the house
And stood there with a helmet and a shield and two spears . . ."

(1.255–56)

Since she works in ways conforming always to Telemachos's own interior needs and predispositions, it is appropriate that he should be able to recognize Athena as the goddess she is, yet he does so only thanks to the transformation she succeeds in working within him. This ambiguity between the human and the divine is then mirrored in Telemachos's actions, as is underscored later by the herald Medon, speaking to Penelope:

"I do not know whether some god incited him
Or his own spirit roused him to go to Pylos to learn
If his father will return or has met his fate."

(4.712–15)

It is possible to interpret Athena as wholly immanent to Telemachos's psyche. Of course, she is represented externally to him as an objective entity, yet all she does works strictly in coordination with his own psychological states and their intrinsic propensities. The divine is understood as an inner dimension of human consciousness and at the same time is represented on an outward, objective plane. This overlap and continuity is pointed out explicitly by Athena herself:

"Telemachos, some thoughts you will have in your mind,
And a god will suggest others."

(3.26–28)

The same applies to human actions and events generally. A certain powerful kind of rumor (κλέος) can be a message from Zeus. News without any identifiable human source counts as coming from heaven, especially if it comes from unaccountably far and comes very fast (1.282–83). Similarly, a particularly potent thought is liable to being a thought from God (3.26–27; 1.200–201). This is recorded as quite a common assumption of people generally, as is suggested even by Antinoos's sarcastic, yet ironically true remark: "Well, Telemachos, the gods themselves must be teaching you / To be presumptuous and speak courageously" (1.384–85).

This kind of superimposition of human agency upon divine—the divine being a heightened degree of the human—enables human will to be really free (or for the first time freed) in relation to the gods' action, for example, Athena's action in the guise of Mentes. There is no conflict or even divergence between divine initiatives and human motives and agency when they interpenetrate in this way. Acting under divine influence frees the human agent to realize all of his own powers to the full and even to exceed what would normally be considered his human limits. Telemachos responds to what could have been the advice of any friend. It is the extraordinary significance of his resolution that justifies conviction that indeed a god has intervened. A superhuman force attained by a man actually *constitutes* divine presence and activity in human affairs.

Athena instigates his plans, but Telemachos acts freely—he becomes free through acting. After the departure of Athena, who has imparted into his spirit strength and courage, Telemachos is empowered to use an authoritative tone that amazes his mother: "'the power in the house is mine.' / She was amazed at him, and back into the house she went" (1.359–60). Next, calling for an assembly, Telemachos threatens the suitors, who are similarly astonished: "they all set their teeth on their lips / And wondered at Telemachos that he spoke so courageously" (1.381–82). He even begins, true son of his father, dissembling—not letting on that his visitor was a god and had announced the immanent return of Odysseus. He repeats to them Athena's cover story of being one Mentes, ruler of the Taphians: "So Telemachos said, but in his mind knew the immortal god" (1.420). Thus the stage has been set for book 2, where Telemachos, with scepter in hand and taking his father's place at the assembly, acts decisively to resolve the dilemma caused by the uncertainty as to whether Odysseus is dead or alive.

In books 3 and 4, the pathos of the journeys Telemachos makes to Pylos and Sparta depends on his discovery there of images of his father and on how he appropriates them: they enable him to grow up into a man of the world, the world that they imply and project. From Nestor he hears that "all men have need of the gods" (3.48). He thus learns of a crucial aspect of his father's world, and the visit climaxes in a sacrifice to his father's divine patroness, Athena (3.380–473). Yet Nestor represents a merely conventional and pious relation to the gods: he is introduced doing obeisance to the god whom

Odysseus defies, namely, Poseidon (3.1–341). Moreover, having arrived home as quickly as possible, Nestor is not experienced and open to experience like Odysseus: "So I arrived, dear child, with no news. I know nothing" (3.184). Nevertheless, Telemachos is able to learn from him the details of Orestes's revenge upon Aigisthos for the murder of his father, Agamemnon, and this is transparently a model for him in his present plight.

Menelaos, on the other hand, has wandered much (4.81) and suffered much (4.95). His own self-descriptions echo, often verbatim, those we have already heard concerning Odysseus. His men, too, hungering like Odysseus's men when they killed the cattle of the sun god, think first of their stomachs (4.369). Yet the result of all his vicissitudes is anti-heroic. He remains disappointed and passive, and his suffering is deadened by Helen's drug, which dehumanizes a man to the point that

> whoever swallowed it down when it was mixed in the bowl
> Would not shed a tear down his cheeks the whole day long,
> Not if his mother and his father were both to die,
> Not if right in front of him his brother or his dear son
> Were slaughtered with a sword, and he see it with his own eyes.
> (4.222–26)

Indeed, the treachery described here fits all too closely the fate of Agamemnon, Menelaos's brother. Menelaos suffers, but he does not triumph in suffering the way Odysseus does: he rather deadens it, and for this purpose Helen herself is his drug. Her beauty kills pain and makes men forget themselves. Menelaos will inherit immortality through his marriage to Helen, daughter of Zeus, thus escaping the pains of mortal existence (4.561ff.). He is only waiting for release rather than living the mortal life to its limit, as Odysseus does. As a foil for Odysseus, he is as hollow as "hollow Lacedaemon," where he sits in his shiny palace with its "well-polished bathtubs."

The twin pieties of sacrifice and hospitality to guests are harped upon over and over again in the visits to Pylos and Sparta, yet this submissive attitude toward the gods is not all that Telemachos has occasion to learn. His potential for growing into the role of his father's son is dangled in front of him as comparisons are made and his likeness to Odysseus is observed, for example, by Nestor in 3.120–25 and by Helen in 4.141ff. Most importantly, he encounters, even if he is not yet prepared to understand and accept it, the image of his father as inflictor of pain. This comes across most pertinently in Menelaos's description of Odysseus:

> "As when a deer in the thicket of a mighty lion
> Has put her newborn milk-sucking fawn to sleep,
> And goes questing over the spurs and the grassy gorges
> For grazing, and just then he comes into his own lair

> And upon the two of them brings a wretched fate;
> So upon these men will Odysseus bring a wretched fate."
> (4.335–40)

The prophecies of Odysseus's return always leave much room for doubt, with the result that it is the Odysseus that they can imagine and desire that his loved ones retain. A dream figment inspired by Athena in the shape of Penelope's sister, Ipthime, answers Penelope's urgent pleas for information by saying,

> "About that man I shall not tell you in full detail
> Whether he is dead or alive. It is bad to utter windy things."
> (4.836–37)

This repeats the evasions offered to Telemachos by the Old Man of the Sea (4.497), Menelaos (4.390), and Nestor (3.216). Revelations from the *other* world concerning *this* world are consistently ambiguous, and precisely this ambiguity is what opens a space for human engagement—not just with facts but also with possibilities, values, and ideals—and consequently for human reflection and growth. Penelope is constrained to live from her own inner faith in Odysseus and to sustain her proverbial faithfulness without external support. This knowledge of Odysseus from within her may open vistas that otherwise would remain undiscovered. It may reveal possibilities of being for Odysseus that she otherwise would never have dreamt of and could not accept.

The unceasing predictions and prophecies precede and condition Odysseus's actual, miraculous reappearance. The psychological conditioning of all that can be revealed from the gods is thus foregrounded by Homer, and this in fact opens insight into the human reality undergirding divine revelation. The introjected psychological dimension, so startling and remarkable in the highly individualized protagonist of this second of the Homeric epics is the sign of a greater awareness of the psychological dimension of all reality and in particular of that which is communicated from the gods. The psychological (from *psyche*, "soul") bases of religious revelation are in this manner wondrously illuminated by the superimposition of divine upon human agency from the poem's beginning.

The first four books taken together have been a deferral of Odysseus's own story, which is nevertheless indicated as central from the very title of the work. This deferral of the main action and protagonist turns out to reflect the structure of the poem as a whole—and of romance narrative in general—as turning on strategies of deferral designed to augment suspense. But it is also a technique for stretching out a space in mind and spirit, a space of waiting and expectation. This is the dimension in which the gods are active, a dimension of attention to what is not fully actual and objective but rather springs from latencies of mind and creative memory, where the gods invisibly are astir and the muses murmur.

Accordingly, an underlying inspiration of Western literature, as we move from the Bible to Homer, continues to be the idea of poetry as revelation. The *Odyssey* as a whole is about revealing the divinity that dwells in human life, especially at its most sublimely heroic and most intimately human. Conversely, the fact that the gods are portrayed so anthropomorphically casts divine life in a human light. In both of these ways, mortals and immortals are seen to mirror each other: their poetic representation in objective forms serves to reveal a theological dimension at the invisible heart of human life.

II. Secularization: The Struggle for Human Autonomy against Invasive Divinity (*Odyssey*, Books 5–8)

The ambiguity between human motivations and divine interventions is further illustrated by the pliant, young character of Nausicaa. All that is supernaturally imparted to her is just what she is coming to realize herself in the natural ripening of her years and inclinations. She serves as an open vessel for divine promptings and puts up no resistance. Her people as a whole, the Phaeacians, are analogous to her in this respect. Close to the gods, they are maximally receptive. Yet they can also come off as less humanly concrete and vital for that very reason. Odysseus strives *against* the gods in order to hew out a sphere of human autonomy. This makes him a first great hero of secular humanism, although he still eminently embodies the divinely inspired world from which a break is just beginning to be made at this stage.

We observed how, in the first four books, divine agency is superimposed upon the human in such a way as to create a continuity and synergism, or even confusion, between the two.[26] In books 5–8, the lack of an absolute abyss between gods and mortals comparable to the divine transcendence in the Bible results in a struggle for freedom within the phenomenal sphere of action that gods and mortals share in common. This struggle is carried out paradigmatically by Odysseus, and it makes him into the prototype of the Enlightenment hero that Adorno and Horkheimer have so suggestively analyzed in *Dialectic of Enlightenment*.[27]

26. The figure of the hero or demigod further underscores continuities between the human and the divine. This subject is pursued by Wolfgang Kullmann, "Gods and Men in the *Iliad* and the *Odyssey*," *Harvard Studies in Classical Philology* 89 (1985): 1–23.

27. Max Horkheimer and Theodor W. Adorno, *Dialektik der Aufklärung: Philosophische Fragmente* (Frankfurt: Fischer, 1969; originally 1947), especially Excursus I, "Odysseus oder Mythos und Aufklärung," 58–83.

Horkheimer and Adorno were able to discern in Odysseus the lineaments of a bourgeois individual emerging from the mythic sphere of universal archetypes. In this perspective, the *Odyssey* is about "secularization"—about making a realm free from constant, direct manipulation by the gods, whose presence and influence invades all the earth. This newly secularized world is a place where a man can freely act and reap the natural fruits of his own actions. But the will to secular, worldly life also means acceptance of mortality. And precisely this consequence is accepted by Odysseus without flinching, thanks to his characteristically remorseless courage. Yet even in portraying the unrelenting striving of Odysseus to escape the higher powers, so as to be able to live his human life on its own human terms, the *Odyssey* nevertheless shows how pervasive the presence of the higher powers is: they operate within human agency itself and are often practically indistinguishable from it.

This epic is about the struggle for human autonomy, yet portraying this struggle reveals precisely the ineluctable influence of the gods. The gods are revealed everywhere that something extraordinary is achieved in human action and experience. Of course, it is the specific virtue of tale and song—or epos and poetry—to make manifest just this quality of the preternaturally marvelous. And therefore the revelation of divinity is once again inextricably bound up with literature and its capacities of disclosure—just as in the Bible. Paralleling the biblical doctrine of the Creator Word is the notion of the inspiration of the poet by the divine Muses: thanks to their inspiration, he is the revealer of the world and its deeper truth.[28] This understanding of revelation in literature is expressed in the legend of the blind seer: the poet receives the gift of song, including a sort of extrasensory perception, in compensation for his lacking the physical sense of sight. Thus Homer is traditionally represented as blind. This marks him as possessed also of extraordinary, prophetic, inspired insight. He embodies this condition within his poem in the figure of the "singer" Demodocos:

> Then a herald came near, leading the trusty singer
> Whom the Muse loved dearly and gave both good and ill.
> She blinded him in the eyes but gave him a sweet song.
> (8.62–64)

Human autonomy has to be won by revolt and resistance—past all common endurance—against the gods. But it must also be granted by the gods.

28. On Truth and the Muses, see Silvio Accame, "L'invocazione alla Musa e la 'verita' in Omero e in Esiodo," *Rivista di filologia classica* 91 (1963): 257–79 and 385–415; and Ruth Scodel, "Bardic Performance and Oral Tradition in Homer," *American Journal of Philology* 119, no. 2 (1998): 171–94. Qualifications concerning an inherent connection between poetry and truth are registered by Louise H. Pratt, *Lying and Poetry from Homer to Pindar: Falsehood and Deception in Archaic Greek Poetics* (Ann Arbor: University of Michigan Press, 1993).

The whole story of Odysseus's coming home to himself in Ithaca begins with the decision of Zeus, procured by Athena, to allow him to return. Strikingly, when Odysseus builds the raft on which his return is to begin, demonstrating his demiurgic power to shape and guide his own life by the skill of his own hands, we are nonetheless never allowed to forget that even this means of autonomy is granted him by the gods. It is the goddess Calypso who gives him all the necessary tools, as the text points out with unmistakable insistence:

> Then she took thought about sending great-hearted Odysseus away;
> She gave him a great axe fitted to the palms,
> . . .
> Then she gave him a well-polished adze and led the way
> To the verge of the island where the tall trees were growing,
> . . .
> Meanwhile, the divine goddess Calypso brought along augers,
> And he then bored them all and fitted them to one another.
> (5.233–47)

This demonstrates concretely how the cooperation of the gods is necessary even in engendering human autonomy. It also turns out, conversely, that once this autonomy is granted, the opposition to the gods loses its edge—as can be seen in the case of Odysseus and Calypso. Once it is decided that he will be set free, Odysseus literally loves this goddess, whom he has been resisting. Up to this moment, he has been "an unwilling man with a willing woman" (5.155). Before Hermes's intervention, he is described as being in a state of despair, and he is unable to enjoy Calypso, but as soon as he knows that he is going to set sail for home, his autonomous, human identity revives, and he can engage in sexual enjoyment with her:

> The two of them went into a nook of the hollow cave
> And took pleasure of love, abiding with one another.
> (5.226–27)

Previously she had robbed him of his identity as a mortal man, bound as this identity is to his wife and home. But with his eventual homecoming secured, the divine nymph again becomes for him an enticing erotic adventure.

Odysseus's human identity is secured especially through *techne*—the arts and techniques that are characteristic of human beings and distinguish them from brutes.[29] This is true also of Homer's artistry, which is based on imitation

29. For some of the far-reaching philosophical implications of *techne*, see David Roochnik, *Of Art and Wisdom: Plato's Understanding of Techne* (University Park: Pennsylvania State University Press, 1996), particularly 18–23 on Homer, and Marcel Detienne and Jean-Pierre Vernant, *Les ruses de l'intelligence: La mètis des Grecs* (Paris: Flammarion, 1974).

and is not without parallels to Odysseus's famous talent for simulation. A particular technique displaying the artifice that becomes a conspicuous hallmark of Odysseus's and Homer's humanism alike in book 5 is that of the simile. The similes do not just present the nearest or most obvious likeness. They are deliberately calculated to remove one from the literal intensity of the action. They introduce a distanced perspective upon the narrative and offer a moment of relief from its overpowering immediacy. They also suggest the coherence of the cosmos, for they indicate how all things, however far removed from one another, share common principles and can be brought together into relation so as to illuminate one another. Yet this work of synthesis and comparison, as a work of art, introduces a human factor into the order of things. This can be illustrated by assembling and comparing some of the remarkable similes in which book 5 in particular abounds. Several of them use scenes on land and at home as foils for Odysseus's struggle to survive on storm-tossed seas:

> As when a blustering wind shakes up a heap
> Of dry husks, and scatters them in all directions,
> So it scattered the raft's long beams.
>
> (5.368–70)

> As when it appears delightful to sons if their father
> Lives, who lies in sickness and undergoes strong pains,
> Long wasting away, and some dread god has assailed him,
> Whom now the gods have delightfully freed from misfortune;
> So delightful did land and forest appear to Odysseus.
>
> (5.394–98)

> As when an octopus is pulled out of its den,
> Numerous pebbles are caught in its suckers,
> So against the rocks the skin from his stout hands
> Was stripped off.
>
> (5.432–35)

> As a man may cover a torch with black embers
> At the edge of a field, where no neighbors may be by
> And save the fire's seed, so he need not light it from elsewhere.
> So Odysseus covered himself with leaves.
>
> (5.488–91)

The intricate artistry of these similes, with their calculated contrasts reaching to registers removed from the immediate action, is symptomatic of an at least implicit new awareness of human autonomy, particularly vis-à-vis the gods, that appears in the *Odyssey*. Of this, Odysseus becomes a veritable emblem. Paradoxically, however, what is most characteristically human is nevertheless still made in the image of the gods. *Techne* itself, after all, is particularly associated with the artisan god, Hephaestus, in 8.286, 327, 332.

Odysseus attempts to carve out a space for autonomous action in order to be human in the midst of the gods. And yet to do so he still needs the help and cooperation of several goddesses. All that happens to him in his life is potentially a revelation of the doings of the gods, and the latter can reduce his own efforts to naught. Nevertheless, the world is revealed to him as a field in which his own action can be continuous with that of the gods and can prosper as well as be annulled thereby. The ambiguity of this help from the immortals registers when Odysseus's raft is swamped and he remains half under water for a dangerously long time: "For the clothes weighed him down that divine Calypso gave him" (5.321). Odysseus knows that help from anyone besides himself, including especially the gods, may be rather a hindrance, and he is at first suspicious of the aid Leucothea offers him, even though she was once Ino, daughter of Cadmos, and thus "earlier had a mortal voice" (5.334). She instructs him to abandon the gifts of the immortals—

> "Take off these clothes and leave the raft for the winds
> To carry; and swim with your hands, and strive . . ."
> (5.343–44)

But at the same time she gives him a veil to tie on his chest, instructing him to discard it as soon as he is on land again (5.348–50). Leucothea herself then plunges back into the sea like a wave. Against the divine rage of the sea, divine protection is necessary—though it comes, in this instance, with a bond of human sympathy from this former mortal. Yet still Odysseus is striving to gain the ground where he can stand on his own two feet. He chooses to calculate the chances, relying as long as he can on himself, nevertheless knowing that he is ultimately at the gods' mercy. His characteristically tenacious and vigilant "presence of mind" (ἐπιφροσύνην), which enables him to land in the river, escaping being crushed on the rocks, is also Athena's doing:

> Then surely wretched Odysseus would have died in excess of fate
> If bright-eyed Athena had not given him presence of mind.
> (5.437)

Thus even his own consciousness is not really sealed off from divine intervention. He then prays to the river as a god and is heard and rescued.

The same direct dependency of human initiative on divine instigation—or perhaps rather the complete coincidence of the two, particularly when human beings act beyond any calculable powers of their own—registers likewise in Nausicaa as she faces Odysseus in the next book: "Athena / Had put courage in her mind and taken fear from her limbs" (6.139–40).

Book 6 moves from open strife on the sea—and *against* the sea, a hostile divinity—to the atmosphere of an intimate encounter, beginning with Nausicaa. Odysseus finds himself in a place apparently free of all conflict, though we hear that it has been displaced from original proximity with violent Cyclopes (whom Odysseus has already had to confront) to Scheria, "far from haunts of men," with a wall around it. This land is (now, at least) a kind of civic idyll, a civilized paradise without enemies. Remote on the sea, dear to the gods, it is isolated from men.

> "There is no man so vigorous and no mortal born
> Who would come to the land of the Phaeacian men
> Bringing hostility. For they are very dear to the gods.
> And we dwell far away in the much-surging ocean,
> The remotest of men. And no other mortal has congress with us."
> (5.201–5)

Thus, curiously, Odysseus's finding refuge and escaping persecution by an enemy god brings him to a place that is peculiarly protected by the gods: it seems there is just no escaping them. This protectedness, furthermore, implies also a certain effeminacy. The queen, "Arete" (her name means "best"), rules here. It entails, furthermore, a peculiar kind of self-enclosure: the royal couple is itself incestuous (7.54–66).

Norms of civility, and the evocation of Artemis rather than Aphrodite, govern Odysseus's exchanges with Nausicaa, even though the situation suggests some wilder, more passionate possibilities for a sexually awakening girl outside the city and momentarily left alone by her maidservants in the presence of a rough-looking, desperate man who fascinates her. Odysseus decides not to grasp her knees and shows delicacy in dealing with her and her maidens, who balk from bathing him, prompting him to say that *he* would be embarrassed not to bathe himself alone. In this encounter between the battered, fully experienced hero and the fragile, innocent young girl, paradoxically Odysseus is the one in need of aid and protection. His speech is a model of tact and craft, for example, in reassuring the girl by evoking her father and kinsmen as a psychological shield set up to render more secure the danger zone of their dialogue.

For exactly similar reasons, Odysseus also invokes on this occasion the image of conjugal happiness and domestic harmony, but, tellingly, he seems able to conceive happiness only together with the pain it causes to the envious, its damage to the feelings or fame of others: Odysseus describes the highest happiness to Nausicaa as a domestic bliss that—for all its peaceful amity—entails necessarily also chagrin for one's enemies.

> Nothing is better or higher than that,
> When a man and wife have a home who are sympathetic
> In their thoughts. It gives many pains to their enemies
> And joys to their friends. And they know it best themselves.
> (6.183–85)

We learn later from his mother in Hades, and from those who live still in Ithaca, that even at home every one suffers for Odysseus. This strikingly negative method of establishing all positive values evidently reflects the mortal lot of suffering. All human value is created only in and by suffering. This is written into the meaning of Odysseus's name, as we shall see, and is even more broadly his "vocation."[30]

The Phaeacians, by contrast, are exempt from pain: they promise also to spare Odysseus further pains on his journey home:

> . . . then let us take thought
> For a convoy, so this stranger without pain or distress
> Under our convoy may arrive at his fatherland,
> And speedily rejoice, even if he is from very far away.
> May he undergo no evil or suffering in mid-passage
> Before coming upon his land; but then he will suffer
> Whatever his fate and the grave Spinners have spun for him
> With his birth thread at the time when his mother bore him.
> (7.191–98)

The Phaeacians represent a temporary suspension of the harsh laws of mortal existence. That it be temporary is necessary, unless Odysseus's firm election of mortality is to be abandoned. The Phaeacians are shown in many respects to be *too* civilized—they are an inversion of the Cyclopes, who are subhuman and bestial. Odysseus's human identity is chiseled out in a space of relative and circumscribed autonomy that is won from the gods ensconced in their sphere of overpowering action. Accordingly, as a mortal identity, it must necessarily be compounded of suffering. This is the distinctive mark of the truly human as against the divine. But the Phaeacians's "ships are as swift as any wing or thought" (7.36), without the weight of the world, just as

30. This point is developed exquisitely by Dimock, both in his article "The Name of Odysseus," *Hudson Review* 9, no. 1 (1956): 52–70, and more at large in his book *The Unity of the Odyssey*. See also E. Risch, "Namensdeutungen und Worterklärungen bei den ältesten griechischen Dichtern," in *Eumusia: Festgabe für E. Howald* (Zurich: E. Rentsch, 1947), 72–91; and Jenny Strauss Clay, "The Name of Odysseus," in *The Wrath of Athena: Gods and Men in the Odyssey*, 54–68.

Alcinoos "had his thought from the gods" (6.12 and 4.712). The Phaeacians are indeed close to the gods, as Alcinoos explains—

> Always before have the gods appeared to us plainly
> . . .
> Even if some wayfarer meets them when he is alone
> They conceal it not at all, since we are close to them . . .
> (7.201–5)

They are too close to be mortally real or at least fully self-aware, and therefore Odysseus must escape them. Odysseus retorts with the certainty of his own mortality:

> Alcinoos, concern yourself with something else. As for me,
> I am not like the immortals who possess broad heaven,
> Either in body or form, but am like mortal men.
> (7.208–10)

Odysseus needs to escape from this enchanted isle, where all are held spellbound by the gods, in order to take charge of his autonomous mortal life. The human dimension here opens up a space of heartfelt sentiment and sustained attachment over time that is a stranger to the immediacy of the gods acting always in the passion of the moment—in the elan of their eternal present. Stronger than erotic passion for mortals, as it turns out, is the motive of remembrance. This is the dimension of the truly human. The immortal gods are often highly erotic, but time and remembrance—the substance of Odysseus's relationship with Penelope in particular—construct a newly and uniquely human sphere. Not the reckless immediacy of divine exploits, but patience and suffering endured, construct the significance of a human life. This is demonstrated also by Nausicaa's and Odysseus's farewell from each other with vows of remembrance. Tellingly, however, in creating this human reality, Odysseus turns it back right away into an image of being divine: asked by Nausicaa bidding him farewell to "remember me," Odysseus prays to Zeus that "I may pray to you as to a god / Forever all my days" (8.462–68). Human remembrance, it seems, leads to thoughts of the divine—and perhaps the gods, too, at some level, emerge out of human remembrance.

This same quintessentially human element of remembrance may be felt also in Odysseus's weeping over the past recalled by the songs of Demodocos. Odysseus requests that the bard recite the story of the wooden horse rather than the fiction of Aphrodite and Mars. He cannot but remember who he is. That is why, in book 8, Odysseus's honor is outraged and his anger aroused by Euryalos's taunts about his supposed weakness. Thus provoked, Odysseus shows himself willing to make trial and to face all dangers in order that the Phaeacians experience something of who he truly is.

Indeed, the Phaeacians represent the counter-image to the manly autonomy that Odysseus so strenuously asserts. We have already seen that they are portrayed as an effeminate society, where the queen bee rules, and that they live in the lap of the gods. They do not normally even have to mess with a recalcitrant material world: their ships glide across the sea like thoughts guided by the gods. Yet their privileged status stands under the threat, enshrined in a prophecy, of its being revoked. Concerning his convoy ships, which are steered by mere thought without rudders, Alcinoos says:

> "There is no fear
> At all for them that they suffer harm or be lost.
> But once I heard my father Nausithoos
> Say this: he asserted that Poseidon bore a grudge
> Against us, because our convoys are safe for all men.
> He said a well-made ship of the Phaeacian men
> Coming back sometime from an escort on the murky ocean
> Would be dashed, and a great mountain would hide our city
> round."
>
> (8.562–69)

In any case, the Phaeacians prefer hearing about life to actually living it as Odysseus does, for that would mean also facing death. Alcinoos says of the Trojan War:

> "That did the gods fashion, and they spun the thread of death
> For men, so that it would be a song for those to come."
>
> (8.579–80)

Indeed life is reduced to a song among the Phaeacians, a dream which Odysseus, the heroic bearer of human woes, cannot help but escape—and even break up and destroy. Thus he makes his mark in human history. The Phaeacians, in contrast, incur the fate of oblivion, of erasure from the record of human history.

III. Narrative Identity and the Revelation of the End: *Odyssey*, Books 9–12

Books 9 through 12 are a *mise en abyme*, a narrative within the narrative: Odysseus himself becomes like a singer (ὡς ὅτ᾽ ἀοιδὸς, 11.368), as he narrates his adventures, his story of woes both suffered and inflicted, woes by which he has come to be what his name says he is—Odysseus or "sufferer and inflicter of pain." The nexus between human and divine agency is negotiated in these books still in terms of the creation of poetry, but the human invention of the poet supplants the divine revelation of the Muses, who are not invoked. The poem thereby asserts most audaciously the encroachment of human skill upon divine power in the making of poetic song. A clever stage director as well, Odysseus has waited for this strategic moment in which to divulge his identity to the Phaeacians so as to do it with maximum effect. In declaring his name only now, he is able to amplify its impact. He symbolically embodies its greatness in the image of the imposing landscape of his home:

> "I am Odysseus, son of Laertes, who for my wiles
> Am of note among all men, and my fame reaches heaven.
> I dwell in sunny Ithaca. A mountain is on it,
> Neritos, with trembling leaves, conspicuous."
>
> (9.19–22)

In thus stating his name and recounting his journey, Odysseus convincingly establishes his identity—as based both on action and on his telling about it. His name—implying suffering and inflicting of pain—gives the keynote for both. For it is in discourse that fate, "fatum," which means literally "the spoken," and freedom, particularly that of the tale-teller, fully coincide. But they are in any case inseparable, to the extent that the way history happens and how it is told cannot be completely separated. The emotional participation in an event through its retelling opens the past to being realized in its full significance, as if for the first time, in being recounted. Odysseus uses a rhetorical technique destined to become a model for Aeneas and Dante, and even for Dante's Francesca, of declaring how it grieves him to retell his grievous tale, since it entails reliving his misadventures right before his audience's eyes:

> "But your heart turns toward me to ask of my woeful cares,
> So that I may grieve still further as I lament."
>
> (9.12–13)

This narrative account, in which Odysseus freely invents himself in the telling of his tale, is an exercise that prepares him for reestablishing his identity in Ithaca. His self-definition as sufferer and survivor, as experienced in woe and yet finally triumphant, will be definitively accomplished only with his homecoming. He remakes himself in narrating his story, and this verbal inventiveness is integral to his being able to reclaim himself and his own in life as well. To make his life's reality coincide with the tale, with what has been spoken, becomes his task after this narrative interlude concludes.

Odysseus's answers to Alcinoos's questions about his name and about where he comes from also strike the note of his nostalgia for home—than which "nothing is sweeter" to a man. Still, this tenderness is hemmed in by a fierceness that is even more fundamental to defining who Odysseus is. That he is defined by the pain he inflicts is patent from the first adventure he recounts with unvarnished brutality. The sacking of the city of the Cicones, in its extreme concision, reads as an accelerated repetition of the siege of Troy, where Odysseus, in fact, first made his name:

> "There I sacked the city and killed its men.
> From the city we took the wives and many possessions
> And divided them so none for my sake would lack an equal share."
> (9.40–42)

After sacking the city of the Cicones, however, many of Odysseus's men delay escaping, and they are killed when allies from the neighboring cities supervene:

> "Then I gave the order for us to take rapid flight,
> But the men, great fools as they were, did not obey . . ."
> (9.43–44)

This emphasis on human responsibility for disaster and one's own demise is constant right from the proem and throughout the whole epic. Yet what mortals do has typically been predicted already by prophecy. Alcinoos recalls the prophecy that Poseidon would isolate his city round with a mountain, turning his ships to stone (8.567–69), which is exactly what happens to the returning ships of the Phaeacians, after they have given safe convoy to Odysseus. Polyphemus has already heard that a man by the name of Odysseus would come to deprive him of his sight (9.507–12). Circe, too, recognizes Odysseus as the one about whose coming she has heard time and again in prophecy (10.330–32).

This lends a kind of necessity or fatality to the results of events, even when they are achieved only through the exceptionally heroic action of individuals, or are brought on by human faults and are justified by their guilt. Indeed, the trajectory for Odysseus's remaining life is foretold him by Tiresias. This interview is even supposed to be necessary for him to find his way home. We have, then, a model of predestination and prophecy at work in tandem with the strongest efforts of the individual to achieve autonomy and become the master of his own fate. The two are not conceived of as incompatible: there is not even any particular accentuation of the tension between them. Rather, the revelation of fate serves as a means of freeing the hero to take up his task and achieve it—to succeed in actually going home. Prophecy reveals what happens because of, rather than in spite of, human action and effort.

Odysseus's "striving for his life" enters into crisis many times over in the course of his wanderings. He is tempted repeatedly to renounce life. His triumph over this temptation is, in the end, his greatest claim to heroism. He comes to represent life against death, in spite of the fact that his living encroaches on the domain of some of the gods, particularly Poseidon and

Helios. The claims of the human are asserted and these claims themselves reveal a vitality of their own only in this antagonistic relationship with the gods, but nevertheless as distinguishing and separating humanity from the regime of total subordination to the will of divinities. It is in this agonistic relationship that divinity—including the divinity of life in this world as immanent within human living—is most originally disclosed. Like Jacob with the angel, the human wrestles with the divine and reveals itself thereby as mantled with a world-transcending worth of its own.

The final challenge to identity is death, for in death identity is apparently extinguished. Yet death is actually also the final way of defining and establishing identity. Death's kingdom is where Odysseus must go. He is sent to the kingdom of death by Circe in order to find his way "home"—to himself. This is where he is able to come into possession of his life—through looking death in the face. To come home to oneself is to grasp one's life and identity, and to do this a mortal must confront death. In Phaeacia, the painful realities of death and even adultery are confronted only as amusing tales, "a song," but Odysseus will disturb the Phaeacians' suspension of reality. As foretold by the prophecy (8.567–72) cited at the end of the last section, he will establish his identity among them, just as he does elsewhere, by inflicting pain.

The constant danger to identity is that of oblivion. This is clear again with the Lotus eaters, who are totally peaceable and unthreatening, and yet eating the lotus makes men "forget about a return" (9.97). The risk here is that of forgetting who they are and where they are from, and thereby of obliterating their identity. This theme is demonstrated dramatically in relation to the Cyclops, to which the long story in book 9 is dedicated, following the two brief episodes of the Cicones and the Lotus eaters. This establishes a pattern of two short narratives followed by a long one that will be repeated four times in the course of the books devoted to Odysseus's tale of himself.

In his duel with the Cyclops, Polyphemus, son of Poseidon, Odysseus is locked in mortal combat with primitive forces that destroy identity as a distinctively human characteristic. The story illustrates the superiority of the human, with its technologies and definitions, to brute nature and its raw, immediate, unmastered impulses. The Cyclopes are subhuman, as is underscored by the negative rhetoric used for describing everything about their life and land—or rather everything that they *lack*. They are a

> "law*less* people, who, trusting in the immortal gods,
> Do *not* sow plants with their hands and do *not* plow
> But everything grows for them *un*plowed and *un*sown . . .
> They have *neither* assemblies for holding council *nor* laws . . ."
> (9.107–12)

Tools and human industry, the arts of civilization, as well as artful manipulation of speech, of which Cyclopes are deprived, are the means by which

Odysseus triumphs. Even the fertile, wooded island, "*not* near and *not* far away," where Odysseus harbors his ships, is described in purely privative terms, which continue the intensive rhetoric of negation that qualifies everything having to do with the Cyclopes:

> "And it is *not* held, either, with flocks *or* with plowed lands,
> But it lies *un*sown and *un*plowed day after day
> Bereft of men, and it nourishes bleating goats.
> There are *no* vermilion-prowed ships for the Cyclopes,
> As there are *no* shipwrights among them who might work . . ."
> (9.122–26)

This is no-man's land, and the Cyclopes themselves are conceived of negatively as not-human: "The wild man who had clear in his mind *neither* justice *nor* laws" (9.214). Although conspicuous and obviously a formidable opponent, the "monstrous man" is described in terms closer to those for inorganic elements:

> "He looked
> Not like a grain-eating man but like a wooded crest
> On lofty mountains that appears singled out from the others."
> (9.190–92)

Whereas men eat grain, the Cyclopes live in isolation from one another, pasturing sheep, but without the arts of agriculture. All this constitutes an essential contrast to Odysseus's human, and even highly civilized, identity.

Yet Odysseus's all-too-human curiosity and desire to experience everything becomes his nemesis here. His companions beseech him to escape with the stolen cheeses to no avail:

> "But I did not listen—that would have been far better—
> So I might see the man and he give me the gifts of a guest."
> (9.228–29)

Odysseus vainly appeals to human customs, such as gift-giving and hospitality toward guests and piety toward the gods. The Cyclops threatens him and stupidly asks where his ships are harbored, giving the lame reason "so I may know" (9.280), and forthwith devours two of Odysseus's companions.

Odysseus has to exercise self-control ("another spirit restrained me," 9.302) not to strike back immediately and thereby condemn himself and his men to die within the cave, since they would never have been able to remove the huge stone blocking its entrance. He has rather carefully to craft his revenge, which he does by converting the Cyclops's massive club into a weapon "as large as the mast" of a twenty-oar ship refined, as by a shipwright's art, for intelligent use. These technological metaphors then become crucial to the scene of the blinding of the Cyclops:

> "I myself, leaning on it from above,
> Twirled it around as a man would drill the wood of a ship
> With an auger, and others would keep spinning with a strap beneath . . ."
> (9.383–85)

The tools Odysseus had used to make his raft (5.234–37, 46) are taken up again in simile: "As when a smith plunges a great axe or an adze" (9.391). These images emphasize how he triumphs over brute force and stupidity by his human industry and technique. But the supreme human technology is language, and hence the stratagem of the name, "my faultless device" (9.414), as Odysseus gloats in recounting the Cyclops's vain, self-defeating appeal, "Friends, Noman [*ou tis* (οὔ τις), literally "no one"] is murdering me by craft, not by force" (9.407).

The triumphant blazoning of Odysseus's real name comes in the taunts with which he jeers at the Cyclops, telling him to say that he was blinded by "Odysseus sacker of cities." Odysseus thereby jeopardizes his own life again and those of his companions. Not only does this boast enable the blind Cyclops to take aim with a boulder that nearly crushes the ships; it also provokes the curse heard and heeded by the Cyclops's father, Poseidon, a curse that dogs Odysseus ever afterward all across the sea, so that he finally arrives home on strangers' ships only after untold troubles, having lost all his men, and only to face still more trouble there. Narrowly considered, this is very stupid of Odysseus, and we might judge that he loses control of himself at least in this instance. Yet it is also only by enduring the full extent of the wrath of Poseidon that he becomes truly "Odysseus." The measure of rashness that he displays here may also be indispensable to his identity as Odysseus.

Odysseus, in fact, comes extremely close to regaining hearth and home immediately after this episode, but he is overcome by sleep just as the shore of his fatherland appears on the horizon (10.29)—almost as if he were suddenly bored and longed for yet more adventure. This is what gives occasion to his envious companions to open the bag of the winds given him by Aeolos, which results in their being blown way off course again. This brings him incalculable chagrin, and Odysseus at this point entertains suicidal thoughts:

> "And I,
> As I awoke, wondered in my own blameless heart
> Whether I should drop from the ship and perish in the ocean
> Or endure silently and stay among the living still.
> But I endured and waited, and lay with head covered
> In my ship."
> (10.49–54)

The covering of the head (καλυψάμενος) becomes a symbol for eclipsed identity, such as is the immediate consequence of his crushing defeats. He is spurned by Aeolos upon arriving back at Aeolia ("Go quickly from the island, most shameful of living men," 10.72) and falls next into the hands of the man-eating giants, the Lestrygonians. Their ruler is named "Antiphates," "anti-fame" or "anti-renown" (10.106), and this name indeed expresses the balance of what happens in this disastrous encounter, where no one hears the name of Odysseus. He loses all of his ships except the one he is himself on, the only one which he had taken the precaution of anchoring outside the "famous harbor" (10.87).

This is truly the nadir of Odysseus's identity in its widely oscillating vicissitudes. The men sail on "grieving in their hearts" (10.133)—a line that frequently recurs as a refrain. The recovery begins only when one of the gods pities Odysseus and sends a stag in his path. Odysseus fells it, reasserting his identity as inflicter of pain by assuming the posture of a predator. He employs once again his technological expertise to twine a rope, in order to haul the meat back to his men and offer them a meal around which they are able to restore their spirits and reconstitute their community. He then addresses them with words hopeful of life:

> "My friends, though we are grieving, we shall not yet go down
> To the halls of Hades before the fated day arrives."
> (10.174–75)

"Uncovering their heads" (10.179), the men gaze in joy on the stag and set upon the "glorious feast."

Thus they are readied for the main adventure of book 10, the meeting and competing in craft and cleverness with Circe. Although it is another triumph for his autonomy, Odysseus needs the help of the gods in order to prevail. Hermes gives him the drug that enables him to withstand Circe's enchantments.

> "The gods call it moly. It is difficult to dig
> For mortal men. But gods are able to do all things."
> (10.305–6)

When Circe attempts to cast her spell on Odysseus, it is by assuming the threatening posture of the aggressor again that he successfully resists her and asserts himself:

> "So she said, but I drew the sharp sword from along my thigh
> And rushed on Circe as if intending to kill her,
> She gave a great shout, ran up under and took my knees . . ."
> (10.321–23)

This gesture divulges him to Circe as the Odysseus whose name indeed has preceded him by prophecy:

> "Surely you are the Odysseus of many turns, who,
> The gold-wanded slayer of Argos always told me
> Would come on his way out of Troy in a swift black ship."
> (10.330–32)

Odysseus wins back their humanity for all his men who had shown themselves perilously close to permanently losing their human identity and regressing to the state of brute animals. Eurylochus, however, revolts. Not all men are willing to follow Odysseus through the pains incumbent upon his living as fully human. This revolt foreshadows Eurylochus's destiny: he will prove to be a life-denying renegade in the end, when he stirs the others up to eat the cattle of the sun god.

Indeed, more seems to be demanded of the men than can be comprehended without blind faith in their leader: they must descend into the regions of the dead. Circe outlines the visit to Hades that Odysseus is going to have to make in order to find out the way home by consulting Tiresias. Odysseus is shattered at this disclosure and for a second time expresses suicidal thoughts:

> "So she said, and my own heart was shattered within me.
> Seated on the bed, I lamented, nor did my heart
> Wish still to live and to see the light of the sun."
> (10.497–99)

Here he sinks to the level of Menelaos, the one who actually does forsake mortal life and who expresses himself very similarly in book 4: "And I wept as I sat on the sand, and wished in my heart / Not to live any longer and see the light of the sun" (4.539–40). Odysseus's men, too, lament and tear their hair, when they hear this news. And yet it is the revelation received on the visit to Hades that will deliver the definitive answer that finally overcomes the recurrent impulse to forsake this life. Life and identity in *this* world are revealed *there* as the only values worth cherishing and striving after.

Nekuia:[31] *Visit to the Underworld*

The *Odyssey*, as a romance of exotic wanderings and an intricate textual maze full of disguises and plot redoublings and circlings back to go forward,

---

31. A necromantic summoning of souls of the dead from the underworld is the original meaning of this Greek word, which is later commonly conflated with "katabasis" or "going down" into the underworld.

is not a very likely candidate for apocalyptic revelations. Yet something like that is what we have, at least incipiently, at the center of this work in the descent to the underworld. The moment of apocalypse that is so vital for defining the whole drift of Western humanities tradition receives here a rendition that will remain paradigmatic throughout subsequent epic literature in the West, thanks especially to Virgil and Dante. The apocalyptic revelation in question here is centrally that of Odysseus's mortality. Tiresias's prophecy culminates in a description of Odysseus's future death. It is this anticipatory vision of his death that enables Odysseus to see the final meaning and purpose of his life and to know definitively who he is. However, the *Odyssey*'s disclosure of the end of human life, and even of the world to come, momentously emphasizes the realization of the value of existence immanently within mortal human life itself rather than in any transcendent realm beyond.

The focus on Odysseus's end is all concentrated on the significance it lends to his life. This life is revealed as significant in and of itself and by its own making. The adventures Odysseus recounts in books 9 through 12 turn on the vicissitudes of his quest for affirmation of his autonomous human identity. The tale itself in its well-craftedness is a masterful construction of identity. His host Alcinoos acknowledges this skill:

> "As a singer would, you have skillfully [ἐπισταμένως] told the tale
> Of all the Argives' sad troubles and of your own."
>
> (11.368–69)

What Odysseus's tale shows is how suffering and inflicting pain on others is essential to establishing a human identity that is fixed in its lineaments finally by death. This is an identity that reveals humanity in its distinctness from divinity and in particular from the divine immunity to suffering and death. The descent to death is itself, in the first place, a revelation of what it means to live life as a mortal. To embrace one's mortal existence as a human being, one needs autonomy, yet such autonomous existence is not without relation to the gods: it is, on the contrary, a further revelation of divinity in the human sphere. It is precisely in this mortal sphere that the divinity and holiness and lasting worth of life can be realized and made manifest in and to and by humans.

Vital to the significance of a human life is its being remembered after death. This is explicit and clamoring in the request—backed up by threats of bringing down the wrath of the gods—made by Elpenor's ghost for burial and a tomb on the strand.

> "Hapless man that I am, so that those to come learn of me
> Do this for me, and set my oar fast on the mound
> With which when alive I rowed among my companions."
>
> (11.76–78)

The token of Elpenor's toil in life becomes the sign of his life's meaning even in death. It is his own doing, the work of his hands, as emblematized by the oar, which constitutes his life's significance in the end. His case may be unheroic: certainly his falling drunk out of bed is a ridiculous more than a tragic end. Nevertheless, even he is to be heard of among men, and to this extent he is only a more mediocre version of Odysseus, who establishes by autonomous action a human meaning for his life. In either case, we create the significance of our lives by our own actions: it is not simply foreordained by the Fates. It is not granted by the gods so much as achieved by acting godlike and so distinguishing oneself as much as possible in one's mortal life on earth. For this purpose, one's actions have value directly in proportion to their effects and the impression they make upon others, ensuring that they be remembered. Value in human life is experienced in terms of pleasures—and especially of pains—for others. This is indeed how Odysseus's significance registers, beginning with his effects on his own parents, one of whom has already died from longing for him (11.202). The other lies at home in great sorrow, grieving and longing for his son's return (11.195–96), a report that is later corroborated by Eumaeos (15.353–60), who adds also his own inconsolable grieving for his master.

It is from the end-point that the final significance of a life, as of any temporal sequence, can be understood. The *Odyssey* is perhaps the earliest extant articulation of the idea that no man can know whether he is really happy before knowing the end of his life.[32] This is what Odysseus is given to know by his visit to the underworld:

> "Far from the sea will death come,
> Ever so gently to your person and slay you
> When you are worn out with sleek old age. And the people about you
> Will be happy. I tell you this unerringly."
>
> (11.134–37)

This is evidently a happy ending to Odysseus's story and a happy conclusion to his life. As he leaves the scene, Odysseus leaves happiness as a heritage to those around him.

It is striking that from this point of view outside of and beyond life, it is enough to affirm the happiness of one's own people and no longer necessary also to stress symmetrically the pain imparted to others. Moreover, Odysseus is instructed to travel inland until he is among people who do not recognize his oar and take it to be a winnowing fan instead. There he is to sacrifice hecatombs. This results in a complete metaphorical transformation of his life

---

32. Herodotus shows that this topos had attained classic status already in the sixth century. He evokes it in staging the admonitions of Solon to Croeusus: "we must wait till he [a man] be dead, and call him not yet blest, but fortunate" (1.32). *Historiae*, vol. 1, ed. A. D. Godley (Cambridge: Loeb Classical Library, 1920–96).

and in distancing it from its literal meaning—which is bound up with hardships at sea: hence the oar. By means of this metaphorical displacement, he is to become able to reconcile himself to the gods and to give his life finally a happy significance. By contrast, in actual living, significance and even bliss prove always inextricable from pain and conflict.

Odysseus sees his own end and knows from Tiresias that he is truly blessed—even in his hardships. He sees, moreover, the souls of a great number of women and men whose stories are complete and can therefore be assessed as to their final significance. He is led to understand that all of the individual souls who come forward for interviews with him are not nearly as happy as he. He, the man of pains, paradoxically attains the height of human happiness possible on earth.

The express motivation on the narrative level for his visit is to hear from Tiresias how he may return home, but this purpose is not very precisely realized in the actual encounter with the prophet. He receives no definite information with regard to the route he must take. Tiresias's words are a strange mix of claims to authority, to "speak unerringly" (11.96), on the one hand, and on the other rather vague uncertainty:

> "I do not think
> You will elude the earth-shaker . . .
> You may get there yet, even so, though you suffer ills;
> If you are willing to check your spirit and your companions. . . .
>
> And even if you escape yourself
> You will return late and ill . . ."
>
> (11.101–5; 113–14)

The deeper psychological motivations for the descent concern the need to see beyond the veil of time in order to know quite generally whether and why one should go on in life: this is achieved presumably by gaining some sense of where it is all going. Yet the answer Odysseus receives to these questions is not the assurance that the end will justify the means because the pains of mortal existence will be compensated for and his efforts will be rewarded in some glorious afterlife. Instead, he hears earthly life commended for just the opposite reason, namely, that it is itself all that is worth living for. Hence his mother's urging him to get back to the world of the living, to "be eager to go to the light as fast as you can" (11.223). The same message is implicit in Tiresias's greeting him with the words:

> "Zeus-born son of Laertes, Odysseus of many devices,
> Why, hapless man, have you left the light of the sun
> And come here to see the dead and a joyless place?"
>
> (11.92–94)

Already before the descent, stripped of his possessions and of his train of men, Odysseus had almost renounced life. Here, in the underworld, he is given the elements that enable him eventually to learn to love it again fully. What Odysseus still has to learn has already been learned by each of the souls of the dead whom he encounters. Elpenor wants a monument in order to be remembered among living men. Agamemnon and Ajax, too, are completely concentrated on earthly existence. But it is Achilles who most poignantly expresses this nostalgia of the dead for earthly life, notwithstanding its most terrible pains, as we shall see shortly.

Odysseus's death is described explicitly by Tiresias, though Tiresias's prophetic revelation is couched, as prophecy frequently is, in the dark language of enigma. What is most fascinating is that Tiresias reveals Odysseus's end in such a way as leaves it completely open to interpretation. Even the end is, in some sense, to be Odysseus's own doing. The symbol of it—his oar (as already for Elpenor)—is the human tool by means of which he travels, accumulating his world-famous adventures and making a name for himself. This tool, moreover, as a result of how it is seen by mortals, is susceptible of metaphorical transfiguration into another instrument for quintessentially human work—the winnowing fan, a tool for reaping what we sow. The apocalypse here is very much do-it-yourself. It reveals not the gods breaking in from above to assign human life a meaning so much as a secular sphere for human self-determination. This, nevertheless, is a revelation of the divine—or rather of the divinity of human life in its essential freedom. Odysseus must consult Tiresias in order to know his way home. But what the prophet reveals to him is, above all, the divine creativity invested in human activities of self-shaping and world-making. This, precisely, is what Odysseus becomes the hero of, most of all in his role as poet: at the center of this disclosure is the divine revelation that by confronting and comprehending his own death he can grasp his life as a whole and become truly free. His life thereby may assume infinite or divine significance. Such is the revelation of fate, his own fate or portion—*moira*—as the *Odyssey* presents it.

Tiresias discloses to Odysseus not so much how he is to get home as how he is to die. Deeply considered, maybe it is *knowing* that he will die that brings Odysseus "home" to himself and to his mortal condition. For any mortal, to be at home in life is to know and accept death as a fundamental fact of existence. This knowledge also opens a space for human autonomy independent of the rule of fate. By learning to accept the necessity of death for the meaning of his life, Odysseus acquires his motive for turning down Calypso's offer of immortality. The significance of human life is revealed paradoxically in mortality, in dying, not in the mythical existence of the immortals. Human freedom, in its very finitude, realizes the infinite significance of existence, its "divinity." The Gospels ultimately bear a hauntingly similar message. Jesus is revealed as God on the Cross: his divinity is revealed in dying freely out of love without limit for humankind.

Secularization in the *Odyssey* is not the rejection of the world of the gods, which the poem so vividly relates in myth, but its fuller revelation in the very concreteness of human existence, which includes an interior, psychological dimension. The full meaning and relevance of the gods as revealing a transcendent dimension to human life and creativity is brought into the open in a way that makes divinity no longer merely myth but rather the very substance of human self-fashioning and creation: they are not apprehended as self-contained but as a privileged way of participating in the creative life of the gods. Secularization in this case reveals itself to be an interpretation and transposition of theological revelation. In this regard, it is possible to discern here a development in some sense parallel to that realized in Christianity with the doctrine of the Incarnation—of God becoming man.[33]

Odysseus passes from the colloquy with Tiresias and the revelation of his end to an encounter with the mother who gave him birth. Her name, Anticlea, means anti-fame, and she stands, in some way, for the womb from which he must emerge in order to make his name. He originates in his separate and incomparable identity by causing pain to his mother: indeed she tells how her sorrow over his apparent loss, while he was on the odyssey of adventures that would make his name renowned forever, is what dragged her down to the grave. The catalog of famous women that follows suggests many more instances of how the lasting significance of human lives is established through pain and violence. The fame of violated virgins is secured by what happens to them in becoming lovers of gods and mothers of heroes who emerge violently from the obscurity and protective enclosure of the womb.

An intermezzo shows how much Odysseus has gained in esteem among the Phaeacians by the telling of his tale. He is loaded down now with gifts. Queen Arete had previously urged that Odysseus's gift-box be lashed down quickly (8.443–45), but now she exhorts her fellow Phaeacians to lavish gifts upon him and not to stint (11.339): she declares that he is *her* guest (11.338). Moreover, the delight of the Phaeacians (and of the reader) in this marvelous

33. The modern world is presented as a secular realization of Christian revelation by Karl Löwith, *Weltgeschichte und Heilgeschehen* (1949), trans. as *Meaning in History* (Chicago: University of Chicago Press, 1957), and Carl Schmitt, *Politische Theologie: Vier Kapitel zur Lehre von der Souveränität* (Berlin: Duncker & Humblott, 1922), trans. George Schwab as *Political Theology: Four Chapters on the Concept of Sovereignty* (Chicago: University of Chicago Press, 2005), both taking cues from Max Weber's famous theories, notably in *The Protestant Ethic and the Spirit of Capitalism* (1904). I review recent work, including Charles Taylor, *A Secular Age* (Cambridge, Mass.: Harvard University Press, 2007) and David Martin, *On Secularization: Towards a Revised General Theory* (Hants, U.K.: Aldershot, 2006), recasting secularization as itself the result and a kind of fulfillment of religious and particularly of Christian worldviews in "Dante and the Secularization of Religion through Literature," *Religion and Literature* 45, no. 1 (2013): 1–31, especially 2–3. Now in *Secular Scriptures*, chapter 1.

tale of adventures has a certain capacity to transcend the ordinary constraints of time. Alcinoos exclaims: "This night is prodigiously long. It is not yet time / To sleep in the hall. Do tell me your wondrous deeds" (11.373–74). Time is suspended and indeed dilated by song. By this means, the art of narrative crafts a world all its own. This, too, is a measure of its vital, revelatory power, as it flows from a human creativity that has become autonomous.

After the intermezzo, Odysseus takes up the fates of men, starting with Agamemnon, the unhappiest of all, slaughtered like an ox at the trough by his treacherous wife and her lover. Agamemnon's bitter fate represents the worst death for a man, and he warns Odysseus that "there is no longer any trust in women" (11.455). Odysseus's ultimately happy fate can be perceived only by contrast with the unhappy fate of others: even those fates reputed to be happy seem to pale in comparison with his. Achilles is hailed by Odysseus as the happiest of men: "Achilles, / No man in the past or hereafter is more blessed than you" (11.481–82). While alive, he was given more honor than all other men; now among the dead, he rules as a king. In contrast to Agamemnon, Achilles represents the best death, that of a hero with highest honors. The supposition, however, that he is therefore happy, Achilles himself emphatically rejects:

> "Noble Odysseus, do not commend death to me.
> I would rather serve on the land of another man
> Who had no portion and not a great livelihood
> Than to rule over all the shades of those who are dead."
> (11.488–91)

It is only in relation to and on account of the living—namely, his son Neoptolemus, praised as illustrious by Odysseus—that Achilles is able to stride off in pride and joy over the asphodel meadow. And this only makes Odysseus's superior happiness the more evident, for he is on his way home to see his living son and comfort his aging father, whereas Achilles's father, Peleus, languishes in neglect. It is thus Odysseus, even with his life of pain, who emerges as the happiest of all mortals. That is the testament of Achilles. Ajax, next, is still sulking inconsolably over having lost in the contest with Odysseus for the armor of Achilles, and this fixation of his serves to confirm again that earthly life is the only one that counts for good or for ill. Such valorization of earthly life and of Odysseus's tenacious choice of it represents a tremendous affirmation of mortal existence even in the midst of all the pains it entails. Against all mythical states of supposed immortal fame or of peace and repose after death, this life with its trials is praised as the only true happiness. Such is the *Odyssey*'s radically secular vision of the ends of humankind.

Following these three featured heroes, the catalogue of men, running from Minos to Orion, Tytyus, Tantalas, and Sisyphus, covers a moral spectrum from justice to predation to senseless violence. It climaxes in the image of Hercules. He is only a phantom here, "For he himself with the immortal gods / Enjoys abundance and has Hebe of the fair ankles" (11.602–3). Might Odysseus, too, as one who is allowed to leave Hades once, likewise enjoy some such freedom even from death's changeless kingdom? Like Hercules, Odysseus has endured many sufferings and gone to the underworld under the protection of Hermes and Athena (11.626), and then, exceptionally, has succeeded in leaving again (11.625). Furthermore, the image of Hercules is that of a predator and, as such, an alter ego for Odysseus.

> There was shrieking about him of the dead as of birds
> Terrified on all sides. And he like the gloomy night
> Held his bare bow with an arrow on the string,
> Peering dreadfully like one who is ever about to shoot.
> Terrible was the sword strap circling him round the chest,
> A golden belt on which wonderful things were fashioned,
> Bears and savage boars and lions with glaring eyes,
> Battles and combats and slaughters and murders of men.
> (11.605–12)

The recognition between Hercules and Odysseus is immediate: "He knew me at once when he saw me with his eyes" (11.615). Hercules points out that Odysseus, like him, is burdened by hard fate and "boundless woe," but in both cases this turns out to be an exceptional privilege. Even in the underworld, Hercules retains his character as a man of action, poised between life and death. He does not pass beyond the crucible of decision between life and death, but dwells eternally in the tension between them. Hercules thereby limns in perpetuity the violence and death that are crucial to life and to the very meaning of mortal existence, which is thereby infinitely affirmed. Hercules, free from death, nevertheless abides forever freely in face of it. Analogously, Odysseus, by facing death in life, gains a certain kind of freedom vis-à-vis death. Whether or not Odysseus might share such privileges in the afterlife, what he shares with Hercules is principally an unlimited passion for earthly life in all its fierceness.

The afterlife here appears as an *alter-imago* of this life—as an image by which this life is haunted. The souls (ψύχη) or ghosts are like mental images of the living: the underworld as a whole obeys the laws of mental experience. Odysseus controls the coming of the ghosts, who remain passive, until he gives them attention. They appear as if in the theater of Odysseus's mind, welling up from unconscious motives and becoming a nightmare over which he loses control:[34]

34. Odysseus is presented as a hero of consciousness, defending his personal and human identity from unconscious, particularly chthonic forces by Charles H. Taylor, Jr., "The Obstacles to Odysseus' Return: Identity and Consciousness in 'The Odyssey,'" *Yale Review* 50 (1961): 569–80. Compare also Dimock, *Unity of the Odyssey*, 149.

> But first numberless bands of the dead came on
> With a tremendous shout, and sallow fear seized me
> Lest noble Persephone send the Gorgon head
> Of the dread monster from the hall of Hades against me.
> (11.632–35)

There is a limit to how much vision beyond the veil of death and the threshold of consciousness Odysseus can endure. So, at this point, he must wake up and go back above ground. But, from now on, for him the meaning of his life is essentially determined by this disclosure of death.

Although the *Odyssey* is *not* a text explicitly about transcendence and apocalypse, it nevertheless exposes an underlying reality of divine activity operating interactively in mortal life. Book 11 transcends ordinary mortal vision in the most thematically explicit way in order to suggest how even this otherworldly vision belongs to the human capacity for self-transcendence. Such transcendence of the ordinary, given, finite world is integral to fully human choosing. Even after the revelation of his fate, Odysseus is nonetheless called upon and challenged to be the forger of his future. In outlining the future course of his trials after his reemergence from Hades, Circe emphasizes to Odysseus that he is solely responsible. His fate is not merely imposed, but must be freely chosen:

> "At that point I shall no longer tell you in full detail
> Which one of the two ways will be yours, but you yourself
> Must decide in your heart. I will tell you the alternatives . . ."
> (12.56–58)

The stories she tells do not determine his fate but rather place the fully conscious hero before his choices: even after the otherworldly revelations, he still must choose, yet now he chooses cognizant of the ultimate value of his life.

Book 12 comprises another series of stories consisting in two shorter adventures (Scylla/Charybdis and the Sirens) followed by a longer one (the cattle of the Sun), repeating the structure we discerned in books 9 (Cicones, Lotus Eaters, and Cyclops) and 10 (Aeolos, Lestrygonians, and Circe). But this structure in Book 12 is doubled by each story's being told twice—once by Circe in a prophetic forecast and forewarning of what he will encounter (lines 21–141) and then by Odysseus himself, as he relates to the Phaeacians what he actually experienced. Thus a certain symmetry is built up around the pivotal disclosure of book 11. This contributes to giving the climactic visit to the underworld a central position as enclosed by two series of tales, before and after the descent.

Books IX	**X**	**XI**	**XII**
Cicones	Aeolos	**Visit**	Scylla/Charybdis
Lotus Eaters	Lestrygonians	**to**	Sirens
Cyclops	**Circe**	**Underworld**	**Cattle of Sun**

In book 12, all the perils involve knowledge of life and death. Odysseus's visit to the underworld has been a symbolic death, as Circe's greeting suggests:

> "Rash you are, who have gone alive into the hall of Hades,
> Dying twice, when other men die a single time . . ."
>
> (12.21–22)

Accordingly, on his return to Aiaia, it has become an isle of the "risings of the sun" (12.4), which is another way of symbolizing the motif of resurrection to life that Odysseus now embodies. This resurrection is first and foremost of the will and resolve to live. Odysseus must summon up all his courage to choose life, since despair and wishing rather for death repeatedly threaten him and his men, who, as a group, succumb.

Ability to resist the temptation to give up on life comes to Odysseus in the wake of the revelations of the end of life in his visit to the underworld. It comes to him, as also to us, his readers, in the retrospective reflection of his narrative in books 9–12. These books narrate events chronologically prior to those related in Books 5–8, yet they are revisited here in the mirror of poetic tale-telling, which becomes a revelatory medium. The tale is provoked by Demodocos's song about Troy, which moves Odysseus to tears. Out of this emotional catharsis comes the re-visioning in which he puts his story together as a whole. Centered on the visit to the world of the dead, this reexperiencing through retelling enables Odysseus to realize an overall significance for his life. This disclosure eventually enables him to hold out in enduring pain and to persevere in choosing life over death, even through dire adversity. In contrast, Eurylochus, the mutinous rebel who leads and abets the hungry crew in their fatal eating of the sun god's cattle, in effect incites the men to choose death, for he is concerned only to choose the least painful among alternative deaths:

> "Hear my speech, companions, though you have suffered ills.
> There are all kinds of hateful deaths for wretched mortals,
> But most piteous is to die and meet one's fate by hunger.
> . . . .
> I would rather gasp once into a wave and lose my life
> Than to be starved a long time on a desert island."
>
> (12.340–51)

The reaction of the sun god, Helios, to the outrage committed against him parallels precisely this choice of death over life. The god threatens to choose the realm of the dead over that of the living and to shine rather in Hades:

> "If they do not pay fitting recompense for the cattle,
> I will go down to the place of Hades and shine among the dead."
> (12.382–83)

This, of course, would be disaster for the whole earth: it would mean the death of life on the planet.

The choice of death over life is perhaps the only really unforgivable sin that can be committed in the world of the *Odyssey* (paralleling the sin "against the Holy Spirit" in the Gospels; see Matthew 12:32)—not stealing another's property or disobeying the gods: such lawlessness fully belongs to that world and characterizes even its most esteemed heroes. It is a far greater offense that Odysseus's men prefer death to discomfort and suffering: they thereby become deserving of it. Like Aigisthos, who murdered Agamemnon, "knowing he would be destroyed, since we told him beforehand" (1.36–37), Eurylochus and those who follow him choose death over life at all costs. They thereby make themselves worthy of it and unworthy of Odysseus. Odysseus is himself no stranger to this temptation in extremes, but he heroically resists it and always rises to the challenge of fighting for his life and for the lives of his companions.

When the ship is thunderbolted in order that the day of return for these men be taken away, Odysseus, on a raft made out of the ruins by binding mast and keel together, is swept back to Charybdis:

> "And she sucked back the salty water of the sea,
> But I raised myself high up against the tall wild fig tree
> And held myself fastened to it like a bat."
> (12.431–33)

This image of Odysseus clinging to the fig tree for dear life symbolizes his desperate yet unrelenting struggle to survive. He is here the epitome of human striving for life, whereas his foolish companions throw life away willfully.

The *Odyssey* is a call to consciousness of a new order in which human existence realizes its inestimable value. Odysseus's men, like the suitors after them, are lost because they are deficient in the consciousness that rises above their physical needs and greed. They lack the capacity of self-abnegation, of becoming "no man," by virtue of which, paradoxically, Odysseus becomes fully human and even godlike. By this negative capability, the human is realized in the image of the divine, which is capable of being everything—and nothing.

After his tale is complete, Odysseus's last words to Arete emphasize the end of mortal existence in decrepitude and death, which he has seen and accepted:

> "May you constantly fare well, my queen, till old age
> And death come upon you, which do exist for men."
> (12.59–60)

This acknowledgment seems to be missing from the rather mythic existence of the Phaeacians, and for this they pay the price. Following hard upon the end of Odysseus's narrative—and because of the escort they accord him—the prophecy against them is fulfilled (3.178). The ship returning from Ithaca to the Phaeacian port is turned to stone (stone is at least perpetually safe), and Poseidon also buries the Phaeacians' city beneath a mountain. They are, in effect, swallowed up by oblivion in the same way that Odysseus had seemed to be, even though by fighting for his life he is able rather to reemerge into prominence and glory—like the massive mountain Neritos that conspicuously marks his place of origin, his beloved Ithaca (9.22).

IV. Gods and Guidance: Freedom and Slavery of Mind (*Odyssey*, Books 13–16)

Book 13 begins the second part of the *Odyssey*. Odysseus has won his life for himself, having snatched it from the clutches of death, and he has blazoned his fame abroad in autobiographical narration to the Phaeacians, but he is still far from being recognized and received by his own people. He is thought dead and is therefore going to have to be resurrected in the minds of all who knew him before he will be able to reassume his place at the head of his household and kingdom. He himself does not even recognize Ithaca, when he first awakes upon his native soil: "But godly Odysseus woke up / From sleeping on his fatherland soil and did not recognize it, / For he had been gone a long time" (13.187–89). Now that he is home, a new struggle begins, a struggle for recognition.

Odysseus's return must be prepared for psychologically within him and within his people before it can be accomplished in deed, and this proves to be as challenging in its own way as the voyage home over hostile seas. It is this inward, psychological odyssey of reestablishing his identity in the minds and hearts of his household and people that now becomes the theater of divine interventions. This mental dimension has always been near to the nexus with divinity, even when the activity of the gods was described as taking place in a purely physical dimension of external space. The inner, psychological space that opens up in the *Odyssey* as such a distinctive part of its new outlook foregrounds human freedom and motivations, but at the same time it manifests their dependency on an intelligence and drama beyond themselves and figured as belonging to the gods. The self-transcending and even "divine" character of human existence, at the psychological level, is thereby made fully concrete.

In particular, after his visit to the transcendent realm of the underworld, Odysseus's death has become part of his life and mind. It inhabits his sleep, as he is ferried to Ithaca by the Phaeacians ("a balmy sleep, / Unwaking, most sweet, nearest in semblance to death," 13.79–80), so that he can now for once forget his pains ("at this time he slept without a tremor, forgetting what he had suffered," 13.92). He need no longer be conscious of them, for they are built into what he is. They make him fully human and thereby also ambiguously divine as he, figuratively, comes back from the dead in order to begin a new life, as if resurrected in his own old land and body politic. He is placed on Ithaca, in the cave of the Naiades in the harbor of Phorcys, as in a tomb from which his new life will emerge:

> First they raised Odysseus out of the hollow ship,
> The linen sheet and the glistening blanket and all . . .
> (13.117–18)

The initial description of the cave of the Naiades in the harbor of Phorcys, where Odysseus lands in Ithaca, maintains an exquisite ambiguity between the natural and the supernatural: the looms of the Naiades are described in such a way that natural formations of the rock are transparent beneath them. A superimposition of imagined divine activities on the natural rock formations of stalactites and stalagmites makes this womb in the earth of Ithaca at the sea's edge wonderfully equivocal:

> And in it there are mixing bowls and two-handled jars
> Of stone. And the bees store up their honey in them.
> There are very long stone looms in it, where the nymphs
> Weave sea purple mantles, a wonder to behold,
> And ever-flowing waters are there.
> (13.105–9)

Not without reason, the scene has been read since ancient times as an allegory for the rebirth of the soul as it is reincarnated in a new body.[35]

All the scenes involving the gods are described *as if* they could also concern only nature and mortals—yet mortals grasped in their capacity to overreach themselves and mere nature and so attain to something inexplicable, godlike. As at the beginning with Telemachos, so in this second beginning with Odysseus, Athena acts in ways that make her, in effect, the exact objectification of his own deepest mind, the part of his psyche beyond that which can be consciously accessed and publicly represented. Even when Athena is in front of him in disguise, Odysseus is right to be mistrustful, just as he was

35. Porphyry, *On the Cave of the Nymphs*, trans. Robert Lamberton (Barrytown, N.Y.: Station Hill, 1983).

all through his wanderings, and not to rely blindly on the help of the gods (which could be an equivalence for good luck) or of concerned sea nymphs, for all this has no certain value—except in relation to what he can do for himself. As Dimock puts it, "in the *Odyssey*, the gods help those who are capable of helping themselves and in just those ways in which they are most capable" (*Unity of the Odyssey*, 8). No wonder the action and assistance of the gods reads so naturally as a figure for extraordinary human effort and achievement.

Odysseus has even become in some respects the equal of Athena: his own initiatives now coincide with hers, and he can therefore presume to point out where she has perhaps been remiss. He invents a story about himself as a Cretan fugitive, having killed the son of Idomeneus "because he wanted to deprive me of all my booty" (13.262), implicitly warning the young shepherd (actually Athena in disguise), lest he set greedy eyes on the tempting treasure piled high on the beach. By such ruses, Odysseus proves himself Athena's match in craft and in the use of disguises. He is not her pawn but rather begins working with the goddess as a peer. He collaborates with her, and she accepts him as co-conspirator:

> "Come, let us say no more of this, as both of us are skilled
> In shrewdness, since you are by far the best of mortals
> In plans and in stories, and I among all the gods
> Am famed for planning and shrewdness . . .
> And now I have come here so I may weave a plot with you . . ."
> (13. 294–303)

The plan that Odysseus and Athena together hatch is exactly what Odysseus himself, at his best, would have resolved upon: it expresses in every way his character and approach to matters, and it is based on exactly such facts as he already knows, or at least suspects. As Dimock remarks, "Athena's telling Odysseus face to face about the suitors is simply an extreme case of what her help to him usually is anyway, a heightened version of what he would naturally have done himself" (*Unity of the Odyssey*, 187). Yet he attributes the knowledge all to her, perhaps out of guileful tact, as calculated flattery, or perhaps as a figurative way of expressing his own heightened human intelligence and a resolve that acknowledges its divine provenance:

> "Well now, I might surely have perished in my halls
> By the evil fate of Agamemnon, son of Atreus,
> If you, goddess, had not duly told me the details.
> Come, devise a plan, that I may do vengeance on them.
> Stand beside me yourself, putting in me such courageous might
> As we had when we undid Troy's shining diadems."
> (13.383–88)

Still, all of Athena's help has not sufficed to remove risk or to spare him pains. Even with her help and vigilance, Odysseus has had to fight with all his human strength at every step of the way. He even sounds sarcastic in reproaching Athena for not sparing Telemachos the journey in search of news concerning his father, since the suitors attempt to take advantage of it in order to ambush the young man:

> "Why did you, who know all in your mind, not tell him?
> So that he too might wander and undergo pains
> On the barren sea and others eat his livelihood?"
>
> (13.417–19)

He questions her as he would an equal. Such presumed partnership between man and god is revealing of the whole secular thrust of the *Odyssey*, for it reveals not the disappearing or banishing of the gods (as has often been assumed to be the case from a narrowly modern perspective), but rather the opposite. The secular world is discovered in cooperation, and sometimes even in competition, with the gods—rather than in their denial. This is a kind of humanism that recognizes the place of the human within a larger scheme of things reaching beyond its own power and control.

The human stories of Odysseus's relations with each individual of his household are in various ways revealing of some sacred bond of relation that transcends the purely human sphere and makes "superhuman" actions possible. But such actions are always also eminently human efforts. Odysseus's encounter in book 14 with Eumaeos, his slave, features tales showing that we are all slaves and yet can all achieve mastery. In fact, even Eumaeos has bought himself a slave (14.450). We are all in subjection to the gods, but we can still define free human identities for ourselves, particularly through enduring and mastering the power of pain. Precisely this lesson needs to be imparted and accepted in order for Odysseus to win Eumaeos as an ally in his homecoming.

Odysseus is frankly cruel to his enemies, and Eumaeos's conventional piety condemns this kind of behavior:

> "For the blessed gods are not fond of cruel deeds;
> No, they reward justice and the righteous deeds of men."
>
> (14.83–84)

Eumaeos is accordingly convinced that "the gods have hindered the return of the man" (14.60). Indeed, for Eumaeos, the Odysseus who challenged the gods is quite dead, and although he is the loyal slave of his master, Eumaeos will have nothing to do with any reports that Odysseus is near (14.122–30). He "wholly denies" the possibility of his master's return and even confesses,

"I am in awe to speak his name" (14.145). This indicates why it is not possible for Odysseus to be received back home immediately as himself. He is forced to gain support for himself in the guise of someone else. His tale of himself as a Cretan—hinting at the truth of its own falsehood, since Cretans were proverbially liars—is craftily adapted in the version he tells Eumaeos (14.191–359) to gain the understanding and support of his despairing servant, for it resembles Eumaeos's own life story. Both Eumaeos and the invented Cretan were sons of wealthy noblemen and were kidnapped by Phoenicians and reduced to rags and slavery.

Yet Odysseus also strategically insinuates into his tale elements of dissimilarity aimed at converting Eumaeos from his pacifist piety because very different virtues are going to have to be called on for the task at hand. The Cretan persona is also a conqueror and a city-sacker. He is, in fact, made in the image of Odysseus as predator:

> "Such was I in war. Labor was not dear to me
> Or household-tending, that raises glorious children.
> No, ships with good oars were always dear to me
> And battles, and well-made javelins and arrows,
> Woeful things, that for others are to be shuddered at.
> But to me things are precious, I think, that a god put in my mind,
> For one man delights in one task, one man in another."
>
> (14.222–28)

One of the main lessons for Eumaeos in the tale Odysseus tells is that the gods, and in particular Zeus, are friends even of a very violent man. Against Eumaeos's conviction that his master "has been very much hated / By all the gods" (14.366–67), the stranger's tale emphasizes the favor of Zeus and the gods at each critical juncture. This favor is what saves him finally in the shipwreck in which his Phoenician captors all perish:

> ". . . Zeus himself
> Put the enormous mast of the dark blue-prowed ship
> Into my hands so I might still escape from distress."
>
> (14.310–12)

When bound in slavery by the treacherous Thesprotian sailors, the "stranger" relates, "the gods themselves bent the bonds back for me" (14.348), and during the ensuing manhunt again "the gods themselves concealed me" (14.457).

Eumaeos, in fact, responds very positively to Odysseus's tale: the "unbelieving spirit" in his breast (14.391) has been moved, and he has been made receptive to marvels that he previously would not have believed. This change is registered by his open, enthusiastic hospitality and his more open mind about the inscrutable will of the gods:

> "Eat, marvelous stranger, and enjoy these things
> That are here. A god gives one thing and lets another go
> As he wishes in his heart. For he can do all things."
> (14.443–45)

As they sacrifice and feast together, Eumaeos no longer seems so sure that city-sackers are automatically punished by the gods.

The story of Eumaeos's hosting of Odysseus resumes, after the scene of Telamachos's departure from Sparta, in book 15.301ff. This is when we hear Eumaeos's own story of being kidnapped from his father's royal house by a Phoenician servant seduced by sailors from her own country, and of how he eventually was sold as a slave to Laertes (15.403–84). By dint of being repeated in various forms, this story of noble origins and of being sold into slavery becomes an allegory of the universal human condition: indeed, the Phoenician servant in Eumaeos's story has herself been kidnapped from a wealthy father and sold into slavery. We are, in effect, all called to return home to our native freedom out of the inevitable entrapments and enslavements of life in the world.

This type-story of wanderings and concomitant pains matches Odysseus's story, which is reflected and enhanced by each new version that he fabricates. This fertile inventiveness also provides another occasion to eulogize the magic dilation of time by narrative: "These nights are immense" (15.392), marvels Eumaeos, much like Alcinous previously. And this creative, transforming power of narrative is constantly exploited as Odysseus reconstructs and reinvents himself in the minds of others by the stories he tells. Indeed, as a result of these inventions of narration, Odysseus has begun to be recognized again, and in book 16 he discloses himself to and is accepted by Telemachos.

> "But I am your father for whose sake you are grieving
> And suffer many pains, receiving the assaults of men."
> (16.187–88)

Tellingly, when they recognize each other, their reunion is placed under the aegis of predatory animals, fierce birds of prey.

> Telemachos
> Embraced his noble father and moaned, shedding tears.
> In both of them there arose a longing for lamentation.
> They wailed piercingly and more incessantly than birds.
> Sea eagles or falcons with hooked claws whose children

> Farmers have snatched off before they were fully fledged.
> (16.213–18)

This fierceness focuses Odysseus's identity at this threshold in particular, where ruthless violence will be necessary for him to reestablish himself in his own household as lord and master.

V. From Anonymous Disguise to Named Identity: *Odyssey*, Books 17–19

Why are eight more books necessary after Odysseus has returned home and been recognized by his son? What remains is the climax of Odysseus's "striving for his life": for this means not just his struggle for survival but also reestablishing his identity and winning back the respect, recognition, and authority due to him both as a private individual and as king. What happens on Ithaca is a much more elaborate and definitive version of the scenario already played out more briefly with the Cyclops and the Phaeacians. In each case, the protagonist starts from the non-identity or anonymity of No-man in order to emerge resoundingly as "Odysseus," the sufferer and inflicter of pains.

Odysseus goes through a series of recognition scenes that start with his own recognition of Ithaca, his home, and converge upon his being recognized by his own household in the culminating scenes. This restoration of identity requires of Odysseus an inner transformation and conversion, beyond the physical fact of being back on his native soil. This inner, psychological dimension is interpreted as embodying and manifesting the power of the gods: whatever cannot be accounted for by external circumstances, but only in terms of Odysseus's miraculous inner strength and resources, suggests divine intervention.

We have already observed how each time he tells his Cretan story it is different, depending on his auditor. It is calculated to conceal—and at the same time reveal—him in the most strategic way in each different circumstance: in book 13, to Athena disguised as a shepherd who might be inclined to contemplate stealing some loot, he emphasizes that he has killed to defend his treasure; in book 14, to Eumaeos, who thinks him dead by divine judgment as punishment for his violent deeds, he portrays sacking cities as something acceptable to the gods; in book 17, to Antinoos, he emphasizes change of fortune, alluding to the retribution in store as this suitor's immanent fate; in book 19, to a despairing Penelope, he forcefully presents an image of her husband as presently home and plotting revenge.

Odysseus uses fiction and disguise in order to reestablish himself as a real presence in Ithaca. His identity has to be regained via use of disguises not only for pragmatic, logistical reasons but also because of a sort of ethical requirement that he first experience pain from the position of the underdog. His heroism is one of bearing pains, not of being above them. He is, in this, strikingly like the man of sorrows, and acquainted with grief, of biblical tradition (Isaiah 53). He alternates and unites this figure of the sacrificial victim with a predator identity that is its diametrical but complementary opposite.

Paradoxically, Odysseus's human essence as sufferer is revealed only by disguising his exterior social identity as king. The same goes for Christ the king revealed as divine through kenotic self-emptying even unto the death on the Cross (Philippians 2). It is ironic that dissembling his identity is precisely the means whereby Odysseus establishes it, just as living out a destiny of pain is shown to be the only way to attain to genuine human happiness. From the lowly non-identity of a beggar, Odysseus gradually rises, by means of suffering and inflicting suffering, toward the revelation of his identity and restitution of his authority at the head of his household. These books (17–19) portray Odysseus continuing to suffer and cause pain and to be recognized for it in his conflicts with Melanthios, Antinoos, Iros, Melantho, and Eurymachos. From Melanthios he receives insults and a kick in a typical instance of an underling taking cruel advantage of whomever he deems to be still lower even than he. Odysseus considers whether to kill him immediately, "but he braced himself and checked his mind" (17.238). He fulfills his essential role, as he himself describes it, by accepting pain and hostility:

> "For I am not unacquainted with tosses or with blows.
> My heart is enduring, since I have suffered many ills
> On the waves and in war. Let this one be added to them.
> There is no way of concealing an eager stomach,
> The accursèd thing that gives many evils to men,
> On whose account also well-rigged ships set out
> Over the barren ocean, carrying evils for enemies."
> (17.281–89)

This constitutes acceptance of the human condition, even in its wretched dependence, bound by material needs, and even with the implication of inevitable aggression against other people. Odysseus recognizes that he, too, is conditioned by this economy of pain and accepts and even affirms it. It enables him to share something in common with even the humblest inhabitant of all at his home in Ithaca, namely, his dog, Argos. In the very moment in which he recognizes his master as having returned home after twenty years, the old hound expires pathetically on a dunghill, but with the dignity of undying faithfulness (17. 301–4). In this way, recognition of Odysseus begins with and proceeds from the lowliest member of his household, for that is where his own sympathies also remain rooted.

But apart from such rare and touching moments of sympathy, mainly what Odysseus has to confront is hostility. The insults and injuries that he will be forced to endure are anticipated emblematically by his scuffle with Iros in book 18. The offense is at bottom a denial of identity to the other as a person instead of recognizing him either as friend or as foe. For having attempted to obliterate Odysseus's identity, Iros loses his own, as is pointed out by the suitors: "Soon Iros, un-Irosed, shall have an ill he brought on himself" (18.73), and Antinoos says, "You ought not to exist now, ox-braggart, or have been born" (18.79). Antinoos himself hits Odysseus with a stool. Such injuries are, he says, dealt him "on account of my woeful belly" (17.473) or again "my criminal belly" which "urges me on" (18.53). Someone points out that the guest may be "some heavenly god" and that Antinoos's act is sacrilegious (17.483–87). It is, indeed, the judgment of the gods that is being secretly prepared in Odysseus's return incognito. Odysseus's avowal at least recognizes human life as needy and vulnerable, whereas denying the beggar food is to refuse recognition of this meanest level of need in human beings. And that is an offense against the gods.

As night draws on, Odysseus offers himself symbolically to enlighten others—"I myself shall furnish light to all these people" (18.318). Even Eurymachos's attempt to tweak Odysseus for being bald ironically alludes to his giving off light:

> "Indeed, the light of the torches seems to me to be his own,
> From his head, since there are no hairs on it in the least."
> (18.355–56)

He names himself "Aithon" ("red") to Penelope and melts her to tears by vivid evocation of the memory of her husband.

> Tears flowed from her as she listened and her flesh melted.
> Just as snow melts down upon the peaks of the mountains . . .
> (19.203–4)

But the fierce and menacing side of his personality is at least as necessary, especially at this point in the story, on the threshold of the battle against the suitors, and so he also takes a step toward emerging as himself when he ferociously threatens the maid-servant Melantho (18.337–41), though without yet divulging who he is.

The process of recognition and of reinstating his identity in relation to his loved ones, and particularly in relation to his wife, necessarily takes an indirect course. Disguised, he tells Penelope of an article of dress worn by Odysseus upon his mantle, which proves that he has indeed seen her husband. Bearing an image of predation—a dog throttling a fawn—it is an emblem of the man. The testimony of this "stranger" is thus authenticated by his description of the brooch that accurately characterizes Odysseus, depicting the decisive thing about him in this dangerous world:

> "And the brooch upon it was made of gold,
> With twin sockets. And on its face it was skillfully wrought:
> In his front paws a dog was holding a dappled fawn
> And gazed at it while it writhed. All men marveled to see
> How the one, being of gold, gazed at the fawn he throttled,
> And the other strove to get away as he writhed with his feet."
> (19.225–30)

This image is then immediately qualified by another, that of a soft onion skin, suggesting the other, complementary side of Odysseus's character as it manifests itself to his own people and appeals particularly to women:

> "I noticed the tunic over his flesh glistening
> The way the husk does on an onion that is dried,
> So soft it was, and it was shining like the sun.
> Many women indeed looked with wonder upon him."
> (19.231–34)

The other key mark of recognition, of course, is Odysseus's scar. The recognition of the scar by Eurycleia has been immortalized as one of the great moments in the *Odyssey* and in world literature.[36] It is a poignant climax of the drama of recognition that occupies the whole second half of the poem, and it concerns the disclosure not only of the fact of Odysseus's return but also of his deepest personal identity, his essential significance as a human being. This epiphany is preceded by a flashback opening upon a memorable scene in Odysseus's youth that marks his coming of age. A parenthesis opens as Eurycleia, while washing Odysseus's feet, notices the scar on his leg:

> The scar which once a boar dealt him with its shining tusk
> When he had come to Parnassos to see Autolycos and his sons,
> His mother's noble father who excelled among men
> In trickery and oath making.
> (19.393–96)

A scene of hunting—and, in the event, of being hunted—scars Odysseus for life. The maternal grandfather's name, Autolycos, means "himself a wolf,"

36. Erich Auerbach, "Die Narbe des Odysseus," in *Mimesis: Dargestellte Wirklichkeit in der abendländischen Literatur* (Bern: Francke, 1946), trans. as "Odysseus's Scar" in *Mimesis: The Representation of Reality in Western Literature.*

and he is a model of the predatory nature which Odysseus himself must assume. Well-endowed by the god Hermes, the man excels literally at "thieving" (κλεπτοσύνη). It is he who gives Odysseus his name:

> "My son-in-law and daughter, give him the name I say.
> I myself come here as one who has been enraged [ὀδυσσεὺς] at many,
> At men and at women, throughout the much-nourishing earth,
> And let him be named Man of Wrath: Odysseus."
>
> (19.406–9)

The exact meaning of this name is elucidated by verbs with which it is cognate, particularly ὀδύσσομαι, meaning to be wroth against or to hate another.[37] The word can take on various meanings, including to be angry, to hate, to vex, to trouble, or to offend. According to Jenny Strauss Clay, "Autolycos derives the name Odysseus from the verb *odysasthai*, which means 'to have hostile feelings or enmity toward someone.' "[38]

Odysseus manifestly fulfills his name when he grows up and returns to Parnassus to take part in the hunt. He shows himself eager to inflict pain on the wild boar and consequently suffers the pain of being gashed by the boar, which he nevertheless kills. This incident is the epitome and the prefiguration of all the exploits that are inextricably associated with the name of Odysseus, notably the wooden horse at Troy, the maiming of Polyphemus by "No-Man," and the final bloody victory over the 108 suitors. Dimock suggests that this is "the wry solution which the *Odyssey* offers to the problem of evil: Pain creates value. Odysseus is the living embodiment of that solution" (*Unity of the Odyssey*, 223).

We might amplify this by remembering that being remembered is the ultimate goal of the hero, the source of value for his life and for his society. Pain should be viewed in this context as a mnemonic instrument. Social cohesion and the whole ethical system depend on heroes who are remembered after their deaths for their glorious acts. They become models of civic virtue, and certainly their having caused pain to some contributes to their being memorable. This trait is crucial to the portrait of Odysseus, man of pains, as he lives eternally in the memory of his people through epic song.[39]

After the inset story illuminating the meaning of his name, Odysseus is shown threatening Eurycleia: "Odysseus groped for her / With his hands and

37. *Liddel & Scott's Greek-English Lexicon* (Oxford: Clarendon, 1975), 7th ed.

38. Clay, "The Name of Odysseus," in *The Wrath of Athena: Gods and Men in the Odyssey*, 59.

39. Compare David Bouvier, "La Mémoire et la mort dans la poésie homérique," *Kernos* 12 (1999): 57–71. See, further, J.-P. Vernant, *L'Individu, la mort, l'amour: Soi-même et l'autre dans la Grèce ancienne* (Paris: Gallimard, 1989), specifically chapter 3: "Mort grecque, mort à deux faces," 81–89.

took her by the throat with his right hand" (19.480–81). This aggression shows us his nature in action. He threatens her even with her life. Although his intentions are obviously benevolent, they are inseparable from his assuming hostile postures and being ready to unleash savage violence. Such is the reality of the world that is here revealed, and Odysseus unflinchingly faces it and accepts all the consequences.

In the world of the *Odyssey*, we are made to face pain and to endure it, if we wish to be born, to emerge into the world rather than be swallowed up by the sea or smothered in the womb-like caves of Calypso. To be eaten alive, even if last, as "no man," by the Cyclops, is another version of the same fate of anonymity, of falling victim to the brute force of nature that obliterates human identity. Odysseus's mission, consonant with his name, is to make us recognize this pain or trouble at the root of human value:[40] that is why he must carry his oar far from the sea, even to where it will be misrecognized as a winnowing fan by men ignorant of the sea and the salt of life. Thus he bears the emblem of struggle and conflict and pain as sources of human value all through his life and escapes its rigorous exactions only in death.

Techne is the characteristically human way of triumphing over the threat of amorphous non-entity, of being engulfed by the formless flux of nature. By technical devices, and especially by language and names, humans establish themselves and their culture enduringly. Odysseus masters a variety of techniques, all of them leveraged fundamentally from language as the master *techne* that enables and accesses all the others. Technology in this sense is revealed as the motor of the secularizing trend followed by human culture perhaps universally. And yet the power of *techne* leaves unanswered the questions of ethics that the *Odyssey* raises. Odysseus's prodigious empowerment cannot but be admired. However, can it be justified and embraced in its ultimate consequences? Only divine revelation—by signs—can tell.

VI. Human Vengeance and the Signs of Divine Justice: *Odyssey*, Books 20–24

Toward the end of the *Odyssey*, the crucial scenes all turn on the reading of signs. Odysseus's identity is deciphered repeatedly only with the help of signs. Reading signs reestablishes Odysseus as husband and king, and finally as son, and when certain manifestations are read as the gods' will and express command, such deciphering is instrumental likewise to reestablishing the peace. Knowing that the merciless, unsparing slaughter of the suitors is just also

40. Again, it is Dimock who expounds with exemplary lucidity these far-reaching insights of the critical tradition, bringing them to focus in his essay "The Name of Odysseus," *Hudson Review* 9, no. 1 (1956): 52–70.

requires signs from the gods.[41] In some sense, signification as such constitutes the presence of a higher or even a divine meaning in human existence.

Significance, as an effect of signs, might be seen as the basic unit or medium of any secular manifestation of divinity in human consciousness and experience. Interpreting signs is based on a certain givenness of things and claims to interpret what things signify of themselves. Yet significance, at least as it is apprehended in language, is not simply given in the nature of things; it must rather be attributed to them by interpretation and therefore as supervening upon them from some other, intelligible, arguably higher sphere or agency. This event of interpretation may be viewed as a purely subjective act, but it also lends itself to being construed as a sort of divine revelation. We have observed such ambiguity between the divine and the human throughout the *Odyssey*.

Signs may be considered the first and the most universal of human technologies and even as coinciding with language itself, but at the same time they must perhaps always be recognized also at some level as given by the gods. Reading signs is the job especially of divines and augurs. Interpreting signs is also one of the original functions of poetry as a making of sense and, simultaneously, an interpretation of the significance of all things and their relatedness together. To this extent, poetry functions as a sort of theological hermeneutic. Poetry, as an art of making signs, marks the intersection of divine revelation with human art or *techne*. The thematics of the sign, accordingly, extends what has been treated here as the secularizing movement of the poem as a whole.

Book 20 develops the sequence of omens foreboding the suitors' demise and Odysseus's revenge. This development has been anticipated by Penelope's dream, at the end of Book 19, of an eagle from the mountains breaking the necks of twenty geese feeding at her house and then identifying himself to her as her "husband" (19.536–55). This is one indication of how the actual event of meeting and recognizing Odysseus must be carefully prepared for by an inward readiness to receive and recognize him. Affected by the dream, Penelope begins to metamorphose inwardly in anticipation of the unveiling of Odysseus. She is stirred to take the initiative, as she sets up the contest of the axes, assuming a more active posture vis-à-vis her pain than she has taken previously. She does, nevertheless, express—one last time—her death-wish, praying to Artemis to take her life away on the streams of Oceanus (20.62–68), since this she presumes has been Odysseus's fate.

At the beginning of book 20, on the threshold of his terrible revenge, Odysseus, who is wakeful in the night, needs assurance that the gods are on

41. For an extensive treatment of the pervasive role of signs in the *Odyssey* set in a broad context of the intellectual and cultural history of the West, see Jeffrey Barnouw, *Odysseus, Hero of Practical Intelligence: Deliberation and Signs in Homer's Odyssey* (New York: University Press of America, 2004).

his side. He prays to Zeus to give him an omen both outside and inside the house. The skies' thundering from Olympus and the cry of a serving woman who sees it as a portent of his revenge and lifts up her voice in the mill room (20.97ff.) presently oblige. He also picks up another needed ally in Philoitios, the cowherd, who recognizes Odysseus, even in his beggar's rags, as king-like. Unlike Eumaeos, Philoitios interprets the misfortunes of "blameless Odysseus" as injustice, thereby proving himself a worthy and reliable ally for the terrible (and perhaps not so obvious) justice that Odysseus is preparing. He shows that he is fully prepared mentally for what is about to happen:

> "But still I think of that hapless man, if from somewhere
> He may come and make the suitors scatter through the halls."
> (20.224–25)

The immanence of this event heightens the dramatic irony as Philoitios says of Odysseus unwittingly to the man himself, "I believe he too / Wanders among men wearing such tatters as these" (20.205–6).

The insults and violence of the suitors against Odysseus continue to crescendo as Ktesippos throws an ox foot at Odysseus. The gods seem to be setting up Odysseus's revenge in such a way that it may explode onto the scene out of the full measure of his pain and outrage:

> And Athene by no means allowed the bold suitors
> To refrain from grievous outrage, so that still more pain
> Might enter the heart of Odysseus, son of Laertes.
> (20.284–86)

The sense of foreboding becomes eerily intense as the suitors are spooked in a surreal scene, revealing imminent death, engineered again by Athene:

> But Pallas Athene aroused
> Quenchless laughter in the suitors and set their wits astray.
> They were already laughing with the jaws of other men,
> And they were eating meat spattered with blood. Their eyes
> Filled up with tears and their hearts sensed an anguish coming.
> (20.345–49)

At this point, Theoclymenous, whose name means "called by the god," declares his apocalyptic vision interpreting the signs of impending doom:

> "Wretched men! What evil is this you suffer? Your heads
> And faces are shrouded in night, and your knees beneath;
> Wailing blazes up, and your cheeks are covered with tears,

> The walls and the lovely pedestals are sprinkled with blood.
> The porch is full of phantoms; the courtyard is also full
> Of those eager for Erebos under the dusk. The sun
> Has perished out of heaven, and an evil mist has rushed in."
> (20.351–57)

The suitors continue to laugh and mock and prepare a sumptuous dinner despite such ominous warnings. Their comportment is an evasion, a choosing of illusory comforts over real life, a choice comparable to that of Odysseus's men, who also died for eating someone else's cattle. The suitors' behavior represents a refusal to accept life with all its pains by responsibly participating in giving and taking them and attempting rather to profiteer from an ambiguous situation and go "scot free." They do not take a stance as mortal men pitted in hostility against another mortal. Instead, they exploit the absence of Odysseus, as if they were his guests, while actually taking advantage of his property. They shirk assuming clear signification, but just that is demanded by the order of signs and its divine sanctions. Such a demand for clarity is itself a sign of the secular, which characteristically circumscribes an ambit from which the vague and mysterious can be exorcised.

This fundamental evasiveness of the suitors' behavior, whereby they avoid taking a clear position as friends or enemies, misrecognizes the nature also of mortal life. Odysseus realizes that he must choose one or the other attitude. The suitors pretend to honor and court Penelope, though really they devour her husband and son's estate. They pretend to be friends in order to act like enemies. Nor is this a wily device on their part, an adroit exploitation of ambiguous signs, but rather a failure to recognize reality and a shirking of responsibility for one's role in it—for good and for ill. As a result of their denial of it and shrinking before it, the reality of individual responsibility rears up as a menace before them and becomes a fateful destiny.

The evasive mind-set of the suitors, blurring the difference between friend and foe, avoiding and deferring such fateful choice as mortal existence and the gods' demand, manifests itself further in the instance of the bow-stringing contest. Antinoos invents a face-saving fiction to avoid the painful reality that none of them can string Odysseus's bow: he announces that it is a "feast day of that god, / The holy one" (21.258–59) and so not a time when anyone would be capable of bending bows. So they put it off till the morrow and return to their carousing. However, when Odysseus makes a bid to try stringing the bow, they are hostile and apprehensive, showing that they do not really believe Antinoos's explanation and excuse. It is a false manipulation of signs designed to dissemble reality rather than reveal it.

Telemachos has to intervene, asserting his authority ("For the power in the house is mine," 21.353) and threatening even Eumaeos, after the suitors protest against his bringing the bow to Odysseus.

> "Uncle, bring the bow out. You will soon not do well to heed all,
> Lest, though younger than you, I drive you to the fields
> And throw stones at you. I am mightier than you in strength."
> (21.369–71)

This aggressive, threatening posture portrays Telemachos, at last, living up to the model of his father, whom he is coming to resemble more and more.

Odysseus's actual stringing of the bow is presented as an apocalyptic event marked by thunderings from the sky and cosmic showing of signs (21.413). For the bow is set up to separate the saved from the damned: it is the instrument of heaven's wrath and vengeance.

> As when a man skilled at the lyre and at singing
> Easily stretches a string over a new peg,
> Tying at both ends the flexible gut of the sheep—
> So without effort did Odysseus string the great bow.
> (21.406–9)

The bow is, metaphorically, a musical instrument, a lyre. The lyre is itself a metaphor for such technical means as Odysseus has used to reveal his identity in his tale, for which he is praised by Alcinoos: "As a singer would, you have skillfully told the tale" (11.368). It now becomes the instrument of a universal revelation. Based on universal harmonies, music embodies the principles of justice in the universe. The lyre of dancing and feasting, moreover—especially when it is feasting on the guts of another man's sheep—turns suddenly and appallingly into a weapon of death. It invites the suitors to act like suitors indeed and dance: it makes them dance the dance of death, the death that they have now come to deserve.

Symbolically, it is Odysseus's bow that discriminates between the doomed and the justified, between illusion and reality. Athena puts it into the head of Penelope (heightening what could also be a human stroke of genius) to set up its stringing as a contest among the suitors for selecting one worthy to become Odysseus's successor. The various suitors range in culpability from the violent Antinoos to the soft Leodes, who sincerely loves Penelope and wants to have her rather than to exploit the situation on the pretext of suing for her hand in marriage. Still, "both share in the suitors' prime fault, an irresponsible attitude toward reality" (Dimock, *Unity of the Odyssey*, 283).

What is important here is not any conventional morality of rights and wrongs, since the worst atrocities are committed also by the greatest heroes, but an attitude that either recognizes and confronts or else distorts and evades reality—reality as more than material, as significant and therefore as entailing obligations to men and gods. Leodes is "son of Oinops" (21.144), that is, "wine eye," and though he is gentle and sensitive, not violent, he colludes in the suitors' fatal misprision of reality. The ethics of the *Odyssey* are founded on the value of life, on its acceptance and affirmation. This affirmation is inclusive of and is even based on life's mortality and pain. Life involves predation and war and raids and slaughter. Simply life itself, particularly in its boundedness by death, is the only—or at least the supreme—value: everything, including sacking cities and inflicting pain on enemies, is condoned on the condition that it belong to life as Homer knows it. But the suitors are in a position that dissembles and confounds all clear definition of mortal existence and its constitutive pains and hostilities.

The suitors are in fact like Odysseus in "hostile-mindedness," as the name of their leader, Antinoos (*anti-nous*), hints. This belongs, tragically, to the human condition. They fail, however, to realize the deathly struggle they are engaged in: living in the ambiguity of their position as guests/profiteers, they exploit the ambiguity of Odysseus's life/death. They fail to accept and face the consequences of the hostility they themselves live by. Odysseus is not necessarily an essentially better or more moral character, but he lucidly realizes what it is to be a mortal man, to give and take pain, and he embraces this human identity fully and achieves the human excellence that it represents. The hostility that this entails is at the same time the condition of his mildness and generosity.

The ethics of the *Odyssey* are thus centered very much on the sense of personal identity, of the individual life that Odysseus is striving to preserve all along—both his own and those of his companions—as signaled from the opening sentence (1.5). The suitors' non-recognition of Odysseus either as dead or alive is worse than any open offense towards an acknowledged enemy. As Odysseus himself fulminates just before opening fire on them:

> "Dogs, you thought I would no longer come home in return
> From the land of the Trojans; and so you wore my house away
> And slept alongside my serving women by force
> And underhandedly courted my wife while I was myself alive,
> And you did not fear the gods who possess broad heaven,
> Or that there would be any vengeance of men in time to come.
> Now the bonds of destruction are fastened on you all."
>
> (22.35–41)

After Eurymachos's attempt to pin all the blame on Antinoos, Odysseus adds:

> "And now it lies with you either to fight face to face
> Or to flee, whoever would avoid death and destiny."
>
> (22.65–66)

This is not a moral condemnation so much as a clear recognition and announcement of the fight to the death in which the enemy parties are now engaged. Ironically, it is Odysseus who ends up enacting, against Melanthios, the equivalent of the horrible threats of Antinoos to send Iros to King Echetas for unconscionably cruel punishments and maiming (22.474–78). He is certainly no less ruthless than his antagonists. The maids, too, are hung by Telemachos in another act of calculated cruelty—in order that their deaths not be "clean" (22.462–73). Only Phemios and Medon are spared—because they recognized all along without fail the place of Odysseus.

This criterion of recognizing human, mortal reality and especially of recognizing Odysseus, dead or alive, and his rights, is presented very much in material terms. As mortal and physical beings, we are constituted by our material needs, and thus we are responsible for what we eat because this has implications for others and even for the whole of society. The neediness of the stomach is immediately connected with the exercise of power in the world at large. Odysseus realizes and reveals this in and from his role as beggar. He is, in fact, privileged in insight by this lowly station, not unlike the fool in Elizabethan drama. To Eumaeos's warnings about others likely to take advantage of the beggar, he replies:

> "I know, I see. You say this to an understanding man.
> Go forward now, and I shall remain here behind,
> For I am not unacquainted with tosses or with blows.
> My heart is enduring, since I have suffered many ills
> On the waves and in war. Let this one be added to them.
> There is no way of concealing an eager stomach,
> The accursèd thing that gives many evils to men,
> On whose account also well-rigged ships set out
> Over the barren ocean, carrying evils for enemies."
> (17.281–89)

Odysseus makes a similar avowal concerning his mortality and the "hateful belly" to the Phaeacians in 7.208–24. For finite, mortal beings, eating is an act with social implications. Appropriating anything for ourselves to relieve our physical neediness involves relations to others. Conflicts and hostility will inevitably arise. We have to recognize and accept all this, if we want to affirm mortal life for what it is.

These values are shown, moreover, to be divinely sanctioned. Such is the business of the theodicy at the end of the *Odyssey*. The similes for the slaughter present it as a kind of natural justice. The images of birds of prey that have been used all along, especially in omens and dreams, as likenesses for Odysseus in his coming wrath and predictable vengeance, recur again in the representations of Odysseus and Telemachos accomplishing their savagely natural revenge:

> . . . as falcons with bent claws and hooked beaks
> Come down from the mountains and dash upon the birds . . . .
> (22.302–3)

So also the image of the lion for Odysseus returning home:

> Bespattered over with blood and gore like a lion
> Who goes along when he has eaten from an ox of the field . . . .
> (22.402–3; see also 4.335–40)

But it is especially the image of the sun of justice shining in full strength over the suitors lying slaughtered in the halls that conveys, poignantly, this impression:

> . . . like fish that the fishermen
> Have drawn up on the curved beach out of the hoary sea
> In a net that has many meshes; and all of them
> Are heaped up on the sands longing for the waves of the sea;
> But the sun in his shining is taking away their life;
> So then the suitors were heaped up on one another.
> (22.383–89)

The divine sanction for slaughter operates, then, also as a curb on human gloating. Odysseus, though victorious, is not exultant over the "huge deed." He acts to restrain Eurycleia's exultation, for it is to be seen not as a deed of human self-glorification and triumph but as a work of the gods and as necessary to reestablish a moral equilibrium:

> "Old woman, rejoice in your heart; hold back and do not exult.
> It is not holy to boast over men who have been slain.
> The gods' fate has worsted these men, and their cruel deeds,
> For they honored no one of the men upon the earth,
> Either evil or noble, whoever encountered them."
> (22.411–15)

Penelope's disbelief at the news of the slaughter and her statement that "some one of the immortals has killed the bold suitors, / Offended at their heart-hurting insolence and evil deeds" (23.63–64) confirm the sense that so huge a deed can only be the doing of the gods. Accordingly, her recognition of Odysseus as a mortal man and her husband is still delayed, even after justice has been dealt out to the suitors.

The reunion of Odysseus with Penelope in book 23 presents still more obstacles and yet another recognition scene. Even so intimate a knowledge as that between husband and wife must be mediated and proved by signs. Human identity itself is a construction depending on the art of interpretation of signs. And then, even after being recognized objectively, Odysseus is still not immediately accepted by her. She must first pain him and make him angry in order that he return to being truly "Odysseus," and so become able to reclaim her emotionally. When "testing her husband," she proposes that

Odysseus's bed be prepared for him outside the bedroom, and at that suggestion "Odysseus / Grew angry" (23.181–82). It is his anger that reveals him to her as fully himself and without disguises, as well as laying bare his love for her, deep-rooted like the immovable olive tree that is their bed. The description of Odysseus's construction of their bedroom around the olive tree taken as bedpost again shows how skill in crafts or *techne* adapted to nature is vital to defining human identity. Odysseus's comment that the bed could not have been moved unless a god had done it evokes once again the mysterious threshold connecting what humans can achieve by their own utmost endeavors to what must be attributed to the gods.

After lovemaking, the couple take delight in telling stories to one another. Odysseus tells of "the many cares he had brought / Upon men, and the many he had suffered himself in his woe" (23.306–7). They reap pleasure from this pain viewed in retrospect (see also 15.400), while the night is prolonged by narrative, suggesting a suspension of time (Athena actually keeps the dawn from appearing, 23.244–45)—just as when Odysseus told his tale to the Phaeacians. Narration is another—and a fundamental—human *techne* attaining to godlike powers.

Odysseus's struggle for his life and his quest for identity end only with the recognition by his father in book 24. It is a painful recognition scene, made deliberately so by Odysseus and his narrative feints: he presents himself as a guest-friend of Odysseus named "Eperitos" (from "to test"). As heartless as it seems, he resists the impulse to pity his old father that overtakes him for a moment under a pear tree (24.234). Odysseus apparently aims to call the pain to mind in order to dramatically realize its meaning and thereby his own identity vis-à-vis his father as the source of his own being. In this manner, he brings the pain round to a happy result rather than just canceling it out, as if it should never have been at all. The greatest danger from the beginning of the epic and throughout is that his disappearance should simply cancel his identity, whether as dead or alive. The despair Laertes struggles against expresses itself pathetically in his reference to "Your hapless guest, my son, *if he ever existed*" (24.289). The worst, once again, is that Odysseus's presumed death is nameless and unknown, so that he could not be properly mourned by his kin and his identity be at least fixed secure and ineffaceable in death (24.291–96). When the pain reaches its limits—a "piercing throb had already / Struck through his nostrils" (24.318–19)—Odysseus finally relents and reveals himself.

After incredulity, signs, solace, and joy, Laertes exultantly praises the justice of the gods. As if in answer to Eurycleia's (19.363–69) and Philoitios's (20.201–3) earlier impugning of the justice of Zeus, he exclaims:

> "Father Zeus, you gods are still on tall Olympus, if truly
> The suitors have paid for their reckless insolence."
>
> (24.351–52)

Later, in the assembly of the Ithacans, Medon testifies that "Odysseus has not / Planned these deeds against the will of the deathless gods" (24.443–44).

Indeed, direct glimpses of the deliberations of the gods both at the beginning and the end of Book 24 show them behind the events that have transpired at Odysseus's hands. The council in heaven decides to restore order. There is here, of course, again a superimposition of divine upon human action. The spearing of Eupeithes by Laertes, spurred by Athena, is also stirred on the natural level by his pride at seeing his son and grandson "contending over excellence" (24.515). In this way, once again, Athena's intervention is transparent to and simply seconds already existing human motivations. Such double layering and overdetermination has been observable in the relation between gods and men constantly from the beginning of the poem. Zeus finally places a limit on the proliferation of vengeance and reciprocal violence, demanding a cessation of hostilities signaled by a thunderbolt in the path of Athena, who in turn checks Odysseus. But just this is what Odysseus himself wants: "He obeyed, and rejoiced in his heart" (24.545). For the action of the gods still represents his higher mind.

In general, in the *Odyssey*, human action has followed its own course, seconded by the gods who do, however, set a limit and impose peace in the end. And yet the justice done is very personal on Odysseus's part. Not just generic "divine justice," this is the full realization of Odysseus's character as sufferer and inflicter of pain—the indispensable means of establishing human value and identity. Our pain is what defines us as humans. This suffering can itself become a sort of divine revelation: in this respect, it is not so completely unlike the revelation of the Cross in biblical tradition. By following their own intrinsic logic as human events, both "holocausts" are ultimately expressed also as ethical, secular enactments of divine justice.

The *Odyssey* is a revelation of human life as possessing value immanently within itself. Finite, mortal existence is all that is worth living for. This is secular, worldly revelation, but a revelation nonetheless: it is not itself just the world as perceived on its surface, for it first emerges against the backdrop of the other world, that of the gods, and through the art of poetic imagination that they inspire. The gods are present in and among human beings: in fact, acts of these two kinds of beings are practically confounded with one another. Yet revelation is not only from above; it is also from within. Revelation at all levels of form and content, moreover, is mediated and constructed by signs, which open an order of significance beyond the world in its immediacy. Stripped down to bare secular terms, this significant order is what poetry is apt to represent as divine. Signification itself embodies a dimension of transcendence that lends itself to such representation.

In the course of history, following the trajectory first traced by the *Odyssey*, the revelation of imagination becomes progressively secularized. Already in this inaugural text, revelation is discovered as inherent in the immanent resources of language and art, as well as being accomplished in deeds of extraordinary prowess, where divine and human are not finally distinguishable. Odysseus, himself a poet who no longer invokes the Muse, stands as an emblem of this process of secularization, which is underway in the epic from its earliest beginnings. And yet this secularization realizes itself through a religious vision: the epic remains stubbornly revelatory as irreducibly religious memory.[42]

42. Compare David Bouvier, "L'Aède et l'aventure de mémoire," in *La Mémoire des religions*, ed. Philippe Borgeaud (Geneva: Labor et Fides, 1988), especially 76–77. See also Michèle Simondon, *La Mémoire et l'oubli dans la pensée grecque jusqu'à la fin du Ve siècle av. J.C.* (Paris: Les Belles Lettres, 1982).

Chapter 3

✦

Virgil's Invention of History as Prophecy

I. The Secondariness of Virgilian Epic and Its Unprecedented Originality

Proceeding from Homer to Virgil means moving westward from Greece to Rome and advancing 700 years to just about three decades before the birth of Christ. After having worked for three years on the pastoral poetry of the *Eclogues* and for seven years on the philosophical poetry of the *Georgics*, Virgil (born 70 B.C.) composed his epic, the *Aeneid*, during the last decade of his life, from 29 to 19 B.C. These were times of transition from republican to imperial Rome, times still troubled by the civil war that broke out between Julius Caesar and his rivals, chiefly Pompey, his son-in-law, with Caesar's crossing of the Rubicon in 49 B.C. Caesar defeated Pompey at Pharsalus in 48 B.C. but was assassinated by Brutus and Cassius and other senators in 44 B.C. The war continued between his assassins and his avengers, with Brutus and his senatorial allies being defeated by Caesar's first lieutenant, Marc Antony, and Octavian, Caesar's nineteen-year-old great-nephew and heir apparent, at Philippi in 42 B.C. Further internecine strife erupted subsequently between Octavian, later to be called Augustus, and Marc Antony, who was routed together with his Egyptian consort, Cleopatra, at Actium in 31 B.C. In such tumult and travail, the imperial age was born.

This historical background concerning Virgil's own times proves crucial for understanding the prophetic purport of his work. Although Virgil is writing about the same mythic-heroic age as Homer—specifically, the aftermath of the Trojan War—the weight and role of history have become decisive in his epic, and the turbulences of his own contemporary period take on a new kind of significance for all his representations of the historical and legendary past. The tormented interpretation of his lived present can be seen to infiltrate all his re-creations of the purportedly heroic past as well as his prophetic projections of a destined future.[1]

The transition from Homer to Virgil also means moving from what can be called primary to secondary epic.[2] For the first time, we are confronted with a highly self-conscious composition by an individual writer. The formulaic, oral style of primary epic is largely conventional and relentlessly repetitious. Recited extemporaneously at solemn occasions, it is designed to be taken in as a rapid succession of verses, with no one verse standing out from the rest. Secondary epic, in contrast, is more intricate and eloquent. As exemplified by Virgil and later in English tradition by Milton, secondary epic prefers a grand, elevated style. This reflects its fundamentally different mode of composition as written rather than as orally recited discourse—and as produced, furthermore, by an individual author rather than by a collectivity of bards.

Primary epic, moreover, is unreflectively and uncritically heroic in content, as exemplified by *Beowulf* or the *Chanson de Roland*, as well as by Homer. Secondary epic generally reinterprets raw heroic content from the point of view of a more sophisticated culture and civilization. This allows also for bringing heroic action into different kinds of historical and literary contexts, making for more self-reflectiveness and complexity. And it creates novel possibilities for parody and irony.

The reflection on itself as secondary strongly characterizes secondary epic's own self-presentation in the case of Virgil.[3] The trope of secondariness resounds in searingly regretful, plangent tones throughout the *Aeneid*. At many turns, Virgil's epic shows itself to be acutely conscious of being a reduction and diminution with respect to its Homeric prototype. This systematic inferiority is betokened most grossly by the fact that the *Aeneid* consists in

1. Some type of incidence of mythic past and mythic future upon present politics in the construction and cohesion of culture may be intrinsic to society itself, as suggested in a widely comparative perspective by Bruce Lincoln, *Discourse and the Construction of Society: Comparative Studies of Myth, Ritual, and Classification* (New York: Oxford University Press, 1989).

2. A distinction between primary and secondary epic is drawn by C. S. Lewis, *A Preface to Paradise Lost* (London: Oxford University Press, 1961), 12–31, and is adopted, for example, by Cecil M. Bowra, *From Virgil to Milton* (London: Macmillan, 1963), 1–32. Something similar can be found already in Charles-Augustin Sainte-Beuve, *Étude sur Virgil*, 3rd ed. (Paris: Librairie Nouvelle, 1878 [1857]), 83–90. Account should also be taken of the influence of intermediary epics on Virgil, as argued by Damien P. Nelis, "Vergil's Library," in *A Companion to Vergil's Aeneid and Its Tradition*, ed. Joseph Farrell and Michael C. J. Putnam (Chichester: Wiley-Blackwell, 2010), 13–25.

3. The view of Virgil as imitative and inferior, as a perhaps unfortunate consequence, has dominated German classical philology, with its characteristic exaltation of Hellenic culture, especially since Lessing's *Laokoon* (1766), chapter 18. It is reproduced by Herder, Goethe, A. W. Schlegel, and so on.

only twelve books—as against the twenty-four of each of the Homeric epics. The sense of being dwarfed by its unsurpassable predecessor becomes audible in frequent notes of futility and despair that make for a conspicuous contrast with the exuberantly unself-conscious tone of Homeric epic. As if in compensation for the loss of Homer's splendidly uncomplicated self-confidence, the greater narrative and emotional reflectiveness of Virgilian epic creates a distinctive kind of pathos that is interiorized and self-lacerating.

When Homer tells the story of Odysseus's scar, the scene with the maternal grandfather, Autolycus, in Parnassus moves into center stage and all else is forgotten.[4] Virgil's narrative, in contrast, is layered, being structured by complex framings that impinge upon the narrative present and infuse it with meaning deriving from the past and future, tingeing it with subjective tonalities. His scenes are almost invariably laden with emotion flowing from nostalgic reflection upon non-present realities rather than concentrating only on what is being immediately represented. The different tenses in this way bleed into and color one another.

While the *Odyssey* remains focused predominantly on the sensuous present, the *Aeneid* opens a reflective space of often melancholic reminiscence. If the *Odyssey* is concerned chiefly with pain and its meaning, the *Aeneid*'s central concern is with meaning and its pain.[5] Virgil has, accordingly, been considered the early inventor of a symbolic poetic trained upon expression of a private dimension of feeling.[6] This faculty can be apprehended at its most powerful, for example, in the scene describing the fatal moment of rolling the wooden horse into the city of Troy. It depicts above all a mood. How the narrator, Aeneas (and indirectly Virgil), feels about this event takes the foreground over against the event itself:

> "Rolling on, it cast a shadow
> Over the city's heart. O Fatherland,
> O Ilium, home of gods! . . .
> Yet on we strove unmindful, deaf and blind . . ."[7]
> (2.321–28)

---

4. Auerbach, "Die Narbe des Odysseus," in *Mimesis: Dargestellte Wirklichkeit in der abendländischen Literatur*, 5–27, trans. by Willard Trask as "Odysseus's Scar," in *Mimesis: The Representation of Reality in Western Literature*, 3–23.

5. See Harold Bloom's introduction to *Virgil's Aeneid: Modern Critical Interpretations*, ed. Bloom (New York: Chelsea, 1987).

6. See Viktor Pöschl, *Die Dichtkunst Virgils: Bild und Symbol in der Äneis*, 2nd ed. (Darmstadt: Wissenschaftliche Buchgesellschaft, 1964 [1950]), trans. by Gerda Seligson as *The Art of Vergil: Image and Symbol in the Aeneid* (Ann Arbor: University of Michigan Press, 1962).

7. Virgil, *The Aeneid*, trans. Robert Fitzgerald (New York: Random House, 1983). Latin texts are cited from P. Virgili Maronis, *Opera*, ed. R. A. B. Mynors (Oxford: Oxford University Press, 1969).

This interior space of the city's "heart" opens up through an interiorization of the surrounding landscape, which is suffused with an atmosphere that is above all psychological and impregnated with subjective feeling:

> ". . . Night from the Ocean stream
> Came on, profound in gloom on earth and sky . . ."
> (2.336–37)

Homer uses symbolism, of course, but as inherent in his world of objective realities rather than as the expression of any distinct personal point of view or consciously inner, subjective sensibility. Whereas Homer is the paragon of the impersonal poet, Virgil imprints his own sentiments on his poem. This is the crucial difference that formed the axis for Schiller's theory of a fundamental polarity between "naive" and "sentimental" poetry.[8] Already in the fifth century, Macrobius had emphasized the "pathos" characteristic of Virgil's style ("pathos quo tenore orationis exprimitur").[9] This distinction, too, can function to separate both ancient and modern epic into primary and secondary phases.

In Homer, the medium through which symbolism is conveyed is nonappearing: "Homer" is just a name for the mouthpiece through which the world, "nature itself," speaks—to echo Goethe's formulation of this commonplace.[10] But in Virgil the individual sensibility of the poet is felt everywhere and entirely imbues the world that is represented. Even prior to Macrobius, Virgil's fourth-century commentator, Servius, called attention to the poet's expression of his own emotion ("ex affectione sua posuit poeta") through personal interjections ("interiectionem ex sua persona interposuit").[11] Little wonder, then, that the protagonist, too, should have a private viewpoint and express emotions irreconcilable with the march of events in the objective world that the poem represents. This margin of divergence for a personal point of view or "vision," a subjective synthesis and peculiar outlook, which gives everything a new and previously unsuspected meaning, opens the dimension in which the unprecedented poetic of the *Aeneid* unfolds.

---

8. Schiller, *Über naive und sentimentalische Dichtung.*

9. Macrobius, *Saturnalia*, 218.

10. Johann Wolfgang von Goethe, *Briefwechsel zwischen Schiller und Goethe* (Jena: Eugen Diederichs, 1905), ed. H. S. Chamberlain, no. 424 (February 16, 1798), vol. 2, pp. 48–49.

11. *Servii Grammaticii qui feruntur In Virgilii Carmina Commentarii*, ed. Georgius Thilo and Hermannus Hagen (Hildesheim: Georg Olms, 1961), vol. 1. The import of these phrases is discussed by Gianpiero Rosati, "Punto di vista narrativo ed antichi esegeti di Virgilio," *Annali della Scuola Normale Superiore di Pisa*, 3rd ser., 9 (1979): 539–62. See, further, Gian Biagio Conte, *Virgilio: L'epica del sentimento* (Turin: Einaudi, 2002) on Virgil's dramatic pathos and sublime style.

The epic typically tells a story of national origins and the founding of a civilization.[12] In the case of the *Aeneid*, this tale did not arise spontaneously from folk tradition, nor was it developed and passed down orally for generations. Instead, Caesar Augustus commissioned Virgil to write a poem exalting the Roman state, and Virgil obliged, with all the grandiloquence that he alone was able to command. His own personal point of view is poignantly expressed, moreover, especially in the highly subjective style of the poem, which is often at variance sharply, even painfully, with the public program: a private voice of regret and doubt whines through the official public rhetoric of the work.[13] Thus Virgil is the poet of quavering melancholic emotion and elegiac wistfulness, as well as of triumphal marches and state propaganda. The question of its real, human, and even acutely personal meaning keeps coming back to haunt the author of the official epic scenario. The magnificence of this great Empire is weighed in the balance against the personal sacrifices it exacts. With all the pathos of nagging doubt that these sacrifices engender, the tormenting question—Is it worth it?—refuses to be laid to rest.[14]

From the outset, Aeneas is presented as a man burdened with a destiny and overshadowed by his task. As the conclusion of the proem has it, "so hard and huge / A task it was to found the Roman people" (1.48–49). Aeneas and his Trojan companions are not only mercilessly buffeted on the sea by higher powers—

> For years
> They wandered as their destiny drove them on
> From one sea to the next . . .
>
> (1.46–47)

—they are also confronted with war, after reaching their destination.

---

12. Compare Gary B. Miles, "The *Aeneid* as a Foundation Story," in *Reading Vergil's Aeneid: An Interpretive Guide*, ed. Christine Perkell (Norman: Oklahoma University Press, 1999).

13. Seminal to this line of interpretation, which influences my reading at several points, is Adam M. Parry, "The Two Voices of Virgil's *Aeneid*," *Arion* 2 (1963): 66–80. Rpt. in *The Language of Achilles and Other Papers* (Oxford: Clarendon, 1989), 78–96.

14. The split between "rival traditions" distinguished by David Quint, *Epic and Empire: Poetics of a Generic Form from Virgil to Milton* (Princeton, N.J.: Princeton University Press, 1993) and associated respectively with Virgil and Lucan, who writes the epic of the defeated in protest against Virgil's epic of victors, is discerned here as a fissure within Virgil's epic itself (as Quint himself also argues in his second chapter).

And cruel losses were his lot in war,
Till he could found a city and bring home
His gods to Latium, land of the Latin race,
The Alban lords, and the high walls of Rome.
(1.9–12)

Indeed, the raising of the "high walls of Rome" ("altae moenia Romae"), for all their glory and majesty, at the same time entails the sacrifice of Aeneas's individual will and personal happiness. This tale of troubles by land and sea is reminiscent of the *Odyssey*, but whereas the *Odyssey* was about the assertion of personal identity, the *Aeneid* is about its effacement. Unlike Odysseus, Aeneas must abnegate his own will in order to fulfill his historical mission. Destiny, *fatum*, by which he came to Italy, as stated in the opening sentence, is for Aeneas a crushing burden of responsibility: it altogether eclipses his own personality. The whole destiny of the world is placed upon his shoulders, and the weight of the mission overwhelms the man. Every individual act is voided as Aeneas's own and is subsumed into a higher historical purpose of far-reaching symbolic significance.

All this is what makes it difficult to refrain from understanding *pius Aeneas*—"duty-bound," but more literally "pious" Aeneas—as the "prototype of a Christian hero."[15] His characteristic virtue of "pietas" in crucial ways seems a quintessentially Christian virtue of self-abnegation. Indeed, already in antiquity Tertullian had christened Virgil an *anima naturaliter christiana* ("soul by nature Christian"), and throughout the Middle Ages Virgil was seen as something of a pagan prophet of the coming of Christ.[16]

This claim was most obviously tied to the Fourth *Eclogue*'s announcement of a prodigious birth, a new progeny ("progenies nova"), under the sign of a Virgin ("virgo") that would lead to a renewal of the Golden Age of peace on earth ("iam redit et uirgo, redeunt Saturnia regna"). These lines (6–10) lent themselves to being interpreted as a prophecy of the birth of Christ. This has

15. T. S. Eliot, "Virgil and the Christian World," in *On Poetry and Poets* (London: Faber, 1986 [1957]), 144. The "proto-Christian" Virgil of other modern authors attributing him a providential mission is reviewed by Theodor Ziolkowski, *Virgil and the Moderns* (Princeton, N.J.: Princeton University Press, 1993), 48ff. One should add also G. K. Chesterton, *The Everlasting Man*, pt. 1, c. 4. Among contemporaries, Louis Markos, *From Achilles to Christ: Why Christians Should Read Pagan Classics* (Downers Grove, Ill.: InterVarsity, 2007), provocatively reads Virgil's "sacred history of Rome" in a Christian apologetic and typological key.

16. Domenico Comparetti, *Virgilio nel medioevo*, ed. Giorgio Pasquale (Florence: La Nuova Italia, 1955; originally Livorno, 1871), trans. E. M. F. Benecke as *Vergil in the Middle Ages* (Hamden, Conn.: Archon Books, 1966), assembles this tradition. For the earliest Christian appropriations of Virgil, see Pierre Courcelle, *Lecteurs païens et lecteurs chrétiens de l'Énéide* (Paris: Institut de France, 1984).

seemed far-fetched from the perspective of modern philology, yet Virgil's invention in the *Aeneid* of a new form of envisioning Roman history as prophetic of a just and even utopian world-order, a sort of kingdom come, is nevertheless an astonishing anticipation from within classical tradition of the sort of historical-prophetic hermeneutic that was shortly to develop in Christian interpretation of the Messianic expectations of what then became "the Old Testament."[17]

Prophecy in this sense is connected with the poetics of reflective self-consciousness that turns back upon itself and dwells on its own history and searches there for meaning. This self-reflectiveness constitutes another yet deeper difference of Virgil from his predecessors—one that defines even more momentously the astonishing originality of the *Aeneid*. The heroic and mythic-epic narrative of Homer is transformed into an allegorical history structured as a prophetic revelation of Virgil's own time and its future prospects. To fully appreciate this, it is necessary to consider very carefully what the claim to prophecy in Virgil entails.

The question of whether Virgil foresaw the birth of Christ concerns prophecy only in the ordinary and relatively banal sense of being able to foretell the future. In this, Virgil would be no different from the myriad seers and sorcerers and divines with which the ancient world was rife. But the originality of Virgil, his particular claim to being an authentic prophet rather than simply to have incorporated prophetic *topoi* into his works like many other major Roman authors, rests on his surpassing prophecy in precisely this sense. It is Virgil's single-handed invention, as if out of nowhere, of a genuinely prophetic mode of understanding history that is the seeming miracle on which his justly deserved fame as a prophetic poet has every right to rest.[18]

Whereas the certainly rather forced Christian interpretation of the Fourth *Eclogue* concerns "prophecy" only in a surface sense of factually foretelling the future, the profound meaning of prophecy as it develops in Virgil and in Dante and in the whole lineage of prophetic poets they foster down through Tasso, Spenser, Milton, and Blake concerns rather the interpretation of history from its end-point and seen as a whole, so that every moment in that history receives new meaning in light of a synoptic vision. In the biblical prophetic

17. Patristic allegorical exegesis of Scripture is compared with classical allegoresis by Jean Pépin in *Mythe et allégorie: Les origines grecques et les contestations judéo-chrétiennes* (Paris: Montaigne, 1958). Pépin pursues Christian figural interpretation of Scripture further in *La tradition de l'allégorie: De Philon d'Alexandrie à Dante* (Paris: Études Augustiniennes, 1988).

18. Illustrious Latinists confess themselves baffled by the phenomenal new use of history as prophecy by Virgil. According to Robert Fitzgerald, "to enfold in the mythical action of the *Aeneid* foreshadowings and foretellings of Roman history" is "drastically original." In other words, "So far as we can see, there are no comparable historical resonances in the Homeric poems; this dimension of meaning is entirely Virgilian." Postscript to *The Aeneid*, 405 and 406.

tradition, this perspective extends even beyond history and time altogether, and this marks a crucial difference from Virgil, whose end-vision is envisaged as primarily intra-historical rather than as eschatological or as beyond the end (*eschaton*) of history. Still, in Virgil, just as in the Bible, the prophetic vantage point is granted supposedly by divine inspiration. Whether this claim to inspiration is understood in purely human terms or as supernatural in character, Virgil discovers the purely poetic, interpretive means that make it humanly possible. Failing an appropriate appreciation of this interpretive revolution, Virgil's prophetic gift, power, and achievement, even as it becomes normative for Western tradition, thanks especially to Dante, remains quite obscure in its essential significance and world-historical purport.

"Prophecy" in common parlance seems to us to be closely akin to a magical power and therefore something no longer to be believed in earnestly, or even perhaps honestly. Virgil's claim to prophecy may be tolerable to the extent that he is kept in his place as a writer of fiction, but this is a place made only by very modern consciousness and literary categories. To do justice to this claim we need a more adequate interpretation of "prophecy" as it can be used to qualify Virgil's poetry and, by consequence, also the tradition of "prophetic poetry" that follows in his wake. Much of the burden of the following reading of the *Aeneid*, especially as it hinges from book 6, will be to make its "invention" of this new poetic-prophetic mode emerge as a momentous and practically unprecedented revelation of imagination.

Prophetic poetry is prominent in Western literature, a cardinal strand, if not indeed the chief thread of coherence that distinguishes this tradition down to our own epoch even in its radical secularization, for example, by James Joyce. Our own historical age, moreover, has distinguished itself also by novel, radically searching speculations about the nature of time, history and interpretation, and I intend to point out the relevance of these researches, as formulated particularly by Martin Heidegger, to a contemporary understanding of Virgil's creation of a poetic art of prophetic interpretation of history (especially in the last subsection, "Prophecy and *Poiesis*," of section V).

Virgil has been very widely acclaimed as a prophet, but the grounds of this acclaim have shifted in the course of history. From ancient and especially from medieval times, this recognition was traditionally accorded him first and foremost, if not exclusively, on the basis of the passage from the Fourth *Eclogue* purportedly prophesying the birth of a Messiah. Historical research reveals Virgil to have, in all probability, intended in this text rather to hyperbolically hail the birth of a son to a particular Roman consul.[19] Yet,

19. Although identification of the *nascenti puero* is not certain, it seems likely that this is the Consul Asinius Pollio's son, Asinius Gallus, welcomed as a prodigy somewhat in the image of Alexander the Great. Virgil was personally indebted to Pollio for the attempt to preserve his lands near Mantua from confiscation, which nevertheless came to pass in 39 B.C., when Pollio was succeeded as governor of Transalpine Gaul.

even apart from historical intentions and inevitable doubts concerning them, to pin Virgil's claim to being a prophet to this text is to miss the momentous discovery that makes him truly a prophet in a way otherwise unparalleled in pagan antiquity.

Modern treatments of Virgil as prophet have not remained beholden to this Christian medieval framework and have opened suggestive avenues for more accurate elucidation of Virgilian prophecy, particularly in terms of its own historical context and the role of the Latin *vates* in Imperial Rome.[20] What I wish to propose, however, is not a more accurately historicized understanding of prophecy in Virgil, but rather a philosophical interpretation of the conception of history as prophetic that is realized in the text of the *Aeneid*. This is actually analogous to the medieval Christian misprision of Virgil in that it focuses on Virgil's potential significance in a new and different historical context: our own. The justification for this approach lies in the fact that historical research into prophecy during the Augustan Empire cannot exhaustively explain the significance of Virgil's text in its astonishing creation of an original conception of history as prophetic; nor can such research explain this text's potential to illuminate the nature of prophecy as it may concern us still today. Study of Virgil can help make the concept of prophecy vital to philosophical reflection on history and the structure of time in our own post-Heideggerian era.

II. A Man or a Destiny: *Aeneid*, Book 1

Within this new Virgilian framework of history as prophecy, Aeneas finds himself used as nothing but a token in dramas reaching far beyond any personal concerns of his own. When he is first seen in the throes of a storm at sea and threatened with shipwreck, wishing that he had died at Troy like the other heroes "thrice and four times blessed" ("O terque quaterque beati . . ." 1.94), he is, of course, echoing Odysseus's despairing lament in the *Odyssey* 5.306ff. in face of the threat of being swallowed up by the sea. More typically, his speech holds back all genuine expression of himself. He encourages his men with the promise that even these hardships will be remembered one day with pleasure. But in articulating this perfunctory encouragement, he is secretly choking back his own real sentiments:

20. Important studies focusing on Virgilian prophecy include Denis Feeney, "History and Revelation in Virgil's Underworld," in *Why Vergil?*, ed. Stephanie Quinn (Wauconda, Ill.: Bolchaszy-Carducci, 2000); Elisabeth Henry, *The Vigour of Prophecy: A Study of Virgil's Aeneid* (Carbondale: Southern Illinois University Press, 1989); and James J. O'Hara, *Death and the Optimistic Prophecy in Vergil's Aeneid* (Princeton, N.J.: Princeton University Press, 1990).

So ran the speech. Burdened and sick at heart,
He feigned hope in his look, and inwardly
Contained his anguish.

(1.284–96)

With this sequestering of personal feeling from outward expression, an exclusively inner realm of experience opens up. It is of a kind that we were rarely, if ever, allowed to glimpse in the *Odyssey*. An inner space that can set itself up over against the public sphere of action by means of private refusal and regret begins to take shape. This new self-reflexive dimension of the poem and its hero in the *Aeneid* becomes, from a certain point of view, primary. Aeneas, in his first speech to his companions, says, "Some day, perhaps, remembering even this / Will be a pleasure" ("Forsan et haec olim meminisse iuvabit," 1.277–78). When Odysseus says something similar in *Odyssey* 12.201–2, he is urging comfort simply in the thought that it will all soon be over. Aeneas, by contrast, suggests that pain may in the future be dwelt on for the pleasure it procures. This is to value life for the sake of the art that can be made of it rather than vice versa.

The *Odyssey* exposes certain dangers of making life simply into a song to be enjoyed, as the Phaeacians do, with the result that they lose touch with reality and are consigned to everlasting oblivion. Odysseus emerges heroically in preferring life itself, even with all its pains, to any form of representation that is not instrumental to establishing his actual presence in reality. Odysseus's tale is an overtly personal story: it merges with the manifestation of his personal identity through his achievements as an individual. Aeneas's personal story, in contrast, is submerged beneath the history and destiny of Rome, and there is a jarring dissonance between the hero's own personal reluctance and indifference, on the one hand, and the irrecusable summons to devote himself to his mission, on the other. The quest for personal fulfillment can no longer be pursued through the objective events of the narrative, but appears only as an indirectly expressed disappointment and an often suppressed counterpoint to the public story.

This difference is bound up with a different mode of revelation of the divine in the human. It is no longer the overwhelming prowess of individual human beings in particular situations of crisis acting beyond the ordinary limits of the human, as in the *Odyssey*, so much as the whole structure of history, within which individuals take on strictly delimited roles, that reveals a higher dimension of existence, a divine power. The *Aeneid* proposes, in unprecedented ways, history as revelation. Not momentary, extraordinary, seemingly superhuman feats or phenomena and ad hoc interventions, but the overall shape and design of events is revelatory of the divine hand at work in human affairs.

This overarching architecture of history, of course, cannot be given objectively within history itself. It arises rather from the vision of a subject who retains the past and projects the future in accordance with a significance that is inwardly felt but cannot be delivered as such through outward events. The contemporaneousness of the past with the present—and indeed with the future as well—is felt in this mode of reflection on history, from which historical meaning emerges in a prophetic perspective. The reflections of secondary epic on the primary materials of history and tradition can reveal their meaning in a wholly new and transfiguring light. But there is in this an irreducibly personal—decisional and ultimately "confessional"—aspect of prophetic vision that is constantly pointed up by the glaring disparity between the public exaltation and the personal lamentation that together go into the composition of Virgil's Roman poem.

This new form of divine prophecy is deeply implicated in human and historical interpretation in an epic mode that is also intensely personal and indeed visionary. However, this is no longer immediate or first-degree personal expression such as is embodied exemplarily by Odysseus in primary epic; in Virgil's secondary epic, personal expression is displaced to the overall order of history and the world. This level of vision can be at odds and even enter into conflict with immediate human impulses and personal motives. Whereas Odysseus refuses immortality for the sake of his own personal life as a mortal man, Aeneas's personal life is suppressed in the interest of the immortal glory of Rome. We see him learn to live not as a man satisfying his own vital human passions and propensities, but as a functionary of fate and the state. The program to which he must submit is laid out by the prophecy of the Roman Empire and its eternal greatness—"imperium sine fine" (1.279)—that is pronounced by Jupiter to Venus as reparation for the misfortunes induced by Juno's jealousy. This prophecy is, in effect, an anticipated recapitulation of Roman history, and as such it begins to set up a structure of history as prophecy that is the *Aeneid*'s most original contribution to Western culture.

The prophecy given as a promise on Jupiter's part to his daughter, Venus, Aeneas's mother, describes the various phases of Roman history as a glorious road of triumph stretching from Aeneas's own achievements all the way down to those of Julius Caesar. This scion of Virgil's own time, "Julius" from "Iulus," the new name added to Aeneas's son, Ascanius or "Ilus while Ilium stood" ("Ilus erat, dum res stetit Ilia regno," 1.268), will be taken to heaven and immortalized and "invoked in prayer" like his forebear, great-souled Aeneas, borne on high by his mother to the stars of heaven ("sublimemque feres ad sidera caeli / magnanimum Aeneas," 1.259–60). Yet already deeply ominous at the conclusion of this prophecy is the way that the *pax romana* is to be built upon conquest and upon a coercive imposition of order. The subjugated forces will hardly rest content:

> "Wars at an end, harsh centuries then will soften,
> Ancient Fides and Vesta, Quirinus

> With Brother Remus, will be lawgivers,
> And grim with iron frames, the Gates of War
> Will then be shut: inside, unholy Furor,
> Squatting on cruel weapons, hands enchained
> Behind him by a hundred links of bronze,
> Will grind his teeth and howl with bloodied mouth."
> (1.391–98)

One cannot but sense the violent repression upon which this imperial order sits and divine that the forces of rebellion and chaos are only biding their time before another savage outbreak: they threaten still to drag to destruction all that has been established by their suppression.

Aeneas, "pius Aeneas," "the dedicated man" (1.411), as Fitzgerald translates, is made to serve the imperial purpose. He is not so much a man as a destiny, even as he announces himself—"sum pius Aeneas"—in fittingly formal, impersonal terms:

> I am Aeneas, duty-bound, and known
> Above high air of heaven by my fame,
> Carrying with me in my ships our gods
> Of hearth and home, saved from the enemy.
> I look for Italy to be my fatherland,
> And my descent is from all-highest Jove.
> (1.519–24)

Worlds apart from the wanderer Odysseus, even while retracing some of the same journey, Aeneas is led by signs at every step along the path of his destiny ("viam . . . qua semita monstrat," 1.418). He is guided particularly by his goddess mother, who appears in the form of a Spartan huntress to inform him of the country where he has landed and of its queen. He invariably conforms to the dictates of fate and simply does what divine destiny requires of him.

Yet Aeneas's own heartfelt resistance to this regime is also signaled, especially in his nostalgic longing for his Trojan past, which is incomparably dearer to him than any glorious future prophesied for Rome. Like an official ambassador, he pronounces a formal blessing on Carthage under construction—

> "How fortunate these are
> Whose city walls are rising here and now!"
> (1.505–6)

This people is certainly far ahead of his own in establishing their new civilization, and he envies their being closer to having finished with the burdensome task. Even more tellingly, it is only in seeing the murals decorated with scenes from the Tojan War—his own personal past—that he is really moved inwardly:

> Here in this grove new things that met his eyes
> Calmed Aeneas' fear for the first time.
> Here for the first time he took heart to hope
> For safety, and to trust his destiny more
> Even in affliction. It was while he walked
> From one to another wall of the great temple . . .
> He found before his eyes the Trojan battles
> In the old war, now known throughout the world . . .
> (1.610–20)

At this sight, Aeneas gives way to tears. Venting his intimately wounded feelings, he sententiously moralizes about life and mortality: "they weep here / For how the world goes, and our life that passes / Touches their hearts" ("sunt lacrimae rerum et mentem mortalia tangunt," 1.462). Despite the sorrow of the tale of Troy's defeat, he exults in the immortalization of this past, concluding: "This fame / Insures some kind of refuge" (1.630–31). But immediately this nostalgic interlude of sentimental reminiscence is interrupted and undermined, as the official voice returns with an insinuated criticism: "He broke off / To feast his eyes and mind on a mere image" ("Sic ait atque animum pictura pascit inani," 1.464/632–33). From the point of view of the man (Aeneas) and artist (Virgil), these human feelings and their expression in art are what matter most. That alone can redeem the tragic losses of history, in victory as well as in defeat, and compensate for the ultimate emptiness even of success. But from the standpoint of his historical mission, this nostalgic indulgence is nothing but blamable dalliance and procrastination.

It is at this point that Dido appears in the guise of Diana, just as had Nausicaa in *Odyssey* 6.2, and Aeneas's personal feelings are diverted from aesthetic to erotic enthrallment. Dido has previously been described to Aeneas by Venus strictly in terms of family relations and religious duty, making conjugal love itself more religious than erotic:

> "Her father had given her,
> A virgin still, in marriage, her first rite."
> (1.471–72)

Because of her wicked brother, Pygmalion, the murderer of her husband, she had to flee, and it is even suggested that her whole tragedy has been provoked by her exodus from the patriarchal sphere of authority. A certain incongruousness, for example, attends her assuming of masculine roles herself: "And captaining the venture was a woman" (1.498). Her patriarchal background is highlighted again later when she celebrates and feasts Aeneas on plates "engraved with brave deeds of her fathers, / A sequence carried down through many captains / In a long line from the founding of the race" (1.874–76). Little does she know how this fragile familial loyalty is going to be eaten away and devoured by her entertaining of Aeneas.

Aeneas, too, at this stage, is intensely mindful of family bonds: "paternal love would not allow / Aeneas' mind to rest" (1.877–78). The vertical lineage descending from ancestry to progeny has not yet been traversed by the horizontal shock waves of *eros* that will sweep him off course. A hint of this threat in the offing comes with Aeneas's gifts to Dido of a robe and a veil. They were "both adornments / Worn by Argive Helen when she sailed / For Pergamum and her forbidden marriage" (1.885–87). Helen's transgressive and internationally disastrous love affair thereby insinuates its egregious example into the minds of the protagonists and into the imaginative furnishings and accoutrements surrounding their encounter.

The dangerous power of *eros* is then personified in the form of Venus's son, Cupid, called into action expressly to ensnare Dido, to "pin her down in passion," by taking the shape of Ascanius, son of Aeneas. In this disguise, Cupid comes to Dido in order to

> . . . use his gifts to make the queen
> Infatuated, inflaming her with lust
> To the marrow of her bones.
>
> (1.899–901)

Venus's address to him brings out both the obsessive character of *eros* and its propensity for subverting—its impulse to make sport of—paternal authority:

> "My son,
> My strength, my greatest power, my one and only,
> Making light of our High Father's bolt,
> His giant-killer!"
>
> (1.907–10)

Venus summons Cupid to "breathe invisible fire into her / And dupe her with your sorcery" (1.939–40). Cupid comes as a substitute for Ascanius/Aeneas in order to dissemble erotic desire in the guise of child-love, so as to snare Dido. What looks like fondness for an infant and love of lineage will reveal itself really to be the violent force of *eros* that confounds family control of genealogy and flies in the face of filial piety.

Already, at this preliminary stage, sympathy for "luckless" ("infelix," 1.712) Dido as victim can clearly be discerned beneath the dominant narrative line as a voice of protest against its implacable drive toward destiny and empire. The little Cupid disguised as Ascanius makes Sychaeus, her deceased husband, fade from Dido's memory and awakes in her "a new love, a living love" ("vivo temptat . . . amore," 1.721). This makes it sound irresistible, and so makes us, too, dissent from the overbearing regime of genealogical piety and public glory.

The theme of Aeneas's success in fulfilling his mission, for which he must first overcome the temptation posed by Dido, is paralleled by the theme of Rome's glory in achieving greatness and empire, principally through its struggle against Carthage, but also against Cleopatra, for whom Dido serves as a prefiguration. At a yet higher level, cosmic order is vindicated, justifying the ways of God to men, by the victory of order over chaos and over the demonic forces impersonated particularly by Juno.[21] Of course, the victory is far from being free of ambiguities, and in certain ways that have remained troubling ever since, Fury will be given the last word. Nevertheless, from the first book of the epic, a piggybacking structure can clearly be discerned, whereby the causes of order must struggle to prevail by subduing the disorder arising from passion in the individual soul, rebellion in the political world of the state, and storm in nature, not to mention dissension in heaven. There is, moreover, a clear gendering of this universal struggle, since it is always insubordinate females who threaten to obstruct males in their mission of establishing order: Juno, at the cosmic level; Cleopatra, in Roman history; and Dido, in Aeneas's personal life and mind. This construction of parallel spheres creates a complex, layered plot that enables different levels of the narrative to reflect and comment on each other, often ironically.

The first scene of the epic presents a hierarchy of authorities exercising rule over the elements and determined to subdue their violence. Yet the epic also places into relief how these authorities are themselves, at some level, governed only by violence. The goddess queen Juno's violent passion flares up into high dudgeon over her slighted divinity and takes her to Aeolia to summon the winds as elemental forces of chaos against Aeneas's fleet:

> Here in a vast cavern King Aeolus
> Rules the contending winds and moaning gales
> As warden of their prison. Round the walls
> They chafe and bluster underground. The din
> Makes a great mountain murmur overhead.
> High on a citadel enthroned,
> Sceptre in hand, he mollifies their fury,
> Else they might flay the sea and sweep away
> Land masses and deep sky through empty air.
> In fear of this, Jupiter hid them away
> In caverns of black night. He set above them

21. For more comprehensive treatment of this theme, see P. R. Hardie, *Virgil's "Aeneid": Cosmos and Imperium* (Oxford: Oxford University Press, 1986).

Granite of high mountains—and a king
Empowered at command to rein them in
Or let them go.

(1.76–89)

Natural forces are imagined here in political terms of empire and prison ("imperio premit ac vinclis et carcere fremat," 1.54). This seems to suggest that in nature and in society alike control over subordinates is maintained by the imposition of violent force. Aeolus sends his winds "in ranks / As though drawn up for battle" (1.116–17). This complicates and even contradicts a certain will to place the violence on the side of disorder only. When order among the natural elements is restored through a higher authority, that of Neptune, it takes on a political, specifically counterrevolutionary significance. This registers especially in the simile—the first in the epic—drawn from the political arena of the pacification of a civic revolt that is used to describe the allaying of the winds.

When rioting breaks out in a great city,
And the rampaging rabble goes so far
That stones fly, and incendiary brands—
For anger can supply that kind of weapon—
If it so happens they look round and see
Some dedicated public man, a veteran
Whose record gives him weight, they quiet down,
Willing to stop and listen.
Then he prevails in speech over their fury
By his authority, and placates them.

(1.201–10)

In civilization and in civilized epic, reason and speech prevail over elemental force. This little political allegory, with its imagery drawn from history used for describing phenomena of nature, is an index of the higher degree of self-conscious artifice that characterizes Virgil's secondary invention of epic. Notwithstanding the secondariness of society with respect to nature, here the social is really nearer to the poet and his readership, and the natural is figured in terms of it. Throughout this epic, nature is no longer seen in its immediacy with anything like the naivety for which Homer was so famously praised. Civilization is the framework from which even nature is perceived, and art—often rhetorically inflated art—is self-consciously infused into all that is represented, including nature itself. Accordingly, in this epic, action will be revealed as being for the sake of art. To this extent, all that is represented exists primarily as symbol.

The song of Iopus, with which book 1 closes, is an interesting reflection on the kind of symbolism that characterizes Virgil's own song. Iopus's song is not a celebration of heroic action but rather a somber meditation on the causes of natural phenomena, a kind of philosophical wisdom literature:

> He sang the straying moon and toiling sun,
> The origin of mankind and the beasts,
> Of rain and fire; the rainy Hyadës,
> Arcturus, the Great Bear and Little Bear;
> The reason winter suns are in such haste
> To dip in Ocean, or what holds the nights
> Endless in winter.
>
> (1.1013–19)

Iopas's song is in some ways more akin to the *Georgics* than to the *Aeneid*, and as such it represents a foil to epic. By contrast with the knowledge peculiar to poetic epic, a knowledge that imaginatively interprets the gods and history, Iopas reasons in terms of natural causes. He omits the gods altogether. "Through these omissions, Virgil suggests the limitations of human knowledge, rationality, and good intentions."[22] In Virgil's own work, epic singing takes on a new dimension of revelation, a revelation that enables historical, heroic epic to become cosmic and providential in scope. Didactic poetry, even Virgil's own previous philosophical poetry, could never attain to this new and ultimately religious dimension of significance.

III. Ashes of Ilium and Odyssean Wanderings: *Aeneid*, Books 2–3

Aeneas's sentimental attachment to and mourning of the past, expressing his personal regret over the events of destiny, expands into the whole of his account of the Fall of Troy and of his sea wanderings in books 2 and 3 respectively. Taken together, they form a miniature *Iliad* and *Odyssey*: first the war, then the wandering. This narrative is all an empty space of memory and elegy, where loss of love and glory in Troy are mourned. The historical-allegorical significance of events and their mental-emotional rememoration supplants the immediate meaning they have in the sensuous present of Homeric narrative.

Books 2 and 3 comprise a flashback told by Aeneas in his own voice charged with lament over all that has ensued upon Troy's demise. This voice distinguishes itself from the public voice of the epic devoted to recounting the earliest ante-facts building up to Rome's glorious founding. It tells a story not of Roman glory but of human catastrophe, hardship, suffering, and personal loss:

---

22. Christine Perkell, "*Aeneid* 1: An Epic Program," in *Reading Vergil's Aeneid: An Interpretive Guide*, 49.

> "Sorrow too deep to tell, your majesty,
> You order me to feel and tell once more . . ."
> (2.3–5)
>
> ("Infandum, regina, iubes renovare dolorem")

A similar grief is expressed by Odysseus as he begins his story in *Odyssey* 9.12–13, on which these lines are modeled, but the elegiac mood is new. For what triumphs in the *Odyssey* is the intensely sensuous present—even though it is fraught with pain—not the nostalgic, melancholy rumination that prevails in the *Aeneid*.[23] The entire epic of the origin of Rome, starting from book 2, is based upon Aeneas's personal tale of sorrow; the public and the private tales, even though they contradict each other, are in fact the same story experienced from different emotional angulations.

Beneath all the propaganda and pageantry of the story told in a public voice celebrating Rome's glorious establishment, this poem is more deeply and intimately about an inner realm of nothingness filled chiefly by tormented memory and remorse. The present of the poem is this interior space of lament. We hear this not only as a tale of sorrow, but as a sorrowing tale, to re-echo Chaucer's reiteration of the *Aeneid* in *Troilus and Criseyde*: "This woful vers, that wepen as I write" (1.8). Placed before such a woeful task of narratively imitating his past woes, Aeneas himself shrinks back in horror:

> "However I may shudder at the memory
> And shrink again in grief, let me begin."
> (2.16–17)
>
> ("quamquam animus meminisse horret luctuque refugit /
> incipiam," 2.12)

The sorrow is really suffered again just in the retelling. Borne through life with Aeneas and enshrined in his personal history, his pain is perhaps more humanly significant than the however great but abstract goal of Rome.

Aeneas re-creates an image of himself as great but hollow because overshadowed by his mission. He tells of his being wrenched from every impulse of his own in order to become entirely subservient to destiny. Officially, he is a success, but not humanly. We hear this as a tale of woe, and the woe,

23. This line of interpretation, stemming from Adam Parry, is elaborated especially by the so-called Harvard school of "pessimistic" interpretation of the epic, comprising, among others, Wendell Clausen, *Virgil's Aeneid: Decorum, Allusion, and Ideology* (Munich: K.G. Saur, 2002); and Michael Putnam, *The Poetry of the Aeneid: Four Studies in Imaginative Design* (Ithaca, N.Y.: Cornell University Press, 1988 [originally 1965]).

which is suffered again in the telling, is more humanly compelling than the putatively redeeming purpose of it all. We hear, thanks especially to Adam Parry, the personal melancholy voice that insinuatingly saturates with regret the official narrative of how Roman greatness was achieved.

There is in Aeneas's voice a note also of protest against the violence of the gods—or of revolt against destiny and its price. The protest is audible, for example, in the description of the destruction of Laocöon, who is carried off by the twin snakes together with his sons, "sending to heaven his appalling cries" (2.300), or again with respect to Cassandra, whose warning goes unheeded "by a god's command" (2.331), as well as in Sinon's lying tale's being favored "by what the gods unjustly had decreed" (2.345). Aeneas obsessively questions the justice of the gods (further hints of this protest can be detected in lines 361, 697, 792). This is the private voice of regret decrying the *unjust* destruction of Troy that can never be made up for by Rome and all its promises. Nevertheless, in the public sphere, Aeneas submits wholly to the gods' plan, renouncing his own self and will.

A leitmotif of Aeneas's account—or rather its argument—is that Troy was conquered not by superior valor but by the sneaking guile of Greeks like Ulysses and Sinon: "Knowing their strength broken in warfare" (2.18), "on the sly" they devised their treacherous deception. Aeneas's story of Troy's fall implies that the Greeks triumphed unheroically, by fraud, signally by Sinon's "tall tale and fake tears." Genuinely heroic Trojan (and thus proleptically Roman) virtue is portrayed as being more straightforward, as suggested also by Aeneas's complaint against his mother's disguises in book 1. But then we must ask: how does Aeneas himself measure up to the standards of heroism to which he appeals? Together with his band of six dressed up like Greeks, Aeneas too resorts to disguise and deception, "lying arms" ("mentitaque tela," 2.422), just like Sinon. An inescapable question that hangs obscurely over the whole account is that of how to justify the fact that Aeneas stole away from Troy in its hour of crisis. His historical mission, of course, is the official reason, but it seems to be carried out at the cost of his heroism and his very self-respect. His tale is, after all, a tale of yielding to the unheroic logic of "the end justifies the means." Even fleeing is justified in this manner. Idealism becomes a calculation rather than an instinct such as characteristically beguiles Odysseus's better judgment, notoriously in the conflicts with Polyphemos and Scylla.

This suggests why Aeneas is on the defensive about having left Troy. He seems to feel that it was a betrayal of his own heroic ideals. Striking out for a new land is naturally justified by the imperial program, but he is perhaps never so proud again as he was in Troy. He becomes "pious" instead. The somewhat too strenuous justifications of his departure give an index of the discomfort of his conscience. Aeneas's defensiveness is felt in his impassioned swearing to Troy's ashes that he did not spare himself but leapt into the flames to fight (2.451):

> "Ashes of Ilium!
> Flames that consumed my people! Here I swear
> That in your downfall I did not avoid
> One weapon, one exchange with the Danaans,
> And if it had been fated, my own hand
> Had earned my death."
>
> (2.567–72)

Aeneas's best impulses were all to stay and die fighting, as he anxiously underscores: "To arm was my first impulse—not / That anyone had a fighting chance in arms" (2.421–22). Even after the apparition of Hector's ghost to him in a dream, urging, "Give up and go, child of the goddess, / Save yourself, out of these flames" (2.387–88), he still feels compelled to die in combat like a hero: "So fury drove me, and it came to me / That meeting death was beautiful in arms" (2.425–26). That such a heroic death was not, in fact, the outcome haunts him still.

Aeneas observes helplessly from a roof the exactions wrought by Greeks within Priam's palace, in particular Politēs's being slain before his father's eyes (2.526–32). The organic continuity of a noble line of descent is thus broken, just as a majestic ash is felled (6.179–81). And for this sacrilege no political propaganda about empire can possibly compensate. Aeneas's personal indignation and rage flare up against traitorous Helen. However, his impulse to kill her is checked as Venus reveals the gods at work destroying the city, and he submits to their will. In this manner, individual feeling cedes to the demands of destiny. The gods no longer solicit and stimulate exceptional human intensities of thought and action, but rather enjoin passivity. No longer an expression of inexplicable heights of human achievement, the gods now are external to human action and restrain it from the outside rather than motivating and heightening it from within. In this more abstract conception of the gods, the logic of action is either/or: either human or divine.

The secularization of divinity that could be seen nascent in the *Odyssey* has now become a freezing of the gods into fates that stand over against human wills and check and rein them in rather than enhancing and fulfilling them. Thomas Greene is succinctly to the point: "Virgil's gods, tending as they do to embody abstract principles or forces, court the risk of transparency, and Homeric mystery starts to fade into Virgilian machinery."[24] The

24. Thomas Greene, *The Descent from Heaven: A Study in Epic Continuity* (New Haven, Conn.: Yale University Press, 1963), 88. Greene continues, drawing the contrast between Virgil's gods and Homer's: "Of all the celestial descents in the classical epic, none symbolizes so strong a pressure on the human will as Mercury's descent to Aeneas at Carthage. In the *Iliad* the celestial messengers commonly intervene to prompt or suggest, and seldom represent a categorical imperative. . . . Hermes as a guide is gentleness itself. His descent in the *Odyssey* simply removes an obstacle from the path of the free human will" (99).

progressive objectification and solidification of divinities has resulted in their being represented simply as positive factors in the action and no longer also always translucently as poetic figures for humans exceeding their own limits. Hence their severance from the human impulses and actions in and through which they were revealed in the *Odyssey*. And where humans are no longer godlike, the gods become inhuman. Hence the question of theodicy that subtends the epic from beginning to end: how can "anger / black as this prey on the minds of heaven?" (1.19). This tendency will be further unveiled in later epic, where the gods function more as abstract principles reified into personifications.[25]

Numerous portents from the gods foreshadow the imperial mission and, consequently, urge Aeneas to escape. Hector's specter reaffirms the world-historical program that has already been prophetically divulged to readers in book 1 through Jupiter's promises to Venus. And the portent of Iulus's hair aflame, followed by a thunderclap and comet, convinces even Anchises of the necessity to follow fate and escape into exile. The wrench from personal attachments that this entails for Aeneas is most acutely embodied in the loss of his wife Creusa. This loss climaxes in the scene of the threefold failed embrace of her wraith modeled on Odysseus's meeting with his mother in the underworld. Aeneas suffers personal anguish at the death of Creusa. Her ghost, "larger than life," prophesies the Roman future, including his destined Italian marriage, but that is no compensation for the human companion he desperately misses, and he remains inconsolable in his sorrowful lament. This regret is expressed in poetry, where Aeneas's human reality finds a voice—necessarily a voice of bereavement, emptiness, remorse, but at least it is something humanly tangible and is charged with the painfulness of real grieving.

Book 2 concludes, "So I resigned myself, picked up my father, / And turned my face toward the mountain range" (2.1045–46). Still wracked by his attachment to Troy, Aeneas takes up his father on his back to bear him away, symbolically carrying his past into his future on what is for him a most anguished journey. Book 2, in effect, represents how Aeneas resigns himself to losing his identity, situated as it is in the particular social fabric and historical context of Troy. He learns not to assert himself after the manner of Odysseus but rather to renounce personal identity in submission to forces greater than himself. "*Obstipui*" ("I was dumbfounded") becomes his constant confession (2.560, 774; 3.48, 298). All his attempts to assert himself and act like a hero fail. Only in assuming a voice of sorrow does Aeneas manage to express a genuinely personal self—with the authenticity not of action but of reflection and lament.

25. C. S. Lewis, *The Allegory of Love: A Study in Medieval Traditions* (Oxford: Oxford University Press, 1973 [1936]), 49–56, traces this process forward into later Roman epic, signally Statius.

Book 3 is Aeneas's book of Odyssean adventures, but none is really for the sake of adventure, as were Odysseus's. All of Aeneas's "adventures" serve to reveal the future or to elegize the past: they are important as symbolic figures rather than as action and event.[26] In place of Odysseus's sensual present of pain, they feature rather sorrow in an emptiness of nostalgic memory and longing: "Weeping, I drew away from our old country" (3.14). In fact, unlike Odysseus, Aeneas regularly avoids danger and adventure. He takes the long way around Sicily rather than risking an encounter with Scylla or Charybdis. He manifests no such spirit of daring as Odysseus evinces by contriving to actually hear the Sirens and so transgress with impunity the limits of ordinary mortal experience. His cutting a poor figure in comparison with Odysseus fits with a pervasive sense of inferiority of everything in this epic as measured against its incomparable Homeric nonesuch.

It seems doubtful whether history is building up to the greatness of Rome or rather winding down from the once great days of the Homeric heroes. This comes through especially in Virgil's sense of belatedness and secondariness with respect to all that comes after the Homeric age.[27] The secondariness of this epic finds its emblem in the references to "little Troy" ("parvam Troiam," 3.350), a simulation ("simulata"):

> I saw before me Troy in miniature,
> A slender copy of our massive tower,
> A dry brooklet named Xanthus . . .
> (3.477–79)

Helenus and Andromachë have reiterated Troy in Epirus, but as scaled down to a meager replica, more word than reality, considering the way Hector's name is invoked over an empty tomb:

> And, as it happened, at that hour she,
> Andromachë, in a grove outside the city
> Beside a brook, thin replica of Simoïs,
> Was making from a ceremonial meal
> Her offerings and libation to the dust,
> Calling the great shade at a tomb called Hector's

26. This shift inward from event to meaning is emphasized effectively by Pöschl, *Die Dichtkunst Virgils*, 44.

27. Philologically sophisticated analyses of Virgil's multi-valenced allusions to Homer are offered by Alessandro Barchiesi, *Traccia del modello: Effetti omerici nella narrazione virgiliana* (Pisa: Giardini, 1984), and Stephen Hinds, *Allusion and Intertext: Dynamics of Appropriation in Roman Poetry* (Cambridge, Eng.: Cambridge University Press, 1998). See especially pages 91–98 on "'Secondary' epic" and pages 107–119 on "Epic repetition: remakes, sequels, doubles."

> Made by her—an empty mound of turf
> Where she had blessed twin altars for her tears.
> (3.407–13)

Andromachë, bereaved widow, embodies a condition of living death, of surviving her own world and reality, the state of mourning and melancholy that characterizes Aeneas himself and the poem's own mood. She is shocked and terrorized when she actually finds herself in the presence of Aeneas and the Trojans. In the habit of taking ghosts to be her daily companions, here she takes this flesh and blood reality rather for a ghost: "gazing at this ghostliness in terror, / She stood there pale and rigid . . ." (3.416–17). She can only stutter:

> "Your face,
> Can it be real? And you real, messenger,
> Coming before me? Goddess-born? Alive?"
> (3.420–23)

Aeneas, too, is overcome in the presence of this evocation of the past and by the obsession with its ghosts that he shares very deeply with Andromachë:

> "I had difficulty
> Forcing a few words out amid her passion,
> So overcome I felt . . ."
> (3.426–28)

He affirms that he is "alive, oh yes . . . Be sure that what you see is real" (3.419–21), but these formal assurances ring somewhat forced and hollow, especially when his condition is brought into close contact with that of the living death of Andromachë.

Andromachë's husband, the prophet Helenus, prophesies "far distant lands" as the goal for Aeneas:

> "That Italy you think so near, with ports
> You think to enter, ignorant as you are,
> Lies far, past far lands, by untraveled ways."
> (3.520–22)

This seems to hint that Rome might be a dream that will never be realized. Aeneas is inconsolable as he leaves Helenus, directed toward the Ausonian coasts that seem to be receding always further into the distance ("semper cedentia retro," 3.658). Aeneas dwells nostalgically on this episode; he would have preferred this replica of Troy that is already built, even though it is a lifeless "effigy" ("Effigiem Xanthi Troiamque," 3.497), to the seemingly impossible task of building the new city and civilization that is demanded of him. In his farewell speech to his fellow former Trojans as he sails on from Epirus, Aeneas says,

> "Here is your quiet rest: no sea to plow,
> No quest for dim lands of Ausonia
> Receding ever. Here before your eyes
> Are replicas of Xanthus and of Troy . . ."
>
> (3.657–60)

The motif of secondariness, of being a mere replica, teasingly belittles the narrative of Rome's greatness. This narrative is betrayed by a voice of regret that may be heard as an indication of Virgil's own participation in Aeneas's experience of nostalgia and grief. Rome may be just such a pipe dream for Virgil, too. His epic is, in any case, likewise turned, despite its prophetic program, back toward the past. It subtly bewails its own being inevitably imitative in nature as a repetition and diminution of its Homeric model: more than a sanguine new incarnation, it is an elegiac memorial to lost Homeric vitality. Even its high seriousness may be understood as a compensation for this loss—and so as covertly expressing regret over a no longer attainable Homeric spontaneity and visionary liveliness. Aeneas's tale ends in a way summing up its overall meaning of grief over the loss of his roots and origin: "here, alas, I lost my father" (3.938). This is Aeneas's "final sorrow," ironically and bitterly designated as "the goal / Of all my seafaring" (3.945–47).

Beyond this story of irremediable loss, which it continues, book 3, like book 2, is a maze of oracles and portents. It focuses entirely on a future that as yet has no substantial existence. This is the counterpart of its nostalgia for the past. Aeneas's present is emptied out in two directions, toward past and future, and consequently he cannot be fully present to anything. Everything real eludes him. Indeed, most remarkable about the prophecies and portents is, first of all, their ambiguousness. They open up vast geographical and interpretive regions of error. Prophecy remains generally at sea: rather than a secure anchor for Aeneas and for narrative, it is an invitation to inconclusive, open-ended interpretation. For example, when Aeneas sees four white horses (not exactly the snow-white sow promised in 3.529) and declares them "our first portent" (3.711), Anchises's interpretation of the portent points to its essential ambiguity:

> "It is for war that horses are caparisoned.
> These herds mean war for us. Yet the same beasts
> Are sometimes trained to take the chariot pole
> In harmony, to bear the yoke and bit.
> There is, then, hope of peace."
>
> (3.715–19)

Confirming this sort of confusion, Helenus's words about Sibyl are a devastating statement concerning prophecy presumably at its most reliable and revered:

> ". . . You'll see a spellbound prophetess, who sings
> In her deep cave of destinies, confiding
> Symbols and words to leaves. Whatever verse
> She writes, the virgin puts each leaf in order
> Back in the cave; unshuffled they remain;
> But when a faint breeze through a door ajar
> Comes in to stir and scatter the light leaves,
> She never cares to catch them as they flutter
> Or to restore them, or to join the verses;
> Visitors, unenlightened, turn away
> And hate the Sibyl's shrine."
>
> (3.593–603)

The first ambiguous prophecy followed by the Trojans misdirects them to Thrace. In Thrace, this "shore of greed," Aeneas encounters the "gruesome prodigy" of Polydorus and learns that he cannot stay there, for "fate opposed it." The oracle at Delos then tells him to go back to his origin, which Anchises indicates as being Crete, where their ancestor Teucrus had settled. On Crete, however, the Trojans are stricken with plague. Returning to Delos for a reinterpretation, Aeneas has a vision of the sacred images of the Phrygian gods he has brought with him from Troy: glowing on the hearth they speak of other forefathers, Dardanus and Iasius, who hailed from Hesperia (in the West, for the Greeks), or Ausonia, now called Italy. Anchises now recognizes the ambiguity of the double Trojan ancestry. On the Strophadës, whereto the Trojans are next blown off course, the harpies, too, prophesy, ominously, predicting famine in Italy as revenge for their slaughter.

As these examples indicate, the significant structures of this book are all stretched between past precedents serving as paradigms and future possibilities projected as ideals. The entire epic is conceived in this historical dimension. For example, the "legend" (the inscription) on the shield nailed to the temple columns at Actium by Aeneas ("Aeneas from victorious Greeks these arms," 3.387) alludes proleptically to Augustus's victory over Marc Antony and Greek armies. A few years before the writing of the *Aeneid*, Augustus had defeated Antony and Cleopatra at Actium and instituted games such as those in which Aeneas's Trojans engage. The episode is thus set up by Virgil as prefiguring the triumph of Augustus. Virgil turns his narrative with its examples, in effect, into "types" that will be fulfilled by actual Roman history as he knows it to have unfolded long after Aeneas's time. This involves a highly original understanding of prophecy that seems unprecedented in Greco-Roman tradition. It finds plausible parallels rather in biblical tradition, with its typological references and correspondences. Aeneas's prowesses illuminate Augustus's *res gestae* similarly to the way the giving of the Law to Moses on Mount Sinai sheds its light on Jesus's Sermon on the Mount, where Sinai shows up as a type looking to be fulfilled by the new covenant in Christ, which in turn acquires deeper significance as a fulfillment and completion of the Old Testament event.

Prophecy, to the extent that it is conceived merely as foretelling the future, is deceptive.[28] Much more than in predicting the future, prophecy consists in interpreting history in a way that reveals its true and final meaning. This, of course, also gives the key to telling the shape of things to come. It means transcending the temporal dimension of an isolated present cut off from past and future and rather seeing time in its wholeness—what in Scripture is termed "the fullness of time" (Galatians 4: 4). Books 2 and 3 show us how limiting and misleading the conventional kind of prophesying as telling the future is. As the epic itself, in its next book, laments: "Alas, what darkened minds have soothsayers!" (4.91). This repudiation of popular soothsaying sets the epic's historical-prophetic infrastructure into relief. Against such widespread and dubious arts, prophecy in another sense is going to emerge as the very foundation of Virgil's artistic originality. Virgil's epic proffers a new form of secularized revelation through the prophetic interpretation of history, which supplants the mythic revelation of gods as present and acting within human deeds in the furthest reaches of human endeavor—the miracle that was apprehended by Homer. This new form of prophetic poetry emerges conspicuously especially in books 6 and 8 (to be discussed in section V).

IV. Love Tragedy and Epic Destiny: *Aeneid*, Books 4–5

In book 4 the conflict between public and private becomes an explicit theme and comes to a dramatic crisis, precipitating within the epic narrative of Aeneas's success the tragedy of Dido's demise. Ostensibly, the *Aeneid* represents the triumph of civilization, of public values—exemplarily *pietas*, *humanitas*—over personal passion turning to furor and madness, such as are illustrated by Dido's uncontrollable, self-destructive rage ending in suicide. In order to achieve this purported victory, however, Aeneas needs prompting

28. The deceptiveness of prophecy in the *Aeneid* is a major emphasis of O'Hara, *Death and the Optimistic Prophecy in Vergil's Aeneid*, summarized on 176–84. O'Hara documents the ways in which "the surface optimism of the poem or prophecy is undercut by darker material partially suppressed" (3). He maintains that "Vergil uses these deceptively optimistic prophecies to depict a world where man cannot know or face the truth, where perception is clouded by misinformation, and where hopeful expectation is repeatedly frustrated by grimmer reality" (4).

from the outside, specifically from his father, who reappears in visions and, in a sense, as his conscience, as well as from Mercury, sent as a legate from the "almighty father" ("Pater omnipotens"). These interventions are necessary in order to fortify Aeneas against the female lures placing obstacles on the path of his civilizing mission. Incarnated especially by Dido and Juno, insubordinate female passion must be subdued and made subject to the law of the father. And yet it lingers ominously still in the terrible curse of the queen (4.868–75) imploring perpetual war between Rome and Carthage.[29]

The interference of the gods in the human sphere can be felt here as intrusive: it does not respect and enhance but rather overrides human motivations, crushing and even reversing them. Dido is herself fully resigned to chaste widowhood, until she is wrought upon from without by demonic powers imaged as bewitching her and overpowering her will. A tragic vision emerges precisely to the extent that the inner unity between divine and human life is broken, or at least is no longer discernible. The gods are no longer perceived as mysteriously immanent in human acts; they are posited, rather, as countervailing forces deployed on the same objective plane of action as human will and annulling it. Their influence does not mirror and reinforce but rather runs counter to the deep-seated motivations of the human actors. An emblematic example is Palinurus, the helmsman, who is overwhelmed by the god of sleep *in spite of* his unwavering resolution to keep wakeful watch (5.1091–1141). Rather than being a miraculous surplus of energy seconding and heightening the human, divine power is manifest as a cold and abstract Fate rising up against human will and prevailing over it.

Jupiter becomes principally Fate (literally, what is spoken). Although he is depicted with lively anthropomorphic colors, Jupiter's role is essentially defined by the destiny he speaks, starting with his first pronouncement outlining the course of events in store for Aeneas and his Roman successors. The life of Olympus is reduced essentially to this "divine machinery," and thus Gordon Williams stresses the gods' "unreality" by comparison with the "real world" of humans.[30] However, Denis Feeney rightly disputes his inference that this undermines the authority of the epic fiction. The gods still operate as an authenticating convention to illustrate how divine reality impinges on human experience, even if mostly in a negative way. The contrariness particularly of Juno stands for a malevolent power in the universe and as a "sign of a fundamental dislocation in the providential natural order."[31]

29. This conflict is laid out well by Brooks Otis, *Virgil: A Study in Civilized Poetry* (Oxford: Clarendon, 1963), 264ff.

30. Gordon W. Williams, *Technique and Ideas in the Aeneid* (New Haven, Conn.: Yale University Press, 1983).

31. D. C. Feeney, *The Gods in Epic: Poets and Critics of the Classical Tradition* (Oxford: Clarendon, 1991), 134.

A heavenly will and power now stand over against human agency, which is condemned to struggle in vain and not to fulfill itself but to be forever at variance with the authority that controls the universe. The separation of human and divine spheres, which are now no longer superimposed and mutually transparent but rather connected through the mechanical laws of fate, releases the human, for the first time, into a sphere of autonomous solitude in a hostile cosmos in which it can become truly tragic. We see this in Dido, who, as such, is more akin to characters in tragedy than to anything in the *Odyssey*. As such, she represents a later age and a more autonomous mode in the evolution of the ways of imagining the human in relation to the gods.

For related reasons, this book is also where Virgil's subjective style comes into full swing. The author's participation in the stories of his characters is felt more intensely than ever in the tragedy of Dido. The emotional backdrop of the tragedy is set up from the opening of book 4:

> The queen for her part, all that evening ached
> With longing that her heart's blood fed, a wound
> Or inward fire eating her away.
>
> (4.1–3)

Wounding and fire, these twin images of destruction, orchestrate everything that follows, starting with the dawn of the fatal day of the hunt on which Dido is going to become the wounded victim. The daylight first flares up as "Phoebus' torch" that "burned away / Night-gloom" (4.9–10). On Dido, maddened lover that she has become, the effect is that

> The inward fire eats the soft marrow away,
> And the internal wound bleeds on in silence.
>
> (4.93–94)

The dread day's fatality is anticipated by yet another description that combines the wounding and the flame images:

> Unlucky Dido, burning, in her madness
> Roamed through all the city, like a doe
> Hit by an arrow shot from far away
> By a shepherd hunting in the Cretan woods—
> Hit by surprise, nor could the hunter see
> His flying steel had fixed itself in her . . .
>
> (4.95–100)

The hunter, of course, alludes to Aeneas, who shortly thereafter appears dressed for the hunt (4.181ff.). The wounding and burning imagery is set up here from the beginning of this brilliantly staged tragic drama in order to flare up again climactically in the scene of Dido ablaze on her funeral pyre, once she has run herself through with the blade of Trojan Dardanus given her by Aeneas.

As a widow ignited to new love, Dido avows to her sister Anna that she recognizes "the signs of the old flame, of old desire" ("adnosco veteris vestigia flammae"). This flame of desire, fanned by Anna's encouraging counsel, provokes the ominous outbursts from the narrator concerning the tragedy that is in store and concerning Dido's deliberate blindness to the fate to which she is delivering herself, as she seeks only reassurance, not warning, from augury:

> Alas, what darkened minds have soothsayers!
> What good are shrines and vows to maddened lovers?
> (4.91–92)

The empathetic involvement of the narrator is patent in myriad such exclamations and asides.

The narrator can be heard editorializing on Dido's transgression in a number of different voices, both impassioned and moralizing. He works silently, too, for instance in his arrangement of the scene of carnal union between Dido and Aeneas as a cosmic marriage, by displacing all representation of physical passion into stormy weather in a symbolic landscape. The coupling of the lovers is, in effect, apprehended as an act of nature decked out with the adornments of a religious rite:

> Primal Earth herself and Nuptial Juno
> Opened the ritual, torches of lightning blazed,
> High Heaven became witness to the marriage,
> And nymphs cried out wild hymns from a mountain top.
> That day was the first cause of death, and first
> Of sorrow
> (4.229–32)

But having himself called this a "marriage" witnessed by heaven ("conscius aether / conubiis"), in the next lines the narrator takes up another point of view and says that *Dido* called it marriage, weaving pretexts: "under that name, / She hid her fault" ("coniugium vocat, hoc praetexit nomine culpam," 4.238–39). This pronouncement speaks from the official public condemnation of Dido rather than from the personal sympathy expressed for her elsewhere in a more private voice. In this official vein, furthermore, the narrator shows that the effects are not only fatal for Dido: the building of Carthage, too, grinds to a halt. The public interest suffers and is even suspended on account of this private passion: "Towers, half-built, rose / No farther . . . . Projects were broken off" (4.121–24).

Dido is later willing to back off from this claim and to be called simply Aeneas's mistress ("amanti"), pleading

> "Time is all I beg,
> Mere time, a respite and a breathing space
> For madness to subside in, while my fortune
> Teaches me how to take defeat and grieve."
> (4.559–602)

She complains not of the inevitable—of what fate decrees—but rather of Aeneas's total subjection of his personal feelings to public duty and his suppression of all emotion:

> "Sigh did he, while I wept? Or look at me?
> Or yield a tear, or pity her who loved him?"
> (4.509–10)

He has surrendered his very humanity in sacrifice to his public duty, she insinuates, charging: "Some rough Caucasian cliff / Begot you on flint. Hyrcanean tigresses / Tendered their teats to you" (4.505–7). She realizes that she cannot compete with fate, but her personal drama is played out at a different level. She demands only recognition for human emotions and vulnerability, at least to the extent of enabling a certain balance with stoic Roman virtues. There is a warning here and in her curse that any mission and historical purpose, however high, will be rendered sterile by complete suppression of what they stereotype as feminine weakness.

Aeneas is torn and indeed sighs inwardly, feeling the power of her words in his great heart, yet he remains firm to his purpose of submission to the gods' commands and utterly fails to show genuine compassion for his lover, who is grieved to distraction. He is like an oak tree buffeted by gales, yet withstanding them. In spite of the powerful imagery used to describe his choice of duty, as an actor in this scene, he cuts a sorry figure. Aeneas pales against the tumultuous energy of Dido and the impassioned rhetoric of her speeches, pleading with him in the highest tragic style, but also deigning to accuse him frontally as "liar and cheat,"

> Leaving him at a loss, alarmed, and mute
> With all he meant to say.
> (4.541–42)

The sublime imagery of duty counterbalances Dido's majestic passion, but it does not originate from within Aeneas. It is rather necessary to prop him up against the overwhelming hurricane of her wrath and rhetoric, which buffet him from without. In steadfastness to epic purpose, Aeneas is unbeatable, but in dealing with this human tragedy he is a catastrophe. How we read and judge the claims of these characters depends on whether we view the narrative in terms of epic teleology or tragic theatricality. The generic ambiguity becomes another way in which Virgil's inner division and ambivalence about the whole purport of his work is expressed. Divine purpose and human passion no longer seem to be naturally linked, as they are in Athena's collaboration with Odysseus: a more abstract interpretation of divine providence in history now becomes necessary to reconcile Aeneas's actions with heavenly decrees.

The sympathy of the narrator for Dido enlarges to a generalized sympathy for humanity and a cry of dismay over our pathetic vulnerability to love:

> . . . Unconscionable Love [*Improbe Amor*]
> To what extremes will you not drive our hearts!
> (4.571–72)

As a final prompt for our sympathy, the book closes with heaven's mercy upon Dido, pitied as a beautiful victim, when Iris, sent by Juno to deliver her soul to death, cuts the thread of her life with a lock of hair.

Beyond these intensely empathetic feelings, there is nonetheless the official judgment against Dido. She represents the snare of female allurements that Aeneas must resist and combat in the interests of defending civilization: Dido and Juno both, in their different spheres, are threats dangerously disruptive of patriarchal order and destiny. From this point of view, Dido is in error, however compellingly human she is and however apt to arouse our sympathy. We saw already in book 1 how Dido chooses—or is destined to choose—the fury of passion over the devotion of *pietas*. Her being thwarted in love and driven to rage actually likens her to Juno. As Otis observes, "Dido and symbolically Juno choose the way of *furor* rather than that of *pietas*" (*Virgil: A Study in Civilized Poetry*, 229). Juno's "love" for Carthage is a vainglorious jealousy. Similarly, Dido's love is erotic in the sense defined by Plato's myth in the *Symposium* concerning our androgynous composite ancestors split apart and ever after seeking their other half. Such love aims to fill some lack in the lover rather than to sacrifice self for the sake of one's people and in answer to the call of destiny.

In this manner, Dido's passion shows itself to be pathological. She identifies with a priestess "of Massylian stock" who has powers to derange the universe,

> ". . . to arrest
> The flow of rivers, make the stars move backward,
> Call up the spirits of deep Night."
> (4.675–77)

Her discourses reveal that she is at least lucid as to her own madness.

The behest of Jupiter to Mercury to intervene upon the lovers, who have become "careless of their good name" (4.301), opened this act of the drama pivoting on the condemnation and deliberate stifling of an illicit love. The figure of Atlas shouldering the earth, whom Mercury passes by on his descent from heaven, depicts a rigid model of Roman virtue and heroic self-denial. Exposed to and braving the elements, Atlas stands sharply in contrast to Aeneas's present wallowing in self-indulgence. The freezing temperatures of this image—

> Snow lay upon his shoulders, rills cascaded
> Down his ancient chin and beard a-bristle,
> Caked with ice . . .
>
> (4.341–43)

—feel like cold water thrown on the hot flames of love, even before Mercury verbalizes the reproach that he is going to deliver to Aeneas.

What Aeneas is being called to is a different kind of love. As Otis stresses, Aeneas must become a devout and even a divine man, a *theos aner*. He must become God-centered, not self-centered like Odysseus. Aeneas's *pietas* is manifest especially in a devotion to his father and his people, and to that extent it is an alternative to erotic love: ultimately it is a divine love, *agapé*.

And yet, the countercurrent to the official program is as strong here as anywhere else in the epic. Powerful mechanisms make us identify with Dido in her plight and draw back aghast at her human tragedy. This dimension of participation is crucial to the workings of prophecy. It is by participation in the future and, inseparably, by reactivation of the past in the present that the poem is able to attain to prophetic vision. This requires specifically poetic capabilities of empathetic participation that are especially acute in tragedy. It entails, furthermore, the sort of vicarious application of the story to oneself that results in what Aristotle analyzed in terms of the purging or purifying emotion of "catharsis."

This subjectively moving dimension of all genuinely interpretive experience is developed particularly in book 4, thanks to Virgil's staging it as a magnificent tragic drama contained within the overarching epic framework. This part of the epic was typically taken to be its center in numerous medieval adaptations. Chaucer's reading of the *Aeneid*, for example, in the *House of Fame*, as well as in *The Legend of Good Women*, makes the whole of the epic revolve around the questions of love and sexual ethics that are treated in book 4. A kindred focus can be found in certain feminist readings today.[32] Such readings highlight the irreducibly subjective and self-referential aspects

32. See, for example, Marilynn Desmond, *Reading Dido: Gender, Textuality, and the Medieval "Aeneid"* (Minneapolis: University of Minnesota Press, 1994).

of interpretation as an impassioned and involved activity, and these aspects concern the epic as a whole.

With Carthage behind him, Aeneas's voyage is once more diverted by the gods' will (5.75) and takes him not to Italy but to Sicily again. He is not yet spiritually ready to go to Italy. Sicily is where he lost his father, which loss he describes at the end of book 3 as his "final sorrow" (3.938, 946). Yet it is only through a return to his father that he will be enabled to resume his destined mission. For, morally as well as physically, he has lost his relationship to his father through his detour in Libya and his involvement with Dido. He must now return to his father, which means that he must confront his own conscience.[33]

This becomes yet more evident retrospectively at the outset of book 6, when Aeneas becomes nostalgically absorbed in looking at the images of Daedalus on the doorpost of the temple at Cumae. Faced with the images of Pasiphae and her monstrous passion for the bull, which is censured by the narrator as reprehensible lust ("Veneris monumenta nefandae," 6.26), Aeneas is forced to recall his own guilty erotic past. The father-son pathos inhering in the story of Icarus and Daedalus, the architect of the labyrinth built to contain the Minotaur, "get of unholy lust" (6.40), makes these images the more pertinent to Aeneas personally. The encounter with these images serves as the equivalent of a rite of contrition. It entails Aeneas's facing his guilt before acceding, repentant and purged, to the presence of his father, who in effect confers upon him his sacred mission.

Aeneas arrives in Sicily just in time to celebrate the anniversary of Anchises's death (5.62–63) with elaborate funeral games. This observance will actually result in a directive from his father to come to Hades in order to seek him out in filial piety. There his father will formally invest Aeneas with the task of founding a new civilization. For the rest, book 5 represents an interlude between the action at Carthage and the arrival in Italy. It is something of a divertissement, and it shows a rather unheroic, even slapstick and funny, side of Aeneas's cohorts. It is, nevertheless, revealing in its own way of the poem's major issues. The games display, for example, how chance and luck come greatly into play (as noted explicitly in lines 418, 261, 296 in English) now that the link with the superior world has become mechanical and the translucency of the divine in the human has been extinguished.

The narration of the games again evinces in particular the intensely participatory style of Virgil's poetry. The psychological emphasis of the preceding Dido episode carries over naturally into a description of games that markedly contrasts with Homer's description of the funeral games in the *Iliad* book 23,

33. Otis suggests that "Aeneas' escape from Dido is also the renewal of his bond with Anchises" (*Virgil: A Study in Civilized Poetry*, 272) and thereby sets up a framework that remains crucial for reading books 5–8. See, further, Joseph Farrell, "*Aeneid* 5: Poetry and Parenthood," in Perkell, ed., *Reading Vergil's Aeneid*.

particularly in point of Homer's poetic impersonality. Virgil's description is punctuated with editorial intrusions expressing the author's own participation in the contests.

Virgil's games, furthermore, are moral allegories of action in the world.[34] The first, the boat race, is oriented, like Aeneas's mission, toward a final goal and glory—a certain rock, a "happy sunning place for gulls": "Aeneas / Made a green goal here" (5.171–72). After many vicissitudes, including a nasty, cruel, unsportsmanlike turn, "chance" confounds all the best efforts of the contestants. Finally, Cloanthes's piety, his appealing to the gods, who give his boat an edge, clinches the race. One of the prizes, moreover, is a cloak woven with a scene picturing the Trojan prince, Ganymede, "the royal boy amid the boughs of Ida." Ganymede ravished by Jove to heaven to be his beloved cupbearer already figured in the poem's prologue among the reasons why Juno hates the Trojans. The depiction parallels the prophecy regarding Aeneas, who is to be escorted to heaven. Here, however, stress falls on the peremptory violence of the rapture: "Then Jove's big bird, his weapon-carrier, / Whisked him aloft from Ida in his talons" (5.324–33).

The foot race features apparently gay lovers, Nisus and Euryalus "whom Nisus dearly loved" (5.380), "his beloved" (5.427). It prefigures their fighting as a couple willing to sacrifice their lives for one another in book 9. In boxing, the brute strength, the massive bulk and berserk "fury" of Entellus is not allowed to prevail: Aeneas breaks up the combat in the interests of defending a humane and civil code of conduct. Out of the archery contest comes another kind of sign, "an omen of great import" (5.673): the arrow shot by Alcestës catches fire and leaves a track of flame like shooting stars "Trailing their blown hair" (5.680). This is an allusion to the previous omen of Iulus's hair aflame (2.904) and constitutes a confirmation of Anchises's decision at that time to go onward. It is a decision that Aeneas must now reconfirm, in spite of the women's setting the ships on fire. This last setback, which is alluded to as well by the flaming "hair," presents a final obstacle causing a division within Aeneas's people—and within himself—between the part that chooses to remain nostalgically fixated on the past and the part that takes courage to venture into the future that has been promised in prophecy.

As in the storm in book 1 and the cave in book 4, Juno has intervened, sending Iris to persuade the women against journeying any further. This provokes counter-interventions by Mercury (as already in books 1 and 4) and by the shade of Anchises (book 5), both acting for Jupiter against his consort's attempts to thwart his will. Each time, Aeneas wavers and questions his mission. Here he wonders, "Should he forget the destiny foretold / And make

34. Richard Heinze, *Virgils epische Technik* (Leipzig: Darmstadt, 1972 [1915]) shows the structural, stylistic, and psychological complexity of Virgil in comparison with the Homeric model in these terms.

his home in Sicily?" (5.911) Each time Aeneas needs outside help to resist temptation and threats: some emissary from Jupiter intervenes. In the last case, it is Anchises's image ("I come by Jove's command," 5.943). The image endorses Nautes's encouragement—"Whatever comes, / All Fortune can be mastered by endurance" (5.921–22)—and sound counsel (5.945).

Anchises's image then informs Aeneas that he must come to visit his father among the dead (5.950–52). To become fully autonomous in *pietas*, he must pass through the ordeal of book 6—the descent to the underworld. He must symbolically die to himself. Here, at the end of book 5, Aeneas must put off his own weakness, together with the faint-hearted among his people. The women only express outwardly the despair Aeneas himself harbors inwardly and had betrayed earlier in his *terque quaterque* speech. Aeneas is not yet ready to face Juno's most menacing intervention—her use of Allecto to ignite the Latin war (book 7). He still needs to be reborn and empowered to exercise *pietas* from within. This will be achieved only with his conversion to the future and to the destiny he has so far been only reluctantly following: hence the necessity of his visit to the realm of the dead.

Already the death of Palinurus, his falling overboard by the violent stroke of the god who attempted to lull him to sleep in effect signals that with the arrival in Cumae Aeneas has no more need for a helmsman: he can steer his own ship now (compare Farrell, "*Aeneid* 5: Poetry and Parenthood," 104). The references to Palinurus at the beginning and end of the book make an envelope structure out of this minor character who, nevertheless, assumes an important role as sacrificial victim: "One life given for many" (5.1066). No psychological motive is adduced for his being seduced by sleep, which he endeavors to resist. It is just the heavy hand of fate that casts him down. Described as "duty-bound" (6.473), and fearing less for himself than for the ship (6.475–77), self-sacrificing and public-minded, he is a proxy for Aeneas. Only less dramatic than Dido, he is another reminder to Aeneas of the personal costs of completing his mission. The price of empire and its glory in personal loss for Aeneas is sounded yet again with the death of his trumpeter, Misenus. The elaborately described felling of trees for his funeral (6.300–330) multiplies and magnifies the sensation of the severance of life. Such a burial ceremony and ritual insist once more on the pathos of sacrifice on which civilization is founded. This sacrifice of life to ideals is a central theme of the epic that finds a haunting emblem in the Golden Bough.

V. Descent to the Dead and Conversion to Life: *Aeneid*, Books 6 and 8

Prophecy as an institution in the world of the *Aeneid* is generally portrayed in a way that emphasizes its unreliability and ambiguity. Sibyl's prophecies conveying the oracles of Apollo are notorious for their obscurity ("obscuris vera involvens," 6.100):

> . . . the Sibyl of Cumae from her shrine
> Sang out her riddles, echoing in the cave,
> Dark sayings muffling truths, the way Apollo
> Pulled her up raging, or else whipped her on,
> Digging the spurs beneath her breast.
> (6.149–53)

This frenzied ecstasy (not unlike epilepsy) interprets the pronouncements of the god, which echo

> In a cavern perforated a hundred times,
> having a hundred mouths, with rushing voices
> Carrying the responses of the Sibyl.
> (6.67–69)

The oracles, furthermore, are written on leaves by the prophetess and scattered by the winds that blow through the cave, endowing it with divine voices, so that Aeneas pleads,

> "But now commit no verses to the leaves
> Or they may be confused, shuffled and whirled
> By playing winds: chant them aloud, I pray."
> (6.117–19)

This is evidently not an authoritative model of prophecy that Virgil would be interested in associating himself with. Sibyl serves rather as a foil for the new and different practice of prophecy that Virgil wishes to inaugurate.

The ambiguity endemic to prophecy as it is commonly encountered in this world is symbolized by the Golden Bough. Everything about this marvelous branch is double and even duplicitous, starting from the twin doves ("geminae") that guide Aeneas to it, as it hangs on a "two-hued tree / Where glitter of gold filtered between green boughs" (6.290–91). A life-preserving talisman against death, ironically the Golden Bough is itself a lifeless, inorganic object consisting in glitter rather than growth and parasitical rather than vital in its connection with the tree it is wrapped around. It is the opposite of Odysseus's great-rooted olive tree made into his bed and thus embracing his most intimate life. It even sounds deathly:

> Like mistletoe that in the woods in winter
> Thrives with yellowish berries and new leaves—
> A parasite on the trunk it twines around—
> So bright amid the dark green ilex shone
> the golden leafage, rustling in light wind.
> (6.292–96)

The ghostly sound of the gold leaf in the wind provokes Adam Parry's characterization of the bough as a symbol of "splendor and lifelessness" and Thomas Greene's likening it to the "sounding brass" of 1 Corinthians 13 ("If I have not love . . ."). By its golden gleam, it is also a symbol of the Golden Age of Augustan Rome, and as such it reflects the ambiguities of the Empire, a strangely exalted, glorious collective life "without end" ("sine fine") built, nevertheless, on death and oppression for individuals and on the deathly abstractions of an ideology that rings tinny and hollow. Even the sound of the word "golden" (*auri*) rustles emptily and homophonically with the word for air (*aura*), but without organic, semantic connection with it, in the line describing the glittering of gold refulgent in the air between branches ("discolor unde *auri* per ramos *aura* refulsit," 6.204).

Sibyl had said to Aeneas:

> "Pull away the bough. It will come willingly,
> Easily, if you are called by fate.
> If not, with all your strength you cannot conquer it . . ."
> (6.213–16)

But this is not the way it happens. Rather,

> Aeneas at once briskly took hold of it
> And, though it clung [*cunctantem*], greedily broke it off,
> Then carried it to the Sibyl's cave.
> (6.297–99; Latin: 211)

This hint of difficulty in breaking the branch seems deliberately calculated to render Aeneas's fate equivocal. The ambiguities of the Golden Bough symbolize, after all, the ambiguities of the Golden Age such as it had supposedly been realized by the Augustan Empire. Though it is supposed to be God-given, as presented in the epic and its prophecies, the Empire is in fact built upon what men have seized in greed.

Like Odysseus, Aeneas goes to Hades to consult with the dead. What the dead know that we do not is the end of life, its final meaning: the end gives meaning to the whole of a life, confers a final shape on the story, even as history's meaning is determined from its end or telos.[35] The significance of book 6 within the program of the poem as a whole is that it opens directly to Aeneas's view the goal of future glory that is the reason for all his labor and the compensation for his personal loss. This vision has been anticipated to him by his dream of Hector, the phantom of Creusa, the oracle at Delos, the visions of the household gods on Crete, the words of the Harpies and

35. These ideas, as general insights into time and narrative, have been explored philosophically by Paul Ricoeur, *Temps et récit* (Paris: Seuil, 1983), 3 vols.

of Helenus, and the visitation of Mercury at Carthage. But it has so far remained obscure and has only goaded him to reluctant acquiescence rather than inspiring him to resolute action. Now that he sees the whole vision that had previously been vouchsafed from the mouth of Jove only to Venus and Mercury, he is finally able to make it his own and dedicate himself to it wholeheartedly.

From any point within history, this end is always only futural, but from a prophetic perspective, the end can be revealed and can even begin to be enacted now. Such revelation inspires present acts aimed at realizing in its premises what has been seen as a future prospect. The end of history is revealed not to seal it off as a fate to be passively awaited, but in order that it may be freely willed and anticipated. To be free is to freely will one's fate—*amor fati.* Aeneas needed a new structure of meaning in order to acquire a new kind of freedom. The revelation to him of the final end of his struggles frees him to will the imperial Roman future as his *own* future.

Freedom *for* the future requires also freedom *from* the past. Aeneas must overcome the bondage of his past so as to gain freedom with respect to his fate—which is then perhaps best called rather his "destiny." His confrontation with his past climaxes in book 6 with his visit to the underworld in order that he might "learn his destiny." In book 4 he sails for Italy "not of his own free will" ("Italiam non sponte sequor"). Not only does he leave Dido unwillingly, but he does virtually everything else against his own heart. We have been shown "pius Aeneas" dragged along by fate against all his personal inclinations and desires from his very first speech, "O terque quaterque beati . . . ," pronouncing thrice and four-times blessed those who died at Troy. He finally manages to escape from this predicament in book 6. For here he gains a vision in which *pietas* will become his own possession and even passion: it is finally, from this juncture forward, no longer imposed on him from without by external interventions. He rises to a prophetic vantage point from which he will assume the whole fated unfolding of history as his own free achievement. By seeing the end toward which it is all moving, he learns to embrace the purposes of providence, to make them his own, and to act freely, willingly, in accordance with them rather than reluctantly and in mere compliance. Aeneas achieves freedom and transcendence of individual selfhood by fully and willingly identifying with the fate of his people and of history as a whole. In this manner, fate and freedom come to coincide.

The vision given Aeneas is not a matter of objective knowledge but of a conversion of will and even, more broadly, of faith. He has to *decide* to make it happen. That is why it is not accorded him without certain teasing ambiguities. Besides being the place of prophecy, the underworld, the world of the dead, is also, of course, full of illusions, chimaeras, "false dreams," "Dis's homes all void, and empty realms" (6.371) ("domos Ditis vacuas et inanias regna," 6.269). Aeneas cannot even challenge and fight them:

> How faint these lives were—empty images
> Hovering bodiless—he had attacked
> And cut his way through phantoms, empty air.
> (6.400–402)

As in the Christian theodicy that identifies evil with nothing, so this Hell is a region of unreality. Yet this is also where Aeneas is given a dazzling prophetic revelation of the future. In this flickering visionary reality, Aeneas has first of all to face the ambiguities of his past.

Aeneas's previous life passes before him in review in the shapes of the characters he encounters here: signally Palinurus, Dido, and Deiphobus. Each is a figure out of his past, and they are known to the reader from books 5, 4, and 2 respectively. They appear to Aeneas in reverse order with respect to his past experience, and each is totally fixated on a past of his or her own. "They can therefore stand for the dead past that Aeneas leaves behind him."[36] In each case, Aeneas's encounters are modeled on Odysseus's in the eleventh book of the *Odyssey*. Palinurus pleading for burial is reminiscent of Elpenor. Dido's unforgiving anger and her refusal to say a word to Aeneas recalls Ajax's smoldering resentment over the shield of Achilles. Earless, noseless, mutilated Deiphobus, with his story of being the victim of Helen's treachery, sets up a parallel to Agamemnon slaughtered like an ox at the trough by his wife and her lover.

Similarly, the threefold attempted embrace of Anchises repeats Odysseus's vain attempt to embrace his mother, Anticlea. But the attempt is also charged with Aeneas's peculiar nostalgia for his past. The pessimism, furthermore, of Aeneas that makes him wish to turn away from the future altogether is poignantly expressed one last time in his question as to how the "poor souls" awaiting reincarnation "can crave our daylight so" (6.968–69) ("quae luci miseris tam dira cupido," 6.721). After this, Anchises unrolls the vision of future glory that is finally going to convert Aeneas and bring him round from being a nostalgic defeatist: this vision lets him emerge as the man of the hour, pursuing (rather than being pursued by) the promise of his future.

In the philosophical Hades—based on Plato's myth of Er, with its belief in metempsychosis[37]—that immediately follows, the souls have no ostensible past. That is what has been erased from their minds by the waters of Lethe. They are about to be reincarnated and are wholly oriented to the future. In passing from the mythological to the philosophical Hades, Aeneas turns from the past to the future, from a backward-turned to a forward-looking

36. Otis, *Virgil: A Study in Civilized Poetry*, 290, clearly expounds the fundamental dynamic of conversion from past to future, and I am indebted to him throughout this discussion.

37. For the sources of book 6, I rely chiefly on Eduard P. Norden, *Vergilius Maro Aeneis Buch VI*, 4th ed. (Stuttgart: Teubner, 1957 [1903]).

orientation. At this point, his futurity becomes his fate or destiny, which now no longer hangs around his neck like an albatross. His embracing this revelation of the final order of history frees Aeneas to act. For the end is, theoretically considered, the origin of all constructive, rationally willed action and grounds it in a vision of the whole.

Anchises's speech begins in a Stoic and Platonic mode by positing the inherence of all things in the *Animus Mundi*: it explains how human souls, based on their conduct in the body, merit reward or punishment after death. This discourse discloses to Aeneas the ends of human life in general before turning to the revelation of Roman history as futural. This revelation embodies the specific purposes for which Aeneas is to act, the purposes with respect to which his whole world of significance can be ordered. This is where Anchises "teaches" Aeneas his "destiny" (6.1020), so that when he has been shown all future times up to the Roman Empire under Augustus Caesar, Aeneas's soul is on fire with love of the glory to come ("incenditque animum famae venientis amore," 6.889).

This revelation of the future has as its axis the line of kings that is to descend from Aeneas, although it includes also Republican heroes and a repertoire of legends about Roman origins, including the story of Romulus and Remus. At its center, Anchises indicates:

> Caesar Augustus, son of the deified,
> Who shall bring once again an Age of Gold
> To Latium, to the land where Saturn reigned
> In early times.
>
> (6.1064–67)

Most importantly of all, this preview is a goal that Aeneas himself must begin to make possible. And then, whether it is achieved in the Augustan Age or proves to be an illusory pipe dream depends entirely on what Augustus and Virgil's own contemporaries themselves accomplish. This opening of the future and of fate as a possibility to be realized—and indeed as an imperative not to be shirked—alone gives its full sense to Anchises's exhortation:

> Do we lag still in carrying our valor
> Into action? Can our fear prevent
> Our settling in Ausonia?
>
> (6.1084–86)

The exhortation to action at the climax of this revelation of a glorious goal applies not only to Aeneas but also to Augustus himself and to Virgil's Roman contemporaries. The Golden Age is equally a project for them to achieve. In this way, the epic poem about national origins and imperial foundations, which is focused on the mythic image of Trojan Aeneas and his exploits, embodies an injunction impinging also on Virgil's own times in imperial Rome. The vision of the Golden Age constitutes a challenge to Virgil's own present, and likewise the idealized heroic past is implicitly a summons to action in the name of a yet-to-be realized future. Just as in the Bible, so here prophecy issues in an imperative to be acted upon. The depiction of a triumphant society begins with a warning against the horrors of civil war, which had recently ravaged Rome, especially in the strife between Caesar and Pompey. Anchises apostrophizes and urgently admonishes these "sons" of his, themselves related as father- and son-in-law, who marched against each other:

> "Sons, refrain! You must not blind your hearts
> To that enormity of civil war,
> Turning against your country's very heart
> Her own vigor of manhood. You above all
> Who trace your line from the immortals, you
> Be first to spare us. Child of my own blood,
> Throw away your sword!"
>
> (6.1120–26)

On the positive side, Anchises's prophecy contains a prescription for the future. Romans are to excel in arts of government. That is how their mission of civilizing the world, of bringing the whole globe to peace within one imperial order, is to be realized. It is set into relief over against what we cannot but suspect that Virgil as a poet prized most highly (as suggested by Parry, "The Two Voices of Virgil's *Aeneid*")—the artistic talents which are handed over to others:

> "Others will cast more tenderly in bronze
> Their breathing figures, I can well believe,
> And bring more lifelike portraits out of marble;
> Argue more eloquently, use the pointer
> To trace the paths of heaven more accurately
> And accurately foretell the rising stars.
> Roman, remember by your strength to rule
> Earth's peoples—for your arts are to be these:
> To pacify, to impose the rule of law,
> To spare the conquered, battle down the proud."
>
> (6.1145–54)

This image has a strongly prescriptive valence. It delineates the Romans' truly distinctive talent for ruling and Rome's moral purpose, its world-historical significance. Aeneas is being summoned to lay the foundation stone for all this. That is what those who continue in his tradition and mission are to aim to achieve.

In book 6, Aeneas is turned around to the future as something he makes, something, therefore, with respect to which he is free—and not by getting out from under fate and defying it, which would be an Odyssean gesture, but rather by fully identifying himself with it. He no longer reluctantly submits, crushed in his own will under the burden of the past: projected into the future, this same fate or destiny becomes his very own purpose, the source of his eager activity. The consequences of this conversion to the future are played out fully in books 7–12. However, as these books show, obedience to freedom, just like obedience to fate, still has its price. It means renunciation: to be free is to be disinterested. Can Rome be willed even at the cost of the personal sacrifice that it is shown to exact?

To freely act in history requires, furthermore, assuming responsibility for tragedies such as war waged in the making of empire. Regret toward the past and its tragedy, which Aeneas must overcome in order to become the model of an empire builder, the civilizer of the world, is not simply cast off like an old garment. Tragedy overshadows, even at its very climax, the revelation of the Roman glory that is to come. An acute tragic sense is intrinsic to, and fundamentally conditions, the meaning of the whole of history in which it is to be transfigured. Last in the long line of triumphant descendents who will sacrifice themselves for Rome is one who looks dejected, one whose temples are surrounded by black night. Aeneas craves to know who this mysteriously compelling figure is. This "immense sorrow" ("ingentum luctum") of his people, as Anchises tells him, is Marcellus, whose funeral rites are invoked: Anchises anticipates heaping lilies upon his descendant's grave in futile gestures of inconsolable grief:

> "For you
> Will be Marcellus. Let me scatter lilies,
> All I can hold, and scarlet flowers as well,
> To heap these for my grandson's shade at least,
> Frail gifts and ritual of no avail."
>
> (6.1098–1102)

The hopelessness and vanity of it all is captured in the sense of this vain ritual commemorating the too terrible sacrifice demanded. It might be meaningful, after all, if only a truly just and peaceful Rome could be pointed to as making good this sacrifice. Then perhaps even the fated death of Marcellus might be willed as the price of peace. However, that prospect seems to remain a counterfactual, since triumphal exultation is not the sentiment that prevails at this climactic juncture.

As already observed, this prophetic vision designed to fire Aeneas with love of future glory and thereby motivate his enthusiastic embrace of destiny has been undermined even from its outset: it was framed by Aeneas's disbelief that souls could wish to be reborn, that they could crave to return again to "bodies' dead weight" (6.968). Anchises's answer to this incomprehension is that the souls' memories have been erased by Lethe. The souls come to Lethe stream,

"That there unmemoried they may see again
The heavens and wish re-entry into bodies."
(6.1007–8)

Whereas the vision of history afforded Aeneas via prophecy is supposed to assure and confirm him in his courage to endure all trials, this amnesia implies that one can have heart to participate in life thanks only to ignorance and blindness toward what history holds in store. Even in devising the narrative mechanism of reviewing history proleptically as projected toward its outcome in order to engender the motivation for history-making action, Virgil manages at the same time to hint that precisely the vision of the whole from the end-point—the vision enjoyed by purged souls with clear perceptions—can also be supremely demotivating. After all, this is his own perspective as creator of the poem and its tragedy ("l'alta mia tragedia," as Dante has him say in *Inferno* 20.113): we sense him dolorously mourning throughout the work. At any rate, both perspectives—and their contradictoriness—are woven together in making up the pathos of the poem.

Ambiguities aside, in the center of the epic at the end of book 6, the Roman destiny which has structured Aeneas's quest from book 1 onward is fully revealed as not just an ideological but also a moral and religious goal. What is revealed is not just the glory of the Roman state but the meaning of life itself as futural. Aeneas is called upon to become a *theios-aner*, a divine man, and to enter upon a kind of transcendent life beyond his merely singular selfhood. This vision is fragile and perhaps will never again be so vividly glimpsed, given the progress of hostilities that stretches almost without relief across the following six books. But here, momentously, the meaning of human life is revealed as historical—not as the one-dimensional, sensuous present of pain that was the reality so tenaciously and heroically lived out by Odysseus.

In the new historical perspective of the *Aeneid*, meaning in human experience accrues over an expanse of time. It concerns not the moment alone, but the whole structure of a sequence of events, events that are themselves built up each one out of component moments that are moving toward a goal. There is a faint anticipation of such a historical sense in Odysseus's being allowed to foresee his death in sleek old age, but this is not the constitutive center of the *Odyssey* as a whole, not overtly anyway. In the *Aeneid*, history is grounded in a purpose that transcends the present and gives it its significant structure. History thereby becomes providential. For the Greeks, anyone who dies as horrendously as Agamemnon did cannot be considered to have been happy.[38] Only the present moment fully exists, and if the last moment of a person's life is calamitous, so also is the final significance of their life. There is no redemption for archaic Greeks in the meaning of a life as a whole, neither in the final goal and order of history.

38. See Herodotus, *Historiae* 1.32.5–6, and the choral conclusion to *Oedipus Rex*.

My use of the Christian-theological language of "redemption" here points not only to Aeneas's death to self through renunciation in order to acquire new life at a higher spiritual level, but also to Virgil's discovery of a narrative structure uncannily close to that of prophetic history (or "typology") in revealed, biblical religion. Roman destiny, as Virgil interprets it, is providential, a divine dispensation that calls human beings to their historical task, granting them grace, particularly in the form of prophetic revelation. This granting, in turn, indicates why Virgil was enthusiastically embraced and assimilated by Christian writers, preparing the way for Dante.[39]

*The Original Site of the Future: Pallanteum-Arcadia (*Aeneid, *Book 8)*

In book 8, the consequences of Aeneas's conversion brought about by the prophetic revelation at the end of book 6 are outwardly dramatized. Up to this point, Aeneas has proved reluctant and uncertain about his destiny. He has needed encouragement from others in order not to give up at every difficult or daunting juncture. Now he introduces himself to Evander, speaking confidently of his own valor ("me virtus") and the sacred oracles of the gods ("sancta oracula divom," 8.131) that "have brought me here by destiny, and gladly" (8.177–80). The next day, when the grim inevitability of war is contemplated and the general gloominess is pierced by a red glare and by thunderous crashes in the heavens, it is Aeneas himself who spontaneously interprets these signs as omens of the destiny that he now lays claim to as his own:

> The others
> Sat still, mystified, but Troy's great captain
> recognized the sound, and knew the promise
> Made by his goddess mother. Then he said:
> "My friend, you need not, truly need not ask
> What new event's portended. I am the man
> Whom heaven calls . . ."
>
> (8.719–25)

Aeneas's resoluteness here demonstrates how the future becomes free. For this revelation of "fate," so far from being an onerous imposition or constraint, is empowering: it reveals a purpose that is to be acted upon rather

---

39. For the history of reception of Virgil by early Christian authors, see Courcelle, *Lecteurs païens et lecteurs chrétiens de l'Énéide*. On Virgil as foundation stone for Christian culture, see the classic study by Theodor Haecker, *Vergil, Vater des Abendlands* (Bonn am Rhein: Wahlband der Buchgemeinde, 1933), trans. A. W. Wheen as *Virgil, Father of the West* (London: Collins, 1934).

than inevitable facts to be just passively endured. Immediately following this speech,

> He rose from his high seat and first revived
> The fires for Hercules on slumbering altars,
> Gladly revisiting, as yesterday,
> The guardian Lar and humble household gods.
> (8.735–49)

By this symbolic action, Aeneas identifies himself with a heroic past, reviving it and transmitting it into a future for which he himself becomes the heroic model. It is in microcosm the same story of triumph of rational order over fury that lies at the heart of Virgil's whole Aenean epic of the founding of Rome. Hercules, the legendary liberator celebrated on this feast day, is exalted in the hymn sung to him for his victories over the Nemean lion, Cerberus, Typhoeus, and the Lernean hydra; he is praised as "not lacking in reason" ("non te rationis egentem," 8.299). Nevertheless, Hercules's triumph over Cacus in his bestial, half-human form (8.260) and in the madness of his furious mind ("At furiis Caci mens effera," 8.205) is achieved by the force of a "knotted massy club" (8.204). Hercules himself is depicted raging "with black bile of anger" and grinding his teeth in fury and heaving mountain cliffs (8.291–326). These are hints of the equivocations attaching in Virgil's eyes (and heart) to perhaps any civilizing mission. All this violence is necessary for conquering monstrous forces and brute nature, even in the interests ultimately of civilized peace among meek fellows.

This builds ambiguity into the mythological origins of Rome, which are explored and pondered on this visit with "King Evander, founder unaware / Of Rome's great citadel" (8.413–14) to Pallanteum, the future site of Rome with its seven hills. This is the place to which Saturn fled from Jove's rebellion to rule over unschooled men sprung from tree trunks, true rustics in a peaceful, archaic age offering an idyllic image of the past (8.424–33). Evander himself comes originally from Arcadia in Greece, enshrined by Virgil's *Eclogues* as the paradigm of an idealized bucolic society living in peace and amity. Such is the Golden Age of Saturn. Simplicity and naivety are its keynotes, and yet this mythic past, too, already has a violent history at its back, according to Evander's account:

> "In that first time, out of Olympian heaven,
> Saturn came here in flight from Jove in arms,
> An exile from a kingdom lost; he brought
> These unskilled men together from the hills
> Where they were scattered, gave them laws, and chose
> The name of Latium, from his latency
> Or safe concealment in this countryside.

In his reign were the golden centuries
Men tell of still, so peacefully he ruled,
Till gradually a meaner, tarnished age
Came on with fever of war and lust of gain."

(8.423–33)

The legendary past of Rome is gathered together for its evocation of the monumental vestiges still in evidence in Augustan times projected from this Arcadian perspective as futural. Indeed, the landscape alludes equally to the future, to the places that are to be hallowed by history: the Carmental altar and gate, the Lupercal grotto, the Roman forum. Evander is Aeneas's tour guide around the settlement whose rustic sites foreshadow those destined to be famous one day in Rome. Their names (including also "Argiletum," "Janiculum," "Carinae") are anachronistically resonant for Virgil's Augustan audience:

He led to our Tarpeian site and Capitol,
All golden now, in those days tangled, wild
With underbrush—but awesome even then.

(8.459–61)

After these revisitations of the mythic, Arcadian past prefiguring the Roman future, Aeneas departs in arms with his new allies to Etruria to seek yet more allies, leaving "mothers with quaking breast" (8.802) watching from the walls behind. Book 8 then climaxes by turning directly toward the future in another major rehearsal of Roman history cast in the form of prophecy (third after Jupiter's promises to Venus in book 1 and Anchises's revelations to Aeneas in book 6): here the Roman past is narrated prophetically by the enormous epic ekphrasis engraved on the shield forged by Vulcan. Like the apocalypse of book 6, this prophetic revelation comes to Aeneas meeting with a parent in a secluded vale, but this time it is Venus who brings him history prophesied in pictorial form:

There the Lord of Fire,
Knowing the prophets, knowing the age to come,
Had wrought the future story of Italy,
The triumphs of the Romans . . .

(8.845–52)

The shield is brought to Aeneas by Venus with a motherly embrace (8.834) that communicates his God-given mandate to set into motion this whole preordained history building up to dominion and world empire.

The focus on the Augustan age as destined future is patent in the shield's design: it centers on Caesar Augustus's crucial military victory at Actium as ending over a hundred years of civil war (since 146 B.C.). Each of the ekphrastic narratives revolving around this center in some way points to the triumph of rational order over savagery, which is, of course, the central meaning attributed to the Augustan imperial triumph: the wolf suckling human twins; the rape of the Sabines atoned for by a pact and offerings ending hostilities; Roman soldiers patriotically sacrificing their lives to counter Etruscan King Porsenna's menaces; Cato giving laws, and so on. The images also recall how perilously close to one another swing the poles of civilized conduct and bestial behavior in the heat of action during the crises of history: Mettus's breaking faith with his Roman allies is punished by savage excoriation; Rome is saved from a surprise attack by Gauls at night through an animal warning given by a goose; religion is expressed by a leaping dance of naked priests; Catiline, an enemy of the state, is pinned to a cliff and made to tremble by the Furies' glare.

This history is the future destiny that Aeneas now shoulders in place of the burden of the past in the shape of his father, whom he had carried away from Troy literally on his shoulders. Having borne the past of pain, he has now exchanged it for the future of promise, though he is not himself conscious of all that this implies:

> All these images on Vulcan's shield,
> His mother's gift, were wonders to Aeneas.
> Knowing nothing of the events themselves,
> He felt joy in their pictures, taking up
> Upon his shoulder all the destined acts
> And fame of his descendants.
>
> (8.987–92)

Aeneas must enact or perform—and not only see—the future. This prophetic future will become real only thanks to him and to the resoluteness with which he acts at this crucial juncture. He anticipates this projected future greatness by beginning to act in accordance with it. He thus embodies resoluteness that lives already out of the future—and to that extent he begins to realize it in the present. Books 5 through 8 as a group have all concerned Aeneas's being turned around from the past toward the future. By this point, his action is truly futural, in the sense of being geared to a revealed end that directs all his efforts in the present. Aeneas must make himself worthy of divinization, and he is enjoined to do so in the manner of a poet's making or fashioning—*fingere*: "shape yourself, / You too, to merit godhead" ("te quoque dignum / *finge* deo," 8.364–65; Latin: 483–85).

Yet the ambiguities of the imperial mission are tellingly registered here, too: the luminous revelation from the gods is in danger of darkening to a history of Realpolitik and so of becoming a prophetic dream-vision degenerated into an ideological nightmare. Just as the revelation from Anchises in book

6 was at risk of being all a false dream, as suggested by Aeneas and Sibyl's passing through the Gate of Ivory immediately afterward, so this vision of a glorious future, in which Aeneas takes such joy, is presented as ambiguously susceptible to being confounded by the lies of Roman political propaganda. It is splendid and matchless as an artwork, but the images on the shield hint that their art may be mere ideology. There is constant contamination of the triumphs of empire by its terrors: for instance, Augustus's helmet vomiting flames ("cui tempora flammas / laeta vomunt," 8.680) recalls Cacus imaged as a fire-breathing dragon ("ore vomens igne," 8.199). The slaughtered bullocks ("caesi iuvenci," 8.972) of the triumphal celebration are actually a sign of the end of the Golden Age (which was without killing) and of the onset of a post-lapsarian state of man, as *Georgics* 2.536–38 would suggest.[40]

The arts were deployed grandly by Augustus on behalf of his imperial program, but art is in fact an image and, as such, potentially false, a golden sheen or veneer that can obstruct accurate knowledge of historical truth. The poem's rhetoric stresses that Aeneas *ignorantly* pleases himself with an *image* ("miratur rerumque ignarus imagine gaudet," 8.730). Art absorbs the mind in glittering, Golden-Age images so that it overlooks the troubling reality beneath and behind them, particularly the devastating consequences of war. The shield is a paradigm of art, even of divine art, but its glorified representation of history is belied by the battle in the books that immediately ensue (books 9–12) and that show the price of empire in blood and tears and tragedy for the human beings involved.

According to the Augustan ideology, which this and the other prophetic passages reflect, civilization was to be achieved through warfare. Aeneas's shield represents the triumph of civilized virtues over monstrous barbarism, but the depictions are riddled with paradox. Aeneas armed with this shield becomes, in effect, a new Achilles: he regresses to all the fraud and violence characteristic of the old heroic code that was supposed to have been overcome and supplanted by his more civilized, rational ethic. Aeneas constantly slips back into the ways and means of warfare judged as immoral according to the new civilized ideal. The ambiguities, as we have seen, are inscribed on the shield itself. It is modeled, moreover, on the shield of Achilles, which was likewise wheedled for him by his mother, Thetis, from Hephaistos (Vulcan) in *Iliad* book 18. Seduction and trickery are employed similarly by Venus as means of persuasion to procure Aeneas's shield in a scene reminiscent of Hera's seduction of Zeus in *Iliad* book 14.

---

40. See Anthony J. Boyle, "*Aeneid* 8: Images of Rome," in Perkell, ed., *Reading Vergil's Aeneid*, 157–58. More generally, the vast literature offering both positive and negative interpretations of the poem's imperial ideology is reviewed by S. J. Harrison, "Some Views of the *Aeneid* in the Twentieth Century," in *Oxford Readings in Vergil's Aeneid* (Oxford: Oxford University Press, 1990), 1–20, and again by Perkell, *Reading Vergil's Aeneid*, 14–22.

Roman civilization from its inception is in violation of the very codes that it creates. The deceptiveness that is accepted as natural and innocent behavior in Homer's world is condemned as immoral by Aeneas. Symptomatic of this hypocrisy is the fact that Aeneas becomes the quintessentially hesitant hero, thus prefiguring Hamlet. The emphasis on the overcoming of "hesitation" ("cunctatio") by subterfuge or force or other unworthy means is a Leitmotif that can be traced from the scene of Vulcan yielding reluctantly (*conctantem*, 8.388) to Venus, to the Golden Bough's giving way only with resistance (*cunctantem*, 6.211) and to Dido's lingering (*cunctantem*, 4.133) in her halls before joining the hunt that will be fatal to her. It reaches all the way to the final lapse into violence of Aeneas hesitating to kill Turnus against his better judgment and against the moderating influence of the word ("cunctantem flectere sermo," 12.940; compare Boyle, "*Aeneid* 8: Images of Rome," 156).

In the end, it is impossible to decide between the optimistic and the pessimistic readings of the *Aeneid* as either pro- or anti-Augustan. The sense of history as prophecy lies necessarily in and between such oppositions. Duncan Kennedy has suggested how the two valences are inseparable, due to the nature of language as a social act in which both poles necessarily operate in any evocation of Augustus.[41] I would add that it is also the nature of Virgilian prophecy as oriented to action, and thereby as open to the future, which positions it between two alternatives: that which is to be chosen and that which is to be avoided. Both are necessary for its signifying this choice, and so Virgil's vision *must* encompass both the positive and the negative aspects of empire. This empire must still always be *made* worthy of being chosen in every successive moment of time in which one lives and acts.

Prophecy—as an interpretation of history in the light of its final significance as disclosed by divine revelation—leads to a resoluteness that makes things happen, that proactively shapes history. For this reason, the knowledge of revelation and prophecy is never given simply as a fact: it cannot be merely a detached, theoretical knowing, but demands decision and a commitment of belief. Such commitment arises only as part of an act or praxis. Accordingly, the knowledge involved in prophecy is inextricably engaged in its historical moment. Prophecy opens a perspective in and for a humanity which it orients in its practical, moral, and historical endeavors. It is this history-making activity that is the condition of possibility of the knowing bestowed by prophetic revelation. The way Virgil has inserted the panoramic revelation on the shield into the crisis of the epic action, as it builds to a climax full of suspense, tells us that this pictorial prophecy does not resolve but rather opens events in progress to their most far-reaching possibilities.

---

41. Duncan F. Kennedy, "'Augustan' and 'Anti-Augustan': Reflections on Terms of Reference," in *Roman Poetry and Propaganda in the Age of Augustus*, ed. Anton Powell (London: Bristol Classical, 1992), 26–58.

Prophecy and Poiesis *in the* Aeneid

It has become clear, then, that prophecy reveals not what necessarily and automatically will happen to passive humans but rather a general order of significance to be freely appropriated and enacted. At the crux of the prophetic revelations in book 6 from the spirit of his father Anchises in the underworld and again in book 8, as depicted on the shield forged by Vulcan, Aeneas is called upon to *act* with resoluteness on the basis of a vision revealing the significance of history as a whole. Prophecy opens a dimension of freedom and meaning, a dimension that enables one to act not blindly as the slave of fate but rather freely toward a future goal shaped by one's own understanding of it. Both history and the future need to be *achieved*, and prophecy opens a perspective that is instrumental to achieving them freely and meaningfully, that is, with the vision of an end and purpose in view.

It is to Virgil's own time that the prophecies of the *Aeneid* most essentially and urgently speak, for they are meant to inspire present action, to incite sacred "labor" to realize what they reveal as the true meaning and mission of Rome. From the beginning of the work, in book 1, the prophecy of Rome as an eternal Empire ("imperium sine fine") has been unfolded not just to the characters within the epic but also to its Roman readers. *They* are the ones to whom prophecy can effectively speak in the present tense and as proposing, indirectly and allegorically, real possibilities for action. Only so does it speak *as* prophecy in the full sense—that is, as leveraged from presently pending decisions. This suspense is what gives prophetic revelation its crucial relevance for free human beings.

The actual *facts* of a prophecy and their fulfillment can even be past because its essence is to interpret the *significance* of life and history for a people at a certain decisive moment within its ongoing historical life. Indeed, from the point of view of Virgil's audience, almost all the prophecies of this epic are after the fact: the facts they prophesy have already occurred and are history. To this extent, the prophecy in question is retrospective. The same can be said generally of the historical prophecies of the Hebrew prophets. For example, Second Isaiah (chapters 40–55) prophesies the campaigns of Cyrus the Persian after they had, to a large extent, already taken place, leading to the fall of Babylon in 539 B.C. This may seem to make prophecy too easy. With hindsight, anyone can "prophesy" events that have already become fact. Yet prophecy, fundamentally, is concerned to reveal not a series of objective facts but rather an order of significance that enables those who receive it to confront the exigencies of the present.

The fact that Virgil's prophecy is retrospective does not make it spurious or sham. In the order of significance, time is reversible: the future remakes the past by changing the significance of its events and rearranging its bypassed possibilities, just as the past prefigures, informs, and eventually "makes" the future. Whether prophecy refers to past, future, or present (and the three actually come to coincide in prophetic perspective), its essential purpose is to reveal in each of these dimensions a way of living an authentically historical existence in the here and now. It projects a horizon within which alone the truly pertinent facts can come to light. In prophetic perspective, past, present, and future are no longer seen as successive and external to one another, but rather as all simultaneously and eternally present. Each of the tenses affords a perspective on the central meaning of the historical world as it appears in the crisis of the present.

To this extent, prophecy is based on transcending one-dimensional time and on achieving a point of view sub specie aeternitatis. Only from outside and beyond the sequence can the final goal of a series of events be apprehended. Only from the standpoint of eternity is the meaning of time revealed. Still, it is only within time, as situated within and among human actions and events, that any such disclosure can be concretely conferred and apprehended. It is not as if the Golden Age as such could ever actually arrive and be present as a fact. That would be to mistake myth for reality. The point of myth as employed within prophecy is to break open the present toward possibilities that it can never encompass but can nevertheless strive after in a movement of ecstatic self-transcendence. Prophecy achieves this by its envisioning a (w)hol(l)y other order of significance breaking into the present and breaking it open toward a future already impinging upon it, riving it asunder.[42] In this sense also in prophecy, even in the eschatological prophecy of apocalypse, the revelation of the other world, the eternal world, is generally, at the same time, a revelation of the essence or truth of *this* life.

The fusion and flexibility of the tenses in poetic narrative, with its potential for prophecy, is incipient already in Homer, where ordinary, external time is suspended and dilated by song in the endlessly open, magic moment of poetic creation: "This night is prodigiously long!" exults Alcinous on the night in which he hears the narrative of Odysseus's adventures (*Odyssey*, 11.373). The same point is made about Odysseus's narration of his odyssey to Penelope: the turning of night and the dawning of day are delayed by Athena, so that the temporality of narrative, with its suspending of outer,

42. A modern hermeneutic thinker who powerfully illuminates this aspect of history as prophecy is Walter Benjamin, especially in his notion of a messianic "Jetztzeit" (now-time), as expounded in "Geschichtsphilosophische Thesen," in *Illuminationen: Ausgewählte Schriften* I, ed. Siegfried Unseld (Frankfurt: Suhrkamp, 1977), 268–81. In "Der Erzähler" (1936), sec. v, Benjamin further emphasizes as essential to epic storytelling the implication of its images for practical action in the present. Karl Barth, in *Kirkliche Dogmatik*, envisages very differently such a breaking-in of revelation as a totally other time—the time of God's self-revelation in salvation history, the only non-illusory basis for human action in time.

worldly time, might unfold free from external constraints (23.244–45). The narrative of the *Odyssey*, furthermore, pivots on a descent to the underworld, and this topos belongs thenceforth essentially to the prophetic enterprise in epic tradition. As exemplified again by Dante's journey to the Christian afterlife, it is from the other world, the eternal world, projected as transcending the universe of time, that our protagonists can gain an understanding of the true and final significance of their lives—revealed prophetically in the mirrors of past, present, and future.

So Homer, too, after all, demonstrates an awareness of how time can be contracted or dilated—and is in any case shaped—by the art of narrative. But Virgil takes this germ of insight to another level of vision in his full-scale reconstruction of Roman history in prophetic perspective, inventing a new narrative art replete with allegorical types and their fulfillment. In developing and exploiting this power of narrative to disclose history and to make it interact with the future through the present of free action and interpretation, Virgil first fully discovers the constitution of human and historical time by prophetic *poiesis*. The poetic construction of a whole narrative discloses possible purposes and trajectories for history. Such narratives are instrumental to the realization of specific projects by historical peoples.

Time, as it is humanly experienced, is to this extent poetically produced. Virgil thus becomes a pioneer of prophetic poetry as an overarching structure of Western cultural tradition laying claim to an all-embracing vision of truth. Homer, too, is a seer, and all things are present to him through the assistance of the Muses. Of course, what he sees is not so much a significant structure of history as a visionary present. Nevertheless, he, too, has his vision of the other world, eternity, particularly in seeing the world of the gods, as well as that of the dead represented in *Odyssey* book 11 (and again in book 24). Time, for the first time, is grasped and can be spoken of as a whole, particularly by the dead or by the gods. In this respect, even Homer's poem has a prophetic dimension. Still, it remains fully in the present, which is what the dead lack, whereas Virgil's historical vision sees the future as mirrored in the past and as to be actualized in the crisis of the present.

Virgil's is a vision of truth for all time—yet just as much a disclosure of truth as inextricably rooted in time. For this truth is itself radically temporal: it happens only in the disclosure of future and past as transpiring in the present of action that decides fate freely. Moreover, as poetic disclosure, it is truth as what is said: literally "fatum."[43] Such saying is poetry and at the same time prophecy. It is where the two meet in revealing the truth of history and

---

43. Theodor Haecker, in the penultimate chapter of *Vergil, Vater des Abendlands*, expounds the far-reaching significance of this term. See also chapter 9, "Fate and the Gods," in Cyril Bailey, *Religion in Virgil* (Oxford: Clarendon, 1935).

history as truth—in the sense of disclosure.[44] This truth is for the present, in which we act and interpret our past in order to reappropriate and actualize it, so as to open up the horizon of our future.

The future is a vision: it can be grasped in the form of prophecy, but its ideals become true and real only through the resoluteness of those who act in the present and carry out the transition from past to future. Aeneas's example is one of carrying the past on his shoulders, in the shape of his father Anchises, toward a future that he takes up depicted on the shield from Vulcan's forge in the images of Roman history, beginning from his son Ascanius and proceeding down the generations of his descendents. These images center on Augustus Caesar, who himself first and foremost needs to strive toward achieving the future peace that the *Aeneid* as a whole heralds.

Criticism of Virgil has noticed the astonishingly original conception of time underlying Virgil's epic. Otis, for example, comments, "It is his ultimate identification of himself with the future that constitutes the psychological meaning of his resurrection" (*Virgil: A Study in Civilized Poetry*, 290). Aeneas struggles toward understanding the human condition through an understanding of its history, and his resulting actions are crucial for enabling the past and its meaning to react on the future, and vice versa. Virgil, by this means, recuperates from the past the Golden Age in order that it may reach into and determine the future, just as that future vision reaches back to shape the present and the past—revealing them in a perspective that transcends the limitations of linear time.

The revelation Aeneas receives from the dead empowers him finally to be resolute in embracing his mission. As such, he serves as a role model for Caesar Augustus. For resoluteness anticipates the future and makes it possible to realize the possibilities of the past, including those of the Age of Gold. Resoluteness is what transforms Fate into Freedom. Resoluteness in the present reaches out and shapes the future, bringing into being the possibilities that have been revealed in the past, possibilities which are grasped as having led up to this resoluteness into which they are gathered and in which they are finally fully activated.[45] It is Virgil's own resolute interpretation of the history

44. This notion of truth as dis-closure or bringing out of hiding, "*a-letheia*," according to its classical root, is crucial to phenomenological philosophy, particularly as expounded by Martin Heidegger, "Vom Wesen der Wahrheit" (1930), in *Gesamtausgabe I. Abteilung: Veröffentlichte Schriften 1914–70*, vol. 9, *Wegmarken* (Frankfurt: Klostermann, 1977), trans. as "On the Essence of Truth" in *Basic Writings*, ed. David Krell (New York: Harper and Row, 1977).

45. The idea of "anticipatory resoluteness" ("vorläufige Entschlossenheit") is developed philosophically by Martin Heidegger, *Sein und Zeit* (Tübingen: Max Niemeyer, 1986; originally 1927), sec. 61, trans. J. Macquarie and E. Robinson as *Being and Time* (New York: Harper and Row, 1962).

of Rome that enables him to project its meaning into the future envisioned as a universal reign of peace.

This historical perspective articulates a view of time as a human making, an ordering into universal significance and empire, a *poiesis*. What is the history Virgil composes, if not his projection of an ideal future? The reign of Saturn in Arcadia in Greece is maybe a myth that never really took place. Nevertheless, it prefigures the future age of peace that Virgil ardently desired to be inaugurated by Augustus. In this vein, toward the end of the epic, Aeneas enjoins his son Ascanius to recollect the past as a model for action looking toward the future:

> "Learn fortitude and toil from me, my son,
> Ache of true toil. Good fortune learn from others.
> My sword arm now will be your shield in battle
> And introduce you to the boons of war.
> When, before long, you come to man's estate,
> Be sure that you recall this. Harking back
> For models in your family, let your father,
> Aeneas, and uncle, Hector, stir your heart."
> (12.595–602)

All his personal virtues and resoluteness, together with those of his race, find their lasting value in being re-actualized by future generations.

This valedictory address illustrates how prophecy, as a call for action in the present, opens a dimension of freedom toward the future. It is not the declaration of an inevitable fate that operates externally to, and in spite of, human will and effort. So far from belonging to a deterministic outlook, in which the future is already present as decided and closed by fate, prophecy is what first opens the way for a human freedom that forms the future and reforms the past, refusing to be confined to a time that can ever be *merely* present. Prophetic temporality in this way reaches backward and forward, actually changing past and future through modifying the fundamental coordinates by which history can meaningfully happen—and have taken place. Past, present, and future communicate freely and openly, impinging upon and revising one another in this uncanny temporal dimension of prophecy, where time is reversible. This temporality exceeds objective analysis and calculated control. It *must* do so because it is inextricably connected with and open to human freedom. This connection of prophecy with freedom has been realized convincingly—and apparently without classical precedents—by Virgil in his epic.

The prophetic revelation centered in book 6 and engendering in Aeneas the resoluteness that enables the future to react upon the past and present, making them instrumental to his fulfilling his final destiny, must pass through the crucible of the present and through the personal commitment of the protagonist. Indeed, the attainment of the prophetic perspective takes place through a personal appropriation that actually exacts a disappropriation of the self. In order to realize his prophetically revealed mission, Aeneas must renounce his own intensely felt personal attachments—starting with the loss of his wife, Creusa, before his departure for Italy. This creates a tension that threatens to upset the poem's official imperial program and expose it as hollow propaganda. The narrative of famous exploits that are instrumental to building a glorious empire can suddenly appear in a sinister light, disfigured to a history of senseless sacrifice that shows through from just below its surface.

The ambiguity of everything revealed about the future belongs to the openness of what is not yet achieved fact but rather a destiny *to be* achieved: its fulfillment is subject to contingency, to all the possible peripities of history—the many ways in which it may still go awry, however certain the rightness of the final goal may be. Virgil, especially in his personal voice of frustration and regret, which insinuates itself whiningly from underneath the official Roman voice of public triumph and success, lets us feel all the burden of this ambiguity.

Nevertheless, the future can be anticipatively grasped as a vision in the form of prophecy, and to the extent that this vision can effectively motivate action, everything in the past, present, or future can really change by being subject to the significances that prophecy projects. Prophecy becomes true and real only through the resoluteness of those who act in the present, that is, in the transition from past to future. Aeneas's example, as we have seen, is one of carrying the past on his shoulders, symbolically in the form of his father, and bearing it toward a future that he also takes up symbolically in the images on the shield from Vulcan's smithy depicting his descendents and the glories that are in store for Rome. The present is the going-over from past to future, and on it falls the burden both for shouldering the past—figuratively one's father, who is also one's moral guide to future prospects—and for forging the future, one's posterity, emblematically chased on the shield. On the shoulder of the present rest "all the destined acts / And fame of his descendents" (8.991–92), for only acts in the present can make possible the future that will in fact turn out to have been not just an illusory figment.

Of course, the present in turn is inhabited by past and future intrinsically and cannot be isolated from them. So the point here is not to privilege the present over the other tenses, but to call attention to their inextricable plaiting together in mutual dependence of precedent, project, and event. It is from this point of intersection that all three time dimensions are leveraged. And it is from precisely this point of intersection and interaction that prophetic poetry such as that of the *Aeneid* proceeds and sets about its work of revelation.

The historical destiny revealed in the poem is an interpretation of history and, as such, a "making" or *poiesis*. This very act or event of interpretation transcends all predetermination of facts by erecting the overarching structures of significance that enable facts first to come to light as significant.[46] Virgil's poetic-prophetic vision gives a general form of meaning to the whole of history placed in a cosmic context: every particular fact comes to light in its supposedly true and final meaning within this eschatological framework. Whatever can meaningfully happen is circumscribed poetically by this projection of destiny. Poetry makes possible the future that can be meaningfully experienced, and in this sense poetry is prophetic.

Numerous prophecies operate as particular instances within the poem, but latent in its very narrative structure is a stronger claim concerning the form of poetry, at least poetry of the order of Virgil's epic, as being per se prophetic. Such poetry's shaping in language of possibilities of existence and of world is the enabling condition of any future that we are going to be able meaningfully to live. Virgil's original poetic technique brings into the open this prophetic character and capability intrinsic to poetry. It highlights especially the way poetic narrative gives a dynamic order of temporality to events. This ordering enables a vision of time as revelation and as unfolding a transcendent meaning—that is, a significance that transcends all actual events. Indeed, Virgil's poem creates such an order of significance in which the future can meaningfully happen as the fulfillment of a destiny prefigured by a mythic-heroic past.

To this extent, history is prophecy, and the past is the future, for the order of significance that we project upon the one is structured by what we are actually bringing about in the present with reference to the other. Virgil's poem, of course, announces a prophecy of the future: it features an ideal world government and postulates that the purpose of history and humanity is to achieve a universal order of peace—the *pax Romana*. At the same time, Virgil's poem foresees how fragile and costly that order is and how endemic the forces of fury are to the human heart. The potential of human nature and therefore the design of things to come are revealed in history as interpreted by the *vates*. Equally in the case of the Hebrew *nabhi*, prophecy, as interpretation of the essential meaning of history from the viewpoint of God, reveals the goal to which events should be made to conform via the active participation of free human beings. To be a holy people unto the Lord, for example, in Deuteronomy, is no mere sterile fact but a pregnant meaning to be realized ever anew in community life. The prophet bases his interpretation of history and the present on a transcendent view into the future, but conversely he prescribes the necessary means of living and realizing that future in and for present life and action.

46. Heidegger's essay on poetry as the setting-to-work of truth in the work of art provides a philosophically penetrating analysis of this dynamic. See *Der Ursprung des Kunstwerkes* (Stuttgart: Reclam, 1960; originally in *Holzwege*, 1936), trans. A. Hofstadter as "The Origin of the Work of Art" in *Poetry, Language, Thought* (New York: Harper and Row, 1971).

In reality, all time and history are always (eternally) present and in process of being decided in every moment. Was the past a catastrophe foreshadowing doom, or rather, even with all its downsides, a springboard toward a brighter future? Is the future futile and foreclosed, as pessimists perennially argue, or does it beckon with promise of inconceivably greater realizations? Both possibilities remain perpetually open, and we decide always again now *what* past and *which* future are going to turn out to be real and true for us. We live both of these contradictory destinies simultaneously and successively, following the swings of mood between despair and the taking of heart that characterize historical epochs no less than individuals in their alternating embrace of one or the other of these mind-sets and its accompanying scenario. Our lives unfold forever oscillating and suspended between these poles.

VI. War and Tragedy and the Fate of the Spoken: *Aeneid*, Books 7, 9–12

The *Aeneid* has long been appreciated for its outstanding qualities as a prophetic poem. Virgil was canonized by Dante as his great pagan precursor in the transmission of divine revelation by means of epic poetry. The locus classicus of this extraordinary rhetorical invention is the descent to the underworld, which climaxes in the prophetic preview (in fact, a review) of Roman history in the form of a revelation of Aeneas's future destiny: Aeneas sees in an ecstatic vision a lineage of sacred Roman rulers running from himself down to Augustus Caesar. This inspired vision comes at the center of the epic, at the end of book 6. The remaining books, 7–12, which are occupied by the war in Latium, have traditionally received much less attention, particularly with regard to this issue of the possibility of prophetic revelation in poetry. Yet the problematic is central to the poem as a whole and demands to be followed all the way through to the end of the work.

Indeed, Virgil uses the word *vates* or "prophet" of himself *first* in the invocation to the Muse at the beginning of the second half of the poem: "tu vatem, tu, diva, mone. dicam horrida bella" ("You, goddess, prompt the prophet. I will tell of frightful wars," 7.41). Here, prophecy and revelation are profoundly transformed in their modalities, and our appreciation of the unity and complexity of the epic depends on our apprehending the permutations of the prophetic project across the entire expanse of the work. My purpose at present is to bring to light the quite different means of producing and conveying prophetic insight and the very different forms assumed by "revelation" in the second half of Virgil's epic poem.

The interpenetration of fate and freedom, which is the upshot of the Virgilian concept of prophecy as we have discovered it so far, is written into the narrative and made practically explicit by the Council in Heaven at the beginning of book 10:

> "The effort each man makes
> Will bring him luck or trouble. To them all
> King Jupiter is the same king. And the Fates
> Will find their way [*fata viam invenient*]."
> (10.154–57)

What can be represented by being spoken, even before it comes into being, is literally and etymologically a "fate." It gives a definite significance to events, which per se are indefinable in their fluidity. "What is spoken"—"fatum"—is the enabling condition of significant intention, and, to this extent, it is equally the condition of free, consciously chosen action. Without language, there can be no free, rational action but only a concatenation of material causes. Virgil's imagination of Fate mythically formulates the presupposition of a secular understanding of history in which it is recognized as being merely a discursive construction. He does so, however, without renouncing the dimension of divine revelation, no matter how profoundly this dimension is transformed by secularization.

Throughout the war scenes, Virgil focuses especially on the freedom of speech as an instrument for conscious decision and rational reflection. But speech is also, paradoxically, a means of "fatalistic" determination that gives precedence to irrational powers. They can be found sedimented and crystallized in words themselves. Indeed rational, human freedom persistently seems to be undermined and destroyed from within by the irrational, angry passions that storm in the human breast and blow the best intentions off course by invading and distorting reasoning itself. The ambiguity of human action—as rational and as determined by passion—is directly reflected in discourse as an artificial and controlled construction of language and at the same time a manifestation of power and even of unconscious force. This is evident most immediately in the power of names.

Virgil's proper names are very often, if not always, charged with significance and laden with the fate of the individuals they name. The proper name is itself the expression of the essence or nature of the individual and thereby the key and index to all that happens to them. We saw how often this was so in Homer, and Virgil develops the technique in both implicit and explicit etymological glosses.[47] "Iulus," added as "cognomen" or nickname to Aeneas's

47. James O'Hara, *True Names: Vergil and the Alexandrian Tradition of Etymological Wordplay* (Ann Arbor: University of Michigan Press, 1996) inventories and analyzes Virgil's use of etymologies. Virgil's adaptation of this "Alexandrian," scholarly technique in poetic composition is pursued also by Nicholas Horsfall, *Virgilio: L'epopea in alambicco* (Naples: Liguori, 1991) and by Michael Paschalis, *Virgil's Aeneid: Semantic Relations and Proper Names* (Oxford: Clarendon, 1997) in one particularly rich vein of Virgilian research. On Homer, see Steve Reece, *Homer's Winged Words: The Evolution of Early Greek Epic Diction in the Light of Oral Theory* (Leiden: Brill, 2009).

son Ascanius, is expressly a reminder of "Ilium" (1.361–62; Latin, 267–68) and therewith inevitably also of Troy's sinister fate. Generally, the etymological histories of words contain roots and residues that are not easily governed by their rational concepts or definitions. There is thus a dark side to the name buried in its history, a side that its etymology still dimly remembers and reflects. This etymological memory harbors half-forgotten, obscure meaning that can threaten to overwhelm or subvert the consciously intended surface meaning of words.

It is Virgil's prophetic-historical vision and method of composition that provides the infrastructure for the extraordinary layering of meaning that distinguishes this peculiarly elegiac epic in which almost every name becomes an epitaph. Programmatic examples are the cape named for Palinurus (6.512 [Latin, 377]; see also 6.327 [235]) and the town named for "nurse Caieta" (7.1–5). Typically memorializing sacrificial victims, such names serve as monuments and indeed as altars erected to an overarching Cause or Purpose that supposedly justifies the sacrifices exacted. As such, names are instruments of rationalization. On the other hand, the pact at the end, which preserves the historical language of the indigenous people (12.1131–36 [834–37]), highlights a stratum of meaning that all the discipline of empire erected to face the violence of war cannot erase or regulate. It grows from the soil and is autochthonous. Even though Virgil's whole epic gives a global meaning to history and forges a general system of all signs, such root meaning at the same time indirectly acknowledges and signals a counter-meaning manifest as the tug from beneath it of what this system cannot subsume, of what underlies and even potentially undermines it.

Aeneas's own name can be derived from the Greek verb *aineo* (αἰνέω), meaning "I consent," as well as "I praise or extol God," and indeed Aeneas becomes the epic's hero only by learning to consent to fate and renounce his own will and life. Language, Virgil is well aware, is a domestication of reality and even its doing to death. Partly the elegiac tone of the whole epic derives from the fact that as a linguistic work it cannot but deal with the dead. The awesome discipline and order of epic and empire alike must kill their subjects in order to keep them in place. At the very least, a regime of strict control is required, which Virgil then counterpoints with his personal, elegiac strain of complaint. Indeed, the imperial ideal that undergirds the epic at all levels is realized, first of all, as an empire of signs. Greene gives us some hints of this:

> *Empire* is the key idea—empire over the world, over nature and peoples, over language, and over the heart. The respective struggles for command over these various realms imitate and illustrate each other. In the end it is hard to say which *imperium* shows the strictest control—the government of Caesar Augustus, or the hexameters which celebrate it, or the terrible moral discipline which Caesar's ancestor is brought to obey. (*Descent from Heaven*, 85)

Revelation in Virgil comes within the framework of an ordered system—an "empire." Yet order and system, at the same time, tend to obliterate revelation, which rather bursts out through the eruptions of history that stand in contradiction to all artificially imposed orderings.[48] It is in this tension between system and history that truth, as this epic understands and conveys it, especially in its second half, is revealed. Language itself becomes revelatory, when opened to an etymological perspective on its own history, even though this may contradict its official, conceptual meaning. There is here a kind of counter-revelation at work, a revelation more material in nature, hidden in the roots of language itself and exposed indirectly through the language of poetry. An analogous structure of irony can be found in the work's narrative logic, which creates a kind of counterpoint to its overt, official revelation.

The *Aeneid* is based on a narrative logic that pivots on a grasp of the whole from the end-point as the condition for rational action: the reason for an act is the end at which it aims. This type of action is what is made possible for Aeneas through the prophetic revelation of the goal of history vouchsafed by Anchises to his son (book 6), and it is ratified in the ekphrastic revelation on the shield procured for Aeneas by his mother (book 8). However, we cannot but see how such rational action breaks down in the event of war, as well as of love. Raging, whether martial or erotic, is contrary to the rationality of the word. The breakdown of the word condemns us rather to irrationally enact our own utter destruction. And yet we have just considered how the word itself can also become a fatality that inhibits freedom. We must question more deeply the relation between freedom and fate in the sense of *fatum*, the spoken. How is freedom in history found—or rather founded—but perhaps also impeded, by the inescapable "fate" of the spoken?

The imagination—particularly in Virgil's imagery of passion—reveals the inextricable interpenetration of *pietas* and *furor* in the work of conquest and civilization. In Aeneas himself, as well as in Hercules and in other figures of his civilizing mission, the noble and rational purposes of universal order assert themselves and are eventually able to prevail only on the strength of intensely personal passion. The imaginative fabric of the poem thus knits together a subtext that is curiously at odds with its official theses and imperial propaganda. This is the revelation of imagination, and it is not capable of being controlled by any rigid or rational sort of ideology. In the end, the imagination compounds and mixes the rational and the passionate, the public and the private, and reveals an order of meaning that embraces both but

48. A theoretical framing of this issue could start from Walter Benjamin's conception of the Messianic as a rupture in history. See particularly his "Geschichtsphilosophische Thesen," in *Illuminationen: Ausgewählte Schriften*, trans. by Harry Zohn as "Theses on the Philosophy of History," in *Illuminations* (New York: Schocken, 1968).

escapes exhaustive explanation in either register and remains at least partially opaque.

In their main focus, books 7–12 move from the private to the public sphere, from the personal to the social. Featured is the struggle for *pietas* against *furor*. A fundamental problem with the "Iliadic" half of the *Aeneid* is that for Virgil war is not heroic, not as in Homer an opportunity to exercise and display human excellence or *arête* (ἀρετή). War is only an instrument of pacification, of *imposing* peace ("pacique imponere morem," 6.852). Aeneas is upstaged when it comes to fighting because his *pietas* is fundamentally opposed to war: war is seen as a terrible necessity that requires Aeneas, against his better nature, to lust for conquest and plunder.

The onset of war in book 7 indeed shows female passion breaking out again, after the episode of Dido (the favorite of Juno and a precursor of Cleopatra), in ways that endanger Aeneas's historical mission. The goddess Juno, who has obstructed this mission three times before, takes it upon herself to whip up fury in order to bring to naught the peace pact agreed upon by Latinus and Aeneas. She uses the queen, Amata, for this purpose and uses yet another female divinity, Allecto, as an instrument for arousing destructive passion in the breast of Amata. The scene is sinister and infernal, evoking the darkest powers of the psyche from the underworld of both myth and emotion:

> Without delay Allecto,
> Dripping venom deadly as the Gorgon's,
> Passed into Latium first and the high hall
> Of the Laurentine king. She took her place
> On the still threshold of the queen, Amata.
> Burning already at the Trojan's coming,
> The plans for Turnus' marriage broken off,
> Amata tossed and turned with womanly
> Anxiety and anger. Now the goddess
> Plucked one of the snakes, her gloomy tresses,
> And tossed it at the woman, sent it down
> Her bosom to her midriff and her heart,
> So that by this black reptile driven wild
> She might disrupt her whole house.
>
> (7.467–80)

The assault works on Amata like an infectious poison, setting the marrow of her bones on fire. The simile of a top depicts her passion spinning out of control. This is the first in a series of similes, including also the boiling cauldron (7.536–40) and a crescendo of waves (7.725–28), which convey the escalating violence that leads to civil war. The war is actually touched off by the slaying of Silvia's stag, a sentimentally pathetic scene. This hints at how war logically begins from the least rational and most vulnerable elements of society. From there, it works its way up to the king. Latinus, though he stood like a sea cliff (7.806), relinquishes the reins of state in a situation that lurches out of his control. The internal upheaval and sedition that overwhelm his authority are now expressed by natural imagery: "I am breached by fate, / Wrecked, swept away by storm" (7.816–17). This inverts the imagery of social strife used to depict the natural violence of the storm in book 1.201, suggesting how civilized order is but a delicate artifice in the face of the overwhelming destructive force of nature.

The last third of the epic (books 9–12), with its focus on fighting, is dominated to a considerable extent by Turnus. Book 9 features Turnus furious and raging, "as a wolf on the prowl," "beside himself." The Rutulian "flared up with helpless rage" and "he, himself enflamed, / Took up a blazing pine torch in his hand" (9.83–102), in the intent to burn Aeneas's ships, which, however, are miraculously metamorphosed into nymphs by the goddess Cybele. But Turnus does not understand this: he misinterprets it as an omen that Jove is helping him. His thoughtlessness becomes increasingly evident, as he commits strategic errors. For example, he misses his chance to defeat the Trojans, when he is in their camp and fails to open its gates to his own men because

> . . . high rage and mindless
> Lust for slaughter drove the passionate man
> Against his enemies.
>
> (9.1054–56)

There is, of course, also a more human side of war, with its costs and losses. Virgil focuses on this in book 9 through the story of Euryalus and Nisus. Here the friends (lovers) remain bonded unto death, as each one dies for the other. And this elicits Virgil's elegiac vein in the lament for youth that is doomed to be cut off like a beautiful and delicate flower that bows its head to the butchery of inclement weather (9.617–20). The aestheticization of violence and death is not new, yet Virgil gives it a new dimension of subjective pathos and, furthermore, opens major questions about the reader's relation to and enjoyment of the war narrative. In particular, he makes us look up toward the imperturbable gaze of the gods. The reader's involvement and yet also detachment from the fiction is reflected in the attitude of the gods, who share a similarly sovereign perspective from outside and above the mêlée.[49]

This episode, featuring also the pathetic keening of Euryalus's mother, occasions expressions of regret about the whole tragedy of history. The

49. Denis Feeney, "Epic Violence, Epic Order: Killings, Catalogues, and the Role of the Reader in *Aeneid* 10," in Perkell, ed., *Reading Vergil's Aeneid*, 178–94, suggests that the countercurrent provokes self-reflection on the reader's status as voyeur, commiserator, and so on, with omniscience.

human story constantly counterpoints the history of public events and their official meaning. Throughout Virgil's epic, a civilized code vies with a heroic code and its warlike values. Jupiter's decrees signal governance not by blind fury but by conscious, deliberate, rational virtue—Aeneas's *conscia virtus*. Turnus's rage and fury, on the other hand, betray him into acts of deception and even savagery. In Turnus, all passions—his erotic passion for Lavinia and his warrior passion alike—merge into a kind of indistinct, undiscriminating violence:

> Desire stung the young man as he gazed,
> Rapt, at the girl. He burned yet more for battle . . . .
> (12.99–100)

It is especially in his slaying of Pallas, son of Evander, that Turnus's utter barbarity and disregard of morality are revealed. In claiming his victim, he deliberately blasphemes against all filial piety:

> "I take Pallas,
> Pallas falls to me. I wish his father
> Stood here to watch."
> (10.613–15)

After achieving this perfidious deed, he boasts,

> "Arcadians, note well
> And take back to Evander what I say:
> In that state which his father merited
> I send back Pallas."
> (10.685–88)

The other side of this coin by which the heroic code in the figure of Turnus is devalued, however, is the symmetrical devaluation of the supposedly civilized virtue of Aeneas. Aeneas's own passionate involvement becomes the motivation for his valor in avenging the death of Pallas. When Aeneas sees Turnus triumphing over the slain young prince,

> Pallas, Evander, all
> Their history rose before Aeneas' eyes.
> (10.724)

It is at this point that Aeneas is personally stirred, cut to the quick, but the result is that he becomes a pitiless butcher himself. His killing is no longer routine and mechanical, performed out of obedience to a command, as before the death of Pallas, when the weapons themselves seem to do the killing: it becomes rather impassioned and excessive. The unmeasured retributive violence unleashed here in Aeneas himself seems to be without law or limit. Aeneas scornfully mocks the brothers Liger and Lucagus begging for pity as he slays them:

> And deaths like these all over the battlefield
> The Dardan captain brought about, in fury
> Wild as a torrent or a dark tornado.
>
> (10.846–48)

The fury and violence of nature are exactly what the civilizing mission of Aeneas, as symbol for Rome, has been defined against up to now, but here we see Aeneas completely overcome and contaminated by uncontrollable rage and by repugnantly "heroic" haughtiness.

The noble, civilizing mission of Rome is thus accomplished, right from these supposedly heroic beginnings, by means of horrifying war (*horrida bella*, 7.41; see also 6.86). The hypocrisy latent in civilized and indeed in human values surges insistently to the surface in the last segment of the poem detailing the ravages of war. Aeneas himself is by no means exempt from bloody passions. When he meets Lausus, "now in the Dardan captain / Anger boiled up higher" (10.1139–40), and Aeneas himself becomes the slayer of a noble son in the act of sacrificing himself for his father, Mezentius, who is shown to be stricken in turn by mortal grief and to go to his own death directly as a consequence. Aeneas, as son of Anchises, shows himself to be acutely sensitive to the contradiction:

> But seeing the look
> On the young man's face in death, a face so pale
> As to be awesome, then Anchises' son
> Groaned in profound pity. He held out
> His hand as filial piety, mirrored here,
> Wrung his own heart . . . .
>
> (10.1148–54)

The personal rage and impassioned fury to which even Aeneas yields appear thus to be bound up at their roots also with his human attachments of love and commiseration. This peculiar closeness of contradictory passions, their seemingly inextricable mix, makes for a certain continuity of motives from the most terribly destructive to the most tenderly fostering and preserving. From the death of Pallas onward, Aeneas is no longer a disinterested, detached commander: he is viscerally involved. His slayings become personally vindictive, expressive of his own animus. He denies the plea of Magus, who appeals to filial piety, and retorts by running the suppliant through:

"Turnus has already done away
With all such war-trade, Pallas being lost.
My father Anchises' ghost feels as I say,
And so does Iulus."

(10.745–50)

This display of the contradictory nature of human motivations at their source-springs becomes itself a revelation, one that literature is peculiarly apt to capture, for its concrete representations can embody ambiguities and make them humanly believable, whereas abstract statement would simply court impossibility and incoherence. The founding of order on fury, of empire on violence, of peace on pitilessness is disclosed unflinchingly. These brutal truths concerning the bases of social power, which reason cannot guide or account for, become a crucial part of the secularized revelation of the imagination that Virgil's epic pursues in connection with the unconscionable contradictions of war.

The unheroic atrocity of war becomes most evident and horrendous in book 11. Aeneas pathetically expresses a wish to avoid loss of life: in making a truce for the burial of the dead, he sardonically remarks that he would have wished to grant this peace to the living (11.153). Pallas's funeral at the beginning of book 11 is an occasion for dwelling on the tragedy of war and the nearly unbearable pain of loss of individual lives. Aeneas presses for peace, and Turnus's obstinacy in provoking war creates a clear polarity in which Aeneas seems to be in the right, although the imagery has suggested that their motivations can also converge and become practically indistinguishable. In book 12, the "two assailants" turn out to be both like fire and then like flood waters from mountain rivers (12.708ff.). In 12.972, they are "two bulls" charging each other with lowered heads and horns. Aeneas is also depicted as a hound pursuing Turnus as stag. Aeneas is burning with rage and terrible fury ("furiis accensus et ira / terribilis"), violent, passionate, fervid, and savagely raging (*acer, arduus, fervidus, saevus*).[50] This is exactly the sort of raging passion that is found also in Turnus—

In that one heart great shame boiled up, and madness
Mixed with grief, and love goaded by fury,
Courage inwardly known.

(12.904–6)

Generally the similarity between Aeneas and Turnus is stressed by the elemental and bestial behaviors into which they both are sucked by the vortex of passion and violence.

---

50. This terminology of war is studied in detail by K. W. Gransden, *Virgil's Iliad: An Essay on Epic Narrative* (Cambridge, Eng.: Cambridge University Press, 1984).

Is history a moral chaos and consequently *arête* or valor and heroism but misleading names for bestiality gone berserk? Or is there some way to bring the apparently mad course of history into conformity with a rational purpose and moral goal? To make it do so is the hard and huge task laid on Aeneas's shoulders from the beginning of the epic. It involves renunciation and self-sacrifice and even morality in a virtually Christian sense of dying to self. Such morality is far removed from the self-assertion of the strong or deviously clever that triumphs in Homeric heroes and even becomes instrumental to divine justice—notably at the end of the *Odyssey*.

Yet Aeneas himself proves prone, in the highest degree, to ceding to the sort of irrational, vengeful violence that his mission in principle aims to stem and stomp out once and for all:

> At this attack,
> A tide of battle-fury swept the Trojan,
> Overcome by Rutulian bad faith. . . .
> Many times, then into the mêlée
> He raced, most terrible to see, with Mars
> Behind him, rousing blind and savage slaughter,
> All restraints on wrath cast to the winds.
> (12.670–79)

The war is waged and, in effect, won by madness without morality even on the part of Aeneas. The poet himself seems shocked by Aeneas's utter lack of restraint and has to appeal to the gods for an explanation. The symmetry in slaughter between Turnus and Aeneas provokes an invocation to the gods that harks back to the question of theodicy raised in the prologue and placing the whole epic within a theological framework. We hear Virgil's own agonized questioning of providence and of the war that the divine Will seems inexorably to require:

> What god can help me tell so dread a story?
> Who could describe that carnage in a song—
> The captains driven over the plain and killed
> By Turnus or in turn by Troy's great hero.
> Was it thy pleasure, Jupiter, that peoples
> Afterward to live in lasting peace
> Should rend each other in so black a storm?
> (12.680–86)

Virgil has constantly emphasized the interpenetration of love and fury, good and evil, in his hero and in his opponents and even in the gods who function as counter-fates—namely, Juno, with her love of Carthage, and Allecto, with her demonic passion. Turnus's love of Lavinia and Amata's love of Turnus are further examples of the destructive potential of erotic love-passion to pervert peace and overturn order. Even more provocatively, "Jupiter himself is subject to the furor of the same eternal wound"[51]—the love-wound that drives him to rape women like Juturna. She denounces him for the immortality he gave her in exchange for her virginity (12.875–84), for she is condemned by it to suffer eternally for the loss due to her human attachment to her brother. Passion certainly has a vital place in human affairs, yet it must be tamed and civilized. Only then can personal feeling be in harmony with public purpose. Since this turns out to be always a costly struggle, tragedy is ineluctably inscribed into triumph. And all of this has an obvious bearing on Virgil's own war-torn times. The war intended to end all war had been waged by Octavian (later Augustus Caesar) in order to unify the Empire, but then, alas, this Empire was itself perhaps still primarily an engine of violence.

The end of the epic demonstrates conclusively the inevitable relapse into fury that dominates even Aeneas, the civilizing hero himself. The defeated Turnus, on the ground before his conqueror and spreading his hands, beseeches Aeneas to "go no further / Out of hatred" (12.1275–76). Aeneas is practically swayed to clemency, until by chance he sees something—Pallas's sword belt on Turnus—that arouses uncontrollable passions within him which cannot but be compared with Achilles's passion for his lost comrade Patroclos. And by this reference, the concluding scene harks back all the way to the beginnings of the martial epic tradition:

> For when the sight came home to him,
> Aeneas raged at the relic of his anguish
> Worn by this man as trophy. Blazing up
> And terrible in his anger . . .
> He sank his blade in fury in Turnus' chest.
> (12.1287–96)

This is a frightful stroke on which to end, and as Turnus's spirit slithers down to the underworld "with a groan for that indignity," the curtain falls on a very somber and disturbing scene, a tragedy indeed. The voice of protest and of personal pain beyond indemnity seems to have been accorded the last word.[52]

The contradictions of Aeneas's motivation in this last scene are patent: love for another man betrays him as protagonist into venting his own fury and thereby blemishing the war for universal peace with an intensely personal

---

51. See Eve Adler, *Vergil's Empire: Political Thought in the Aeneid* (Lanham, Md.: Rowman and Littlefield, 2003), 213.

52. See the influential development of this view by Putnam, *The Poetry of the Aeneid: Four Studies in Imaginative Design.*

and arbitrary act of senseless violence. This act inaugurates in a most ambiguous and unpropitious manner the Roman peace that is supposed to last forever.

This disconcerting revelation is what raises yet again the rankling question of divine malignancy that was posed at the outset of the poem in a prelude to the storm scene: "Can anger / Black as this prey on the minds of heaven?" (1.18–19; "Tantaene animis caelestibus irae?" 1.11). Jupiter is accused at the end of the epic by this question echoing in the query as to whether it could be his pleasure that eternal peace should be inaugurated by such a violent concussion ("tanton placuit concurrere motu, / Iuppiter, eterna gentis in pace futuras?" 12.503–4).

The reader, too, is split between comprehension of the whole, with the providential justification of war from the height of the divine vantage point ("aethere summo," 1.223 = 12.853), and passionate revulsion from the way of the world as it is revealed in this universal travesty.[53] For even Jupiter, the supreme Judge, is susceptible of savagery: his "cruel" will demands the death of Camilla ("et saeva Iouis sic numina poscunt," 11.901). And he is able now to recognize Juno as his sister and as the daughter of Saturn on account of the vast waves of anger in his own breast ("irarum tantos voluis sub pectore fluctus," 12.831).[54]

The rhetorical question of theodicy defies an answer. But it is not as if we were left simply clueless in the dark. There is, after all, a revelation: it is history. We observed in the *Odyssey* a strong sense of original unity between the acts of gods and mortals. At a presumably more advanced stage of reflection, Virgil is discovering a similar coincidence between the divine and the human in the rational structure of significance that confers meaning on history. Material (or natural) causes and rational (or discursive) causes meet in history. Each encounters there its limit and spills over into the other. Virgil is deeply interested in how this ambiguity enfolds a potential for regression.

Virgil, of course, repeats Homer's frequent questioning of the ambiguity of our action in his asking, for example, "whether a god stirred him, or his own spirit," concerning Telemachos's decision to go to Pylos (*Odyssey* 4.712–13). Nisus puts just such a question to Euryalus:

> "This urge to action, do the gods instill it,
> Or is each man's desire a god to him . . . ?"
> (9.252–54)

---

53. See Denis Feeney, "Epic Violence, Epic Order: Killings, Catalogues, and the Role of the Reader in *Aeneid* 10," in *Reading Vergil's Aeneid*, as well as *The Gods in Epic*, 155ff.

54. The dark, irrational forces in charge of Virgil's universe are compellingly expounded by W. R. Johnson, *Darkness Visible: A Study of Vergil's Aeneid* (Berkeley: University of California Press, 1976).

> "*Dine hunc ardorem mentibus addunt,*
> *Euryale, an sua cuique deus fit dira cupido?*"
> (9.184–84)

However, in this formulation by Virgil's character, the use of "god" as metaphor for human emotion or impulse becomes deliberate and conscious. There is no longer a mysterious, implicit continuity between the human and the divine so much as a simple resort to expressive hyperbole. In any case, it is not in the particular acts so much as in the overall design of the narrative of history that the question of divine guidance is most relevant for Virgil.

Virgil's epic thus constitutes another step toward the secularization of divine revelation in epic poetry. What was represented by the ambiguous significance of things as portrayed in poetic language by Homer becomes a split into two worlds in Virgil, the human and the divine, of which one is real and the other symbolic. Divine revelation by the invocation of the Muses, a convention still honored at the outset of this poem and in certain of its key transitions (1.13–19; 7.47–59; 9.223–26; 12.680ff.), is consciously and completely transferred to the faculties of poetic language and imagination.

History's purpose can be projected by the construction of narrative, and this invention is shown by Virgil to have great prophetic force. Poetic language becomes "fatum," the "spoken" that scripts future possibilities. Even the inherent ambiguity of poetic language becomes part of its capability of becoming revelation to humans, for they have to choose on their own responsibility the future that they will work to realize.

Revelation of a providential purpose, as if heaven-sent, for human history remains intact in the poem. This revelation is disclosed as deeply implicated in Virgil's poetic construction of narrative in a way that enables the tenses to interpenetrate with one another. Historical vision becomes theological revelation for Virgil, but history makes this revelation equivocal and even contradictory. The ambiguities of poetic language and representation express the contradictoriness that Virgil finds deeply seated in the human heart. This is thus a "revelation" that is immanent to human experience and therefore fraught with all the enigmatic ambivalence of everything human. Revelation involves an orientation toward the future in the present of action which repeats the past. But what is revealed, then, is no longer abstract and pure: it is rather imbued with all the compressed tension of the present in which decisions are made on conflicting impulses and in constraining circumstances. Virgil's vision is not just a revelation of a utopian ideal but also an expression of present passion in all its murky viscosity. And only this explosive emotion can motivate (or undermine) ideals.

Virgil has become painfully aware that revelation of a divine purpose in history is a product of the construction of narrative—and so of the art of poetic interpretation. This makes prophecy not "true" so much as "fictive," which he signals by having Sibyl and Aeneas pass through the gate of ivory, the gate of false prophecies, at the conclusion of the prophetic revelations in book 6.[55]

He is no less aware of how the visions of poetry as prophecy can motivate action and inspire valor, of how they become effective in shaping historical reality. Yet they do so only immanently, on the basis of human power and emotion, not by some divine force from above or outside. This entails the insight that prophecy and the history it reveals are fraught with all the ambiguity and contradictoriness of the human heart itself.

Virgil, in prophesying, looks deep into the heart of passion for civilization and its ideals and discovers this passion in its virtual identity, or at least its tight entanglement, with destructive desire for bloody vengeance and death-directed *eros*. Revelation by the imagination is rooted in this ambiguous human reality, and Virgil's evocations of glory, accordingly, are intoned elegiacally and with painful cognizance of their ultimate impotence and vanity vis-à-vis death. Even while revealing a divine purpose for history that transcends the foul human struggles out of which Roman glory arises, building upward, Virgil knows that his prophetic revelation interprets poetically a human tragedy that inexorably ends in death and destruction. Revelation is imagination, splendid and alluring, but ultimately also a phantasmatic construction—out of the gate of ivory.

At some level, precisely the construction of a vision of the whole as justifying acts of conquest and violence is what Virgil is putting into question. That kind of calculated violence, where one has a total explanation in terms of the end that justifies the means, is what creates the tragic undertow that threatens finally to swamp the poem's official ideology. The theological framework becomes a political ideology and an instrument of violence precisely when it makes this claim to sufficiency and wholeness of vision.

Belying all pretenses to total justification by panoptic vision and rational control, passionate acts in defense of others, though violent, may be morally necessary: at any rate, they are humanly inescapable. In the end, this "free" submission to blind necessity is where the authentically theological must be found—it occurs only in the transcendence and negation of all human calculations and justifications. *Because* of its ambiguity and uncertainty the *Aeneid does*, after all, open a space of theological revelation—it opens upon the Unknown. The attempt to unify history in the imagination and to bring it into one order is also necessary. But in the end, the *Aeneid* deplores the

55. There are alternative readings, according to which instead of questioning the authenticity of the vision, Aeneas's exit through the ivory gate would signal simply that he is not a true resident of the underworld, as proposed by Nicholas Reed, "The Gates of Sleep in *Aeneid* 6," *Classical Quarterly*, new series, vol. 23, no. 2 (1973): 311–15, or that the *poem*'s underworld is in any case a product of Virgil's artistry. These ideas are not incompatible with my emphasis on the revelatory capabilities of fiction.

tragedy of war and discloses a situation in which humans are called upon to act in faith, in the face of mystery, with no sure legitimation for their acts.

From the beginning, we have noted that Virgil not only celebrates events in an official, public voice, but also laments over them in an unreconciled personal voice of protest. Prophecy becomes an organ for personal expression, and what the personal voice expresses is sorrow over the tragedy of human history. This has long been felt by readers of the poem, memorably by Tennyson in his stirring salute to "Roman Virgil," "Thou majestic in thy sadness / At the doubtful doom of humankind."[56] The poet's personal involvement, in the form of recurrent editorial commentaries, personalizes prophecy and makes it a moral rather than just a metaphysical revelation of another world. Such prophecy is read from the heart as much as from the heavens:

> The minds of men are ignorant of fate
> And of their future lot, unskilled to keep
> Due measure when some triumph sets them high.
> (10.701–3)

This suggests that knowing the future is a moral knowledge of human fate that would constitute a defense against ruinous *hubris*. Divine prophecy merges with human wisdom in this most Virgilian type of insight.

In the economy of Virgil's writing, the revelations of divine purpose and providence are made for the sake of revealing the human passions that spring up as a result around them and give them their meaning and motivation. The prophecies do not trump human agency or eclipse it by jumping to a higher level at which human aspirations and feelings become irrelevant or at least secondary in importance. Rome's historical mission is divinely revealed, but what divine revelation really discloses to Virgil is the ultimacy of the meaning of his own human endeavors as felt deeply in the heart and as prescinded from all abstract ideals. This is the meaning, at one level, of Jupiter's declaration that "the effort each man makes / Will bring him luck or trouble" (10.154–55). The meaning of prophecy as revealing a transcendent order of history registers in its purely human implications. That is why prophecy must speak into the present of action; only there can it have its meaningfulness. The devastating action of the second part of the epic is indeed the realization of prophecy in the secularizing historical mode that remains in the end as the peculiar mark of originality of the second half of the *Aeneid*.

In order for this action-oriented emphasis of prophecy to be developed further, it will be necessary to open explicitly a dimension of transcendence from within individual consciousness, and this will be the revolutionary work

56. Alfred Lord Tennyson, "To Virgil: Written at the Request of the Mantuans for the Nineteenth Centenary of Virgil's Death," in *Works*, ed. H. M. McLuhan (London: Macmillan, 1891), 421.

of Saint Augustine's "confessions." Virgil has discovered through prophecy a private or a personal dimension of freedom basically as opposition to (or, equivocally, identification with) a public destiny or fate. Augustine then pries wide open this infinite freedom intrinsic to individual self-consciousness as a locus of prophetic revelation.

Chapter 4

✦

Augustine's Discovery of Reading as Revelation

I. The Act of Invocation and the Personalization of Prophecy (Prologue, *Confessions*, Book 1.i–v)

Augustine's *Confessions*, often touted as the premier work of autobiography in Western literature, does not begin with his birth in 354 A.D., and it does not simply narrate the events of his life. The work opens, instead, with a prayer and is framed in its entirety as a conversation with God. It is enunciated in the first person and in the present tense as discourse addressed directly to a "Thou": this addressee becomes identifiable as God, the God of the Bible and specifically of the Christian faith, to which (for countless later readers) *Saint* Augustine famously converted. By this device, the whole work is spoken out of a presumed presence of or to God in an act of prayerful self-consciousness. God is discovered as immanent within the self-reflection of an individual self: he is made consciously present by the speech act of invocation or direct address. Augustine thereby constitutes the element of subjectivity—and of the word in which subjective self-consciousness is realized—as theological revelation.

By its own account, the narrating consciousness owes everything, even its very being, to God: "You are already in me, since otherwise I would not be." This form of consciousness reaching out in the act of address to God understands itself to be dependent on and already inhabited by God. Paradoxically, God is already present in consciousness and in its very invocation imploring him to vouchsafe his divine Presence: "And if You are already in me, since otherwise I would not be, why do I cry unto You to enter me?" ("quid peto, ut venias in me, qui non essem, nisi esses in me?" 1.i).[1]

What is revealed by this word of address reflecting on itself in relation to God is purportedly the transcendent ground of consciousness and, consequently, also of all that comes within the range of consciousness.

1. Augustine's Latin text is quoted from *Confessions*, ed. James J. O'Donnell (Oxford: Clarendon, 1992), vol. 1: *Introduction and Text*. English translation by F. J. Sheed, *Confessions* (Indianapolis, Ind.: Hackett, 1942), slightly modified.

Consciousness is itself the proximate ground of everything of which it is conscious. The entire universe is thereby gathered together as *for consciousness* and as the object of its discourse.[2] Yet, at the same time, Augustine's consciousness constitutes itself as grounded by God, the ground of consciousness itself and of every other being as well. The very discourse in which this consciousness self-reflectively articulates itself is directed to God as its necessary condition.

The doctrine that God is the Creator and Ground of all things is, of course, basic to Christianity and is therefore automatically accepted by Augustine. But to discover this Ground in and through his own act of subjective reflection is a revolution wrought by Augustine in his way of thinking through the relation of beings, and particularly of human being, to the Ground of existence. Charles Taylor calls this "radical reflexivity" and remarks: "Augustine shifts the focus from the field of objects known to the activity itself of knowing; God is to be found here," that is, "in the intimacy of self-presence" more than in the exterior world.[3] God, for ancient philosophy, is typically the ground of all that is, but for Augustine "God is also and for us primarily the basic support and underlying principle of our knowing activity" (Taylor, *Sources of the Self*, 129). In "taking a stance of radical reflexivity or adopting the first-person standpoint" (130), Augustine effects a revolution that is decisive for modern thought: "It is hardly an exaggeration to say that it was Augustine who introduced the inwardness of radical reflexivity and bequeathed it to the Western tradition of thought" (131).[4]

What I wish to focus on is the incarnation in language and specifically in the word of address to divinity of this radically reflexive knowing turned toward itself and through itself toward its Ground in God. Such radical reflection is achieved in the *Confessions* as an irreducibly linguistic act and, at the same time, as inextricably theological: self-conscious reflection in speech addressed to God is discovered by Augustine to be theological revelation. This is a rather astonishing claim that I am attributing to Augustine, and it needs to be carefully examined.

The opening words of the *Confessions* place us in the midst of a dialogue with God, the one who is addressed from the very first utterance in words

2. These points are explored later in the analysis of mind and "Memory" in book 10 (see section V of this chapter).

3. Charles Taylor, *Sources of the Self: The Making of the Modern Identity* (Cambridge, Mass.: Harvard University Press, 1989), 134 and 130.

4. Taylor's views have been criticized by Richard Sorabji, *Self: Ancient and Modern Insights about Individuality, Life, and Death* (Oxford: Clarendon, 2006) for neglecting Plotinus's contribution. However, Augustine's originality as the inventor of a concept of "private inner space" or of an "inner self" is demonstrated in detail by Phillip Cary, *Augustine's Invention of the Inner Self: The Legacy of a Christian Platonist* (New York: Oxford University Press, 2000).

of prayer and praise: "Magnus es, domine, et laudabilis valde" ("Great art Thou, O Lord, and greatly to be praised"). The question of how this address and the presumed dialogical situation in which it is embedded are made possible asserts itself from the opening paragraph and, in fact, becomes the thematic thread that this discourse uses to sustain the dialogue and weave itself together textually. This discourse presupposes God's existence and presence to the purported conversation, while at the same time the reality of God as interlocutor is not given except in and through this discourse itself. There is a circle between Augustine's invocation of God and God's presence, so far as it is evidenced in and by this text. "For it would seem clear that no one can call upon Thee without knowing Thee . . . . Yet may it be that a man must implore Thee before he can know Thee?" (1.i).

God is not a physical presence sitting in front of Augustine. There is no empirically manifest being whatever to be identified with this express addressee. From a skeptical point of view, Augustine's words would seem to be spoken into a void, or to the speaker himself, or to the overhearing reader in the role essentially of an eavesdropper. In any of these cases, the intended addressee, God, would have no real presence outside the presence projected by Augustine's discourse itself.

Yet Augustine's way of addressing God personally and questioningly provides what he is seeking by his very asking: for he asks that he be given to converse with God, to invoke and so to know him. This self-validating conjuring of divinity by an apparently autistic linguistic act is tantamount to a discovery of God immanent within the self-reflexive faculty of self-consciousness in language. Such self-consciousness becomes the privileged locus of a theological revelation. However theologically skeptical it becomes, the modern age remains indissolubly indebted to Augustine for his discovery of self-consciousness as this immanent sphere of disclosure of reality together with its unifying ground. God is the focal point for Augustine's revolutionary invention of subjectivity as a unified field for disclosure of the entire world as a phenomenon of consciousness. This inchoate phenomenology of consciousness is worked out later in the meditations on Memory and Time in books 10 and 11, but its essential structure is set up from the very beginning by Augustine's mode of discourse itself—that of a self-reflecting subjective consciousness in dialogue with God as its ultimate Ground.[5]

5. Edmund Husserl's *Phenomenology of Inner Time Consciousness* (*Vorlesungen zur Phänomenologie des inneren Zeitbewußtseins*, 1928) acknowledges this debt of modern phenomenology to Augustine. Ludwig Wittgenstein's *Philosophical Investigations* (*Philosophische Untersuchungen*, 1953) likewise begins with quotations from Augustine's *Confessions*, even if in order to reject his theory of language acquisition. *Augustine and Philosophy*, ed. Phillip Cary, John Doody, and Kim Paffenroth (Lanham, Md.: Lexington, 2010) bears witness to this continuing influence.

Peter Brooks, drawing on the linguistics of Émile Benveniste, points out that a speaking *I* creates a situation that implicates a listening *you* and that these poles are reciprocal and can be reversed, so that "the expression of subjectivity takes place in the context of intersubjectivity."[6] Augustine's speaking *I* implicates a divine *You* and takes place in a context of intersubjectivity with a transcendent Subject. This would be mere projection, if the human pole were primary, but for Augustine the situation is just the reverse. Although his discourse projects its divine interlocutor, it also recognizes the divine interlocutor as the Source of everything, including Augustine's own being and very words, his own reflections and most intimate motivations. Rhetoric and ontology interpenetrate vertiginously to produce a discursive reality that cannot be adequately assessed except from the first-person point of view opened up uniquely by interior reflection that addresses itself in faith to God as its enabling Ground.

One way to describe Augustine's maneuver is to say that he adopts the fiction of a conversation with God that realizes itself not as a fiction but as the reality of a discourse of prayer: it is real within the language of faith that he proposes and actually performs.[7] Thus, by his own act alone, Augustine's dialogue with God becomes a discursive reality. He is, in fact, carrying on a conversation with God. That is the reality presupposed by this discourse, whether it has any reality outside the discourse or not.[8] It can be a reality also for others who read Augustine's *Confessions*, who enter into his discursive world and who can, at least in a suspension of disbelief, accept his postulate of faith in the authenticity of his language and in the reality of its object or addressee.

His discourse is thus itself the only manifest "embodiment" of the relationship with God that Augustine establishes through his invocation in this very

---

6. Peter Brooks, *Troubling Confessions: Speaking Guilt in Law and Literature* (Chicago: University of Chicago Press, 2000), 95.

7. M. B. Pranger, "The Unfathomability of Sincerity: On the Seriousness of Augustine's *Confessions*," in *Actas de Congresso International As Confissoes de santo Agostinho 1600 Anos Depois: Presenca e Actualidade* (Lisbon: Universidade Catolica Editora, 2001) explores Augustine's use of "prayer as a performative" to support "the author's efforts to reflect the depths and heights of addressing himself to God" (224).

8. In general, whether there can be access to a reality altogether outside discourse seems doubtful, as has been rediscovered in challenging ways by poststructuralist thinkers like Jacques Derrida, Michel Foucault, Jacques Lacan, and numerous literary theorists in their wake today. Jean-François Lyotard's *La Confession d'Augustin* (Paris: Galilée, 1998) is similarly oriented. For contemporary philosophical reactions to Augustine's *Confessions* as refracted especially through Derrida's "Circonfession" (1991), see *Augustine and Postmodernism: Confessions and Circumfession*, ed. John D. Caputo and Michael J. Scanlon (Bloomington: Indiana University Press, 2005).

opening passage and in the reiterations of such direct address throughout the *Confessions*. The language itself is what comes forward to vouch for the God who is not concretely or objectively present—except to the extent that concreteness and objectivity are redefined as themselves projections of language. This, indeed, is implicitly the case, since the linguistically invoked Presence is not presented as secondary or substitutive but rather as the most immediate manifestation of the very God who is the source and ground of the speaker himself—and so also of his discourse, as well as of every possible object of this discourse.

The very conversation in which God is presumed to be intimately present itself becomes the primary revelation of the Source of Augustine's own being. It is, moreover, an a priori experience of divinity—prior to any empirical attempts to question and verify the existence of God or the possibility of knowing him. The dialogical projection by which Augustine constructs his address to God is itself a reality not to be considered inferior in its ontological degree to empirical presence: the dialogue with God is experienced as a direct revelation of the enabling ground and condition of all reality. Augustine's discourse takes itself as such a revelation, to the extent that it claims to be communicating immediately with God.

This suggests, furthermore, why Anselm's formulation of his famous ontological argument in *Proslogion*, chapter 2, might have been prompted by his intensive reading of Augustine: Augustine's discovery of God's existence as necessary a priori is simply transposed by Anselm from a rhetorical to an explicitly ontological register.

The resolution of Augustine's opening paradox—essentially, that we cannot invoke God before we know him, but neither can we know him unless we first invoke him—comes, then, in the action he sustains of communicating with God in and through the speech enacted by his text. The paradox itself and the perplexity it engenders are offered up to God in prayer: "Grant me, O Lord, to know which is the soul's first movement toward Thee—to implore Thy aid or to utter its praise of Thee; and whether it must know Thee before it can implore Thee" ("Da mihi, Domine, scire et intellegere, utrum sit prius invocare te an laudare te et scire te prius sit an invocare te," 1.i). This dialogue (or, at least, dialogical address) actually fills in for the God who is not manifestly present—except as the one who is addressed. He is addressed as the one who necessarily sustains the conversation, just as he sustains Augustine's very being in the moment of speaking and in every moment. This, however, makes God a transcendental condition of the discourse rather than just a discrete, concrete presence and participant within it. Yet Augustine confounds, or at least challenges, exactly such a distinction by displacing the empirical, substantive reality of an individual as a presumably concrete presence and by implicitly redefining presence as a phenomenon appearing primarily in and through discourse and as consisting in a relation enacted by language.

Augustine thereby focuses attention on discourse as the locus of revelation by virtue of its performative powers. As realized by the speech act of invoking divinity, Augustine's discourse becomes the event of a greater Mind and comprehension breaking into finite human consciousness and speech. This all happens in the speech act itself as an act of consciousness and self-transcendence toward its source and Ground. Augustine's discourse is circular and self-validating, but the circle is not encompassed by him and his consciousness. He projects himself into a circle that surpasses him. This seems to be all only his own doing, and yet he negates himself and all his own doings in self-abandon to an action and event that exceeds him. His own act of speech is reinscribed within the Mind and consciousness of God—the eternal Word. He thereby realizes the dynamic of self-reflexivity of his discourse as a self-negation and transumption into a transcendent sphere, where action is no longer confined to finite agents.

The presence of God in the *Confessions* is, to this extent, essentially linguistic: God is there in and through being invoked as present. Augustine questions how this is possible, for it seems that God would have to be known in order to be invoked, but he also sees that in some sense it is necessary that God be invoked in order for him to be known. For he cannot be known by humans at all unless they first open themselves to him and seek him, asking that he give himself to be known. Hence the question, "Yet may it be that a man must implore Thee before he can know Thee?" (1.i) The search itself can be sustained only with the help of God, to whom Augustine must plead: "Let me seek Thee, Lord, by praying Thy aid, and let me utter my prayer believing in Thee: for Thou hast been preached to us" (1.i).

This last remark points to Scripture as the revelation of God's being that makes knowing and imploring or invoking him alike possible. It is because God has been preached ("praedicatus enim es nobis," 1.i) that Augustine knows how to seek to know him and invoke him. Indeed, God's part in the conversation throughout the *Confessions* is consistently adapted and even "ventriloquized" from Scripture, the Word of God. Accordingly, Augustine's personal questions blend into Scripture in the question, "But how shall they call upon him in whom they have not believed?" from Romans 10:14, and they are answered in Augustine's text by a quotation from Psalm 21:27: "they shall praise the Lord that seek Him." Here we might also hear echoes of the invitation "Seek, and ye shall find" in Matthew 7:7.

Augustine's discourse is thereby linked to and encompassed by the discourse of a tradition, a language that is already familiar and validated as the language of a community, a faith community. In this context, Augustine's discourse reaches out and links to the wider discourse of Scripture and tradition, through which it connects further to a transcendent God that comprehends him as a portion of the Creation (*aliqua portio creaturae tuae*, I.i). This is what supports Augustine's discourse even in its circularity. By inscribing itself into this larger discourse of Christian revelation, Augustine's *Confessions* becomes a relay of tradition—it stands or falls with this tradition and with the witness of this tradition to an experience of God in his self-revelation, in which Augustine also participates.

What Augustine adds to this tradition is an acute analysis of God's presence within self-conscious reflection as it is borne upon the stream of discourse. He discovers God as immanent within the self-reflexive capacity of self-consciousness realized in and through speech. For, in the word, the mind is present to itself: it is made present, at least momentarily, even as it escapes into absence, which already inhabits perhaps every presence. This self-presence is then projected onto the plane of the infinite Word and Mind of God.[9] And this projection understands itself to be possible only because God has first made it, like all things whatsoever, possible. It is possible only on the basis of the infinite transcendence of divinity, an infinite dimension that Augustine projects and thereby also internalizes. Only an infinitely conscious God can completely encompass Augustine's mind, so as to precede this mind's own most spontaneous motions and grant it its very own freedom.

This unlimited power and knowledge, which is the Mind of God, encompasses the whole universe and becomes active upon the inner world, the microcosm, of the human mind. Human consciousness is not complete and unified like God's; nevertheless, it is a reflection of God's consciousness. And through this relation, consciousness is itself a kind of whole that contains all that it fragmentarily surveys—including its own ground, namely, God. This shifts the locus of reality to another axis, one that will be fundamental to Descartes's remapping of the real, or being, onto the substrate of consciousness instead of material substance. Augustine's anticipating this transition from material, substance-based metaphysics to a metaphysics of consciousness positions him as a precursor of modern philosophy. And yet Augustine does not isolate this "I" as its own ground and foundation in the manner that will become characteristic of modern thought in the wake of the Cartesian *cogito*. Rather, the discourse to and about God, questioning whether and how it can reach or refer to him, understands itself as possible only within God and re-inscribes itself into God as the source of all that is. Ontological dependency makes the circle inescapable but also hardly confining or vicious: for all that is—all being, together with the very source of being—in a certain manner passes through this circle. Still, the presence of God is given within and not prior to the act of seeking and believing in God (even if it may be given *as* prior). And these acts are linguistically realized and guided.

Taken on its own terms, Augustine's discourse, as it propagates itself over the space of the thirteen books of the *Confessions*, reveals God as a party to

9. Augustine elaborates theoretically the mirroring of infinite in finite subjectivity especially in his treatise *De Trinitate*. See Johannes Brachtendorf, *Die Struktur des menschlichen Geistes nach Augustinus: Selbstreflexion und Erkenntnis Gottes in "De Trinitate"* (Hamburg: Felix Meiner, 2000).

the dialogue. Of course, this "revelation" is a conjectural projection, yet it is nonetheless real as a discursive experience, and it becomes the framework for organizing a comprehensive outlook embracing in its vision all beings—and even Being itself (*ipsum esse*) beyond them all as their ground. This vision is, by hypothesis, that of an infinite, transcendent consciousness, the one who is addressed and who sees and knows all. This, finally, is the perspective from which everything in the *Confessions* is revealed. Only this divine point of view, as projected by the prayerful address of the dialogue, unites and realizes the total vision on the basis of which Augustine's comprehensive phenomenology of all that can be perceived or conceived is elaborated in the concluding books of the work, and especially in book 10.

This unitary perspective of divine vision thus lays claim to opening a truly prophetic outlook on reality, and Augustine has found the resources for projecting it latent within his psychological powers of self-reflection and particularly in his discursive powers of address or apostrophe. Such apostrophe to God, what is in effect prayer, opens the way to "prophecy": indeed prophecy should perhaps always be understood as, at some level, spoken by a voice of prayer. This is to see prophecy from the perspective of its subjective ground, its intimate involvement with the psyche of the prophet.[10]

Prophecy, as interpretation of history and existence from the point of view of God, offers a synoptic vision rendering it possible to see things whole, which means also truly. This inspired, holistic type of vision is typical also of epic narratives inspired by the Muses, but as such it remains at the level of a *muthos*. It may still pass through the ivory gate of false dreams or visions. However, a more interior probe into the sources of prophecy and a more philosophically sophisticated claim for true revelation in literature are lodged in Augustine's self-reflective discourse cast into the mode of prayer. Of course, these are not Augustine's express claims but rather the far-reaching implications of his unprecedented speculative employment of certain literary forms.

The total vision of the divine Mind, in which all exists as a whole, cannot be comprehended by any human mind or in human language. And yet human mind and language can address themselves to the higher, infinite instance of Mind and Word that, as divine, *are* capable of comprehending all that is.

---

10. The subjective ground of prophecy as a state of consciousness that is nevertheless connected with the Transcendent is explored by Abraham Heschel, *Die Prophetie* (Krakow: Plska Kademja Umeijetnosci, 1936). Heschel treats Old Testament prophecy as an act that transcends the prophet's own psyche serving as receptor for inspiration from a divine source. In a vocabulary of phenomenological philosophy that is most appropriate for Augustine, he writes that "the prophet experiences the act of prophecy as an event transcending consciousness" ("Der Prophet erlebt den Akt als bewußtseinstranszendentes Ereignis," 55). In English, see Heschel's *Prophetic Inspiration after the Prophets: Maimonides and Other Medieval Authorities*, ed. Morris M. Faierstein (Hoboken, N.J.: Ktav, 1996).

Dialogically, then, this hypothesis of total vision is projected from the finite mind's discourse. The whole is not an actual object of vision but is nevertheless present in and to finite consciousness, in so far as this consciousness relates itself to one who exceeds its comprehension and surpasses all human possibilities. This consciousness remains bound to a point of view based on human resources of word and reflection—but as reflected beyond themselves into God as an unconditioned and infinite consciousness that exceeds all such limitations.

Augustine cannot comprehend the divine all-comprehensiveness, but he can nevertheless contact it discursively in the verbal act of address. Discourse thus reaches out toward a completeness that it cannot encompass; it does so by addressing another, an infinite Mind in which the whole of sense—glimpsed always only in part by the finite mind—would be gathered together into one. This requires an unlimited scope that the human mind lacks, yet the human mind is nevertheless regulated by this principle of wholeness that transcends it. And relating himself and his discourse to that complete, comprehensive Mind is a crucial motivation for Augustine's ongoing apostrophes to the divinity he assumes as his partner in dialogue throughout the work. These apostrophes become the means of structuring his whole discourse as communicating with the infinite knowledge or omniscient consciousness of God. They give Augustine's representations of concrete fields of experience the status of revealing—or in any case refracting—this higher reality of whole and total cognition.

From this vantage point, Augustine's work realizes the aspiration to prophetic vision that can be found as a constant—in constantly changing forms—throughout the tradition of the humanities and particularly in epic texts. In this vision, everything connects together, and the universe is opened and made susceptible to bearing coherent sense that establishes a comprehensive order.[11] Such vision has been revealed to the imagination, which is understood to be divinely inspired, in the major works of poetic prophecy in the classical Western tradition moving from Homer and Virgil.[12]

In the case of epic, poetry involves the attempt to "see" a unified order or pattern in things, a *uni*verse. It might not be rationally graspable, but it can be imaginatively projected. In epic poetry, the invocation of divinity (the Muses) is crucial to the imagination of a wholeness beyond the compass of the finite

---

11. This order, of course, does not exclude eruptions of disorder, such as marked Augustine's troubled times, as is stressed particularly by Peter Brown, *Religion and Society in the Age of Augustine* (New York: Harper and Row, 1972), and by R. A. Markus, *Saeculum, History and Society in the Theology of Saint Augustine* (Cambridge, Eng.: Cambridge University Press, 1988).

12. Such a "transcendent horizon" is traced through epic tradition by Joachim Küpper, "Transzendenter Horizont und epische Wirkung: Zu *Ilias*, *Aeneis*, *Chanson de Roland*, *El Cantar de mío Cid* und *Nibelungenlied*," *Poetica* 40, nos. 3–4 (2009): 211–68.

human mind. In like fashion, Augustine sees wholly, and even truly, only to the extent that his vision is granted him by the Divinity whom he invokes.

Augustine will strain his powers of intellection to the utmost, for example, in the attempt to understand eternity as the wholeness of time. But his efforts will collapse always into offering praise to the Mind above his own, whose perspective he cannot quite share and adopt. Neither, then, can he represent it imaginatively in the manner of the inspired prophetic poets. Nevertheless, he can imagine himself to be conversing intimately with this divinity. His own ideas are thus under the surveillance of the total vision of God. With grace, they can be guided by, and even be made to reflect, this transcendent vantage point.

If a book like the *Confessions* can be comprehended in terms of a single stroke of genius, then it must be found in the insistent recourse to invocation and specifically to self-reflective conversational address of God. In precisely this apostrophic mode, Augustine offers all of his reflections on the story of his life, as well as on truth in every domain of knowledge on which he touches. And this mode of discourse changes the tenor of absolutely everything in Augustine's narrative. The narrative he produces is not just his memory of his life and thought to date. It is rather a placing of all that he remembers in the purview of the one Power and Consciousness who is the source and ground of it all and who comprehends it infinitely better than Augustine himself ever could. The incidents and reflections Augustine expresses are themselves mere reflections from a much larger, more meaningful story that is not actually told by Augustine, but is nonetheless adumbrated: it is the story as it would be told by the other partner to the dialogue, the Divinity to whom Augustine constantly addresses himself, having himself been addressed by the Word.

In recurrent passages, Augustine evokes God as knowing more than he himself does about what he tells. Humans are generally blind and vainly attempt to evade the all-knowing divine Presence:

> Where indeed did they flee to when the fled from Thy face? Or where dost Thou not find them? The truth is that they fled, that they might not see Thee who sawest them. And so with eyes blinded they stumbled against Thee—for Thou dost not desert any of the things that Thou hast made. . . . Plainly they do not know that Thou art everywhere whom no place compasses in, and that Thou alone art ever present even to those that go furthest from Thee. Let them therefore turn back and seek Thee because Thou hast not deserted Thy creatures as they have deserted their Creator. Let them turn back, and behold Thou art there in their hearts, in the hearts of those that confess to Thee and cast themselves upon Thee and weep on Thy breast as they return from ways of anguish . . . But where was I when I sought after Thee? Thou wert there before me, but I had gone away from myself and I could not even find myself, much less Thee.
>
> (5.ii)

Augustine is not able to encompass this divine, overseeing Presence, but he reflects or refracts it from his own limited point of view. For Augustine's own account inscribes itself into the all-comprehending vision of his divine interlocutor. The effect of his mode of discourse as a form of address to God is to continually project his own partial knowledge of himself and his life onto this virtual horizon of God's complete cognizance of his life and heart sub specie aeternitatis. While no narrative and no temporal organization of experience can comprehend this perspective, Augustine's narrative can, nevertheless, constantly evoke it, and so Augustine's discourse presents itself as, in a sense, conversant with this perspective as realized by God in eternity.

This helps to clarify the status of the *Confessions* as "prophetic" in the broadest sense. Saint Augustine is interpreting his own life from a standpoint anchored in God's unlimited cognizance. Our definition of prophecy as interpretation of history from the standpoint of a revelation of its final meaning is here applied to the history of an individual life. Augustine's work may become paradigmatic for the genre of autobiography, yet it is not simply autobiography as this genre is commonly understood today. For Augustine's story reveals a meaning beyond the meaning of his life itself. His story is exemplary of a truth that is presented as eternal: it represents the whole human story as prophetically revealed. The *Confessions* are "an epic of the soul struggling to admit the Word."[13] They lead from a narrative of self to the exegesis of Scripture, specifically of Genesis: the self is thus made to originate together with the biblical epic of universal history. That Augustine's historically concrete existence should become exemplary is in itself a momentous innovation. Not the Platonic universal form, but the individual life in its social context, with all its enmattered particularity and misery, becomes the locus of revelation and truth. This is now possible for Augustine, thanks to his Latin realism and historical sense, in ways that were not possible, or at least not natural, for the Greeks.

Building on the paradigm of life experience leading to crisis and issuing in prophecy, as encountered already in epic poetry such as the *Aeneid*, Augustine deepens it into the articulation of a personal conversion experience. This is what divides his story into an old life and a new one and redeems the former retrospectively. Hence, for example, his mother's prophetic dream envisioning her son on the yardstick she herself is on and the promise: "where you are, there will he be also" (3.xi). In books 1–9, he retells his life from the standpoint of his conversion. Books 10–13 then relate a kind of ascent of the mind to God on the basis of the conversion that has been accomplished, completing the earthly pilgrimage and opening the way toward the heavenly. This itinerary furnishes knowledge of all things in memory, but then transcends

13. Eugene Vance, "Augustine's *Confessions* and the Grammar of Selfhood," *Genre* 6 (1973): 21.

all things and memory itself toward their origin, namely, God. In principle unknowable because incommensurate with a finite, human mind, yet known miraculously through the Incarnation, God in his self-humbling to the level of man raises man to God's own level, that is, into a relationship with Himself, into being directly in communication with the divine in a way that had been lost ever since the rupture with Adam.

The originality of the discourse Augustine invents in the *Confessions* emerges strikingly when we consider the question of genre. The generic paradigms for the work include not only autobiography but also theology, philosophy, exegesis, and most importantly and originally "confession." *Confiteri* in Augustine's late-antique Latin means primarily to acknowledge one's faith and praise God's glory.[14] This may well include "confession" in the sense of owning up to one's sins, as is certainly done throughout the *Confessions* through constant contrast between God's generous acts toward Augustine and the latter's stubbornly perverse refusal to abandon his self-will to the divine Will. Augustine consistently portrays himself as needing to be taught the hard way—by suffering for his sins and being mercifully punished for his disobedience.

Yet even more important to defining the generic originality of this discourse is the way Augustine's autobiographical story is cast into the form of a dialogue with God that is essentially a confession—or, more exactly, what we would call a *profession*—of his faith. The life story, with all its "confessions" unfolding in a succession of anecdotes, forms a horizontal axis that is traversed by and wholly subsumed under and suspended from a vertical axis along which Augustine places himself directly into conversation with God. The point of view evoked through dialogue with God about Augustine's life and its development toward its goal is not a temporally finite point of view but rather the *totum simul* vision that is actually possible only for divinity. Nevertheless, this humanly unattainable point of view can decisively shape, in ways beyond his control, Augustine's own self-comprehension, and he seeks to let it do so by hewing as closely as possible, in prayer and praise, to the divine Mind with which he engages in dialogue.

This structure projects the temporality of the narrative into the eternity of the divine Mind and sets Augustine's whole life into a prophetic dimension and framework. Beyond his own grasp, the meaning of his whole life is in the

---

14. As William Mallard, *Language and Love: Introducing Augustine's Religious Thought Through the Confessions Story* (University Park: Pennsylvania State University Press, 1994) notes, "a confession in the early church meant confessing the glory and wonder of God, and only secondarily confessing one's sin" (12). Pierre Courcelle, *Recherches sur les Confessions de Saint-Augustin* (Paris: Bocard, 1950), 13ff., details three current meanings for *confessio* and *confiteri*: confession of sins, confession of faith, and confession of praise. He traces them through the work as the "theological scheme" of the *Confessions*.

hands of God, the God whom he addresses in his "confession," and this God sees everything Augustine records prophetically—or in light of the revelation of its final end. This form of prophecy is revealed as enabled by a certain negation—the negation of human finitude. So prophecy, or prophetic revelation, again as in epic, is the ultimate generic frame of reference, the genre of genres that can be discerned at work beneath this narrative. God's consciousness, which is continually evoked as present by direct address—even though, of course, it cannot be represented in its infinity—grasps Augustine's life as a whole, and this virtual, panoptic, divine vision is what gives ultimate meaning and unity to Augustine's story.[15]

Everything that happens to Augustine in the vicissitudes of the narrative takes on a final significance in the light of this revelation of the whole from the perspective of the end. There is a sufficient reason for everything that happens to him, a providential reason, even though this may be fully understood only by God. By communicating with God in prayer, Augustine is in touch with this providential rationale, which he can attempt to interpret and can in any case acknowledge—whether he understands the why of it or not—as willed by the One whom he directly speaks to as "Thou." To this extent, as revealed and yet veiled, divine providence, by being invoked in prayer, is mysteriously operative in Augustine's life as he narrates it.

My choosing to call this vision, which belongs properly to God and is only refracted in Augustine's discourse, a prophetic "revelation" could be contested. Nicholas Wolterstorff does not accept calling just any kind of divine discourse "revelation."[16] He sharply distinguishes between "illocutionary act" (employing J. L. Austin's term) and "propositional content" in

15. Augustinian studies have been very much preoccupied by the question of the *Confessions*'s unity. The epic motif of the *peregrinatio animae*, or the soul wandering back to its origin, established especially by Neoplatonic interpretations of the *Odyssey*, serves as a key for solving this enigma in Robert J. O'Connell, *St. Augustine's Confessions: The Odyssey of the Soul* (Cambridge, Mass.: Harvard University Press, 1969). O'Connell defends his interpretation in *Soundings in St. Augustine's Imagination* (New York: Fordham University Press, 1994) and in *Images of Conversion in Saint Augustine's Confessions* (New York: Fordham University Press, 1996). He acknowledges as precursor the outstanding essay by Georg Nicolaus Knauer, "*Peregrinatio animae*: Zur Frage der Einheit der augustinischen *Konfessionen*," *Hermes* 85 (1957): 216–48. He is himself in turn a basis for further work by Roland J. Teske, *To Know God and the Soul: Essays on the Thought of Saint Augustine* (Washington: Catholic University of America Press, 2008).

16. Nicholas Wolterstorff, *Divine Discourse: Philosophical Reflections on the Claim That God Speaks* (Cambridge, Eng.: Cambridge University Press, 1995), chapter 2: "Speaking Is Not Revealing," 19–36. See also his "God's Speaking and Augustine's Conversion," in *Augustine's Confessions: Critical Essays*, ed. William E. Mann (Lanham, Md.: Rowman and Littlefield, 2006).

God's speaking. For Wolterstorff, an illocutionary act, such as commanding or promising, cannot per se be revelation. It demands or projects some event that may or may not take place and that may even depend on human choices. My point is that Augustine's discourse puts pressure on such an analysis and suggests how speaking with God, even where the content cannot be clearly divided into divine speech and human reflection, "reveals" God as in any case present to the discussion. Obviously, this is not revelation in the strong sense intended by Wolterstorff—revelation specifically *that* such and such is the case. Thus, I am fully in agreement with Wolterstorff in discerning divine speech as something other than propositional discourse and its content. We disagree only as to whether or not such divine speech should be called "revelation."[17]

In the dialogue of the *Confessions*, the content comes all from Augustine's own reflections, and God speaks only through them. But this, too, can be an indirect revelation or unveiling of God, with the proviso that such revelation is at the same time also a *re-veiling*. The divine manifests itself as present to this speaking or "confessing," even if it is revealed only as *veiled*—in the effects it produces upon Augustine and in the utterances that he, as a consequence, proffers. God's "own" voice derives, of course, also from Scripture, but scriptural revelation, too, as a poetic rendering into words and images, is just as much a re-veiling as a supposedly authoritative revelation of the divine. In either case, we do not have pure presence of the divine, but rather a purported presence refracted in and through human consciousness. In Augustine, this consciousness becomes more specifically the self-reflective activity of consciousness in language. Humanities tradition thus owes to Augustine the momentous discovery of this extraordinary dimension of revelation inherent in self-reflective consciousness as it is enacted in the word.

II. The Story of a Life in Language: *Confessions*, Books 1–2

The opening paragraphs of the *Confessions*, then, show Augustine's awareness that our knowledge of God is relational, not objective: it is about us, too, and about God not in himself but rather in relation to us. In this dialogue,

17. More congenial to my approach to Augustine's speech act in the *Confessions* as mediating divine revelation are the speech act-based reflections of Jean-Louis Chrétien, *Saint Augustin et les actes de parole* (Paris: Presses Universitaires de France, 2008). Current French religious phenomenology lends support to finding God revealed in and through human self-reflection also in Jean-Luc Marion's *Au lieu du soi: L'approche de Saint Augustin* (Paris: Presses Universitaires de France, 2008). "Revelation" emerges here as having a phenomenological meaning—akin to "manifestation" and even "gift"—that stands as independent of its more metaphysical meanings as involving supposedly supernatural knowledge.

God identifies himself as Augustine's salvation: "Ego salus tuum" (1.i). While the invocation of God seems to place him within the circle of Augustine's own discourse and consciousness, Augustine discovers that this very invocation already presupposes God as its own ground and as the ground of all that is. The invocation thus places itself within God's Mind and Word rather than the other way around. The human being is always already related to God. Everything Augustine recounts has its meaning relative to the God whom he addresses, and the medium of this relation is language: the relation is made manifest in and by his invocation of God.

Augustine's life itself, moreover, is a sort of language that is ordered to an overarching significance: the meaning of everything that happens to him is found in God. The same holds in principle for all of history, starting from the Creation story in the Bible. In book 10, Augustine begins to interpret this story as if it were the epic of the universe revealed from a prophetic vantage point. At that point it becomes clear that Augustine's self-reflective discursive mode in the *Confessions* transfigures epic as well as autobiographical narration into theological revelation: all is told in and through the presence of God in human, speaking consciousness.

The key theme of Augustine's account of his infancy and childhood thus turns out naturally to be language. The whole content of the story revolves around language as the fundamental axis along which his life develops. This is not by accident, since language is the condition that enables him not only to narratively relate, or to author, his life's story but also to relate to the Author of his life. He sets up this discourse by the opening prayer as a linguistic construct that, nevertheless, comes to coincide with reality in the largest and richest sense, indeed as reaching even to the transcendent reality of God the Word. Both generically and thematically, Augustine's discourse self-reflectively emphasizes its own immanence to language, an immanence that is also the very act and realization of transcendence—of a relation to and communication with the divine.

We have already noticed in discussing the prologue that Augustine discovers language as the engine of his self-transcendence. He directs every word and thought to God, but this God is projected from within the immanence of radically reflective language. We cannot fail to notice also how in relating his life he arraigns and condemns the abuse of language for worldly and egotistical purposes. Yet even this rejection of language transpires within the element of language and is itself a self-conscious rhetorical performance. It is through the self-critical, self-negating capacities of language that Augustine in his life-experience discovers an opening toward transcendence, toward something other, and this means also something theologically Other. He moves from invoking God to telling of his own origin, his "ortus et infantia," in chapter vi of book 1, with the question "Whence am I?" God's eternal self-identity is conceived here as the negation of Augustine's discontinuous identity. God's eternal being is apprehended only as a negation of Augustine's temporal being, beginning with his infancy, which is now dead and has been followed by successive selves that are now forgotten and unknown.

What remains of these selves now is the language proffered by his text: this language is a reverberation of the divine Mind that holds the keys to the mystery of Augustine's origin. Augustine tells the story of his origin as centered on his being and having become endowed with language, and language he understands as having been bestowed on him originally by God. He learns it not from teachers or from anyone else's deliberate efforts, but by his own mind's spontaneous insight—his "genius," which he acknowledges as God's gift ("ingenio meo, munere tuo," 1.xvii). The human factors in language acquisition are all relativized, since Augustine recognizes God as its one true source and origin, and this divine origin then gives him a criterion for moral evaluation of the various uses of language.

Augustine tells the story of his life as pivoting upon the various ways he has learned, from infancy through adulthood, of using and abusing language.[18] Language can be used either for or against God's purposes. Its first use by the infant originates from desire in the sense of egotistical interest. Augustine's first words were formed "in order to get my own way" (1.viii), and this type of motivation must constantly be resisted and corrected. Augustine does so by offering up to God all knowledge expressed in language. In this way, his distorting, self-interested motives can be overcome, so that language becomes a true reflection of beings and of their truth, ultimately the truth of Being itself. As Augustine elsewhere stresses, Being is the proper name of God—indeed the name God gives himself in Exodus 3:14. The proper employment of language is necessary for human beings to fulfill God's will, but at the same time the pursuit of language for its own sake is sinful and signals from early on Augustine's liability to sin.

His learning of letters, accordingly, is judged by the standard of its usefulness in leading to knowledge of God and, consequently, virtuous living. In this connection, Augustine's rejection of literature becomes significant and paradoxical. There is a tension between the literary vehicle he employs to such effect in writing his *Confessions* and their goal—namely, serving God ("tibi serviat quidquid utile," 1.xv). Much better than the enjoyment of literature is the "doctrine" it disguises ("melior est prorsus doctrina illa prior," 1.xiii), and yet his conveying doctrine efficaciously is surely helped much more than it is hindered by the enjoyment that his own narrative procures as literature.

Augustine's story is a revelation in and of language, and accordingly the work gives an account of how language as this organ of revelation actually

18. Of the vast bibliography on this topic, concise and useful is Philip Burton, *Language in the Confessions of Augustine* (Oxford: Oxford University Press, 2007), together with O'Donnell's commentary in vols. 2 and 3 of his edition of the *Confessions*.

develops in a human being. The story turns on the ambiguities with which this extraordinary faculty is fraught. Augustine is caught between the devotional discourse of his mother at home—where God can be evoked in simplicity of heart in prayer—and discourse used in public institutions for morally indifferent or downright deleterious purposes. He laments the greater solicitude for conventional laws of grammar than for God's covenant that reigns in the world and, as a result, dominates any man seeking success: "Such a man will be most vigilantly on guard lest by a slip of the tongue he drop an 'h' and murder the word 'human': yet worries not at all that by the fury of his mind he may murder a real human" (1.viii). And yet the law of God is itself described as linguistic in nature by Augustine's metaphor of the interior writing of conscience ("non est interior litterarum scientia quam scripta conscientia," 1.xviii) that forbids doing to others what one would not bear to have done to oneself.

The division within discourse between serving or else denying truth, morality, and God is replicated by a division in his parents' attitude toward him and his development: his mother's solicitude for Augustine's morality and for the salvation of his soul, on the one hand, and, on the other, an overweening ambitiousness for his public success, with consequent indifference toward or neglect of his moral education. A certain hypocrisy comes out even in his mother's decision to defer his baptism when, as a boy, he begins to recover from what had threatened to be a fatal illness. This decision implies an expectation that he will fall back into sin, and in fact no attempt was made to offer him what he needed in order to live virtuously: "It would have been far better had I been made whole at once and had so used my own efforts and the aid of my friends that the health brought to my soul should be safe in Your keeping, by whose gift it was given me" (1.xi). Augustine finds himself caught in a discourse that to him is absurd. It says, in effect: "do not become healthy because you might then become ill." And this cannot but lead him to rebellion.

Closely related to such duplicity is language's function of manifesting thoughts in an outward way that can make them perceptible to others. It is thus predicated on rupture of one's immediate presence and sufficiency unto oneself. Language is per se a condition of separation and exile, and in fact the whole *discourse* of the *Confessions* transpires in precisely such an element. Nevertheless, language is the means necessary for reconstituting a relation of unity with oneself and with the ground of one's being, namely, God. Augustine's own unity now passes through his relation with others, and the medium of this passage is language. Language stands between us and the world of others, as well as between us and the ground of our being, but it is also what connects us and makes us ultimately one with others, as well as one with God and ourselves.

Guided from beginning to end by the theme of language, the first book of the *Confessions* inaugurates whole branches of knowledge ranging from developmental psychology and philosophy of consciousness to linguistics.[19] The book describes with unprecedented insight and detail the acquisition of language by a child: it charts the transition from being *infans*, literally "without speech," to being a *puer loquens*, a "prattling boy." Augustine presents learning the meaning of words as proceeding basically by ostension—by pointing to the objects associated with specific significant sounds. In this manner, he conceives of language as founded on the naming of objects. Tellingly, this language of conventional names for substances can actually be learned only by the instrumentality of other signs, such as gestures of pointing, that Augustine classifies as a natural language common to all people ("tamquam verbis naturalibus omnium gentium," 1.viii).

To this extent, language must already be possessed in order to be acquired: there must be a basic ability to understand signs—and some signs must in fact be understood—in order for the significances of words to be learned. As remarked earlier, this innate capability is not learned from others, but is given directly from God into the possession of the individual's intelligence: "I did not learn by elders teaching me words in any systematic way, as I was soon after taught to read and write. But of my own motion, using the mind which You, my God, gave me" ("sed ego ipse mente, quam dedisti mihi, Deus meus," 1.viii).

Likewise pointing to God as principle and source, the resolution of the inquiry as to whence he came has already been anticipated and hinges on his faculty of signifying. The extraordinary ability to signify is evidence that he, like life and being itself, could only have come from God: "Clearly then I had being and I had life and signs: and by them toward the end of my infancy I tried hard to find ways of making my feelings known to others. Whence could such a living being come but from You, Lord?" ("Eram enim et vivebam etiam tunc, et signa, quibus sensa mea nota aliis facerem, iam in fine infantiae quaerebam. Unde hoc tale animal nisi abs te, domine?" 1.vi).

This last question hints that the existence of a signifying being cannot but come from God: to be in the dimension of signification is perhaps already, in some sense, to be communicating with God. The idea contained *in nuce* here is developed extensively in Augustine's mature theory of signs, especially in *De doctrina Christiana* and in his several commentaries on Genesis. Augustine proposes a universe of signs, in which all things are linked in an order of love directed to the one Being and one Love, which are not transitive, not for the sake of some other, namely, God. Augustine begins here to establish signification in the order of love as an overarching axis of his thought.

By telling his life in terms of language, Augustine can understand and grasp it as all directed toward a single end and purpose that is gradually

19. Psychologist Paul Bloom's reflections, "Word Learning and Theory of Mind," in *Augustine's Confessions: Critical Essays*, ed. Mann, 17–29, illustrate this range.

uncovered through his peregrinations. He can judge his youthful errancy from a prophetic perspective focused on a goal that is revealed only later and is fully embraced through his conversion in his mature years. To project everything onto this teleology is the work of narrative, but it is also made possible more basically by the signifying function of language. The sign enables one thing to be for the sake of another and even allows all things to stand and be for One—one goal, one beginning and end of desire. As a signifying being, Augustine discovers this capacity of his to live in relation to One as the source of all the facts and circumstances of his life, which in his immediate experience appears only as fragmentary and meaningless and therefore vain and inevitably painful. Augustine's whole metaphysical and theistic vision of the universe and its transcendent Ground is an enactment of the resources of discourse that he discovers in his capacity to signify himself and his world and to address this signifying speech to God—as revealed in the wider discourse of the faith community to which he elects (or is elected) to belong. The power of gathering together all things, starting from his own life, into a unified significance is what analogically gives him some inkling of God as the unifying significance of the universe and of its history as a whole.

Book 1 of the *Confessions* thus opens a genetic perspective into the vision underlying Augustine's theory of signs. Quite generally, Augustine's vision consists in seeing all things through the lens of language and language through the theological lens of the divine Word. His story of a life in language makes it, by its very nature as language, a testimony to the God whom he "confesses." In language, everything is related to everything else; all becomes unified and a sign ultimately of God as the only ultimately intransitive signified: consequently, the key to making his life a testimony to God is interpreting it through language. Augustine does this not only by using language as form and instrument, but also by making it the central thematic thread of his story.

God as ground of the order of signs is not just postulated as an end-term in the series, but is believed in or projected in such a way as lends a superior level of significance to everything in our life and world. This projection or belief is based on analogy: we see many convergences to unity of sense among things in the temporal world, and this alone offers the key to reading their intrinsic order. Of course, the whole order of signification as hinging on some ultimate source of significance not dependent on any other can be ignored and denied in innumerable all-too-human ways. Thus Augustine tells how as an infant he began to use signs in order to communicate to others outside him the wishes otherwise contained within the interiority of his mind. Language is an invaluable instrument of communication; indeed, it is necessary to survival. It is, however, at the same time, revealed here as an instrument of manipulation and self-will. Language, from its very first inception, arises from human desire in all its ambiguity.

Language is, furthermore, devalued in book 1 as a mere form without content. As such, it is susceptible to becoming a deception and distraction from the moral imperatives of life and from the purposes of God, which lie far above human conventions such as language. Particularly the study of literature is taken by Augustine as emblematic of the vanity and immorality that drives the institutional learning of language. The passion with which, as a boy, Augustine was able to invest himself emotionally in the dying of Dido as told in Virgil's fiction contrasts glaringly with the insouciance with which he speeds to his own ruin—in effect, the dying of his own soul through its separation and distancing of itself from God. He is applauded at school for his imitation of Juno's wrath in the *Aeneid,* and basking in gratification at such approval he completely overlooks his own endangered moral state.

These stories told by Virgil, of course, never really happened. They are poetic figments ("figmentorum poeticorum"), smoke and wind ("fumus et ventus," 1.xvii). Augustine admits that learning letters can have a useful purpose, for it is necessary for the success of all serious teaching. Nevertheless, his enthusiasm as a child was rather all for the sweet, vain spectacles of literature, whereby all its potential usefulness was traduced. Language learned in this manner is rather an inducement to sin, as exemplified by the character in Terence's *Eunuch* who is spurred on in his adulterous desires by a picture of Jove in the form of a golden rain falling in Danae's lap and ravishing her. But especially the *Aeneid* is referred to repeatedly in the *Confessions* as the epitome of literary vanity and as luring Augustine to morally debilitating enjoyments.

It is not words per se that are at fault. In themselves, they are precious vessels and useful particularly for moral edification and religious instruction. The problem is the immoral use made of them by men drunk with the wine of error ("Non accuso verba quasi vasa electa atque pretiosa, sed vinum erroris, quod in eis novis propinabatur ab ebriis doctoribus," 1.xvi). Augustine wishes, therefore, that he could have learned letters from the study of Scripture alone and so have avoided the frivolous and filthy entanglements to which his literary studies enticed and induced him. Of course, Scripture, too, is poetic, especially as Augustine himself reads it. Ironically, Augustine's very critique of literature remains itself within the order of the literary and becomes a literary classic, indeed a best-seller.[20] Augustine himself separates content from form, story from grammar, in order to salvage what may serve God, namely, the grammatical form of language, while condemning the rest, particularly the fabrications of fancy used to make immorality seductive, and he consigns this part to perdition. He performs a similar operation on his own life prior to conversion, condemning the substance but preserving a

20. *The Confessions*'s popularity through the ages specifically *as literature* is highlighted by *Augustine and Literature*, ed. Robert P. Kennedy, Kim Paffenroth, and John Doody (Lanham, Md.: Lexington Books, 2006).

linguistic residue in the form of the narrative of a sinner's misery, which is useful for its exemplary value in modeling a conversion to Catholicism.

Yet how he, nevertheless, preserves his life in all its suggestive sinfulness by this sublation! Language signifies by opposition, by differential terms, as both medieval sign theory and modern structuralist linguistics following Saussure clearly recognize. And likewise Augustine's life signifies God and the human good only by contrast, that is, through its very profanity. Augustine writes from the point of view of the true moral sense of everything, including all his sins, extricated from the web of words and their ambiguities. God alone enables him to assume this superior vantage point. Yet even as he writes, he uses writing to condemn mere writing and so to lift it to a higher plane of vision above itself. Paradoxically, he invokes the wholly transcendent God in the sheer immanence of his own language. Not surprisingly, the descriptions that can be given of God are all contradictory, as Augustine himself insists: "O Thou . . . utterly hidden and utterly present . . . never new, never old . . . ever in action, ever at rest, gathering all things to Thee and needing none . . . ever seeking though lacking nothing" (1.iv).

Language is indeed deeply ambiguous, for it is what destroys the unity with God and with oneself, breaking what is one in conception into the multiplicity of articulated speech, as well as being the necessary means of (re) constituting this unity. By reviewing his past life, as he makes his confession in the present and in the sight of God, Augustine is able to collect himself out of dispersion ("colligens me a dispersione"). He explains:

> I do it for love of Thy love, passing again in the bitterness of remembrance over my most evil ways that Thou mayest thereby grow ever lovelier to me, O Loveliness that dost not deceive, Loveliness happy and abiding: and I collect my self out of that broken state in which my very being was torn asunder because I was turned away from Thee, the One, and wasted myself upon the many.
>
> (2.i)

The self-reflection and self-recollection that language makes possible is the precondition of unifying himself with God through addressing him and so being consciously related to him. It makes possible also the effusive praise of God: in meditation, language becomes rapturous enjoyment and express love of God, whom Augustine celebrates.

Augustine finds unity always only in God. Relation to God is the enabling condition of his psychological examination of himself. The centering of consciousness that enables him to comprehend his whole life story from its central meaning depends on a principle transcending that life and consciousness. It is God alone who can unify Augustine's life and mind and recollect him out of the dispersion of the many, to which his being is otherwise delivered over.

The last chapter of book 1 and the first chapter of book 2 (just quoted above) share this Neoplatonic theme in common: "even so early I had an instinct for the care of my own being, a trace in me of that most profound Unity whence my being was derived; in my interior sense I kept guard over the integrity of my outward sense perception . . . Yet all these were gifts of my God, for I did not give them to myself . . . because even that I exist is Thy gift" (1.xx). Augustine is ontologically dependent on God to such an extent that his separation and exile from God constitutes a loss of unity not only with God but even within his own self.

The linguistic dimension of this state of disintegration is epitomized by the concept of Babylon as *confusio linguarum*. In 2.iii, Augustine inveighs against the decadent civilization of the Carthaginian metropolis, and at the same time, by evoking the biblical story of the tower of Babel (Genesis 11:1–11), he interprets his own ruin—and the disrupted unity of mankind along with it—as specifically linguistic in nature.

Book 2 pursues the theme of language and loss of unity with God (who is revealed as Logos), shifting the focus to adolescent sexual life. That Augustine learn rhetorical eloquence proves to be the chief concern of his parents, who neglect his more important moral development for the sake of fostering mere skill in verbal art, given the material advantages it can procure in society. Language, so used, becomes instrumental to his exile from unity with self and God rather than an instrument of recollection of self and of centering on God. This ambiguous role of language occurs within a discourse in which the self in its dispersion and divinity in its unity are both irreducibly linguistic. Augustine's thought is thus the apotheosis of the Word, together with and in and through its being also a critique and even a sort of exorcism of human words.

And yet, in chapter iii of book 2, a moment of writerly self-consciousness about who he is addressing brings to articulation another ambiguity in this direct address to the divine Word. The intimacy of his prayer directly to God is interrupted at its very inception by its being published—or its being *for* publication—among men.

> But to whom am I telling this? Not to Thee, O my God, but in Thy presence I am telling it to my own kind, to the race of men, or rather to that small part of the human race that may come upon these writings. And to what purpose do I tell it? Simply that I and any other who may read may realise out of what depths we must cry to Thee.
> (2.iii)

> (cui narro haec? neque enim tibi, deus meus, sed apud te narro haec generi meo, generi humano, quantulacumque ex particula incedere potest in istas meas litteras. et ut quid hoc? ut videlicet ego et quisquis haec legit cogitemus de quam profundo clamandum sit ad te.)

Augustine is conscious of himself in his conversation with God as being overheard by his fellow human beings. And this makes for a radical ambiguity in the addressee of the *Confessions*. While he is expressly speaking *to* God ("tibi"), Augustine is also, in effect, speaking *for* fellow humans ("apud te narro haec generi meo, generi humano"). It may even be that in some deep sense his conversation vertically with God is actually sustained and motivated, on a horizontal plane, by his communication with humans. He admits to being conscious that he is being overheard by humans, and this cannot but influence—perhaps even, in some ways, underwrite and instigate—the address to God.[21] In an extension of this self-consciousness vis-à-vis others, in chapter vii Augustine actually melds together his discourse of conversation with God as You or Thou ("Tu") with words of caution addressed to his human readers. His readers, if they hearken to God's voice, ought not to scorn him for his sins: "If any man has heard Thy voice and followed it and done none of the things he finds me here recording and confessing, still he must not scorn me" ("qui enim vocatus a te secutus est vocem tuam, et vitavit ea, quae me de me ipso recordantem et fatentem legit, non me derideat," 2.vii).

When book 2 enters into the psychology of sin, which it dramatizes in recounting the stealing of the pears, here again language is in some sense the protagonist, figuring as the "law of conscience written in the heart." What motivates Augustine's theft? He answers: love of the theft itself and of sin ("ipso furto et peccato," 2.iv) and his own consequent self-annihilation: "I loved my own undoing, I loved the evil in me—not the thing for which I did the evil, simply the evil" ("amavi perire, amavi defectum meum, non illud, ad quod deficiebam, sed defectum meum ipsum amavi"). This love of his own nullity ("defectum") is expressed in his usurping a false identity with or as God, so as to have no higher standard above him, nor any limit placed upon his own will. As such, he is omnipotent, is in effect God: "getting a deceptive sense of omnipotence from doing something forbidden without immediate punishment" (2.vi). Imitating God in his omnipotence, however illusorily ("tenebrosa omnipotentiae similitudine," 2.vi), is Augustine's motive for stealing. Sin is a denial of God, just as all is good when it is acknowledged as being from God. This relation of self to God, in affirmation and denial, is pursued by Augustine throughout the balance of his *Confessions*: the potential of words for deception, as well as for relation to God, makes them vehicles of transcendence of the whole finite, human order.

21. Erich Feldman, *Augustinus-Lexikon* (Basel: Schwabe, 1986–), 1: 1157–93, classifies the *Confessions* generically as a "protreptikos" aiming to convert its readers. Annemaré Kotzé, *Augustine's Confessions: Communicative Purpose and Audience* (Leiden: Brill, 2004) makes the "protreptic" purposes of the work in its orientation to its readers central.

III. Growth of the Self in and through the Word: *Confessions*, Books 3–4

Augustine's account of his early private and professional life is overshadowed by his reflections on sin and specifically on its expression in certain perversions of language. Book 3 charts Augustine's development in adolescence, ages sixteen to eighteen, traversing stormy and dangerous seas, as moving between the poles of good and bad language. Bad is the language of law and rhetoric—for it is prostituted to professional advancement and is terribly adept at deceit. Likewise the language of the theater is condemned, for it arouses unwholesome passions (3.iii). In particular, tragedy arouses feelings of sorrow that are—paradoxically—enjoyed: this involves taking pleasure vicariously in the suffering of the protagonist, who is at once both hero and victim. There is nothing compassionate or charitable in such enjoyment of another's destruction. Contrary to Aristotle, Augustine does not see the reaction to tragedy as cleansing and purifying—a catharsis—so much as corrupting and as productive of dissoluteness.

In observing his mother Monica's devotions, in contrast, and by participating in the Christian prayers that he himself learns to recite, Augustine has already experienced at home the good language leading to God. He also, observes, however, that prayers do not save him from his beatings at school. More to his immediate purpose, Augustine momentously discovers at eighteen years of age the language of truth in philosophy, the love of wisdom, and this opens the way for him toward a new orientation to God. He has a species of conversion experience in reading a now lost work of Cicero, the *Hortensius*, exhorting to the love of philosophy: "Suddenly all the vanity I had hoped in I saw as worthless, and with an incredible intensity of desire I longed after immortal wisdom. I had begun that journey upward by which I was to return to You" (3.iv). This last phrase casts Augustine as the prodigal son, who decides: "I will arise and go to my father" (Luke 15:18). In fact, this model echoes all through Augustine's conversion narrative (again, for example, in 3.vi.11). Still, there is something, one thing, lacking in this new discovery: "the only thing I found lacking was that the name of Christ was not there" (3.iv). Since he had drunk that name down with his mother's milk, no doctrine without it could fully satisfy him as being the Truth. He knows instinctively what Scripture says, namely, that "there is no other name under heaven given among men, whereby we must be saved" (Acts of the Apostles 4:12).

Augustine needs the Name of Christ and, more broadly, the language of Scripture. However, he is not yet prepared to fully appreciate it, for it requires a humble mind and heart to be understood, and he is still far too puffed up with pride.

> So I resolved to make some study of the Sacred Scriptures and find what kind of books they were. But what I came upon was something

> not grasped by the proud, not revealed either to children, something utterly humble in the hearing but sublime in the doing and shrouded deep in mystery. And I was not of the nature to enter into it or bend my neck to follow it.
>
> (3.v)

It is, then, precisely the form of its language that prevents Augustine from embracing the Scriptures as revealing what he will later recognize as the true faith. "My conceit was repelled by their simplicity," he says, and he avows that he was not able to become a little one, a child in whom Scripture might grow up in tandem with his own growth ("cresceret cum parvulis," 3.v) as a reader.

Augustine's pride prevents him from accepting that such humble language could actually be speaking the exalted Truth he seeks. He turns instead to a Christian heresy that uses the name of Christ, as well as those of the Father and Holy Ghost, with great rhetorical flourish, even to the point of absurdity. Manichaeism indulges in material imaginations of divinity and in a dualistic conception of the universe as contended over by opposing forces of light and darkness. The Manicheans attribute their absurdities to Scripture and even bring Augustine to blame the holy patriarchs of the Old Testament. Although it will take him nine years to finally break away from his association with this religion, Manichaeism turns out to be just another form of linguistic deception. The Manicheans ensnare Augustine by using all the names of the Christian Trinity, yet in effect they abuse these names merely as sound, as syllables empty of truth ("Haec nomina non recedebant de ore eorum, sed tenus sono et strepitu linguae; ceterum cor inani veri," 3.vi)—Truth, which is God's name and, in fact, his very being.

In truth, it is by his language of address, of "te, te ipsum, solo te" ("you, you yourself, only you"), rather than by any names, that Augustine evokes an unmistakable and yet unrepresentable divine identity. God is distinct from all creatures: he is the immaterial, uncreated source of all beings. Yet even so, he has only been defined conceptually, and he is of course infinitely beyond any concept. He cannot be approached by any identifications but only through the address, which leaves it to the addressee, to God, and him alone, to truly know the One who is addressed. "Theology," in the strict sense of "doctrina sacra" defined later by Thomas Aquinas, working out the consequences of Augustine's legacy, is *God*'s knowledge *of himself* (*Summa Theologica* 1a.1). *Our* theology is only a faint, imperfect reflection of the true theology that exists in the Mind of God. By invoking God in his addresses, Augustine relates his own discourse to this one, true, divine Logos.

Augustine employs a form of address that does not objectively delimit the identity of the addressee in any finite form of concept, but rather calls upon the addressee to recognize himself as the one addressed. The mode and presuppositions of the address may not be adequate to the one being addressed, but the address nevertheless communicates a belief that someone can and will answer to the address and recognize himself as the one intended, even if not adequately. Augustine amply describes God in addressing him: He is Truth, Fountain of Life, Creator and Ruler of the universe ("fons vitae, qui es unus et verus creator et rector universitatis," 3.viii), but in the discourse of address these descriptions serve to focus our human attention on what transcends all such terms—on the otherness of the irreducible "You"—so as not to circumscribe God or his nature.

This intimate mode of conversing with God as the principle and ground of his own being leads Augustine, moreover, into a novel relation of self-reflection upon himself. Augustine's story from beginning to end is a search for some stable truth in the midst of the illusions and shifting deceptions of life in the late and declining Roman Empire. He meditates much on God's justice versus the justice and customs of men, recognizing that all relative judgments presuppose some absolute principle of judgment even to justify their relative views. This search for an Absolute is borne by words as its vehicle all throughout: it is, moreover, a search for the true discourse. And Augustine reviews how he became dupe to a number of discourses, such as academic or skeptical philosophy and Manichaeism, along the way, even though he kept on testing and finally rejected them. This search relies on words, but also deeply distrusts them.

Augustine begins to theorize topics such as perception, memory, and imagination in a new way based on the self-reflexive consciousness of an individual self. He adumbrates something that will later be recognized as akin to the "Cartesian" cogito, the certainty of "I think, therefore I am." However, Augustine, in effect, deconstructs the Cartesian subject *avant la lettre* by rephrasing the cogito as "I doubt, therefore I exist."[22]

The crucial difference between Augustine's formulation and most modern, Cartesian versions of self-certain consciousness is that the Augustinian self-consciousness is inhabited by an Other: in its deepest core, it does not possess itself, but is possessed by what transcends it, by God. For God is within and

22. This point is made nicely by Jean Bethke Elshtaine, "Why Augustine, Why Now?" in *Augustine and Postmodernism*, ed. Caputo and Scanlon, 246. Moreover, Descartes himself recognized Augustine as precedent very much in these terms. He wrote to a correspondent that he was quite pleased to be in agreement with Saint Augustine in his inference that he exists from the fact that he is doubting: "I am obliged to you for calling to my attention the passage of St. Augustine to which my *I think, therefore I am* has some relation. I have been to read it today in the town library, and I find he does truly use it to prove the certainty of our existence." I translate from Descartes, *Oeuvres de Descartes*, ed. C. Adam and P. Tannery (Paris: Cerf, 1897–1910), 12 vols., 3: 247–48. Descartes refers to *City of God* 11.26. Other important Augustinian formulations of the cogito principle include *De libero arbitrio* 2.3.7: "Si fallor, sum"; *Contra Academicos* 3.26; *De Trinitate* 10.10, 15.21. The topic is exhaustively researched by Emmanuel Bermon, *Le cogito dans la pensée de Saint Augustin* (Paris: Vrin, 2001).

above any essence of the self: "You were more inward than the most inward place of my heart and loftier than the highest" ("tu autem eras interior intimo meo et superior summo meo," 3.vi). By turning within, Augustine finds God above.[23] In 4.xii, Augustine writes, "And He withdrew from our eyes, that we might return to our own heart and find Him. For He went away and behold He is still here." And yet, by turning within, Augustine does not immediately find true being, for "Man is a great deep, Lord" ("grande profundum est ipse homo," 4.xiv). The human psyche is itself the image and homology of the infinite abyss of divinity. There is a void in the midst of the human self: there must be, in order that the self be opened up in self-transcendence toward God. It is rather in looking above, to the God whom he does not grasp but can nevertheless address, that Augustine is able to unify and return to himself.

The perennial philosophical interest of the *Confessions*, with their phenomenological tenor and method, depends on the fact that they derive the fundamental principles of Christian metaphysics directly from Augustine's personal experience. This provides an existential grounding for Christian theology. However, it has been interpreted, notably by Martin Heidegger, as a philosophical anthropology that is existential rather than specifically Christian.[24] The doctrine of God, and of everything else in relation to God, is grounded quite simply in the human experience of the search for a love that can satisfy. Following Heidegger, Hannah Arendt is captivated by the infinite abyss that opens up in the unsoundable depths of the human heart as interpreted by Augustine.[25] She opens the thinking of the final limit of death in her

23. On Augustine's theory of interiority as key to his continuing relevance for philosophy, see Luigi Alici, "Agostino e il futuro dell'interiorità," in *Agostino e il destino dell'Occidente*, ed. Luigi Perissinotto (Rome: Carocci, 2000), 119–38. Setting limits to this detachment and escape into a private, interior sphere, Charles Mathewes, in *A Theology of Public Life* (Cambridge, Eng.: Cambridge University Press, 2007) argues in Augustine's name for a theology of worldly engagement.

24. An existentialist philosopher, Heidegger treats Augustine's analysis of "facticity" as a practical experience of Being beyond all objective knowledge in his 1921 Freiburg lecture "Augustinus und der Neuplatonismus," in *Einleitung in die Phänomenologie der Religion*, *Gesamtausgabe* 60 (Frankfurt: Klostermann, 1993), 157–302. Instructive commentary is found in Friedrich-Wilhem von Hermann, "Die 'Confessiones' des Heiligen Augustinus im Denken Heideggers,"*Quaestio* 1 (2001): 113–46.

25. Arendt began her thinking in dialogue with Augustine from her 1929 Heidelberg dissertation "Liebesbegriff bei Augustin," later revised and published as *Love and Saint Augustine*, ed. Joanna Vecchiarelli Scott and Judith Chelius Stark (Chicago: University of Chicago Press, 1996). This conversation continued all the way to her last work, *The Life of the Mind* (New York: Harcourt, Brace, Jovanovich, 1978), vol. 2: *Willing*, particularly in its section "Augustine, the First Philosopher of the Will," 84–124.

teachers Heidegger and Karl Jaspers to an experience of infinity in the charitable bond of political community. Augustine thus becomes a bridge from premodern to postmodern outlooks on society: in both these perspectives, the human is not sufficient unto itself but rather infinitely open to the other.[26]

Everything in his life up to this point is understood by Augustine as a spiritual rearing leading him along the way to being able to speak the Word of God. Again, Augustine reminds us that it is God who really brings him up, using parents and teachers as instruments.[27] God's prior agency within Augustine's life and even in his very own acts is confirmed by the answer Monica receives from a certain bishop, whom she consults in her desperation about how to disabuse her son of his Manichean errors. He answers that Augustine will turn from his errors himself through his own reading, which the bishop understands to be providentially guided: "he will himself discover by reading what his error is and how great his impiety" ("ipse legendo reperiet, quis illa sit error et quanta inpieta," 3.xii). This had been the anonymous bishop's own experience of eventually growing unconvinced by the discourses of the Manicheans, whose books he had assiduously learned and copied. He thus prophesies Augustine's conversion by reading. This is fundamentally how the saint will be recuperated for Catholic Christianity.[28] In the intimacy of reading, his conversion takes place as a transaction between him and the divine Word directly.

By virtue of his addressing God, who sees all, the wholeness of Augustine's life as in the eye of God is present and governs his narrative from its inception. It thereby becomes a narrative of his return to origin, of his responding to a call to come back to himself ("redeas"). This may seem less adventurous than the open road envisaged along the axis of modern, secularized time, but actually the mystery of a projected destiny can first open definite possibilities and instigate a desire to seek them out and achieve them. This sort of determinism—or, better, determination—can be every bit as risky as the open road: by determining itself according to some definite end and purpose, it becomes open to adversity. Moreover, it may well be that there is some sort of virtual or negated goal, however vaguely defined and however much contradicted by events, that oversees any possible narrative, however minimal.

26. See Michael Scanlon, "Arendt's Augustine," in *Augustine and Postmodernism*, ed. Caputo and Scanlon, 158–72.

27. See Marsha L. Dutton, "'When I Was a Child': Spiritual Infancy and God's Maturity in Augustine's *Confessions*," in *Collecteana augustineana*, ed. Joseph C. Schnaubelt and Frederick Van Fleteren (New York: Lang, 1990), 113–40.

28. The pervasive and pivotal role of reading in Augustine's life and thought is studied meticulously by Brian Stock, *Augustine the Reader: Meditation, Self-Knowledge and the Ethics of Interpretation* (Cambridge, Mass.: Harvard University Press, 1996).

Beyond the idea of an end that is prophetically revealed, Augustine explores the idea of revelation in and by self-consciousness and the language in which it is realized. Can we imagine that human self-reflective awareness—as realized in discourse directed ultimately to the Word—itself reflects the divine destiny to which human beings are called? The words of Augustine's "confessions" all lead to the revelation that "the Word Himself calls to you to return" ("verbum ipsum clamat ut redeas," 4.xi). Augustine's self-reflective discourse is the story of a journey to precisely this realization in his embrace of faith in the Trinitarian God revealed as divine Word.

Book 4 covers nine years, from ages nineteen to twenty-eight, during which time Augustine taught rhetoric and law at Thagaste and Carthage. He denounces rhetoric as an art of deception. He also denounces his interests in divination and astrology. Such superstitions are dangerous, especially to the extent that they deny human responsibility and blame the stars for human beings' sins. But a still deeper renunciation is learned from Augustine's experience of the death of his anonymous friend. It is for him a hard lesson in the difference between loving mortal versus immortal things. The only true friendship is one that is anchored in God. The death of his friend teaches him to renounce attachment to all earthly, mortal things. All things, including language, literature, and friendship, are good only in relation to God and as directed toward Him as end. God alone is the answer to all human longings, for God's friendship cannot be lost, except by the one who leaves it.

The experience of death leads Augustine in this way to discover the horizon of eternity. God already is everything in its full and perfect being: he is the ground and perfection of all being. Everything else is nothing, except to the extent that it is from God: "For these lovely things would be nothing at all unless they were from You" ("quae tamen nulla essent, nisi essent abs te," 4.x). "Wherever the soul of man turns, unless toward God, it cleaves to sorrow, even though the things outside God and outside itself to which it cleaves may be things of beauty" ("Nam quoquoversum se verterit anima hominis, ad dolores figitur alibi praeterquam in te, tametsi figitur in pulchris extra te et extra se," 4.x).

Particularly death is the revelation to Augustine of the vanity and unreality of all mortal being: "I was wretched, and every soul is wretched that is bound in affection to mortal things" (4.vi). The only true being is God's. Mortal beings are rather forms of disappearing. Their only being is in becoming, which is a ceasing to be, a becoming nothing, a perishing. Only what is loved in God can last: "For he alone loses no one that is dear to him, if all are dear in God, who is never lost" (4.ix).

Augustine begins here to expound this ontology of love (as all for and from God) in terms of time and language. Of mortal things, as mere parts of a whole, he says, "the more haste they make toward fullness of being, the more haste they make toward ceasing to be." And language is like this too. Its particular parts must disappear in order to give place to the sense of the whole: "For there never could be a whole sentence unless one word ceased to be when its syllables had sounded and another took its place" (4.x). In the sentence and in discourse generally, each successive part must pass away to give place to what follows it in the whole so that sense at the end may be achieved ("nonenim erit totus sermo, si unum verbum non decedat, cum sonuerit partes suas, ut succedat aliud," 4.x).

In order that the whole and total may be all in all, whatever is partial must cease to be. In this manner, his meditation on human mortality modulates into a metaphysical reflection on how the part is necessary to the whole—with special emphasis on the analogy of language. This is also where Augustine mentions his lost work *De pulchro et apto*, which is concerned with the aesthetic justification of the universe as a whole. And, of course, vision of the whole, as Augustine understands it, is necessarily a theological perspective, for God is the unifying Ground of all.

At the end of book 4, Augustine boasts of his autodidacticism—of what he achieves himself by means of reading. At twenty years old, he reads Aristotle's treatise on the categories and understands it on his own ("legi eas solus et intellexi," 4.xvi). Scholars are able to teach him no more than he has already understood himself by reading ("nihil inde aliud mihi dicere potuerunt, quam ego solus apud me ipsum legens cognoveram," 4.xvi). His self-referential language here emphasizes the independent nature of this activity, though of course this independence from others exterior to him only deepens his dependence on the divine ground within and above him. He portrays himself as a prodigy of learning and talent in the liberal arts, but he laments that they were vainly learned because not learned with a view to knowing and serving God, the only Truth. "And what did it profit me that I read and understood for myself all the books of what are called the Liberal Arts that I was able to get hold of, since I remained the vile slave of evil desires? I enjoyed the books, while not knowing Him from whom came whatever was true or certain in them" (4.xvi).

Augustine excels in the liberal arts, but in vain, because this excellence does not yet direct him toward God. It only fills him the more with pride and with himself, making him like the dwellers in Plato's cave, who see but shadows of reality, and like the prodigal son of Luke 15. God's absolute ontological superiority, his being unique in being fully for his own sake, entails that morally all value—and consequently action—must be oriented to him alone. It is God who reveals to Augustine even his own heart: "Behold my heart, O my God, look deep within it; see how I remember, O my Hope, You who cleanse me . . ." ("ecce cor meum, deus meus, ecce intus. Vide, quia memini, spes mea, qui me mundas a talium affectionum immunditia," 4.vi). His very own thoughts are nothing but God's action in and through him and must by rights be offered up to God: "You know, Lord my God, because swiftness of understanding and keenness of perceiving are Your gift. But none of this did I offer in sacrifice to You" (4.xvi). Total ontological and even conscious psychological dependence on God is a fact that needs also to be realized as an ideal by perfect conformity to the divine Will.

The books Augustine reads and writes are essential for defining the new relationship to the world and reality that he inaugurated and established as canonical for the Christian Middle Ages. Reading and writing open a space of auto-affection and self-reflection. They enable Augustine to know himself, but his emphasis is constantly on their reference to an Other beyond him. Auto-affection and self-reflection become solipsistic acts in the modern age of narcissism that drives hard upon Nothing. But in Augustine they are rather theological revelations of the unfathomable depth of Being that opens up in the depths of human being ("grande profundum est ipse homo . . . Domine," 4.xiv): this is none other than God himself, who infinitely transcends the human individual, yet is present in and sustains all finite existence. Access to this transcendence is achieved by Augustine essentially by address through the word, but not without the mediating agency of the letter.

IV. Conversion by the Book

Interpretive and Philosophical Conversion: Confessions, *Books 5–7*

Book 5 recounts Augustine's life at age twenty-eight, the beginning of a phase of decisive developments eventually culminating in his conversion. Deceiving his mother about his going, he departs for Rome, in the hope of finding less insubordinate students. Upon arrival, he has a bout with a deathly illness, which he understands as due to his moral sickness, which is figuratively his going to hell ("ibam iam ad inferas," 5.ix). He seeks truth in vain from philosophers, particularly from Academics and Skeptics. His life in public likewise continues to be turbulent. He finds that Roman students, although they are not riotous like the Africans, abscond without paying for their lessons. His anger is assuaged by his being chosen—quite a coup for a North African—by the Roman prefect Symmachus for a post teaching rhetoric in Milan. This north Italian capital had, in effect, become the Western center of the Roman Empire. Most importantly for Augustine, as it turns out, the church there was presided over by Ambrose.

Augustine listens to the sermons of Ambrose at first for their rhetoric alone rather than for their theological content. Their message does not interest him, since he is convinced, along with the Manicheans, of the untenability of the Catholic faith. "His words I listened to with the greatest care; his matter I held quite unworthy of attention. I enjoyed the charm of his speaking, though for all his learning it was not so pleasing and captivating as that of Faustus" (5.xiii). Although sweet, Ambrose's speeches are not as enchanting as the Manichean orator's in their rhetorical style and manner. Yet Augustine soon remarks, in spite of himself, that in their matter and substance they are incomparably superior, and gradually he cannot but be affected by this.

> Yet along with the words, which I admired, there also came into my mind the subject-matter, to which I attached no importance. I could not separate them. And while I was opening my heart to learn how eloquently he spoke, I came to feel, though only gradually, how truly he spoke. First I began to realize that there was a case for the things themselves, and I began to see that the Catholic faith, for which I had thought nothing could be said in the face of the Manichean objections, could be maintained on reasonable grounds.
>
> (5.xiv)

Most significantly, Augustine learns from Ambrose to distinguish between the spirit and the letter of Scripture, or in other words to read figuratively, and so to be able to refute those who mocked the law and the prophets. This is a tremendous breakthrough, and yet he is at first still not able to conceive of God as spirit: "If only I had been able to conceive of a substance that was spiritual" (5.xiv). Catholic solutions to problems such as God's being and the nature of evil seemed paradoxical to Augustine. Unable to conceive of a substance that is spiritual and not material, he remains undecided between Catholic and Manichaean metaphysics. He becomes a skeptic, resolving to leave the Manicheans. However, neither is he fully convinced of the skeptical philosophies that he now sees as superior to Manichaeism, for they lack the name of Christ. "Yet I absolutely refused to entrust the care of my sick soul to the philosophers, because they were without the saving name of Christ" (5.xiv). So he resolves to become a catechumen in the church and to wait for a light to appear.

Book 6 tells of Augustine's life at twenty-nine years of age. Most significantly, he continues to learn Christian methods of reading and interpretation. Closely connected with the revelation of the spiritual or inner sense of Scripture that is so different from the outward sense of its letter is Augustine's discovery of a form of reading which is interior and immaterial. He describes how he observed with astonishment one day Ambrose reading silently: "But when he was reading, he drew his eyes along over the leaves, and his heart searched into the sense, but his voice and tongue were silent" (6.iii). The purely intellectual sense of the text, as opposed to the sensuous production of sounds by the voice, is highlighted by Ambrose's method of silent reading.

This interiorization of the practice of reading constitutes a watershed in Western culture: it effects a revolution in the conception of truth. The interior space of reading opens into a world-transcending dimension of subjective, confessional truth. No longer necessarily sounding aloud in the public forum of the ancient city, literature enters upon a silent, interiorized mode of existence that will be concretized in the bookish culture of the Middle Ages. Its emblem is monks practicing *lectio divinis* (an interior praying of Scriptures) and copying manuscripts in the scriptorium so as to preserve the classics for posterity. This revolution reaches in its ramifications all the way to the modern individual reading novels in private and potentially experiencing a personal epiphany or enlightenment through them.

The discovery of silent reading concretely illustrates how Augustine began to learn from Ambrose to seek more profoundly the spiritual sense of Scripture. He learns that there is also a hidden, interior mystery together with the immediately accessible sense of the letter (6.v). Augustine ponders Ambrose's interpretations of Scripture based on the principle that "the letter killeth, but the spirit giveth life" ("Littera occidit, spiritus autem vivificat," 2 Corinthians 3:6), and his eyes begin to be opened to the deeper meaning of the Bible and of Christian doctrine. These discourses no longer sound logically absurd—as they had been made to do by the Manicheans—once he learns the secret of reading spiritually. Such spiritual reading enables the Scriptures to speak on two levels simultaneously:

> Indeed the authority of Scripture seemed to be more to be revered and more worthy of devoted faith in that it was at once a book that all could read easily, and yet preserved the majesty of its mystery in the deepest part of its meaning: for it offers itself to all in the plainest words and the simplest expressions, yet demands the closest attention of the most serious minds.
>
> (6.v)

The distinction between letter and spirit is also the breakthrough that enables Augustine to understand God not as a finite body, as the literal sense of Scripture sometimes seems to imply, but rather as infinite spirit. For example, he understands man's being made in the image of God, as affirmed by Genesis, no longer in a crudely physical sense as ascribing features of the human body to God. It is rather by virtue of his intellectual nature that man can be said to bear a likeness to God. Augustine begins to comprehend God as purely spiritual, yet his life remains still a good deal more complicated and vexed than the pure, intellectual truth that he can now discern.

While he is making these discoveries, Augustine is living in community with Alypius, Nebridius, and Romanianus. He and his friends make far-reaching projects, but they founder on the question of how to accommodate the wives or future wives of certain members of this male community. Women pose an insuperable obstacle for such communal, monastic life. Augustine himself is planning at this point to be married, even if only for social advantages. His faithful concubine of over a decade, the mother of his son, is sent back to Africa, evidently at Monica's insistence, in view of his betrothal to a not yet nubile girl who is still two years under the required age of twelve (6.xiii). But Augustine also confesses that, within two months of his concubine's departure, he has a new mistress who is not his fiancée. This is one of the most delicate and potentially damning points in his moral biography.

To draw near to the Catholic faith and to total abandon to God, Augustine also needs to be weaned away from his worldly ambitions for success, and to this end an unexpected encounter with a beggar proves to be providential. Walking through the streets of Milan, he chances upon a drunk who by virtue of his bottle has already attained the happiness and freedom from cares that Augustine and his friends have assiduously sought for so long in vain. Augustine is struck by the sense of his own misery as a seeker after a happiness that he attains not nearly so quickly or easily as this drunken mendicant (6.vi). He nearly despairs of finding any other way.

However, in book 7, relating his thirty-first year of life, Augustine describes an intellectual conversion that will be followed by full conversion of his heart and whole existence in book 8. His intellectual search is resolved by attaining to a vision of immutable Truth, Beauty, and Being that is essentially Platonic. By identifying Platonic Being with God, he is able to connect this philosophical revelation of an eternal Truth and Being with the Scriptural revelation "I am that I am" (Exodus 3:14). The Platonic theory of Being as Goodness and as, equivalently, all intellectual perfections (such as Oneness, Truth, Beauty), gives Augustine a key for understanding the enigma of evil (xii–xiii), which previously had seemed to him to require a Manichean dualistic solution. He explains that all that is, to the extent that it is, is good ("ergo quamdiu sunt, bona sunt. ergo quaecumque sunt, bona sunt," 7.xii), as well as true ("omnia vera sunt, in quantum sunt," 7.xv). There is nothing in the order of Creation that to God is evil, nor anything that can harm it from outside ("Et tibi omnino non est malum, . . . quia extra non est aliquid, quod inrumpat et corrumpat ordinem, quem inposuisti ei," 7.xiii). It is only free will that can defect from this order and introduce an experience of lack, or of something being less good than it could be. Only in this relative sense does evil exist. The various facets of this core doctrine of the inherent goodness of being as such are subsequently refined with care and curiosity in relation to the diverse areas of Augustine's thought.

Augustine has at this stage reached intellectual certainty about God as Being and Truth and Goodness thanks to the changeless light ("lucem incommutabilem") that illuminates him from within, but also from above, since it infinitely transcends him and transcends every intensity or immensity of physical light, just as the Creator incommensurably transcends every creature. He describes a Platonic ascent from beings or bodies to a vision of Being itself which, however, remains momentary and epiphanic, not truly incarnate (7.vxii). He knows now, with his intellect, the true God whom he has been seeking all along. Nevertheless, his rational mind does not yet govern his body or his existence as a whole. And to this extent, he is still in need of redemption. "And I marvelled to find that at last I loved You and not some phantom instead of You; yet I did not stably enjoy my God, but was ravished to You by Your beauty, yet soon was torn away from You again by my own weight, and fell again with torment to lower things. Carnal habit was that weight" (7.xvii). He sees the truth of eternal Being, but he cannot yet completely embrace it and live by it. Although his mind attains to this Truth, he is unable to sustain and to embody it contrary to the pull of old desires:

> Thus in the thrust of a trembling glance my mind arrived at That Which Is [et pervenit ad id, quod est, in ictu trepidantis aspectus]. Then indeed I saw clearly Your *invisible things which are understood by the things that are made*; but I lacked the strength to hold my gaze fixed, and my gaze was beaten back again so that I returned to my old habits, bearing nothing with me but a memory of delight and a desire as for something of which I had caught the fragrance but which I had not yet the strength to eat.
>
> (7.xvii)

Augustine's intellectual conversion is catalyzed by what he interprets as a providential encounter with certain books of the Neoplatonists ("quosdam Platonicorum libros," 7.ix). He reads in them of the Creation by the divine Logos—the Word which was in the beginning and which was with God and which *was* God—the Word by whom all things were made. He remarks their agreement with Holy Scripture. Indeed, he quotes and paraphrases the prologue to the Gospel according to John up to the point where the true light that enlightens every man actually comes into the world in the flesh and dwells among men. Just before reciting this, he stops. Despite the large measure of uncanny agreement up to that point, the revelation of the Incarnation—"that the Word became flesh and dwelt among us" (John 1:14)—was not to be found in the books of the Platonists ("sed quia verbum caro factus est et habitavit in nobis, non ibi legi," 7.ix).

Furthermore, the idea of kenosis, or the "self-emptying" of Christ articulated in the hymn in Philippians 2:5–11, was likewise not to be found in those books. For Platonism does not know the wisdom of humility. A token of this is that the books had been procured for him by a certain one "puffed up with a most unreasonable pride" ("inmanissimo typho turgidum," 7.ix) Platonism, accordingly, cannot comprehend the sacrifice of Christ, his submitting to death, nor his declaration that he is meek and lowly of heart (Luke 11:29), for "professing themselves wise they become fools" ("dicentes se esse sapientes stulti fiunt," 7.ix), as Paul writes in Romans 1:22.

Augustine does, nevertheless, receive from this philosophy an indispensable orientation that directs him to return to himself. This *conversio* turns on his receiving intellectual illumination from pagan philosophy. It is like taking gold from the Egyptians, following the example of the people of Moses in the Exodus. By this means, Augustine enters into himself. And within himself he finds the unchanging light of truth that is over him and his changing mind ("inveneram incommutabilem et veram veritatis aeternitatem supra mentem meam commutabilem," 7.xvii). Entering into himself, with God as his guide ("intravi in intima mea, duce te"), the eye of his soul sees above itself an immutable light above his mind ("intravi et vidi qualicumque oculo animae meae supra eundem oculum animae meae, supra mentem meam, lucem incommutabilem," 7.x).

Nonetheless, Augustine still remains far from his God, finding himself lost in the region of dissimilitude ("et inveni longe me esse a te in regione dissimilitudinis," 7.x). All externally proffered language belongs to this region, which is alien from God, who is Truth that is not extended in either finite or infinite space, or again Being that is without speech in time and space and yet is interiorly present as Word. This interior, true speech of Being calls from afar "I am that I am" ("ego sum qui sum").

Augustine, in this phase of Platonist philosophical enlightenment as yet lacks an existential, relational Logos: in other words, he lacks Christ. He must still learn to humble himself before God rather than making his own rational power the standard by which everything else is to be measured. The Platonist ascends on the strength of his own intellect toward the divine light. But this is to idealize himself and to ignore the less divine parts of human being that, without grace, have not the intrinsic power to rise up: they rather drag him down. To overcome this downward moral drag, he needs the humility of Christ, the mediator between God and humans ("mediatorem dei et hominum, hominem Christum Iesum," 7.xviii). He sees the goal, the divine light, but he does not know and accept the way of humility that is necessary to get there, the way demonstrated by the Incarnation of Christ: "I was not yet lowly enough to hold the lowly Jesus as my God" ("non enim tenebam deum meum Iesum humilis humilem," 7.xviii). For the Platonic writings do not contain the face of pity, the tears of confession, the spirit of sacrifice and tribulations, and the heart of contrition and humility ("non habent illae paginae vultum pietatis illius, lacrimans confessionis, sacrificium tuum, spiritum contribulatum, cor contritum et humiliatum," 7.xxi). Although intellectually he has discovered sound metaphysical principles, morally he is still in the mode of presumption rather than of confession (7.xx).

In literary terms, Augustine must learn to accept the humility of biblical prose and prefer it to the polish of eloquent men's words. The Incarnation turns out to be the solution to this problem. Christ incarnate as the baby Jesus is a Word given in weakness and without speaking: it abides simply in silent humility. Incarnation of divinity as silent Word beyond all that sounding words can express is a paradox that can provide the key to many other paradoxes relating to God.

But Augustine is still beaten back from untrammeled contemplation of supreme Being by the infirmity of his flesh. Bereft of this eternal presence, he is left with only memory and desire, with missing and longing for the Good, for God, whom he does not possess. He can only glimpse the supreme Good or God as that from which or whom his purely contemplative gaze is thrust back ("et pervenit ad id, quod est in ictu trepidantis aspectus . . . sed aciem figere non evalui et repercussa infirmitatate redditus solitis," 7.xvii).

Once Augustine sees that God is truth and that only God truly *is*, his *understanding* of the world, of all the things that are, is revolutionized. All things besides God *are* only because they are *from* God, and otherwise they would not be at all. They have no being of their own. The fact that they are at all depends on God, who alone *is* in and of and through himself. It is God who made them and who still, in every moment, sustains them in their being. There is an ontological gulf between Creator and creature, between unchanging and mutable being. "Then I thought upon those other things that are less than You, and I saw that they neither absolutely are nor yet totally are not: they are, in as much as they are from You: they are not, in as much as they are not what You are. For that truly is, which abides unchangeably" (7.xi).

Augustine will go on to "flesh out" this ontological lack in terms of attachment to lower things which are not in being to the same degree as the higher. The will is prevailed upon by the weight of flesh and carnal habit, and so we enter into a Pauline arena of combat within the will between flesh and spirit. On this same basis, it becomes possible from another angle to understand how the new ontological insight acquired from Platonism revolutionizes Augustine's understanding of evil. Evil cannot really be, since only God *is* in the truest sense, and God is wholly good; he is indeed Goodness itself. What is evil is really (ontologically) nothing: evil things, in so far as they are absolutely evil and in no way good, simply are not at all. "If they were deprived of all goodness, they would be altogether nothing: therefore as long as they are, they are good. Thus, whatsoever things are, are good; and that evil whose origin I sought is not a substance, because if it were a substance it would be good" (7.xii). For God and for his creation considered as a whole, there is no evil, for whatever is is good, and it is good that even less excellent things are. The whole is better than it would be if the lesser things were not at all: "To You, then, evil utterly is not—and not only to You, but to Your whole creation likewise, evil is not. . . . I realized that while certain higher things are better than lower things, yet all things together are better than the higher alone" (7.xiii).

What is evil, then? Augustine can now answer that it is only a perversion of the will that turns to lower things and their lesser good and away from God, the supreme and absolute Good. It is only this breakdown in the right order of loving within the free, rational will that is evil. "So that when I now asked what is iniquity, I realized that it was not a substance but a swerving of the will which is turned toward lower things and away from You, O God, who are the supreme substance: so that it casts away what is most inward to it and swells greedily for outward things" (7.xvi).

The insight into incorruptible being as the origin of all material and corruptible being that Augustine acquires from Platonism gives him the key to resolving the problem of evil without resorting to the Manichean postulate of a world created evil. It is through the discovery of the books of the Platonists that Augustine is able to break free of the hold of Manichaeism. However, it should not be thought that Augustine overlooks or underestimates evil, blinded by Platonic idealism. Mallard suggests how profound Augustine's apparently empty conception of evil really is:

> Beyond Manichaean mythology lay the subtlety of real evil, alluring in its promises, its dynamism, and its freedom. The profundity of evil as "nothing" then appears. . . . the evil will, eroded by "nothingness," is capable of countless horrid, aggressive scenarios. Furthermore, evil as nothing also rightly means that no one can scrutinize the essence of evil in itself: the dynamic effects of the breakdown can be seen, yes; the thing itself, no. Evil as nothing is all the more disturbing in this active hiddenness. By the time its effects come to view, the evil lack within the will may already be undermining other matters, not yet suspected. Augustine in his evil as "nothing" had come beyond Manichaean passivity into the true challenge of aggressive evil.
>
> (Mallard, *Language and Love*, 99–100)

Evil is not a mythic "force," such as Manicheans of all ages simplistically imagine. It is insidiously at work in the disconnects and incoherencies of our own practical everyday engagements with the world. These lacks and gaps are where evil's "nothing" insinuates itself. It is especially when we do not really know what we should be doing with ourselves, for loss of a general vision of the order of things, such as genuine humanities learning inculcates, that evil can work within us in the name of nothing. The energy to act is there; it is in itself good, but if nothing directs it, nothing that brings it into relation with the order of things that permits them to be in peace and to harmoniously develop and fulfill their being, the result will be an active production of nothingness and destruction. We cannot judge being, but we can let it be, and this demands active participation in promoting and contributing to the order of being. This is how the divine "Let there be . . ." is carried out concretely in every moment.

It is a new language, that of Platonic philosophy, which gives Augustine the key to this new outlook on the world and on being as intrinsically and absolutely good. In yet another way, and in terms of another tradition and vocabulary, Augustine thus discovers language as revelation. It is from the moment that one can formulate a world linguistically that unified sense can be made of it and commitment to its harmonious wholeness be engendered. This is the miracle in which the world truly comes to be—it originates in and with language. Augustine comes into possession of a language for God as incorruptible and immaterial, simple Being. As a consequence, his whole world emerges from confusion into clarity.

Complete Moral and Existential Conversion: Confessions, *Books 8–9*

Book 8 portrays Augustine as convinced but not yet truly converted. He has seen the Truth and knows that only God can satisfy his desire, yet his will is still enslaved by habits that prevent him from renouncing his earthly attachments and from fully embracing and living out what he already knows. He knows the eternal Good, the whole Truth, but he cannot yet wholly will it. He faces the enigma of a will that cannot fully will itself. Even when obeyed by the body, it seems impotent to command *itself* to will *resolutely* what it wills. This quandary leads Augustine to Scripture and through it to developing a classic Catholic understanding of deficiency in the will that can account for his bondage to sin and his difficulty in converting completely, even after he has become certain of the Truth. The Manichean theory of two souls, one good and one evil, vying for control within the human breast, echoing the cosmic conflict between Good and Evil, would relieve the individual agent of moral responsibility, but Augustine now refuses it and insists that the weak and contradictory will is his *own*. The division is *within* him, inasmuch as *he* wills not entirely what he would will: "it was I who willed to do it, I who was unwilling. It was I. I did not wholly will" ("ego eram, qui volebam, ego, qui nolebam, ego, ego eram. nec plene volebam," 8.x).

What Augustine experiences is not a Manichean dualistic conflict between primordial good and evil in the universe but rather the Pauline interior conflict between the will of the flesh and that of the spirit: "the flesh lusts against the spirit and the spirit against the flesh" (Galatians 5:17). Even so Augustine: "My two wills, one old, one new, one carnal, one spiritual, were in conflict and in their conflict wasted my soul" ("ita duae voluntates meae, una vetus, alia nova, illa carnalis, illa spiritalis, confligebant inter se, atque discordando dissipabant animam meam," 8.v). After his intellectual illumination, the unachieved moral conversion issues in this scene staging the combat between flesh and spirit, just as in Paul's archetypal scenario.

Concerning these two conflicting wills which are emphatically within Augustine himself, he observes that any finite will cannot but engender a counter-will. This belongs to the nature of human will as divided from itself and scattered across time. Unification of the will can come only from its abandon of itself to a higher Will, to God. God is more myself than I myself am (3.vi). He is, moreover, himself a Trinitarian unity of multiple persons. The solution to the problem of the human will divided inevitably into antagonistic counter-wills comes through a transcendence of human will toward the divine Will. Only turning to God repairs the division within the will. The divine Will finally unifies the human faculties of memory, understanding, and will—not by willing as such but by an all-encompassing act, and this act is Love.[29]

---

29. Illuminating here is John Burnaby, *Amor Dei: A Study of the Religion of Saint Augustine* (London: Hodder and Stoughton, 1938).

Given its obvious exemplarity and its conformity to a Scriptural paradigm, the question can be raised as to whether this account of the conversion of the will to God is a true story of Augustine's own experience.[30] Whatever historicity the event may have, it is plain from the account itself that Augustine's conversion is all literarily mediated. It is elaborately framed by several layers of preliminary conversion *narratives* that provide literary models. The first is the one about Victorinus that is related by Ambrose's spiritual father, Simplicianus. Augustine seeks him out for help in carrying through the moral conversion necessary to enact his newfound conviction, his certainty concerning eternal life and God conceived Platonically as incorruptible, spiritual being. Simplicianus tells Augustine of Victorinus, a famous Roman orator covered with honors of state who converted to Christianity and humbled himself to make public profession of his faith, scandalizing high society thereby but also winning the hearts of simple believers. The story is told in order to serve as a model for imitation, and this is precisely the effect it has on Augustine, as he confesses to God: "Now when this man of Yours, Simplicianus, had told me the story of Victorinus, I was on fire to imitate him" ("exarsi ad imitandum: ad hoc enim et ille narraverat," 8.v). Augustine wants to follow Victorinus in giving up the teaching of worldly rhetoric in order to devote himself wholly to the service of God. Nevertheless, his will is still encumbered.

Such conspicuous literary mediation highlights how language and narrative are constitutive of the construction and of the very experience of Augustine's exemplary religious conversion. Augustine's conversion is made possible fundamentally by his new interpretation of his life, and it is specifically narrative discourses encountered at a critical moment, in which they can illuminate the meaning of his own life, that provide the necessary impetus for his metamorphosis. The stories, together with their pathos and their poetry, are not just decorative or edifying picture frames: they are indispensable catalysts in bringing about Augustine's conversion. To this extent, narrative art is intrinsic to the revelation that is accomplished concretely by Augustine's act of converting.

Augustine emphasizes how he does not recollect the cause ("non recolo causam," "nescio quid a nobis volebat") for which Ponticianus, his fellow countryman, an African in imperial employ, on a certain day ("Quodam igitur die"), came to his house, where he sighted a book, a compendium of the epistles of Paul, lying on the table "by chance" ("forte"). This narrative account explicitly emphasizes the role of contingency in conversion. Where

30. Pierre Courcelle's classic study, "La valeur historique des *Confessions*," in *Recherches*, 29ff., suggests that the conversion is literary fiction rather than historical reality. The question is approached historically by J. J. O'Meara, *The Young Augustine* (London: Longman, 1954), and Gerald Bonner, *St. Augustine of Hippo: Life and Controversies* (Philadelphia: Westminster, 1963), 42–52.

there is no other calculable, human motivation, chance functions as the marker of an otherwise indiscernible divine providence. Likewise in the story Ponticianus tells about two imperial legates wandering around a monastery somewhere outside Milan, the book recounting the Life of Saint Antony is stumbled upon *by chance*. "One of them began to read it, marvelled at it, was inflamed by it. While he was actually reading he had begun to think how he might embrace such a life, and give up his worldly employment to serve you [God] alone" (8.vi). Even within the story of Antony's conversion, the same thing happens in order to catalyze his exemplary conversion. Antony hears by chance, as he passes in front of a church with its door open, a certain quotation from the Gospels—"give away what you have and come, follow me"—which he immediately applies to his own life. The one imperial legate who has been converted by stumbling on the book of Antony's life communicates his change of heart to the other, who decides to imitate him in exchanging the service of an earthly emperor for that of the heavenly one. The two then further convey their resolution to their respective betrotheds, to whom it proves similarly contagious, so that they in turn take vows dedicating their virginity to God alone.

Augustine's own conversion, like those in these frame stories, is mediated by an encounter with a book, indeed with a specific passage hit upon at hazard. There are distinct moments in this event: first, he hears a solicitation from the outside urging him to take a decisive step; this is then followed by his own reading of a text in silence. In addition to echoing the scene of Ambrose reading silently, the description of this moment—"I snatched it up, opened it and in silence read the passage upon which my eyes first fell" ("arripui, aperui et legi in silentio capitulum quo primum coniecti sunt oculi mei")—is modeled on the discovery by Ponticianus of the book of Paul's epistles on the table in Augustine's house: "He picked it up, opened it, and found that it was the apostle Paul" ("tulit, aperuit, invenit apostolum Paulum," 8.xii). By these literary structures of enframement, chance occasions are shown to have been providential.

The story of one conversion leading to another in a chain reaction, moreover, prefigures what Augustine's own conversion—which is memorialized in this very narrative and projected toward the future—is going to do. Augustine's text sets itself up as a link in an ongoing transmission of conversion experiences. Immediately following and modeled upon his own conversion is that of Alypius. Rather than only recounting a conversion that has already taken place and is simply history, the *Confessions* open an opportunity to the current reader ("you") to continue the series by becoming the latest convert. Such "verbal action" in the *Confessions* calls to be understood, among other ways, in terms of its rhetorical basis and implications.[31]

31. See Kenneth Burke, *The Rhetoric of Religion: Studies in Logology* (Berkeley: University of California Press, 1970), 43–171.

But neither is verbal action alone enough. Augustine is still trammeled by the lusts of the flesh and its sinful habits. He stages a contest in persuasion between pleasures and lust plucking at his fleshly garment and Lady Continency before him in chaste dignity (8.xi). Of course, it is God who finally moves him. Consequently, rhetoric is sublated by grace to religion and speaks to him with the power of the divine Word. The actual moment of conversion features a text speaking directly to Augustine: it is recognized by him as meant for him in particular and as directing him to apply it to his own life. The mysterious childlike voice bids him to "take up and *read*"—*tolle, lege*—thereby voicing explicitly the indispensable role that reading has in triggering his conversion (8.xii). Augustine reads a passage from Paul come upon by chance, reading it, like Antony, as if it were addressed specifically to him at just this moment:

> I snatched it up, opened it and in silence read the passage upon which my eyes first fell: *Not in rioting and drunkenness, not in chambering and impurities, not in contention and envy, but put ye on the Lord Jesus Christ and make not provision for the flesh in its concupiscenses.* I had no wish to read further, and no need. For in that instant, with the very ending of the sentence, it was as though a light of utter confidence shone in all my heart, and all the darkness of uncertainty vanished away.
>
> (8.xii)

The rest is silence. Shortly after conversion, Augustine resigns from his profession of rhetoric, retracting his tongue from the marketplace of words (9.i). Yet he turns first to literary activity: thus literature and conversion again turn out to be contiguous and in fact inextricably intertwined. Verecundius's country villa at Cassaciacum enables Augustine and his little community of friends to enjoy a spiritual life of contemplation and cultivation of the liberal arts. The love of letters and the desire for God: such is Augustine's idyllic dream of beatitude in this life (9.i–v). His ideal model for a monastic life was destined to be pursued long afterward by deeply indebted devotees.[32]

This makes a fitting conclusion to the story of a conversion that comes about thanks to the mediation of reading. Augustine's whole life has been a process of learning to read aright, which means learning to see the hand of God everywhere in everything and thus to believe in God's revelation of himself to humanity. Reading, moreover, is a process of gathering elements together into a meaningful whole. The Latin word for reading, *lego, -ere*,

32. See Jean Leclerq, *L'Amour des lettres et le désir de Dieu: Initiation aux auteurs monastiques du Moyen-Âge* (Paris: Cerf, 1957), trans. Catherine Misrahi as *The Love of Learning and the Desire for God: A Study of Monastic Culture* (New York: Fordham University Press, 1982).

literally means "picking out" and "gathering." Etymologically, the word implies also "binding together." This is indeed what Augustine's *Confessions* do with his life and thinking, in order to make them a revelation that is both literary and theological. This binding into wholeness—for which the structure of the sentence serves Augustine as paradigm—is the basic function of language that makes it revelatory. Expression in language and particularly in literature can be per se revelatory, and Augustine analyzes its resources for wholeness of vision such as that enjoyed and possibly granted by God. God is addressed as all-knowing (*Domine tu scis*) and as the truth itself, always present—"praesentem veritatem, quod tu est" (9.x)—and such truth makes itself present specifically in reading.

This vision of his life as a whole, including all that it was before it merged with the eternal life which he begins to share in from the moment of his conversion in 386, is realized at the culmination of the autobiographical portion of the work. This part is the story of his earthly life and errancy, and it turns out to be coextensive with the life story of his mother in the flesh. Monica's life for all practical purposes concludes with her son's conversion, and Augustine, in effect, ends his autobiography of his wayward youth with his mother's death in 387. Book 9, accordingly, includes also a miniature biography of Monica (chapters viii–ix). Both his own and his mother's biographies are made to culminate in the mystical vision at Ostia, in which mortal life in time is momentarily suspended in a being beyond time and beyond language. After this, Augustine's mortal life is eclipsed by a wider horizon opening to eternity. The experience at Ostia is one of transcending beyond the reach of language. Nonetheless, it is through language that he and his mother approach this experience of the ineffable: "Our conversation had brought us to this point."[33] It is in surpassing language, by opening into a realm beyond verbalization, that this language achieves its goal. Augustine's express purpose is to use language in order to evoke the experience of silence:

> So we said: "If to any man the tumult of the flesh grew silent, silent the images of earth and sea and air: and if the heavens grew silent, and the very soul grew silent to herself and by not thinking of self mounted beyond self: if all dreams and imagined visions grew silent, and every tongue and every sign and whatsoever is transient—for indeed if any man could hear them, he should hear them saying with one voice: We did not make ourselves, but He made us who abides

33. Brian Stock observes similarly in *Augustine the Reader*: "The medium through which the pair's ascent takes place is human language (*sermo*, 9.10.14; *dum loquimur*, 9.10.27). Their words to each other are the steps of their mutual ascent beyond all corporeal things (including the sun, the moon, and the stars; 9.10.14–19), just as Augustine's reading of the Psalms is a *canticum graduum*" (118).

> forever: but if, having uttered this and so set us to listening to Him who made them, they all grew silent, and in their silence He alone spoke to us, not by them but by Himself: so that we should hear His word, not by any tongue of flesh nor the voice of an angel nor the sound of thunder nor in the darkness of a parable, but that we should hear Himself whom in all these things we love, should hear Himself and not them: just as we two had but now reached forth and in a flash of the mind attained to touch the eternal Wisdom which abides over all: and if this could continue, and all other visions so different be quite taken away, and this one should so ravish and absorb and wrap the beholder in inward joys that his life should eternally be such as that one moment of understanding for which we had been sighing—would not this be: Enter Thou into the joy of Thy Lord?"
>
> (9.x)

This long passage is all one uninterrupted sentence, notwithstanding the shifts from declarative to conditional to optative and imperative moods. The contemplative experience it describes is buoyed up and sustained on the very language from which it essentially distinguishes itself. Moreover, the vision of God himself as beyond representation of any kind remains, nevertheless, an experience of God as Word. His presence is a speaking that he himself *is*. The unmediated presence of God as Word emerges out of conversation between Augustine and his mother in a language that is nearly telepathic thought and finally merges with the truth or Wisdom of God:

> And higher still we soared, thinking in our minds and speaking and marvelling at Your works: and so we came to our own souls, and went beyond them to come at last to that region of richness unending, where You feed Israel forever with the food of truth: and there life is that Wisdom by which all things are made, both the things that have been and the things that are yet to be.
>
> (9.x)[34]

This transcendence into the ineffable presence of the divine Word or Wisdom, of course, can be made explicit only before it starts—or else when the vision finishes, when Augustine and his mother enter back into the dimension of speech: "And while we were thus talking of His Wisdom and panting for it, with all the effort of our heart we did for one instant attain to touch it;

34. "et adhuc ascendabamus, interius cogitando et loquendo et mirando opera tua, et venimus in mentes nostras et transcendimus eas, ut attingeremus regionem ubertatis indeficientis, unde pascis Israel in aeternum veritate pabulo, et ibi vita sapientia est, per quam fiunt omnia ista, et quae fuerunt et quae futura sunt" (*Confessions* 9.x).

then sighing, and leaving the first fruits of our spirit bound to it, we returned to the sound of our own tongue, in which a word has both beginning and ending" (9.x).

Indeed, the eternal Word becomes audible only in creatures and their speech. Nonetheless, it is in the silencing of their speech that the Word Itself speaks. Augustine imagines all things growing silent, and in their silence their very being would speak. Their being spoken into being by the Word, their creatureliness, would then be articulated and become audible. In their silence, it is the eternal Word that is heard. If all physically audible speech and sound were silenced, and even the representations of the soul to itself were to grow still, all transient creatures would be heard saying with one voice that they are creatures, and this saying of their being would be the voice of the Word that is Being itself, which is not made but rather makes all things that are made:

> We did not make ourselves, but He made us who abides forever: but if, having uttered this and so set us to listening to Him who made them, they all grew silent, and in their silence He alone spoke to us, not by them but by Himself: so that we should hear His word, not by any tongue of flesh nor the voice of an angel nor the sound of thunder nor in the darkness of a parable, but that we should hear Himself whom in all these things we love, should hear Himself and not them: just as we two had but now reached forth and in a flash of the mind attained to touch the eternal Wisdom which abides over all.
>
> (9.x)

In this experience of the silence of all things, God Himself, the Word, can be heard. This is an experience of eternity and of the resurrected life, when "we shall all be changed" (1 Corinthians 15:51).

In this manner, it is through words that Augustine and Monica attain to the experience of the eternal Word. And yet it is only by suspending and transcending all temporal speech of any kind that the experience of eternity takes place. This becomes clear when, after that instant of contact with divine Wisdom, Augustine writes, "we returned to the sound of our own tongue, in which a word has both beginning and ending." There is a Word that infinitely transcends all finite words and that gives itself to human experience through discourse, yet as infinitely beyond it. Augustine's own discourse is a rhetorical weave that is designed to draw a reader into openness toward the sort of transcendent experience it describes as silence. Thus revelation is curiously linguistic and yet, at the same time, a revelation of the silence beyond language. This is the nature of poetry—to be words reaching beyond words into silence. For the order of experience with which Augustine is dealing, there is no language but poetry.

As a transcendent vision in the company of his parent now at the end of her life, this culminating vision has a function comparable in some respects to Aeneas's revelation from his father in the afterlife: as such, it is a revelation of destiny. And in this case, it is clearly not just a historical but also an eternal destiny. The parent who gave him life is now again instrumental in giving him new life, eternal life.

Reaching this prophetic vision of eternity through a personal relation with a parent has been made possible by Augustine's conversion, his turning to God, as accomplished in the preceding book (8). In the following books, Augustine's conversion is registered concretely as a conversion of his language. He is now able to withdraw his tongue from the service of worldly eloquence ("subtrahere ministerium linguae meae mundinis loquacitatis," 9.ii). The silence discovered as beyond language, but also as its transcendent ground, prepares for a new life of language and thus for Augustine's rebirth as the consummate Christian rhetor in his role as bishop of Hippo until his death in 430.[35]

V. Syntheses of Mind and Time—in Language: *Confessions*, Books 10–11

The end of book 9 and the beginning of book 10 reactivate the restless questions about Augustine's addressee in the *Confessions*. This extraordinary dimension of his discourse comes back under examination here as his "confession" shifts its focus from past to present and thence to timeless verities concerning creation as an eternal act. Augustine admits again that from one point of view all he says, even in confessing himself to God, is for his fellow men ("ego quoque, Domine, etiam sic tibi confiteor, ut audiant homines"). Yet their hearing his discourse as true can occur only by their hearing it through love and through God ("quibus demonstrare non possum, an vera confitear; sed credunt mihi, quorum mihi aures caritas aperit," 10.iii). In other words, not only does Augustine confess to God in order that men may hear, but conversely his communication with men is meant to pass through God: other men cannot in principle see what Augustine is divulging of his inner soul except through charity and through what God reveals in their own hearts about themselves. They can know only from Truth working directly in them, not from Augustine, that what Augustine says about himself is true. This opens an inner dimension of personal knowledge and testimony to which human witness can only be indirect: God alone sees it directly and totally.

Thus even the relation to the reader is mediated by the relation to God. In this way, Augustine is able to strategically undermine the readers' own

35. Calvin L. Troup, *Temporality, Eternity, and Wisdom: The Rhetoric of Augustine's Confessions* (Columbia: University of South Carolina Press, 1999) argues for the essentially rhetorical inspiration of the *Confessions* as a whole. He contrasts the rhetorical model of the incarnate Word with the Neoplatonic paradigm of intellectual ascent.

standards of judgment by appealing to God as silent addressee whose judgment nevertheless trumps that of the human reader, in whatever way the latter may choose to understand what Augustine has written. "But now, O Lord, I confess to You in writing, let him read it who will and interpret it as he will" ("et nunc, domine, confiteor tibi in litteris. legat qui volet et interpretetur, ut volet," 9.xii). This construction connecting the author directly to a divine Author and inscribing his relation to his readers into his dialogue with divinity is key to Augustine's transfiguration of a highly personal and interpersonal discourse into discourse with a genuine claim to being religious revelation.

Whatever Augustine can say to his fellow men has already been confessed much more deeply and completely before God tacitly, in the cry of the heart—before any articulation in words. This is, in fact, crucial in order for Augustine's work to become a total revelation of the truth about himself as reflected in God and not only as he subjectively experiences it. All that he himself knows, even about himself, is complete and perfect only in God's mind.

> For You, O Lord, are my judge, because though no man knows the things of a man, save the spirit of a man that is in him [as Paul says in 1 Corinthians 2:11], yet there is something of man that the very spirit of man that is in him does not know. But you, Lord, know all of him, for You made him.
>
> (10.v)

This is a lucid acknowledgment of the unconscious, of a region within man that is unknown to his own mind or spirit. Augustine infers that his knowledge of himself can be true and total only to the extent that it is knowledge in God, for it is not really grasped by Augustine except through his faith in God.

> I will confess therefore what I know of myself and what I do not know; for what I know of myself I know through the shining of Your light; and what I do not know of myself, I continue not to know until my darkness shall be made as noonday in Your countenance.
>
> (10.v)

The claim to revelation rests on a gesture of totalizing experience and knowledge through this appeal to the mind of God. This repeats the gesture of prophetic revelation based on the totalizing of knowledge of history from the end-point that we have discerned in epic tradition as its decisive pivot. However, in Augustine this total knowledge has become interiorized and has been projected beyond human comprehension altogether into God, since "I cannot totally grasp all that I am" ("nec ego ipse capio totum, quod sum," 10.viii). In spite of its elaborate, outwardly expansive expression, the whole meaning of the work is in principle interior and unexpressed. The essential confession, therefore, remains tacit: "And so my confession, O my God, in Your sight is made silently: and yet not silently, for if it makes no sound, yet it cries aloud in my heart" ("confessio itaque mea, deus meus, in conspectu tuo tibi tacite fit et non tacite. tacet enim strepitu, clamat affectu," 10.ii). In his treatise on the Trinity (*De Trinitate*, book 15.10.19—xii.22), Augustine fully develops his theory of the "interior word," which is eternal, true, and total. The persons of the Trinity correspond to the human faculties of Memory, Intellect, and Will. Phenomenologically speaking, in Augustine's *Confessions*, it is through memory that this interior space opens to a dimension above it, where God is eternally present.

Speculations of Memory

Augustine's autobiography has built up to his conversion, the story of which is really complete after the vision at Ostia and the death of his mother at the end of book 9. He continues for four more books on a rather different tack, one no longer focused on his personal experience, but pitched on a more universal plane of philosophical and theological inquiry. This progression could be seen as parallel to the sequence of books that make up the Bible in the shift from the historical narrative of the Pentateuch to prophecy and Wisdom literature. The work becomes speculative and also exegetical rather than narrative in nature, but it is still "confessional" in the sense of redounding to the praise of the Creator for all his wonderful works.[36]

The turn toward philosophical speculation and theological doctrine, as well as to Scriptural exegesis, that the *Confessions* takes in its last four books makes patent that the autobiography has not been told for its own sake alone but rather in order to lead to contemplation of more universal, indeed everlasting truths—and so for the sake of doctrine in the highest and purest sense. Indeed, in its last four books the *Confessions* turn into a sort of encyclopedia measuring the whole extent of human experience—all that can be contained by the human mind. This encyclopedic form welds together the story of Augustine's life as totalized in the moment of his conversion and consequent vision—from which everything in his life takes on its definitive meaning—with the more explicitly philosophical and theological portions of his work.

In this regard, the *Confessions* are actually similar to the other works we have treated so far: the classical epic has served as an encyclopedic form, and the Bible too, perhaps more than any other book, has been taken to contain the sum of all wisdom, human and divine. Augustine uses an encyclopedic form to sum up all of Creation, but this gathering into synthesis of creatures

36. For comprehensive evaluation of the unity of the work based on intricate patterns of correspondence between the last book (13) and books 1–9 and 10–12, see Robert McMahon, *Augustine's Prayerful Ascent: An Essay on the Literary Form of the Confessions* (Athens: University of Georgia Press, 1989).

also reaches beyond them to the Creator. All creatures speak of God and bid us to love him (10.vi). And yet, emphatically, they are all not God. In the way of a *via negativa*, all the creatures whom Augustine interrogates reply, "We are not your God; seek higher" (10.vi). Augustine is led thus from the highest echelons of the outwardly visible Creation into his own soul and thence even beyond toward the ultimate object of his love. In God, all things are gathered into one.

Already on the human plane, memory furnishes a key for totalizing mind and soul. It forges a simultaneity of all experience and knowledge, and yet at the same time opens into an unfathomable abyss. The moment all is gathered into one and synchrony is achieved in memory, it becomes glaringly evident to Augustine how the whole is dependent on what it does not contain—how it all collapses toward what transcends it.

Memory is not just an indifferent storage room for materials. It integrates all experience and history into unity. It is precisely the recomposition of events in memory, and the forging of their union into one, that projects an image of eternity. Book 10 gives the first intimations of how humans attain to a consciousness of eternity through their experience of time. They do so by cultivating a grasp of continuities and of the connectedness of all experience. Memory is marvelously fertile in producing such connectedness. The logic of this production, for Augustine, is linguistic: the Word is what makes the connection between time and eternity that is investigated in book 11.

This gathering into unity is not only a summation of facts; it is a revelation of original unity in a Mind higher than any human memory and its limited unifying powers. Memory, through making possible a unity of our experience, is a bridge to Augustine's own Maker: "I shall mount beyond this power of my nature, still rising by degrees toward him who made me. And so I come to the fields and vast palaces of memory" (10.viii). This self-transcendence toward God, as built into the structure of memory, is signaled by the fact that human memory (or mind) cannot contain itself:

> Great is this power of memory, exceedingly great, O my God, a spreading limitless room within me. Who can reach its uttermost depth? Yet it is a faculty of my soul and belongs to my nature. In fact I cannot totally grasp all that I am. Thus the mind is not large enough to contain itself: but where can that part of it be which it does not contain? Is it outside itself and not within? How can it not contain itself?
>
> (10.viii)

These reflections open up an abyss within the mind itself, and that is where Augustine finds God always already present and containing all that his own mind cannot contain. This power of self-transcendence in the mind is so marvelous that Augustine launches into exclamations that would inspire many, including eventually Petrarch in his epoch-making letter on the ascent of Mount Ventoux.[37] Petrarch took the following passage as if it had been written *for him*:

> Here are men going afar to marvel at the heights of mountains, the mighty waves of the sea, the long courses of great rivers, the vastness of the ocean, the movements of the stars, yet leaving themselves unnoticed and not seeing it as marvelous that when I spoke of all these things I did not see them with my eyes, yet I could not have spoken of them unless these mountains and waves and rivers and stars . . . had been inwardly present to my sight: in my memory . . . (10.viii).

Memory is a prodigious power of making even absent things present (10.xv). There is a representative presence within the mind of all external things, including those that are most vast—mountains, rivers, stars, plains. The mind, though of no apparent dimension itself, and seemingly localized in a single human body, can encompass them all. Not only external realities, but knowledge, such as arts and sciences (10.ix), and general and abstract truths, such as make up mathematics (10.xii), are contained in memory, as are also affects beyond all facts: "My memory also contains the feelings of my mind" (10.xiv). There is even memory of remembering itself (10.xiii), as well as of forgetting (10.xvi). For even forgetting presupposes remembering of what is forgotten, since it can be missed and searched for only if it is remembered—at least as having been forgotten.

This discussion of memory is thus a revelation of the mind's powers of self-reflection. They are crucial to memory as a power of gathering, of collecting out of dispersion, and this activity of synthesis is practically the essence of thought. Of his scattered memories, Augustine observes: "they must be collected out of dispersion, and indeed the verb to cogitate is named from this drawing together" (10.xi). He then points out that *cogito* (I think) is based on *cogo* (I collect).

As the power of synthesis, memory is identical with the mind and its activity (10.xiv). Not only does it store up images, received from without, of sense objects and feelings produced from within the mind itself, along with the propositions of the arts and sciences that it learns; and not only does memory also have a power of self-transcendence so that it proves unable to contain itself: memory is able, furthermore, to transcend time, and it reaches even beyond itself to the eternal, to God.

Previously Augustine's analysis of his whole historical life as present in his memory had implicitly relied on a synthetic process of self-reflection. Now

37. Valuable reflection on the letter's originality is found in Francesco Petrarca, *La lettera del Ventoso: Familiarium rerum libri 4.1*, ed. Maura Formica and Michael Jakob (Verbania: Tarara: 1996), preface by Andrea Zanzotto.

that power of synthesis itself becomes his express theme. There is no limit to what the mind can take in. This infinity is a sign of some higher reality. Imagination—the mind's faculty of representing things—becomes a revelation to itself and even from beyond itself. Augustine's explorations highlight mainly the fact that memory does not contain itself but reposes rather in God. It finds its source and ground not in any innate idea of God that it contains in itself but rather above and beyond itself in God *himself*: "In what place then did I find You to learn of You? For You were not in my memory, before I learned of You. Where then did I find You to learn of You, save in Yourself, above myself?" (10.xxvi).

Through the mind's synthetic power, Augustine mounts to the source of all that is, the ultimate point of synthesis in the source of all: "In my ascent by the mind to You who abide above me, I shall mount up beyond that power of mine called memory, longing to attain to touch You at the point where that contact is possible and to cleave to You at the point where it is possible to cleave" (10.xvii). The search for completion and happiness of the self is likewise a search for God (10.xx). All pursue happiness and therefore must all possess it in their minds, for "we should not love it unless we had some knowledge of it" (10.xx). In fact, we even "remember" what we have never known or possessed, namely, the total happiness of the *vita beata*.[38] Memory is ultimately memory of God. For memory entails a searching and a desire for what satisfies the soul, for happiness, but the truly happy life is nothing other than rejoicing in and for God only (10.xxii).

Augustine reworks the opening paradoxes of the *Confessions*, in which immanence and transcendence both require and exclude each other, in declaring that the blessed life could not be sought and loved unless it were known ("sed quaero, utrum in memoria sit beata vita. neque enim amaremus eam nisi nossimus," 10.xx), and thus already in memory, yet neither can it be there or it would not be sought.

The extraordinary thing in the vision of the *Confessions* is that the sum of all knowledge can be experienced immanently within memory or the human mind. The principle of subjective synthesis emerges clearly as the unifying principle of all knowledge and experience. Nevertheless, this principle is not autonomous and self-grounding. It is turned toward the divine transcendence at its own core and center. This turn marks out a crucial direction for the secularization of religious revelation to be pursued in the ensuing centuries. The total vision of history through prophetic revelation as the fulcrum of epic tradition in Virgil is extended by Augustine's Christian and biblical vision so that it now passes through the self-reflective consciousness of the individual subject. Reality, human and divine, just as in the epics, is revealed through

38. In his treatise *De vita beata* (386), Augustine reflects on how he can seek a blessedness that he has never known. Desiring itself can constitute a sort of knowing of the Unknown.

a discursive synthesis, but now the individual life and mind of the author is probed as the locus of revelation. All things are gathered into the miraculous synthesis made possible through "memory." Memory or mind, a secularized version of Mnemosyne, the mother of the Muses, now steps forth as a principle of subjective unity and identity.

Memory is the thesaurus of knowledge, and from the beginning of book 10 the theme of knowledge is treated from within the desiring relation to God. Augustine prays: "Let me know Thee who knowest me, let me know Thee even as I am known" ("Cognoscam te, cognitor meus, cognoscam, sicut et cognitus sum," 10.i). Augustine's self-reflective "I" is poles apart from the autonomous, self-grounding cogito ("I think, therefore I am") of the modern subject. Clearly, for him the foundation of knowledge is not the self, but in God. God's knowledge of me is superior to my knowledge even of myself: rather than being a sovereign act of judging all in its purview, knowledge is first of all a submission to being judged, and is thus a humbling. This is also a guiding principle of Augustine's metaphysics. Knowledge of oneself is not a matter of sovereignly inspecting oneself by one's own lights and power but rather of humbling oneself so as to let the Light shine on the blind spots that our pride otherwise prevents us from seeing (10.v).

Not only man but all things are known truly only in God. Augustine, having found God, is now prepared to sketch an encyclopedia of human knowledge—a task he will carry over into numerous further works. Yet here he already begins by raising basic philosophical questions. In particular, Augustine anticipates many of the chief problems of philosophy of mind down to the present: sense-perception as origin of knowledge versus innate ideas; the ambiguous status of objects of cognition as mental representations and as extra-mental entities or referents; the mental status of the peculiarly formal being of mathematical entities.[39]

All of these questions can be raised for Augustine only within the framework of divine knowledge, and indeed they all point to what transcends the merely human. Augustine emphasizes particularly the terrifying greatness of memory (from 10.viii onward), yet it is above memory that God must be sought. God is not an innate idea inherent within the mind but rather a truth over and above it. Thus the mind is aware of judging by a standard superior to itself.[40]

Memory finds in itself God as the sign that it is itself contained by what is above it: "Where then did I find You to learn of You, save in Yourself, above myself?" ("ubi ergo te inveni, ut discere te, nisi in te supra me?" 10.viii). Yet this being above is experienced not as an object but as the rule of the mind's

---

39. See Gerard O'Daly, *Augustine's Philosophy of Mind* (London: Duckworth, 1987).

40. Augustine develops this idea of *summa veritas* intensively in *De vera religione* (391).

own activity. Augustine, accordingly, expresses the relation of the mind to God by maintaining that God is not exactly an innate idea but rather a truth, that is, Truth Itself, by which we can judge and are ourselves judged: "You were not in my memory, before I learned of You. Where then did I find You to learn of You, save in Yourself, above myself? . . . You, who are truth" (10.xxvi). In chapter xxiv, Augustine had already said, "For where I found truth, there I found my God, who is Truth Itself, and this I have not forgotten from the time I first learned it." It was indeed by transcending all creatures toward the Creator that Augustine was led to memory or mind in the first place, at the very peak of all created things, in order to mount still beyond (10.viii).

Again, as in the preamble of the *Confessions*, it is the very activity of searching for God that constitutes his reality for the human mind. Not being an innate idea in the mind, as in Platonic theories, God is found in the search of the mind for the rule that grounds and unifies it and that gives it a coherence beyond its own disparate impulses and fragmentary, dissipated recollections. Augustine's activity of "confessing" presupposes a prevenient act of God, as he continues to say in various ways throughout the work: "Receive the sacrifice of my *Confessions* offered by my tongue, which Thou didst form and hast moved to confess unto Thy name" (5.i).

The constant pattern is that God himself gives first what Augustine then offers: "Let me offer in sacrifice to Thee the service of my mind and my tongue, and do Thou give me what I may offer Thee" (11.ii). God alone guides Augustine's inward seeing with his memory and unifies Augustine's self: "Nor in all these things that my mind traverses in search of you, do I find any sure place for my mind save in You, in whom all that is scattered in me is brought into one, so that nothing of me may depart from you" ("neque in his omnibus, quae percurro consulens te, invenio tutum locum animae meae nisi in te, quo colligantur sparsa mea nec a te quicquam recedat ex me," 10.lx).

In this way, memory or, more broadly, mind ("mens"), as a power of synthesis, of constituting and so of transcending time is possible only through an instance above it, namely, God, who unifies all things. Our mental power of reflection and synthesis is in the image of God and, in effect, operates as the instrument of God's unifying power working in our own being. This empowers it to be the juncture between time and eternity. While receptive to temporal flux, still mental synthesis confers permanence upon things perishable. For mental synthesis totalizes the world and the soul. It creates a synchronic unity of all experience and knowledge—and yet, at the same time, opens them to an unfathomable abyss above them. The mental synthesis of temporal moments creates a unity but also presupposes a higher unity. It must itself be held together in a unity beyond itself and beyond time.

Memory thus enables the function of a subjective synthesis of a temporal manifold into a continuum. Augustine treats it as the place of the holding together and preserving in presence of the passing realities of the world, which otherwise vanish without trace. However, so conceived, memory is but "the subjective form of time."[41] And Augustine goes on to treat time also as a worldly phenomenon beyond all subjective or personalized orderings and structurings of the past. This is how he inaugurates the phenomenological research into time that aspires to philosophical or even to scientific validity still in modern phenomenology as founded by Edmund Husserl.

Time and Eternity

Augustine's *Confessions* articulate the juncture between time and eternity through deployment of narrative together with other types of discourse. This juncture is structured into the work by its shift from autobiographical narration in the form of a confession of the sins of Augustine's past to a discourse professing the glory of God in the present. This latter mode, expressing Augustine's consciousness of (and to) God in the present, takes diverse shapes including an encyclopedia of the human mind (memory) and an exegesis of the first few verses of Genesis. This exegesis enfolds, furthermore, an extended philosophical meditation on the nature of time. Kenneth Burke understands the two parts of the *Confessions*, the autobiographical, on the one hand, and the exegetical (and speculative), on the other, as embodying, respectively, time and eternity: "the contrast between the first nine books and the last four is clear, and clearly involves the distinction between 'rectilinear' and 'circular' terminologies . . . . The turn from a Narrative of memories to the principles of Memory is itself a technical, or 'logological' equivalent of a turn from 'time' to 'eternity.' "[42]

The question of eternity is raised expressly in relation to the beginning of time in the Creation. Whence is it, and when? Augustine's answer is: the Word. All things were created by the Word. As in the order of Creation, so in the order of revelation, only the divine Word, co-eternal with God and yet also incarnate as man, can bridge the unfathomable abyss between time and eternity. This is, of course, an index of the role of language in affording an account for human understanding of matters eternal that otherwise exceed its grasp altogether. Human language is the closest analogy to the divine Logos, and the experience of language makes possible the nearest thing to a kind of natural knowledge of divinity. Although in its proper nature divinity transcends human understanding, language provides the otherwise missing

41. Jaroslav Pelikan, *The Mystery of Continuity: Time and History, Memory and Eternity in the Thought of Saint Augustine* (Charlottesville: University Press of Virginia, 1986), 26.

42. Kenneth Burke, *The Rhetoric of Religion: Studies in Logology* (Boston: Beacon, 1961), 124.

link: God as Word reveals his infinite nature in a form that can be grasped by finite human minds.

Still, the *eternal* Word is not as such within our grasp. In Augustine's philosophy of mind, what permits synthesis of a vision of the whole that is presented in memory—the divine Word—stands outside the vision. It is a point of reference for memory in the infinite, truly all-encompassing view of God, who can be addressed, but the divine Word as such is not accessible as a phenomenon within the purview of the human mind. It is a transcendental condition of possibility that can be seen or rather verified only in what it makes visible. Prophecy—or vision from the point of view of God—was discovered in classical epic to entail seeing things whole, the whole trajectory and unfolding of history to its end, which makes the purpose of it all manifest. But this whole can be represented by language only illustratively, in images and myths. Augustine similarly relates to a whole beyond representation, yet reflected in language. Language is the mirror of synthetic vision. Language cannot state the whole, which, as God, is infinite. But language can reflect this whole, as the infinite is reflected in the finite.

Language is the preferred analogy for eternal vision because language is a whole that precedes its parts, inasmuch as every part depends on the sense of the whole to be meaningful. Moreover, the whole sentence depends on the whole of language for the complete determination of its sense, and since language is infinite, this makes meaning depend on an infinite whole. These "theological" aspects of language, as an indivisible whole and as open to an Infinite (or as infinitely open), can still be found in more secular terms in the "Romantic" linguistic philosophies of Wilhelm von Humboldt (*Über die Verschiedenheit des menschlichen Sprachbaues*, 1836) and Friedrich Schleiermacher (*Hermeneutik*, 1819, 1828). The latter discovers language's infinity in its endless openness to interpretation. But already the insight into language as what enables us to understand how time is bound together into a whole that opens upon an inexhaustible infinity was the basis for Augustine's interpretation of the theological doctrine of the eternal Word.

By the end of book 10, Augustine has identified the incarnate Word as the link between the temporal and the eternal that alone makes knowledge of God humanly possible. Yet the juncture between Creator and creature remains still virtually impossible to think. For one cannot help asking, *When* did the Word create the heavens and the earth? Any conceptualization of this moment seems doomed to fall into paradox and to having to blur the difference between time and eternity. From the beginning of his autobiography, Augustine had emphasized the role of language—of both the word and the Word—in forming and in effect creating him, along with his whole world, at every stage, for better or worse. It is the projection of this theme onto a cosmic scale that leads to the discussions of books 11–13 revolving around Creation by the divine Word. Augustine, at least on the strength of his own efforts, cannot know God directly as he is in himself, but must search for him in the form of vestiges of divinity in the Creation. Augustine's search leads him from creatures to the Creator, but precisely this juncture remains to be interrogated: it can only be understood in terms of language and time and their conjunction in Creation by the Word.

Beginning in the Word

While memory, from the side of humans, reaches toward divine permanence, from the other side it is God who reaches toward humans through the revelation of his Word. Already the fact of Creation by the *Word* means that the whole created universe is a divine revelation. In 11.iii, Augustine begins an exegesis of the opening chapters of Genesis and of their premise that God created all things by his Word: "You spoke and heaven and earth were created; in Your word You created them." This affirmation, derived from Scripture, specifically Genesis 1, forms the background for Augustine's speculative discussions throughout the concluding three books of the *Confessions*. He devises a theology of the Word, in which God reveals himself in and by and *as* the Word—the Word that grounds and guarantees and redeems all the words through which Augustine, since the beginning of his life and in this very literary work itself, has been seeking God and, through God, his own self.

Yet when and where can this speaking, as the original act of Creation, have taken place? It cannot have been in any physical universe. On the contrary, it is necessary to explain Creation in a way that does not presuppose any created beings such as vibrating substances or air as the necessary medium for words to sound in. God had first to create via a purely incorporeal Word, since the existence of any bodies would presuppose that he had already created something. Even more difficult to conceive, this original creative act cannot have occurred in time, for any order of time would presuppose a creative act as already having taken place. Time is itself created—it has no part in God himself, who is eternal. The Word, God's divine Son, by whom "all things were made," is "before" every creature (Colossians 1:15, 17), fully co-eternal with God, and thus prior even to time itself.

This view of God's Word as eternal is prompted also by Isaiah 40:8: "But the Word of God will remain forever" ("Verbum autem Dei manet in aeternum"). Augustine must posit the eternal Word's creating act not only as "before" there is time but also as fully eternal and therefore as going on at all times. This is a Word that says all Creation all at once and always ("simul ac sempiterne omnia," 11.vii.9). Otherwise, it would be limited in time. But an eternal act can never be past—any more than it can be future. Without any successiveness, such as characterizes all human language in time, all things are eternally spoken into existence by God the Word ("et eo sempiterne dicuntur omnia," 11.vii.9).

Given God's eternity, his Word cannot transpire in time like ours. It cannot be divided up into a sequence of syllables. His Word holds together in a perfect unity without differences of time, unlike all our spoken words, which are parsed out in time. Nonetheless, the only way of understanding God's eternity is through the analogy of his Word to our words in the discursive experience of language. There is a certain premonition of the eternal, a certain moment of quasi-transcendence of time in the human experience of *language*, precisely in the synthesis of sense, when the last syllable is uttered and the meaning of the whole sentence finally flashes across the mind and is grasped. This is what undergirds Augustine's discussion of time and its connection with eternity in the eleventh book of the *Confessions*. The analogy has already been broached in book 4, where the decease of his friend moved Augustine to lugubrious meditations on the difference between love for transient beings and an eternal love. There already he resorted to the analogy of language to explain this difference: the successiveness of syllables in time contrasts with the simultaneity of the sense of the whole sentence, even though in the actual event of language the two fuse into an indivisible unity.

Augustine thereby brings us to consider explicitly and philosophically problems that have been implicitly raised by poetic prophecy all along: how can a vision that claims to be of eternity be rendered in temporal terms? This is what language does, according to Augustine, and he explains how it does so in terms of the theological model of the divine Word, the Creator of all things, eternally present with God ("apud Deum") and yet making all things to be, beginning from a certain time. In interpreting Genesis 1:1 ("In the beginning God created the heaven and the earth"), Augustine appeals to the Gospel of John 1:1 and its teaching of the Word that was with God and that *was* God (11.vii.9). In Genesis, God speaks all things into being ("And God said . . . and it was so"), and John renders this fact fully explicit: "all things were made by *him*"—that is, by the Word, the Logos—"and without him was not anything made that was made" (John 1:3). The Word is God, and through its act of Creation it unfolds a temporal and material universe that remains, at the same time, its speech. As Scripture says: "The heavens *declare* the glory of God and the earth shows forth his handiwork" (Psalm 19:1).

In the eternal Word, all is one. There are no parts; there is simply a perfect synthesis or oneness of all Creation preexisting in its Cause. This is to be understood through analogy with the properties of language. Augustine conceives of the divine Word through the human word as the capacity to contain interiorly, intact, and in a purely mental synthesis all that it articulates externally in physical forms and sounds.[43] This is why language is a revelation of eternity. Such a conviction has been operative all through the

43. The linguisticality of this interior word, the *verbum interius* (or *intus*), is effectively underscored by Hans-Georg Gadamer, *Wahrheit und Methode* (Tübingen: J. C. B. Mohr, 1960), part 3, section 2b.

Confessions, beginning with the discursive invocation of God in the preamble that refracted Augustine's own life and inner psyche from an omniscient point of view. The whole work has been, through God, its first addressee and interlocutor, in communication with a total knowledge of self in all its temporal intricacies. Augustine has had to painstakingly gather this knowledge out of multiplicity and fragmentariness, but he has been enabled and guided in doing so by God the Word who knows all about him already and who searches into his heart more deeply than Augustine himself can do.

Augustine's meditation on time is a sublime peak in the visionary tradition of texts that we have been probing, with their strong insistence on claims to prophetic vision in poetry. Augustine investigates how any vision of time or history must, in effect, be grounded in the synthesis of temporal moments from the standpoint of eternity. He thinks out the philosophical and theological grounds of possibility of such a synthesis. Eternity, that is, the "now" which is present to all times, is presupposed in any vision of the intelligibility of life in time. This eternity is the presupposition for any possibility of narrative as a connected sequence of events such as Augustine has achieved in the preceding books that recount his life up to his conversion followed by the vision with his mother, just before her death, of eternal life. Narrative creates a kind of eternal present. It records a past which, nevertheless, remains present—in memory. The order of events and meaning that make up a narrative holds together past moments, which would otherwise have vanished, in the simultaneity of a present that never passes away. The narrative fixes in an enduring and changeless present the elapse of time that it recounts. Narrative creates a kind of eternal "now" that is given a concrete content.

Augustine's transition from narrative time to contemplation in the concluding four books of the *Confessions* brings into the arena of philosophical analysis the structural underpinnings of poetry as prophecy. Augustine elucidates theoretically the interpretation of history from the point of view of God that we have found imaginatively realized in each of the epic works examined up to this point. At certain exceptionally self-conscious moments, the eternal vision implicit in prophetic poetry was articulated by that poetry itself, particularly in its claims to see the final end of things. But Augustine gives us by far the most philosophically reflective account of the vision of eternity as the necessary foundation of any experience of time as an integrated whole, and just such an experience is what our narrative works aspire to confer, most explicitly and deliberately in their prophetic transports. The whole of history, seen in the focus of a unified meaning, reveals a time-transcendent, providential purpose that abides in an eternal now.

What Is Time? The Enigma of the Present

Although he feels intuitively that he knows it, time proves impossible for Augustine to explain discursively. His analysis unfolds as an elucidation of *aporiae* or "knots." Since past and future *are* not at all, how can they be long? Only the present *is*. However, the present is without extension. We say that it is "now"? But is it when I begin to say this word, or after I have said it, or rather while I am saying it? It can be truly "now" only while I am actually saying it, but, then, at which point precisely during my saying it? If this point has any duration at all, it too can be divided into before and after and so is never actually present all at once. And since any duration or segment of time, no matter how small, is infinitely divisible, there is no extent of time that can ever be present as a whole. It is always divisible into a time that is no longer and a time that is not yet. This points out how time has no objective existence as such and how it is but a subjective mode of apprehension of what is either no longer or not yet present. This is the conclusion that Augustine reaches through this and some other related reflections that remain landmarks in the philosophical analysis of time.[44]

How can what is not at all (that is, the past and the future) or what has no extension (the present) be measured? Yet we do measure times, past and future, as well as present. But we can measure time only when it is passing. That is, we measure the extension or "stretching" of the soul ("distentionem animi"), its synthesis of a segment of time in memory and expectation or attention. Such a segment is never existent altogether as such, but only in passing. Thus only the presence of the past (memory) or of the future (expectation) or of the present (attention), as perceived by the soul in an extended present moment of apprehension, can be measured. Only this subjective synthesis makes time perceptible at all. Augustine anticipates Kant by almost a millennium and a half in this philosophically revolutionary insight that time is a structure of subjective experience of the world.

Is not the possibility of synthesis, and therefore of the measuring of time, already grounded in eternity? In any case, the soul and its synthesis of time furnishes us our only image of eternity, in which all times are present. In order for time to be measured or to have any duration and continuum, it

44. Thus Edmund Husserl begins his *Vorlesungen zur Phänomenologie des inneren Zeitbewußtseins*, ed. Martin Heidegger (Tübingen: Max Niemeyer, 1980), which first appeared in 1928 in *Jahrbuch für Philosophie und phänomenologische Forschung*, vol. 9, with an acknowledgement that no substantial advance in understanding time consciousness has been made since Augustine: "The analysis of time-consciousness is an age-old crux of descriptive psychology and of the theory of knowledge. The first one who deeply felt the powerful difficulties that reside here and exerted himself over them almost to the point of despair was Augustine. Chapters 13–28 of Book XI of the *Confessions* must be thoroughly studied still today by anyone who is occupied by the problem of time. For modernity, for all its proud knowledge, has not made any substantial advance over this great thinker who seriously struggled with these matters. Still today we can say with Augustine concerning what time is: *if no one asks me, I know; if I wish to explain to an inquirer, I do not know*" (2).

must be present to the soul, for the presence of the past, future, and present can be apprehended only in the soul—indeed they can be apprehended only *as* modifications of the soul (*distentionem animi*). Yet the soul is not itself the ground of the Presence that it must rather presuppose and be sustained by in order to synthesize the times that it remembers and anticipates by its attentiveness in the present. This grounding in a presence that does not pass makes eternity the condition of time, or at least of any intelligible temporal order and duration. Of course, the soul's consciousness of presence passes, but even this can be perceived only from the standpoint of a present that does not pass, precisely the absolute present of eternity. This is a present which the human soul never possesses, but which it must nevertheless fleetingly image or reflect in order to perform the synthesis of times that are not present, being either no longer or not yet. This synthesis of past and future times is possible only on the basis of an ever-abiding present that they pass through and in which they are retained or anticipated as present in the form of memory or expectation. All time, which is eternally present to God, is present to the human mind only as memory, or as expectation, or as a vanishing present.

The whole of any present or presence transcends the temporal sequence that makes it up. Augustine discovers this wholeness as synthesis precisely in discovering that in itself it is ungraspable and never present except in parts that disintegrate ad infinitum. Yet the experience of the present is real. This analysis of time is experiential for Augustine: it defines the fundamental character of his existence. It is the very brokenness of time as he experiences it and its intractability to his conceptual attempts to understand it that raise Augustine's sights toward the eternity that transcends time: "and behold my life is but a scattering," "I am divided up in time," "and my thoughts and the deepest places of my soul are torn with every kind of tumult until the day when I shall be purified and melted in the fire of Thy love and wholly joined to Thee" (11.xxix). Radical experience of rupture and of existential incompleteness leads Augustine to apprehension of transcendent wholeness and an orientation to the unity in God that transcends this existence in time yet is ardently desired and, to that extent, already efficacious as a goal in unifying his existence.[45] "Nor in all these things that my mind traverses in search of You, do I find any sure place for my mind save in You, in whom all that is scattered in me is brought into one, so that nothing of me may depart from You" (11.xl).

45. On this dynamic of desire, see Margaret R. Miles, *Desire and Delight: A New Reading of Augustine's Confessions* (New York: Crossroad, 1992). The paradoxical juncture of time and eternity in desire is treated insightfully by Virginia Burrus, Mark D. Jordan, and Karmen McKendrick, *Seducing Augustine: Bodies, Desires, Confessions* (New York: Fordham University Press, 2010), 84–98, 112–14.

Time is dispersion; it can be gathered and unified only in an intimation and intuition of eternity (11.xxix). How this is possible is explained in terms of language and its synthesis of sense. After being utterly baffled and running up against one aporia after another, near the end of book 11 and of his discussion of time, Augustine returns to the analogy that he has used before of reciting a song: in xxvi he spoke generically of a line of verse, and in xxvii he cited by way of example Ambrose's hymn "Deus Creator omnium." Such a hymn is a whole, yet it transpires in time. The whole must transcend each of its component moments, which must individually pass away in order that the other parts may occur and enable the whole to be completed. For any part to have sense, it must be bound into the synthesis of the whole. In this way, each temporal moment is dependent for its sense or meaning on the temporal synthesis of sense in the whole. This is, then, an image of time's dependency on eternity.

The key role of language as an indispensable analogy and even concrete realization of the nexus between time and eternity has been stated lucidly by Kenneth Burke: "From a logological point of view, there is one area in which we do experience, *formaliter*, in principle, the relation between 'time' and 'timelessness.' This is in the relation between the words of a sentence and its 'meaning.' The syllables of the words are 'born' and 'die.' But the meaning of those syllables 'transcends' their sheer nature as temporal motions. It is an essence, not reducible to any part of the sentence, or even to the whole of it" (Burke, *The Rhetoric of Religion*, 142). John Freccero develops Burke's reading of Augustine in terms of the syntax of the sentence and its movement toward the unity of sense as dominated by a drive to realize the "principle of perfection" in a constant movement toward absolute unity.[46]

Augustine's intuition that language in its synthetic (and thereby also creative) power transcends time is bound up with his idea of Creation and his theological understanding of eternity. He champions Creation by the Word, but not in time. God's creative speaking is not like his pronouncement in time at Jesus's baptism: "This is my beloved son, in whom I am well-pleased" ("Hic est filius meus dilectus . . . ," Matthew 3:17), in which the words sound in the air and transpire in time. Not a temporally passing word but an eternal Word creates the universe. And Creation occurs in the Word in no time at all, since time, too, must be created and does not exist in the beginning. Augustine compares the words sounding in time ("haec verba temporaliter sonantia") with the eternal Word of God in silence ("aeterno in silentio verbo tuo") and declares: "these words are far beneath me, nay, they are not at all, because they flee and pass away; but the Word of God is far above me, and abides for ever" (11.vi). God's Word truly *is* because it is eternal, not successive: "For

46. John Freccero, "Logology: Burke on St. Augustine," in *Representing Kenneth Burke*, ed. Hayden White and Margaret Brose (Baltimore: Johns Hopkins University Press, 1982), 52–67.

that which was spoken was not spoken successively, one thing spoken ended that the next might be spoken: but all at once, and unto everlasting" ("simul ac sempiterne omnia," 11.vii).

All time is a little unreal and nonexistent on Augustine's (as also on Plato's and Plotinus's) account.[47] Only in the unity of a now (for us) unattainable eternity is the true and complete reality of things manifest. Time is a passing out of being, which is understood as presence. "But now my years are wasted in sighs, and Thou, O Lord, my eternal Father, art my only solace; but I am divided up in time" (11.xxix). Yet there is a crucial difference for Augustine with respect to his Neoplatonic sources. Time is not only negative and a falling away from the eternal and ideal. Augustine also conceives of history as a progression toward fulfillment. He understands time as redeemed by the Incarnation of Christ. He tells his own life story as a temporal development toward conversion and salvation and sanctification. In his vision, time can be the realization of eternity and of its wholeness and perfection. However, this requires relativizing the temporal point of view and seeing it as dependent on an eternal reality that it does not encompass, but to which it can, nevertheless, relate and from which it can receive wholeness.

If we start with the conviction that our temporal experience alone is real, we come at the end of the history of metaphysics to identify being with time.[48] But Being, in Western thought since Parmenides, has just as often been understood to be what is above time and therefore not subject to change. Do we throw this off as sheer illusion? Would we not thus risk falling into the reverse dogmatism? Being (as opposed to beings) is what we do not have command over, so we ought not to reduce it to time or to anything else. To say that Being is "eternal" is to qualify it negatively by what we do not understand and cannot grasp within our mental framework. Nonetheless, there is a revelation that can instruct us about how being is made enduring, and this is literature. Our thought takes place in the sphere of the fictive—of the weaving together of words by the imagination. This process of production does not exhaust what is produced in it, but is itself a product of creation that it cannot exhaustively account for. We do not master the creations of sense that such invention manifests. It opens toward a reality beyond itself. Our thought can be only the adumbration of this reality beyond, which mysteriously guides it and manifests itself miraculously in the synthesis of meaning in the text. If we approach this problem literarily, or as readers, we must allow time and eternity to remain reciprocally in play with each other and active as producing representations of the unrepresentable.

47. Jean Guitton, *Le temps et l'éternité chez Plotin et Saint Augustin*, 3rd ed. rev. (Paris: Vrin, 1959 [1933]).

48. The thesis of Heidegger's *Sein und Zeit* (1927), trans. J. Macquarie and E. Robinson as *Being and Time* (New York: Harper and Row, 1962).

VI. *Legere*—Reading as Binding Things Together in Unity: *Confessions*, Books 12–13

Having in the autobiographical part of his "confessions" told his life as the story of a conversion to God in and through reading, in the non-narrative—the exegetical and speculative—portion of the book Augustine takes up the task of considering reading in the most important instance of all, that of reading the Word of God. Confessing no longer his personal life and sins, he rather "confesses" the faith of the church universal. For this purpose, he has had to learn to speak in the language of Scripture, the language of Truth which, from the opening lines of the work, supervened and buoyed up his uncertain searchings by way of his invocations of God. In possession now of a truly grounded language, Augustine discovers that all his human language is actually devoid of stable meaning unless God infuses it with meaning by direct inspiration from above. Words merely as expressions of human thought can be no more than a *docta ignorantia*, a learned ignorance: "Thus speaking, the human mind can but aim at a sort of lightless knowledge—or, if you prefer, enlightened ignorance" ("dum sibi haec dicit humana cogitatio, conetur eam vel nosse ignorando vel ignorare noscendo," 12.v). The human authors of Scripture themselves often did not understand all that was meant by the words they transmitted.

Returning, then, from philosophical speculation to Scriptural exegesis, book 12 resumes the interpretation of Genesis that had been initiated in 11.iii but was interrupted by the question of *when* the Creation could have taken place. Creation by the Word must be outside of time, since there is no such thing as time before the Creation (11.vi). This forces Augustine to an unexpected interpretation of the first verse of Genesis ("In the beginning the Lord created the heaven and the earth"). He posits a Creation first outside of time, one that is not within the enumeration of the seven days of Creation. In the beginning, that is, in his *Word*, God created the "heaven of heaven," *caelum caeli*, or the purely spiritual Creation that is always the same (12.ix). In this first verse, "heaven" is the spiritual Creation, the heaven of heavens, and the "earth" is sheer formlessness—the prime matter that God would use in creation of the material universe. This, then, is prior to the creation of the physical heaven and earth, which includes the sky we see above and the forms of things we perceive all about us on earth. Both this spiritual heaven and primordial matter are outside of time: they are not absolutely unchangeable like God, since they are created, but they are not in temporal flux either (12.xii). They can be called "sempiternal," since they have an origin but no end.

This exegesis brings to the surface Scripture's *mira profunditas*, its "marvelous profundity" (12.xiv), and its multiple, indeed inexhaustible meanings. Such spiritual interpretation opens the larger question of the basis of the meaning of Scripture and of how it should be read. Moses's meaning does not exhaust Scripture's meaning. He could not possibly have comprehended all that the Holy Spirit intended in the words he wrote, when he was inspired to author Genesis and the other books of the Torah. Therefore:

> What harm is it to me, I ask again, if I think the writer had one meaning, someone else thinks he had another? All of us who read are trying to see and to grasp the meaning of the man we are reading: and given that we believe him a speaker of the truth, we should obviously not think that he was saying something that we know or think to be false. While therefore each one of us is trying to understand in the sacred writings what the writer meant by them, what harm if one accepts a meaning which You, Light of all true minds, show him to be in itself a true meaning, even if the author we are reading did not actually mean that by it: since his meaning also, though different from mine, is true.
>
> (12.xviii; see also xxiii)

Reading strives to determine the author's intent, but it may also profitably gather other truths beyond what the author himself saw in his words. God, as the ultimate author of Scripture, intends infinitely more than what Moses or any other human writer of any of the books of the Bible would have been able to understand in what he wrote. Anything whatever that is true might, after all, be revealed by God to the reader. And in any case, whether Moses intended a certain meaning or not, one cannot know that what he says is true from Moses himself but only from an inward illumination, in which truth validates itself to the judgment of a thinking subject. Truth can be given only directly and inwardly by God, who is Truth:

> But how should I know that what he said was true? And if I did know it, would it be from him that I knew it? No: but within me, in the inner retreat of my mind, the Truth, which is neither Hebrew nor Greek, nor Latin, nor Barbarian, would tell me, without lips or tongue or sounded syllables: "he speaks truth": "You speak truth." Since, then, I cannot question him, I ask Thee, the Truth filled with whom Moses spoke truth: I ask Thee, my God: pardon my sins, and as Thou didst grant to Thy servant to speak those words, grant me to understand them.
>
> (11.iii)

This direct inspiration of the divine working in each individual reader results in diverse apprehensions of the truth, even if all are inspired by one Truth. Augustine affirms diversity of interpretations through the image of God's truth as a stream out of which every person draws some portion suited to him or herself. God's narration "sets flowing in its brevity of utterance torrents of clear truth from which each may draw such truth as he can, one man this, another that, but with far lengthier windings of words" (12.xxvii). In these terms, Augustine affirms that there are many truths in Scripture: "Thus different meanings are extracted from these words by different enquirers. Among so many meanings—each of them true in itself—can any of us find one of which he would dare to affirm that Moses meant this, or wished that to be understood from what he wrote, as confidently as he would affirm that this or that is true, whether Moses meant it or not?" (12.xxiv). In fact, it is possible to be certain about what God reveals in the Scriptures to oneself, though not about what Moses meant. Truth can be decided more definitely than the author's intent, for it comes in a direct illumination from God. This direct inspiration of the reader by God makes reading itself the locus of what is, in effect, prophetic revelation. The *Confessions* issue in a conception of inspired, prophetic reading that we will see developed further by Dante.

In this situation of uncontrollably multiple readings, Augustine enjoins all interpreters to love truth rather than their own opinions, and so to avoid factiousness. Thus charity is introduced as the supreme hermeneutic principle. Whatever one's interpretation, it must be promulgated only with charitable intents and purposes (12.xxv), avoiding contentiousness and offense against others. Such is the condition even of its truth.

This truth grasped by understanding, moreover, must be free of the contingent circumstances of historical languages ("neither Hebrew nor Greek, nor Latin, nor Barbarian"). It seems that the divine light that enlightens Augustine is indistinguishable from the light of universal reason by which he can be certain of truth. Yet reason is not thereby made wholly autonomous: it is the shining of *God's* Word in the human mind. Thus the communication of truth occurs intuitively as the voice of the eternal Creator in Augustine's inner ear ("mihi veritas voce forti in aurem interiorem dicit de vera aeternitate creatoris," 12.xiv; see also 12.xi or 12.xvi). In other words: "all these things are true which Your Truth has uttered inwardly in my mind." Augustine speaks, furthermore, of this inner uttering of Truth in terms of inspiration: "With Your inspiration I shall utter the truth You have willed me to say of these words. For I do not think that I could utter truth save by your inspiration" ("vera enim dicam te mihi inspirante, quod ex eis verbis voluisti ut dicerem," 13.xxv).

Inspiration of the individual reader in an event of reading, such as brought about Augustine's own conversion as described in book 8, implies also that the biblical text is open to all true meaning that readers can find there. He avows, "I should prefer so to write that my words should mean whatever truth anyone could find upon these matters, rather than to express one meaning so clearly as to exclude all others" (12.xxxi). This statement is a powerful endorsement of the open nature of humanities texts as living truth in an ongoing tradition.[49] Augustine interprets this transmission of truth through individual discovery in reading as divinely guided and inspired.

---

49. Charles T. Mathewes, "The Liberation of Questioning in Augustine's *Confessions*," *Journal of the American Academy of Religion* 70, no. 3 (2002): 439–60, stresses that Augustine's dialogical reflections aim to remain infinitely open, even after the *Confessions*'s last word, which is in fact "opens" ("aprietur").

Book 13 continues the exegesis of the first chapter of Genesis. In fact, book 12 has covered only the first two verses about the creation of the spiritual heaven and prime matter. The emergence of a physical universe in time is dealt with only beginning from Genesis 1:3, with the creation of light on the first temporal day of Creation followed by the rest of the days. Book 8 of the *Confessions* is a continuous stream of Scriptural quotations. Augustine seems to have lost his sense of narrative direction and to have delivered himself up to an orgy of Scriptural citation, yet in doing so he has found a language that frees him to expatiate, without limits, upon his own understanding of the truth. The language of Scripture has become his own language. The first verses of Genesis allegorically enfold in themselves all of Christian doctrine. The principle here is that every part of the Bible contains the whole:[50] in this way, it is analogous to God's indivisible being—a true expression in words of the Word.

This whole meaning applies, moreover, directly to Augustine as reader. In fact, Augustine reads Genesis 1 as implicitly the background to his conversion: understood figuratively, it is calling him to turn to God. Everything in the Genesis account turns out to mean something about the ways of reading and interpreting truth, which also happens to be the key to Augustine's own life story and conversion. The "heavens" are the Holy Scripture rolled out like a parchment, its authority established securely like the firmament; the waters above the heavens are the angels who have immediate access to the Truth in an unobstructed gaze; the waters gathered below the firmament are the pagan world; the dry land and its fruits are the faithful and their works; the sun, moon, and stars are spiritual activities; reptiles produced from the water are the sacraments, beginning with baptism.

Everything in Creation encloses some reference to Augustine's own being re-created or regenerated as a Christian out of the sea of pagan beliefs by the power of the Holy Spirit in the Word of Scripture. The "living souls" mentioned in the creation of man and woman are believers in the Word; they thereby live from the life of God. Man's being made in God's image means that he is regenerated. Animals are symbols of good affections, instincts, and sentiments. "Be fruitful and multiply" refers not to physical procreation but to fecund engendering of significations and interpretations. Grass and trees are aids for evangelists. From the chaos of the sea to the dry land and the flying fowl, all details serve to outline a moral order in which things are signs: "Thus the waters of the sea are filled, and their waves stand for the various

50. This point is crucial to Augustine's interpretation of Scripture generally in the context of the techniques of medieval exegesis, which he does so much to establish, as is shown by de Lubac, *Exégèse médiévale*, 2 vols. (Paris: Aubier, 1959–64); Ceslas Spicq, *Esquisse d'une histoire de l'exégèse latine* (Paris: Vrin, 1944); and Beryl Smalley, *The Study of the Bible in the Middle Ages*, 3rd ed. (Oxford: Blackwell, 1983).

meanings of signs; and the land is filled with new generations of men: its dryness is shown in its thirst for truth, and reason dominates it" (13.xxiv). All beings stand for meanings and their interpretations.

Everything in time, moreover, is a figure of something in eternity. The purely spiritual realm is for Augustine the primary reference of the Creation story. Most significantly, as just suggested, Augustine takes the command to "increase and multiply" as an invitation to multiply senses of Scripture and become prolific in interpretations. Such spiritual reading is the exegetical method that Augustine develops, having first learned it from Ambrose. Nature is all basically a symbol for spirit. In this way, Augustine interprets everything as relating in some sense to the act of reading. Reading Scripture thus figuratively or spiritually, he offers an exemplary illustration of reading in the self-reflexive mode of applying everything to one's own existence—even in the very act of reading. Such reading is fundamental to the life of the humanities tradition and to the continual renewal of its particular type of truth, especially as we have discovered it in our study.

This hermeneutic dimension of application to oneself as intrinsic to texts and reading is the premise for a prophetic-poetic program of revelation. Holy Scripture's meaning grows with its readers' own growth.[51] The meaning is alive in the present and open to the future. This is the principle that we have observed at work beginning with our first readings from the Bible: the truth of humanities texts is apprehended ever anew in their application in a constantly changing present. Augustine's reading Scripture allegorically as addressed to him personally enables him to explore it with freedom and boundless fascination. Scripture presents not just *a* story but *his* story in symbolic language that he must learn to decipher. He is guided in this interpretive endeavor by projecting his relation to a God with whom he directly converses.

This relation with divinity, too, passes through the lens of reading. Reading as *legere* is literally the binding together of things. Through reading, we realize temporally the unity of all as it exists eternally in God. Augustine's interpretation of the evolution of his life in terms of his progressive discovery of ways of reading apotheosizes in these final books into a universal theory of reading. Reading, as it follows in the tracks of the divine Word, emerges as directly reflecting and realizing the unifying principle of all things.

This apotheosis entails the discovery of another kind of reading emancipated from the limits of words in time and space. It is a "reading" by contemplation in the eternal present of the Word ("verbum tuum") that is God himself. Its model is the angels' contemplation of God in an unbroken, timeless reading ("semper legunt") of him. Of the angels, Augustine writes,

51. An excellent exposition can be found in Cesare Bori, *L'interpretatazione infinita: L'ermeneutica cristiana antica e le sue trasformazioni* (Bologna: Il Mulino, 1987), 44 and section 1, passim.

> For they ever see Your face, and in Your face they read without syllables spoken in time what is willed by Your eternal will. They read it and they choose it and they love it; they read it without ceasing, and what they read never passes away. For by choice and love they read the very immutability of Your counsels. Their scroll is not closed, their book is not folded together, for their book is Yourself and You eternally are.
>
> (13.xv)

Striving after this uninterrupted, whole vision, human reading does not see God except in a glass darkly. We must pray for illumination from the God we cannot see but can nevertheless invoke and thereby discursively relate to and reflect. "These are the things You discuss with us most wisely, O our God, in Your Book, Your firmament, that in the wonders of contemplation we may distinguish all things, though we are still under *signs and seasons and days and years*" (13.xviii). Within this discourse, it becomes possible to read God from the book of nature and the heavens above us.

Of course, already at the end of book 10, the shortcomings of direct mystical vision as an avenue to God were made perfectly plain. Augustine realized that, instead, God must come to him in sensible form—particularly in the Incarnation. And this is communicated to us by the Gospels. In its most sustained form, the vision or contemplation of God turns out to be neither purely mystical vision of the universe nor direct intuition of the Godhead so much as inspired *reading* of the Word of Scripture.

Augustine's story all along has pivoted on reading. In book 12, he finally evolved an explicit theory of how to read Scripture. Scripture is full of many very different meanings. It accommodates many different readers' diverse truths and ways of thinking. Reading thus emerges in its subjective and psychological reality. It is also a means of relating to an Author whose intention is infinitely more than we can grasp or imagine. The fact that we can read this intention at all implies that by interpreting sensible signs we are able to fathom something of a spiritual reality transcending the finite sphere. Spiritual reading, in this respect, is a form of vision that is incarnate: it sees the transcendent in the sensible.

Augustine's search for—and with and by—Truth leads him through the external world of sense and the interior world of memory. He is led not only by his own power but by Truth, that is, by "You"—God—teaching and commanding, enabling him to judge whether and what things are, and of what weight. Through his search he is placed in touch with another Power, whereby his scattered self is unified and is, moreover, united with a transcendent Consciousness. Yet this mystical vision proves impossible to sustain, and he turns by the end of book 10 to the Mediator manifest in the Incarnation. Since he is unable to ascend with his mind directly to God, but is dragged down by the weight of his sin, he has to be saved by God descending into the flesh and redeeming it. It seems, however, that his ability to recognize God in the flesh depends on his mental exercises in unifying his consciousness by the discipline of language leading him from the temporal to the eternal, from mere words to the one Word, in which alone they have their true and inexhaustible sense.

In exploring how his own experience is related to and always already anticipated by the eternal Mind of God, particularly as manifest in the act of Creation, Augustine opens up the dimensions of subjectivity and creative interpretation as channels of divine revelation. These avenues will be explored further by Dante and taken to some of their most marvelous and audacious disclosures. The self-reflexive focus on the subject and on the subject's own creative act of reflection in reading is a key to opening the humanities tradition as a journey of self-discovery. This journey has typically been oriented toward the wholeness represented by the book, even though it gives itself to experience only in inevitably fragmentary texts. The fragment is what breaks open and creates room for the transcendent vision of the Word that is never adequately encompassed by our words. The provocatively fractured text of Augustine's "confessions" (split, as it is, between autobiography and doctrine in books 1–9 and 10–13) qualifies as paradigmatic of precisely this sort of creative endeavor of knowledge to transcend itself.

Chapter 5

✦

Dante's Poetics of Revelation

I. Introduction: The Coordinates of Divine Vision

The Visit to the World of the Dead as the Origin of Apocalyptic Prophecy

We come to Dante's *Inferno* as the culmination of a series of visits to the underworld. Dante's most direct precedent is Aeneas's journey to meet his father in Hades, as told by Virgil in book 6 of the *Aeneid*. Aeneas's voyage is modeled in turn on Odysseus's encounter with shades of Hades in book 11 of the *Odyssey.* The epic quest in each of these models pivots on a visit to the domain of the dead, a *discensus ad inferas*, as a climactic episode at its center. However, Dante makes this episode the general framework of the whole poem: from beginning to end, Dante's poem narrates a voyage through the world beyond the grave. In this respect, Dante's *Inferno*, and in fact the whole of the *Divine Comedy*, is conceived primarily as an expansion of the ancient epic motif of the *katabasis* or "going down" of the protagonist to the underworld for a revelation of his destiny from beyond the threshold of death. Like Virgil, Dante interprets history prophetically, finding in it the essential pattern of things to come. But this projection now reaches to an eschatological future beyond history altogether—to an uncannily dynamic realization of eternity.

The other world that is visited by Dante asserts itself unequivocally as ultimate reality. It is not just some shadowy world of bloodless phantoms like the shades that approach Odysseus, nor is it vacuous and inane, as are Virgil's "houses void and empty realms of Dis" ("domos Ditis vacuas et inania regna," *Aeneid* 6.269). Dante's "other" world shows up as even more vivid than the world of ordinary sense perception by virtue of a strikingly realistic, indeed surrealistic imagery. Dante heightens the mythological topos of the visit to the underworld that he inherited from Virgil and Homer. He uses it to represent the true and eternal life: *la vera vita*. Dante's world of the dead, moreover, is not just one in a series of episodes befalling the protagonist: it is rather the final and definitive experience, the apocalypse that reveals the true meaning of all possible experiences and thereby the meaning of the cosmos as a whole. This is perhaps implicit and incipient in Homer, or at least in Virgil, since the journey to the underworld in each case frames a revelation that illuminates the meaning of everything else and orients the protagonist's entire subsequent journey through life up to death. But Dante's other world is more than just the place for a miraculous glimpse into the true meaning of life: it transposes the essence of *this* life on earth into actual existence in a transcendent dimension.

Of course, Virgil had interpreted the whole of Roman history through the optics of prophecy, but his prophetic history was directly disclosed only at privileged moments within his poem. Dante's poetic narrative transpires wholly in an eschatological register disclosing the final ends of human life. It aspires to reveal, beyond the limits of history, a full-blown vision of eternity—history as projected into the eternal world that it is taken to prefigure. While at the level of content Dante expands the theme of a visit to the underworld into an entire poem of epic proportions, more deeply, at the level of genre and in terms of its mode, Dante's whole poem is prophetic in character. In it, history and narrative become themselves prophetic rather than only forming a background or a frame for prophecy.

So the descent to the dominion of the dead—a symbol for the revelation of the ultimate meaning of life—is more than just a thematic thread that runs through each of the works we have examined so far. In Dante it becomes the central axis of a poetic text that is per se religious revelation. Moreover, Dante greatly intensifies self-consciousness of the revelatory function of poetry. His work represents an unprecedentedly powerful theoretical reflection on poetry as revelation in the modes of prophecy and apocalyptic, in as much as the customary *literary* means of poetic expression are now revealed in their intrinsically prophetic and apocalyptic potency.

From the *Aeneid*, Dante could learn that prophecy reveals not so much fated facts as an order of significance that opens within history and activates a dimension of human freedom. We observed an allegorical dimension in the *Aeneid*, in which the heroic actions of the past were spoken into the present—so as to impinge on the moment of decision for Virgil's contemporaries in Augustan Rome. The poem indirectly challenges the Romans to realize a future prefigured by their heroic past, particularly in their founding father, Aeneas. This sort of implicit interpellation mutates to an explicit form of address in Dante's poem, specifically in its addresses to its readers.

The First-Person Protagonist and the Address to the Reader

In general, prophetic discourse is never merely descriptive or predictive; it is always also *prescriptive*, and as such it is addressed to a public. The hearers or readers of prophecy are involved in a future that is revealed, yes, but revealed as *to be achieved* by their own efforts. Virgil and his contemporaries, Augustus Caesar foremost among them, who see along with Aeneas the prophetic revelation of the glory that is in store for Rome, are at least subliminally called upon to act worthily of their noble ancestors. Moving beyond this, Dante writes the reader right into the text consciously and explicitly through his use of direct addresses.[1] The poem calls the reader to conversion as a consequence of its eschatological revelations. There is even—in marked contrast to his epic models—a hidden form of address to the audience from the very first line: "In the middle of the way of *our* life" ("Nel mezzo del cammin di *nostra* vita").[2]

The reader accompanies Dante on his journey through the afterlife, and in a certain sense everything that happens to him is to be realized by his readers in its pertinence to *their own* lives and in the *now* of their act of reading. It is their acts of interpretation *of themselves* as they confront interpretive challenges such as those presented by the poem that will be decisive for the readers' own lives—and even for their afterlives. Sin and salvation in Dante's afterlife stem from how one interprets oneself, and the reading of the poem can be crucial to determining the outcome of this drama: how we read is, at any rate, *symptomatic* of how we live and act morally. The poem can thus reveal us to ourselves and can even become instrumental to our salvation through the insight it provokes.

Dante's prophetic discourse is different from Virgil's and from his other models, which are principally biblical. In crucial ways, he personalizes prophetic address, dramatizing his own role as first-person prophet-poet addressing himself directly to his reader. Dante's whole personal experience and history are now vehicles of the divine Word. This is not exactly the direct speech of God as it was conveyed by the biblical prophets: they functioned purportedly as simple mouthpieces, intoning "Thus saith the Lord . . ." Dante offers rather a personally mediated experience to which poetry, language, culture, and reflection all contribute: his historical intellectual baggage and even his personal biases become overt mediators of a revelation of the divine.

The first-person protagonist thus becomes the fulcrum for realizing the poem's truth in the present of each individual reader's personal experience. The address to the reader, with its injunction to interpret, extends the exercise in self-reflection from the poet-protagonist to the reader: each is engaged in a realization of revealed religious truth by personal appropriation in terms of their own life and experience. This self-reflective, subjective locus of revelation owes as much to Augustine's unprecedentedly personal story in the *Confessions* as to the invention of history as revelation in Virgilian epic. Augustine had foregrounded *reading* as the means and medium of a divine revelation understood as an inner illumination in the life of the

1. I further sift the significance of this in "Dante's Address to the Reader and Its Ontological Significance," *MLN* (*Modern Language Notes*) 109 (1994): 117–27.

2. Dante's Italian text is quoted from *La Divina Commedia secondo l'antica vulgata*, ed. G. Petrocchi, 4 vols. (Milan: Mondadori, 1966–67), with my own translations.

individual. Dante now addresses himself expressly to the individual reader, who is enjoined to become the living center of a dramatic actualization of his poem's prophetic truth. The poem's pretensions and projections become reality in and through the interpretive responses of the reader, whose life becomes potentially a locus for the operation of divine grace—through poetry!.

Dante's Journey and the Augustinian Itinerary through Self to God

Augustine forms a vital link from the ancient epic, as well as from the Bible, to Dante. The *Confessions*, too, situate themselves symbolically on the trajectory of a descent to the world of the dead. This happens expressly when Saint Augustine writes "ibam iam ad inferos" ("I was going to hell," 5.ix) to describe his moral disease, the death of his soul ("mors . . . animae meae"). The *Confessions* adumbrate an existential descent into the depths of Augustine's own sinful self and into the abysmal heart of a fallen humanity as the precondition—and the necessary path—of his conversion. This existential descent into the self and its personal hell is dramatized on an epic scale by Dante.

Dante combines classical tradition with Christianity, and Augustine is a major precedent, even though Augustine, in his *Confessions*, rejected pagan literature and specifically the *Aeneid*. Augustine guides Dante to a fundamentally Scriptural rather than a classical poetics.[3] Nevertheless, Dante places his emphasis on synthesis rather than on disjunction between classical literary tradition and Christian revelation. We know that Augustine saw Virgil's fictions as temptations. Pagan literature distracted him from the serious challenges of his own life. The classics and the rhetorical institutions within which they were studied are of this world and, at least at first, an impediment to gaining the next. Given this imposing precedent, it is striking that Dante, in a bold symbolic gesture, should make the pagan author, Virgil, his guide to salvation specifically in a religious sense. More broadly, he brings biblical and pagan traditions together in his unique creation of a poetic-prophetic vision. He thereby reverses the prejudices and moralizing objections expressed by Augustine and other church fathers that inhibited full appreciation of pagan literature, the *auctores* used in the course of a Christian education. Building on revivals of classical literature in humanist schools like Chartres from the twelfth century on,[4] Dante envisages a full integration of all human learning

3. Simone Marchesi, *Dante and Augustine: Linguistics, Poetics, Hermeneutics* (Toronto: University of Toronto Press, 2010). For a nuanced assessment, see Peter S. Hawkins, "Divide and Conquer: Augustine in the *Comedia*," in *Dante's Testaments: Essays in Scriptural Imagination* (Stanford, Calif.: Stanford University Press, 1999), 197–212.

4. Marie-Dominique Chenu, *La théologie dans le douzième siècle* (Paris: Vrin, 1957); Charles Homer Haskins, *The Renaissance of the Twelfth Century* (Cambridge, Mass.: Harvard University Press, 1978 [1927]).

in a Christian-prophetic perspective. And yet, notwithstanding this radical revaluation of pagan letters, Dante remains profoundly Augustinian.

An Augustinian itinerary is mapped out from the opening of the *Inferno* in the "prologue scene." This scene stages Dante's failed attempt to scale the mountain mantled by the light of the sun, a natural symbol of divinity, as Dante explains elsewhere (*Convivio* 3.xii.7). This hill is identified, at least symbolically, with the mountain of Purgatory, at the summit of which lies the Earthly Paradise, the original place of human happiness on earth. But Dante's attempt to directly ascend the slope proves abortive, and he is constrained to take a detour that leads him all the way to the bottom of the Inferno. This recalls Augustine's descriptions of his experience of *intellectual* conversion to the certainty of the Truth, spurred by his reading of "certain books" of Platonist philosophy, and consequently his attempt to ascend directly to the Light, as recounted in book 7 of the *Confessions*. His will, nevertheless, remained unable to follow suit by conforming itself to the Good until his complete *moral* conversion as described at the climax of book 8.

Augustine's account is itself modeled on Saint Paul's drama of the divided will in Romans 7. At the literal level of the narrative, Dante is in fact impeded in his ascent by the three beasts that emerge to deter him from progressing upward. The leopard, the lion, and the she-wolf can perhaps be decoded as allegories of envy, pride, and greed (see *Inferno* 6.74), or of lust, pride, and avarice, the devastating threesome rehearsed again in *Inferno* 15.68. Such moral corruptions inhering in Dante's will prevent him from reaching happiness, even after his intellect has been able clearly to see the way to it. These figures, moreover, exemplify some of the more traditional, didactic features of Dante's poem that are surpassed as it distinguishes itself from the medieval context of symbolic-allegorical literature by the power of its new idiom of realistic representation.

Dante, like Augustine, then, seems to have experienced, first, a conversion of the intellect on a Neoplatonic model. This would correspond to the period of his philosophical work, the *Convivio*, abandoned unfinished, perhaps in view of the new Christian-moral perspective inaugurated by the *Commedia*. Dante's flirtation with philosophy as a substitute for authentic Christian salvation would be allegorically encoded into his attempt at the beginning of the *Inferno* to ascend the hill cloaked in the light of the sun, the planet that "leads men straight along every road" ("pianeta / che mena dritto altrui per ogne calle," 1.17–18). In fact, Virgil, for whom, as a pagan, direct philosophical ascent to enlightenment would be possible and indeed the right way to go, asks Dante why he is returning to so much suffering rather than simply ascending the delightful mountain ("dilettoso monte") that is the source of all joy (1.76–78). He proposes an alternative route only after he sees Dante weeping ("poi che lagrimar mi vide," 1.92) and evidently understands something about his moral condition.

We learn that Dante had been climbing in a spiral because his "left foot was always the lower" ("'l piè fermo sempre era 'l più basso," 1.30). This line has been ingeniously elucidated as meaning that the protagonist's will drags along behind his intellect in the process of conversion. John Freccero shows this by drawing on exegetical literature by the church fathers, including Ambrose (from whom Augustine learned to interpret Scripture spiritually), concerning the two feet—or wings—of the soul, of which one, the will, lags behind the other, namely, reason.[5]

The Platonic dialogues are predicated on the principle that virtue is knowledge, but Dante, like Augustine and Paul before him, discovers that knowing the truth, or seeing the light, is not enough. Indeed, in the biblical view, virtue and moral reform are not matters purely of the mind. As Paul avowed, "The good that I would I do not: but the evil which I would not, that I practice" (Romans 7:19). Likewise for Augustine, intellectual illumination by Platonic metaphysics may give certainty about God and his sovereignty, but it does not give him the power to realize the good that he now *would* do. And Dante similarly finds in *Inferno* 1 that he is unable to ascend the mountain, even though he sees the light. This is what forces him to take "another way" ("altro viaggio," 1.91) passing through all the hazards of Hell. It means going through excruciating moral self-examination by facing up to sin always also in himself, as he views his own woefully fallen humanity mirrored in others at each step of his way. Read in this perspective, the prologue scene to Dante's epoch-making poem is about the necessity, beyond merely intellectual illumination, of a more thoroughgoing moral and existential conversion such as Augustine undergoes finally in book 8 of the *Confessions*.

Didactic Poem and Summa of Truth

Dante lived from 1265 to 1321 and wrote at the height of the Middle Ages, just after the high-water mark of the Scholastic synthesis, in which the metaphysics of Aristotle were wedded to Christian theology in the doctrine of God as Being (*esse*) by philosopher-theologians like Albert the Great (1206–1280) and Thomas Aquinas (1225–1274). It was, moreover, a great age of encyclopedias such as the *Speculum maius* of Vincent de Beauvais (1190–1264) and the *Legenda aurea* of Jacopo de Voragine (1230–1298). In its own very different way, like Aquinas's *Summa Theologiae*, Dante's *Commedia* represents a grand synthesis of the knowledge available to his age of culture.

5. John Freccero, "The Firm Foot on a Journey without a Guide," collected as chapter 2 of his *Dante: The Poetics of Conversion*, ed. Rachel Jacoff (Cambridge, Mass.: Harvard University Press, 1987). For Freccero's Augustinian framing of the poem, see further "The Prologue Scene," chapter 1 in the same volume. A forceful challenge to this interpretation is launched by Gregory B. Stone, *Dante's Pluralism and the Islamic Philosophy of Religion* (New York: Palgrave, 2006), 60–61.

From early in antiquity, as we have seen, poetry was often considered to be the original and comprehensive form of knowledge in general, and Dante revives this humanistic ideal and the claim it makes for poetry. Virgil and Beatrice, his guides, are also his teachers on a journey that is always fundamentally a gnoseological journey traversing the whole known world—past, present, and future—as it could be conceived in Dante's times. The encyclopedic aims of the poem become conspicuous early on, in Limbo, with its extensive, immensely learned catalog of philosophers and poets, among other great and famous personages (*Inferno* 4.70–147).

Homer was esteemed to be the summa of Greek culture and the encyclopedia of all significant knowledge of the world. He was imitated by Virgil, in whom these "epic" ambitions became more self-conscious. Saint Augustine, too, turned his *Confessions* into a kind of encyclopedia, especially from book 10 on. At that point in the aftermath of his conversion story, Augustine begins interrogating Memory as the place where all knowledge is stored. He turns from a personal story of individual redemption to the interpretation of universal philosophical truths and to exegesis of the story of Creation. The Bible, of course, for Dante and his Christian medieval culture is the book of books and the book of the universe. It contains preeminently, as divinely revealed, all that can be learned from any other source. Dante's work, in its encyclopedic scope, is thus an imitation and dissemination of the Bible.

This means also that the *Divine Comedy* is a didactic poem in the broadest and deepest sense. Its lesson is the most important one humanly conceivable. "Mark well my words," it insists, like the bard in Blake's *Milton*, for "they are of your eternal salvation." Indeed, the literal subject of the poem is the afterlife, which consists of souls in Hell, Purgatory, and Heaven all revealed in the eschatological light of their eternal destinations. The knowledge in question is not just a knowledge of facts and culture but, much more vitally, a knowledge by revelation of the ultimate ends of life and history. In this regard, the poem fits into and, moreover, brings to its culmination the tradition of poetry as religious revelation that we have been tracing from Homer and the Bible. Of course, this would not forestall further elaborations of the tradition of prophetic poetry subsequently by the likes of Milton and Blake.

The Figural Method of Representation

The basic interpretive technique used by Dante to perform this revelation of ultimate, saving truth is a species of allegory known as "figuralism."[6] This is

6. See especially Erich Auerbach, "Figura," in *Gesammelte Aufsätze zur romanischen Philologie* (Bern: Francke Verlag, 1967 [1944]), trans. R. Manheim in *Scenes from the Drama of European Literature, Six Essays* (New York: Meridian, 1959). I define Dante's art by this term in "Figuralism," in *The Dante Encyclopedia*, ed. Richard Lansing (New York: Garland, 2000), 376–79.

the key to the poem's working as a prophetic revelation. Dante represents the souls in the form of bodies and as performing actions that epitomize the sort of action they freely chose to engage in on earth. Their earthly lives in this way serve as "figures" for what each soul has become in eternity. The souls represented as already in the state in which they will remain for eternity are the "fulfillment" of the condition that their earthly lives have prefigured. By this device, the eternal state of souls after death is made poetically palpable and graphic through realistic representation of the fateful moment and decisive act of their mortal existence: this moment figuratively represents their eternal destiny.

In its figural dimension, Dante's poem is modeled on the Exodus. If this were not already evident from the text itself (especially in *Purgatory* 2.43, which cites Psalm 113: *In exitu Isräel de Aegypto*), we could nevertheless infer it from Dante's discussions of theological allegory in his theoretical writings, particularly the *Convivio* 2.i, along with the Letter to Can Grande (*Epistle* 13.7–8). We have already considered (in chapter 1, section III) Exodus as a model for the prophetic interpretation of history in the Bible. In Dante's prophetic poem, the Exodus becomes a general paradigm of escape from the enslavement of sin followed by an arduous journey to the promised land of Christian salvation. From the other side of its cultural heritage (the classical), the journey is also quasi-Odyssean or "Ulyssean," in Dante's Latinized rendering.

This itinerary to hard-won freedom starts from a key passage in the prologue scene, in which Dante begins his ascent up the Mountain. He has just figured himself as a survivor narrowly escaped from shipwreck:

> poi ch'èi posato un poco il corpo lasso,
> ripresi via per la piaggia diserta,
> sì che 'l piè fermo sempre era 'l più basso.
> (*Inferno* 1.28–30)
>
> (When I had rested a little my tired body,
> I began again the way along the deserted slope
> so that my left foot was always the lower one.)

As Charles Singleton pointed out, the immediately preceding verses referred to Dante's mind ("animo") as looking back like a shipwreck over the perilous pass that he has managed to survive (1.22–27), but it is Dante's *body* that rises up out of the simile of the shipwreck in order to embark on the journey to the other world.[7] By bringing the body of the protagonist that is

7. Charles S. Singleton, *Dante Studies I: Elements of Structure* (Cambridge, Mass.: Harvard University Press, 1957).

going to make the journey out of a poetic simile in this way, Dante's poem produces, out of its own powers of poetic figuration, an incarnate revelation. In this bodily resurrection of the poem's protagonist from a symbolic shipwreck, poetic language and metaphor themselves produce a type of figural embodiment that is destined to become the bearer of the revelation of the poem.

Redemption, like revelation, is emphatically incarnate in the perspective developed by Dante's poem, and this is one of the deeply distinguishing features of the whole Christian understanding of revelation. That is one reason why poetic representation, alongside pictorial and plastic arts, has such a prominent place in transmitting and achieving revelation throughout the cultural history of Christianity. Poetry, with its figurative, pictorial powers and its sensuous sonorities, is peculiarly apt to give an incarnate rendition of the intellectual contents of language. The language of poetry can even be defined, as it was by Roman Jakobson, as "sense made sensuous." Poetry in the Western tradition following Dante, from Metaphysicals to Romantics to Symbolists, has often exhibited a propensity to interpret itself as, in effect, an incarnation of the divine Word in the form of some higher Truth or Meaning. Of course, the very strength of this proclivity inherent in poetic language generates many attempts precisely to interrupt and counter it, especially among modern poets, starting from Baudelaire and Rimbaud, for example, with their anti-idealist and sometimes satanic insistence.

Poetry as Prophetic Vision of History

Poetic prophecy, as a superior sort of vision, as inspired insight of the kind to which poets since Homer have continually laid claim, is deliberately raised by Dante to a new level of seriousness and self-consciousness. Beyond the conventional gesture of the invocation of the Muses, Dante, assuming an authoritative attitude and prophetic tone, directly addresses himself to a reader in the name of Truth. A distinctive new accent in Dante's re-creation of the office of prophecy, within the parameters of poetry and specifically of epic narrative, is the literal truth claim he makes. We have already seen the extent to which prophecy is interlocked with history, so that in the case of the Bible we were able to define prophecy as the interpretation of history from the point of view of divine revelation. Even Homer purported to relate the true history of the Trojan War and its aftermath, and he claimed to do so assisted by the divine Muses, to whom all history was perpetually present. But Dante claims to have been there historically himself and to have seen with his own eyes all that he relates of the eternal worlds. Moreover, at the outset of his journey, he invokes the Muses *together with* his own ingenious mind or memory, to assist him in making all that he has experienced manifest:

O muse, o alto ingegno or m'aiutate;
o mente che scrivesti ciò ch'io vidi,
qui si parrà la tua nobilitate.
(2.4–6)

(O muses, o high genius help me now;
o memory that wrote what I saw,
here your nobility will show itself.)

The basis for prophecy here is direct personal witness—"what I saw" ("ciò ch'io vidi," 2.8)—which regrounds the conventional appeal to the Muses for help in representing what is beyond normal, mortal vision. This appeal takes an especially telling turn when Dante invokes his own "memory" and invites it to show its nobility by manifesting what it *wrote*. Writing is thereby recognized not only as an external medium but rather as intrinsic to the experience. To the extent that the experience as recorded in memory is already "written," the literary medium by which Dante poetically conveys his vision is brought into—and becomes constitutive of—the making of the visionary experience itself.

Such reflective concentration on his poetic art and its capability of modulating into prophecy, in order thereby to reveal a higher reality, characterizes Dante's work throughout its whole extent. The theoretical reflection on writing, poetry, and prophecy as all co-implicated in his act of literary creation *and* religious vision marks Dante's poem with a distinctive character that earns it its preeminent place in the history of prophetic poetry, as well as of literature generally. In Dante, the question of poetry as prophecy becomes a central and conscious preoccupation. Poetry is not simply assumed as the necessary vehicle for a message of purportedly divine import. Nor are prophetic strains and utterances occasionally interjected into what otherwise would remain merely an artful display of human talents in poetic composition. In Dante, poetry becomes programmatically prophetic. It is prophetic *as* poetry, which becomes, then, not just the rhetorical dress for a religious message. The poetic act itself is discovered in all its intrinsically prophetic potential.

History, Eschatology, Apocalypse

In this respect—as a peculiarly intense and self-conscious instance of the communication of poetic tradition as prophetic or as religious revelation—Dante's *Divine Comedy* marks the culmination of the developments that we have been tracing all through the Western humanities tradition. Poetry becomes prophecy in Dante's magnum opus more programmatically and explicitly than ever before. Poetry as prophecy, and finally as apocalyptic, coincides with the injunction to remake one's history through reinterpreting it in the present: poetic prophecy issues in an urgent call to conversion. This is a call to conversion of religious faith, of course, but first and foremost of interpretive outlook. Interpretation is the decisive locus of revelation of the meaning of life—of individual as well as collective sense or meaning as deposited in tradition. The origination of tradition and its truth—and so also of history and its meanings—in the act of interpretation is realized by Dante more deliberately and intensely than by any of his predecessors. Although he is for the most part only bringing out into the open the far-reaching implications of their works, he also radically transforms the scope of what prophecy as interpretation in poetic literature—epic, dramatic, and lyrical—ultimately entails.

Dante, moreover, represents the terminus, or at least an apex, of Western tradition in its development toward a unified vision of reality as the total vision of apocalypse, wherein all things are revealed in their final truth. Such unity of vision has presumably become impossible in the modern world. It is often held to have been realized as never before or since by Dante in the *Divine Comedy*. The modern Italian poet Eugenio Montale remarks that this unity was still possible in Dante's age, after which the historical conditions for such a synoptic vision of reality never existed again.[8] Dante is an icon of this totalizing, unitary outlook, and the visionary mode of his poem expresses its claim of access to ultimate truth. And yet he also shows how even apocalyptic revelation relies on the dynamics of interpretation—the interested appropriation of meaning by individuals in historically specific circumstances. To this extent, individual interpretation and even creative appropriation are recognized as key to unlocking the secret sense and the final truth of human lives and of life as a whole. This truth, as it is revealed in Holy Scripture and in texts, including Dante's own, which mediate and renew Scriptural revelation, is always in need of further interpretation in order to remain actual and operative in the minds and hearts of individuals.

Prophecy in the narrower sense of foretelling the future is already largely surpassed by Virgil. The grand vision of the Roman future at the center of his epic is actually an interpretation of the past as itself a prophecy of a future destiny that is *to be enacted* in the present. Dante, by grasping the importance of such prophetic-historical interpretation to the shaping of human destiny by the epic enterprise, and heightening the vocation of poetry to the level of apocalyptic revelation, makes the announcement of immanent redemption for the world the central message of his poem. According to his prophecy, the

8. Eugenio Montale, "Discorso su Dante" (1965), in *Atti del Congresso Internazionale di Studi danteschi*, vol. 2 (Florence: Sansoni, 1966), trans. Jonathan Galassi in *The Poet's Dante: Twentieth Century Responses*, ed. Rachel Jacoff and Peter Hawkins (New York: Farrar, Straus and Giroux, 2001), 94–117. See also *T. S. Eliot, Dante, and the Idea of Europe*, ed. Paul Douglas (Newcastle: Cambridge Scholars, 2011) on the unity of "sensibility" achieved paradigmatically by Dante in European tradition.

veltro ("greyhound") will come not devouring land and wealth ("Questi non ciberà terra né peltro") but nourished by wisdom, love, and virtue ("sapienza, amore e virtute," 1.103–4) from a land "between Feltro and Feltro." The *felt* suggests, among other overtones, medieval writing implements, specifically a felt blotter, and thereby hints possibly that the poem itself, as a prophetic revelation, may play a messianic role in the event of salvation that it announces.[9] This cryptic code for identifying (or rather failing to unambiguously identify) the Redeemer belongs to the allegorical nature of Dante's prophecy. It is not explicit but rather disguised in figures whose true meaning calls for interpretation, perhaps for unending interpretation. Indeed, scholarship on the *veltro* prophecy has never been able to satisfactorily resolve the question of the identity of the expected savior.[10]

This anticipation of an apparently historical savior modulates into an apocalyptic expectation of the renewal of the world, for which Dante mobilizes the classical myth of the return of the Golden Age. The poem lays claim to being nothing short of an eschatological vision.[11] That this prophetic revelation of a final End should be realized expressly in and through the experience of reading poetry is rather extraordinary. In crucial ways, it inaugurates the sense of self-reflectiveness as an ultimate revelation characteristic of modern consciousness. We have already sounded its premises as they are set down in decisive ways by Augustine. But in Augustine, writerly self-consciousness still understood itself as a reflection of Transcendence, of the infinite consciousness of God. And Dante likewise writes before the modern severing of consciousness from its ground in the Divine Mind. Yet he does so with a vivid and startlingly modern sense of discovery of himself through poetic invention as a unique, concrete human person: he grasps his humanity as participating in divine revelation in the historical sphere. Nevertheless, Dante's awakening to new consciousness as an individual is conspicuously marked by traditional apocalyptic signs: the passage into Hell occurs between his swooning at the end of *Inferno* 3 (verses 130–36) in terror at an earthquake, with a flash of vermillion light, and his being reawakened from "deep sleep" by the sound of thunder at the beginning of *Inferno* 4 ("Ruppemi l'alto sonno ne la testa / un greve truono"). By such means, Dante's unprecedented, newfound self-consciousness is inscribed into age-old traditions of religious revelation.

9. Compare Claudia Rattazzi Papka, "'Tra feltro e feltro': Dante's Cartaceous Apocalypse," *Dante Studies* 107 (1999): 35–44.

10. Jean Hein, *Enigmaticité et messianisme dans la "Divine Comédie"* (Florence: Olschki, 1992), for one, acknowledges this.

11. The most comprehensive treatment remains Nicolò Mineo, *Profetismo e apocalittica in Dante: Strutture e temi proefetico-apocalittici in Dante dalla Vita Nuova alla Divina Commedia* (Catania: University of Catania, 1968). Among more recent treatments, see Robert Wilson, *Prophecies and Prophecy in Dante's Commedia* (Florence: Olschki, 2008).

The work's prophetic, eschatological meaning is closely bound up also with a political vision that is intelligible only in light of the contemporary political scene. The two great powers of world history, emperor and pope, are bitter rivals fighting for hegemony in medieval Europe. Dante's own city, Florence, is riven asunder by two parties, the Guelfs, allied with the papacy, and the Ghibellines, in league with the emperor. Dante himself is exiled as a result of internecine party politics, leaving the city in 1301, never to return. He writes his poem in exile and in relentless protest against the injustice that reigns in his own city and in the world at large. At the same time, he prophetically envisages an apocalyptic event that will overturn this reign of wickedness and restore justice upon earth.

The political vicissitudes of Dante's life and times are brought to focus, first, in cantos 6 and 10 of the *Inferno* in relation to fellow Florentines, Ciacco and Farinata degli Uberti, with their prophecies of Dante's exile. The events alluded to are, in fact, important background for reading Dante's poem. In 1260 the emperor's party, the Ghibellines, had gained control of Florence through their victory at Montaperti near Siena. But in 1266, a year after Dante's birth, the defeat of imperial forces at Benevento, near Naples, by Charles of Anjou, brother of the French king, Louis IX, and favored also by Pope Clement IV, ushered in an era of Guelf power in Florence in which Dante himself participated.

Dante was a Guelf, even though his ideology was to develop along imperialist lines. Ironically, with the demise of the Ghibellines, the Guelf party itself split into white and black Guelfs, reproducing the ideological divide between champions of the empire versus supporters of the papacy. The death of the imperial heir-apparent, Manfredi, at Benevento, together with the demise in 1268 of the grandson of Frederick the Great, Conradino, captured at Tagliacozzo and beheaded at Naples, sealed the fate of this imperial dynasty and therewith of the Holy Roman Empire: it was condemned to be ineffectual in Italy for the remainder of Dante's days. The defunct status of the empire was proved again by the unsuccessful, in fact fatal campaign of Henry VII of Luxembourg, who descended into Italy in 1310. This claimant to the imperial throne was enthusiastically hailed by the poet (*Epistola* 7) with an impassioned call to arms (*Epistola* 5), but in vain: by 1313, Henry was dead.

Considered with hindsight, Dante's visionary apocalypse projecting a restoration of unified rule to the world under the aegis of the Holy Roman Empire appears thus to have been anachronistic and politically unrealistic. As apocalyptic vision, however, it represents an ideal of world government as the only effective guarantor of peace and justice on earth among inevitably fractious human beings. And as such, Dante's vision of a unified world order remains compelling as a possible and perhaps necessary ideal in our own age of globalization, with its distressing sectarianism—its fragmentation into rivalrous and often warring ethnic and religious identities.

II. The Interpretive Journey and the Allegory of Reading: *Inferno*, Cantos 1–8

Humanities traditions, as we have seen, live by being interpreted, which means being constantly *re*interpreted, and the truth they bear and disseminate depends on how they impinge on the present—on the historical and institutional and personal situations *into* which they are interpreted. Their representations of the past reveal a meaning that can become prophetic, to the extent that it represents a challenge to the present to realize its own highest possibilities as these are disclosed by the past. Energized in this way by relation to the present, the past can become prophetic of the future, which it then actually contributes to shaping. This happens especially in epic poems, which interpret the past in accordance with a claim to divine revelation that is expressed in the appeal to the inspiration of the Muses. Epics typically address this interpretation specifically to a historical people.

In this sense, every text in the humanities tradition—on the model of the epics that, to a considerable degree, found it—is not only about the past that is being recounted but also about the present, in which its meaning is sifted, and about the future, which begins to be realized by anticipation as its promises are turned into active projects. Humanities texts live by continually projecting the old stories into new historical contexts in which they take on new meanings and thereby interpret the present, illuminating it, revealing it to itself in ways that would never be possible without the historical perspective that tradition affords. Conversely, the past is revised in the light of the present and its possibilities: new, previously invisible or neglected aspects of it move into the foreground as prophetic of a possible, newly emergent future.

We have observed this reshuffling of tenses—which reverses time and anticipates it—taking place within Greco-Roman tradition in the epic, as well as in the context of the Judeo-Christian tradition in the Bible. We dwelt, for example, upon how Adam is us all, as even his name suggests, and on how the Exodus from Egypt is memorialized in order to be repeated and relived in each new, successive generation. The text itself insists, with reiterated injunctions, that the story be told and retold to "your sons and your sons' sons." This demand for reliving by retelling, or by narrative rumination, re-actualizes and can even encroach upon the "original" event. Retelling becomes a retrospective, even a retro*active* realization of the original events: these events are revealed and realized in their enduring meaning and truth through the process—not to say the "progress"—of tradition.

This faculty of tradition to expose and challenge the present, to address itself to us as readers, by contemporizing the past and future in the present, becomes especially intense in prophetic poems. By virtue of some extraordinary access or uncanny insight into the meaning and destiny of things, prophetic poets lay claim to delivering nothing short of divine revelation.

The claim to prophetic knowledge through inspired interpretation of the past in the present and in the incandescent light of an envisioned future becomes more conscious and explicit in Dante than ever before.

For Dante, the prophetic meaning of his narrative is actualized in an event of interpretation expressly enjoined upon his poem's readers—particularly in the poem's addresses to its readers. The address to the reader thus becomes the locus for revelation and for the realization of truth in self-consciously interpretive experience. Everything that supposedly happened in the past that is recounted by the poem in a certain sense happens all over again in the present of the poem's telling as an event of interpretation, and it is here that its vital meaning and truth are revealed. The narrative as such assumes the status of an allegory of reading. The story is, in this respect, about the interpretations enacted by the reader and the conversion of life that these interpretations (can) inspire and embody. Explicitly through these addresses, the reader's interpretation is integrated into the poem itself, just as the poem becomes part of the reader's life.[12]

The emphasis on repetition of past events in the present time of poetic interpretation and reading is palpable from the first verses of the poem in the insistence on the prefix "ri" in "ritrovai," "rinova," "ridir": it is so hard for Dante to retell what happened to him that fear is renewed in merely thinking of it ("nel pensier rinova la paura"). Everything is being reenacted, and it is in this literary reenactment that the full charge of emotion can perhaps for the first time register and, accordingly, the crucial meaning of events be comprehended. Then, and perhaps only then, their saving significance can be realized and result in conversion. This possibility of "conversion" is precisely what is at stake in the first canto of the poem, right from the proem, with its rhetoric of reenactment and its emphasis upon poetry as the site of an original experience of truth, inasmuch as poetry involves the reactualization of events, their being relived in poetic interpretation:

> Ahi quanto a dir qual era è cosa dura,
> esta selva selvaggia e aspra e forte,
> chè nel pensier rinova la paura!
>
> (1.4–6)

> (O how difficult a thing it is to say how it was,
> this wild wood, bitter and oppressive,
> that fear renews in thinking about it!)

---

12. Throughout this chapter, I am building on the interpretation of Dante's poetics first worked out in *Dante's Interpretive Journey* (Chicago: University of Chicago Press, 1996), beginning with its opening chapter on "The Address to the Reader."

Thus literary repetition presents itself from the outset as the origin of the conversion experience that the poem invites its readers to participate in and make their own. Participative reading can validate Dante's conversion experience, for the latter is potentially reenacted by the reader every time the text is read. This gesture of bringing the drama and its emotion into the moment of interpretation as a repetition of Dante's original experience in the underworld is frequently revisited throughout the *Inferno*. It is the extreme intensity of Dante's encounters that provokes this emotional osmosis from the original experience to the experience of interpreting it, or from the narrated temporality to the temporality of the narrating, which is itself already an act of interpreting (see, further, 3.132; 5.25–27; 6.1–9; 8.56; 16.12; 17.115–23; 22.31; 24.84; 26.19; 28.113–14; 32.71–72; in different ways also 4.145–47; 10.1; 7.19–21; and 14.16–18; 13.25, "dico," "I say" in 8.1 and 14.8).

In this sense, the journey realized by Dante's poem is an interpretive journey as much as a literal journey through the other world. The latter journey has some traits of fiction; the former is in every sense real. To the extent that Dante's claims to truth may not be believable at the literal level of a journey through eternity, still there is a literal journey in interpretation that is manifestly realized in and through the poem by its being read. When transferred onto this journey of interpretation on which Dante takes the reader, the imperious claims to truth are no longer far-fetched: they become plausible and even compelling. The reader need only believe his or her own experience of poetry.

This aspect of the poem—its built-in interpretive dimension and its character as a script for interpretive acts performed by Dante himself and by the reader in his wake—is announced from the opening verses and is called back to mind repeatedly throughout the poem by the shifts into the present tense: the present is the tense of interpreting and, in this sense, of reenacting the incidents that are narrated. What the poem as a whole relates is not only the past action of Dante's visit to the afterlife in 1300 but also his reactions to it as he relives the whole journey in the experience of writing it, which is the act of interpreting it poetically. And at this level, the reader, too, can directly share with Dante in the journey of interpretation that the poem re-creates and *is*.

Part of this fantastic poem's insistence on its own literal truth—as in the invocation in *Inferno* 2: "O memory that wrote what I saw" ("O mente che scrivesti ciò ch'io vidi")—is to be accounted for by Dante's new and acute apprehension of the literariness of truth, of the way that truth is produced in and by the event of reading and writing. This was already patently the case, though it remained still largely unacknowledged, in Augustine's conversion narrative, with its multiple framings by narrations of other exemplary conversions. But Dante exploits all the resources of literature—the subtle suggestions of poetic language, the dramatic effect of graphic description, a savant design of narrative structure—in order to enact a religious revelation that occurs in the present tense of the reading of the poem. He produces thereby a text that actually performs the revelation it conveys rather than only telling about it. Any mere telling *about* can tend to conceal more than it reveals. But as inducing an interpretive experience—one that can be as much religious as literary in character and that, in any case, converts its reader to a new sense of existence and its possibilities—the poem itself becomes a revelatory event. The human reality of the poem as an interpretive event thus can become the revelation of a putatively transcendent, theological truth. The experience of poetry discloses what claims to be the ultimate meaning of things, and in this sense poetry becomes religious revelation.

The first fully developed dramatic episode of the poem demonstrates this interpretive-revelatory dynamic in exemplary fashion. From its first highly individualized representation of sinners, namely, Paolo and Francesca, the poem is explicitly about reading. Their sin of lust is mediated by reading and is shown to be inextricable from it. Likewise Dante's reading of their story—together with the way he provokes his own reader's interpretations of it—is laden with implications about how sin is itself basically an act of false self-interpretation, a misreading of one's own life and its meaning. In some way or other, all these false readings fail to acknowledge God as the Lord of life. They are self-interpretations of individuals who obstinately opt for a view of themselves that is sequestered from divine revelation. Francesca's interpretation of herself and Paolo contradicts God's manifest judgment revealed as the final truth about their lives by the evidence of their condition in the eternal world.

What we see directly are the punishments, but these are transparent to the sins which they, in effect, interpret and reveal in their ultimate meaning. In general, the punishment simply makes explicit and permanent the life-choice that is elected in committing the sin. The first in the series of sensual sins is lust: the sinners are being driven by a tempest that externalizes the inner state of turmoil of "those who subject reason to desire." The punishment reveals the nature of the sin and fulfills its true intent by fully and manifestly realizing its inescapable consequences. This understanding of sin makes the punishment intrinsic to the sin rather than a condition externally imposed by a punishing God.

In the case of the neutrals, who in canto 3 are actually barred from Hell and so not under the same law of retribution, this logic is reversed: the sinners are subjected to the very state that they attempted to avoid, and it is intensified so as to become unbearable. Since their sin is not exactly what they chose but rather their refusing to make any choice whatever, they are being painfully spurred into motion behind a banner, and so are goaded into a perpetual parody of partisanship. Their being forced to run around frenetically makes mockery of their having preferred inaction, showing that that, too, has consequences and is, in itself, an adherence simply to themselves ("per sé fuoro," 3.39) rather than to any greater cause. And this is deemed even more reprehensible than any of the choices they might otherwise have made. The price of passivity is made painfully tangible in their being stung or bitten by wasps and giant flies and noisome worms. Crucial is that what these sinners experience be, in any case, directly the result and, in effect, the true realization of their failure to choose for one party or the other, for good or for evil. The moral: you get what you choose, but if you do not choose at all, this refusal ("rifiuto," 3.60) will itself become your inescapable fate and will sting and torture you unremittingly.

Deeply considered, each of the punishments externalizes the corresponding sin and thereby makes the sin transparent to the false interpretation of self that it results from and embodies and enacts. Whatever the specific nature of the sin in question, it entails some sort of positioning of oneself vis-à-vis God and others, and it is this self-understanding that issues in concrete acts. Sinful acts are the expression of erroneous, willful interpretations of self as autonomous and separate from God. There are as many sins as there are ways of alienating oneself from God. All are forms of distorted and willfully false misinterpretation, pivoting always on some misinterpretation of *oneself*. As forms of mistaken self-interpretation, the sins represented are applicable not only to the characters but also potentially to the reader. This is especially so because reading is an activity of self-interpretation par excellence. In order to interpret each character, readers cannot but interpret themselves and project onto the characters their own possibilities of being. The reader, as reader, is able thus to participate, at least potentially, in each sin as at bottom a possible mode (however covert or latent) of their own self-(mis)interpretation.

The self-reflexiveness of the poem, the potential application of its implicit moral sense to the reader, applies in some way to each representation of sin in the *Inferno*. But the first detailed description by Dante of an act of sin, namely, Paolo and Francesca's sin of adultery, demonstrates this emblematically by focusing explicitly on reading as the locus of self-interpretation and misinterpretation: it suggests how sin per se is symbolically bound up with "reading" understood in just this sense of self-interpretation. For at the source of Francesca's sin with Paolo and, inseparably, her self-misrepresentation is the reading of a book: the Arthurian romance of Lancelot is presented literally as literature pandering to lust. The name of the book's author, Gallehaut, is made to serve, somewhat anachronistically, as already synonymous with pandering: "Gallehaut was the book and the one who wrote it" ("Galeotto fu il libro e chi lo scrisse," 5.137).

It is the reading of this romanticized tale of courtly love, or rather of adulterous passion, that induces Paolo and Francesca to cede to a falsely idealized interpretation of their lust for each other. And Francesca is continuing still to pander this false interpretation by recounting her sin to Dante in the rapturous measures of the love lyric, indeed by echoing just such love lyrics as Dante himself wrote in his youth. Her "Love, which swiftly takes the gentle heart" ("Amor, ch'al cor gentil ratto s'apprende," 5.100) rehearses the love poetry of Guido Guinizelli, on whom Dante's own amorous verse was modeled. This line cites specifically "Foco d'amor in gentil cor s'aprende" ("Fire of love in noble heart is kindled") from Guinizelli's sonnet "Al cor gentil rempaira sempre amore," which Dante imitated in chapter 20 of his *Vita nuova*. However, this exalted and refined language notwithstanding, some of the less polite terms, like "bocca" ("mouth") or "questi" ("this one here") for Paolo, betray the cruder, more sensual motives of this discourse by a bourgeois dame out of contemporary chronicle assuming pretentious airs of nobility.[13] Heard in this conjunction, her first address of Dante as gracious "living creature," literally "O animal" ("O animal grazïoso e benigno," 5.88) may have also a brute overtone unintended by Francesca and jarring within the classical rhetoric of her *captatio benevolentiae*.

Dante construes the sin of the lustful as a "subjecting of reason to desire" ("peccator carnali, / che la ragion somettono al talento," 5.38–39), and he shows how exactly this is what threatens him and all who listen to Francesca—all those who read his text. The infectiousness of Francesca's sin of interpreting herself in a way contrary to the truth revealed by the judgment manifest in her is demonstrated by Dante's own reactions. He literally falls for Francesca and her seductive story, as the last verse of the canto says: "and I fell as a dead body falls" ("e caddi come corpo morto cade").

Dante (as poet, but not as character) understands this surrender to sensuality as a sort of death, the death inherent in the body per se. In Dante's Christian medieval and moral understanding, a human body, to the extent that it is infected by sensuality, is already dead and fallen. If we listen soberly, discerningly, and even a little suspiciously, Dante's own interpretation of himself as "tristo e pio" ("sad and full of pity," or "sad and compassionate") in his reaction to Francesca sounds like a moralization and Christianization of what is actually his libidinous interest in her intriguing story. Despite his affecting a religious detachment and compassion, a much more passionate sort of involvement is betrayed by the eager accents with which he solicits the juicy details of "how?" and "when?" she fell into the forbidden embraces: "at what point and in what way did love grant / you to know the dubious desires?" ("a che e come concedette amore / che conosceste i dubbiosi disiri?" 5.119–20).

From the beginning of his encounter with the lustful, Dante understands his own reaction in terms of the Christian virtue of "pity" or "compassion" ("pietà," 5.72). This term is suggested to him by Francesca herself (5.93). But his initial perception of these souls as "ancient ladies and knights" ("le donne antiche e' cavalieri," 5.71) hints that he may be dupe to a romanticized misinterpretation of this company of sinners. He is like them in having his reason placed into subjection by desire: he is involved emotionally and

13. Compare Renato Poggioli, "Tragedy or Romance? A Reading of the Paolo and Francesca Episode in Dante's *Inferno*," *PMLA* 72 (1957): 313–58.

cannot extricate himself and in the end literally faints and falls, which symbolically is to die.

The readers, in turn, are presented with the question of how to react to Francesca and her story. Should we recognize her high citations as shabby artifices employed to disguise sneaking lust and to seduce unwary readers by their romantic rhetoric? Her own idealizing misinterpretation of her carnal sensuality, which rubs off on Dante in his perception of the lustful as noble knights and ladies, tempts the reader as well. Indeed many critics and readers have glorified Francesca into a Dantesque heroine. This was the case particularly in the Romantic age, and such a strain resonates still, for example, in Puccini's opera *Francesca da Rimini* (1914, Teatro Regio, Turin). But precisely this sort of reading is exposed as an interpretive trap, as itself exactly the sin for which Francesca is punished. What she does right here in the encounter with Dante, in proffering the misinterpretation of herself within which she continues to live—or rather to eternally die—*is itself the sin* for which she is being punished. She performs it ever anew in the eternal present of Hell and in the endless repetitions of this text. It is, we have seen, fundamentally a sin of self-misrepresentation, of interpreting herself in a way that denies God and his judgment on her sin. The divine judgment reveals her as blinded by the lust that she legitimizes in her tale. And this is precisely what she does in the encounter with Dante, specifically in the way she presents herself thus also before the eyes of his readers: they, in turn, are tempted in their own imagination of the scene to cede to sensual lust aroused by her seductive words.

This case shows exemplarily how the true sense of the characters' histories is presented in and through their modes of interpreting themselves presently in the text. The sinners are punished not just for what they have done in the past but for what they continue to do as we encounter them presently in our reading: their sin is an ongoing reality in the way they constitute themselves by self-interpretation in the text we read. Francesca's sin consists not only in one past act of passion and adultery or in any other facts and events of her personal history. It is constituted much more essentially by her self-(mis) interpretations performed in the text as we read it. And *this* specific misinterpretation may well implicate also the reader. The chain begins with Dante himself as the first reader of his Francesca, vulnerable as he is to the seductions of her story and its poetic language. The incipit of the following canto confirms that Dante's emotions of "pity" and compassionate "sadness" fully confused him, so that he lost his mind and judgment—just like the lustful, who "subject reason to desire":

> Al tornar de la mente, che si chiuse
> dinanzi a la pietà d'i due cognati,
> che di trestizia tutto mi confuse, . . .
> (6.1–3)

(At the return of consciousness, which closed
in view of the pity of the two in-laws,
who completely confounded me with sadness . . .)

Francesca's power of attraction is unmistakable, as Dante's sympathetic reaction demonstrates. Yet there is something equivocal about her seductive blandishments and about the idyllic description she gives—even from the midst of the maelstrom that now devours her!—of her native land as the place where the river Po descends to the "peace" of the sea (5.99). For she, in contrast, is forever consumed by the winds of passion to which she willingly abandoned herself, surrendering her power of rational self-control. If we understand her sin, and each sin, as a form of self-(mis)interpretation, the deeper sense of justice in the *Inferno* surfaces. It becomes glaringly evident in Francesca how sin is its own punishment and how the punishment, too, is nothing other than a perpetuation of the self-misinterpretation in which the sin consists.

The pains of Hell are to be understood as eternalizing the willful desires that constitute the corresponding sins in the first place. In Hell, these willed desires are simply followed out to their natural and necessary consequences. One's freely chosen way of being is the decisive act of will that alone can be sinful. It is the only basis for one's fate in eternity. For God does not vengefully punish: he rather gives each soul only what it has freely chosen. The punishments are not just externally imposed: they are rather manifestations and intensifications of the state chosen by those who sin. This state flows from each soul's free interpretation of itself and of the sense of its existence. Fundamentally, sinful souls choose to understand themselves as separate from God. They prefer to believe a conceit of their own fabrication rather than to accept the divine Will that created them with a specific purpose for their lives. The damned, furthermore, persist in such a choice beyond the point of no return, the point at which their will is no longer capable of reversing itself. We see Francesca even in eternity still resisting seeing herself in accordance with the divine Judgment.

Through persistent sin, free will is eventually lost, as Saint Augustine taught, notably in *De libero arbitrio*. Free indulgence becomes habit and eventually results in loss of the ability *not* to sin. What we once chose freely becomes addiction, compulsion, necessity: we *become* it. Eventually we no longer know how to understand ourselves otherwise than in terms of the sin—or, more precisely, of the self-interpretation that a certain sin entails. We die morally, and at that point it is too late to change. This is demonstrated in the punishments of the gluttonous (canto 6), of the avaricious and prodigal (canto 7), and of the slothful and wrathful (canto 8). In each case, the punishment *is* the sin presented as involving a specific misinterpretation of being human, one that distorts and eventually destroys human nature in its original state as created by God.

III. Deep Hermeneutics of Complicity and Conversion: *Inferno*, Cantos 8–17

Self-interpretation, which is so crucial to the fate of the souls in the afterlife, is made manifest as a crucial structuring principle of the poem in the segment that begins with Dante's entry into the city of Dis. This transition directly involves the reader as interpreter by means of the poem's explicit addresses to the reader.[14] The first explicit address to the reader occurs in canto 8 before the Gate of the City of Dis, where the difficulties for Dante in his descent through the Inferno become humanly insurmountable. Demons and furies gather to make him remain ("rimarrai," 8.92) there, separating him from Virgil, his guide. The address comes in the form of a direct meta-narratological intervention that interrupts the narrative, which has reached an impasse (8.94–96). Recalling his fear that he might never return, Dante turns to his reader:

> Pensa, lettor, se io mi sconfortai
> nel suon de le parole maladette,
> ché non credetti ritornarci mai.
> (8.94–96)
>
> (Think, reader, if I did not panic
> at the sound of the accursed words,
> since I believed I'd never again return.)

This express involvement of the reader throws into focus a whole new field of reference for the realization of the narrative's meaning.

The significance of this dimension, in which the reader is brought directly into the poem, begins to become clearer when a similar interruption occurs again, but much more dramatically, in canto 9. Here the address to the reader follows upon the appearance of three infernal furies that block the Gate and threaten to show the Gorgon's head that would petrify Dante, forcing him to remain in that place forever. By close proximity and association with the address to the reader, these threats are made to figure the risk also to the reader of remaining fixated upon the literal level of the narrative and consequently failing to penetrate to its deeper doctrinal meaning. Precisely such hermeneutic penetration is expressly enjoined by the address to the reader in canto 9:

> O voi che avete li 'ntelletti sani,
> mirate la dottrina che s'asconde
> sotto 'l velame de li versi strani.
> (9.61–63)

---

14. Eric Auerbach, "Dante's Addresses to the Reader," *Romance Philology* 7 (1953–54): 268–79, focused attention on the topic.

(O you who have sound intellects,
look at the doctrine which hides itself
beneath the veil of the strange verses.)

At this point, "the veil of the verses," that is, the story which serves as vehicle for the allegory or doctrine of the poem, has become particularly riveting and tends to arrest attention upon the visual surface of the narrative, where the furies are described in graphic detail, with their blood-flecked female limbs and snaky hair. Only Virgil's naming of them with traditional mythological names—"Megaera," "Allecto," "Tisiphone"—exerts some measure of control over the hallucinatory visual intensity of this scene. Without Virgil's verbal mediation, Dante's (and the reader's) gaze would be liable to remain fixated, petrified forever by the Medusa. However, the figures of the furies and the Medusa are typical of the sort of myths that were routinely interpreted in accordance with allegorical meanings in medieval exegesis. By literally blocking the protagonist's further progress through Hell, they serve as figures for blockage of the hermeneutic process of interpretation on the part of the reader.

Stumbling blocks at the literal level force the interpreter to dig deeper in order to find the rational, allegorical meaning that is masked beneath the mythic exterior. The interpreter must avoid becoming obsessed merely with the story and its images and rather pass beyond the literal sense. The *face* of Medusa, whose beholders turn to stone, emblematizes this tendency to remain fascinated and frozen or literally *petrified* by the aesthetic-erotic surface. Virgil, representing the better part of rationality, rescues Dante also by putting his hands over his protégé's eyes and turning him around, so that he not remain petrified when the Gorgon's head (Medusa) appears.

. . . ed elli stessi
mi volse, e non si tenne a le mie mani,
che con le sue ancor non mi chiudessi.
(9.58–60)

(. . . and he himself
turned me, and did not rely on my hands,
but with his own also closed my eyes.)

This act directly precedes the injunction to the reader. Virgil does this in a coercive manner that concretely imitates the author's intrusive intervention into the text by direct address to call the mind of his reader away from the literal narrative and its dangerously engrossing action. The call to allegorical penetration beyond the veil of the verses warns the reader not to be absorbed by what simply appears in its immediacy on the narrative's surface. Virgil's action *within* the narrative in this way figures the interpretive action performed by the author *upon* the narrative: the abrupt breaking off of the narration (diegesis) with the sudden switch to the discourse of address (appellation) invasively interrupts the reader's involvement in the story on its literal level. Made in the image of Virgil turning Dante about and covering his eyes, the address to the reader forcibly turns the reader away from the literal surface of the narrative and demands reflection searching rather for its allegorical meaning.

The prompting of the readers to look beyond the letter of the text and to find a hidden, allegorical meaning, inevitably by application of the text to themselves, thus becomes perfectly explicit in cantos 8–9, in the transition from upper to lower hell ("basso inferno," 8.75) and into the City of Dis. We noted that this sequence is subtly prefaced by the encounter earlier in canto 8 with Filippo Argenti, who, like the other damned souls, *remains* where he is in hell (the word "rimani" in various declensions reverberates in lines 34, 38, 92, 116). Argenti's condemnation to remain is confirmed by Dante's curse. He stays in the Styx, whereas Dante himself passes over it and into further depths of the nether world, as Dante curtly remarks: "If I come, I do not remain" ("S' i' vegno, non rimango," 8.34). Even more significantly, the poem leads Dante, together with his reader, into further depths of revelation, into a space of interpretation where the true journey beyond the fictive one unfolds. The forward motion through hell thus becomes a figure for passage beyond the poem's literal sense to its "doctrinal"—its educative and prophetic and ultimately apocalyptic—meaning. Dante's going deeper into hell within the narrative becomes an image for the interpreter's looking beneath the letter of the narrative to its deeper figural and salvific meaning, as is enjoined expressly in canto 9 by the address to the reader.

Already at the end of canto 8, Virgil recalled the "dead letter" ("la scritta morta," 8.127) that Dante saw inscribed over the Gate of Hell as he entered (canto 3). Dante was not able to understand this inscription when he saw it immediately before his eyes. The sense of the words was "hard" for him ("il senso lor m'è duro," 3.12), since his understanding was, in effect, petrified by being confined to the literal level. Only by entering into hell—and seeing not just the literal landscape but seeing *through* to its figural meaning—is he able to understand the sense of this inscription, which is presented with literal immediacy to him at the entrance. This inscription appears also to the reader at the head of canto 3 as a "dead letter" whose meaning, if it remains merely literal rather than becoming the gateway to deeper "doctrinal" understanding, will spiritually kill him: "For the letter killeth, but the spirit giveth life" (2 Corinthians 3:6).

Contrary to this dead letter, Christ is the key to all true interpretation, and the sprung bolts on the Gate of Hell mentioned at this juncture allude to him (8.126). The traces of Christ's descent are inscribed unmistakably in Hell in the form of the Gate left unsealed ("sanza serrame") by the earthquake that was caused by his descent into Limbo. The evidence of this quake is also seen in ruined bridges and debris of landslides pointed out along the way, most conspicuously at 12.4–10 (see also 5.34; 11.2; 21.108; 23.136). Passage through the lower Gate to the city of Dis is secured for Dante and Virgil by a figure who descends from heaven in the track through Hell opened previously by Christ. This "one" sent from heaven ("un . . . da ciel messo," 9.85) indeed crosses the Styx and "walked as if on land and with dry soles" (9.81) like Christ (Matthew 14:24–33). The celestial "messenger," which is the literal Greek meaning of "angel" (ἄγγελος), is in effect repeating Christ's descent into and unsealing of Hell. Hell is opened now for Dante as protagonist, as well as for his reader, both of whom enter into "secret things" ("cose segrete," 3.21), in order to emerge with new and supernaturally enhanced understanding.

Christ is the interpretive key that clears away all impediments to Christian understanding for the reader. He unveils allegorical meaning behind the mere letter of the "fatal text" ("la scritta morta," 3.127) that kills. Classical myths of descent into Hell by heroes such as Hercules and Theseus, alluded to in lines 98–99 and 54 respectively of canto 9, were similarly taken in medieval exegesis to be allegorical prefigurations of Christ's descent. Illuminated according to their spiritual or allegorical sense, these descents, too, reflect the light of Christ that lightens the way through Hell for the protagonist, as well as for the reader on the path of life. In this manner, the events in the narrative ensuing immediately upon the injunction to the reader in canto 9 read coherently as figuring an event in the interpretive journey of the reader.

The violent descent of the "heaven-sent messenger," causing the great disruption that is drawn out in detail in verses 64–105 of canto 9, is homologous to Dante's abrupt interruption of his own narrative. Dante's intervention by direct address forces the reader to break away from the literal narration in order to reflect upon and decipher its meaning in allegorical terms. The angelic figure is a sort of Hermes, the god of interpretation, whose name actually lies at the root of the word "hermeneutics" for the theory and practice of interpretation. The messenger's descent recalls the descent of Hermes (in *Aeneid* book 4.146ff) intervening to free Aeneas from an erotic attachment potentially fatal to his world-historical mission. The celestial messenger's intervention is now necessary to unblock the way for Dante and Virgil to descend deeper into the Inferno and to allow the deeper allegorical sense of the poem for the reader to emerge from beneath its surface. Paralleling the action of the messenger within the narrative, the intervention of Christ from outside upon the reader's mind is necessary to enable the reader's understanding to penetrate deeper into the meaning of the poem.

Interpretation, like the Christ event itself, and specifically the descent to Limbo that caused so much visible structural damage in Hell, is often inevitably a violent activity. Interpretation must disturb the surface in order to penetrate the depth of an experience or a text. And in this, too, the text of

Inferno canto 9 strikingly mimes and highlights the essential elements of the hermeneutic process. Since Dante enters into the circle of the violent (the seventh circle) just beyond this juncture, it is no accident that the violent side of interpretation should be foregrounded with particularly impetuous imagery such as is used to describe the descent of the celestial messenger. He breaks on the scene with a frightful fracas of wind and storm that provoke a scattering of branch and beast and herdsmen (9.64–72). He is a Christ figure (we have already seen that he walks on water), but in this world of threats he also ambiguously possesses some demonic traits: the terrified souls flee before him like frogs from the "enemy snake" ("la nimica / biscia," 9.76–77).

The violence Dante focuses on is never exclusively that of the characters and events represented in his poem, but always also that perpetrated by the interpretive event that the poem itself *is*, which includes also, by anticipation, the interpretive act of the reader that is proleptically folded into it. This is demonstrated by Dante's own interpretive violence, which is underscored throughout this circle, for example, against his beloved teacher, "Ser Brunetto." Dante's poem in this manner realizes its meanings *performatively*—in the event of poetry as an interpretive act.

The realization of the journey in an interpretive dimension is then carried to the level of the reader programmatically by Dante's explicit metanarratological addresses to the reader. These begin, as we have seen, in *Inferno* 8 and establish themselves as key to the poem as a whole in canto 9. But just as strikingly, *within* the narrative the characters themselves are all involved in acting out dramas of self-interpretation. In fact, their sins are presented by Dante most fundamentally as forms of self-misinterpretation, and we see such self-misinterpretation enacted by them directly as they appear in Dante's text. Particularly compelling instances of this can be found in the first and last extended first-person narratives of damned souls in the *Inferno*: Francesca da Rimini's in canto 5 (as we saw in section II) and Conte Ugolino's in cantos 32–33 (as we will see in section VI).

Another telling example of sinful self-misinterpretation can be found in canto 10. The insinuations concerning Guido Cavalcanti have proved confusing to commentators. Nevertheless, they make a clear statement that he refused the necessary support of grace and guidance from above and beyond himself. His very name, "Guido," means "I guide," and Dante pronounces it in answering Guido's father, telling him that his son held God or Beatrice in disdain ("forse cui Guido vostro ebbe a disdegno," 10.63). Whoever Guido disdains, it is a mark of lack on his part of openness to guidance from above and therewith to transcendence. Guido flies rather by his own "high genius" ("altezza d'ingegno"), exactly as his father's words suggest. This constitutes a self-centered rather than a God-centered interpretation of his life's journey. He has no guide but his own conceit of genius, and that marks his essential difference from Dante and from the type of journey that the latter is on. Like Guido, whose fate is evoked here, so the heretics, with whom his father is punished, are condemned by their misinterpretations of Christian doctrine and therewith of their own existence. Most flagrantly, this is the case of the Epicureans, who "make the soul die with the body" ("l'anima col corpo morta fanno," 10.15).

*Linguistic Self-Interpretation and Sins of Rhetorical Violence (*Inferno*, Cantos 13–17)*

In Pier de la Vigna, Capaneo, and Brunetto Latini, the poem continues to offer perspicuous examples of how self-understanding and self-interpretation determine the eternal state and destiny of each individual Dante meets. The history of each, with respect to their fateful nemesis, is seen realized *in nuce* in their present encounters with Dante and in the compressed dramas of self-presentation that they act out before him. They all, as we encounter them, actually *do* whatever it is that they are condemned for, showing this to be in no way incidental or over—and, to that extent, forgivable. Rather, their sin is manifest as the very essence of who they are for all eternity as a result of their own free and fatal choices. Capaneo says as much explicitly: "Such as I was alive, so am I dead" ("Tal fui vivo, tal sono morto," 14.51)—at the beginning of a blasphemous speech defying the gods that reenacts in Dante's presence the very sin for which this Greek king (one of the *Seven Against Thebes*) is being punished.

A more complicated and elaborate display of sin as erroneous self-interpretation is folded into the verses presenting Pier de la Vigna. Pier's tortuous rhetoric exposes one type of interpretive fallacy, that of becoming tangled up in his own neurotic self-consciousness and its excessive verbiage, which is "knotty and convoluted" ("nodosi e 'nvolti," 13.5) like the branches of the shrub into which he has been turned. Indeed such a destiny seems to be written into his very name "de la Vigna," meaning "of the vine." This characteristic involution is realized tellingly in Pier's own self-reflexive language and twisted logic, obscuring the natural and normal function of language. This function, according to medieval logic and semantic theory, is primarily *to refer*, to designate objects in the world. And it cannot do this well if it gets all wound up around itself. The presumably proper function of language is perverted disastrously by the courtier who becomes enmeshed in viscous verbal formulations that show up as impenetrable like the twisted and knotty wood of the vine.

A vertiginously convoluted pattern of language is patent in Pier's description of how the "meretrix" or "courtesan," allegorically Envy, worked against him when he was the loyal privy counselor of the emperor, Frederick II. He protests that she "inflamed all minds against me; / and thus the inflamed inflamed Augustus" ("infiammò contra me li animi tutti; / e li 'nfiammati infiammar sì Augusto," 13.67–68). A likewise doubly-folded, opaque verbal style inflects again Pier's description of his "injustice against his own just self" ("ingiusto fece me contra me giusto," 13.72). The same thick, self-reflexive rhetoric, moreover, is dangerously reflected into Dante's own language from the outset of this very canto: "I believe that he believed that I believed" ("Cred'io ch'ei credette ch'io credessi," 13.25).

The tendency of highly rhetorical language to become self-involved, thereby interfering with transparency and obscuring reference beyond itself, is signaled from the beginning of Pier's speech, in his pleading for indulgence for what is about to become a woody or viscous ("inveschi") discourse:

> ". . . e voi non gravi
> perch' io un poco a ragionar m'inveschi."
> (113.56–57)
>
> (". . . let it not burden you
> if I dilate a little in discoursing.")

This is the first hint of how speech can thicken into a substance and cease thereby to properly serve its purposes with reference to the world, and so become a tangle and a trap. The intrigues of the imperial court, which led to Pier's demise, are all wound up with language taking on a disproportionate weight in and for itself: it thereby becomes a sticky bird lime (the most literal meaning contained in "m'inveschi") rather than a transparent medium. All the descriptions of speech in this scene insist on its becoming physicalized, its being turned into a thing and thereby being made into a mechanical production rather than a natural human expression of thought and spirit:

> Come d'un stizzo verde ch'arso sia
> da l'un de' capi, che da l'altro geme
> e cigola per vento che va via,
> sì de la scheggia rotta usciva insieme
> parole e sangue . . .
> (13.40–44)
>
> (As a green branch that is burned
> at one end, that from the other groans
> and squeaks from wind that passes through,
> so from the broken stump words and blood
> came out together . . .)

The mixing of words and blood is a palpable carrying out to an extreme of the degradation and befouling of speech by an overly conspicuous rhetoric. In Pier's punishment, words actually become concrete things: his language and its immaterial meaning metamorphose into blood and words mixed together, and his speech is mechanically generated like the hiss of a burning log (13.40–45).[15] This artificial concoction and simulation of human speech is spooky, but it is also uncannily close in its results to the familiar artifices of rhetoric. For this is what rhetoric tends to do: it dwells upon the sensuous, material qualities of language and draws attention to words as things in their own right.

Turned to bloody substance or mechanical sound, the intellectual quality of speech is corrupted; it becomes completely mired in the material world. This sort of hypostatization is tantamount to a denial of the referential function of proper language to point beyond itself. In fact, rhetoric tends to take language as a substantial medium to be molded into shape by purely formal means. Having denied to language transcendence of the world that it should, rather, reflect and represent, Pier then denies transcendence to life itself—through his suicide. He acts as if the soul possessed no transcendence of the material world but could die along with the body. Pier's rhetoric and his suicide constitute a negating of the transcendence of language and of the human soul respectively, and the two are shown to be tightly intertwined.

The power of language to negate real things is placed into evidence from the opening of the canto, with the insistently negative grammar used to describe the pathless forest:[16] "No green foliage . . . no smooth branches . . . no fruits were there . . . . No such thickets harsh and dense" ("Non fronde verde . . . non rami schietti . . . non pomi v'eran . . . Non han sì aspri sterpi né sì folti," 13.4–7). This is rather like the description of the island of the Cyclops in the *Odyssey*, which similarly specified only what was lacking and what things were *not*. Rhetorical language, by virtue (or vice) of its inner-linguistic density and self-referentiality, is at some level the negation of real beings. Such language readily induces also the inverse negation or category-mistake of reducing language—which is arguably that by which humanity is made in the image of God and transcends nature—to a thing. From treating language as if it were a thing without intellectual transcendence, it is a short, slippery step to treating one's own soul and its immortal life as if they were a mere thing that could be snuffed out, broken off, extinguished.

The dupe of his own rhetoric, Pier takes himself, just as he has taken words, to be a thing—and so he actually becomes one, a mere thing, and for all eternity. Befuddled by the instrumentalization of language reified into mere material to be manipulated through rhetoric, he takes also his own life as if it were a material thing that could be destroyed. Misunderstanding the spiritual nature of the soul as much as of the word, he tries to break off his own life as one would break a branch off a tree. Such is the crude misinterpretation of himself with which he is condemned thenceforth to live in an

15. Groundbreaking here is Leo Spitzer, "Speech and Language in *Inferno* XIII," *Italica* 19 (1942): 17–44.

16. Luigi Scorrano, "*Inferno* XIII: Un orizzonte di negazione," *Deutsches Dante-Jahrbuch* 73 (1998): 99–125.

eternal death. This curiously disarticulates all natural relation of the soul to the body, as is grotesquely illustrated by the hanging, after the Last Judgment, of the bodies of the suicides on the trees into which their souls have degenerated and metamorphosed. Nature is thus perverted to a macabre metaphor for instrumentalizing words and bodies, as if they were external, dead material rather than animated spiritually from within.

Pier, as a rhetorician, molds language like a malleable substance, yet precisely its susceptibility to manipulation allows rhetorical language to be used against him by the court flatterers who undermine the emperor's trust and confidence in him. Concrete experience, such as Virgil affords Dante in bidding him to break the branch of Pier's shrub rather than relying only on the text of the *Aeneid* about Polydorus, is a sounder basis for true belief. But Pier turns to and believes in rhetoric more than in reality itself. He becomes therefore eternally entangled in rhetoric's intrinsic negativity and involutedness. Dante, too, is susceptible to falling prey to such deceptions, especially being a poet and finding himself lost in a dense, pathless forest. But to Pier, such belief in mere words becomes fatal: he is mortally wounded and envenomed by words of calumny to the point of physically annihilating himself.

This concentration on the pitfalls of rhetorical language hints at how, in this case again, the sins Dante sees are virtually and potentially his own, for Dante himself inevitably and self-consciously employs rhetoric in the making of his poem. Its seductions and deceptions represent aspects of his own self-interpretation, aspects that he must guard against, lest they become the fatal motions of his soul and fix how his will is determined for eternity. The reader, moreover, is in nearly the same case as Dante vis-à-vis each of the *exempla* of sin, since what readers make out of the *Commedia*'s characters is intimately related to how they understand themselves. It is symptomatic of how they are able to understand human beings generally and therefore of how they interpret themselves also—for good or ill, salvation or damnation.

Canto 13, seen from this perspective, is about the horror of reification of the human, of the human becoming a thing, and this involves particularly the reification of language. Language, in the humanist tradition to which Dante so decisively contributes, particularly in his *De vulgari eloquentia*, is the essential vehicle and sign of a transcendence of mere nature. Language is what distinguishes humans from beasts in the classical humanist outlook reflected in *De vulgari eloquentia* (see particularly book 1, chapter 2) and enshrined in the Aristotelian definition of man as an "animal endowed with speech" (ζῶον λόγον ἔχον, *Nichomachean Ethics* 1.13). But language can also be perverted into the negation of this transcendence. This happens through the corruption of language by mendacious, self-serving rhetoric, whenever language is detached from its civic purpose and content and becomes mere form and flattery. Pier has fallen victim to the deceptions of his own style of intricate, rhetorically elaborated speech. This negative potential of language is insisted upon from the opening lines of canto 13, and Dante's own rhetoric is in jeopardy of becoming all for naught, as suggested by its homologous mirroring of Pier's patterns of rhetorical convolution: it, too, could become suicidal for his mission by becoming an end unto itself.

Dante's critical examination of rhetorical humanism continues in the encounter with Brunetto Latini. This episode, however, inverts the lesson imparted in connection with Pier de la Vigna. This encounter develops an indictment of rhetoric as inducing not to a materialization of speech but to the illusion of a final transcendence of matter and time through man's own works and words. Brunetto interprets himself as a winner of eternal life betokened by the ever-green banner he runs after in the concluding verses (15.121–24) of the canto. He sees himself as immortalized through his own rhetorical achievement in his *Li Livres dou Tresor* or "*Tesoro*," literally his "treasure":

> "Sieti raccomandato il mio Tesoro,
> nel qual io vivo ancora, e più non cheggio."
> (15.119–20)

> ("May my *Treasure*, in which I still live,
> be commended to you, and I ask no more.")

Since "where your treasure is, there will your heart be also" (Matthew 6:21), this indeed becomes his self-willed lot and portion for eternity. He substitutes a self-created image, an artifact, in effect, an idol, for what should have been rather a living soul blessed eternally in the sight of the living God.

Nonetheless, Dante represents himself as still somewhat under the spell of his great teacher. This sentiment is attested by his expressions of deep affection and attachment, as well as respect signaled by the formal "you" ("voi"). Yet Dante's reminiscing upon the way Brunetto taught him "how man eternalizes himself" ("come l'uom s'etterna," 15.85) shows up as tragically ironic in this scene blazoning Brunetto's eternal damnation. Brunetto reenacts precisely this sin and its damnation again here and now in this very text by the manner in which he still interprets human being, particularly his own, humanistically. Specifically, the desire for eternity, for personal immortality, is pursued by Brunetto, as by a certain breed of humanists generally, through merely human channels rather than by submitting to God as the ultimate and only Lord of life. The humanist dream of self-immortalization through an artifact of one's own creation, one's literary work or oeuvre, is exposed as really an illusory evasion of time and death through an idolatrous sort of false transcendence.

Of course, Brunetto is actually condemned to the seventh circle of Hell for the sin of sodomy, but this too may be understood as falsely interpreting one's mortal, worldly, and physical life as perennial and even eternal. The specific form of sodomy in question here, namely, pederasty, can be analyzed as a self-deluded form of pretending to be ageless and eternal. Through amorous liaison with a youth, the pederast perhaps seeks an illusory escape from his own mortality. The sodomite's indulgence in sterile sex—especially the pederast's passion for infertile sexual relations with a young boy—constitutes, from a certain Christian moral perspective, a self-deceptive denial of time, to which all are nevertheless subject. Pederasty is a use of sex that dissociates it from the death of the old and the birth of the new and denies its implication of ceding one's own place to the next generation. Reproductive sex defines the limits of our personal life: it entails the succession of generations and therewith our own mortality, whereas pederasty perverts sex in its refusal to recognize these limits.

The pederast remains spellbound by a fascination with apparently ageless, ideal beauty. Just such a passion is explored by Thomas Mann in his story "Death in Venice": the aging protagonist's love for the beauty of a youth proves fatal to him.[17] In this way, sodomy and humanism, which were closely linked historically in educational institutions based on the relationship between young boys and masters of the liberal arts, are exposed together as both forms of seeking a false transcendence. Each mirrors and reveals the other.[18]

Brunetto Latini is, furthermore, a deeply individual and personal version of the "old man" of New Testament resonance (Romans 6:6 and Ephesians 4:22), of fallen humanity, that Dante also treats on a historical-allegorical level as the "Old Man of Crete" in canto 14. "Erect" ("sta dritto," 14.103), like Capaneus, the "veglio" embodies iconographically the pride through which humanity falls in its very attempt to raise itself in defiance of the divinity it wills to supplant. An allegory of the succession of empires, as in Daniel 2:31ff., this figure tells the story of humankind as a history of progressive decline—from gold, to silver, to bronze, iron, and clay. Its tears, forming the four rivers of Hell, concretize the flow of history and its tragedy into eternity, with ineffaceable consequences.

All of these examples, moreover, point out how absolutely central language, as interpretive medium, is to the sins and fates of the characters in the *Inferno*. That sin and indeed human action per se should be fundamentally linguistic in character is in itself an index of the extent to which Dante is conscious of human life as interpretation through and through.

---

17. John Freccero made such a connection in a course taught at Stanford University.

18. For historical context, see Michael Rocke, *Forbidden Friendships: Homosexuality and Male Culture in Renaissance Florence* (Oxford: Oxford University Press, 1996). The sterility of sodomy was frequently compared to rhetorical impropriety in the form of indulgence in metaphor already by familiar medieval sources such as Alain de Lille's *De planctu naturae* and Jean de Meun's portion of the *Roman de la rose* (especially Genius's sermon, verses 19463ff.).

Self-interpretation—construing ourselves in one way or another—constitutes the very essence of what we, as free agents, do and are, and it takes place preeminently in the medium of language. Accordingly, Dante analyzes all the ways that language can be employed and perverted by interpretation for sinful purposes. Practically every sin is understood as basically linguistic in nature, or at least from the standpoint of its linguistic manifestation. As Robin Kirkpatrick suggests, "the speeches Dante attributes to the damned represent a pathological display of the many ways in which words can die or become, quite literally, immoral."[19] Directly dependent on language is not only the essentially human power of rationality, specifically perverted in graver sins, but also freedom, a necessary prerequisite for the possibility of any sin whatsoever. Only an animal endowed with speech is capable of sinning.

This linguistic emphasis of Dante's outlook takes on particular importance through a kind of recursive twist, inasmuch as language is also the medium of Dante's poem. The poem, therefore, constantly calls itself into question as a linguistic act and artifact. The poem and Dante's act in writing it are themselves vulnerable to being marred by all the sorts of sins that are manifest linguistically and inventoried in the course of the journey. As poet, he can directly participate in the sins he represents specifically under the aspect of their linguistic manifestations. Dante's examination of sin and of how it infects human language constantly reflects on himself and his own dilemmas with language in attempting to write a prophetic poem, a human work of art that will somehow communicate the Word of God, even from the depths of damnation in Hell.

Throughout the *Commedia*, Dante is in search of a new sort of language, a language with an authority that is not that of philosophy, which is liable to being corrupted by intellectual pride or "presumption," as Augustine warned, nor just that of poetry and its rhetorical brilliance. He ruthlessly impugns all language that depends on his own capabilities or on any merely human resources whatsoever. The *Inferno* is a relentless undermining of all the conventional sanctions of human and institutional authority that Dante might turn to for legitimation and validation of his language. The solution he finally adopts is that of a *sermo humilis*,[20] a humbly sublime Christian prophetic word that lets divinity speak by disavowing and discrediting its own human authority and prestige. He goes so far as to *humiliate* his own human speaking and persona. Dante's artistically self-conscious production of poetry is merely human, and he prominently highlights and exposes its limitations as such. Dante's model is, ultimately, the Bible, which speaks from beyond its

19. Robin Kirkpatrick, *Inferno: Difficulty and Dead Poetry* (Cambridge, Eng.: Cambridge University Press, 1989), xiii.

20. See Erich Auerbach's historical-stylistic analysis, "*Sermo Humilis*," in *Literary Language and Its Public in Late Latin Antiquity and in the Middle Ages*, trans. Ralph Manheim (New York: Pantheon, 1965), 25–66.

human authors and their individual voices as the Word of God. But he can approach this model only to the extent that he effaces his own authority and delivers his text up to be used for a higher purpose by another Author.

In canto 16, the noble Florentines indirectly confirm Brunetto's prediction that Dante is destined for greatness by recognizing the privilege of his descent while living into the world of the dead. They entreat this marvelous man traversing hell safely on living feet ("vivi piedi," 16.32) to tell them who he is. The extraordinary fact of his presence among the dead is immediate evidence of his enjoying the special favor of God. To this extent, Dante's authority as poet and prophet in the interpretive journey is directly grounded on the corporeal journey of Dante as protagonist that demonstrates his election by grace for a world-historical mission. That is why all the vicissitudes to which Dante is subjected as a pilgrim cannot but reflect upon his status as poet-prophet. What happens to the character also happens to the author, even if somewhat indirectly, since the character is represented as in the process of becoming the author. Even the indignities to which he is subjected are necessary to strip away the merely human bases of his authority: Dante's human capacities are compounded of a corrupt admixture needing to be purged away in the course of his descent for the sake of his divine calling. These capabilities are indeed foregrounded, yet not as reliable resources assuring him the mastery necessary to achieve his goal but rather as offered up to a higher Author and Person and Purpose, in order that they may be made genuinely fruitful.

Dante's first and most indispensable human resource as a poet is, of course, his language. And the scene with the sodomites is one of myriad scenes that point up the essentially linguistic status of the past and of every spiritual condition in the present. Time and language are inextricable. This is suggested by the reply the sodomites give to Dante's ringing denunciation of the Florentine nouveaux riches:

> "Però, se campi d'esti luoghi bui
> e torni a riveder le belle stelle,
> quando ti gioverà dicere *'I' fui,'*
> fa che di noi a la gente favelle.
> Indi rupper la rota, e a fuggirsi
> ali sembiar le gambe loro isnelle.
> Un amen non saria possuto dirsi
> tosto così com' e' fuoro spariti . . ."
> (16.79–89)

> ("Therefore, if you make it out of these dark places
> and return to sight of the lovely stars,
> when it will please you to say *'I was,'*
> do make mention of us to the people.

Then they ruptured the wheel, and fleeing
their legs seemed wings for speed.
An *'amen'* could not have been said
as fast as they were gone . . .")

Past time is identified as the tense that says "I was," and a minimal moment of present time is measured by saying "amen." These hints of the essentially linguistic definition of the past and present highlight the power of language to determine our reality particularly in its temporality. This power will prove fundamental to Dante's attempt to use language to prophesy the future.

But immediately after this demonstration of appreciation for Dante's high-minded, prophetically intoned speech delivered "with face upraised" ("Così gridai con la faccia levata," 16.76), which is recognized right away as "the truth" (16.78), speech is drowned out by the waterfall of the Phlegethon tumbling down to the next lower circle of the *Inferno*, where indeed vision will take over from discourse, the eye from the ear. The sound of rushing water now deafens Dante and Virgil so that they can hardly hear each other speak:

che 'l suon de l'acqua n'era sì vicino,
che per parlar saremmo a pena uditi.
(16.92–93)

(for the sound of the water was so near us
that we would scarcely have heard ourselves speaking.)

The simile used to describe this falling water compares it to "Acquacheta"—literally "Quiet Water"—in the Apennines by "Monte Viso" (16.95), which can be taken to mean "Mount of Sight" ("viso" is, in fact, used in this sense a few lines later: "al tuo viso si scovra"—"be uncovered to your sight," 16.123). This hushing up or drowning out of speech signals the transition—which is imminent—to a region where disclosure will depend more on the power of the image than on the word. Dante is building toward his thoroughgoing and devastating indictment of speech, in its turn, as chief among the all-too-human means of interpretation.

Precisely at this point the transfer to the Malebolge takes place, with Dante and Virgil on the back of Geryon. It is a transfer from the circle of violence to that of fraud and, at the same time, an exposure of fraud in Dante's own poetic interpretations. This parallels the transition from the circles of incontinence to those of heresy and violence (cantos 10–17), in which Dante's interpretations themselves tend to become violent. By swearing to the literal truth of his *comedía* in one of the most obviously preposterous moments of the whole poem, Dante deliberately provokes the question, Can we take all this seriously? Obviously not at face value. Rather than being any sort of natural creature, Geryon, that "filthy image of fraud" ("quella sozza imagine di froda," 17.7) with the face of a just man ("faccia d'uom giusto," 17.11), is a literary pastiche, a production of high artifice like a Turkish tapestry or like Arachne's virtuoso web. The many colors of his hide suggest "colors" of rhetoric, just as the knots and convolutions painted on his surface ("dipinti avea di nodi e di rotelli," 17.15) make him an emblem for textuality and for some of the more far-fetched literary inventions that have been woven into the text of the *Inferno*. Both knots ("nodi") and scrolls ("rotelli") are terms suggestive of writing and written artifacts.[21] Geryon's symbolizing, in these respects, Dante's poem itself suggests that the poem is "a truth having the face of a lie" ("ver c'ha faccia di menzogna," 16.124).

The claim to straightforward literal truth, to actually having seen this very beast come rising up out of the depths of hell, conspicuously invalidates and ironizes itself. It thereby forces us to interpret the poem's nonetheless serious claim to truth on a different level. Ingeniously, Dante manages to impose the authority of his text precisely by exposing its extravagant fictiveness. For exactly this sort of self-ironic interpretive twist is what is necessary to reverse the fraud of fiction and turn it into an instrument of prophetic revelation. Dante's prophetic authority can be asserted only at the expense of the human poet's authority and voice, for the latter can be but a purveyor of fictions and therefore, in strict medieval rationalist terms, of lies. Still, the episode affirms the truth of fiction in its very preposterousness, since fiction, by exposing its own falsehood, becomes, paradoxically, true. In this sort of interpretive self-consciousness resides fiction's capacity to tell truths indirectly that otherwise cannot be told at all, so as to grasp what otherwise remains ungraspable about real life.

The actual descent, with the blocking of Dante's sight and the concomitant concentration of attention on the sense of hearing, enacts the drama of another hermeneutic transition: it figures interpretive penetration to a new depth of sense, thus taking up the relay from canto 9. Canto 16 concludes with the image of a diver returning to the surface, after having freed an anchor snagged on something beneath the sea. This may hint that Dante, too, has had to make some adjustments in the depths of his own poem, helping it to become unstuck from too rigidly literal an interpretation of the deep truth to which it is indeed anchored. So the "bark" of his poem is freed to sail on.

In this transition from the circle of the violent to that of the fraudulent—and thus from the second to the third major structural division of the *Inferno* (the first being incontinence) according to the classes of sin outlined in canto 11—Dante again emphasizes ways in which his own poem is complicit in the type of sin it portrays. Behind the face of a just man, Geryon has the body

21. Franco Ferucci, "Comedía," *Yearbook of Dante Studies* 1 (1971): 29–52, and Teodolinda Barolini, *The Undivine Comedy: Detheologizing Dante* (Princeton, N.J.: Princeton University Press, 1992), chapter 3, develop the textual connotations of Geryon.

of a serpent (17.12)—recalling the first prevaricator in the Garden—and a sharp tail that menaces unseen (17.1 and 84). Also, its descent in one hundred circles ("per cento rote," 17.131) is a figure for the poem's one hundred cantos. Throughout the eighth circle, Dante will concentrate on how poetry itself is apt to become a sort of hermeneutic fraud. Only by just such a self-aware admission and open exposure can the fraud inherent in poetic fiction be neutralized and even be corralled into serving indirectly as a disclosure of divine truth.

In his descent to the eighth circle, Dante registers, through his references to two notoriously over-audacious voyagers in heaven, Phaethon and Icarus, his worry over trespassing upon territory where as a living human being he does not belong. Both are emblems of the risk Dante runs of encroaching upon a realm that is off-limits to him. As a human being and particularly as a poet, he is liable to producing a representation of the other world that cannot but be fraudulent. It is a risk that he is able to contain only by admitting the absurdly arduous, mad undertaking on which he has embarked in his poem. By clinging close to Virgil as father figure, an all-too-fragile delegate of ultimately divine authority, Dante corrects for the transgressiveness of the temerarious sons who ignored their fathers' warnings. By calling attention himself to his dangerous proximity to such figures, he claims to be in conscious control of the risk and thereby differentiates the program of his poem from their disastrously deluded enterprises. While his poem is inextricably complicit in the very fraud and violence it denounces, sins which prove to be his characters' eternal damnation, this diagnosis and conscious denunciation opens a possibility of being saved by grace for Dante and for those who follow him on his journey of self-interpretation.

IV. Dante's Deconstruction and Reconstruction of Prophetic Voice and Vision in the Malebolge: *Inferno*, Cantos 18–25

In the Malebolge especially, we see Dante subjecting himself to scathing self-critique and even becoming a comic figure. As the protagonist climbs down deeper into the pit, the poem itself descends a declining scale of genres and stylistic registers all the way to the crude realism and burlesque of cantos 21 and 22. Here Dante's epic poem sinks to the level of Latin New Comedy, perhaps alluded to in Dante's phrase "nuovo ludo" (22.118), replete with lewd displays, comic gags, and sadistic games.[22] Dante's poem resorts especially to cooking imagery and proverbial wisecracks such as, "In church with saints and in the taverns with drunkards" (22.14–15). Prophecy itself, insofar as it

22. Zygmunt G. Baranski, "Dante, the Roman Comedians, and the Medieval Theory of Comedy," in *"Libri poetarum in quattor species dividuntur": Essays on Dante and 'Genre,'* supplement 2 to *The Italianist* 15 (1995): 61–99.

is the invention of a human poet, must be subjected to ridicule and affronts to its dignity. We see, in the Malebolge, a relentless critique of the prophetic voice, to the extent that it represents the presumption of a human poet. This is necessary to categorically distinguish prophecy as divine revelation from every merely human counterfeit made of persuasive and perhaps deceiving rhetoric.

The authentic language of prophecy cannot be any proud, self-confident Ciceronian rhetoric but only a *sermo humilis*, such as is forged in the Bible, eminently by Christ himself, for example, in parables drawn from the common run of experience and quotidian life. Paralleling Augustine's progression from the language of "presumption," which is characteristic of philosophy and classical literary models, to acceptance of the humble language of Scripture, Dante dramatizes his own coming into such a language by representing himself as undergoing a series of humiliations that force him to relinquish all his own human resources, including his personal pride and self-reliance. Dante's existential descent into the self enacts a destitution of his own self-sufficiency and self-centeredness, his being grounded in himself, and issues in an unconditional openness toward a transcendent or divine ground for his existence. Only by such self-ironic exposure of the inevitable deceptions of literary language and self-representation can Dante's all-too-human poem actually attain to the transcendent heights of authentic prophecy.

Such self-irony may be the deeper sense of "comedía" as the generic description Dante adopts for his poem in *Inferno* 16.128 and again in 21.2. Indeed, only as "comedy" can it become "divine." The best that any human effort can do, finally, is to confess its own insufficiency. A poem can, furthermore, unmask the false pretensions of more purportedly solemn attempts to prophesy that, without comic qualifiers, take themselves absolutely seriously, as if they were Gospel. This is seen by Dante to be the case even with the prophetic claims of the *Aeneid*. Virgil's "high tragedy" (20.113) lacks the self-ironizing capacity of comedy that alone can allow human literature to become truly divine revelation. Of course, modern readings of the *Aeneid* go a long way toward discovering already in Virgil's text an ironic current running counter to its own presumable imperialistic program. The triumphalistic story of Rome's founding through glorious martial victory yields to a tragic tale of irreparable human loss, of becoming embroiled in a war of conquest and eventually in bloody civil war. Yet precisely such self-undermining serves in Dante's text not just to render the poem ambivalent but to spark a higher realization of truth. By systematically undermining his own autonomous pretensions to communicate the truth, Dante's comic irony catalyzes a conversion to a divine Truth that can emerge from beyond the lie of artifice inherent in the literary.

Only as comedy in this sense can literature attain ultimate truth. The *Commedia*'s comedy, deeply considered, is its irony, its exposure of literature as dissimulation. The insinuation of tragedy in Virgil's ostensibly optimistic epic—its communicating a tragic truth only by way of its irony—may well be among the essential lessons that Dante learned from the *Aeneid*. However, as "high tragedy" Virgil's epic remains essentially a dissimulation of its own ironic truth. Dante, in contrast, discovers in comedy the self-ironic mode necessary to let a truth break through what otherwise would remain human mendaciousness and fraud disguised behind the face of a just man (17.7–12). By ironic exposure of its own inherent fraud as a literary fiction, Dante's poem overcomes or at least neutralizes this fraud in order to become "the truth that has the face of a lie" ("quel ver c'ha faccia di menzogna," 16.124).[23]

This strategy of self-subversion in the *Commedia* is carried out particularly through its demolition of language. The development of the poem through the Malebolge, starting from canto 18, demonstrates the devastating breakdown of language, rhetoric, prophetic pronouncement, authorial integrity, and so on. Here "ornate speech" ("parole ornate," 18.91) becomes an instrument of perdition in the mouths of seducers like Jason. This ironizes Virgil's supposedly saving "parola ornata" (2.67), called on for Dante's rescue at the outset of the poem. In fact, here the power of Dante's speech is in its being not ornate but *clear* ("la tua chiara favella," 18.53), and his *eyes* become more potent than any verbal eloquence. Pimp Venedico Caccianemico finds that he cannot hide from Dante's gaze (18.45–46), and Alessio Interminei da Lucca cries out in protest over being *eyed* more than the other flatterers (18.118–19).

At this stage, it is the dialectic between seeing and saying that becomes most revealing. Canto 18 presents the sin of pandering in the act of being performed, as if it were to capture the culprit precisely at the moment of saying "yes"—just as the word operates in the execution of this sin. Dante uses *sipa*, an affirmative in Bolognese dialect (18.58–61), for local coloration of this linguistically characterized sin. Similarly, barrators or grafters are identified in the dialect of Lucca as changing "no" to "yes" for money ("del no, per li denar, vi si fa *ita*," 21.42).

This sort of crystallization of a sin by its linguistic expression can be found almost everywhere in the *Inferno*. In 23.7, two words for "now" in different dialects, *mo* and *issa* (from Latin *modus* and *ipse* respectively), are used to point out a difference in the sensible signs used as signifiers, even where the signified meaning remains the same. Such arbitrary interchangeability of linguistic signifiers is intimately bound up with fraud, here specifically in the form of hypocrisy. Sin is inextricable from language right from Eve's

23. Massimo Verdicchio, *Of Dissimulation: Allegory and Irony in Dante's Commedia* (Warsaw: Wydawnictwo Energia, 1997), chapter 5, insightfully analyzes the *Comedy*'s comedy as its use of irony to expose acts of deceit, though he does not see this as enabling the poem ironically to surpass even its own merely human assertions and lay claim to a truth beyond what it can itself authenticate.

being beguiled by the serpent's deceptive discourse in the Garden. The sins' linguisticality also renders them susceptible of bleeding into Dante's text, of participating in the poem itself as a linguistic act. As a writer, Dante inevitably presents all sins and sinners through linguistic constructions and representation, even when he does not explicitly make language his theme. Sin is realized in the poem linguistically, not only in the linguistic acts of the sinners, but also in the poem itself as a form of self-interpretation in language. The poem's language cannot escape, and will even own up to, being sensual, violent, fraudulent, and finally treacherous—following the sequence of general categories of sin progressively punished in Hell.

Pitfalls of Prophecy: Inferno, *Cantos 19–23*

In canto 19, Dante claims a prophetic authority for himself surpassing the priestly authority of the popes, but at the same time he begins to become a comic figure in his own poem. Standing over the popes, who are rammed upside down into the ground, he is ironically on the high ground vis-à-vis these high priests: he is in the position of the confessor with whom a condemned criminal was allowed to communicate just before the earth was filled in from above, so as to cause death by suffocation. Yet Dante himself may also be seen to be undermined in this exchange: in reprimanding the writhing feet, he cannot but come off as a little ridiculous. The poem oscillates subtly, but persistently, between affirmations of prestige and acceptance of ridicule with respect to its protagonist.[24]

Here it becomes crucial to see how what happens to the pilgrim, at least indirectly, reflects also on the poet: they are both, after all, "Dante," this personality that is created essentially by the poem. The savant artistry of the *Commedia* exploits this ambiguity between Dante as protagonist and as poet to its own immense advantage rather than dissembling it as a secret condition which, if exposed, would invalidate the fiction. Dante writes fiction and makes the reality of this very act of writing into an underlying theme of the poem. The self-reflective act of the imagination as opening another world, a glimpse into eternity, has been implicit in poetic prophecy all through ancient and medieval tradition, but it becomes fully self-conscious and identified with the act of writing first in Dante.

24. Kirkpatrick, *Inferno: Difficulty and Dead Poetry*, 253, develops this line of interpretation in exquisite detail. Throughout this section and the next, my reading is indebted to Kirkpatrick's in general and specific ways. Another treatment that adroitly shows how the checks and setbacks of the protagonist inevitably reflect on the progress or peril of the poet is that of Giuseppe Ledda, *La guerra della lingua: Ineffabilità, retorica e narrativa nella Commedia di Dante* (Ravenna: Longo, 2002). See particularly chapter 6: "Scacchi e indicibilità infernali," 177–210.

In setting up this scene of his preaching to the popes, Dante as narrator refers to an episode in his own life in which he claims to have broken a baptismal basin in San Giovanni, the baptistery in Florence, in order to save the life of someone who was drowning (19.16–21). This odd allusion may well be concerned with justifying Dante's apparent usurping of priestly authority in this canto attacking the popes. In fact, Dante's whole poem constitutes an assertion of his prophetic authority in his role as poet over and against the official, sacramental authority of the clergy, who are criticized scathingly throughout the work. And yet the canto of the popes (19) depicts Dante being reduced from the self-confidence manifest in the opening denunciation of Simon Magus ("O Simon mago . . .") to a state of helplessness and insecurity. For he himself has no authority to stand on. When Pope Nicholas III mistakes him for Boniface VIII, his successor in office and in sin, Dante's identity is so shaken that he is incapable of responding until Virgil feeds him a response that he meekly repeats, stuttering: "I am not he, I am not he whom you think" ("Non son colui, non son colui che credi," 19.62)—a response that is purely negative and defensive.

After hearing the pope's story, however, Dante recovers and again preaches vehemently against the greed of simony that so provokes his moral indignation. In presuming to denounce the church's official heads, Dante is, by his own admission, perhaps again too temerarious, "troppo folle" (19.88). He uses the word *folle* that elsewhere describes the rash venture of Ulysses (26.125), as well as his own perhaps too rapid resolve to enter into the underworld (2.35). But this time he also cleaves to the word of Scripture, with a reference first to 2 Maccabees 4:7–8, which concerns the buying of priestly offices from the emperor. He then alludes further to the selection by lot rather than for money of Matthias to replace Judas in Acts 1:26 and to the great whore of Babylon in Revelation 17:1–5. This reliance on Scripture seems to make the essential difference. In accusing the popes of making gold and silver their gods, Dante is repeating the characteristic denunciation of idolatry leveled by the prophets of the Old Testament against religious authorities. In particular, he is echoing Hosea: "of their silver and their gold have they made them idols" (8:4).

It is no longer a foolish self-confidence of his own but rather the language of Holy Writ on which Dante relies in rebuking the popes. This allows the voice of the divine Other to break into his text, and this Voice alone is able to make Dante's poem truly prophetic. For all that is said in his own voice is the work of a man, a rhetorician; it is an instrumentalization of language for interested, egotistical purposes, as is illustrated eminently by the eloquence of Francesca, Pier, Brunetto, and Ulysses, and it is therefore subject to damnation. Against such self-serving rhetoric, Scripture breaks in with its magnificently unrhetorical and yet commanding and irresistible authority in a phrase like "Follow me" ("Viemmi retro"), or again in the inverted echoes of the *Magnificat* (Luke 1:52): "calcando i buoni e sollevando i pravi" ("treading under the good and exalting the wicked," 19.105). This echoing of God's Word enables Dante to transcend his own human limits in making his poem the mouthpiece of a moral authority beyond that of his own confessedly sinful self.[25] By this means, the "sound of words truly expressed" ("lo suon de le parole vere espresse," 19.123) reverberates through his text, which thereby becomes genuinely prophetic. For Dante, in effect, admits his own inadequacy and the inadequacy of his own poetic rhetoric to be a vehicle of the divine vision. But he suggests that in exposing its inadequacy, in retracting its own claim to truth, the poem can become instrumental to allowing another more adequate, truer Voice to be heard.

The problematic nature of Dante's language in the poem is brought to thematic focus with ever increasing intensity in the Malebolge. Starting in canto 18, the eye assumes the ascendancy. The potency of the eye cuts through the entanglements of language and rhetoric to reveal the naked truth of hell. Moreover, as language is increasingly revealed in the depths of its fraudulence, the guidance lent to Dante by Virgil depends more and more on his physical and emotional presence and less on the rhetorical style ("bello stilo," 1.87) that initially was relied on in forming the relationship between the two poets. Virgil carries Dante on his hip down to the perforated turf in which the popes are plunged (19.43–45, as promised in 34). And at the end of canto 19, in order to bring him into the fourth division (or "bolgia") of the Malebolge, Virgil takes Dante into his arms and lifts him onto his breast ("Però con ambo le braccia mi prese; / e poi che tutto su mi s'ebbe al petto," 19.124–25). In canto 23.37, Virgil will clutch Dante like a mother escaping with her infant in arms from a house afire.

Canto 20 is ostensibly an encomium of Virgil, who is presumably Dante's guide and model as prophetic poet. But actually the canto pursues further the interrogation and indictment of claims to prophecy on the part of human poets specifically in relation to Virgil. Virgil waxes loquacious in his story of the founding of Mantua by Manto, begging indulgence as he sets out on what he perhaps half realizes is too lengthy a disquisition ("onde un poco mi piace che m'ascolte," 20.57). Nevertheless, Dante assents unconditionally to his authority when Virgil enjoins him to believe no other account of his home town's origins, in order that "no lie be allowed to defraud the truth" ("la verità nulla menzogna frodi," 20.99). The irony here is that Virgil, in his story of the founding of Mantua on the bones of Tiresias's "virgin" daughter, Manto, has contradicted his own account in *Aeneid* 10.198–201. The *Aeneid* makes Mantuans descendants from a *son* of Manto, Ocnus, presumably in accordance with Manto's divination. Is Virgil's account as poet of the

25. Kirkpatrick elaborates on the way Dante allows the "authority of his text to be broken through by urgent simplicity of scriptural voices" (Inferno: *Difficulty and Dead Poetry*, 424). See, further, Stanley Benfell, "Prophetic Madness: The Bible in *Inferno* XIX," *Modern Language Notes* 110, no. 1 (1995): 145–63.

Aeneid then a fraud? The word "defraud" ("frodi") renders irrepressible this possibility. Prophetic-poetic authority here demonstrates its susceptibility to contradicting itself. Indeed, the ambiguities of this type of authority are the central issue of this canto and of the *bolgia* that it covers.

All of the sinners punished here, including classical figures like Amphiaraus, Tiresias, Aruns, and Eurypylus, have been self-proclaimed prophets, but false ones, in their various ways. All were "seers." What distinguishes Virgil, nevertheless, from the soothsayers, augurs, astrologers, haruspices or omen readers, mantics, and divines in this circle is that his prophesying is an interpretation of history. The false kinds of prophesying that are punished here consist in foretelling facts by presumably magical means rather than in rationally interpreting the significance of things as revealed in history. Virgil's account of the founding of Mantua after Manto's death is based on the natural ecological and strategic advantages of the site chosen rather than on any supposed divination or omens. Virgil, in effect, interprets natural history, bringing out what would make this place an ideal site for a fortress city. This sort of use of interpretive intelligence, unlike mechanical and superstitious techniques of fortune telling, can form the basis for an authentic exercise of prophetic faculties quite different from those of the sinners punished in this *bolgia*.

Nonetheless, by dint of its intensive discursivity, Virgil's own brand of prophecy also risks falling into error. That is what becomes conspicuous in this most intensely visual area of hell: as one index, the word "vedi!" ("see!") is constantly repeated throughout the canto. Virgil's idyllic interpretations, loaded with blessings and picturesque charm and names bespeaking benevolence (like "Benaco"), gloss over the harsher realities written into the deceptive landscape, which are also inadvertently exposed—including rivalry between bishops and a garrison set for war that is aestheticized as a "beautiful and strong fortress" ("bello e forte arnese," 20.70). Even more subtle is a mutation of the river's name, as it begins moving into the real world, to "Menacio" (20.74), connoting loss (*meno*, less) and badness (*-accio*) and perhaps also threat (*minaccia)*. Upon investigation, Virgil's serene words turn out to be mined with hints of violence and treachery; they are even liable to becoming fraudulent. Presumably all merely human, rhetorical claims to prophecy are thereby likewise placed under a shadow of suspicion.

The visual immediacy of Dante's Hell is at a maximum in the Malebolge and particularly in cantos 21 and 22, which depict the barrators boiled in pitch and the escape of Ciampola, the corrupt official from Navarra. Immediate action completely absorbs all attention, with an at least momentary loss of any further dimension of significance. The opaqueness of the pitch perfectly reflects the lack of penetrability, the occulting of interpretive depth in this part of hell. Even the *Discensus Christi* is here reduced to a brute fact of dates: "1266 years less five hours ago" (21.112–14). Ironically, we receive this vital information from an unreliable source, Malacoda, who lies concerning the ridge that he says remained intact and would allow Dante and Virgil to cross over to the next *bolgia* (23.136). Alas, as is pointed out by the jovial friars, the devil is a proverbial liar and father of lies (XXIII. 139–44). In this way, the poem again flags its own complicity—as a work of fiction—in fraud.

The narrative here is full of implicit questionings of the veracity of Dante's deed in narrating. This apparently problematizes his claim to prophetic authority, and worry about such a claim is reflected back into the narrative itself: it is felt again in the way in which Dante's confidence as protagonist is also destroyed. After having adopted a prophetic tone in denouncing the popes and in his clear speech ("chiara favella") exposing the procurers, Dante is portrayed here as ludicrous and himself a butt of the farce. He is told by Virgil to crouch down behind a crag out of sight (21.58–60). A little later, he is told that it is all right for him to come out now:

> "O tu che siedi
> tra li scheggion del ponte quatto quatto,
> sicuramente omai a me ti riedi"
> (21.88–89)

> ("O you who sit squatting
> among the jutting rocks of the bridge,
> in safety now you can come out.")

This seems much like the familiar ploys of farce, with its quickly improvised makeshifts. As literature, Dante's work at this point belongs inextricably together with low comedy of the most raw and unedifying sort. The slapstick slams and blows dealt by the demons also menace an extremely vulnerable Dante: "Let him have it in the rump!" ("in sul groppone," 21.101). In this manner, language can suddenly plummet to the vernacular profanity of street slang and sarcasm. Indeed, "Here is no place for the Sacred Face!" ("Qui non ha loco il Santo Volto!" 21.48). The allusion is to an ebony icon in "Santa Zita" (literally "Holy Hush," 21.38), a church in the city of graft and corruption, Lucca, where mum is the word. Nether "cheeks" blackened and bobbing up to the surface of the pitch here blasphemously evoke this icon of the Holy Visage.

The mixture of styles and even of stylistic registers is seasoned, furthermore, with a generous dose of cooking imagery ("Non altrimenti i cuoci," 21.55), and this, too, is part of Dante's strategy to make mockery of the prophetic pretenses of his own poem, to ironize its solemn tone and high seriousness. Such sudden sinkings from the sublime to the grotesque and scarcely decent are among the indirect ways in which Dante exposes the vulnerability of his poetic project—its potential for collapsing into mere presumption and even to become demonically deceptive. If its exalted purpose is to be fulfilled, its artifices, even those of the lowest sort, must be exposed and seen through, just as the literal meaning of the narrative must be transcended. But that is exactly what Dante has trouble doing here, as he looks into the boiling pitch: "I saw it, but I did not see *into* it" ("I' vedea lei, ma non vedëa in essa," 21.19).

Ultimately the penetration of the meaning of all history is possible only thanks to Christ. Underlining Virgil's hermeneutic limitations once again, the next canto brings out precisely Virgil's inability to understand the Christ event and its significance. This absolutely unique event cannot be comprehended by any pagan discourses constructed on however perfect rhetorical principles, for language and rhetoric are inherently general and universal. Every word in language is made to be reiterated in an unlimited variety of situations. Before the sight of "one, crucified" ("un, crucifisso"), Virgil is at a loss for words. Dante sees him perplexed and uncomprehending:

> Allor vid' io maravigliar Virgilio
> sovra colui ch'era disteso in croce
> tanto vilmente ne l'etterno essilio.
> (23.124–26)

> (Then I saw Virgil marveling
> over him who was stretched in a cross
> so vilely in eternal exile.)

But more than just Virgil's limitations are in question here. Dante, too, is tested, and his own poetic-prophetic pretensions are in danger of showing up as blatant presumptuousness by the test of Christ's uniqueness and the incomparable, singular event of the Crucifixion. Specifically at this juncture, there is a hint that perhaps he is implicated in hypocrisy through his fiction posing as prophecy. The possibility that he is an impostor seems to invade his consciousness subliminally and to check him as he begins to excoriate the jovial friars (*frati godenti*) for their hypocrisy. His speech is called up short by the *sight* of Caiaphas, the "one, crucified" on the ground in front of him and Virgil:

> Io cominciai: 'O frati, i vostri mali . . .';
> ma più non dissi, ch'a l'occhio mi corse
> un, crucifisso in terra con tre pali.
> (23.109–11)

> (I began: 'O brothers, your ills . . .';
> but I said no more, because my eye was struck by
> one, crucified in the earth with three stakes.)

Throughout the Malebolge, Dante's (like Virgil's) repeated resort to prophetic elocution and its presumed authority is punctured and deflated by the immediacy of sight. Here the uniqueness of the fact of an individual in front of Dante—an individual alluding to *the* individual and unique event at the center of all history—asserts its absoluteness against the inherent generality of all discourse. This immediate presence gestures toward the revelation of a truth external to the digressive meanderings and weavings of Dante's text, a truth that no human discourse can possibly comprehend.

All this points up the ingeniously indirect strategy by which Dante's poem asserts its prophetic authority: it does so through undermining all of its own merely human pretensions to precisely such authority. By exposing itself as fiction, it becomes true. Its self-deconstruction of its own assertion of authority enables it to be informed from beyond itself by an authority not just its own. It thereby opens the way for divine grace to bring about a revelation of truth within the reader's heart and intellect trained on the doctrine hiding beneath the veil of the strange verses (9.60–63). Its truth may thus be discerned by individual readers aided by divine action of grace working in and through interpretation carried out in the light of Christ—in whose tracks Dante follows on his own descent into Hell. The apex (or nadir) of infernal irony is that Dante's *Inferno* becomes prophetic revelation of truth by undermining its own merely human claim to be capable of delivering just such a revelation.

Writing and (Anti-)Revelation: Inferno, *Cantos 24–25*

The general breakdown of all human interpretive means, signally language, in the *Inferno* is analyzed particularly with regard to writing as a medium in cantos 24 and 25. Canto 24 opens with an image of the frost's ephemeral writing on the earth and its fading soon away: "but not for long does its pen's sharpness last" ("ma poco dura a la sua penna tempra," 24.6). Tellingly, the canto closes with images of black and white that clearly refer to the vicissitudes of contemporary Black and White Guelf politics. Pistoia will first grow thin of Blacks ("Pistoia in pria d'i Neri si dimagra," 24.143), but then Mars will bring turgid clouds and tempest and suddenly disperse the mist "so that every White will be wounded" ("sì ch'ogne Bianco ne sarà feruto," 24.150). At the same time, these images also suggest black ink on white paper, and as such they are woven into the metaphorical fabric of allusions to phenomena of writing that runs through these cantos.

Writing is in theory an instrument of stability, but here it becomes an emblem of turmoil and transience. Writing had traditionally been relied on as the means of stabilizing and fixing an indelible memory of oneself: witness, for example, the epigraphs on ancient tombstones. But in these cantos Dante reveals writing to be an eminently erasable trace of a human, mortal reality that is quintessentially vanishing. Particularly poets endeavor to achieve immortal fame by their writings. Dante's own aspirations for his writing are patent, for instance, where he boasts over outdoing Lucan and Ovid by his virtuoso description of metamorphoses of thieves into snakes and vice versa (25.94–102). Such a claim for writerly rank with or even above the Latin classics, however, is ironically undercut by being placed in the midst of a demonstration of how impermanent all human identity is—particularly insofar as it is entrusted to effaceable written tokens or inscriptions.

The central action of Canto 24 is the instantaneous reduction to ashes, in order to be restored and start over again, like the phoenix, of Vanni Fucci, whose very name rings with vain fugacity (*vanitas*) and the fact that he *was* here (*ci fu*). This predicament of the perpetual disintegration of the self is perceived through a metaphor of writing construed as an impersonal act described by a reflexive verb ("si scrisse"). The instability and volatility connoted by writing are linked with dissolution of personal identity also in the way *io*, the word for "I," breaks down into the sub-semantic particles of its component letters: o and i.

> Né *o* sì tosto mai né *i* si scrisse,
> com' el s'accese e arse, e cener tutto
> convenne che cascando divenisse . . . .
> (24.100–102)
>
> (Neither *o* nor *i* ever was so quickly written,
> as he ignited and burned, and was turned all
> to ashes at the same time as he fell.)

In the same vein in the next canto, the metamorphosis of the thieves into snakes and vice versa, robbing them of personal identity, is consummated metaphorically as the dying of the whiteness of paper turned black by the heat of the flames (25.63–66).

> né l'un né l'altro già parea quel ch'era:
> come procede innanzi da l'ardore,
> per lo papiro suso, un color bruno
> che non è nero ancora e 'l bianco more.
> (25.60–63)
>
> (already neither appeared as he was before:
> as a brown color proceeds
> before the heat when paper burns,
> it is not yet black, while the heat dies.)

This is a subtle reminder of the impotence of writing in the face of physical dynamism. It comes just as Dante boasts of his unprecedented writerly mastery of metamorphosis, with his defiant challenge to classical poets, whom he claims to have surpassed: "Taccia Lucano . . . Taccia di Cadmo e d'Aretusa Ovidio, . . . io non lo 'invidio" ("Be silent Lucan . . . Be silent Ovid concerning Cadmus and Arethusa . . . I have nothing to envy," 25.94–99). The volatility of writing undercuts the interpretive art that is Dante's own vehicle, sending up in smoke even his own illusion of establishing a permanent identity through such a work as the *Inferno*.

If the work is to have enduring value, this cannot derive simply from Dante's own virtuosity, for his writing per se is unmasked as another merely mortal expression of a perishable self. Truly lasting value can only be given rather by a transcendent source. As the property of its author, the *Inferno*, too, is condemned by the dissolution of all supposedly stable identities, the ineluctable obliteration of all merely human form. Dante's writing outstrips Ovid's by entering more deeply into the mystery of metamorphosis that writing cannot describe without fixing (and thereby falsifying) it in static signs. Writing in this way reverses its usual connotation of permanence and becomes emblematic of the instability of unredeemed, mortal, human identity.

Dante, moreover, incorporates into his text the dimension of reading as a factor that inevitably makes the meaning of the written internally unstable and open to shifting interpretations. His own writing is continually opened to new appropriations of meaning through the poem's solicitations of its reader. This is a crucial way in which Dante relinquishes and even undermines his control as author, in order to let loose a power transcending his own. Ultimately only relation to an absolute Other—a transcendent God—can create stable, substantial, and inviolable identity for the human person. Creation of an enduring identity can be catalyzed, but cannot be contained or controlled, by human acts and means such as writing.[26] Indeed, within a few lines of the arrogant boast relegating Lucan and Ovid to silence in face of Dante's matchless virtuosity (25.97–102), these cantos conclude with Dante's confession that he is not in command of his own pen and a consequent appeal for pardon:

> . . . e qui mi scusi
> la novità se fior la penna abborra.
> (25.143–44)

> (. . . and here may the strange novelty
> excuse me, if my pen at times is errant.)

26. A subtle reading of the role of writing in these cantos is James Chiampi's "The Fate of Writing: The Punishment of the Thieves in the *Inferno*," *Dante Studies* 102 (1984): 51–60. Medieval conceptions of metamorphosis as a form of non-being are explored in relation to these cantos by Warren Ginsberg, *Dante's Aesthetics of Being* (Ann Arbor: University of Michigan Press, 1999), 115–59.

This sudden shift typifies Dante's oscillation between bursts of self-confident pride, marked by prophetic pronouncements, and moments of humiliation and retrenchment, in which he (as protagonist) is often reduced to silence.

V. Discursive Traps: False Transcendence and Bad Faith (*Inferno*, Cantos 26–30)

Writing is one of the means that human beings seize upon in order to attempt to establish their identity and confer eternity *upon themselves*—in fact, to steal it, Dante suggests in the cantos on the punishment of the thieves—from the one Author who alone can truly give life and even immortality. In his *Inferno*, this connotation of permanence is reversed, and writing turns into a revelation of the collapse of human identity and its pretended stability. So far from standing for things eternal, writing is made to serve as an emblem of the ephemeral. Dante's demolition of writing in its pretentions to permanence becomes part of a strategy of indicating the way toward the true transcendence that only God can grant. This reversal belongs to a series of ruthless exposures of false transcendence sought by sinners through human works and particularly by means of words. In crucial ways, this series climaxes in the encounter with Ulysses. The series runs through Francesca, with her deceptive poetic rhetoric (canto 5), Pier de la Vigna, who is also duped by his own linguistic dexterity (canto 13), and Brunetto Latini, whose teaching "how man eternalizes himself" ("come l'uom s'etterna," 15.85) through his own work in words—his literary *Tesoro*—is emblematic of false transcendence that ignores the one true Lord of life in attempting to achieve immortality by one's own efforts.

Canto 26 represents the height of Dante's examination, through this series, of the dangers of hubris inherent in his own rhetorical project. Ulysses, the great voyager and rhetorician of antiquity, is an alter ego in whom Dante beholds the image of his own near-damnation. In the presence and proximity of the legendary Greek hero, Dante registers his sense of peril about his own audacious voyage: it is a little too like Ulysses's "mad flight" (his "folle volo," 26.125), which echoes *Inferno* 2.35, where Dante feared that his own journey might be rash or "folle." Here Dante says that he has to reign in his genius, as he depicts himself gripping a rock tightly, without which he would be precipitated down to his own destruction (26.43–45). He is, in his keen empathy and eagerness to converse with Ulysses, bent with desire toward the tongue of flame flickering in damnation ("vedi che del disio ver' lei mi piego!" 26.69).

Ulysses is a chief and, in crucial ways, a culminating symbol of the attempt to establish human identity autonomously. He minds none of the markers put in place by others but rather follows only his own unprecedented audacity. He travels out beyond the limits of language and its domestications into the Nameless. Navigating the world prior to its being charted with names, he reaches Gaeta before Aeneas names it for his nursemaid, and in fact before anyone else living he comes into sight of Mount Purgatory in the southern hemisphere. He ventures past all the limits set for human nature, embarking at an already advanced age, when he is old and slow (26.106), trespassing beyond the columns of Hercules (26.108–9) into the unpeopled world ("mondo sanza gente," 26.117) behind the sun.

Ulysses's mad flight turns his ship's oars into wings ("de' remi facemmo ali al folle volo," 26.125)—a kind of category mistake reminiscent of Geryon's aviation described as navigation that violates and defrauds the natural order of things (17.7). More precisely, here it is a question of artifacts, specifically oars: they are produced by human art for a rational purpose which, however, is perverted in exceeding their natural use since they are made metaphorically into wings for a reckless "flight." Indeed, throughout the Malebolge, it is perversions of reason that are punished. Whereas, from Dante's theological viewpoint, human identity can be secured only through a relationship with the divine source and Creator of all, Ulysses's fully autonomous search for himself, relying entirely on artifacts of his own making, leads him, heedless of his mortal limits, into uncharted seas where no human being belongs. Dante's own unprecedented journey comes perilously close to retracing this wild course, particularly in his ultimate adventure transcending the limits of language into the ineffable sublimities of Paradise in quest of a God who must ultimately remain unknown. It is entirely fitting, therefore, that in *Paradiso* 27.82–83, as Dante crosses the threshold of the fixed stars, moving beyond the planetary universe, he should again recall the "mad passage" ("varco / folle") of Ulysses. That Ulysses's brave new rationality should be exposed as the height of unreason uncannily anticipates the "dialectic of enlightenment" as analyzed by Adorno and Horkheimer.[27]

The voyage of Ulysses is mad and foolish because he attempts, not unlike the humanist Brunetto Latini, a false transcendence based on human faculties, specifically "virtue and knowledge" ("virtute e canoscenza," 26.120).[28] In his unguided journey, he is oblivious not only to the divine Other but also to all others, including his wife and son, his father, and even his companion in arms, Diomedes, whom he does not so much as acknowledge, even though they are eternally bound together in the same punishing tongue of fire. He

27. Theodor Adorno and Max Horkheimer, *Dialektik der Aufklärung: Philosophische Fragmente* (Frankfurt: Fischer, 1969 [1947]), "Excursus I: Odysseus oder Mythos und Aufklärung," 58–83.

28. Ancient Roman *virtus* centered on autonomy and manly glory versus new Christian virtue based on humility and obedience, as well as the correspondingly different value of the senses for knowledge, are finely distinguished by Georg Rabuse, "Die lezte Irrfahrt des Danteschen Odysseus," 99–126, and Hugo Friedrich, "Odysseus in der Hölle," 154–200, in *Geistige Überlieferung: Das zweite Jahrbuch* (Berlin: Küpper, 1942).

himself tells us that no natural bonds to others were able to conquer his lust for experience of the world and of human values:

> "né dolcezza di figlio, né la pietà
> del vecchio padre, né 'l debito amore
> lo qual dovea Penelope far lieta,
> vincer potero dentro a me l'ardore
> ch'i' ebbi a divenir del mondo esperto
> e de li vizi umani e del valore."
> (26.94–99)

> ("neither tenderness for a son, nor pity
> for an old father, nor the love owed
> Penelope, to make her glad,
> could conquer in me the ardor
> I had to become experienced in the world,
> both of human vices and of valor.")

Experience is for Ulysses the highest value ("esperto . . . del valor," 26.98–99), whether it is the immanent, all-too-finite experience of the senses or rather experience following the cyclical eternity of the sun ("l'esperienza / di retro al sol," 26.116–17). In either case, experience is for its own sake and is therefore a type of knowledge that remains within an enclosed circuit. Even in overstepping all the boundaries that he encounters along his horizontal trajectory over the ocean, Ulysses falls far short of true vertical transcendence toward the God above. Only in this direction, moreover, could he transcend the pagan time of cyclical repetition—traced in the circlings of his ship as it founders into the deep—and move toward the radically new time of the absolute Other inaugurated by the Christian Incarnation.[29] In the end, he sees that his destiny is directed by the will of an Other—"com'altrui piacque" ("as pleased another," 26.141)—from *beyond* the horizon of his own experience. This final recognition (*agnitio*) qualifies him as a tragic hero, but his fate is nevertheless sealed.

The human power of self-reliance that Ulysses chooses over anything and anyone else transcending him is manifest most immediately in his language. Yet it becomes for him a trap of self-enclosure. In his own speech, he consigns himself and his companions eternally to the immanent sphere of human life and his own subjective consciousness—"this so tiny vigil of what remains for our senses" ("questa tanto picciola / vigilia d'i nostri sensi ch'è

29. Oscar Cullmann, *Christus und die Zeit: Die urchristliche Zeit- und Geschichtsauffassung* (Zurich: Evangelischer Verlag, 1946), trans. Floyd V. Filson as *Christ and Time: The Primitive Christian Conception of Time and History* (Philadelphia: Westminster, 1964).

del rimanente," 26.114–15). The world of his experience circumscribes his ultimate concern, and he will acknowledge no boundary beyond or above himself.

Ulysses's language, his rhetorical prowess exercised for purposes of deception, metaphorically "robs" him of himself ("e ogni fiamma un peccator invola," 26.42) and wraps him eternally in an ancient flame ("fiamma antica") that shakes "as if it were the tongue that spoke" ("come fosse la lingua che parlasse," 26.85–89). These are not—except in parody—the flaming tongues of the Holy Spirit that descended upon the disciples' heads at Pentecost (Acts 2) but rather the vain tongues of false counselors that burn eternally in Hell. This threat of damnation for whoever becomes wrapped up in his own rhetoric—to the forgetting and exclusion of the one and only transcendent ground of all eloquence and truth—is a great threat for Dante also, as he is himself engaged upon the all-too-willful act of creating his sublime poem.

Countering this risk, a vertical axis pointing upward toward this transcendent ground can be glimpsed in the allusion to Elijah's chariot, with its horses rearing up straight to heaven ("quando i cavalli al cielo erti levorsi," 26.35–36). The allusion is more directly to Elijah's disciple, Elisha, watching his master's chariot ascend. This brings onto the scene, from biblical as opposed to classical tradition, a model of transmission of prophetic revelation to a younger generation, and as such it contrasts with Ulysses's neglect of his son. Dante himself hopes for such sons from among his literary progeny; he describes them as bursting eventually into the "great flame" that he hopes his words will spark (*Paradiso* 1.34). But Ulysses endeavors to transcend all limits himself, leaving nothing for those who, following after, would transcend *him*.

The sublime speech Ulysses delivers is larded with *topoi* of modesty, signally with the recurrent adjective "picciol" ("small"), but this is more strategic than sincere, as his damnation for false counsel suffices to suggest. In keeping with the classical prescription for a tragic hero, Ulysses comes to consciousness of his flaw after he has fallen: this happens at the canto's end in the *peripeteia* of joy turning to sorrow ("Noi ci allegrammo, e tosto tornò in pianto," 26.136). Ulysses's tragic greatness is unmistakable in his attempt to transgress all limits, emblematically the limits of the humanly navigable world. His mistake is to attempt it on his own power rather than in acknowledgment of the divine Other whose good-pleasure is in reality the master of his human fate. This is what makes all the difference between his fate and Dante's. The risks of transgression and prideful impurity inherent in Dante's undertaking are registered all through the *Inferno*. However, Dante's journey transcending mortal limits is based on a vocation accepted in response to the summons of a transcendent Lord God rather than on the quasi-Romantic overreaching of a self-absorbed hero who acknowledges no limits and submits himself to no Other or even others.

In the first canto of the *Purgatorio*, Dante will look back over the sea that Ulysses failed to cross, the sea from which he himself had narrowly escaped as a metaphorical shipwreck in *Inferno* 1.22–27. He will recall, in a thinly veiled allusion to Ulysses, that no man was experienced or expert ("esperto") enough to cross it without losing himself:

> "Venimmo poi in sul lito diserto,
> che mai non vide navicar sue acque
> omo, che di tornar sia poscia esperto.
> Quivi mi cinse sì com' altrui piacque . . ."
> (*Purgatorio* 1.130–33)
>
> ("We came then to the deserted shore,
> which never saw its waters navigated
> by any man expert enough to return.
> There he girded me even as pleased Another . . .")

The last line reiterates verbatim the phrase "as pleased another" ("com'altrui piacque") from the end of *Inferno* 26, where Ulysses finally recognizes, too late, the sovereignty of a divine Will. Dante's journey, by contrast, is divinely sanctioned, not just self-willed, as canto 2.52–114 explains through the account of a relay of three blessed ladies summoning Virgil to Dante's rescue. This is signaled again in *Purgatorio* 1, when Dante is girded with the yielding reed of humility at the foot of the purgatorial mountain. He is guided by an Other—with and through the mediation of others like Virgil and Beatrice—rather than being a self-elected explorer with no transcendent purpose or limits to orient and contain him. For all his perilous proximity to Ulysses, this makes the dramatic difference between his salvation and Ulysses's damnation.

In contrast to Ulysses, who is the archetypal ancient hero, Guido da Montefeltro, "coming a little late" ("perch' io sia giunto forse alquanto tardo," 27.22), epitomizes the modern antihero. Unlike Ulysses, he does not boldly pursue his destiny to infinity without looking back, heedless of all else. Guido, in characteristically self-conscious, modern fashion, calculates the consequences. When he is near death, at the time of life when it is more astute to be pious than ruthless, he turns repentant and confesses. In this respect also, he contrasts with Ulysses, who sets off on his mad flight at that time of life when other men are trimming their sails. Guido believes that he can manipulate his fate in the same way that he attempts to manipulate his own conscience—by making himself believe what he wants to believe—and so win heaven, too. And he really believes, he says, that this would have worked to save his soul, had it not been for the hypocrisy of the pope, that "prince of the new Pharisees" (27.85):

"Quando mi vidi giunto in quella parte
di mia etade ove ciascun dovrebbe
calar le vele e raccoglier le sarte,
ciò che pria mi piacea allor m'increbbe,
e pentuto e confesso mi rendei;
ahi miser lasso! e giovato sarebbe."
(27.79–84)

("When I saw myself come to that part
of my life where everyone should
lower the sails and gather in the cords,
that which pleased me before I regretted,
and I made myself penitent and confessed;
Oh miserable wretch! And it *would* have worked.")

Turning Franciscan after his exploits as a captain in arms, he believes he can make amends for his sins. His bad faith, however—his awareness that he does not really believe what he tries to make himself believe—is betrayed by the fact that he describes this conversion as a mere change of costume from captain to monk. It is no more than an astute maneuver, a trick devised to win him salvation by hook or by crook:

"Io fui uom d'armi, e poi cordigliero,
credendomi, sì cinto, fare ammenda;
e certo il creder mio venìa intero . . ."
(27.67–69)

("I was a man of arms, and then a friar,
believing that, so girded, I made amends;
and certainly my belief would have been fulfilled . . .")

Guido avails himself of a similar device at the climax of his story. He tries to make himself believe that the pope can assure him of absolution for a sin even before he has committed it. Counting on his ability to manage his own conscience, he tricks himself into believing that he needs only to formally repent, ignoring the fraudulence of such a sentiment summoned at will and at the most opportune moment for purely strategic purposes. Such perverse mental meddling turns against him and is mocked by the devil, who comes to vie for his soul, arguing irrefutably against Saint Francis that it is logically impossible to will the sin and repent for it at the same time. Like the artisan of evil who perishes in his own death machine—the "Sicilian bull" evoked at the outset of the canto (27.7–12)—Guido is trapped by his own devious construction of a belief that he does not himself really believe. He finds himself unable to evade the necessary consequences of his beliefs as actions whose implications he cannot simply control at will. In attempting thus to manipulate his own beliefs, in the end he is snared by them.

This sort of dishonest management of one's own beliefs has been analyzed as "bad faith" by the existentialist philosopher Jean-Paul Sartre,[30] and it has been represented in poetry by T. S. Eliot, particularly in "The Love Song of J. Alfred Prufrock." This poem, too, is about the cripplingly over-acute self-consciousness of the modern protagonist, the antihero whose capacity for whole-hearted conviction and sincere commitment has been undermined by excessive self-reflectiveness and self-doubt. Such convoluted consciousness expresses itself tellingly in Guido's opening lines, those chosen by Eliot for the epigraph of his poem:[31]

> "S'i' credesse che mia risposta fosse
> a persona che mai tornasse al mondo,
> questa fiamma staria sanza più scosse;
> ma però che già mai di questo fondo,
> non tornò vivo alcun, s'i' odo il vero,
> sanza tema d'infamia ti rispondo."
> (27.61–66)
>
> ("If I believed that my response was
> to a person who would ever return to the world,
> this flame would remain stock-still;
> but since never from this bottom
> has any one returned alive, if I hear truth,
> without fear of infamy I answer.")

The irony here is that Guido, the fox, for all his renowned cleverness, does not see, as most all other souls in hell do, that Dante is alive and destined to return to the world. Arguably, he fools himself by design, since what he really wants is to relate his story ("e come e *quare*, voglio che m'intenda," 27.72). In this way, he would be caught actually reenacting in the text the bad faith intrinsic to the false counsel for which he is damned. Bad faith—making oneself believe what one really does not believe—is diagnosed here as a characteristically modern syndrome already by Dante. With the emergence

30. Jean-Paul Sartre, *L'Être et le néant: Essai d'ontologie phénoménologique* (Paris: Gallimard, 1943), part 1, chapter 2: "La Mauvaise Foi," 85–114.

31. Robert Harrison, "Comedy and Modernity: Dante's Hell," *Modern Language Notes* 102, no. 5 (1987): 1043–61, starts from this Prufrock citation to draw a contrast between Ulysses and Guido as representative of an ancient, tragic heroism and modern bad faith respectively. The parallels between Ulysses and Guido are explored also by Lawrence V. Ryan, "Ulysses, Guido, and the Betrayal of Community," *Italica* 54 (1976): 227–49.

of a modern, acutely reflexive self-consciousness come specific unprecedented pitfalls that Dante is quick to register and dissect in his examination of the human psyche and its vulnerability to sin. He is all the more anxious about this particular case, since self-reflexiveness is so crucial to his own so highly reflective artistic project—and also so potentially vitiating of it.

Canto 28 begins with a meta-narratological reflection declaring the extreme difficulty of telling what has been seen, serving notice that the poem has arrived very near the limits of its discursive powers:

> Chi poría pur con parole sciolte
> dicer del sangue e de le piaghe a pieno
> ch'i' ora vidi, per narrar piú volte?
> Ogne lingua per certo verría meno
> per lo nostro sermone e per la mente
> c'hanno a tanto comprender poco seno.
> (28.1–6)

> (Who could even in unrhyming words
> and with repeated narration tell
> the blood and wounds galore that I now saw?
> Every tongue would surely fail
> because of our discourse and mind
> that are not apt to comprehend so much.)

This opening announces the obliteration of speech by vision that is then directly realized by the canto's intensive focus on limbs cut off, that is, on isolated and static components of formerly organic bodies. The canto moves from Mohammed to Bertran de Born and Ahitophel, sowers of discord, placing into view graphic images of mutilated and truncated body parts that interrupt the narrative perhaps more violently than ever before up to this point. The word is arrested by startling visual tableaux such as Mohammed's being ripped wide open by a laceration from chin to bowels, or Bertran de Born's carrying his head swinging alongside him like a lantern. A similar effect is produced by Pier da Medicina's cloven throat, chopped-off nose, and single ear ("una orecchia sola"); by Mosca dei Lamberti's handless stumps ("moncherin") raised in the air; and by Curio's slit tongue. The tongue that split Rome and fomented civil war in the body politic, by urging Caesar to cross the Rubicon, has now become literally and visibly the division of a body against itself.

The images of division and mutilation are mirrored in Dante's own narration, with its augmented complexity, its fracturing and overlapping and fragmentation. The narrative is constantly interrupted and its fabric ripped apart. The poetry itself, moreover, partakes of the human form's violability and volatility among the thieves. It is torn asunder, just as Bertran's condition ruptures the unity of the person made in the image of God who is One, producing an unholy "two in one and one in two" ("eran due in uno e uno in due," 28.124).[32] Characters and their successive episodes bleed into and contaminate one another, corrupting the integrity of the individual scenes. Images of amalgamation and adulteration abound—signally among the falsifiers and counterfeiters. This messiness is itself a manifestation of infernal unholiness and unwholeness, in which Dante's own poetry fully participates.

Dante is severely scolded by Virgil at the beginning of canto 29 for having become too absorbed in the chaotic visual spectacle offered by the disseminators of discord:

> Ma Virgilio mi disse: "Che pur guate?
> perché la vista tua pur si soffolge
> là giù tra l'ombre triste smozzicate?"
> (29.4–6)

> (But Virgil told me: "What are you gawking at?
> why is your gaze fixated down there
> on the sad mutilated shades?")

The same sort of reproach is leveled at the end of canto 30, when Dante is threatened by Virgil for looking too intently, as if mesmerized, upon the scuffle between Simon Greco and Mastro Adamo: "Now go ahead and ogle, / I could almost fight with you myself!" ("Or pur mira, / che per poco che teco non mi risso!" 30.131–32). Language, for all its deceptive pitfalls, is nevertheless necessary in order to maintain a certain distance from the fray and mayhem that is displayed before the open gaze of the pilgrim. Thus discourse and sight have at least a negative function of checking one another reciprocally. If sight has been privileged against discourse as revealer of a more immediate truth throughout the Malebolge, at the end of the eighth circle its own risks and inadequacies are brought out, leaving us in a state of epistemological incertitude and without any secure channel for ascertaining truth. The world of the *Inferno* proves rather the unattainability of truth for fallen human nature and its fallen faculties.

Moreover, at the bottom of the Malebolge, a certain trivialization becomes rampant and makes a travesty of truth, whatever the means by which it may be disclosed, whether visual or discursive. The striking thing about most of the falsifiers of metals and of persons punished in the last of the ten *bolge*

---

32. Guy P. Raffa, *Divine Dialectic: Dante's Incarnational Poetry* (Toronto: University of Toronto Press, 2001), explores this imagery as signaling a parody and perversion of the Incarnation—the divine paradigm of unification of two natures in one.

is the frivolousness of their characters. We have come rapidly down from the ancient and modern tragic modes of Ulysses and Guido da Montefeltro respectively to stories of ridiculous frauds from contemporary anecdote. Gianni Schicchi's disguising himself as Buoso Donati on his deathbed in order to change this deceased man's last will and testament proved to be perfect material for comic opera (*opera buffa*) in the hands of Giacomo Puccini. The scuffle between Mastro Adamo, a contemporary counterfeiter, and Simon Greco, mixing up the ancient with the modern, also stoops to new depths of indignity: it transgresses the sense of decorum separating the ancient from the modern that has been invoked as recently as in Virgil's insisting that he alone should speak with Ulysses and Diomedes ("Lascia parlare a me"), since as Greeks they might well balk at Dante's unclassical speech (26.73–75).

On a purely physical and visual plane, Mastro Adamo illustrates a further assault upon the dignity of the human form. Deformed into a shape like that of a lute by his dropsy, he has become a satiric representation of harmony perverted and disturbed. The music of the universe—based on the Pythagorean proportions that hold all things together in unison—is distorted by the counterfeiter's action. Since by counterfeiting he interferes with the flow of currency in the body politic, the circulation within his own body is now deranged. As an individual, Mastro Adamo is a representation of the base and abject condition to which fallen man falls, in spite of—and belying—his idyllic discourse on the pure waters coursing uncontaminated through the valley of Casentino (30.64ff.). As suggested also by his name, he is an archetype of the fallen human condition.

All this cannot help but reflect on Dante's poetic discourse, which must accept showing up as *itself* base and trivial, if any higher purpose is to be accomplished through it. Indeed, Griffolino d'Arezzo's story of a flying man is embarrassingly close to Dante's own unbelievable tale of descending alive into hell, as Virgil summarizes it in 29.94–96. Dante has to debase and discredit and in every way demean his literary means, along with his very humanity, in order that they might be redeemed from above and beyond his own creation and control. Only so can he be reached by a true transcendence that he is as powerless as Ulysses is to reach all by himself.

VI. Freezing of Signification in "Dead Poetry": *Inferno*, Cantos 31–34

In the last major structural division of the *Inferno*, the well of Cocytus, where traitors are punished, the difficulty of progress increases, approaching a zero-point, not only for the pilgrim but also, and expressly, for the poet. The linking of these two kinds of difficulty has been evident before. For example, Dante's weariness and Virgil's exhortations to exert in order to make an enduring mark and achieve fame (24.46–51) apply not only to the pilgrim struggling with difficulty over the rough ridges of Hell but also indirectly to the writer descending even deeper into the representation of yet more unspeakable sin. Here, at the bottom of the universe ("fondo a tutto l'universo," 32.8), Hell becomes explicitly a "place about which to speak is hard" ("loco onde parlare è duro," 32.14). Writing becomes as hard as the rock and ice at the bottom of the pit. The writer can only wish that he had adequately harsh rhymes with which to represent it:

> S'io avessi le rime aspre e chiocce
> come si converrebbe al tristo buco
> sovra 'l qual pontan tutte l'altre rocce . . .
> (32.1–3)
>
> (If I had harsh and grating rhymes
> such as would suit this sorrowful hole
> upon which weigh all other rocks . . .)

Here, apparently, Dante gives up his aspirations toward higher interpretive significance and attempts simply to describe the literal reality before him ("discriver fondo a tutto l'universo"), which is arduous enough, not a task to be taken lightly or in jest ("ché non è impresa da pigliare a gabbo," 32.7–8). The Muses are invoked once again to ensure that the saying not diverge from the facts ("sì che dal fatto il dir non sia diverso," 32.12).

Yet just such plain, literal description of Hell proves impossible, and as Dante descends via the giants of classical fame into the frozen lake of Cocytus, the journey is turned back virtually into myth, which is all that this poetic production of the eternal world can really be, at least in the absence of divine grace. At the same time, myth here is defined in the most factually objective terms, for example, by the comparison of Nimrod's face to the bronze pine cone that once stood outside St. Peter's in Rome. Such reduction of the mythic to the factual signals a deflation and a deadening of the symbolic potential of literary signs. Despite scattered signs of moving toward apocalypse (for example, the trumpet blast announcing war in 31.12), the ultimate disclosure in this circle—and consequently in the conclusion to the *Inferno* as a whole—is disclosure only of sound and fury signifying nothing. Satan, like the evil he perfectly personifies, is in fact a perfect nullity (echoing Augustine's Neoplatonic interpretation of evil as lack and as in itself nothing). So is all human effort, including writing, in the end, nothing—unless something can be made of this nothing by a wholly other power, a power that declares itself thereby as transcendent and divine.

Already at the end of the Malebolge, Dante represented himself as speechless with shame, after he had been reprimanded by Virgil for being transfixed before the scuffle between Mastro Adamo and Simon Greco (30.130–36). He points out that it is ironically his very inability to excuse himself that excuses him:

> tal mi fec'io, non possendo parlare,
> che disiava scusarmi, e scusava
> me tuttavia, e nol mi credea fare.
> (30.139–40)
>
> (so became I, unable to speak,
> and I desired to excuse myself, and in fact did so
> in spite of believing that I did not do it.)

That he does not and cannot say what he would like to say is the exact expression of the bitter embarrassment and chagrin that overpowers him. Such an expression by negation of expression becomes already at some level Dante's mode, most importantly as a writer, as he bears down on the inexpressible, absolute nullity of Hell. Dante has had to evolve a negative form of expression throughout his journey, and now he must complete and perfect it. The reality he aims to convey, namely, absolute evil, is, strictly considered, nothing. It is therefore without significance and is literally unsignifiable. This makes him impotent as a writer, and paralleling this writerly impotence, Dante as a character, too, is denied speech as he passively submits to the grasp of the giants.

The linguistic impasse Dante reaches at the core of Hell is emblematized in the figure of Nimrod, the main instigator and engineer of the building of the Tower of Babel and thereby of the fall of human language into confusion, according to Genesis 11:1–11. Nimrod presides, with a language that has degenerated into unintelligibility (31.67), over Dante's descent to the ninth and last circle of Hell. Reminiscent of Nimrod's leading role in building the Tower of Babel, the giants appear to Dante in the illusory form of towers: they are seen to "tower" ("torreggiavan," 31.43) above the well of Cocytus. Again, as Dante is lowered by Antaeus, he perceives the giant as a tower of Bologna, "la Garisenda," leaning over him (31.136–38). The "reality" of the literal towers is thereby changed into the imagination's figure for something fantastic—the giants. In the collapse of language to the level of literal fact, literal sense itself tends to collapse back upon the metaphors—technically "catachreses"—lying at the origin of words.

One of Dante's constant techniques throughout the *Inferno* is to literalize the language that he uses to describe features of Hell, taking his cue from the root meaning of metaphors in order to determine the literal reality that is represented. The simonist popes who put money in their purses end up literally "impursing" themselves ("mi misi in borsa," as Nicolas III says in 19.72) in the pouches ("bolge") of the Malebolge. Such cases suggest how language can become most revealing by dint of a kind of failure to signify in the usual way. They reveal a crassly literal, crudely true meaning beneath language's overt meaning as used for conscious purposes of representation and also, inevitably, misrepresentation. This meaning remains as a stubborn residue clinging to the words themselves and resists all motivated manipulations of surface sense. Another more basic level of meaning below the conventional level of signification emerges from the concrete sense of words taken according to their etymological senses based typically on the physical content of images. Such displacement and apparent distortion by improper, metaphorical meaning turns out to disclose a deeper, truer reality beneath what is said by the official, conventional significances of words.

As Dante descends to the last circle of Hell via the giants in 31, he makes much of the optical illusion that they present to him in their guise as towers: the end of the Malebolge emphasizes how sight can be just as deceptive as discourse. This suggests that there is no reliable standard for judgment in the *Inferno* at all. And yet precisely this uncertainty is superlatively revealing about the human condition. When language shakes itself loose from conscious, conceptual control, and meaning spills over into metaphor, the author or authoritative statement may be undermined, but the truth thereby first finds a way to get out. Language in the poem lets us "see" a truth that cannot as such be consciously and deliberately said.

The canto immediately following Dante's being lowered by the giant Antaeus harps on the inadequacy of language to the reality that the poet has to describe: "If I had harsh and grating rhymes" ("S'io avessi le rime aspre e chiocce," 32.1). The dead-wood literalness of language comes to stand for its lack of transitivity, of referential transparency, and especially of transcendence in a theological sense. While the *Inferno* tends to concretize the literal meaning of its own language, in the *Paradiso* language is metaphorical in a sense that points away from the concrete toward infinitely open and ineffable meaning. Here, in Hell, it is not the Infinite and divine that is being contemplated, at least not directly, but fallen, sinful humanity. And language's falling into the dark opacity of the literal expresses this. Here the truth is a matter of facing brute facts: it is most immediately and intimately a matter of facing oneself without the distorting lenses of language. Dante must take the lead in this process of exposure to himself. His actual *viewing* of himself in the *spectacle* of the damned comes to express articulation in the question put to him by Camiscion de' Pazzi: "Why do you mirror yourself so much in us?" ("Perché cotanto in noi ti specchi?" 32.54).

In the last circle of the Inferno, it finally becomes explicit that Dante is viewing himself in the sinners he encounters—here, those frozen in the lake of Cocytus. However, most importantly as writer, and not only as character, Dante has shown himself to be complicit in the sins examined in each region of Hell. His interpretive acts as poet are equivocally adulterated with falsehood in the registers specifically, as we have seen, of sensuality, violence, and fraud. In the last segment of the *Inferno*, Dante accordingly concentrates on writing no longer merely as fraudulent but as outright treacherous. His very act of writing and publishing Hell betrays certain individuals to everlasting reprobation in the minds of fellow humans and in history (canto 32 furnishes two lists of five names each in lines 55–69 and 116–23), and Dante is perhaps somewhat sadistically conscious of this power as a punishing weapon that he can wield. In this vein, he (now as protagonist) reviles Bocca degli Abati, taunting him with the promise to carry news of his damnation back to the living:

> ". . . malvagio traditor; ch'a la tua onta
> io porterò di te vere novelle."
> (32.110–11)

> (. . . wicked traitor; to your shame
> I will bear back true news of you.)

It is striking and really quite shocking to see how Dante is now meting out, with genuinely hateful animus, the punishments of Hell before which previously he had often recoiled in pity and horror. While crossing the lake with sinners frozen solid in it, he kicks Bocca degli Abati in the face—whether by destiny or by fortune he does not know ("se voler fu o destino o fortuna / non so," 32.76). Again, the levels of character and poet interact, and the insinuation of culpability bleeds from one to the other.

The most explicit example of Dante's actually practicing treachery among and upon the treacherous is his treatment of Frate Alberigo. Dante promises to relieve Alberigo of the heavy visor of ice congealed on his brow in exchange for the sinner's story, but he expresses this promise equivocally in a conditional: "if I do not defrost you, let me go down to the bottom of the ice" ("s'io non ti disbrigo, / al fondo de la ghiaccia ir mi convegna," 33.115–17). Since that is exactly where he is going anyway, he can omit performing the favor requested without technically breaking the word of his promise, even while betraying the soul with whom the pact was made.

Dante is seen torturing Bocca, pulling his hair out while the wretch screams, in order to force him to reveal his identity. It is uncannily accurate that the voice that then cries out Bocca's name should ask, "What devil is tormenting you?" ("Qual diavol ti tocca?" 32.108). For Dante himself has assumed the role of a punishing devil in this awful bottom of the infernal abyss. Dante as character, here and elsewhere in the *Inferno*, in this way doubles the writer—the prodigious inventor of so many devilish designs for chastisement. The punishments are inflicted, as if for his own revenge, on many whom he had reasons to hate and, in fact, resented or despised in real life.

Dante the writer's complicity in treachery is scrutinized above all in the justly famous episode presenting Count Ugolino. Here the veritably satanic potential of narrative is terrifyingly exposed. Dante is concerned to show how the art of narrative can become a treacherous instrument for suppressing and killing meaning. This exposé is the more poignant in that it occurs within Dante's own revenge narrative—and thus may bear a sharply self-critical edge. While narrative ideally reveals meaning and discloses truth, it also remakes whatever it reveals in the image of the narrator: narrative inevitably shapes what it tells and molds it to the motivations and character of the teller. But then the true meaning of the story can be buried beneath the infernal purposes of an evil narrator. And in this case, narration itself can be turned into a highly destructive engine of sin.

Ugolino's speech begins with the topos of how the telling of a tale about painful experience renews the pain. He remarks that the experience of pain in a sense can even (re)originate in its verbal imitation in narrative: the thinking about pain, which issues in narrative, renews that very pain. So Ugolino protests:

> "Tu vuo' ch'io rinovelli
> disperato dolor che 'l cor mi preme
> già pur pensando, pria ch'io ne favelli."
> (33.4–6)
>
> ("You ask me to renew
> desperate pain, so that my heart is wrenched
> just thinking of it, before I start to speak.")

This echoes the incipit to Francesca's oration—itself based on the lines of Aeneas to Dido at the beginning of his tale of travels and woe in book 2 of the *Aeneid*, which is, in turn, an echo of Odysseus's proem to his autobiographical narrative of adventures and gruesome ordeals in the *Odyssey* 9–12. Dante began his own *Inferno* the same way with the phrase: "the fear renews in thought" ("nel pensier rinova la paura," 1.6). Here in Cocytus, where traitors are punished, this topos of narrative self-consciousness par excellence signals Dante's attention to the use of narrative for its potential of inflicting pain—and of committing betrayal.

Ugolino's speech—and even more emphatically what he does not say—constitutes a reflection on rhetoric and its fatal traps, its aptitude for becoming treacherous. Dante indicts the art of rhetoric more mercilessly than ever before in an all-out onslaught upon the presumption built into human rhetorical projects, not excepting the *Inferno* itself. Ugolino uses the form of his story as a weapon of revenge upon the bishop against whom he burns eternally in hatred. His aim in speaking is none other than that his words might be seeds bearing the fruit of infamy for the enemy whose temples he gnaws (33.7–9). Yet in the intensity of his malicious purpose, he is devilishly deaf to the redemptive possibilities that are nevertheless present in the situation he describes, however tragic it may be. Concentrated on the hateful aim of his own rhetoric, he closes off and seals this story with a meaning that feeds and satisfies only his own hunger for vengeance. He entirely misses the profounder human meaning and indeed the divine, Eucharistic significance of this agonizing death, which his young sons, in contrast, are able to discern and even to express most movingly. The narrative itself and the events it relates are full of signs of this potentially redemptive meaning, but to Ugolino all other possibilities of meaning besides those serving his own revenge are as dead and frozen as the ice of Cocytus. His all-consuming rage is made incarnate in the "bestial sign" ("bestial segno," 32.133) that he himself has become, gnawing in ghastly, mock-Eucharistic fashion on the flesh of his enemy's skull.

Ugolino's account shows exactly what it means to be imprisoned—not only in the tower that for him has the name of "hunger," but also *within narrative*. After all, this "tower" will continue to enclose other persons ("e che convien ch'altrui ancor si chiuda," 33.24), and it will continue forever to enclose Ugolino in and by his narrative, which he repeats in perpetuity in the text of the *Inferno*. There he remains, eternally obsessed by the unconscionable facts of his demise. He is unable to see beyond them to any higher meaning such as is nevertheless poignantly conveyed particularly by his sons' Christological gestures. They offer their own flesh ("carni") in sacrifice to their father (33.61–63).

The sons offer themselves with the words "eat of us" ("mangi di noi") in express recognition of their progenitor's right over all that they are: "you dressed us with this miserable flesh, so you may strip us of it" ("tu ne vestisti / queste misere carni, e tu le spogli," 33.61–62). They are saying, in effect, "Take, eat, this is my body," as in the sacrifice of the Son in obedience to the Father enacted in the Mass. The Eucharistic rite of the Mass calls—as we can see more clearly than ever from this medieval text—to be understood as a ritual rehearsal of the self-offering of Christ on the Cross. The echo of "My God, my God, why hast thou forsaken me" (Matthew 27:46) in Gaddo's words "My father, why do you not help me" ("Padre mio, ché non m'aiuti," 33.69) is perhaps somewhat subtle. But if we were unsure as to whether they were really meant to recall Christ's cry from the Cross, our doubts should be dispelled by Dante's own voice a few lines later remonstrating with "Pisa" for having "put the sons on such a cross" ("non dovei tu i figliuoi porre a tal croce," 33.87).

We cannot help but observe, furthermore, that Dante's calling upon the islands offshore from Pisa near the mouth of the Arno, where it flows into the Tyrrhenian Sea, to dam up the river so as to drown *every person* ("ogne persona!" 33.84) in the city implicates the poet himself in a vengeful narration of his own. Evidently following his instincts for what is authentic, Dante admits to the virtually murderous passions that drive his own narrative. The islands' names "Capraia" and "Gorgona" mean "Goat" and "Gorgon" island respectively, recalling petrifaction, as with the Medusa (the Gorgon's head), and damnation, as in Christ's separation of sheep from goats in Matthew 25:33. They thus invoke dangers condemning the denizens of the *Inferno* and menacing Dante himself in his descent. It is difficult to know exactly what to do with such violent outbursts of bloodlust on Dante's part, unless they can be seen as part of a strategy of self-subversion and of implicitly admitting that as a human poet he is complicit in the abuse of narrative art for his own vindictive purposes. Having admitted this, Dante's narrative is open to being used from above and beyond his own human control for other, divine purposes: it can then bring an illumination of grace and truth into its readers' lives, to the extent that they are examined in its light and are exposed as to their own worst risks.

The sacramental overtones of the whole passage in Dante's text are there to highlight, by conspicuous contrast, all that Ugolino's own interpretation overlooks and indeed savagely blots out. Ugolino reports only how he "petrified within" ("sì dentro impetrai," 33.49). He is unable to respond with any genuine human emotion to his sons' deeply moving offer of themselves in sacrifice for him. He is, furthermore, unable to envisage any potentially sacramental, redeeming significance in the dire plight of his whole family. As in canto 9, where the Medusa threatens to forever arrest Dante's gaze and his reader's alike, petrifaction serves here as emblem of the death of interpretation and of the inability to see any further sense in events beyond the literal and most immediate one.

Ugolino avails himself of the device of direct address to his hearer—"You are exceedingly cruel, if you do not already grieve" ("Ben sei crudel, se tu non gìa ti duole," 33.40)—that Dante himself often employs to such momentous effect, signally in canto 9. But when Ugolino uses it, the purpose of such address is not to open the text to limitless interpretation by the whole range of readers who may apply it to their own lives. Ugolino's purpose is rather that of locking the receiver into his own fixed interpretation of the event, a judgment without repeal that is, according to his own words, set in stone in his heart ("impetrai"). How ironic, then, that his account itself proves finally to be ambiguous, particularly with regard to the undecidability of its last line. Ugolino's own narrative takes its revenge against him by remaining infinitely open to interpretation despite his obsessive determination to fix its meaning unequivocally. Its last line reads. "Then, more powerful than pain was fasting" ("Poscia, più che 'l dolor poté 'l digiuno," 33.75). This could mean either that, despite his sorrow, hunger drove him to consume the corpses of his sons, or simply that he starved.[33] Given the former possibility, his own inhumanity, as much as that of his enemy, turns out to be the overall meaning or impression perpetuated by his tale.

33. Jorge Luis Borges, whom I take as exemplary of a broadly cultivated reader, in "El falso problema de Ugolino," in *Nueve ensayos dantescos* (Madrid: Espasa-Calpe, 1982), maintains that we must *suspect* Ugolino of cannibalism. Accordingly, the episode's significance remains lodged in the text's ambiguity and in the necessary uncertainty of the purported fact: "Debemus incluir en esa textura la noción de canibalismo? Repito que debemos sospecharla con incertidumbre y temor" (110).

Either way, meaning, as a single, deliberate, intentional act is sacrificed. It is the very *lack* of properly intentional and determinate meaning that becomes the line's linguistic and human significance. It thus demonstrates how linguistic signification is by its very nature open and interpretable. The final meaning of the scene is horribly displayed rather in the *act* of cannibalism that we actually *see* Ugolino performing as he gnaws on Ruggieri's skull—at the point where the brain is joined to the nape—the way one chews on bread in hunger ("come 'l pan per fame si manduca," 32.127). In the "bestial sign" (33.133) of Ugolino's grisly revenge, meaning sinks below the threshold of language and humanity. This contrasts violently with the transcendent meaning of the Eucharist, which signifies the divine beyond the order of the material signs by which it is conveyed. The language of narrative is used by Ugolino no longer to illuminate and convey a transcendent meaning or truth but rather to occult it in the darkness of his blind passion sunk in sin and gorily materialized.

When used with treacherous intent, even prophecy, which is in principle a means of revelation, can become part of a narrative mechanism annihilating true meaning and its intrinsic openness by the attempt to manipulate it. Ugolino's "bad dream" "rips the veil of the future" ("io feci 'l mal sonno / che del futuro mi squarciò 'l velame," 33.26–27) and reveals the horror that awaits him. Nonetheless, he proves blind to the full meaning of his own prophetic dream, which depicts him as a wolf that is being chased along with its little cubs ("il lupo / e ' lupicini," 33.29). He interprets these figures simply as "the father and sons" ("lo padre e' figli," 33.35), ignoring the much more somber and sinister connotations of the wolf as a predator fabled for its treachery and ruthlessness. He is insensitive to the meaning of the prophecy that he himself recounts and that indeed is fulfilled in the sequel, in which he (by an ineluctable implication of his own words) savagely devours human flesh. This exemplifies the gross betrayal of meaning that Ugolino's general practice of the art of narrative embodies. He is hell-bent on using his narrative to manipulate his hearer's sympathies, and as a result he is deaf to its deeper human and even divine significance. As it is repeated eternally in this text, his chilling narration enacts a petrifaction of his understanding, which is forever blinded by his rage for revenge.

The scene is all the more provocative in that Dante, too, produces a narrative that apparently would fix significances permanently, significances which are driven by his own sometimes admittedly unholy passions. At this juncture, Dante could hardly fail to be preoccupied with the pitfalls of his own poem as itself prone to turn into a revenge narrative against his personal and political enemies. It is therefore imperative that his narrative include also a self-critique of narrative, an exposure of its own diabolical potentialities. By this means, Dante's narrative opens to question the specific significances that it also inevitably establishes. It simultaneously suspects itself as narrative, so as to keep the dialectic of meaning open and in motion. It thereby undermines the type of fixity in which Ugolino's damnation is narratively sealed for all eternity. The horrendous presumption of Dante's pronouncing eternal condemnations against others in his poem is to this extent neutralized by the poem's built-in self-reflection on the deceptiveness and treacherousness of narrative, not least its own narrative—by its owning up to the inherent liability of narrative to being instrumentalized for purposes of revenge.

The last stage of the *Inferno* marks a return to the blockage of an impenetrable narrative, such as we encountered first in canto 9 just before its address to the reader, with the threat of petrifaction by the Medusa. Dante now provides an image for this type of impasse in the frozen lake in which the sinners are immobilized. The ice prevents the damned from venting their emotion ("Lo pianto stesso lì pianger non lascia," 33.94–99). They can express virtually nothing, and it is only Dante's representation of this nothing that enables them to take on significance in the poem. Significance is trapped and cannot escape the ice that freezes it at a degree-zero of expression.

All this is condensed and concretized in an immobile, mute Satan. He is the absolutely evil being, an absolute cipher or lack, as Saint Augustine taught. Considered dramatically, this is an anticlimax—hence the ironic incipit, announcing the king of Hell's banners unfurling, as if for a great battle and final show-down: "Vexila regis prodeunt inferni" (34.1). Such dramatic description could hardly be less appropriate for this Satan placed on ice, but theologically such a neutralized, nullified Satan makes perfect sense. Satan is the absolute zero of the universe, an ontological nullity, from which only a cold wind blows, and that is exactly what evil is in a world created good, where everything that is, insofar as it *is*, is good.[34] Evil is exposed as a tale of sound and fury signifying precisely nothing. It can acquire meaning only by being the parody of the Good—that is, of God: hence this "emperor" is a threefold unholy Trinity of heads and mouths punishing the arch-betrayers of Christ (Judas) and Caesar (Brutus and Cassius).

Dante's metaphorical representation of Satan, precisely by failing to be dramatically compelling like Milton's Satan, conveys the nullity of evil that is Hell's reality at its core. After this encounter, Dante is turned around, literally "converted," and prepared to ascend to the stars. The abstract nothingness of evil has been encountered face to face, and from this point on Dante can begin to climb the mountain of virtue, the "dilettoso monte" sighted in vain at the outset of the poem. In the same movement, he can "let dead poetry arise," as he raises his sails to embark on "better waters" ("miglior acque," *Purgatorio* 1.1).

34. In Genesis, at several reprises, God saw what he had made and "saw that it was good" (Genesis 1:12, 25, 31). The church fathers, eminently Augustine, saw this as Scriptural confirmation of the Platonic doctrine that all being is some form of expression of the Good.

How poetry dies is the business specifically of the *Inferno*'s last segment, the ninth and final circle, which occupies cantos 31–34, but also in many ways of the *Inferno* as a whole. In fact, everything human is mortal, and the pride of poetry, which Dante shares in common with the great poets eternally suspended in Limbo (canto 4), is likewise claimed by death. In the invocation of the *Purgatorio*, where Dante calls for a resurrection of dead poetry ("la morta poesì resurge," *Purgatorio* 1.7), he will define the new poetics of Purgatory with reference to the divinely inspired psalms and the angel pilot's "eternal pens [or feathers] that do not mutate as does human hair" ("etterne penne, / che non si mutan come mortal pelo," 2.35–36). But before that can happen, he must complete his denunciation of poetry as one of the humanistic means by which man presumptuously attempts, like Brunetto Latini, to "make himself eternal" (15.84) and consequently loses himself to eternal death. The *Inferno* climaxes in some of Dante's most thoroughgoing and devastating indictments of poetry and particularly of narrative technique as it is actually practiced by fallen humans like Ugolino pursuing their sinful purposes.

Only afterward, upon leaving Hell, will Dante be ready to begin to learn the discipline of a purgative poetry that renounces itself in order to live for God. In the *Purgatorio*, poetry is seen in the process of being punished and purged of its own inevitably flawed, self-serving motivations: this happens most explicitly in the persons of some of Dante's poetic predecessors in the vernacular like Forese Donati, Bonaggiunta da Lucca, Guido Guinizelli, and Arnaut Daniel in cantos 24–26. Then poetry is prepared finally to blossom into a figure of theological transcendence, spectacularly in the Celestial Rose—a transfiguration, among other things, of the profane French poetic masterpiece *Le roman de la rose*. Poetry is transfigured beyond the human and even beyond the articulable altogether in Paradise, since "transhumanizing cannot be signified by words" ("trasumanar significar per verba non si poría," *Paradiso* 1.70). Prophecy outdoes and ultimately *un*does itself in these final gestures of transcending humanity. Dante conducts poetic prophecy to a culmination in self-erasure at the limits of language, which are the limits of the human.[35]

35. I pursue such an interpretation of the *Paradiso* in *Dante and the Sense of Transgression: "The Trespass of the Sign"* (London: Bloomsbury Academic [Continuum imprint], 2013). An epitome can be found in "Scripture as Theophany in Dante's *Paradiso*," *Religion and Literature* 39, no. 2 (Spring 2007): 1–32.

Conclusion

✦

Canonicity, Creativity, and the Unlimited Vision of Literature, or Theology of Literature as Meta-Critique of Epistemology

Literary-critical discussions of classic literary texts such as the Bible, the *Odyssey*, the *Aeneid*, the *Confessions*, and the *Divine Comedy* have often aimed to demonstrate the high degree of creativity at work in such "great books" of Western tradition. This creativity cannot be isolated and made static in formulas and, moreover, proves to be inseparable from the ongoing tradition in which these books continue to live through constant reinterpretation. They thereby assert their "canonicity"—their perennial relevance. Canonicity in this sense is not immobile or exclusive of innovation: it calls rather for continually new, creative interpretations or "applications" of classic texts in contemporary contexts.[1] I have attempted to elicit and display the creativity of the works studied here as, in good part, embedded in and flowing from this type of canonicity. In particular, I stress the re-origination of these works—and the regeneration of culture that they foster—precisely in and through ongoing interpretation in the course of history.[2]

All of the books included in this study are chosen from those commonly recognized as among the most canonical in Western literature. Great Books courses have come under attack in recent decades for enshrining the model of a closed canon such as has been challenged from various quarters, particularly in the name of genders or ethnicities or geographical regions or socioeconomic classes of humanity that have apparently been excluded. I will not

1. "Applications" is intended in the sense that Gadamer in *Wahrheit und Methode* (Tübingen: J. C. B. Mohr, 1960) gives to the term "Anwendung" as generating an "increase in being" through the repetition of interpretive events, including artistic performances, in new historical contexts.

2. Such a dynamic, famously expounded, for example, by T. S. Eliot, "Tradition and the Individual Talent" (1919), in *The Sacred Wood: Essays on Poetry and Criticism* (London: Methuen, 1920), is seen thus to extend from the poems themselves to their interpretation.

undertake an apology for the (or rather *a*) Western canon.[3] I have elsewhere examined the concept of canonicity and the open kind of universality that it ideally embodies.[4] Here I wish to stress that the canon, as we have discovered it, is distinguished precisely by its ability to creatively change and to grow.[5] My main concern is to show how, in a manner of speaking, this creativity hinges from "heaven"—how the claim to inspiration and the hypothesis of divine revelation can be the source of such creativity. The very idea of a literary "canon," after all, derives from the canon of books constituting the biblical revelation by extending this notion to the arena of secular writings.

At the same time, we should not forget that currency was given to the term also by Polykleitos's *Kanon*, his Pythagoras-inspired treatise on sculpture, with its classical ideal of perfect proportions and symmetry as the source of aesthetic beauty. This ideal was embodied most perfectly in Polykleitos's *Doryphoros* (circa 450 B.C.), a male nude sculpture which he named—like the lost treatise whose principles it illustrated—"Kanon."[6] Given this polygeneticism bringing together multiple semantic backgrounds, typically normative terms such as "canon" and "revelation"—as well as "divinity" and "prophecy"—as I use them take on senses that evade the statically traditional. Part of my purpose in what follows is to conjugate classical pagan tradition with revealed, biblical religion by finding their common epistemological grounds in the interpretive work of the imagination. Keeping the kinds of claims to knowledge proper to each of these forms of culture in play and in dialogue prevents them from reducing one another to dogmatic forms of either secular humanism or religious fideism.

A keystone in this arching bridge between cultures is the thesis that the inventiveness of canonical texts in the creative context of tradition is not compromised even by the totalizing structures of the imagination with which it is typically allied and indeed bound together. The *effort* to totalize one's vision, which demands both inner coherence and comprehensiveness *in extenso*, is not necessarily as final and deadening as has often been assumed by common consent in recent criticism: it can also be the vehicle of a continual challenge to always reach out and meet—and so to attempt to enter into dialogue with—every imaginable point of view that is, or might be, advanced. This

3. Such a project has been pursued by Harold Bloom in *The Western Canon: The Books and School of the Ages* (New York: Harcourt Brace, 1994).

4. "The Canon Question and the Value of Theory: Towards a New (Non-)Concept of Universality," in *The Canonical Debate Today. Crossing Disciplinary and Cultural Boundaries*, ed. Liviu Papadima, David Damrosch, and Theo D'haen (Amsterdam: Rodopi, 2011), 55–71.

5. On this tack, see, for example, Robert Alter, *Canon and Creativity: Modern Writing and the Authority of Scripture* (New Haven, Conn.: Yale University Press, 2000); and David Fishelov, *Dialogues with/and Great Books: The Dynamics of Canon Formation* (Brighton, Eng.: Sussex Academic, 2010).

6. Galen, *De placitis Hypocratis et Platonis*, chapter 5.

open sort of universality becomes an ongoing *striving* after completeness and inclusiveness, which is never fully or finally achieved.

The enterprise of imagining, especially on an epic scale, always entails, in addition to figuration of its objects, some idea of our relations with others, since what we imagine defines also *ourselves*. We can imagine ourselves in ways that make us open to and co-participants with potentially all others in a common world, or else we can construe ourselves as fundamentally separate from them and as not sharing in a common destiny. This will determine what type of interpretive process of cultural transmission is fostered by our canons and their "revelations." A totalizing imaginative vision need not be construed as closed and exclusionary; it can rather represent an idiom of unrestricted, universal outreach. Eluding the closure of the concept, this imaginable universality remains always open to re-vision and further inclusiveness because it is itself but a way of relating to undelimited others in the always open structure of our human, historical existence, which we can—and must—nevertheless strive to imagine whole.

From his very different, Marxist perspective, Frederic Jameson likewise protests against the zealous rejection of totalization in any form whatsoever. Jameson uses "totalization" as an equivalent for "praxis" in order to "stress the unification inherent in human action itself." He maintains, accordingly, that "the hostility to the concept of 'totalization' would thus seem to be most plausibly decoded as a systematic repudiation of notions and ideals of praxis as such, or of the collective project."[7] My emphasis is rather on how the refusal of totalization can be tantamount to a refusal of the imaginative nature of human tradition and of the inextricably poetic nature of all our knowledge, which makes it an affair of relations without intrinsic limits—of continual, unbounded "carryings over" ("meta-phor" in its etymological sense).

In the "Introduction" to this course of reflection and study, I observed how, early in the Western tradition, all kinds of knowledge, which today is divided up into different disciplines, could still be grasped together in a comprehensive sort of wisdom that was expressed poetically. This wisdom often entailed a sort of truth that purports to transcend the limits of normal, mortal understanding, and in this sense it asks to be understood as "revealed." Such is evidently the case with the poetry of the Bible and Homer. These works constitute source texts of religion for their native cultures, the Judeo-Christian and the Greco-Roman respectively. Taken to its limits—as, eminently, in the texts selected—poetry endeavors to reveal the *totality* of the real in something of its inexhaustible meaning and pathos. This revelation of imagination, I maintain, overlaps—and at center even coincides—with religious revelation. The concepts of poetic and of religious revelation invade and destabilize each other reciprocally.

7. Frederic Jameson, *Postmodernism: or, The Cultural Logic of Late Capitalism* (Durham, N.C.: Duke University Press, 1991), 333.

Religion (*re-ligio*) can, at the level of origins, perhaps even be equated with poetry as what binds everything together through the "re" of representation. In the mirror of representation—or the reflected image—it is possible to imagine seeing everything whole and to disclose the meaning of life and history in a way that is not possible for us from within our direct involvements in the world. Only in the *re*-presentations of such experience can manifestations of life be imaginatively grasped together as a whole and from their source. Of course, any *representation* of this wholeness is at the same time also illusory. The dialectical counter-truth is that only in the direct engagement of action can we be whole because in that mode we can relate as parts to a larger whole that we never reflectively grasp or conceptually encompass.[8] Nevertheless, the necessarily restricted action of a finite thinking being does not exempt it from the challenge of endeavoring to think beyond all set limits circumscribing its field of cognizance. The notion of a wholeness without bounds and excluding no others obliges us in principle to practice an unrestricted openness to all that is.

A challenging theological interpretation of this predicament of being pragmatically oriented to an inconceivable wholeness that transcends us is proposed by Hans Urs von Balthasar. He, too, calls for acknowledgment of how we are in pursuit of a truth that summons us to imagine ourselves as open to an always greater wholeness:

> The trouble, however, lies always in a drawing of boundaries over against a further truth, in holding fast and absolutizing a finite perspective, which one no longer wishes to see as a part and an expression of an over-arching, infinite truth. Human guilt comes not from the fact that one knows only a piece of the infinite truth but from the fact that one remains complacently with this fragment and closes oneself off from suggestive and supplementary outlooks and so separates oneself from the living source of truth.[9]

---

8. Maurice Blondel emphasizes a transcendence inhering even in the immanence of action in *L'Action: Essai d'une critique de la vie et d'une science de la pratique* (Paris: Presses Universitaires de France, 1950 [1893], trans. by Oliva Blanchette as *Action: Essay on a Critique of Life and a Science of Practice* (Notre Dame, Ind.: University of Notre Dame Press, 1984).

9. Hans Urs von Balthasar, *Theologik*, 3 vols. (Einsiedeln: Johannes Verlag, 1985–87), 1: "Immer aber liegt das Ärgernis in einer Grenzziehung gegenüber einer weitern Wahrheit, im Festhalten und Verabsolutieren einer endlichen Perspektive, die man nicht mehr als einen Teil und Ausdruck der übersteigenden, unendlichen Wahrheit ansehen will. Nicht darin, daß der Mensch nur einen Ausschnitt aus der unendlichen Wahrheit kennt, liegt seine Schuld, sondern darin, daß er sich bei diesem Ausschnitt beruhigt, sich gegen erweiternde und ergänzende Ausblicke abriegelt und sich so von der lebendigen Quelle der Wahrheit trennt" (138).

Imposing limits, as is often done on the pretext of intellectual modesty, can hardly be justified, when finally we must answer to a truth that we cannot in any way delimit. I choose von Balthasar to make this point and to provide a certain theological frame for my reflections on the literary canon and its claim to a kind of totality which evades binary logic, with its inevitable exclusions, in favor of an associative, inclusive logic of the imagination projected to infinity. I do so because he deftly combines a theological aesthetic with a negative theology that draws back from positive assertion of the idea of unlimited vision by which it is nevertheless animated. Aesthetic representation can be theologically revealing—but only on condition of opening toward what finally transcends aesthetic representation. The totality of "vision" in question is not itself of the order of the representable. However, representation has an ability to transcend or exceed itself toward what cannot be represented. Totality, rather than being achieved by representation per se, is operative precisely in representation's failures. Von Balthasar's theological aesthetic highlights beauty among the transcendental properties of Being (including also oneness, truth, and goodness) as what makes a transcendent God present in manifestations of "glory" ("Herrlichkeit")—even while divinity in its essence remains forever out of reach and unrepresentable.[10]

What is particularly telling in von Balthasar's theological aesthetic, and what I wish to emphasize, is the way that poetry in a broad sense functions as an uncanny mediator between purported representation of the whole and the true whole that cannot be represented—the one that lies beyond the reach of representation altogether. What capabilities and resources make poetry the medium of this disclosure of truth, of potentially all knowledge in concrete, particular images and in a perspective that can coincide with religious revelation, bearing witness to what poets from Dante to Blake call "divine vision"? We have paid particular attention to the character of each of the works we have read as "prophetic," as carriers of something on the order of a transcendent vision. The coalescence of the poetic and the religious—the way the one is always at core intrinsically also the other—at this level, at the limits of representation, has been elucidated by the comparative study of the works selected. In this connection, a revelation of truth that is ultimately "religious" in nature, in the sense of an infinite disclosure that would in principle tie all

10. Hans Urs von Balthasar, *Herrlichkeit: Eine theologische Ästhetik*, 3 vols. (Einsiedeln: Johannes Verlag, 1961–69), vol. III, pt. 2–1, p. 13. Although he rejects negative theology narrowly understood as pagan in *Theologik, II: Wahrheit Gottes*, B: "Die Frage der Negativen Theologie," Balthasar constantly employs its insights and formulas such as: "If you understand, it is not God" ("Begreifst du, so ist es nicht Gott," *Theodramatik*, vol. 4: 447–476 [Einsiedeln: Johannes Verlag, 1971–83]), which echo throughout Christian tradition—for example, in Saint Augustine, *De doctrine Christiana*, book 1, chapter 6.

things together, seems essential to a full conception of poetry in the Western humanities tradition.[11]

This study of great books of the Western tradition has focused to a considerable extent on epics, not because of any generic predilection per se, but rather because in their attempt to achieve a certain universality of vision, epics represent this tradition at its most ambitious and comprehensive.[12] All of the texts read here propose a visionary—or what I have called a "prophetic"—outlook on nothing less than the whole of human experience and its place in the cosmos.[13] Each work is somehow predicated on the possibility of transcending the limits of ordinary human perception, which is bound by time and space, in order to see into the final end or destiny, and therewith into the deeper meaning, of existence, which is not manifest to mortal sight but can be revealed from the perspective of divinity—whether God or the Muses.

All of these "humanities" texts have everything to do with religion because, at its origin and in its disclosure of truth, all knowledge is one, or is at least unified, not broken down into separate disciplines. The literary works we have read are all in some sense summas; they embrace the whole field of what counts as vital knowledge in their time. This includes obviously religion and, in fact, privileges religion as the overarching perspective and discourse that ultimately joins everything together.[14] Re-ligion—from *ligo, -are,* to tie or bind, as in "ligament," "ligature," and even "legal," in the sense of something binding[15]—is at work in any discourse or cultural practice that ties us back (re) to our source and origin such as we might imagine it.

---

11. Such is the drift, for example, of Northrop Frye's conception of poetic literature. Illuminating here are the essays gathered in *Northrop Frye on Religion*, ed. Alvin A. Lee and Jean O'Grady (Toronto: University of Toronto Press, 2000).

12. In *Poetry and Apocalypse: Theological Disclosures of Poetic Language* (Stanford, Calif.: Stanford University Press, 2009), I pursue similar reflections in relation to the Christian epic from Dante to James Joyce—thus in relation to the modern continuation of the ancient and medieval tradition examined in the present volume.

13. Something similar could surely be shown for non-Western traditions by focusing on epic works such as the Mesopotamian *Gilgamesh* or the Babylonian *Enuma Elish* or the Indian *Mahabharata*.

14. A recently revived sense of religion as unifying all human knowledge registers, for example, in Amy Hollywood, "On Understanding Everything: General Education, Liberal Education, and the Study of Religion," *PMLA* 126, no. 2 (2011): 460–71.

15. Such an etymology is found in Lactantius, *Institutionum Divinarum* 4.28: "We are born under such condition that, once generated, we should offer our just and due services to God, should know and follow him. By this bond of piety we are tied and bound [*religati*] to God" ("Hac conditione gignimur ut, generati nos Deo justa et debita obsequia praebeamus, hunc noverimus, hunc sequamur. Hoc vinculo pietatis obstricti Deo et religati sumus").

All of these works implicitly ask the question: what is the meaning of human and historical life—what knits it together in its multifarious manifestations and in their temporal unfolding? And all envision this meaning as inhering in some kind of theological revelation in which humanity is seen as existing in relation to God or the gods. The Bible offers a revelation of humanity as created in God's image and as positioned within a hierarchy of beings that forms an ordered and harmonized Creation—but also as fallen. It works out this revelation of a bond between God and humanity in history and calls for its reestablishment through prophecy. The meaning of existence in any case comes from a relation to divinity, even when this meaning seems highly questionable, as it does already within the Bible itself, particularly to the "Preacher" (Qohelet) in Ecclesiastes. The divine meaning of the universe may thus turn out to be disclosed and affirmed through—and not in spite of—human limitations and even lack.

Going much further in this direction, Odysseus's story emphasizes the grounding of life's meaning upon man's mortality. Odysseus chooses his own wife and home and a death that awaits him in sleek old age over an immortality of pleasures with the goddess Calypso. The life chosen is a painful one, as his name itself suggests, especially as this name, "Odysseus," meaning "sufferer and inflicter of pains," is elucidated through the story about the scar inflicted by the wild boar that frames the scene of his naming in book 19 (lines 393–409). But these pains of mortal life are also what give that name and his very life their meaning. Odysseus struggles with the gods, especially with Poseidon, and he has need of a prophetic vision from Tiresias in order to make his way home, for he is passing through the realm of the dead—an unknown, forbidden world. By his mastery of narrative technique, which is also, obviously, the poet Homer's mastery, Odysseus relates his life as a series of adventures directed toward a goal. This gives a minimal teleological structure to the story of his wanderings, but the digressive meanderings of the narrative repeatedly shift this telos out of the foreground. As each separate episode takes on fascination in and for itself, the sensuous intensity of the present and its peculiar adventure are highlighted.

In this manner, Odysseus's mortality, along with its pathos and sublimity, are dramatically relived and reexperienced in each present moment. Yet in choosing "this" life, the poem has raised it to a more exalted plane of significance. His life is no longer simply an indifferently arranged sequence of events. There are certain moments of synthesis of meaning that would seem to transcend the mortality dwelling in each moment taken just for itself. They come in storytelling, in *poiesis*, in magical moments in which objective time is suspended and becomes elastic, so that, as Alcinous observes in listening to Odysseus's tale, "this night is prodigiously long" (11.373–74).

The *Odyssey* on the whole is not prophetic in temperament. Nevertheless, the revelation of a meaning for human life as a whole emerges even here, where the emphasis is on immanence, on human life for its own sake, apart from transcendence. Moreover, the motif of a journey to the underworld, modeled on Odysseus's *nekuia* in book 11, becomes the archetypal matrix for prophetic vision in epic poetry: it reaches an apotheosis in Dante, who expands the visit to the dominion of the dead to encompass his whole narrative, which transpires almost entirely in the afterlife. Dante turns Odysseus's journey home into Ulysses's would-be open-ended quest for unlimited knowledge. Nevertheless, the transcendence of the limits of the living is presupposed already in Homer by Odysseus's journey to the underworld, even if the hero subsequently chooses to live out his life within its ordinary mortal limits. His very refusal of transcendence is itself grounded in a transcendent vision penetrating behind the veil of death that is granted him by the prophet Tiresias.

Virgil's vision of universal history is similarly delimited by a goal: peace for the whole world, the *pax Romana*. Of course, he feels the cost of the sacrifices exacted—one need only think of Dido. But the pathos is repeated in the cases of Turnus, Nisus, Eurialus, Camilla, Pallinurus, Misenus, Creusa, Caïta, and so on—so acutely as to call the whole enterprise of empire into question. Still, in the *Aeneid*, literature identifies itself with prophetic insight and a divine perspective. Poetry, considered as language that realizes its most essential powers, becomes the vehicle of a transcendent vision of ultimate meaning in history. Yet this transcendence does not in essence exceed the temporal, historical order as such—except perhaps in the promise of immortality for Aeneas and for certain emperors succeeding him in his line. The crowning vision received by Aeneas in the underworld emphasizes rather the *historical* destiny of Rome. A further dimension of transcendence in eternal life as the "true" life is centrally envisaged first by the imaginative literature of Christianity.

Augustine condemns poetry (the tradition of classical letters and rhetoric) for its *un*truth, and yet *poiesis* is essential for his realization in the *Confessions* of nothing less than the divine vision in the form of constant dialogue shadowing the point of view of God, who is represented as his interlocutor. From the opening chapters of the book, Augustine's language reflects upon itself in the attempt to reflect the presence and speech of God in his own meditative discourse. Here, again, imagination is exploited for its intrinsic capabilities of effecting revelation of a religious order. Poetry serves as a powerful form of predestination. Augustine "makes"—in the Greek sense of "making" or *poiesis*—his life revolve around his conversion. This poetic shaping is part and parcel of the conversion itself, which, in fact, turns out to be realized through imitation of a series of literary models. Hence the ongoing debates about the literary construction of the conversion scene, since the sense of the work revolves around the way the whole of it reads as a retrospective ordering and in fact a literary reinvention—in accordance with a religious purpose—of the events of Augustine's life.

Dante, finally, is the one who makes theological poetics programmatic and thereby brings to a climax the discovery of the poetic as intrinsically revelatory in a religious sense—the central and defining discovery of the Western humanities tradition as it has been presented here. The imagination is so thoroughly imbued with a visionary transcendence in Dante that poetry becomes self-consciously and programmatically a vehicle toward the experience of the divine culminating in the mystical vision of God, the *visio Dei*, in Paradise.

Mortal sight is bound within the succession of moments in time: it never sees whole. A level of vision superior to this, one that enables seeing eternity from beyond the bounds of time, is proffered by all our exemplary texts, starting from the Bible and its account of what happened "in the beginning" as well as in the end, in the Apocalypse. The Christ event recounted in the Gospels prefigures and actually inaugurates the end, with Jesus's resurrection from the dead, which is also a new beginning of the universal order of Creation. The obvious possible exception is the *Odyssey*, but precisely this text establishes for later epic the paradigm of the journey to the underworld in search of the secret of life among the dead.

Prophecy has had to be defined differently in each case, yet all the texts considered here mediate their prophetic vision essentially by poetic imagination. All are at core about—albeit, for the most part, covertly—the revelation of imagination. Imagination, as the comprehensive framework for our knowledge, has resources that make it the earliest form—in the guise of myth or narrative—of what is typically recognized as divine revelation emergent in budding human culture.[16] And when we focus particularly on the linguistic form of this structure of narrative or myth, then we speak of "poetry." The myths we have dealt with, as conveyed by language, are essentially poetry.[17]

By means of poetry it is possible to realize, to a degree, this visionary knowledge, which is unrestricted as to type and discipline, a wisdom embracing all the manifold variety of life seen whole, all things in their interconnectedness—as in the sight of God. Poetry of the order of the works interpreted here, by forging the conceptual basis in terms of which all things can first be perceived and represented, reveals the groundedness of all human action and history in imagination. Thereby, rather than merely representing the world as an object, poetry actively participates in *making* things what they are. Poetry is a form of mimesis that enables human beings to participate in the act of

16. Such an understanding of imagination was first developed for modern criticism by Giambattista Vico, *Princìpi di scienza nuova* (1744). Its varied elaborations in Continental philosophy today are explored by Richard Kearney, *Poetics of Imagining: Modern to Postmodern* (New York: Fordham University Press, 1998).

17. Northrop Frye, in *Words with Power: Being a Second Study of "The Bible and Literature"* (San Diego: Harcourt Brace Jovanovich, 1990), describes Vico as "the first modern thinker to understand that all major verbal structures have descended historically from poetic and mythological ones" (xii).

creation, which is the divine act par excellence.[18] We have seen over and over again, in the works selected, how poetic interpretation enters into the event that it represents, enabling that event to ground itself in present consciousness that determines here and now what is real and thereby re-creates time as we can apprehend it and as projected from the completeness of an always only imaginable eternity.

The poetic event becomes an ongoing creative revelation, for example, in the Exodus story, which is constantly relived at different stages of Israel's history. We can see the event itself merge with its poetic celebration in ritual and song: the "original" Exodus can hardly be disentangled from the creating of a poetic tradition in the book of Exodus, which in its very telling enjoins relentless retelling to future generations for the sake of continuous re-actualization of the event. Similarly the Creation story, being about "Adam," the common noun for "man" in Hebrew, is about all human beings at any time. Humanities tradition lives from this realization of its truth as present in the experience of every age and of each individual. Thus knowledge in the humanities is continually regrounded in actual experience because it pertains not to plain facts but to values and significances that are made poetically and *re*made every time they are communicated anew. Its grounds are in what can be communicated, for all its changes, from generation to generation in a way that projects an at least hypothetical common ground that can bind historical experience together across successive epochs.[19]

In reality, this common ground is nothing that can be defined as such or ever be objectified. This is why it has been appropriately expressed throughout tradition through figures of transcendence like God and the Muses. Such a grounding can never be anything merely finite and empirical or immanent.[20] It must escape all finite formulation in order to serve as the glue that

---

18. Vico's conception of the analogy between human and divine creation is developed in terms of the *homo creator* topos by John Milbank, *The Religious Dimension in the Thought of Giambattista Vico 1668–1744* (Lewiston, N.Y.: Mellen, 1991). The idea is proposed more familiarly for English-language readers by Samuel Taylor Coleridge, particularly in his discussion of Imagination in *Bibliographia Literaria* (1817), chapter 13: "The primary Imagination I hold to be the living Power and prime Agent of all human Perception, and as a repetition in the finite mind of the eternal act of creation in the infinite I Am."

19. The historicism that stretches from Dante to Vico to Erich Auerbach understands this process poetically in accordance with the thesis that "poetry created modern humanity," as Paul Bové sums it up in *Poetry against Torture: History, Criticism, and the Human* (Hong Kong: Hong Kong University Press, 2008), 40–48.

20. Some, of course, would disagree. Especially concerning Homer, see György Lukács, *Die Theorie des Romans: Ein geschichtsphilosophischer Versuch über die Formen der grossen Epik* (Berlin: P. Cassirer, 1920), trans. Anna Bostock as *The Theory of the Novel: A Historico-Philosophical Essay on the Forms of Great Epic Literature* (Cambridge, Mass.: MIT Press, 1971).

mysteriously holds together contingent, heterogeneous, unpredictable historical experience. Yet even sheer historical continuity postulates—or at least projects—such an ungraspable ground. Understanding humanity and history as a continuing tradition, as all our texts have proposed to do, binds past, present, and future together and creates for them a presumptively common, or at any rate comparable, meaning. Ironically, however, such supra-historical continuity is forged always only from fragments, in a contingent historical moment, and through struggle, as is stressed by Walter Benjamin in his "Messianic" conception of history.[21]

We cannot fail to recognize that, alongside notions such as canonicity, totalizing aesthetic visions have been under heavy fire in recent critical discourse. Bringing out the dangers of totalizing representations has been an overriding preoccupation of criticism now for several decades. But we should also note that the more nuanced and insightful rejections of the aesthetics of totality typically acknowledge some conception of wholeness as part of a dialectic that enters into the production of such knowledge as can and should still be considered valid and desirable. In Benjamin's Messianism itself, there is a sense in which the *whole* of history takes on new meaning through the contingent upheavals that reposition memories in new mutual relations. In *The Arcades Project (Das Passagen-Werk)*, for example, Benjamin endeavors to make historical and philosophical connections concrete so as "to discover in the analysis of the small individual moment the crystal of the *total event*" ("Ja in der Analyse des kleinen Einzelmoments den Kristall des *Totalgeschehens* zu entdecken").[22]

Universality of vision is still quite widely felt to be something necessary to strive for—now perhaps more than ever before, in a globalized world torn asunder by atrocious ethnic wars and rending religious rivalries. As sectarianism seems to have become even more of a threat than totalitarianism in our new global order, a new generation of philosophers is now endeavoring to reclaim universality, and some, including even atheistic thinkers such as Alain Badiou and Slavoj Žižek, have done so specifically in terms of Christian revelation.[23] I wish to focus for a moment on a particular figure

---

21. See particularly Benjamin's "Geschichtsphilosophische Thesen," in *Illuminationen: Ausgewählte Schriften* (Frankfurt: Suhrkamp, 1961), 268–79, trans. by Harry Zohn as "Theses on the Philosophy of History," in *Illuminations* (New York: Schocken, 1968).

22. Walter Benjamin, *Gesammelte Schriften* (Frankfurt: Suhrkamp, 1983) vol. 5, part 1, 575 (my emphasis). I align myself with James R. Martel, *Divine Violence: Walter Benjamin and the Eschatology of Sovereignty* (New York: Routledge, 2012) in emphasizing how, for Benjamin, *all* inevitably idolatrous human political orders are undermined by the theological moment of the Messianic.

23. Alain Badiou, *Saint Paul: La fondation de l'universalisme* (Paris: Presses Universitaires de France, 1997); Slavoj Žižek, *The Puppet and the Dwarf: The Perverse Core of Christianity* (Cambridge, Mass.: MIT Press, 2003).

from this constellation of critics who offer key insights for rethinking universality, one who works also from Jewish matrices and is heavily indebted to Benjamin. Eric Santner develops an ethics of the remnant and an epistemology of the "not-All" that issues in "revelation" based on the "New Thinking" introduced by the remarkable Jewish thinker Franz Rosenzweig. He is crucially inspired also by Hölderlin's fragmentary and yet visionary poetry.[24]

A logic of the remnant appears prima facie to be opposed to anything like purportedly whole vision. Santner, in fact, levels a devastating critique of the metaphysics of "fantasy" and its creation of ideological, holistic formations of symbols subservient to the general order of things upheld by the State. Oppressive political systems are undergirded by the psycho-symbolic order through the all-controlling energy exerted by the superego. Nevertheless, in spite of the manifest evils of the drive to totalize, neither is Santner satisfied to leave knowledge simply in a fragmentary state. What is necessary in the end is surpassing the sphere of knowledge altogether in a move toward an uncanny encounter with otherness—or, more specifically, with the Other in the midst of life. This is a prescription for "revelation" more than for "knowledge" in any narrow sense, and it is drawn from the Judeo-Christian tradition as crystallized in Rosenzweig. It is a mode of vision in crucial ways comparable to that which has been developed also under the rubric of "prophecy" in the broader cultural tradition of the West. The tradition we have surveyed has come to light as a continuous, ever recommencing effort of *re*imagining the world and history as a whole, from the ground up. It is such an effort because it is *involved* knowing—it is forged "in the midst of life," to adopt Santner's shibboleth.

The prophetic viewpoint overlaps with what Santner, following Rosenzweig, terms "revelation," which looks beyond all myths and systems of identity to the singular truth—beyond symbolization—that opens a divine dimension in human life, especially in its singular incomprehensibility. This prophetic perspective forms the basis for a critique of all the ideological appropriations of the imagination. Such, we saw, are the piercing critiques by Virgil of the ideology of Empire in the name of the claims of single individuals (Dido, Camilla, Pallinurus, Misenus, Caieta, Marcellus, etc.) whose sacrifice it demands. And Dante similarly critiques the ideology of humanism: he exposes as tainted by damnable egoistic pride the effort to confer eternity upon oneself through great humanist works, after the manner of Brunetto Latini with his *Tesoro*. The irony is that this humanist master taught Dante "how man makes himself eternal" ("come l'uom s'etterna") through such

24. Eric Santner, *On the Psychotheology of Everyday Life: Reflections on Freud and Rosenzweig* (Chicago: University of Chicago Press, 2001), 140ff. Lacan's "pas-tout" (not-all), elaborated in *Séminaire, Livre XX: Encore* (Paris: Seuil, 1975), exerts influence here, too.

works as his "Treasure," in which he deems that he "still lives" ("nel qual io vivo ancora"), even while we espy him eternally dying in Hell (*Inferno* 15.85, 119–20).

This sort of internal critique of ideologies is intrinsic to the tradition and passes through Augustine, with his acute sense of the limits and potential deceptiveness of signs: it demands reaching finally beyond imaginative constructions to the revelation that animates them from beyond the horizon of all that they can represent. This is where Dante's unsparing critique in the *Inferno* of all the human modalities of representation (reason, writing, narrative, language itself) is exemplary. The constructive mythic work of the imagination and its deconstruction by critique belong equally to the "revelation of imagination" in the novel, negatively couched senses of these words that emerge from the present study.

The indefatigable striving for completeness of vision is in reality what prevents any achieved vision or idea, including that of fragmentariness, from ever establishing itself as definitive or sufficient. Striving to grasp the whole, so far from being an impediment, is actually what motivates attending to the uniqueness or singularity of the Other. It issues in straining to be open to the whole of what another person is, excluding nothing. An open receptiveness to *all* others, without exclusions, is likewise demanded. We should remember that Rosenzweig, who is the source of a rigorous philosophy of the not-All, himself at the end of the *Star of Redemption* embraces what he calls the "true All, the All that does not spring into pieces as in the world of the Nothing, but rather the one All, the All and One" ("das wahre All, das All, das nicht in Stücke springt wie in der Welt des Nichts, sondern das eine All, das All und Eine").[25] Rosenzweig writes also of the "new allness" ("Die neue Allheit"), an All which is infinite ("ein Unendliches," sec. 257). This new All of interrelationality, as differentiated from the Hegelian All (*das Ganze*) and as a new realization of the redemptive unity of the All, serves as fulcrum for a new conception of system which does not eclipse the singular truth of individuals.[26]

Every unique individual is infinitely related to All as to what it *is not*. What is deleterious is not opening one's mind and thoughts to All, that is,

---

25. Rosenzweig, *Der Stern der Erlösung* (Frankfurt: Suhrkamp, 1988 [1921]), sec. 406. From a divergent point of view stressing social differentiation rather than mystical oneness, Catherine Keller, *The Face of the Deep: A Theology of Becoming* (New York: Routledge, 2003), similarly conceives of an All that is "all-relational": "If the All is the 'all-relational,' we begin to see how this discourse may resist its own temptation to a mystical de-differentiation, with its corresponding social indifference" (207).

26. Benjamin Pollock, *Franz Rosenzweig and the Systematic Task of Philosophy* (Cambridge, Eng.: Cambridge University Press, 2009) makes this argument convincingly.

to all others and to what is infinitely other, but rather reducing the world and the Other to representation, as if everything could be represented and thus be made commensurable to oneself.[27] The prophetic perspective of visionary poetry has shown how the total vision of imagination is fundamentally not a self-enclosed system of representation but rather a piercing insight into a fathomless depth: it opens a depth dimension in which the singular becomes manifest in its unlimited relatedness with all. The vision at stake in these works has proved in each case to be a revelation rather than just a system—a revelation of imagination beyond any closed system of representation.

Even the readings, so prevalent today, that warn against the dangers of any pretension to wholeness or to totalizing thought acknowledge this essential moment of opening without restriction to the Other. Santner illustrates how this Other is apprehended essentially through a self-interruption of the One. Following the Heraclitean saying about "the One differentiated in itself,"[28] Santner writes that the beautiful is conceived "not as a harmonization of parts within an ordered whole but rather as the representation of an interrupted whole—or better, a self-interrupting whole—one animated, as it were, by a 'too much' of pressure from within its midst" (*Psychotheology*, 136).

Envisaging a potential—or even an "impossible"—whole as if it were miraculously actual is necessary even for the *refusal* of any achieved, articulated vision as total. Only by negating the holistic vision of "fantasy," which is complicit in coercive ideologies of the state (including the ideology, we must suppose, of global empire), does this vision of the not-All advocated by Santner find its cutting edge and take shape. The whole must be presented at least as a false image or idol even in order to be undermined.[29] Artworks exposing, for example, fascist ideologies penetrate, at their best, to a global interpretation affording a glimpse, however fleeting and elusive, of the driving

---

27. Instructive here are the essays of Elaine Scarry in *Resisting Representation* (New York: Oxford University Press, 1994). We could extrapolate also from Scarry's defense of beauty, in *On Beauty and Being Just* (Princeton, N.J.: Princeton University Press, 1999), to argue that the more complete the aesthetic vision experienced by the likes of Odysseus or Dante (her examples) becomes, the more acute is their sense of inadequacy and the stronger their aspiration to truth and to ever more complete vision. "The whole," in the apprehension of beauty and truth alike, can never be complete: it stands rather for something unlimited, a plenitude that one strives after more and more.

28. The ἐν διφαφερον ἑαυτῳ, which is taken up by Hölderlin ("Das Eine in sich Unterschiedene") in *Hyperion and Selected Poems*, ed. Eric Santner (New York: Continuum, 1990), 67.

29. These issues are expertly probed also by Leora Batnitzky, *Idolatry and Representation: The Philosophy of Franz Rosenzweig Reconsidered* (Princeton, N.J.: Princeton University Press, 2000).

motives and mechanisms behind a whole world order. Furthermore, to close oneself off in an ideology of the fragmentary is equally idolatrous and would eventually prove unproductive, too: as if by grasping only after fragments, one had the truth!

Thus the claim of these epic texts to comprehensive vision is not to be jettisoned. Critical perspectives are parasitic upon the holistic visions purveyed in great works of imagination such as the epic poems that contribute prodigiously to the founding of world cultures. Neither should we reject, of course, the critiques leveled, not least from within these works themselves, against the very ideologies with which they are otherwise aligned. The "total revelation" aspired to in epic is *not* a totality that admits of no addition or revision, but just the opposite: it aspires to always greater inclusiveness, ideally admitting no definitive exclusions and recognizing no final bounds.

The need to deny closure to cosmic vision by returning to the universality inherent in singularity, that of the remnant, we may agree, has been advocated especially effectively by Jewish culture and criticism, particularly in the wake of Walter Benjamin and his crucial predecessor, Franz Rosenzweig. However, it is not unprecedented or unparalleled elsewhere.[30] It belongs essentially to the cultural tradition of the West, even in its most canonical representatives.[31] The shift from a global, imperialist system to a vision that pivots on revelation of the universal in the singular is achieved by Virgil already in the *Aeneid*—with its critique of the ideology of the Roman Empire from the standpoint of the singular persons who are sacrificed for its sake. And Dante does something analogous in spinning the universal Catholic theological vision out of his own unique life-experience: theological doctrine is thereby personalized and historicized in the form of an archetypal and yet unmistakably idiosyncratic journey of a superlatively singular individual.[32]

---

30. A fascinating fusion is wrought by Elliot Wolfson, *Language, Eros, Being: Kabbalistic Hermeneutics and Poetic Imagination* (New York: Fordham University Press, 2005), in which a dialectic of imagination with the unimaginable, also inspired intensively by Rosenzweig, is brought to focus through the lens of Western philosophical thought (Heidegger, Merleau-Ponty, etc.) trained on the Kabbalah.

31. This is demonstrated eminently by Erich Auerbach's criticism of the European tradition, signally in *Mimesis: Dargestellte Wirklichkeit in der abendländischen Literatur* (Bern: Francke, 1946), trans. by Willard Trask as *Mimesis: The Representation of Reality in Western Literature* (Princeton, N.J.: Princeton University Press, 1953).

32. Averil Cameron, *Christianity and the Rhetoric of Empire: The Development of Christian Discourse* (Berkeley: University of California Press, 1994), following up suggestions by Michel Foucault, *Le Soucie de soi* (Paris: Gallimard, 1984), throws light on Christianity's vocation, in its early development, to span the universal and the private.

A blanket refusal of all visions striving for wholeness would effect a mutilation of human imagination and spirit. Unifying visions must, admittedly, be subjected to critique and be reopened to what any closed system inevitably excludes. Yet the critique of totalizing systems, with all its benefits, becomes possible thanks only to these great synthetic projects, and all the "blessings of more life" come as a consequence of the interplay between deconstruction *and construction* of whole structures.[33]

The projective wholeness of vision that is characteristic of certain founding texts of Western humanities has manifested itself in every case we have studied from the angle of vision of what we have been calling "prophecy." As prophecy, humanities knowledge is grounded in a vision beyond the capacity of mortal sight, and in this sense it reveals (at least negatively) a "divine" point of view. Intended in this term "prophecy" is not so much foretelling the future as seeing the whole course of events in the unfolding of time from a standpoint cognizant of its goal and origin. Of course, the goal and origin can only be mythically represented and imaginatively projected. What, after all, do these myths of origin and end represent, if not what no representation can adequately say? The ineffable can be approached only through myth and imagination.[34] This avowal of ineffability is not a denial of revelation but a recognition of its transcendent source and object. Every one of our texts has claimed to communicate a divine vision—to reveal something of or from the divine—in some form of poetic expression that leads to the threshold of the inexpressible.[35]

Every one of the works we have studied proposes in its own way a total (and therefore "unrealizable") vision. The Bible begins "In the beginning" and stretches its narrative all the way to the end of the world, to apocalypse. This pattern of alpha and omega is the most complete and explicit assertion of totality. But Homer's epics, too, were a comprehensive encyclopedia for the culture that created them. The encyclical structure of returning in a full

33. The quoted phrase comes from Harold Bloom's *Ruin the Sacred Truths: Poetry and Belief from the Bible to the Present* (Cambridge, Mass.: Harvard University Press, 1987), 160. It is cited repeatedly by Santner in *Psychotheology*, becoming a refrain and in effect an implicit acknowledgment of indebtedness to the "visionary tradition" that Bloom champions.

34. This paradox has even become something of a popular commonplace thanks to authors like Mircea Eliade, *Myths, Dreams and Mysteries: The Encounter between Contemporary Faiths and Archaic Realities* (New York: Harper and Row, 1975); and Joseph Campbell, *The Mythic Dimension: Selected Essays 1959–1993*, ed. Anthony Van Couvering (New York: New World Library, 2007).

35. Sanford Budick, *The Western Theory of Tradition: Terms and Paradigms of the Cultural Sublime* (New Haven, Conn.: Yale University Press, 2000) offers a searching attempt to ground the creative freedom of tradition in the power of works such as those discussed here to effectuate a suspension of cultural transmission through sublime representation.

circle back to its origin is, in fact, the basic narrative line of the *Odyssey*, the story of Odysseus's return home, his *nostos*.[36] The *Aeneid* very deliberately attempts to follow in Homer's tracks in creating the comprehensive epic of Latin civilization. Its inclusion of the themes of both the *Iliad* and the *Odyssey*, the war and the return home, is already a gesture of striving for completeness. But reaching beyond Homer's horizon, Virgil conveys a powerful sense of history as having a potential fulfillment, which he imagines as coinciding with the Roman Empire. His vision of a final end and a total providential order for the historical world made Virgil irresistible for Dante as the prophet of a Christian world order under the aegis of the Holy Roman Empire.

Augustine's *Confessions*, being initially the story of a single life, may seem less obviously encyclopedic and therefore less of a totalizing vision. Yet the concentration on the existence of the individual proves to be but a displacement of the epic projects that we have followed from earlier tradition. Augustine presents his story not just as the personal "confession" of a self but also as representative of human life in general, both in its slavery to sin and as redeemed. Although its point of view privileges an individual self, the scope of Augustine's work is epic: it interiorizes a universal history and a general interpretation of culture. In its latter books, moreover, Augustine's autobiography takes a sharp turn toward contemplating the whole of Creation as it is summed up in the opening verses of Genesis. Even the literary artifice of the work, for example, its intricate and archetypal narrative framings, can be viewed as not compromising its integrity but rather as fulfilling its true purpose—if only we remember its aim of representing the typical and universally true rather than simply the particularity of Augustine's own existence.

Dante preserves the inwardness of epic vision born of the individual self that is inaugurated by Augustine, making his own life's story central to the narrative, even while he signals from the first line—"Nel mezzo del cammin di *nostra* vita" ("In the middle of the path of our life")—that his life is *our* life, that it is representative of at least a possible and perhaps an ideal pattern for every human life. He deliberately inscribes his work into the epic tradition, following, literally, in the footsteps of Virgil.[37] He invokes the Muses and evokes myriad other epic conventions. The encyclopedic scope of the work, moreover, compels it to exceed even the epic and to become "comedy," which as "mixed" is a universal genre that can subsume all others—or, better,

36. Franco Ferrucci, *L'assedio e il ritorno: Omero e gli archetipi della narrazione* (Milan: Mondadori, 1991).

37. Winthrop Wetherbee, *The Ancient Flame: Dante and the Poets* (Notre Dame, Ind.: University of Notre Dame Press, 2008) traces in filigree this inscription into the epic texts of Virgil, Lucan, Ovid, and Statius.

that can exclude none.[38] Most importantly, Dante's individual life story traverses virtually the whole range of knowledge and culture that was available to him in his day. His journey to the ultimate source of all in God is a gnoseological journey to comprehensive knowledge—a gnosis which is, of course, already present eternally in the divine Word. Conformably to its Scriptural model, the knowledge in question forms not just a summa in the sense of a gathering together of what is variously and diversely known: the knowledge conveyed in Dante's poem is—in a sense through which literature complicates theology—*revealed*.

The synthesis of vision offered by the epic perspective shows everything in a new and different light. Seen as part of a whole which itself, however, is *not* seen per se (any more than God can be seen in his essence), everything in the universe and in history takes on a sense that it otherwise lacks. Still, this heightening of intellectual vision is expressed in every case through some kind of communication with a divine perspective. God or the gods are at least indirectly involved in granting a vision that is revealed. When we consider that this whole vision is also in every instance precisely imaginative vision—imagination being the way, and perhaps the only way, in which human beings can see things concretely in the semblance of a whole—then we are on the way to comprehending the works considered here as representing a revelation of imagination.

The ongoing interpretation of tradition is a way—evidently the only tried and true way—of participating in the whole of our cultural heritage. This whole is always only virtual—indeed the projection of our very efforts themselves. Yet living one's own moment ecstatically, by reaching out to connect with other ages and their different but somehow still comparable experiences, is how we participate in more than our immediate situation: we participate in history as a larger whole. The coming to light of meaning for the universe as a whole, as it emerges at privileged junctures in history, thence to escape back into unintelligibility again, is the miraculous offering brought to us by great books of the Western tradition such as those that we have studied.[39] This vision, which is pieced together here through a comparative, speculative philology or criticism, constitutes what could be called a "philosophy of

38. Authority for this view is found in the commentary by Dante's son, Jacopo Alighieri, who defines the poem's title and style together as "'comedy,' under which generally and universally all things are treated" ("chomedia sotto il qualle gieneralmente e universalmente si trata di tute le chosse," *Chiose*, *Prohemio* 17–19 [Florence: T. Barracchi, 1848]).

39. The very different, but in some ways convergent, approach to Great Books, also highlighting their trans-historical universality, of Mortimer J. Adler, *How to Read a Book* (New York: Simon and Schuster, 1972 [1940]) and Robert Maynard Hutchins, *The Great Conversation: A Reader's Guide to Great Books of the Western World* (Chicago: Encyclopedia Britannica, 1990 [1952]), has resulted in a program of higher education widely disseminated throughout North America.

revelation" in order to highlight certain of its historical and intellectual affinities, including those with German Romantic or American Transcendentalist conceptions of imagination and their theosophical antecedents and spin-offs.[40]

The viewing of history whole and from a point of view that is "divine," such as prophecy hypothesizes, is realized specifically through the imagination in all of the works that we have chosen as touchstones. Imagination is the faculty of synthetic vision that makes it possible to represent a totality concretely—even if porously. Consciousness of the whole of reality is possible only in the world of the imaginary. The image, with the simultaneity among constituent parts that it forges, is what first gives us a totalized view of anything as an object. However, as *re*presentation, this vision is mediated by negation and absence. Being no reality anywhere within the world, the *whole* of reality is the realm precisely of the imagination, and its constitutive *un*reality is the very element of literature, as Maurice Blanchot, in particular, understands it. Literature, as the universe of the imaginary, is the realm of the unreal. Blanchot explains how the writer, precisely because he deals with what is unreal,

> makes *all* of reality available to us. Unreality begins with the whole. The realm of the imaginary is not a strange region situated beyond the world, it is the world itself, but the world as entire, manifold, the world as a whole. That is why it is not in the world, because it is the world, grasped and realized in its entirety by the global negation of all the individual realities contained in it, by their disqualification, their absence, by the realization of that absence itself, which is how literary creation begins, for when literary creation goes back over each thing and each being, it cherishes the illusion that it is creating them, because now it is seeing and naming them from the starting point of *everything*, from the starting point of the *absence* of everything, that is, from nothing.[41]

Blanchot goes on to explain that the unreality of the whole is realized in literature in the concrete particularity of language and thus as having language's peculiar, palpable, and historical reality. The manifest reality of the

---

40. For historical matrices of the notion of a philosophy of revelation as combining the perspectives of history, myth, and metaphysics, bringing them to bear on all reality ("die Gesamtwirklichkeit"), see Peter Koslowski, *Philosophien der Offenbarung: Antiker Gnostizismus, Franz Baader, Schelling* (Paderborn: Schöningh, 2001). The renewed importance of Romantic epistemology for contemporary philosophy is evidenced by *Philosophical Romanticism*, ed. Nikolas Kompridis (New York: Routledge, 2006).

41. Maurice Blanchot, "Literature and the Right to Death," in *The Gaze of Orpheus and Other Literary Essays by Maurice Blanchot*, ed. P. Adams Sitney (Barrytown, N.Y.: Station Hill, 1981), 36.

linguistic medium lends a marvelously detailed, determinate appearance to the unreality of the whole that is represented therein.

> By revealing to each moment the whole of which it is a part, literature helps it to be aware of the whole that it is not and to become another moment that will be a moment within another whole, and so forth; because of this, literature can be called the greatest ferment in history. But there is one inconvenient consequence: this whole which literature represents is not simply an idea, since it is *realized* and not formulated abstractly—but it is not realized in an objective way, because what is real in it is not the whole but the particular language of a particular work, which is itself immersed in history; what is more, the whole does not present itself as real, but as fictional, that is, precisely as whole, as everything: perspective of the world, grasp of that *imaginary* point where the world can be seen in its entirety. What we are talking about, then, is a view of the world which realizes itself as unreal using language's peculiar reality. ("Literature and the Right to Death," 57)

The reality which is represented as whole is fictive or imaginary. Blanchot thus describes how it is possible to obtain a sense of the whole only negatively—in the medium of absence, which language is. And yet language is present as a fact, making the impossible whole that it can only imaginatively project concretely real. Readers such as Virginia Woolf are familiar with the experience, when reading the most compelling literature, of suddenly exclaiming to themselves: Yes, that is how it really is! Yet, paradoxically, this feeling is produced by an unlimited opening in imagination to reality in which everything relates to everything else. This holistic reality can be found everywhere because it is "really" (as a particular thing) nowhere.

Religious prophecy and imaginative literature overlap in proposing such a universal vision of what is not. Tradition in the humanities is the constant re-actualization of the truth of this vision in the present in which it is reinterpreted with a view to the future and as reappropriating the past. Both are modalities of what is *not*, since the past is not (any longer) and the future is not (yet). The historical sense of prophecy and the intuitive sense of imagination marry in the totality of the book based upon the models of the Bible and Homer and their transmission through works such as the *Aeneid*, the *Confessions*, and the *Divine Comedy*.[42] To see the whole in every part—"the world

42. This tradition is charted by Ernst Robert Curtius, *Europäische Literatur und Lateinsiches Mittelalter* (Bern: Francke, 1948), trans. by Willard R. Trask as *European Literature and the Latin Middle Ages* (New York: Bollingen, 1952). See particularly chapter 16: "The Book as Symbol." For metamorphoses of this symbol in modernity, see Hans Blumenberg, *Die Lesbarkeit der Welt* (Frankfurt: Suhrkamp, 1981).

in a grain of sand," as Blake puts it—proves itself to be the aspiration of these texts and their tradition. Of course, this can be expressed temporally as well as spatially. To be in one's time as communicating with every other time and as a moment of all time taken together emerges as the uncanny possibility that the humanities hold out to us.

To live one's present in relation to a past and future and as open to the whole of human experience—and this is what we learn to do in studying the humanities as a tradition of revelation by imaginative vision—can render us freer as agents in and designers of our destiny. This sense of the shape of human history as a whole helps enable human beings to act freely within it. This is a paradox that has been approached repeatedly in the texts we have read. The ability to imagine one's reality whole—to grasp it as *un*real—enables us to engage with effective creative energy in transforming our actual existence.

Prophecy overcomes the antinomy of fate-versus-freedom by introducing a perspective from which one's fate itself is freely determinable, for the ultimate end of history may then be chosen and appropriated in such a way as to make the will conform to—and at the same time creatively shape—its destiny. By identification with the will of God, or with the whole dispensation of the universe, one's own will becomes the means by which fate is achieved. Prophecy is an interpretation of history in which fate, by being freely chosen, becomes destiny. It does so by being spoken (*fatum*) and so being freely appropriated in language. Our scope of action is not thereby restricted or diminished. Rather, our comprehension of what we are doing is expanded by being seen in this perspective of the whole created by the poetry of language. This mode of vision through the lens of language and open to the whole of our reality is eminently the vision fostered by the tradition of the humanities.

INDEX